Lecture Notes in Computer Sci

T0237870

Commenced Publication in 1973
Founding and Former Series Editors:
Gerhard Goos, Juris Hartmanis, and Jan van Leeuwen

Qing Li   Stefano Spaccapietra   Eric Yu
Antoni Olivé (Eds.)

Conceptual Modeling - ER 2008

27th International Conference on Conceptual Modeling
Barcelona, Spain, October 20-24, 2008
Proceedings

 Springer

Volume Editors

Qing Li
City University of Hong Kong, Department of Computer Science
83 Tat Chee Avenue, Kowloon, Hong Kong, China
E-mail: itqli@cityu.edu.hk

Stefano Spaccapietra
EPFL-IC-IIF-LBD
Station 14 - INJ 236, 1015 Lausanne, Switzerland
E-mail: Stefano.Spaccapietra@epfl.ch

Eric Yu
University of Toronto, Faculty of Information
140 St. George Street, Toronto, Ontario, M5S 3G6, Canada
E-mail: eric.yu@utoronto.ca

Antoni Olivé
Universitat Politècnica Catalunya
Jordi Girona 1-3, 08034 Barcelona, Spain
E-mail: olive@lsi.upc.edu

Library of Congress Control Number: 2008935110

CR Subject Classification (1998): D.2.2, D.2.8, D.3, H.1, H.4

LNCS Sublibrary: SL 3 – Information Systems and Application, incl. Internet/Web
and HCI

ISSN   0302-9743
ISBN-10   3-540-87876-9 Springer Berlin Heidelberg New York
ISBN-13   978-3-540-87876-6 Springer Berlin Heidelberg New York

Springer is a part of Springer Science+Business Media

springer.com

© Springer-Verlag Berlin Heidelberg 2008

Typesetting: Camera-ready by author, data conversion by Scientific Publishing Services, Chennai, India
Printed on acid-free paper   SPIN: 12525928   06/3180   5 4 3 2 1 0

Preface

Conceptual modeling has long been recognized as the primary means to enable software development in information systems and data engineering. Conceptual modeling provides languages, methods and tools to understand and represent the application domain; to elicit, conceptualize and formalize system requirements and user needs; to communicate systems designs to all stakeholders; and to formally verify and validate systems design on high levels of abstraction.

The International Conference on Conceptual Modeling provides a premiere forum for presenting and discussing current research and applications in which the major emphasis is on conceptual modeling. Topics of interest span the entire spectrum of conceptual modeling including research and practice in areas such as theories of concepts and ontologies underlying conceptual modeling, methods and tools for developing and communicating conceptual models, and techniques for transforming conceptual models into effective implementations.

The scientific program of ER 2008 featured several activities running in parallel. The core activity was the presentation of the 33 research papers published in this volume, which were selected by a large Program Committee (PC) Co-chaired by Qing Li, Stefano Spaccapietra and Eric Yu. We thank the PC Co-chairs, the PC members and the additional referees for the hard work done, often within a short time. Thanks are also due to Moira Norrie from ETH Zurich, Oscar Pastor from the Universitat Politècnica de València, and Amit Sheth from the Wright State University for accepting our invitation to present keynotes. Fifteen sessions of the conference were dedicated to the seven ER Workshops selected by the Workshops Co-chairs Il-Yeol Song and Mario Piattini. We express our sincere appreciation to the Co-chairs and to the organizers of the seven workshops for the work done. The proceedings of these workshops are published in a separate volume. Three sessions were dedicated to the PhD Workshop, a new activity in the ER Conferences, organized by John Mylopoulos, Jordi Cabot and Giancarlo Guizzardi, whose efforts are highly appreciated. This volume also includes short descriptions of the 18 demos that were selected by a committee chaired by the Demonstration Program Co-chairs Juan Trujillo and Martin Gogolla, whose efforts are also highly appreciated. Thanks also to the Tutorial Co-chairs Jolita Ralyte and Vicente Pelechano, and to the Panels Co-chairs Paul Johannesson and Pericles Loucopoulos for the work done in selecting and organizing the tutorials and the panel, respectively. Special thanks to David W. Embley, the ER Steering Committee liaison for the advice and help he gave to us whenever we needed it.

Likewise we acknowledge the engagement and enthusiasm of the local organization team, chaired by Ernest Teniente and Joan-Antoni Pastor. The members of the team were Maria R. Sancho and Joan-Antoni Pastor (Sponsor Chairs), Jordi Cabot (Publicity Chair), Cristina Gómez (Treasurer), Jordi Conesa and Xavier de

Palol (Webmasters), Dolors Costal (Venue Chair), Enric Mayol and Ruth Raventós (Social Events Chairs), and Anna Queralt, Albert Tort and Elena Planas (Registration Chairs).

October 2008   Antoni Olivé

Program Chairs' Message

The ER International Conferences on Conceptual Modeling aim at providing a leading international forum for presenting and discussing current research and applications in which the major emphasis is on conceptual modeling. Their scope spans the entire spectrum of conceptual modeling. This year it included in particular research and practice in areas such as theories of concepts and ontologies underlying conceptual modeling, methods and tools for developing and communicating conceptual models, and techniques for transforming conceptual models into effective implementations.

In response to the call for papers, ER2008 received a total of 178 submissions. Thirty-three submissions were accepted for presentation, representing an acceptance rate of about 18.5%. Based on a separate call, 18 demo papers were accepted for presentation. The authors of these accepted papers come from 11 countries resulting in a remarkable international diversity. We would like to thank all the reviewers for spending their precious time reviewing the papers and for providing valuable comments that aided significantly in the paper selection process.

The best paper presented at the ER2008 Conference, selected by the PC Co-chairs, received the DKE 25Year Award, given by Elsevier, publisher of the *Data and Knowledge Engineering* journal to celebrate the 25 years of the journal.

A conference of this magnitude involves the work of many people. We would like to thank our General Chair, Antoni Olivé, who served as the main interface between the Program Committee and the local organization team. We also thank the ER Steering Committee Liaison, David W. Embley, for providing directional instructions as well as paper reviewing assistance in cases of need. Our work was made easier by relying on the MyReview conference management system, developed by Philippe Rigaux.

Finally, we would like to thank all the authors of the submitted papers, whether accepted or not, for their contribution in maintaining the high quality of this conference. We count on all your continual support in the future in making significant contributions to the conceptual modeling community.

Qing Li
Stefano Spaccapietra
Eric Yu

ER 2008 Conference Organization

Honorary Conference Chair

Peter Chen   Louisiana State University, USA

General Conference Chair

Antoni Olivé   Universitat Politècnica de Catalunya, Spain

Program Committee Co-chairs

Qing Li	City University of Hong Kong, China
Stefano Spaccapietra	École Polytechnique Fédérale de Lausanne, Switzerland
Eric Yu	University of Toronto, Canada

Organization Co-chairs

Ernest Teniente	Universitat Politècnica de Catalunya, Spain
Joan A. Pastor	Universitat Oberta Catalunya, Spain

Workshops Co-chairs

Il-Yeol Song	Drexel University, USA
Mario Piattini	Universidad de Castilla, La Mancha, Spain

PhD Workshops Co-chairs

John Mylopoulos	University of Toronto, Canada
Jordi Cabot	Universitat Oberta Catalunya, Spain
Giancarlo Guizzardi	Federal University of Espírito Santo, Brazil Laboratory for Applied Ontology ISTC-CNR, Italy

Demos Co-chairs

Martin Gogolla	University of Bremen, Germany
Juan Carlos Trujillo	Universidad de Alicante, Spain

Tutorials Co-chairs

Jolita Ralyté	University of Geneva, Switzerland
Vicente Pelechano	Universidad Politécnica de Valencia, Spain

Panels Co-chairs

Paul Johannesson	Stockholm University and the Royal Institute of Technology, Sweden
Pericles Loucopoulos	Loughborough University, UK

Steering Committee Liaison

David W. Embley	Brigham Young University, USA

Local Organization

Sponsor Chairs	Maria R. Sancho, Joan A. Pastor
Publicity Chair	Jordi Cabot
Treasurer	Cristina Gómez
Webmasters	Jordi Conesa, Xavier de Palol
Venue Chair	Dolors Costal
Social Events Co-chairs	Enric Mayol, Ruth Raventós
Registration Co-chairs	Anna Queralt, Elena Planas, Albert Tort

Program Committee

Carlo Batini	Università degli studi di Milano-Bicocca, Italy
Sonia Bergamaschi	Università di Modena e Reggio Emilia, Italy
Philip Bernstein	Microsoft Research, USA
Alex Borgida	Rutgers University, USA
Boualem Benatallah	University of New South Wales , Australia
Mokrane Bouzeghoub	Université de Versailles, France
Shawn Bowers	UC Davis Genome Center, USA
Isabelle Comyn-Wattiau	CNAM and ESSEC, France
Philippe Cudre-Mauroux	EPFL, Switzerland
Bernardo Cuenca Grau	University of Manchester, UK
Ernesto Damiani	University of Milan, Italy
Mathieu d'Aquin	The Open University, UK
Valeria De Antonellis	University of Brescia, Italy
Olga De Troyer	Vrije Universiteit Brussel, Belgium
Lois Delcambre	Portland State University, USA
Jan Dietz	Delft University of Technology, The Netherlands
Hans-Dieter Ehrich	Technische Universität Braunschweig, Germany

Colette Rolland   Université Paris 1, France
Matti Rossi   Helsinki School of Economics, Finland
Motoshi Saeki   Tokyo Institute of Technology, Japan
Monica Scannapieco   Università degli Studi di Roma "La Sapienza", Italy
Klaus-Dieter Schewe   Massey University, New Zealand
Marc H. Scholl   University of Konstanz, Germany
Keng Siau   University of Nebraska-Lincoln, USA
Il-Yeol Song   Drexel University, USA
Veda Storey   Georgia State University, USA
Heiner Stuckenschmidt   Universität Mannheim, Germany
Rudi Studer   Institut AIFB - Universität Karlsruhe (TH), Germany
Andrei Tamilin   Bruno Kessler Foundation - IRST, Italy
Dimitri Theodoratos   New Jersey Institute of Technology, USA
Guy De Tré   Ghent University, Belgium
Juan Trujillo   University of Alicante, Spain
Holger Wache   University of Applied Sciences Northwestern
                                       Switzerland (FHNW), Switzerland
Gerd Wagner   Brandenburg University of Technology, Germany
X.Sean Wang   University of Vermont, USA
Kyu-Young Whang   Korea Advanced Inst. of Science and Technology,
                                       Korea
Roel Wieringa   University of Twente, The Netherlands
Carson Woo   University of British Columbia, Canada
Jian Yang   Macquarie University, Australia
Dongqing Yang   Peking University, China
Jeffrey Yu   Chinese University of Hong Kong, China
Yanchun Zhang   Victoria University, Australia
Shuigeng Zhou   Fudan University, China
Esteban Zimányi   Université Libre de Bruxelles, Belgium

External Referees

Carola Aiello	Yi-Shiang Chang	Virginia Franqueira
Sofia Athenikos	Po-Chia Chen	Renata Galante
George Baryannis	Chi-Wei Chen	Michael Grossniklaus
Domenico Beneventano	Dickson Chiu	Christian Gruen
Jesus Bermudez	Philipp Cimiano	Francesco Guerra
Serge Boucher	Andreas Classen	Peter Haase
Vanessa Braganholo	Fabiano Dalpiaz	Hakim Hacid
Petra Brosch	Jérôme David	Yanan Hao
Jordi Cabot	Antonio De Nicola	Dat Hoang
Cinzia Cappiello	Giovanni Denaro	Siv Hilde Houmb
Marco Antonio Casanova	Matteo Di Gioia	Horst Kargl
Sven Casteleyn	Ion-Mircea Diaconescu	Zoubida Kedad
Syin Chan	Cédric Du Mouza	Woralak Kongdenfha
Wen-Hsin Chang	Flavio Antonio Ferrarotti	Kiriakos Kritikos

Nadira Lammari
Chan Le Duc
Ki Jung Lee
Jonathan Lemaitre
Mario Lezoche
Sebastian Link
Hong-Cheu Liu
Jung-Bin Luo
Jiangang Ma
Svetlana Mansmann
Leonardo Mariani
Raimundas Matulevicius
Christian Meilicke
Sergio Mergen
Milan Milanovic
Irena Mlynkova
Mirella Moro
Hamid Motahari
Hans Mulder
Kreshnik Musaraj
Vivi Nastase
Martin Necasky
Wee Siong Ng
Oana Nicolae
Mirko Orsini

Matteo Palmonari
Emilian Pascalau
Gabriella Pasi
Bram Pellens
Verónika Peralta
Laura Po
Elaheh Pourabbas
Nicolas Prat
Rodolfo Resende
Marco Rospocher
Raul Ruggia
Seung Ryu
Deise Saccol
Antonio Sala
Ana Carolina Salgado
Yacine Sam
Germain Saval
Anne Schlicht
Martina Seidl
Frédéric Servais
Samira Si-Saïd Cherfi
Tomas Skopal
Stefanos Souldatos
George Stoilos
Ljiljana Stojanovic

Nenad Stojanovic
Francesco Taglino
Puay-Siew Tan
Aries Tao
Rainer Telesko
Linda Terlouw
Bernhard Thalheim
Ornsiri Thonggoom
Thanh Tran
Thu Trinh
Pascal van Eck
Steven van Kervel
Boris Verhaegen
Maurizio Vincini
Gianluigi Viscusi
Denny Vrandecic
Hung Vu
Bing-Jyun Wang
Qing Wang
Yi Wang
Rob Weemhoff
Xiaoying Wu
Zhong-Jer Yeh
Lucas Zamboulis
Jane Zhao

Organized by

Universitat Politècnica de Catalunya
Universitat Oberta de Catalunya

Sponsored by

The ER Institute
Commissionat Universitats i Recerca (Generalitat de Catalunya)
Ministerio de Educación y Ciencia (Gobierno de España)
Elsevier
Universitat Internacional de Catalunya
Universitat Politècnica de Catalunya
Universitat Oberta de Catalunya
Grupo Alarcos (Universidad de Castilla-La Mancha)

In Cooperation with

ACM SIGMIS
ACM SIGMOD

Table of Contents

Keynotes

Conceptual Modeling Meets the Human Genome 1
   Óscar Pastor

Relationship Web: Spinning the Web from Trailblazing to Semantic
Analytics 12
   Amit Sheth

PIM Meets Web 2.0 15
   Moira C. Norrie

Novel Semantics

Developing Preference Band Model to Manage Collective Preferences ... 26
   Wilfred Ng

A Conceptual Modeling Framework for Expressing Observational Data
Semantics 41
   Shawn Bowers, Joshua S. Madin, and Mark P. Schildhauer

Towards a Compositional Semantic Account of Data Quality
Attributes 55
   Lei Jiang, Alex Borgida, and John Mylopoulos

Ontology

A Formal Model of Fuzzy Ontology with Property Hierarchy and
Object Membership 69
   Yi Cai and Ho-fung Leung

What's in a Relationship: An Ontological Analysis 83
   Giancarlo Guizzardi and Gerd Wagner

An Upper Level Ontological Model for Engineering Design Performance
Domain 98
   Vadim Ermolayev, Natalya Keberle, and Wolf-Ekkehard Matzke

Patterns

A Multi-level Methodology for Developing UML Sequence Diagrams 114
   Il-Yeol Song, Ritu Khare, Yuan An, and Margaret Hilsbos

Content Ontology Design Patterns as Practical Building Blocks for
Web Ontologies 128
    Valentina Presutti and Aldo Gangemi

Quality Patterns for Conceptual Modelling 142
    Samira Si-Saïd Cherfi, Isabelle Comyn-Wattiau, and Jacky Akoka

Privacy, Compliance, Location

Automating the Extraction of Rights and Obligations for Regulatory
Compliance 154
    Nadzeya Kiyavitskaya, Nicola Zeni, Travis D. Breaux,
    Annie I. Antón, James R. Cordy, Luisa Mich, and John Mylopoulos

Location-Based Software Modeling and Analysis: Tropos-Based
Approach 169
    Raian Ali, Fabiano Dalpiaz, and Paolo Giorgini

Risk Evaluation for Personal Identity Management Based on Privacy
Attribute Ontology 183
    Mizuho Iwaihara, Kohei Murakami, Gail-Joon Ahn, and
    Masatoshi Yoshikawa

Process mgt and Design

Beyond Control-Flow: Extending Business Process Configuration to
Roles and Objects 199
    Marcello La Rosa, Marlon Dumas, Arthur H.M. ter Hofstede,
    Jan Mendling, and Florian Gottschalk

Value-Driven Coordination Process Design Using Physical Delivery
Models 216
    Roel Wieringa, Vincent Pijpers, Lianne Bodenstaff, and
    Jaap Gordijn

Relaxed Compliance Notions in Adaptive Process Management
Systems 232
    Stefanie Rinderle-Ma, Manfred Reichert, and Barbara Weber

Process Models

On Measuring Process Model Similarity Based on High-Level Change
Operations 248
    Chen Li, Manfred Reichert, and Andreas Wombacher

Recommendation Based Process Modeling Support: Method and User
Experience 265
    Thomas Hornung, Agnes Koschmider, and Georg Lausen

On the Formal Semantics of Change Patterns in Process-Aware
Information Systems 279
Stefanie Rinderle-Ma, Manfred Reichert, and Barbara Weber

Queries

Modeling and Querying E-Commerce Data in Hybrid Relational-XML
DBMSs 294
Lipyeow Lim, Haixun Wang, and Min Wang

Approximate Probabilistic Query Answering over Inconsistent
Databases 311
Sergio Greco and Cristian Molinaro

Conjunctive Query Containment under Access Limitations 326
Andrea Calì and Davide Martinenghi

Similarity and Coherence

Automatic Extraction of Structurally Coherent Mini-Taxonomies 341
Khalid Saleem and Zohra Bellahsene

Analysis and Reuse of Plots Using Similarity and Analogy 355
*Antonio L. Furtado, Marco A. Casanova,
Simone D.J. Barbosa, and Karin K. Breitman*

Discovering Semantically Similar Associations (SeSA) for Complex
Mappings between Conceptual Models 369
Yuan An and Il-Yeol Song

Space and Time

An Adverbial Approach for the Formal Specification of Topological
Constraints Involving Regions with Broad Boundaries 383
Lotfi Bejaoui, François Pinet, Michel Schneider, and Yvan Bédard

Capturing Temporal Constraints in Temporal ER Models 397
Carlo Combi, Sara Degani, and Christian S. Jensen

Temporal Constraints in Non-temporal Data Modelling Languages 412
Peter McBrien

System Design

Integrated Model-Driven Development of Goal-Oriented Data
Warehouses and Data Marts...................................... 426
Jesús Pardillo and Juan Trujillo

Design Metrics for Data Warehouse Evolution 440
George Papastefanatos, Panos Vassiliadis, Alkis Simitsis, and
Yannis Vassiliou

A Domain Engineering Approach for Situational Method Engineering... 455
Anat Aharoni and Iris Reinhartz-Berger

Translation, Transformation, and Search

RETUNE: Retrieving and Materializing Tuple Units for Effective
Keyword Search over Relational Databases 469
Guoliang Li, Jianhua Feng, and Lizhu Zhou

Model Driven Specification of Ontology Translations 484
Fernando Silva Parreiras, Steffen Staab, Simon Schenk, and
Andreas Winter

Dealing with Usability in Model Transformation Technologies.......... 498
Jose Ignacio Panach, Sergio España, Ana M. Moreno, and
Óscar Pastor

Demo

Ontology Coordination: The iCoord Project Demonstration 512
Silvana Castano, Alfio Ferrara, Davide Lorusso, and
Stefano Montanelli

Designing Similarity Measures for XML 514
Ismael Sanz, María Pérez, and Rafael Berlanga

SESQ: A Model-Driven Method for Building Object Level Vertical
Search Engines 516
Ling Lin, Yukai He, Hang Guo, Ju Fan, Lizhu Zhou, Qi Guo, and
Gang Li

HealthSense: An Application for Querying Raw Sensor Data........... 518
Fabrice Camous, Dónall McCann, and Mark Roantree

Visual SQL: Towards ER-Based Object-Relational Database
Querying 520
Bernhard Thalheim

SAMSTAR: An Automatic Tool for Generating Star Schemas from an
Entity-Relationship Diagram 522
Il-Yeol Song, Ritu Khare, Yuan An, Suan Lee, Sang-Pil Kim,
Jinho Kim, and Yang-Sae Moon

Constraint-Aware XSLT Evaluation 524
Ming Li, Murali Mani, and Elke A. Rundensteiner

A Quality Circle Tool for Software Models 526
  Hendrik Voigt and Thomas Ruhroth

Generating and Optimizing Graphical User Interfaces for Semantic
Service Compositions 528
  Eran Toch, Iris Reinhartz-Berger, Avigdor Gal, and Dov Dori

REMM-Studio⁺: Modeling Variability to Enable Requirements Reuse... 530
  Begoña Moros, Cristina Vicente-Chicote, and Ambrosio Toval

A Conceptual-Model-Based Computational Alembic for a Web of
Knowledge 532
  David W. Embley, Stephen W. Liddle, Deryle Lonsdale,
  George Nagy, Yuri Tijerino, Robert Clawson, Jordan Crabtree,
  Yihong Ding, Piyushee Jha, Zonghui Lian, Stephen Lynn,
  Raghav K. Padmanabhan, Jeff Peters, Cui Tao, Robby Watts,
  Charla Woodbury, and Andrew Zitzelberger

MDBE: Automatic Multidimensional Modeling 534
  Oscar Romero and Alberto Abelló

Oryx – Sharing Conceptual Models on the Web 536
  Gero Decker, Hagen Overdick, and Mathias Weske

Providing Top-K Alternative Schema Matchings with OntoMatcher ... 538
  Haggai Roitman, Avigdor Gal, and Carmel Domshlak

Role and Request Based Conceptual Modeling – A Methodology and a
CASE Tool.. 540
  Yair Wand, Carson Woo, and Ohad Wand

AutoMed Model Management 542
  Andrew Smith, Nikos Rizopoulos, and Peter McBrien

QUINST: A Metamodeling Tool 544
  Xavier Burgués, Xavier Franch, and Josep M. Ribó

An Implementation of a Query Language with Generalized
Quantifiers 547
  Antonio Badia, Brandon Debes, and Bin Cao

Author Index 549

Conceptual Modeling Meets the Human Genome

Oscar Pastor

Centro de Investigación en Métodos de Producción de Software –PROS-.
Universidad Politécnica de Valencia
Camino de Vera s/n, 46022 Valencia, Spain
opastor@dsic.upv.es

Abstract. Looking backwards, it makes sense to discuss the value that Conceptual Modeling has provided to the Information Systems Design and Development area. Thinking about the present, the most advanced Software Engineering approaches oriented to producing quality software propose using extensively conceptual model-based approaches. Conceptual Modeling is widely used in the Information Systems domain. Nevertheless, in terms of Conceptual Model Evolution, we should wonder which new application domains will become more challenging for Conceptual Modeling in the very near future. In an attempt to answer that question, one path to follow is associated to the Bioinformatics domain and specifically, to confront the problem of precise understanding of the Human Genome. The problems related to this topic have become first-order issues in which, curiously, the role of Conceptual Modeling has not yet been fully exploited. The comprehension of the Human Genome is an extremely attractive topic for future research taking into account the continuous and increasing interest that is being generated. Therefore, it is worth analyzing how Conceptual Modeling principles, methods and techniques could help to face the problem and how Conceptual Modeling could aid to provide more efficient solutions. The basic goal of this talk will be the introduction and the discussion of these ideas. If we look at the Human Genome as the representation of some Conceptual Model –which is not yet known-, interesting analogies with the modern Model-Driven Software Development principles appear. As a precise interpretation of the Human Genome would be much easier if the underlying model were known, Conceptual Modeling can provide new ways of facing that problem in order to obtain new and better strategies and solutions.

Keywords: Conceptual Modeling, Bioinformatics, Human Genome.

1 Introduction

If we look at the past, it makes sense to discuss the strong value that Conceptual Modeling has provided to Information Systems Design and Development. If we look at the present, we see how the most advanced Software Engineering approaches, which are oriented to producing software with the required quality, extensively use models under the acronyms of Model Driven Development (MDD), Model-Based Code Generation (MBCD), Model-Driven Architectures (MDA), etc. Nowadays, Conceptual Modeling is widely used in the Information Systems domain. If we look

Q. Li et al. (Eds.): ER 2008, LNCS 5231, pp. 1–11, 2008.

at the future, we could wonder what kind of new application domains could become more challenging for Conceptual Modeling.

Specifically, the Bioinformatics domain in general (and the understanding of the Human Genome in particular) are currently considered to be first-order issues, where the role of Conceptual Modeling has not yet been fully exploited. Considering the continuous and increasing interest of this domain, analyzing how Conceptual Modeling principles, methods and techniques could help to improve the current ways of facing the problem and how Conceptual Modeling could help to provide more efficient solutions, is an extremely attractive topic.

The introduction and the discussion of these ideas are the basic goals of this keynote speech. Describing the Human Genome as a representation of some mainly still unknown Conceptual Model, analogies with the main Model-Driven Software Development conventional principles will be analyzed in order to achieve a precise interpretation of the Human Genome.

Current and future scenarios based on these ideas will be introduced. If Conceptual Modeling is being an effective approach for providing a sound linkage between concepts and their associated software representation –facilitating the understanding of where programs (seen as conceptual model representations) come from-, why not conclude that Conceptual Modeling can be equally effective in understanding the Human Genome (seen as a representation of a Conceptual Model) by extracting the concepts that are behind it? Since the interpretation of the Human Genome is a big challenge for the scientific community, the use of Conceptual Modeling-based notions and methods to undertake this problem will open exciting scenarios finding more efficient scientific strategies with their corresponding set of original solutions, tools and subsequent practical applications.

2   Will Genome Conceptual Modelling Really Make Things Better?

Why use Conceptual Modelling for understanding genomic information? How can the application of Conceptual Modeling techniques help to improve the current strategies that are used to confrontfor facing that challenging problem? These are the main questions to be answered in this talk. Firstly, virtually everything that is known about genomes and genome expression has been discovered by scientific research: it is said to be quite normal to learn "facts" about genomes without knowing very much about "why" they happen as discovered. This lack of conceptual understanding is an interesting first problem.

Secondly, understanding requires precise definitions. Too often, vague descriptions appear associated to basic bioinformatics concepts. This imprecise definition of concepts is a second problem. As already commented in [1], the provision of clear and intuitive models is fundamental to be able to have an effective description and management of genomic data. Also, we read in [2] that the idealistic goals of systems and synthetic biology will not be feasible without the engaged contribution of computer scientists. The role of Computer Scientists should not be limited to the implementation level. Indeed, I would like to emphasize that the role of Conceptual Modeling is still more important. We could say that the conventional view of a computer scientist in the Bioinformatics domain is that of an engineer providing more processing power and more refined algorithms intended to process larger and larger amounts of information, normally trying to discover or infer specific patterns in the genome. Instead, a computer scientist should be perceived as a conceptual modeller of reality, in this case, as a modeller of how life works.

That fundamental conceptual perspective is too often just not present. If biological cells are seen as an alternative to current hardware, it is logical to conclude that a software analogy should be engineered to direct cells to produce useful artifacts or substances. However models should play a fundamental role in that scenario, as they are considered to play a basic role in what we could call "conventional" software production methods. Additionally, through the use of models, it would become possible to characterize conceptual patterns seen as modelling primitives related to those human aspects that are represented in that "biological" low-level software that the human genome constitutes. In that case, we could reuse the Model-Driven Development (MDD) "metaphor" of moving from the Problem Space (a conceptual model of the human genome now) to the Solution Space (the human beings that constitute its running implementation).

Conceptual Modeling could provide the necessary basis to have a consistent and integrated representation of genomic data. While the biological community is building and dealing with increasingly complex models and simulations of cells and lots of biological entities, it is our belief that conceptual models can improve communication among the involved actors. Through the use of conceptual models, it will be possible to fix the relevant concepts, abstracting those biological system components that are really required to describe and understand how the human genome works. By having a proper conceptual model, the relevant biological information will be preserved and understood by all the different researchers involved in the challenge of interpreting the human genome. Models are useful to provide different views of the relevant information that are properly adapted to different user needs. Another important issue is that such a conceptual model should include both system structure and system behaviour. On the one hand, a data model must be provided to characterize the static system architecture, specifying the classes and their relationships that make up the structural genome. On the other hand, a process model has to fix the behaviour that is attached to this structure. In most of the text books about biological systems, functional biological information often appears to be drawn with somewhat inconsistent or at least highly complicated nodes and arrows. As a consequence the readers are often confused because a vague view about how a biological system works is provided to them, especially when they do not have enough knowledge about the biological systems. Putting the information in a Process Diagram –which is complementary to the former Entity-Relationship Diagram- will package the precise information required to understand the basic structure and the subsequent behaviour of the involved biological complex system that is analyzed.

In that context, understanding how a genome specifies the biochemical capability of a living cell, and subsequently, the rules that determine our perceived behaviour, is the major research challenge of modern Bioinformatics. Conceptual Modeling can provide extremely attractive and efficient answers to this challenge. In the next section, we are going to explain in further detail that process of conceptual modelling analysis, starting from a basic entity-relationship modelling intended to characterize the structural view of the genome. This view should be complemented with the subsequent process modelling perspective, which is not dealt with in this paper although it will be briefly analyzed in the talk. This behavioural model includes the processes of transcription –in which individual genes are copied into RNA molecules- and translation -where the proteins that make up the proteome (the cell's repertoire of proteins) are synthesized by translation of the individual RNA molecules present in the transcriptome (RNA copies of the active protein-coding genes). According to this genome taxonomy, transcriptome (the result of the transcription process) and proteome (the result of the translation process) ([8]), we are going to focus our next modelling efforts on the Genome, seen as a store of biological information that is in its own unable to release that information to the cell, because the utilization of its biological information requires the coordinated activity of enzymes and other proteins which participate in a complex series of biochemical reactions referred to as genome expression.

3   A Conceptual Schema for the Human Genome

If, for instance, we want to elaborate an Entity-Relationship Diagram to represent the basic genomic concepts, their precise definition will be a need. At least, we are forced to determine in detail what we mean by any given concept. A common agreement in a shared definition for such a fundamental concept as the "gene" concept becomes an extremely interesting issue. We could start saying that the most modern definition basically accepts that a gene is a union of genomic sequences encoding a coherent set of potentially overlapping functional products ([3],[4]). This definition manifests how integral the concept of biological function is in defining genes: they are not characterized by their precise structure, which probably exists, but which is mostly still unknown. What precisely characterizes a gene is what it does from a functional perspective, specifically which protein or proteins it can exactly code.

However, as stated above, things are not so simple. When a Conceptual Modeler enters the game of understanding what exactly a gene is, and when one tries to characterize the "gene" entity, it is surprising to see how many different definitions exist, and how difficult it becomes to fix the subset of observable properties associated to the gene notion, as position (start and end of the DNA chain), sequence of nucleotides, etc. that should allow a gene in a DNA chain to be identified uniquely. These properties can vary in different individual of the same specie. In other modelling domains, if this situation occurs, one external property is added to the object to identify it. For instance, a tree in a forest or sheep in a flock can be labelled. But it is not so easy to label a gene within a DNA chain. In the genomic data repositories, genes are named, but that name is even not unique.

In the literature, there are different gene definitions that come from different prominent authors and works. Currently, there are clear discrepancies between what we could call a previous protein-centric view of the gene, and one that is revealed by the extensive transcriptional activity of the genome. For instance, in [3] and [4], emphasis is placed on genomic sequences at the DNA level and what they do in terms of protein production, while in [5] the point is that at the DNA level, the gene cannot yet be directly identified and the formation of the mRNA and its expression must be analyzed in time and space to characterize the gene function at translation time. Taking into account these works, we could even question whether the gene concept exists as a precise concept! Obviously, when genetists make an experiment and they look for a given gene in an DNA sequence, they find it and they manipulate it with certainty. Furthermore, when they talk about a gene, they know what they are talking about. The immediate conclusion is that observable properties that allow it to be recognized do exist. But which properties we are talking about exactly is not so clear when we enter in further detail. Conceptual Modeling can provide a lot of knowledge in that context.

As an example of these ideas, we now present an Entity-Relationship Diagram to describe a gene. The intention is twofold: i) on the one side, to show how conceptual modelling forces us to understand and to define with precision what we are talking about, and ii) to open the door to implement a concrete database corresponding to the conceptual schema, whose context would be clearly structured and ready to be used as a data repository of reference for further, concrete experimentation. Such a unified database including all the information related with genes, their characteristics and their concise behaviour would constitute a first-order result in the current context, where information is spread in a lot of different repositories, with strong problems of interoperability and often with inconsistencies and useless information.

This problem has been intensively reported in the last years. Ram in [9] discusses how difficult it is to connect all those data sources seamlessly unless all the data is transformed into a common format. Different solutions to try to overcome this problem exist, as those based on using the notion of seed [10], from which an extraction ontology can be generated in order to collect as much related information as possible from online accessible repositories. But in any case all these solutions are always partial solutions, and the underlying problem of lack of uniformly structured data across related biomedical domains is a barrier that is always present.

3.1 A Model for Chromosomes

Even if in this section we restrict ourselves to the gene concept due to obvious size constraints, let us first introduce some basic genome concepts to show the huge amount of complexity associated to the goal of modelling any genome in general, and certainly for the human genome in particular.

In biology, the genome of an organism is its whole hereditary information and is encoded in the DNA (or, for some viruses, RNA). A genome includes all the genetic material present in the cells of an organism. In eukaryote beings – those whose cells are organized into complex structures enclosed within membranes, including a nucleus- genome refers to the DNA contained in the nucleus and organized in chromosomes. A very basic hierarchy of concepts can be seen in Fig.1, where the highest level is constituted by the cell, and the lowest level is made up of chromosomes and genes.

The genome of an organism is a complete genetic sequence on one set of chromosomes. Chromosomes are organized structures of DNA and proteins that are found in cells. A gene is basically a locatable region of genomic sequence, corresponding to a unit of inheritance, although an attempt to define it precisely is the goal of this section.

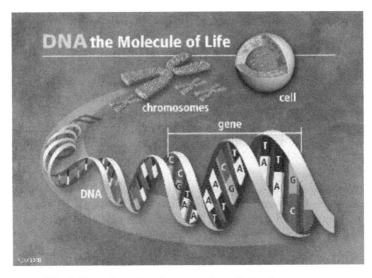

Fig. 1. From the cell to the genes, through the chromosomes

For our modelling purpose, the chromosome segment is the first relevant structure within a chromosome to be specified. By a chromosome segment we refer to i) a set of genic sequences that also includes regulator sequences, or ii) nongenic sequences including other chromosomic elements and intergenic elements. This basic structure is graphically depicted and can be analyzed in Fig. 2.

A chromosome segment could be seen as a DNA sequence constituted by different genic or non-genic sequences. Instead of looking at a chromosome segment as a union of different types of DNA sequences, we will model a chromosome segment as a conceptualization of any relevant type of DNA sequence that is present in a chromosome. From the modelling representation perspective, this means that a specialization relationship will be used instead of an aggregation or association relationship. As we will see later, a parent entity ChromosomeSegment will be specialized in a set of disjoint, descendent entities that represent the different existing, relevant types of chromosome segments. In this way, the chromosomes can be defined as an ordered sequence of chromosome segments that have a precise functionality and that can overlap.

We will refer to these types of chromosome segments as genic and non-genic segments. By a genic segment we mean a DNA segment made up of the following components:

- A Promoter, which is a DNA sequence that controls the start of the transcription process.
- A Transcribed Sequence, constituted by a set of nucleotides that contain the instructions that have to be transcribed and translated in order to synthesize a given protein for a specific gene. It has a precise start and end point defined by particular codons (combinations of three nucleotides with that special function).
- A Terminator, which is a DNA sequence that signals the end of a gene, or more precisely the end of a transcription chain.
- An Enhancer is a DNA sequence that includes the instructions that fix where and how much a gene will express itself.

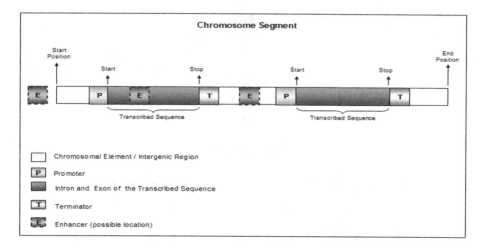

Fig. 2. A chromosome segment can denote either a genic segment (a transcribed sequence, a promoter, a terminator or an enhancer), or a non-genic region which includes non-coding DNA located in between the genic segments

Promoters and terminators are called regulators sequence. To include them in the genic segment is a controversial issue. We have decided to model them in that way, considering that they are an important part in explaining and understanding the gene function. Similarly, how to model the enhancer is an interesting issue. It can be located either within the Transcribed Sequence, or in the non-genic segment, or even it could even be outside of the considered chromosome segment.

The non-genic segments refer to sequences of nucleotides that are considered non transcribable material. Nevertheless, they are part of the chromosome segment as chromosomal elements or intergenic regions, with some particular function probably still unknown. By chromosomal elements we mean the following three different types of regions:

1. ORI, which is are a specific DNA sequence required to start a replication.
2. Centromeres, which are regions that are often found in the middle of the chromosome. They are involved in cell division and the control of gene expression.
3. Telomeres, that constitutes the ending extreme of the chromosomes. They are non-coding DNA regions, which are highly repetitive and which have the main function of assuring chromosome structural stability.

3.2 A Conceptual Schema Proposal for the Human Genome

Taking into account the previous information, we can have an idea of the degree of complexity attached to all the components together with all their interactions involved in the genome structure. In order to understand the genome fundamentals, we propose a Conceptual Schema that could adequately represent all the introduced concepts. This Conceptual Schema, which includes the classes specification, the definition of relationships and the declaration of integrity constraints, provides a basis to fix the main features that are considered relevant to characterize the basic components of the human genome. Fig. 3 presents that proposed schema.

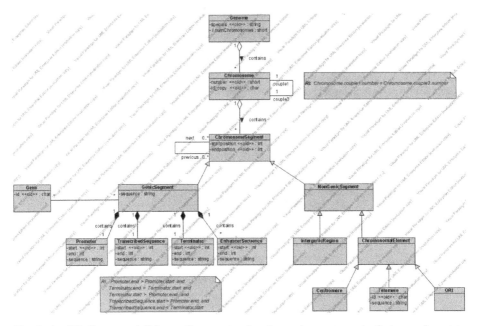

Fig. 3. An ER Conceptual Schema for representing the main components that are relevant to understand the structure of the Human Genome

In this paper, we list the attributes of entities only when these are considered to be important to the understanding of the model as a whole. Obviously, listing all the relevant attributes of all the entities would consume a prohibitive amount of space. Further details will be provided during the keynote address. As usual in the scope of Conceptual Modeling, the final selection of entities, attributes, relationships, cardinalities for relationships, etc. fixes and defines a specific structure that is the result of the modeler decisions, which has direct implications on the intended use of the model in empirical settings. A corresponding database would include the contents according to the model structure. A further characterization of functional products associated to particular genes would have, for instance, a strong impact on the management of biological, biomedical and healthcare knowledge representation. This could, for example, accelerate the development of solutions for the pharmacological and medical industries by benefitting from knowledge reuse and inferencing capabilities.

Many aspects are to be considered, which will be analyzed carefully during the keynote address. The model is full of extremely relevant details. In this short, written presentation, let's mention some of them. For instance, we can observe that:

☐   a genic segment is associated not only with a transcribed sequence, but also with its functionally relevant regulator components: promoter, terminator and enhancer;

☐   inter-chromosome segments do not exist since each chromosome segment only belongs to one chromosome;

☐   chromosome segments are specialized in genic and non-genic segments to represent those parts of the segment that correspond to the genes, and those that represent intergenic regions or chromosomic elements, composed by (at least as far as it is currently known) non-coding DNA sequences;

☐ genes are related to genic segments in a many-to-many way, which covers the gene view as a union of genomic sequences encoding a coherent set of potentially overlapping functional products;

☐ integrity constraints can be specified to declare specific properties. For instance, it appears to be a natural order in the way in which the different types of sequences appear within a genic segment: first, a promoter; then a transcribed sequence; and finally, a terminator. The following constraint based on the start and end attributes of the involved parts could be used to specify that property:

RI: Promoter.end > Promoter.start and
Terminator.end > Terminator.start and
Terminator.start > Promoter.end and
TranscribedSequence.start > Promoter.end and
TranscribedSequence.end < Terminador.start

Broadly speaking, the Conceptual Schema must answer important questions that are present even today in the genomic domain. Is there a distinction between genic and intergenic segments? The Conceptual Schema provides a positive answer by distinguishing between genic and nongenic segments, depending on the coding DNA sequences associated to the rich tapestry of transcription involving alternative splicing. Splicing (including alternative splicing) and intergenic transcription are also some of the most problematic aspects.

Other modeling approaches could be considered. In the works presented in [1] and [6], chromosome segments are specialized in Transcribed and Non-Transcribed regions, instead of the presented specialization of Genic and Non-Genic segments. A Transcribed Region is then associated to a set of Primary Transcripts, while Regulatory Sequences are attached to Non-Transcribed Regions. As regulatory regions are important for gene expression, we suggest that they should be considered as an essential part of the gene, which is in itself a controversial decision. Hence, we assume that regulation is an integral concept in the gene definition, and we adopt the tradition of defining a gene in molecular terms as "the entire nucleic acid sequence that is necessary for the synthesis of a functional polypeptide" ([7])

At the same time, many challenging open problems assure the evolution of the model. It appears that some of the regulatory elements may actually themselves be transcribed. This could mean that promoters, terminators or enhancers could also be seen as transcribed sequences. In that case, integrity constraints such as the one mentioned above would be incorrect. In the extreme, we could even declare the current concept of the gene dead and try to come up with something completely new that fits all the open, not well-solved challenges. Here, we have introduced a tentative attempt to understand the current notion of a gene by means of Conceptual Models. On the one hand, the proposed Conceptual Schema clarifies the currently most accepted definitions, and on the other hand, it leaves the door open to conceptually rethinking and adapting the existing models to the new biogenomic information that is discovered day after day.

4 Conclusions

Imagine for a moment that humans are able to develop to a very sophisticated species of robots, whose specialized behavior is in many aspects a replication of particular human activities. We have seen this kind of fiction in recent, successful movies. Imagine that due to the widely commented current global climate change there is a natural disaster that makes our civilization disappear, while this other silicon-based life –created by humans- persists in time. Imagine for a moment that after centuries of evolution, individuals of that silicon-based species start to wonder about where they come from, and what the fundamentals of their life processes are –which are assumed to be based on binary sequences of 0s and 1s-.

Trying to answer those questions just by exhaustively analyzing the execution model of programs is as difficult as looking for a needle in a haystack. But isn't that just what we humans are doing when we try to understand the working mechanisms of our life by directly exploring our intricate biological-based execution model? In our case, instead of huge sequences of 0s and 1s, we face huge sequences of four nucleotides (A,C,G,T), and we try to discover hidden patterns that should allow us to understand why life processes happen as we perceive them.

How difficult could it be to discover, for instance, the notion of a foreign key –a basic and trivial data modeling concept when it is described at the conceptual modeling perspective- just looking for it in the executable, machine-oriented version of a program? Nevertheless, it is quite trivial to model a foreign key using the DDL of any Relational Data Base Engine. In some sense, within the current Bioinformatics domain, we are looking for the foreign key concept directly in the assembler version of a program. The position of this keynote address is quite clear: this is not the right way.

To understand the program encoded by any genome, we should be able to elaborate and manipulate the models that constitute the source of which a particular implementation is an individual –a human being for the human genome- Conceptual Modeling is consequently a basic strategy that could become the essential approach for guiding the research in Bioinformatics.

We have outlined how a Conceptual Schema can be built to characterize the Human Genome. If such a Conceptual Schema were widely accepted, it would make sense to create a Human Genome database whose contents would include all the essential information to determine which genes synthesize which proteins. As protein elaboration can be associated with particular human behaviors, this will open the door to linking genes with behaviors in order to create a complete catalog of human characteristics. At the same time, this level of understanding can be used to understand the effect of mutations that cause undesired effects –illnesses- and consequently, it would become much more feasible to face and correct them. By applying conceptual modeling-based techniques, we shall not only find ourselves equipped with precise definitions for understanding gene expressions in terms of Molecular Biology, but we shall also be able to devise and apply model-based transformations that could analyze gene storage and expression in terms of information systems processing. This is a real challenge to be overcome by the Conceptual Modeling community in the near future.

References

1. Paton, N., et al.: Conceptual Modeling of Genomic Information. Bioinformatics 16(6), 548–557 (2000)
2. Cohen, J.: The Crucial Role of CS in Systems and Synthetic Biology. Communications of the ACM 51(5) (2008)
3. ENCODE Project Consortium: Identification and Analysis of Functional Elements in 1% of the Human Genome by the Encode Pilot Project. Nature 447, 779–796 (2007), doi:10.1038/nature05874
4. Gerstein, M.B., et al.: What is a gene, post-ENCODE? History and updated definition. Genome Res. 17, 669–681 (2007)
5. Scherrer, K., Jost, J.: Gene and genon concept: coding versus regulation. Theory Biosci. 126, 65–113 (2007)
6. Paton, N., et al.: Conceptual Data Modeling for Bioinformatics. Briefings in Bioinformatics 3(2), 166–180 (2002)
7. Lodish, H., et al.: Molecular cell biology, 5th edn. Freeman and Co., New York (2000)
8. Brown, T.A.: Genome 3. Garland Science Publishing (2007)
9. Ram, S.: Toward Semantic Interoperability of Heterogeneous Biological Data Sources. In: Pastor, Ó., Falcão e Cunha, J. (eds.) CAiSE 2005. LNCS, vol. 3520, p. 32. Springer, Heidelberg (2005)
10. Tao, C., Embley, D.: Seed-Based Generation of Personalized Bio-ontologies for Information Extraction. In: ER Workshops 2007, pp. 74–84 (2007)

Relationship Web: Spinning the Web from Trailblazing to Semantic Analytics

Amit Sheth

Kno.e.sis Center, CSE Department
Wright State University, Dayton OH 45435-0001 USA
amit.sheth@wright.edu

Subject and object convey little without a verb and a few prepositions. Reducing this to the subject-predicate-object representation, subject and object convey little without predicate. Entities are lame without the relationships that associate meaning to them. Concepts can be quite ambiguous without context or domain of discourse. Labels and terms become meaningful when we associate them with a conceptual model or an ontology. Semantics is about meaning and understanding, and relationships are at the heart of semantics. And with semantics we can create more powerful search, achieve interoperability among heterogeneous and multimodal content, and develop more powerful analytic and discovery capabilities.

We believe, as we move from simpler to more demanding activity, from search to integration to analysis and discovery, that the role of semantics becomes more vital and relationships become more central. Dr. Vannevar Bush in his 1945 Atlantic Monthly article outlined Memex, a compelling vision for information processing, in which relationships are pivotal. Describing the human brain navigating an information space in what he called trailblazing, Dr. Bush said, "it operates by association. With one item in its grasp, it snaps instantly to the next that is suggested by the association of thoughts, in accordance with some intricate web of trails carried by the cells of the brain."

Semantic technologies and Semantic Web languages and techniques have opened up a rich playground in which to utilize and benefit from a focus on relationships. There has been substantial progress in entity and relationship extraction from the Web-based text and semi-structured content that builds on longstanding research in IR, information extraction, NLP, statistical NLP, etc. There has also been limited success with entity/object identification from nontextual content. Semantic Web gives us a number of capabilities that enhance our ability to exploit a variety of content and metadata extraction capabilities. These include the following.

- Use of nomenclatures, taxonomies, domain models or ontologies that embody collective understanding and agreements as well as provide factual knowledge to exploit (esp. with populated ontologies), leading to largely automated or semi-automated methods for semantic annotations.
- Use of model reference and microformats to extend XML-based language with semantic annotations (e.g., SAWSDL for WSDL and XML schemas, SA-REST for RESTful services and WebAPIs[1], SML-S for sensor markup language[2]).

---

[1] http://knoesis.org/research/srl/standards/sa-rest/
[2] http://knoesis.org/research/semsci/application_domain/sem_sensor/

Q. Li et al. (Eds.): ER 2008, LNCS 5231, pp. 12–14, 2008.

- Using semantic metadata to enrich links (i.e., HREF) or to define semantic relationships between Web resources. For example, Metadata Reference Links was defined as a method to add semantic metadata or facets to HREF or to define relationships between any Web resources (including entities and concepts within Web pages that may not have been linked a priori by a HREF).
- Ability to express semantic data in RDF, which enables representation of relationships as first-class objects, and richer knowledge representation languages for representing ontologies.
- Support for graph-based and inferencing techniques that deal with manipulation of relationships for the discovery of multi-relational connection patterns between entities.

Capabilities such as those described above support definition and exploitation of a broad set of implicit and explicit linguistic and formal relationships [4] between Web content and resources, independent of explicitly encoded or generated links. This meta-web in which relationships interconnect with Web content and resources is what we call the Relationship Web.

What metadata, annotation, and labeling are to the Semantic Web, relationships of all forms (implicit, explicit, and formal) are to the Relationship Web. The focus on relationships lead in turn to such advanced capabilities as:

- Faceted search: Early this decade we developed a semantic search (also called faceted search) called Taalee Semantic search engine ([7]). A more recent example is that of Power Set's semantic search.
- Semantic Analytics: This includes semantic association discovery that involve finding meaningful paths and subgraphs, similarity, causality and other pattern discovery.3
- Trailblazing: development of an interactive, human-directed, semantic browsing environment in which users can explore heterogeneous content from disparate sources in a kind of stream of consciousness, identifying one item of interest and then following contextually relevant links to another. Our recent work [2] on semantic metadata extraction from text has allowed us to create such a browser for biomedical literature. Combining this with data in existing curated data sources, this vision of Semantic trails can be realized.
- Spatio-temporal-thematic (or spatio-temoral-thematic) query processing and reasoning, leading to EventWeb [1].
- Hypothesis validation: a complementary form of analysis that allows the specification of a complex, potentially underspecified hypotheses composed of entities connected by relationships with constraints on these relationships expressed as edge weights. Corroborating evidence for these hypotheses might be gleaned from textual as well as structured sources. We envision a system supporting piece-meal corroboration of hypothesis fragments, thereby affording the user an investigatory tool for heterogeneous data sources.

In this talk, we will weave a number of explorations focused on relationships and provide several examples from the domains for biomedical research, health care and

---

3 http://knoesis.wright.edu/projects/semdis/

Semantic Sensor Web that have been developed or are being developed in collaboration with the scientists and users. Complementary discussions can also be found in [3, 5].

References

1. Jain, R.: EventWeb: Developing a Human Centered Computing System. IEEE Computer, 42–50 (February 2008)
2. Ramakrishnan, C., Mendes, P., Wang, S., Sheth, A.: Unsupervised Discovery of Compound Entities for Relationship Extraction. In: Gangemi, A., Euzenat, J. (eds.) EKAW 2008. LNCS(LNAI), vol. 5268. Springer, Heidelberg (2008)
3. Sheth, A., Arpinar, I.B., Kashyap, V.: Relationships at the Heart of Semantic Web: Modeling, Discovering and Exploiting Complex Semantic Relationships. In: Nikravesh, et al. (eds.) Enhancing the Power of the Internet Studies in Fuzziness and Soft Computing. Springer, Heidelberg (2003)
4. Sheth, A., Ramakrishnan, C., Thomas, C.: Semantics for the Semantic Web: the Implicit, the Formal and the Powerful. Intl. Journal on Semantic Web and Information Systems 1(1), 1–18 (2005)
5. Sheth, A., Ramakrishnan, C.: Relationship Web: Blazing Semantic Trails between Web Resources. IEEE Internet Computing 11(4), 84–88 (2007)
6. Shah, K., Sheth, A.: Logical information modeling of Web-accessible heterogeneous digital assets. In: Proc. of the Advances in Digital Libraries (ADL 1998), April 1998, pp. 266–275 (1998)
7. Sheth, A., et al.: Semantic Content Management for Enterprises and the Web. Technical report, IEEE Internet Computing, July-August, pp. 80–87 (2002)

PIM Meets Web 2.0

Moira C. Norrie

Institute for Information Systems, ETH Zurich
CH-8092 Zurich, Switzerland
norrie@inf.ethz.ch

Abstract. Web 2.0 refers to a new generation of web applications designed to support collaboration and the sharing of user-generated content. These applications are increasingly being used, not just to share personal information, but also to manage it. For example, a user might use Facebook to manage their photos and personal contacts, a networking site such as LinkedIn to manage professional contacts and various project Wiki sites to manage and share information about publications and presentations. As a result, personal data and its management become fragmented, not only across desktop applications, but also between desktop applications and various Web 2.0 applications. We look at personal information management (PIM) issues in the realm of Web 2.0, showing how the respective communities might profit from each other.

1 Introduction

The term Web 2.0 has been adopted to refer to a new generation of web applications specifically designed to support collaboration and the sharing of user-generated content [1]. Applications commonly classified under Web 2.0 include social networking sites such as Facebook, sites to share and manage multimedia content such as YouTube and sites that support collaborative authoring such as Wikipedia.

Web 2.0 applications are increasingly being used not just to share personal information, but also to manage it. For example, a user might use Facebook to manage personal contacts and photos, networking sites such as LinkedIn to manage professional contacts and various project Wiki sites to manage information about publications and presentations. As a result, personal data and its management becomes fragmented, not only across desktop applications, but also between desktop applications and various Web 2.0 applications.

We propose that there should be a clear separation of concerns between *publishing data* and *managing data* with the former being the task of Web 2.0 applications and the latter the task of personal information management (PIM) systems. Further, the PIM system should provide an *integrated solution* to the management of all forms of personal information management, whether related to social or professional activities of the user, and it should also be responsible for controlling where, when and how information is published to Web 2.0 applications.

Q. Li et al. (Eds.): ER 2008, LNCS 5231, pp. 15–25, 2008.

At the same time, we believe that the developers of PIM systems can learn valuable lessons from the popularity of Web 2.0 applications when it comes to designing systems for the management of personal data. Sites such as Facebook provide simple, intuitive interfaces along with a plug-and-play architecture that allows users to easily select and combine applications. Further, users can even create and share their own applications.

In this paper, we examine personal information management issues in the realm of Web 2.0, showing how the respective communities might profit from each other. We start by examining some of the data management issues related to Web 2.0 applications in Sect. 2. In Sect. 3, we then discuss the recent renewal of interest in PIM systems within the research community and outline the main approaches proposed in various research projects. Following on from these discussions, we present an architecture designed to develop an integrated solution to data management for PIM and Web 2.0 in Sect. 4 and outline our on-going work in this area. Concluding remarks are given in Sect. 5.

2   Data Management for Web 2.0

As mentioned previously, Web 2.0 applications include social networking sites such as Facebook, Xing and LinkedIn, sites to share and manage photos and videos such as Flickr and YouTube, and sites that support collaborative authoring such as project Wikis. While Web 2.0 does not define a particular technology, it is commonly associated with a number of technologies that can support the forms of interaction, collaboration and information sharing characteristic of these applications. For example, Asynchronous JavaScript and XML (AJAX) increases the interactivity and responsiveness of web pages important in many Web 2.0 applications. AJAX toolkits support the development of the required JavaScript and are available for most web scripting languages such as PHP and ASP.NET. To support the development of Web 2.0 applications, Google Web Toolkit (GWT) can be used to transform Java-based applications into AJAX applications.

The term Rich Internet Application (RIA) introduced by Macromedia in 2002 to describe web applications with the same level of interactivity as desktop applications is often used in relationship to Web 2.0 applications. In the early days of web applications, Java Applets were proposed as a technology to support highly interactive applications by downloading Java applications to allow client-side processing. This even included systems where components of a DBMS were downloaded onto the client to improve user interaction [2]. However, later, Java Applets tended to be abandoned in favour of Java Servlets and server-side processing due to various problems such as browser variability, security restrictions and latency. Now that web technologies are more mature, the vision of desktop-style applications being accessible over the web and within browsers is more realistic. Major software companies such as Adobe, Microsoft, Google and Sun Microsystems are all developing tools to make this vision a reality. Examples of technologies that have been developed or extended to support RIA are DHTML, Adobe Flash, Microsoft Silverlight and JavaFX. Based on these technologies, a number of RIA development frameworks have been proposed such as Adobe Flex, Microsoft Popfly and the open-source project OpenLaszlo.

While RIA technologies are designed to support rich interaction which is certainly a characteristic of Web 2.0 applications, they do not specifically support other characteristics such as user participation and collaboration. A Wiki is software that supports collaborative authoring of web sites and the term dates back to 1994 with the emergence of WikiWikiWeb. Wikis have been widely adopted with the best known application being Wikipedia. They are often used nowadays to support research and commercial projects, enabling members of a project team to easily upload and share documents as well as collaboratively authoring design documents and articles.

Another feature of many Web 2.0 applications is the ability to reuse content from existing web sites, often integrating it to provide new or value-added services. Users can create their own applications by combining data from existing web applications through a notion of web mashups[1]. The content is usually generated by RSS or Atom web feeds, screen scraping or public programming interfaces. A common example is to combine data tagged with location information, for example hotels, with Google Maps. Various tools have been developed to allow users to easily combine data from web feeds to create their own mashups, e.g. Yahoo Pipes, Microsoft Popfly and the Google Mashup Editor.

Research within the database community related to Web 2.0, tends to focus mainly on issues of *data integration* of which mashups are one example. A recent joint effort by the University of Illinois and the University of Wisconsin is a project to develop a software platform to set-up and support on-line communities [3]. As a first step, they have developed a community portal DBLife [4] for the database research community that will serve as a driving application for their research. The DBLife systems monitors more than 900 data sources, extracting and integrating data about people, events, publications etc. relevant to the database community. A major research issue that they want to address is how to ensure data quality and part of the proposed solution is the encouragement of user participation.

Having outlined the key ideas and technologies characteristic of Web 2.0 applications, we now turn to consider related research in the field of web engineering. The long-term goal of the web engineering research community is to develop technologies, tools and methods to support the systematic design, development, deployment and maintenance of high quality web applications. This is a major challenge in a field in which new technologies and tools are constantly emerging, but a major influence has been the promotion of model-based approaches. Leading research efforts in this field include WebML [5], Hera [6], WSDM [7], OOHDM [8], OO-H [9], SiteLang [10] and UWE [11]. WebML and Hera stand out as model-based approaches which feature comprehensive implementation platforms. As the requirements of web applications have evolved to deal with features such as multi-channel access, context-awareness and mobility, researchers have

---

[1] http://www.programmableweb.com

addressed how to adapt and extend their models and methods to support these. WebML, in particular, has been enriched several times, using its built-in support for extensibility to introduce additional concepts for the definition of business workflows, web services and context-aware adaptation [12,13]. With the rapid growth in interest in RIA and Web 2.0, a current topic of research within the web engineering communtiy is how to support the design and development of RIA and Web 2.0 applications.

We note that, with few exceptions, research projects in all areas related to Web 2.0 tend to be based on existing data management platforms and there has been little consideration given to how databases could play a more central role in managing all forms of data that define a web application and supporting both the development and operation of a web site. Further, user studies related to Web 2.0 applications have tended to focus on the social networking or collaboration aspects rather than on issues of personal information management. If anything, these issues have only been considered at the level of *data integration* rather than *data management*. Yet, anyone who is a regular user of Web 2.0 applications will be well aware of the rich variety of personal information being managed by these applications and the fact that application support for managing all sorts of data ranging from contacts to photo albums often makes it much more convenient to use a Web 2.0 application than desktop applications. A key advantage of using a Web 2.0 application such as Facebook is the fact that all these applications are integrated in a single, portal-like interface. Also, simple tagging mechanisms allow links to be easily created across applications, for example, between a contact and a photo.

On the down side, personal data often ends up being replicated and fragmented. For example, some personal contacts may be managed using Facebook, while professional contacts are managed using a site such as LinkedIn or Xing. At the same time, a desktop application such as Microsoft Outlook may be used to manage more general contact information including contacts who are not registered on Web 2.0 sites. Photos may be stored on a desktop PC, with subsets uploaded to Web 2.0 sites such as Facebook. Information about publications may be published on one or more project web sites and also personal web sites.

We therefore feel that studies should be undertaken to find out more about *how* and *why* users are managing personal data using Web 2.0 applications. This should include examining the problems of replication and fragmentation of data across Web 2.0 applications as well as between desktop and Web 2.0 applications. Based on these studies, new data management solutions should be developed that will allow personal information to be managed in a convenient, integrated manner and published to Web 2.0 applications as and when required.

3   PIM Systems

Although personal information management (PIM) is a topic that has long been of interest to the research community, particularly with respect to possible replacements for the desktop paradigm, there has been a recent renewal in interest as seen by the series of PIM workshops started in 2005[2]. The workshops are inter-disciplinary, bringing together researchers from various domains including human-computer interaction, information retrieval and databases.

The basic model of managing personal data has changed little over the past decades. Essentially, today's PIM solutions are based on the file system and desktop applications. One problem is the fact that personal information is typically managed by different applications and often stored in different places, making it difficult to handle data uniformly and integrate it in interesting ways. This problem has been referred to as *information fragmentation* [14] or *information compartmentalisation* [15].

The most radical approach is to consider replacing the file system as the basic model underlying PIM with a different model that allows information to be managed and shared in more flexible ways. For example, in the Presto system [16], they developed a notion of shareable document spaces to replace the file/folder means of hiearchically classifying documents within personal spaces. Documents could be freely tagged with properties that could then be used to classify and retrieve documents. One of the major drawbacks of such an approach is the problem of migrating existing data and applications. If applications are to take advantage of the flexibility that new PIM models offer, then they have to be re-designed.

With the dramatic increase in the volume of personal data typically stored by users, researchers in the information retrieval and database communities have become interested in trying to adapt their technologies to the problems of retrieving and processing information stored as personal data. In both cases, they typically build tools on top of existing file systems and applications that can allow data to be extracted and integrated from various documents to meet a user's information needs. For example, in the position paper by Franklin, Halevy and Maier [17], they propose a notion of *dataspace systems* where traditional database technologies such as metadata management, indexing and query processing can be used alongside traditional file systems and applications to support the administration, discovery and enhancement of personal data. This is the approach that has, for example, been adopted in the iMemex system [18].

Both of the above approaches have had limited success to date. One reason for this is that both approaches typically require major efforts in the reengineering of applications or ways of user working. Therefore while they tend to be of theoretical interest, they have had little impact in the everyday use of computers. In the meantime, the development of Web 2.0 applications has caused a dramatic shift in personal information management that has almost gone without remark in the research community. Many users are increasingly shifting away from traditional desktop applications for managing all of their personal information and instead are using Web 2.0 applications. This applies to professional as well as social information since people are increasingly using Web 2.0 applications such as Wikis and community portals not only as a basis for collaboration, but also

---

[2] Information about these workshops, papers and report can be found at http://pim.ischool.washington.edu/

to manage information about publications, articles of interest, bookmarks etc. Also, messaging supported in systems such as Facebook and community portals is now often being used to support asynchronous communication rather than email systems. There are a number of reasons for this trend away from some desktop applications to Web 2.0 applications. One is the nature of Web 2.0 applications to empower the users as information providers and promote information sharing. Thus, a user does not need to create and manage the contact details of friends and colleagues as they do this themselves. By each user providing a small amount of information, the combined effect is a vast information space.

We believe another reason is the very nature of Web 2.0 applications and their portal-style interfaces as discussed in the previous section. Sites such as Facebook provide an integrated solution to the management of all sorts of data through a very simple, intuitive style of interface. While a core set of applications are provided to manage basic information such as contacts, messages, photo albums etc., it is simple for users to install other applications of interest and even to write their own applications. Facebook now offers several thousand applications[3]. This plug-and-play style typical of many Web 2.0 applications makes it easy for users to customise their site in terms of the types of information stored and published, their own visibility, the level of information sharing and also the layout. In addition, Facebook provides a rich networked information space by automatically generating links between information items and applications based on social networks as well as explicit links created by users through image tagging etc. Last but not least, Facebook offers awareness information about the activities of users through status messages and news feeds.

Given the overwhelming success of Web 2.0 applications, we believe that the PIM community could benefit from trying to understand the reasons behind their success and possibly adopting the Web 2.0 paradigm in the design of future PIM systems.

4   Integrating PIM and Web 2.0

Our goal is to provide improved, integrated PIM solutions based on the Web 2.0 paradigm that will at the same time support the publishing and sharing of data through Web 2.0 applications. The information architecture that we aim for is shown in Fig. 1. Each user manages their personal information through an instance of PIM 2.0, a personal information management portal, and users have control over how and when this information is published to one or more Web 2.0 applications. Further, since Web 2.0 applications are about the sharing of user-generated content, it is possible for users to have data published on Web 2.0 applications by other users automatically imported into their own personal information space.

PIM 2.0 has a plug-and-play architecture that allows users to select and even develop their own information management components as and when required.

---

[3] Facebook listed more than 17'600 in February 2008.

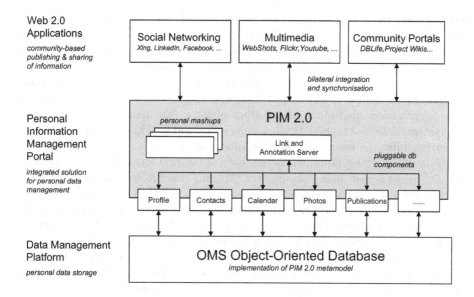

Fig. 1. Information Architecture

We aim to make these *database components* rather than *services* since we want to achieve tight integration at the level of data management to enable us to leverage as much as possible of the database functionality and semantics within PIM 2.0. Also, it should be possible to create links between objects in different database components and to create mashups by integrating data from one or more components. We therefore introduce a general link and annotation server as well as the concept of personal mashups in PIM 2.0.

The concept of plug-and-play architectures at the database level is something that has received little attention to date within the research community. A lot of emphasis has been placed recently on service-oriented architectures and specifically the use of web services, but this is more suited to integration and orchestration at higher levels, especially in heterogeneous environments. We want to be able to integrate components *within* the database in order that we could, for example, introduce constraints and triggers over these components as well as executing queries over them. This in turn would enable the integration of data from different components required for personal mashups to be performed within the database. Currently, we are in the process of formulating precisely a notion of a database component and designing an architecture and mechanism to support this concept. Also, since users should be able to, not only select components, but also develop their own components and personal mashups, we need to investigate how this can best be supported through declarative languages and graphical tools.

To provide improved PIM systems, it is important that the underlying data management platform is based on a semantic data model. Specifically, it should be able to support rich classification structures, versions, constraints, triggers and associations as well as a declarative query language. The ability to support multiple classification is particularly useful as a basic means of specifying which information objects should be published to which Web 2.0 applications. We are using the OMS Avon system [19] as a data management platform for PIM 2.0 since it supports these concepts. OMS Avon provides a semantic data management layer on top of the object database engine db4o[4]. In OMS Avon, all data—application, metadata and system objects—are handled uniformly and the system is bootstrapped from a core metamodel. This provides the basis for its flexibility in being able to integrate new concepts required to meet the demands of emerging domains as has been done previously for web engineering [20], peer-to-peer data management [21] and context-awareness [22,23]. The implementation of the database will be based on a PIM 2.0 metamodel which in turn will take into account the database component concept under development.

An important part of the architecture is the mechanism used to support the various forms of integration and synchronisation required. On the one hand, there needs to be some form of data synchronisation between PIM 2.0 and the Web 2.0 applications that will be the basis behind the publishing of personal information in the Web 2.0 applications. Thus changes to the data in PIM 2.0 should propagate to all Web 2.0 applications that are registered as using that data. We may also want bilateral synchronisation which means that it should also be possible to propagate changes to data in the Web 2.0 applications to PIM 2.0. An example of this would be propagating changes to the contacts information in PIM 2.0 if the corresponding data has been updated in the Web 2.0 application. On the other hand, there also needs to be integration and synchronisation of data within PIM 2.0 across database components. For example, a personal mashup application may integrate data from two or more database components.

The PIM 2.0 architecture that we propose exemplifies the various forms of data integration and synchronisation that are found in many forms of modern distributed information systems, especially those based on web technologies. Therefore it is important to develop general mechanisms that are flexible enough to meet these requirements and can be customised to specific settings. We want to use this project to investigate how we can achieve a general model and associated mechanisms for data integration and synchronisation that can be applied both within object databases and between object databases and external data sources. We therefore propose to investigate how we can generalise and extend the generic proxy mechanism that we recently developed for the integration and synchronisation of OMS Avon databases [24] with external data sources to these more general architectures.

An advantage of the generic proxy approach is that it allows the details of how and when synchronisation takes place to be customised through proxy processes. Also, it supports integration at the database level, which again means that we can leverage database fucntionality and semantics. The generic proxy mechanism was developed for object-oriented databases and we will need to consider how the concept can be adapted and extended to cater for situations where the

---

[4] http://www.db4o.com

data sources are non-OODBMS and possibly heterogeneous. In particular, we need to investigate in detail how we can interface with Web 2.0 applications to achieve bilateral synchronisation. Another key issue is how to ensure that the mechanisms are efficient.

The PIM 2.0 project is in its first phases and there are many open issues. An initial prototype that allows data stored and managed in a personal data space to be published to one or more Web 2.0 applications has already been developed [25]. In the next stage, we will implement a second prototype based on the concept of database components and the plug-and-play architecture. In addition to the issues mentioned above, an important aspect of the project will be the means for users to specify how and where data should be published. Currently we are developing a simple language that can be used to specify the necessary data mappings and also modes of synchronisation. Later, we will design and experiment with various tools to allow these to be specified graphically.

Alongside the technical work, we plan to carry out various user studies. These will cover the use of Web 2.0 applications for personal information management as well as evaluations on the system and tools that we will develop.

5   Conclusions

We have discussed the issue of personal information management in the realm of Web 2.0 and how the problem of information fragmentation has now extended beyond the desktop. We make the case for an architecture that supports a clear separation of concerns between the management of data and the publishing of data. The proposed system PIM 2.0 provides an integrated solution for personal information management based on the Web 2.0 paradigm of a portal with a plug-and-play architecture. The publishing of data to Web 2.0 applications is controlled through a bilateral synchronisation mechanism that also offers the possible automatic importation of data published by other users into a personal information space. Central to the plug-and-play architecture is a notion of database components that allow personal information spaces to be constructed in a modular way.

The concepts presented in the paper are still under discussion and the PIM 2.0 system is in the early stages of design and implementation. However, we are optimistic that significant advances in PIM systems can be achieved by learning from the success of Web 2.0.

Acknowledgements

Many members of the Global Information Systems group at ETH Zurich have contributed to the ideas expressed in this paper. Special thanks are due to Michael Grossniklaus and Stefania Leone who are leading the PIM 2.0 project and Martin Schnyder who has implemented a first prototype.

References

1. O'Reilly, T.: What Is Web 2.0: Design Patterns and Business Models for the Next Generation of Software (2005),
   `http://www.oreillynet.com/pub/a/oreilly/tim/`
   `news/2005/09/30/what-is-web-20.html`
2. Norrie, M.C.: Client-Server Database Architectures for the Web. In: Masunga, Y., Spaccapietra, S. (eds.) Advances in Multimedia and Databases for the New Century, A Swiss/Japanese Perspective (2000)
3. Doan, A., Ramakrishnan, R., Chen, F., DeRose, P., Lee, Y., McCann, R., Sayyadian, M., Shen, W.: Community Information Managemnt. Data Engineering Bulletin 29(1) (2006)
4. DeRose, P., Shen, W., Chen, F., Lee, Y., Burdick, D., Doan, A., Ramakrishnan, R.: DBLife: A Community Information Management Platform for the Database Research Community. In: Proceedings of CIDR 2007 (Demo) (2007)
5. Ceri, S., Fraternali, P., Bongio, A., Brambilla, M., Comai, S., Matera, M.: Designing Data-Intensive Web Applications. The Morgan Kaufmann Series in Data Management Systems. Morgan Kaufmann Publishers Inc., San Francisco (2002)
6. Fräsincar, F., Barna, P., Houben, G.J., Fiala, Z.: Adaptation and Reuse in Designing Web Information Systems. In: Proceedings of International Conference on Information Technology: Coding and Computing, Las Vegas, NV, USA, April 2-4 (2004)
7. Casteleyn, S., De Troyer, O., Brockmans, S.: Design Time Support for Adaptive Behavior in Web Sites. In: Proceedings of ACM Symposium on Applied Computing, Melbourne, FL, USA, March 9-12 (2003)
8. Rossi, G., Schwabe, D., Guimarães, R.: Designing Personalized Web Applications. In: Proceedings of International World Wide Web Conference, Hong Kong, China, May 1-5 (2001)
9. Garrigós, I., Casteleyn, S., Gómez, J.: A Structured Approach to Personalize Websites Using the OO-H Personalization Framework. In: Proc. Asia Pacific Web Conf., Shanghai, China (2005)
10. Schewe, K.D., Thalheim, B.: Reasoning About Web Information Systems Using Story Algebras. In: Proceedings of East-European Conference on Advances in Databases and Information Systems, Budapest, Hungary, September 22-25, 2004, pp. 54–66 (2004)
11. Koch, N.: Software Engineering for Adaptive Hypermedia Systems. PhD thesis, Ludwig-Maximilians-University Munich, Munich, Germany (2001)
12. Ceri, S., Daniel, F., Matera, M., Facca, F.M.: Model-driven Development of Context-Aware Web Applications. ACM Transactions on Internet Technology 7(2) (2007)
13. Ceri, S., Daniel, F., Facca, F.M., Matera, M.: Model-driven Engineering of Active Context-Awareness.In: World Wide Web (2007)
14. Tungara, M., Pyla, P., Sampat, M., Perez-Quinones, M.: Defragmenting Information using the Syncables Framework. In: SIGIR Workshop on Personal Information Management (2006)
15. Bellotti, V., Smith, J.: Informing the Design of an Information Management System with Iterative Fieldwork. In: Proceedings of the Conference on Designing Interactive Systems (DIS 2000) (2000)
16. Dourish, P., Edwards, W., LaMarca, A., Salisbury, M.: Presto: An Experimental Architecture for Fluid Interactive Document Spaces. ACM Transactions on Computer Human Interaction 6(2) (1999)

17. Franklin, M., Halevy, A., Maier, D.: From Databases to Dataspaces: A New Abstraction for Information Management. ACM SIGMOD Record (December 2005)
18. Dittrich, J.P., Blunschi, L., Färber, M., Girard, O.R., Karakashian, S.K., Salles, M.A.V.: From Personal Desktops to Personal Dataspaces: A Report on Building the iMeMex Personal Dataspace Management System. In: BTW 2007 (2007)
19. Norrie, M.C., Grossniklaus, M., Decurtins, C., de Spindler, A., Vancea, A., Leone, S.: Semantic Data Management for db4o. In: Proceedings of 1st International Conference on Object Databases (ICOODB 2008), Berlin, Germany (March 2008)
20. Grossniklaus, M., Norrie, M.C., Signer, B., Weibel, N.: Producing Interactive Paper Documents based on Multi-Channel Content Publishing. In: Proceedings of International Conference on Automated Production of Cross Media Content for Multi-Channel Distribution, Barcelona, Spain, November 28-30 (2007)
21. Norrie, M.C., Palinginis, A.: A Modelling Approach to the Realisation of Modular Information Spaces. In: Bressan, S., Chaudhri, A.B., Li Lee, M., Yu, J.X., Lacroix, Z. (eds.) CAiSE 2002 and VLDB 2002. LNCS, vol. 2590. Springer, Heidelberg (2003)
22. Grossniklaus, M., Norrie, M.C.: Using Object Variants to Support Context-Aware Interactions. In: Proceedings of International Workshop on Adaptation and Evolution in Web Systems Engineering, Como, Italy, July 19 (2007)
23. Norrie, M.C., Signer, B., Grossniklaus, M., Belotti, R., Decurtins, C., Weibel, N.: Context-Aware Platform for Mobile Data Management. Wireless Networks 13(6) (2007)
24. Vancea, A., Grossniklaus, M., Norrie, M.C.: Database-Driven Web Mashups. In: Proceedings 8th International Conference on Web Engineering (ICWE 2008), New York, USA (July 2008)
25. Leone, S., Grossniklaus, M., Norrie, M.C.: Architecture for Integrating Desktop and Web 2.0 Data Management. In: Proceedings 7th International Workshop on Web-Oriented Software Technologies (IWWOST 2008), New York, USA (July 2008)

Developing Preference Band Model to Manage Collective Preferences

Wilfred Ng

Department of Computer Science and Engineering
The Hong Kong University of Science and Technology
Hong Kong
wilfred@cse.ust.hk

Abstract. Discovering user preference is an important task in various database applications, such as searching product information and rating goods and services. However, there still lacks of a unifying model that is able to capture both implicit and explicit user preference information and to support managing, querying and analysing the information obtained from different sources.

In this paper, we present a framework based on our newly proposed Preference Band Model (PBM), which aims to achieve several goals. First, the PBM can serve as a formal basis to unify both implicit and explicit user preferences. We develop the model using a matrix-theoretic approach. Second, the model provides means to manipulate different sources of preference information. We establish a set of algebraic operators on Preference-Order Matrices (POMs). Third, the model supports direct querying of collective user preference and the discovery of a preference band. Roughly, a preference band is a ranking on sets of equally preferred items discovered from a POM that presents collective user preference. We demonstrate the applicability of our framework by studying two real datasets.

1 Introduction

Discovering user preference is an important task in various database applications, such as searching product information and rating goods and services [2,7,8]. Many business activities also rely heavily on estimating overall user preference in order to import user preferred goods and to design appropriate selling tactics. Previous work that incorporates user preference into databases mainly falls into two main categories of approaches. It either assumes that users are able to formulate their preference explicitly in terms of formulas or constraints [2,7,8], which may not be easy in reality, or develops mining techniques to discover implicit users' preference from the log of item selection [9] and then generate an adaptive full ranking of items, which may be too restrictive. However, there still lacks of a unifying model that is able to capture both implicit and explicit user preference information and to support managing, querying and analysing the information obtained from different sources.

We identify three problems that arise from handling preferences obtained from different sources and times. First, individual user preference can be modelled as a partial or full ranking between items [7,8]; but how do we model a large amount of such ranking information, which represents very different, possibly noisy and conflicting user

Q. Li et al. (Eds.): ER 2008, LNCS 5231, pp. 26–40, 2008.

preferences? Second, how do we compare and contrast expected preference and real user preference? This also gives challenges to focus on some target preference data for analysing. Third, how do we rank and classify collective user preference and express the result in some form of simple but useful knowledge?

In this paper, we present a holistic framework shown in Figure 1, which involves a formal model, a set of algebraic operators and various algorithmic techniques to tackle the above problems. The framework aims to manage preference information in a systematic way and to support better analyses of collective user preferences.

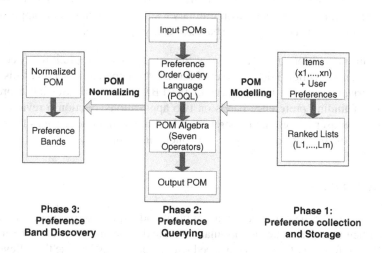

Fig. 1. The framework for managing collective user preference based on PBM

The basic idea of our approach is to convert a collection of user ranked items into a Preference-Order Matrix (POM). An entry a_{ij} in a POM is the frequency that one item x_i (more preferred) precedes another item x_j (less preferred) in the collected information, which captures the fact that users prefer x_i to x_j in a number of choice records.

As shown in the blueprint presented in Figure 1, we classify the process based on our Preference Band Model (PBM) into three phases. In the first phase, the PBM integrates implicit and explicit preference information represented by a set of user ranked lists, each of which is a user preference with possible choice order on target items. The information is modelled within a unifying matrix structure called POMs. In the second phase, we use a high level declarative query language called POQL to support manipulation of preference data and to generate a more effective POM for further analyses. The language is executed and can be optimized via a set of POM operators, which shares the similar spirit of execution of SQL expressions in relational databases. In the third phase, we need to normalize the POM in order to have it run in an adapted PIVOT algorithm [1], which classify and rank items into a preference band. The algorithm is known to be an efficient and effective method for discovering order knowledge from similar matrix structures, which is capable of tolerating noise of order in some reasonable limit [5,4].

Our main contribution in this paper is the development work of the PBM that supports managing user preference information and discovering preference bands.

- We formalise the novel concept of preference-order matrices (POMs) that express collected preference information. POMs support the discovery of preference bands that represent the maximal consistent collective preference obtained from a given set of user preference ranked lists.
- We establish a new set of seven algebraic operators such as the sum, the union, the intersection and the selection on POMs. We develop a new declarative language POQL based on the POM operators.
- We identify efficient algorithmic techniques for discovering preference bands, which shows that the discovery of preference bands from a POM is feasible in practice. Finally, we present the preliminary results of two interesting applications, which show the idea of preference bands is easily applicable.

The rest of the paper is organised as follows. Section 2 gives some preliminary concepts of user preference. Section 3 defines a set of formal POM operators. Section 4 discusses the issues arising from the three phases of the PBM framework. Section 5 presents our results of finding preference bands on two applications. Section 6 reviews some related work on user addressing preference and the algorithmic techniques for finding preference bands. In Section 7, we give our concluding remarks.

2   Preliminaries

User preferences can be expressed in an implicit and explicit order of items. For example, explicit user preference is formulated in a lexicographic order of preference attributes [8]. Preference SQL [7] is equipped with a "preferring" clause that allows user to specify soft constraints reflecting multiple preference terms. All these approaches would result in a preference ranking of items. Implicit preferences are some ranking order that is inferred from users' track record of choosing items against some background of item order [9], which also depends on the interpretation of the chosen items.

We assume that a preference rank list can be obtained via some users' implicit or explicit preference information and formalize the concept as follows:

Definition 1. (Preference Ranked List) Given a set of items $I = \{x_1, \ldots x_n\}$ with an imposed order $<_I$. A choice $C \subseteq I$ is a list of items ordered according to some user preference $<_C$, where $(C, <_C)$ may or may not equal to $(I, <_I)$. We generate a *preference ranked list* T by appending $(I - C)$ into C such that $T = \langle C, (I - C) \rangle$, in which the items of $(I - C)$ are ordered according to $<_I$. We denote by $L = \{T_1, \ldots, T_m\}$ a collection of m preference ranked lists.

Note that in Definition 1, $<_C$ can represent the order of choosing items in C by the user, which is an implicit preference, or it can represent the order according to some explicit preference criteria. L is a collective user preference on I. The following example helps illustrate the ideas of individual and collective preferences.

Example 1. Let $I = \{a, b, c, d, e, f\}$ be the items stored in a database and two customers search some items on the web. Let the items be ranked according to the default order $I = \{a > b > c > d > e > f\}$, which can be interpreted as an arbitrary ranking or a ranking derived from some commercial considerations. One customer explicitly states his or her preference criteria, which result in a preferred ranking $C_1 = \{c > f > e > d > b > a\}$. Another customer does not state any preference and just browses the items ranked by the default order $<_I$. However, s/he only checks a subset of items of I in some different order given by $C_2 = \{d > b > f > e\}$.

We now show in Figure 2 two sets of preference ranked lists L_1 and L_2, each of which contains five preference ranked lists. L_1 and L_2 can represent collective customer preference information obtained from two sources. It can be checked that T_1 and T_8 are the preference ranked lists derived from C_1 and C_2 respectively. T_5 can also be viewed as a precise match between a user's preference and the shop's estimated user preference that is expressed in the default item order.

$$L_1 = \begin{array}{|l|} \hline T_1: c > f > e > d > b > a \\ \hline T_2: a > c > b > d > f > e \\ \hline T_3: a > c > d > b > f > e \\ \hline T_4: d > f > c > a > b > e \\ \hline T_5: a > b > c > d > e > f \\ \hline \end{array} \quad L_2 = \begin{array}{|l|} \hline T_6: c > f > e > d > b > a \\ \hline T_7: a > c > b > d > f > e \\ \hline T_8: d > b > f > e > a > c \\ \hline T_9: d > f > c > a > e > b \\ \hline T_{10}: b > d > f > e > c > a \\ \hline \end{array}$$

Fig. 2. An example of two sets of five preference ranked lists

A collection of preference ranked lists L from a given source can be modelled as a Preference Order Matrices (POMs) M_L, which is a matrix structure derived from L to support further querying and preference band discovery.

Definition 2. (Preference Order Matrix) Given L and let $\mid L \mid = n$. A *Preference-Order Matrix* (POM) M_L with respect to L (or simply M if L is understood) is an $n \times n$ matrix such that each entry $a_{ij} \in M$ is equal to the number of occurrences that item x_i precedes item x_j in L. We define $a_{ij} \in M$ to be $\mid L \mid$ whenever $i = j$. M is said to be *normalized* if each entry $norm(a_{ij}) = \frac{a_{ij}}{n}$ (or equivalently, $\frac{a_{ij}}{a_{ii}}$ or $\frac{a_{ij}}{a_{jj}}$) whenever $i \neq j$, and $norm(a_{ij}) = \frac{1}{2}$ whenever $i = j$.

Clearly, it follows from Definition 2 that $0 \leq a_{ij} \leq \mid L \mid$, $a_{ij} + a_{ji} = \mid L \mid$ for any distinct i, j. The normalization implies that each entry $a_{ij} \in norm(M_L)$ is equal to the probability that item x_i precedes item x_j in L. Given $norm(M_L)$. The entries satisfies the following conditions: (1) (normalization constraint) $0 \leq a_{ij} \leq 1$; (2) (linearity constraint) $a_{ij} + a_{ji} = 1$; and (3) (triangle constraint) $a_{ij} \leq a_{ik} + a_{kj}$.

Normalised POMs are important in this work. For simplicity of presentation we assume all T being a total order. However, we remark that if a partial order is resulted from more general user preferences [7] we still can use a corresponding set of linear extensions to represent the order information of equally preferred items. I.e. two equally preferred items x_i and x_j can still be captured by normalised POMs in the entry $a_{ij} = \frac{1}{2}$. Specifically, a partial order can be directly represented by a normalised POM as follows: $a_{ij} \in M$ is equal to 1 if $x_i \leq x_j$, $a_{ij} \in M$ is equal to 0 if $x_j \leq x_i$, and $a_{ij} \in M$ is equal to $\frac{1}{2}$ otherwise (i.e. x_i and x_j are incomparable). In other words, normalised POMs are flexible enough to capture more general user preference information.

	a	b	c	d	e	f
a	5	4	3	3	4	3
b	1	5	1	2	4	3
c	2	4	5	4	5	4
d	2	3	1	5	4	4
e	1	1	0	1	5	1
f	2	2	1	1	4	5

$\Rightarrow$

	a	b	c	d	e	f
a	0.5	0.8	0.6	0.6	0.8	0.6
b	0.2	0.5	0.2	0.4	0.8	0.6
c	0.4	0.8	0.5	0.8	1.0	0.8
d	0.4	0.6	0.2	0.5	0.8	0.8
e	0.2	0.2	0.0	0.2	0.5	0.2
f	0.4	0.4	0.2	0.2	0.8	0.5

	a	b	c	d	e	f
a	5	2	2	1	2	1
b	3	5	2	2	3	3
c	3	3	5	2	3	2
d	4	3	3	5	4	4
e	3	2	2	1	5	0
f	4	2	3	1	5	5

$\Rightarrow$

	a	b	c	d	e	f
a	0.5	0.4	0.4	0.2	0.4	0.2
b	0.6	0.5	0.4	0.4	0.6	0.6
c	0.6	0.6	0.5	0.4	0.6	0.4
d	0.8	0.6	0.6	0.5	0.6	0.8
e	0.6	0.4	0.4	0.2	0.5	0.0
f	0.8	0.4	0.6	0.2	1.0	0.5

(a) M_1 and $norm(M_1)$ (b) M_2 and $norm(M_2)$

Fig. 3. The POMs M_1 and M_2 obtained from L_1 and L_2, and their normalized counterparts

Example 2. We now continue Example 1 to derive the POMs and their normalized form from L_1 and L_2. The POMs M_1 and M_2 and their normlized forms are given in Figures 3(a) and (b).

One objective of this work is to establish a set of operators that are able to manipulate POMs and support in-depth analyses of collective user preference modelled in POMs. Another objective is to discover preference bands obtained from a given normalised POM. A preference band is intuitively a linear order of sets of equally preferred items taking into collective user preference. The motivation of defining a preference band is that in many adaptive searching applications, modelling the preference with a total order might be too restrictive in the sense that all items in I should be comparable. However, it is also too complex to manage, analyse and present the preference information expressed in general partial order.

We now give the formal definition of a preference band as follows.

Definition 3. (Preference Band) A *preference band* B of I with granularity k is an ordered partition of I given by $\langle P_1, \ldots, P_k \rangle$, where $P_i \subseteq I$ is a non-empty set called a band element in B. A band order of the items in I arising from B, denoted as $<_B$, can be inferred from B as follows: For any pair of items x and y in the same band element P, x and y are incomparable (i.e. $x \not<_B y$ and $y \not<_B x$). However, if x and y are from two distinct band elements P_i and P_j such that $i < j$, then $x <_B y$.

Essentially, a preference band adopts an appropriately low granularity to eliminate noises and ranking contradictions of items among preference ranked lists collected in L. However, there is an inherent cost of losing some information of the preference orders in individual T when putting items in a band element; as an extreme we can put all items in one single band element which is obviously no use. Thus, we need to establish a penalty cost function for measuring the quality of a preference band. A simple one is adopted as below but more sophisticated functions can be studied as a future work.

If M_1 and M_2 are two normalized POMs, we define the distance measure given by $D(M_1, M_2) = \Sigma_{i \neq j} \mid a_{ij}^{M_1} - a_{ij}^{M_2} \mid$.

Given a normalised POM M. We aim to find the best preference band describing M. We now formulate the Preference Band Discovery (PBD) problem.

Definition 4. (PBD problem) Let M_L be a normalised POM on I obtained from L and M_B be a normalised POM obtained from a preference band B of I. Find a preference band such that $D(M_L, M_B)$ is minimized. (Note that B is a partial order and can be represented by POM M_B.)

In other words, the main task of PBD is to find a preference band B on the items of I such that the penalty cost function is minimized, which is equal to the sum of values in the following three cases: (i) $| (a_{ij})_M - 1 |$ if $x_i <_B x_j$, (ii) $| (a_{ij})_M |$ if $x_j <_B x_i$, and (iii) $| (a_{ij})_M - \frac{1}{2} |$ otherwise.

Example 3. Consider our running example L_1 and L_2 given in Figure 2. Suppose there is a preference band $B = \langle \{a, b, c, d\} > \{e, f\} \rangle$ (which may not be the best one according to D). Then, it can be checked that $D(M_{L_1}, M_B) = 6.6$ and $D(M_{L_2}, M_B) = 10$. The difference is reasonable, since it can be checked that L_1 has a noise level of 40% with respect to the preference band B because two of the five preference ranked lists, namely T_1 and T_4, are not the linear extension [5] of B, whereas L_2 has an even worse noise level of 80% with respect to B because only T_7 is the linear extension of B. This motivates us to develop an effective algorithm to generate B from a given M_L.

3   The POM Operators

In this section, we define seven POM operators, namely the sum, the union, the difference, the intersection, the complement, the projection and the selection, each of which takes one or two given POMs as input parameters, and returns a POM.

The POM operators are easy to understand and to compute and their output result serves as a basis for carrying out the discovery of preference band. The sum operator is additive to preference data, that is, the result is incremental with respect to preference information. This gives advantage to handle preference data in a progressive manner, say temporal change in preference can be detected. The overall, change, common, opposite preference can be formalised by the sum, the union, the difference, the intersection, and the complement operations. We can focus on the preference information of a particular set of items by using the projection and the selection operations. On the other hand, matrices are an elegant notion studied in a well-established branch of mathematics. It implies that many interesting results in matrix theory can be used to strengthen the foundation of PBMs as a development work.

We need two binary operators, denoted as *min* and *max*, to represent the usual minimum and maximum of two given integers in defining the POM operators. From now on, we use throughout the paper M_1 and M_2 to represent two POMs defined over the same set of items I. The sum operation is given in Definition 5.

Definition 5. (Sum) The *sum* of two POMs M_1 and M_2, denoted as $M_1 + M_2$, is defined as a POM M_3 over I such that for all $i, j \in \{1, \ldots, n\}$, $(a_{ij})_3 = (a_{ij})_1 + (a_{ij})_2$.

An interesting property of the sum operation is that the sum of two POMs M_1 and M_2, which originates from the two respective preference ranked lists L_1 and L_2, is equal to the matrix which originates from the preference ranked list L_3 containing the combination of the information in L_1 and L_2 (i.e. $L_3 = L_1 \cup L_2$). This implies that we are able to perform analyses on "overall" preference information by summing up "individual" pieces of preference information, in this sense we say that the sum operator is *additive* with respect to the preference data.

Another possibility to combine preference information is to consider the maximum number of occurrences of precedence between items, taking into account the "overlap" effect. We now define this operation by the union operator as follows.

Definition 6. (Union) The *union* of two POMs M_1 and M_2, denoted as $M_1 \cup M_2$, is defined as a POM M_3 over I such that $(a_{ii})_3 := max((a_{ii})_1, (a_{ii})_2)$ for all $i \in \{1, \ldots, n\}$ and for all pairs of distinct $i, j \in \{1, \ldots, n\}$, we obtain $(a_{ii})_3$ as follows:

Let $x := max((a_{ij})_1, (a_{ij})_2)$ and $y := max((a_{ji})_1, (a_{ji})_2)$.

If $x > y$ then $(a_{ij})_3 := x$ and $(a_{ji})_3 := max((a_{ii})_1, (a_{ii})_2) - x$;

otherwise (i.e. $x \le y$) $(a_{ji})_3 := y$ and $(a_{ij})_3 := max((a_{ii})_1, (a_{ii})_2) - y$.

Note that the comparison $x > y$ makes sure that the most dominant precedence in M_1 and M_2 is chosen as the output. In contrast, we can consider the less dominant precedence but it is common to both M_1 and M_2. This becomes another operation called intersection defined as follows.

Definition 7. (Intersection) The *intersection* of two POMs M_1 and M_2, denoted as $M_1 \cap M_2$, is defined as a POM M_3 over I such that $(a_{ii})_3 := min((a_{ii})_1, (a_{ii})_2)$ for all $i \in \{1, \ldots, n\}$ and for all pairs of distinct $i, j \in \{1, \ldots, n\}$, we obtain $(a_{ii})_3$ as follows:

Let $x := max((a_{ij})_1, (a_{ij})_2)$ and $y := max((a_{ji})_1, (a_{ji})_2)$.

If $x < y$ then $(a_{ij})_3 := x$ and $(a_{ji})_3 := min((a_{ii})_1, (a_{ii})_2) - x$;

otherwise (i.e. $x \ge y$) $(a_{ji})_3 := y$ and $(a_{ij})_3 := min((a_{ii})_1, (a_{ii})_2) - y$.

We now introduce the difference operator, which is useful to contrast two preference ranked lists. For example, we can use the difference operator to find the temporal change in preference data obtained at two different time intervals or to compare the preference data obtained from two user groups having different preference profiles.

Definition 8. (Difference) Assume $\mid L_1 \mid > \mid L_2 \mid$. The *difference* of two POMs M_1 and M_2, denoted as $M_1 - M_2$, is defined as a POM M_3 over I such that $(a_{ii})_3 := (a_{ii})_1 - (a_{ii})_2$ for all $i \in \{1, \ldots, n\}$ and for all pairs of distinct $i, j \in \{1, \ldots, n\}$, we obtain $(a_{ii})_3$ as follows:

Let $x := (a_{ij})_1 - (a_{ij})_2$ and $y := (a_{ji})_1 - (a_{ji})_2$.

Case $x > 0$ and $y > 0$: $(a_{ij})_3 := x$ and $(a_{ji})_3 := y$;

Case $x > 0$ and $y \le 0$: $(a_{ij})_3 := min(x, (a_{ii})_1 - (a_{ii})_2)$ and $(a_{ji})_3 := (a_{ii})_1 - (a_{ii})_2 - min(x, (a_{ii})_1 - (a_{ii})_2)$;

Case $y > 0$ and $x \le 0$: $(a_{ij})_3 := (a_{ii})_1 - (a_{ii})_2 - min(y, (a_{ii})_1 - (a_{ii})_2)$ and $(a_{ji})_3 := min(y, (a_{ii})_1 - (a_{ii})_2)$.

Notably, the operator is undefined for $\mid L_1 \mid \le \mid L_2 \mid$. This prevents the happening of meaningless negative entries in a POM. Thus, there is no need to consider the possibility of $y \le 0$ and $x \le 0$ in the definition. It also implies that either x or y is strictly positive as shown in the three cases in Definition 8.

The following is an interesting operator that defines the "reverse" of the preference order for all items in I.

Definition 9. (Complement) The *complement* of a POM M_1, denoted as $\neg M_1$, is defined as a POM M_2 over I such that for all $i, j \in \{1, \ldots, n\}$, $(a_{ij})_2 = (a_{ji})_1$.

Similar to relational algebra, the POM operators are employed to extract a target set of items. The operators projection and selection aim to realise similar objectives. But unlike operating on relational tables, an POM operation needs to preserve the entries of the non-target items in the output, since POM is a matrix. To tackle this problem, we simply fill in the entries of these items according to the default order $<_I$. I.e. All the items in $(I - X)$ in the projection are ordered according to $<_I$ in the output POM.

Definition 10. (Projection) The *projection* of a POM M_1, denoted as $\pi_X(M_1)$ where $X \subseteq I$ is a set of items, is defined as a POM M_2 as follows:

Case $x_i, x_j \in P$: $(a_{ij})_2 = (a_{ij})_1$.

Case $x_i \in P$ but $x_j \notin P$: $(a_{ij})_2 = (a_{ij})_1 + (a_{ji})_2$ and $(a_{ji})_2 = 0$.

Case $x_i, x_j \notin P$: $(a_{ij})_2 = (a_{ij})_1 + (a_{ji})_2$ if $x_j <_I x_i$; otherwise (i.e. $x_i <_I x_j$) $(a_{ji})_2 = 0$.

The tricky point in defining the POM selection is that we should not allow arbitrary entry comparison, since it is difficult to know or seldom need to concern the absolute occurrence of precedence in L. Instead, we choose the relative ratio of precedence between items as the parameter used in the selection predicate, which always falls in a unit interval. This also captures the intuition that how much x is more preferred to y.

Definition 11. (Selection) The *selection* of a POM M_1, denoted as $\sigma_{\theta x}(M_1)$, where θ is a comparator such as $>, <, \geq, \leq$, or $=$, and $x \in [0, 1]$ is a positive number, is defined as a POM M_2 as follows:

For all $i \in \{1, \ldots, n\}(a_{ii})_2 = (a_{ii})_1$.

For all distinct $i, j \in \{1, \ldots, n\}$, if $\left| \frac{(a_{ij})_1 - (a_{ji})_1}{(a_{ij})_1 + (a_{ji})_1} \right| \theta x$, then $(a_{ij})_2 = (a_{ij})_1$;

otherwise (i.e. $\left| \frac{(a_{ij})_1 - (a_{ji})_1}{(a_{ij})_1 + (a_{ji})_1} \right| \bar{\theta} x$) if $x_j <_I x_i$ $(a_{ij})_2 = (a_{ij})_1 + (a_{ji})_2$; or else (i.e. $x_i <_I x_j$) $(a_{ji})_2 = 0$,

where the notation $\bar{\theta}$ denotes the complement of θ (e.g. $\bar{\theta}$ is "$\leq$" when θ is "$>$").

It follows from Definition 11 $\sigma_{\geq 0}(M) = M$, where all entries are trivially selected. The result of "$\sigma_{>1}(M)$" represents the preference being reduced to the default order $<_I$. This can be used as the *identity* POM ID for revealing some interesting properties of the union and intersection operators in the following discussion.

We let $\delta_1 \in \{+, \cup, \cap\}$ and $\delta_2 \in \{\neg, \pi_X\}$ and $\delta_3 \in \{\neg, \sigma_p, \pi_X\}$. The following properties of the POM operations can be verified by Definitions 5 to 11.

Associative Property. The POMs on the same I are associative under *sum, union* and *intersection* which is shown in the equations as follows:

$(M_1 \delta_1 M_2) \delta_1 M_3 = M_1 \delta_1 (M_2 \delta_1 M_3)$.

Commutative Property. The POMs on the same I are also commutative under *sum, union* and *intersection*.

(1) $M_1 \delta_1 M_2 = M_2 \delta_1 M_1$. (2) $\delta_3'(\delta_3(M)) = \delta_3(\delta_3'(M))$.

Distributive Property. *Projection* and *negation* are distributive under *sum, union* and *intersection*.

	a	b	c	d	e	f
a	10	6	5	4	6	4
b	4	10	3	4	7	6
c	5	7	10	6	8	6
d	6	6	4	10	8	8
e	4	3	2	2	10	1
f	6	4	4	2	9	10

	a	b	c	d	e	f
a	5	4	3	1	4	1
b	1	5	1	2	4	3
c	2	4	5	4	5	4
d	4	3	1	5	4	4
e	1	1	0	1	5	0
f	4	2	1	1	5	5

	a	b	c	d	e	f
a	5	2	2	3	2	3
b	3	5	2	2	3	3
c	3	3	5	2	3	2
d	2	3	3	5	4	4
e	3	2	2	1	5	1
f	2	2	3	1	4	5

	a	b	c	d	e	f
a	5	4	3	5	5	5
b	1	5	1	5	5	5
c	2	4	5	5	5	5
d	0	0	0	5	5	5
e	0	0	0	0	5	5
f	0	0	0	0	0	5

	a	b	c	d	e	f
a	5	4	5	5	4	5
b	1	5	1	5	4	5
c	0	4	5	4	5	4
d	1	0	1	5	4	4
e	1	1	0	1	5	1
f	0	0	1	1	4	5

(a)   (b)   (c)   (d)   (e)

Fig. 4. The results of the some binary and unary POM operations (a) $M_1 + M_2$ (b) $M_1 \cup M_2$ (c) $M_1 \cap M_2$ (d) $\pi_{abc}(M_1)$ (e) $\sigma_{\theta > 0.2}(M_1)$

$$\delta_2(M_1 \ \delta_1 \ M_2) = (\delta_2(M_1)) \ \delta_1 \ (\delta_2(M_2)).$$

In general, $\sigma_p(M_1\delta_1 M_2) \neq (\sigma_p(M_1))\delta_1(\sigma_p(M_2))$ and $\pi_X(M_1 - M_2) \neq (\pi_X(M_1)) - (\pi_X(M_2))$. However, $\neg(M_1 - M_2) = (\neg(M_1)) - (\neg(M_2))$ and $\neg(\neg(M)) = M$.

We now let $\sigma_{>1}(M) = ID$ and present the identity property.

Identity Property. *Union* and *intersection* satisfy the identity property.
(1) $M \cup ID = ID$. (2) $M \cap ID = M$.

Example 4. We now make use of the POMs M_1 and M_2 given in Figure 3 to show some of the results of $M_1\delta_1 M_2$ and $\delta_3(M_2)$ in Figure 4.

4 Implementation Issues

In this section, we briefly discuss the techniques and methods that address the challenges arising from the three phases of the PBM framework depicted in Figure 1.

4.1 Phase 1: How to Obtain and Store POMs?

We can construct the POM M by using L in two ways. The first way is to adopt a brute force approach to bookkeep a_{ij} when scanning the total order in which x_i precedes x_j. As the algorithm for discovering preference bands needs to take a normalized POM as the input, we still need to compute the normalized values of the entries in M in the final phase. So we may use a more direct way to obtain $norm(M)$. We can sample possible orderings of the user preference $T \in I$ and in this case $norm(a_{ij})$ is set to be the fraction of L in which x_i precedes x_j, such as Markov Chain Monte Carlo method used in [10]. In this approach, we avoid the heavy computation to track all precedences. In fact it is inevitable to have noise in preference data in real applications. Sampling techniques seem to be more appropriate to generate normalized POMs.

The storage scheme of a matrix greatly affects the performance of POM operators. In practice, there are usually many items to be considered. As I is large and the number of preferred items is small, the POMs may be very sparse with respect to the entries that actually represent user preference data. As the entries of diagonal and lower triangular portion of a POM can be deduced from $| L |$, we may develop a concise version that targets on only those entries that contain preference information. Specifically, we fill in zeros in entry of (i) the lower triangular portion of the POM and (ii) the diagonal running top left to bottom right. The first condition is valid, since we have $a_{ji} = \mid L \mid - a_{ij}$. The second condition is also valid since we have $a_{ii} = \mid L \mid$. There will be more zero entries in the upper triangular portion of M if the ranking order is skew.

4.2   Phase 2: How to Use the POM Operators to Formulate Queries?

We develop a declarative language on POMs in our framework and term the langauge the Preference Order Query Language (or simply the POQL). A POQL expression is executed via the seven POM operators defined in Section 3, which shares the same principle of translating a SQL expression into a sequence of relational algebra operations. We now define the POQL syntax in Backus Naur Form (BNF):

<query> :: = <selectClause><fromClause>[<conditionClause>]
<selectClause> :: = SELECT <itemList>
<queryList> :: = query [, query...]
<fromClause> :: = FROM <matrixIdentifier> | FROM <operator> <matrixList>
<conditionClause> :: = WHERE PREFERENCE RATIO <compOp> a number in [0,1]
<itemList> :: = itemIdentifier [, itemIdentifier...] | *
<matrixList> :: = matrixIdentifier [, matrixIdentifier...]
<operator> :: = SUM|UNION|DIFFERENCE|INTERSECT|COMPLEMENT
<compOp> :: = |<=|>=|<|=

There are three main clauses in a query expression: the *select*, *from*, and *condition*. Among them the *select* and the *from* clauses are compulsory, while the *condition* clause is optional. Similar to SQL, POQL is a simple declarative language but is expressive enough to formulate query on finding preference information stored as POMs.

We execute a POQL expression by translating it into a sequence of POM operations using Algorithm 1. Suppose $X \subseteq L$ is a set of items which appears in the select clause, $\mathcal{M}$ is a set of m POMs which appears in the from clause, where $\mathcal{M} =$

Algorithm 1. Translate POQL Algorithm

Input: A POQL expression q
LET $q = $ <selectClause><fromClause>[<conditionClause>]
$\qquad\qquad$ <selectClause> := "SELECT $X \mid *$"
$\qquad\qquad$ <fromClause> := "FROM $OPER\ \mathcal{M}$"
$\qquad\qquad$ <conditionClause> := "WHERE PREFERENCE RATIO θx"
Procedure:
$\qquad$ **Step 1** : For the fromClause, **CASE** $OPER$ **OF**:
$\qquad\qquad$ $\epsilon : TEMP :=$ "M_1"
$\qquad\qquad$ $COMPLEMENT : TEMP :=$ "$\neg M_1$"
$\qquad\qquad$ $SUM : TEMP :=$ "$M_1 + M_2 + \cdots + M_m$"
$\qquad\qquad$ $UNION : TEMP :=$ "$M_1 \bigcup M_2 \bigcup \cdots \bigcup M_m$"
$\qquad\qquad$ $DIFF : TEMP :=$ "$M_1 - M_2 - \cdots - M_m$"
$\qquad\qquad$ $INTERSECT : TEMP :=$ "$M_1 \bigcap M_2 \bigcap \cdots \bigcap M_m$"
$\qquad$ **Step 2** : For the selectClause:
$\qquad\qquad$ **IF** "$*$" **THEN** $TEMP := TEMP$
$\qquad\qquad\quad$ **ELSE** $TEMP :=$ "$\pi_X(TEMP)$"
$\qquad$ **Step 3** : **IF** there is a whereClause **THEN** $TEMP :=$ "$\sigma_{\theta x}(TEMP)$"
Output: $TEMP$ expression

$\{M_1^*, M_2^*, \ldots, M_m^*\}$ and M^* means either M or $COMPLEMENT$ M, and $OPER \in \{\epsilon, SUM, UNION, DIFFERENCE, INTERSECT\}$. Note that the input POQL query expression is assumed to be syntactically valid. If $OPER = \epsilon$, then $m = 1$.

4.3   Phase 3: How to Generate Preference Bands?

The challenge of this final phase is to tackle the PBD problem in Definition 4. However, the problem is equivalent to the Bucket Order Discovery (BOD) problem, which aims to find a linear order of buckets from a given set of linear orders. The BOD problem has been proved to be NP-hard [1]. Thus, we have to resort to heuristic algorithms. Given a set of full rankings T_1 and T_2 over I. Gionis et al. [5] proposed a heuristic algorithm called Bucket Pivot, which is adapted from Ailon's randomized algorithm Pivot [1] (or simply called the PIVOT algorithm).

Essentially, the PIVOT algorithm starts with a random selected element and then compares the elements with others and finally generates three classes of "left", "same" and "right" classes. To apply the techniques in our context, the PIVOT algorithm can be employed to exploit precedence probabilities stored in the input normalized POM M and then to discover the output preference band recursively, in which a preference band can be regarded as a bucket order B. The three classes of buckets correspond to the lower band (LB), current band (CB) and upper band (UB) elements.

Specifically, the adapted PIVOT algorithm runs in a quick-sort-like manner. In each recursion, a random pivot item x_i is first selected and the following three band elements, $\langle UB > CB > LB \rangle$, are also created for x_i. Other items are then compared with the pivot x_i. An item x_j will be put into CB if the precedence probability a_{ij} satisfies the following inequality: $0.5 - \beta \leq a_{ij} < 0.5 + \beta$, where $\beta \in [0, 0.5]$ is a parameter that describes the degree of precision of precedence probability relative to 0.5. The drawback of using PIVOT is that it is not easy to set a suitable β value and the choice of β affects the final number of band elements in B. Clearly if $\beta = 0$ we cannot generate any approximated band element to provide insight of the collective preference in the input POM. On the other hand, if $\beta = 0.5$ we have a very imprecise (and is likely to be large) band element that contains all x_j having $a_{ij} \neq 1$ (which has a high probability).

Algorithm 2. The Preference Band Discovery Algorithm $PBD(X, M, \beta)$

Input: A normalized POM M of I, $X \subseteq I$ and $\beta = 0.25$ by default
Procedure:
        Step 1 : **IF** $X = \emptyset$ **RETURN** $\emptyset$
        Step 2 : Pick $x_i \in I$ randomly as a pivot **DO**
            $UB \leftarrow \emptyset$
            $CB \leftarrow \{x_i\}$
            $LB \leftarrow \emptyset$
        Step 3 : **FOR ALL** items $x_j \in (X - \{x_i\})$ **DO**
                IF $0.5 + \beta \leq a_{ij}$ **THEN** $UB \leftarrow UB \cup \{x_j\}$
                  ELSE IF $0.5 - \beta \leq a_{ij} < 0.5 + \beta$ **THEN** $CB \leftarrow CB \cup \{x_j\}$
                  ELSE IF $a_{ij} < 0.5 - \beta$ **THEN** $LB \leftarrow LB \cup \{x_j\}$
Output: A preference band given by $\langle PBD(UB, M, \beta), CB, PBD(LB, M, \beta) \rangle$

Fortunately, according to [5], the default value $\beta = 0.25$ is shown to be able to make PIVOT achieve good approximation ratio with respect to the penalty cost function D.

We now present the adapted PIVOT algorithm for PBD problem in Algorithm 2, which adapts PIVOT in our contest. We simply assume $\beta = 0.25$ for running PBD.

5   Applications of Preference Bands

We now present two applications of the PBM to discover the user preference in (1) a real rating movie dataset and (2) a real clickstream dataset. A clickstream is the evidence of user preference in choosing a web page to browse.

(1) Movie Preference. We consider the ranking of movie obtained from MovieLens dataset[1]. The dataset consists of 6040 users, 3900 movies, and 1 million movie votes. Each of the movie votes has a weight and a score, where the weight denotes whether or not the user actually saw the movie, and where the score denotes the user's movie rating. Using Algorithm 2, we ignore the weight and set it to 1 for all users. There are actually very different preference in ranking the movies. We target on the following set of ten movies to find the PB:

$I = \{$Strange Days (SD), Lawnmover Man 2 (LM), Flintstones (FS), Free Willy (FW), Godfather (GF), 3 Musketeers (MU), 101 Dalmatians (DM), Empire Strikes Back (ES), Barb Wire (BW), and Jungle Book (JB)$\}$.

Figure 5 shows the normalised POM for the rankings of the 10 movies. We obtain the best preference band of four band elements of movies as follows: $\langle \{ES, GF\} > \{ JB\} > \{SD, DM, MU\} > \{FW, FS, BW, \} > \{LM\} \rangle$. The band elements are not so trivial to be obtained from the huge amount of data or even from the POM given in Figure 5, which is obtained after the processing efforts in Phases 1 and 2.

(2) Web Page Preference. We consider the user page visits of msnbc.com on a single day. The clickstream dataset is obtained from MSNBC data[2]. Each user has exactly one

$$
\begin{bmatrix}
 & ES & GF & JB & SD & MU & DM & FW & FS & LM & BW \\
ES & 0.50 & 0.32 & 0.78 & 0.92 & 0.90 & 0.92 & 0.95 & 0.96 & 1.00 & 0.99 \\
GF & 0.68 & 0.50 & 0.86 & 0.94 & 0.90 & 0.92 & 0.95 & 0.94 & 1.00 & 0.98 \\
JB & 0.22 & 0.14 & 0.50 & 0.69 & 0.77 & 0.88 & 0.92 & 0.94 & 0.96 & 0.95 \\
SD & 0.08 & 0.06 & 0.31 & 0.50 & 0.69 & 0.71 & 0.77 & 0.92 & 0.96 & 0.91 \\
MU & 0.10 & 0.10 & 0.23 & 0.31 & 0.5 & 0.65 & 0.81 & 0.88 & 0.96 & 0.85 \\
DM & 0.08 & 0.08 & 0.12 & 0.29 & 0.35 & 0.5 & 0.68 & 0.70 & 0.80 & 0.88 \\
FE & 0.05 & 0.05 & 0.08 & 0.23 & 0.19 & 0.32 & 0.5 & 0.64 & 0.77 & 0.67 \\
FS & 0.04 & 0.06 & 0.06 & 0.08 & 0.12 & 0.30 & 0.36 & 0.5 & 0.83 & 0.67 \\
LM & 0.00 & 0.00 & 0.04 & 0.04 & 0.04 & 0.20 & 0.23 & 0.17 & 0.50 & 0.19 \\
BW & 0.01 & 0.02 & 0.05 & 0.09 & 0.05 & 0.12 & 0.33 & 0.33 & 0.81 & 0.5
\end{bmatrix}
$$

Fig. 5. The normalized POM of movie preference to discover preference bands

---

[1] http://www.grouplens.org/node/73#attachments
[2] http://kdd.ics.uci.edu/databases/msnbc/msnbc.html

User 1:	frontpage → news → sports → weather
User 2:	news → politics → weather
⋮ ⋮	⋱ ⋮
User n:	frontpage → politics → weather

Fig. 6. Collective users' browsing habits to form a preference band

sequence of page visits, where each page visit is recorded as a URL category. There are 17 categories in total, and each category is encoded by a distinct integer from 1 to 17. In other words, $I = \{1, \ldots, 17\}$ with usual numerical order and L consists of a set of T sequences, each of which is a permutation of I.

First, we keep the first occurrence of a category in each sequence T and denote the resulting sequence as C. Usually, $C \subseteq I$ and thus $\mid C \mid$ is less than 17. We denote the $(17 - \mid C \mid)$ categories as S and sort the categories in S according to the numerical order of their integer code. Then, we append S to C to form a permutation of I as a result, which is a T sequence. We select a subset of the sequences whose $\mid C \mid$ contains at least 14 categories in order to increase the effect of the user preference in L. In total, we identify 160 such T sequences.

Examples of URL categories are "frontpage" and "msn-sports". The page visit sequence is a total order if we do not consider duplicate page visits. The order of page visits reflects a user's browsing habit. By clustering page-visit orders, we generate a user preferred categorization. For example, in Figure 6, we may use a preference band to indicate the common browsing habits of the set of users, who may usually start from reading some news, either about politics or about sports, and end up with a look at the weather conditions.

The best preference band discovered in MSNBC data is found as follows: $\langle \{frontpage, news\} > \{tech, local, on\text{-}air, misc, weather, msn\text{-}news, health, living, business, sports, summary, travel\} > \{opinion\} > \{msn\text{-}sports, bbs\}\rangle$. It shows that the item "news" is put in the first band element in addition to the "frontpage". The result that both "frontpage" and "news" are in the top band element is not so trivial but seems to match real-life experience: while users can first visit "frontpage" and then go from the "frontpage" to "news", users may have bookmarked "news" and visit "news" directly. In contrast, if we use a preference ranking instead of a preference band to represent such browsing preference, "frontpage" would most likely be put in the top of the preference rank, which wrongly assumes that users normally start with the "frontpage" and then go to the "new". Thus, using a preference band is a more natural and meaningful representation of collective preference.

6   Related Work

Preferences are receiving much attention in querying, since DBMSs need to provide better information services in advanced applications [7]. In particular, preference SQL [7] is equipped with a "preferring" clause that allows user to specify soft constraints reflecting multiple preference terms. Implicit preference has been commonly studied in the area of searching such as using clickthrough data to mine user preference in web browsing [9]. In reality, implicit and explicit user preferences are important but there lacks of a formal basis to accommodate and manipulate both of them.

Our previous work [8] models single user preference as a hierarchy of its underlying data values and formalises the notion of Prioritized Preferences (PPs). We then consider multiple user preferences in ranking tuples in a relational table. We examine the impact of a given set of PPs on possible choices in ranking a database relation and develop a new notion of Choice Constraints (CCs) in a relation.

The PBD problem can be translated into the bucket order discovery (BOD) problem that is studied in recent years. The problem of obtaining a single bucket order from a collection of input total orders has been considered by Fagin et al. [3] in their general framework of comparing and aggregating partial rankings. In our recent work [4], we develop a new algorithm, called GAP, to tackle the BOD problem. The GAP algorithm consists of a two phase ranking aggregation and involves the use of a novel rank gap heuristic for segmenting multiple quantile orders.

7   Concluding Remarks

In this paper, we propose a new PBM framework that consists of three phases of work for managing a collection of user preference data that are modelled as POM matrices. We also establish a set of operations which serve as the formal tool to analyse and manipulate preference data. We further develop a declarative query language based on the POM operators and a new concept of preference band to discover and classify collective user preference. We discuss various technical issues related to the three phases.

There are indeed many interesting issues that deserve further study. In the modelling aspect, we need to clarify if POQL is expressive enough to obtain important preference information from given POMs. In the deployment aspect, we still need to study the efficiency of the POM operators and devise effective optimization strategy for the execution of the operations. The algorithm of finding preference bands is also related to the research work of discovering bucket order in data mining area. In the application aspect, we are exploring more interesting possibilities to apply our framework, in addition to usual databases and web applications discussed in Section 5.

Acknowledgements. Thanks to Qiong Fang for updating the experimental results presented in Section 5 in this published version. This work is partially supported by HKUST grant under grant No. DAG04/05.EG10.

References

1. Ailon, N., Charikar, M., Newman, A.: Aggregating inconsistent information: Ranking and clustering. In: ACM STOC, pp. 684–693 (2005)
2. Chomicki, J.: Preference formulas in relational queries. ACM Transaction Database System 28(4), 427–466 (2003)
3. Fagin, R., Kumar, R., Mahdian, M.: Comparing and aggregating with ties. In: ACM PODS, pp. 47–58 (2004)

4. Feng, J., Fang, Q., Ng, W.: Discovering Bucket Orders from Full Rankings. In: ACM SIG-MOD (2008)
5. Gionis, A., Mannila, H., Puolamaki, K., Ukkonen, A.: Algorithms for discovering bucket orders from data. In: ACM SIGKDD, pp. 561–566 (2006)
6. Goharian, N., Jain, A., Sun, Q.: Comparative analysis of sparse matrix algorithms for information retrieval. Journal of Sys., Cyb. and Inf. 1(1) (2003)
7. Kießling, W., Köstler, G.: Foundations of Preference in Database Systems. In: Proc. of VLDB (2002)
8. Ng, W.: Prioritized Preferences and Choice Constraints. In: Parent, C., Schewe, K.-D., Storey, V.C., Thalheim, B. (eds.) ER 2007. LNCS, vol. 4801, pp. 261–276. Springer, Heidelberg (2007)
9. Tan, Q., et al.: Applying Co-training to Clickthrough Data for Search Engine Adaptation. In: Lee, Y., Li, J., Whang, K.-Y., Lee, D. (eds.) DASFAA 2004. LNCS, vol. 2973, pp. 519–532. Springer, Heidelberg (2004)
10. Puolamäki, K., Fortelius, M., Mannila, H.: Seriation in paleontological data using markov chain monte carlo methods. PLoS Computational Bioglogy 2(2) (2006)
11. van Zuylen, A., et al.: Deterministic pivoting algorithms for constrained ranking and clustering problems. In: ACM-SIAM SODA, pp. 405–414 (2007)

A Conceptual Modeling Framework for Expressing Observational Data Semantics*

Shawn Bowers[1], Joshua S. Madin[2], and Mark P. Schildhauer[3]

[1]Genome Center, University of California, Davis
[2]Dept. of Biological Sciences, Macquarie University, Australia
[3]National Center for Ecological Analysis and Synthesis, UC Santa Barbara
sbowers@ucdavis.edu, {madin,schild}@nceas.ucsb.edu

Abstract. Observational data (i.e., data that records observations and measurements) plays a key role in many scientific disciplines. Observational data, however, are typically structured and described in *ad hoc* ways, making its discovery and integration difficult. The wide range of data collected, the variety of ways the data are used, and the needs of existing analysis applications make it impractical to define "one-size-fits-all" schemas for most observational data sets. Instead, new approaches are needed to flexibly describe observational data for effective discovery and integration. In this paper, we present a generic conceptual-modeling framework for capturing the semantics of observational data. The framework extends standard conceptual modeling approaches with new constructs for describing observations and measurements. Key to the framework is the ability to describe observation context, including complex, nested context relationships. We describe our proposed modeling framework, focusing on context and its use in expressing observational data semantics.

1   Introduction

Scientific knowledge is typically derived from relatively simple, underlying measurements directly linked to real-world phenomena. Such measurements are often recorded and stored in *observational data sets*, which are then analyzed by researchers using a variety of tools and methodologies. Many fields increasingly use observational data from multiple disciplines (genetics, biology, geology, hydrology, sociology, etc.) to tackle broader and more complex scientific questions. Within ecology, e.g., cross-disciplinary data is necessary to investigate complex environmental issues at broad geographic and temporal scales. Carrying out such studies requires the integration and synthesis of observational data from multiple research efforts [1,2]. These investigations, however, are hindered by the heterogeneity of observational data, which impedes the ability of researchers to discover, interpret, and integrate relevant data collected by others.

The heterogeneity of observational data is due to a number of factors: (1) most observational data are collected by individuals, institutions, or scientific communities through independent (i.e., uncoordinated) research projects; (2) the structure of observational

---

* This work supported in part by NSF grants #0533368, #0553768, #0612326, #0225676, #0630033, and #0612326.

Q. Li et al. (Eds.): ER 2008, LNCS 5231, pp. 41–54, 2008.

data is often chosen based on collection methods (e.g., to make data easier to record "in the field") or the format requirements of analysis tools, as opposed to standard schemas; and (3) the terms and concepts used to label data are not standardized, both within and across scientific disciplines and research groups [3]. This need for a more uniform mechanism to describe observational data has led to a number of proposals for observational data models [4,5,6] and ontologies [7,8,9,10]. While many of these approaches provide domain-specific vocabularies for describing data, or data models for storing certain types of observational data, generic and extensible approaches for modeling observational data semantics are still needed.

We present an initial step towards such a generic conceptual modeling framework for observational data. Our framework extends traditional conceptual modeling languages with constructs for explicitly modeling observations, measurements, and observation context. Our approach aims to address challenges associated with the following general characteristics of observational data:

- Observational data are primarily stored as tables within text files, where each data set corresponds to a single table within one file. This situation stems from data being generated for use in common analytical programs, e.g., spreadsheet tools.
- Observational data sets are represented in first normal form (1NF), but are not otherwise normalized, with no integrity constraints given.
- Observational data are not initially created from explicit conceptual models (e.g., ER or UML diagrams).
- Observational data do not represent a set of facts, or "ontological" truths about the world; instead, they represent (possibly conflicting) measurements of phenomena within some broader context.
- Observational data do not use standardized terms for attribute names and coded values (e.g., species or location names). The terms used, however, may be informally described within plain-text metadata descriptions.

We envision conceptual models being created within our framework to describe *existing* observational data, primarily for the purpose of enabling discovery and integration of data sets. That is, while it may be possible to employ a more traditional "top down" modeling approach using our framework, we are primarily focused on the case of supplementing existing data with formal, semantic content descriptions. We call this process *semantic annotation*, whereby annotations referencing an external conceptual model serve to clarify and constrain the interpretation of the original data set.

As others have noted (e.g., [11,12,13]), it is often difficult to represent observations and their context in traditional conceptual-modeling languages. For example, Fig. 1 shows three hypothetical observational data sets together with their corresponding ER diagrams. Fig. 1(a) shows diameter measurements of trunks of different tree species taken in different years. Fig. 1(b) depicts similar yearly measurements of tree trunk diameters, but where trees are located within plots, plots have average daily temperatures, and plots are located within sites. Fig. 1(c) also consists of tree diameter measurements, where trees are located along a transect (a fixed path within an area) and within a particular type of soil, soil acidity is measured, and each transect has a particular type of treatment applied (either a high or low watering regime). These relatively simple examples demonstrate the need for semantic descriptions to clarify similarities

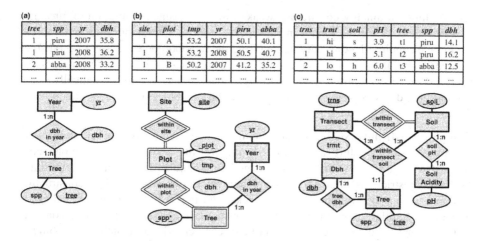

Fig. 1. Three simple observational data sets and example ER representations: (a) diameter-at-breast-height (dbh) measurements per year for tree species; (b) dbh per year for tree species located in plots within sites; and (c) dbh and soil pH (acidity) measurements along transects. The attribute spp* in (b) generalizes the two attributes labeled with species names, *piru* and *abba*. Cardinality restrictions x:y denote the min and max participation of the entity in the corresponding role of the relationship.

and differences among data sets. For example, it is not obvious from the attributes and data values, nor the ER diagrams, whether these three data sets contain similar types of measurements.

While the conceptual models of Fig. 1 help to describe these data sets, they also highlight challenges in expressing observational data semantics that are crucial to the scientific interpretation and potential usage of these data for an integrated analysis:

Implicit context. In each example data set, the same tree entity has different diameter (dbh) values. These discrepancies are explained by the context in which the diameter measurements occur. In general, context describes the meaningful "surroundings" of an observation, such as the other entities observed, their measured values, and their relationship to the observed entity. However, context is only implicitly modeled in Fig. 1: it is unclear which relationships denote context (e.g., "dbh in year", "within plot") and which denote measurements (e.g., "tree dbh", "soil pH"). Similarly, context is only partially specified: it is not explicitly stated that transects and soils are context for trees, or that trees also serve as context for soils. Without an understanding of the contextual relationships within a data set, it becomes difficult to interpret and analyze data. In Fig. 1, e.g., it is not trivial to determine whether it is meaningful to summarize temperatures across years (computing a yearly average), or how to compute average tree diameter by soil type. This in turn has ramifications for data integration, which often requires the aggregation of observations to combine data [10].

Coupled structure and semantics. Although similar, the conceptual models in each of the examples reflect potentially important differences. These differences are primarily due to variation in methodologies used to collect data, and are expressed through relationships, cardinality constraints, weak-entity constraints, promotion of attributes to entities, etc. While the same general types of entities and relationships exist across the three examples, the difficulty of capturing the methodological constraints (such as context) within models impairs the ability to: (1) define domain-specific concepts and relationships (e.g., within a shared ontology) that can be used to semantically annotate *multiple* datasets; and (2) easily compare the semantics of different data sets for discovery and integration.

Complex constraints. Similarly, constructing conceptual models of observational data using traditional modeling languages often requires the combination of complex constraints in conjunction with "advanced" modeling features (e.g., n-ary relationships, cardinality restrictions). Because of the complexity of observational data, constructing appropriate conceptual models is often tricky, and thus a time-consuming and error-prone task. Similarly, these approaches often require knowledge of esoteric concepts that would not be intuitive to most scientific researchers who ultimately need to understand and use the data.

The rest of this paper is organized as follows. In Section 2 we describe our proposed framework for modeling observational data. Our approach addresses a number of the challenges highlighted above: (1) we introduce explicit constructs for modeling observations and their context, thereby allowing domain-specific concepts and relationships to be decoupled from the constraints imposed by data-collection methods; (2) because of this separation of concerns, the complex constraints needed to represent observational data are reduced; and (3) the framework provides a natural approach for data annotation and summarization. In Section 3 we describe related work, and discuss future directions in Section 4.

2   Modeling Observational Data

The basic constructs of our modeling framework are depicted in Fig. 2. We introduce new constructs (left) for representing measurement standards, measurements, observations, and context. These constructs are layered upon "traditional" ER constructs (right), namely, entities, relationships, attributes (called "characteristics" in Fig. 2), and values.

Measurement standards represent the various criteria used for comparing measured values. Examples of measurement standards include units (e.g., meter, gram, square centimeter), nominal and ordinal codes (e.g., location or color names, gender codes), scales (e.g., pH, Richter scale, drought severity index), and date-time standards. Values are combined with measurement standards to form **Standard Values**. Although not described here, measurement standards are often classified by a standard typology that differentiates nominal, ordinal, interval, and ratio measurements [14].

Measurements consist of a characteristic (i.e., attribute) and a standard value.[1] In our framework, each value within an observational data set represents a measurement. For example, the first value in the *dbh* column of Fig. 1(a) denotes a measurement consisting of a characteristic of type 'diameter-at-breast-height', the unit 'centimeter', and the value '35.8'. Values representing categorical and identifying information are

---

[1] Measurements may also have additional information, such as *precision* and *accuracy*.

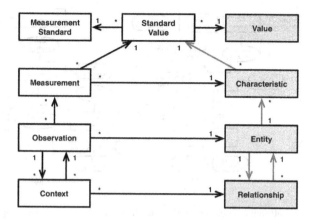

Fig. 2. A metamodel for describing observational data

also considered measurements. For example, in Fig. 1(c), the *trns* column denotes measurements having characteristics of type 'name' according to a local transect naming scheme, and similarly, the *trmt* column represents measurements having characteristics of type 'water-level' and a measurement standard that defines the values 'hi' and 'lo'.

Observations consist of an entity (denoting the entity observed) and a set of measurements. Each measurement associated with an observation applies to the observed entity. That is, an observation asserts through a measurement that a particular value was observed for one of the characteristics of the entity (implicitly shown by the gray arrows on the right of Fig. 2). In addition, an observation can be related to zero or more observations through context. A **Context** consists of a relationship and an observation, and states that an observation was made within the scope of another observation. A contextual relationship between observations asserts that the relationship was observed between the corresponding entities.

As shown in Fig. 2, binary directed relationships are used within the framework for modeling observational data. Binary, as opposed to more general n-ary relationships, are employed for two primary reasons: (1) they allow for ontology languages based on description logics (e.g., OWL-DL[2]) to be easily used within our framework to define domain-specific vocabularies for data annotation (e.g., where entities are expressed via OWL-DL classes, relationships through object properties, and characteristics through datatype properties); and (2) they generally result in models that are simpler and easier to define (although less restrictive). We also use the term 'characteristic' instead of 'attribute' to distinguish the semantic property being described from the particular column label used within a data set. In particular, the process of annotation involves associating the attributes of a given data set with specific characteristics defined in domain-specific vocabularies (described further below).

Fig. 3 shows three observational models for describing the data sets of Fig. 1. Instead of defining entity, relationship, and attribute types (as in Fig. 1), the diagrams of Fig. 3 define the observation, measurement, and context types for the data sets.

---

[2] http://www.w3.org/TR/owl-ref/

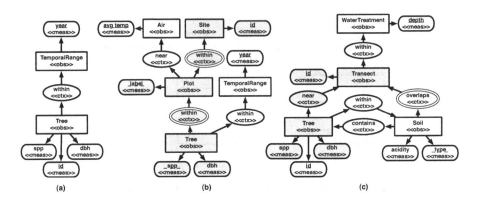

Fig. 3. Example observational conceptual models for the data sets of Fig. 1. Rectangles denote observations labeled with the corresponding entity, rounded boxes represent measurements labeled with the corresponding characteristic, and ovals represent context labeled with the corresponding relationship. To simplify the diagrams, measurement standards are not shown. Closely related concepts of (b) and (c) are highlighted.

These types *reference* the appropriate entity, relationship, and characteristic types defined, e.g., within one or more shared ontologies. As shown, measurements and context relationships can be used to denote distinct entities (via keys, weak entities, and identifying relationships), where the same entity may be involved in multiple observations.

The examples of Fig. 3 demonstrate many of the advantages of our framework for describing observational data. Because observational structures (observations, measurements, context) and semantic structures (entities, relationships, characteristics) are decoupled, the latter can be used uniformly across observational models (e.g., dbh or the 'within' relationship). Similarly, creating models for observational data can be driven by the definitions within standard ontologies, thereby simplifying the annotation process, and lowering the potential for terminological ambiguity. As an example, characteristic and relationship types can be defined within an external ontology to be used only with specific types of entities, thus suggesting entity types for characteristics, and vice versa.

Another advantage is that context is explicitly represented and distinguished from measurements. In contrast to Fig. 1, context relationships are directed, allowing one to easily determine the context hierarchies (or "paths") induced by observations. Similar to summarizability in multidimensional databases [15], context hierarchies can help determine the meaningful summarizations available within a data set. Context relationships also encourage the full disclosure of *what* was observed, which is critical metadata that is often left implicit in observational data. This is demonstrated in Fig. 3(c), where an explicit observation type is used to denote water entities used as experimental treatments, in which the corresponding depth measurement denotes the height of the water level. Similarly, in Fig. 3(b), an explicit air observation type is used to signify that air temperature was measured (as opposed to water or body temperature, e.g.).

Below we further describe the framework of Fig. 2. We first give a formal definition of the modeling constructs, focusing on instance-level descriptions. We then describe types, which are used to construct observational models (e.g., as in Fig. 3). We also show how existing data sets can be annotated with conceptual models defined in our framework, and finally discuss issues related to summarization.

2.1 Observation Instances

An instance of a model is constructed from the following base and derived sets. *Val* is the set of measurement values (integers, doubles, strings, etc.). *Std* is the set of measurement standards (units, scales, etc.). *Ent* is the set of entity objects. *ObsId* is the set of observation identifiers. *Rel* is the set of identifiers denoting binary, directed relationships between entities. And *Char* is the set of identifiers denoting entity characteristics that relate specific entities to standard values. The derived structures are built from these base sets as follows.

$$StdVal \subseteq Val \times Std$$
$$EntRel \subseteq Ent \times Rel \times Ent$$
$$EntChar \subseteq Ent \times Char \times StdVal$$
$$Obs \subseteq ObsId \times Ent \times \mathcal{P}(Meas) \times \mathcal{P}(Ctx)$$
$$Meas \subseteq Char \times StdVal$$
$$Ctx \subseteq Rel \times ObsId$$

A standard value consists of a measurement standard and a value, e.g., $StdVal(5, \text{cm})$ denotes the quantity "5 centimeters" (where cm represents the unit centimeter). The elements of *Rel* and *Char* act as "handles" to specific relationship and characteristic occurrences such that *EntRel* and *EntChar* specify the relationships and characteristics, respectively. If $EntRel(e_1, r, e_2)$, we say e_1 is r-related to e_2, and that r goes from e_1 to e_2. Similarly, if $EntChar(e, c, v)$, we say that e has the standard value v for characteristic c. Entities may have at most one value for a characteristic. Each observation has an explicit identifier and consists of an entity, a set of measurements, and a set of contexts. For convenience, we often write $o = Obs(e, M, C)$ to denote an observation $Obs(o, e, M, C)$. A measurement consists of a characteristic and a standard value. And a context consists of a relationship and a reference to an observation.

Example 1 (Observation instance). A portion of the instance of the observational model of Fig. 3(a) corresponding to the first row of the data set in Fig. 1(a) is given below, where c_1 to c_4 are characteristics of type `Year`, Dbh (diameter at breast height), Spp (taxonomic name), and Id, respectively, and r_1 is a relationship of type `Within`.

$$o_1 = Obs(e_1, \{m_1\}, \emptyset)$$
$$m_1 = Meas(c_1, StdVal(2007, \text{datetime}))$$
$$o_2 = Obs(e_2, \{m_2, m_3, m_4\}, \{Ctx(r_1, o_1)\})$$
$$m_2 = Meas(c_2, StdVal(35.8, \text{cm}))$$
$$m_3 = Meas(c_3, StdVal(\text{Picea rubens, ITIS}))$$
$$m_4 = Meas(c_4, StdVal(1, \text{LocalTreeIds}))$$

Here, e_1 and e_2 denote entities of type `TemporalRange` and `Tree`, respectively; ITIS represents a taxonomic name standard[3]; and LocalTreeIds represents a catalog of tree ids local to the study.

As mentioned above, observations represent assertions about entities. In particular, measurements imply that within a given context, an entity was observed to have the corresponding measured characteristic values. Similarly, observations inherit the assertions of their contextual observations. The assertions of an observation are obtained by "entering" the observation, given by the operation $enter(o)$[4], for an observation o. Let

$$context : ObsId \rightarrow \mathcal{P}(ObsId)$$

be a function that takes an observation and returns its corresponding contextual observations. For an observation $o = Obs(e, M, C)$, we define

$$context(o) = \{o' \mid \exists r \; Ctx(r, o') \in C\},$$

where $context^+$ denotes the transitive closure of $context$. For $context^+(o) = O$, we define $enter(o) = E_m \cup E_r \cup E_c$ such that:

$$E_m = \{EntChar(e, c, v) \mid Meas(c, v) \in M\}$$
$$E_r = \{EntRel(e, r, e') \mid \exists o' M' C' \; (Ctx(r, o') \in C) \land (o' = Obs(e', M', C'))\}$$
$$E_c = \bigcup_{o' \in O} enter(o')$$

For example, Fig. 4 shows the result of entering two different observations corresponding to the first two rows of data in Fig. 1(b). Entering a tree observation (i.e., for the *piru* attribute; denoted by o5 in the figure) results in assertions "up" the context hierarchy of Fig. 3(b), and includes the corresponding temporal, plot, air, and site observations. Entering a plot observation (denoted by o3 in the figure), however, results only in corresponding plot, air, and site assertions.

By providing a semantics for observation context, the *enter* operation can also help verify the consistency of conceptual models and their instances. In particular, for an observation to be consistent, the result of entering the observation must be consistent. The latter is determined by the constraints implied by the corresponding semantic constructs (entities, relationships, characteristics). For example, because entities have at most one value for a characteristic of a given type (such as dbh in Fig. 3), the result of entering an observation must also satisfy this constraint. Adding a new observation o8 to Fig. 4 with observation context o5 and o7 would violate this constraint, e.g., since the union of *enter*(o5) and *enter*(o7) is inconsistent. Similarly, cardinality constraints on relationships must be satisfied after entering an observation.

2.2 Observation Types and Models

As mentioned above, decoupling observational and semantic structures allows semantic types (i.e., the entity, relationship, and characteristic types) to be defined independently

---

[3] Integrated Taxonomic Information System, http://www.itis.gov

[4] The notion of entering an observation is similar in spirit to "lifting" operators in [16].

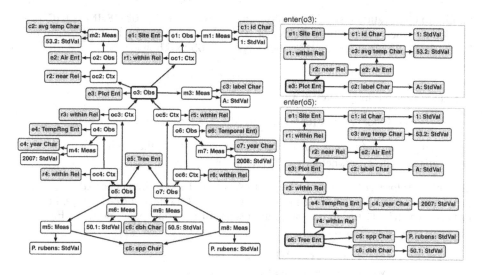

Fig. 4. Example instances of the first two rows of Fig. 1(b), for the *Picea rubens* (*piru*) species (left), and the corresponding result of entering observations o3 and o5 (right). For simplicity, measurement standards are not shown for standard values.

of observations and measurements. Thus, the same semantic types can be used to describe multiple observational data sets. In prior work [3,10], we have used OWL-DL for defining entity, relationship, and characteristic types. However, the framework is not limited to a specific approach (such as OWL), and instead can support the use of a number of different conceptual modeling languages. Here we consider a simple typing language for the purpose of defining observational models such as those of Fig. 3.

We define base types `Std`, `Val`, `StdVal`, `Meas`, `Obs`, `ObsId`, `Ctx`, `Char`, `Ent`, and `Rel` for constructing observational models. We require subtypes τ' of types τ, written $\tau' \sqsubseteq \tau$, to imply subset relations. That is, $\tau' \sqsubseteq \tau$ iff $[\![\tau']\!] \subseteq [\![\tau]\!]$, where $[\![\tau]\!]$ denotes the set of instances of a type τ. If $\tau' \sqsubseteq \tau$ we say that τ' *is-a* τ. Similarly, if x is an instance of a type τ, we write $x : \tau$ such that $x : \tau$ iff $x \in [\![\tau]\!]$. Each base type denotes its corresponding instance-level set, e.g., $[\![\text{Val}]\!] \equiv Val$, $[\![\text{Std}]\!] \equiv Std$, etc. With slight abuse of notation, we define the standard-value, observation, measurement, and context base types as follows.

$$\text{StdVal} \sqsubseteq \text{Val} \times \text{Std}$$
$$\text{Obs} \sqsubseteq \text{ObsId} \times \text{Ent} \times \mathcal{P}(\text{Meas}) \times \mathcal{P}(\text{Ctx})$$
$$\text{Meas} \sqsubseteq \text{Char} \times \text{StdVal}$$
$$\text{Ctx} \sqsubseteq \text{Rel} \times \text{ObsId}$$

These types correspond to the instance-level sets defined above as follows.

$$[\![\text{StdVal}]\!] \subseteq [\![\text{Val}]\!] \times [\![\text{Std}]\!]$$
$$[\![\text{Obs}]\!] \subseteq [\![\text{ObsId}]\!] \times [\![\text{Ent}]\!] \times \mathcal{P}([\![\text{Meas}]\!]) \times \mathcal{P}([\![\text{Ctx}]\!])$$
$$[\![\text{Meas}]\!] \subseteq [\![\text{Char}]\!] \times [\![\text{StdVal}]\!]$$
$$[\![\text{Ctx}]\!] \subseteq [\![\text{Rel}]\!] \times [\![\text{ObsId}]\!]$$

Similar to observation instances, for convenience we write $O = \text{Obs}(E, \{M_1, ...\}, \{C_1, ...\})$ to denote the type $\text{Obs}(O, E, \{M_1, ...\}, \{C_1, ...\})$. In general, a type definition $\text{Obs}(O, E, \{M_1, M_2, ...\}, \{C_1, C_2, ...\})$ implies a type $\tau \sqsubseteq \text{Obs}$ such that:

$$\tau \sqsubseteq O \times E \times \mathcal{P}(M_1 \cup M_2 \cup ...) \times \mathcal{P}(C_1 \cup C_2 \cup ...).$$

This definition similarly states that:

$$[\![\tau]\!] \subseteq [\![\text{Obs}]\!] \cap ([\![O]\!] \times [\![E]\!] \times \mathcal{P}([\![M_1]\!] \cup [\![M_2]\!] \cup ...) \times \mathcal{P}([\![C_1]\!] \cup [\![C_2]\!] \cup ...)).$$

Thus, using these definitions it is straightforward to test whether an instance x is of an observational type τ, or whether $\tau \sqsubseteq \tau'$ for two observational types.

Example 2 (Observation types). Let $\text{DateTime}, \text{ITIS}, \text{Cm}, \text{LocalTreeIds} \sqsubseteq \text{Std}$; $\text{Int}, \text{String}, \text{Double} \sqsubseteq \text{Val}$; $\text{Year}, \text{Spp}, \text{Id}, \text{Dbh} \sqsubseteq \text{Char}$; $\text{TemporalRange}, \text{Tree} \sqsubseteq \text{Ent}$; and $\text{Within} \sqsubseteq \text{Rel}$. The observation types of the conceptual model of Fig. 3(a) can be expressed as follows.

$$\text{DateTimeVal} = \text{StdVal}(\text{Int}, \text{DateTime})$$
$$\text{YearMeas} = \text{Meas}(\text{Year}, \text{DateTimeVal})$$
$$\text{TemporalRangeObs} = \text{Obs}(\text{TemporalRange}, \{\text{YearMeas}\}, \bot)$$
$$\text{SppMeas} = \text{Meas}(\text{Spp}, \text{StdVal}(\text{String}, \text{ITIS}))$$
$$\text{IdMeas} = \text{Meas}(\text{Id}, \text{StdVal}(\text{Int}, \text{LocalTreeIds}))$$
$$\text{DbhMeas} = \text{Meas}(\text{Dbh}, \text{StdVal}(\text{Double}, \text{Cm}))$$
$$\text{TreeObs} = \text{Obs}(\text{Tree}, \{\text{SppMeas}, \text{IdMeas}, \text{DbhMeas}\}, \{\text{WithinCtx}\})$$
$$\text{WithinCtx} = \text{Ctx}(\text{Within}, \text{TemporalRangeObs})$$

An observational **model** $M = (O, K, W)$ consists of a set of observation types O, a set of key constraints $K \subseteq O \times \mathcal{P}(C)$, and a set of weak-entity constraints $W \subseteq O \times \mathcal{P}(C) \times \mathcal{P}(R \times O)$, where C and R denote the set of characteristic and relationship types, respectively. For every $(O, \{C_1, ..., C_n\}) \in K$, we require observation type O to have a measurement type M_i with characteristic type C_i, for $1 \leq i \leq n$. We similarly constrain $(O, \{C_1, ..., C_n\}, \{(R_1, O_1), ..., (R_m, O_m)\}) \in W$, adding the additional constraint that observation type O also consist of a context type having relationship type R_j and observation type O_j for $1 \leq j \leq m$

Example 3 (Observational model). Assume we have the following type definitions for the model of Fig. 3(b):

$$\text{TreeObs} = \text{Obs}(\text{Tree}, \{\text{SppMeas}, \text{DbhMeas}\}, \{\text{PlotCtx}, \text{YearCtx}\})$$
$$\text{PlotObs} = \text{Obs}(\text{Plot}, \{\text{LabelMeas}\}, \{\text{AirCtx}, \text{SiteCtx}\})$$
$$\text{AirObs} = \text{Obs}(\text{Air}, \{\text{AvgTmpMeas}\}, \bot)$$
$$\text{SiteObs} = \text{Obs}(\text{Site}, \{\text{IdMeas}\}, \bot)$$
$$\text{YearObs} = \text{Obs}(\text{TemporalRange}, \{\text{YearMeas}\}, \bot)$$
$$\text{PlotCtx} = \text{Ctx}(\text{Within}, \text{PlotObs})$$
$$\text{AirCtx} = \text{Ctx}(\text{Near}, \text{AirObs})$$
$$\text{SiteCtx} = \text{Ctx}(\text{Within}, \text{SiteObs})$$
$$\text{YearCtx} = \text{Ctx}(\text{Within}, \text{YearObs}).$$

The model $M = (O, K, W)$ shown in Fig. 3(b) is defined as:

$$O = \{\texttt{TreeObs}, \texttt{PlotObs}, \texttt{AirObs}, \texttt{SiteObs}, \texttt{YearObs}\}$$
$$K = \{(\texttt{SiteObs}, \{\texttt{Id}\}), (\texttt{YearObs}, \{\texttt{Year}\}), (\texttt{AirObs}, \{\texttt{AvgTmp}\})\}$$
$$W = \{(\texttt{TreeObs}, \{\texttt{Spp}\}, \{(\texttt{Within}, \texttt{PlotObs})\})$$
$$(\texttt{PlotObs}, \{\texttt{Label}\}, \{(\texttt{Within}, \texttt{SiteObs})\})\},$$

An **instance** $I \subseteq Obs$ of a model $M = (O, K, W)$, denoted $I : M$, consists of a set of observations that are instances of types in O. If $I : M$, then I must satisfy the key and weak-entity constraints of M. These constraints are the same as those of standard ER models, but apply indirectly through observations and context. For example, if $o_1, o_2 \in I$ are of type O in M such that $(O, \{C_1, \ldots, C_n\}) \in K$ and both o_1 and o_2 have the same characteristic instances (implying the same characteristic values, see Fig. 4) for C_1 to C_n, then both instances must reference the same entity instance. Additionally, if $I : M$, we require $enter(o)$ to be consistent for each $o \in I$.

2.3   Annotation

Given a data set D and a conceptual model M, we annotate D with M by relating attributes of D to measurements in M. The result of this process is an *annotation* $A = (D, M, \Sigma)$ consisting of a set of mappings $\Sigma \subseteq V \times O \times C$, where V is a set of attribute names, O is a set of observation types, and C is a set of characteristic types. If $(V, O, C) \in \Sigma$, we require that V be an attribute of D, O be an observation type in M, and C be a characteristic type for some measurement type of O.

Example 4 (Annotation). The annotation $A = (D, M, \Sigma)$ for data set D of Fig. 1(a) and model M of Fig. 3(a) consists of the mappings:

$$\Sigma = \{(tree, \texttt{TreeObs}, \texttt{Id}), (spp, \texttt{TreeObs}, \texttt{Spp}),$$
$$(yr, \texttt{TemporalRangeObs}, \texttt{Year}), (dbh, \texttt{TreeObs}, \texttt{Dbh})\}.$$

Additional rules are often needed to define Σ, e.g., for converting data-set values to allowable values of a measurement standard. Thus, a set Σ is often accompanied by more complex expressions. Observational models may also contain measurements not directly linked to data-set attributes. In Fig. 1(b), e.g., we may know that all plots of the study have a $10m^2$ area, which typically would not be stored in a data set since the corresponding column would contain the same value in every row.

Annotations provide a mechanism to determine the semantics of attributes in a data set. For instance, from an annotation we can determine for each attribute: (1) the corresponding measurement in the conceptual model; (2) the observation in which the measurement was made; (3) the characteristic, measurement standard, and entity associated with the attribute; (4) other attributes of the data set associated with the same observation; and (5) the observations, measurements, and attributes serving as context for the attribute. It is also possible to construct schema mappings (i.e., views [17]) from annotations that map instances of data-set schemas to instances of observational models. Such mappings can be used to generate instances of the model, query data sets via the model, or integrate data sets across models.

2.4   Data Summarization

Meaningful summaries of data are often constrained by the direction of context relation-ships. In particular, similar to "roll-up" operations in multidimensional and statistical databases [15], summarization is often performed over contextualized observations and measurements, where measurements of observations that are "lower" in a context hi-erarchy are summarized by observations that are "higher" in the context hierarchy. For instance, computing an average water-treatment depth by transect in Fig. 3(c) is not meaningful, since each transect has exactly one depth. However, computing average tree-trunk diameter by transect in Fig. 3(c) is a generally meaningful summarization.

The types and constraints defined within observational models can be used to enable summarization testing [18], i.e., to automatically determine and compute meaningful summarizations. For instance, the measurement standard (e.g., nominal, ordinal, inter-val, ratio) determines the kinds of summaries that can be applied to an observation [14]. Cardinality constraints on observations imposed by context relationships also can suggest summaries. For instance, in Fig. 3(b) each plot within a site contains a *single* average air temperature, which can be used to compute average air temperatures by site (via the plots within the site). Key and weak-entity constraints also enable summariza-tion by determining when two observations reference the same entity. For example, averaging soil acidity by tree species in Fig. 3(c) is made possible by first averag-ing acidity for each tree entity, and then aggregating over the set of entities of each species.

Finally, annotations allow summarizations over data-set attributes to be analyzed and computed according to the constraints of the corresponding observational model. For example, given a desired summarization expressed over data-set attributes, the corre-sponding measurement types within the model can be obtained, and then used to check whether the summarization is meaningful, and if so, to determine how it should be carried out (i.e., based on context relationships, key, and weak-entity constraints).

3   Related Work

A number of data models [4,5,6] and ontologies [7,8,9,10] have been proposed to support observational data (see [3] for a general survey). Our approach differs by pro-viding formal and generic constructs for describing observations, measurements, and contexts that are compatible with well-established conceptual-modeling languages (ER, UML, description logics) and suitable for data annotation. Our approach also supports generic context relationships that are either missing or provided only through specific properties in existing approaches (e.g., recording when or where a measurement was taken). In [10], we describe an OWL ontology developed within the SEEK project[5] that includes concepts similar to those presented here. We extend these ideas in this paper by: (1) identifying and formalizing the constructs of Fig. 2; (2) providing a general definition and formalization of context that can reference arbitrary relationships; (3) defining observational models that include key and weak-entity constraints; and (4)

---

[5] Science Environment for Ecological Knowledge: http://seek.ecoinformatics.org

describing a formal approach for annotating data sets with observational models. In [10], we define concept hierarchies and properties for measurement standards including units and unit conversions, which can also be used in the framework presented here.

Approaches for representing context have been widely studied in logic [16,19] and conceptual modeling [20,12,11]. For instance, in [11], an ER model is extended by adding "weak attributes" to support context and data quality; in [12], ORM extensions are proposed to support context-aware applications; and in [20] context is modeled via sets of objects that can be related via classification, generalization, and attribution. In contrast, our approach distinctly separates observations of entities from entities and indirectly assigns context to entities via observations, thus providing additional flexibility for describing observational data and associated context relationships. Similar to context, a number of ER extensions have also been proposed to explicitly support temporal aspects of data [13]. In [21,22,23], approaches for reverse-engineering databases into ER models are proposed, where [21] defines an approach to generate ER models from denormalized relational sources (as in Fig. 1). Many annotation approaches have been proposed, ranging from column-level tagging [24] to query-based mappings [17]. Our approach differs by employing simple annotations to observational models (as opposed to arbitrary ontologies) from which more complex mappings can be constructed. Finally, summarization is well-established in multidimensional and statistical database systems with techniques developed for testing summarizability [15,18], and our framework can directly leverage these approaches.

4   Summary and Future Work

We have presented an approach for modeling observational data that extends existing conceptual-modeling frameworks by adding new constructs for representing observations, measurements, measurement standards, and context. The benefits of our approach include a formal and generic treatment of observation context, the ability to decouple observational models from conceptual descriptions (allowing observational data to be described via shared ontologies), an approach for simplifying data annotation (e.g., based on key, weak-entity, and context constraints), and support for data summarization. These benefits directly address challenges in interpreting and integrating heterogeneous observational data that are critical for supporting broad-scale scientific analyses.

We have implemented a number of prototype tools within the SEEK project based on an earlier version of the framework presented here. These tools support semantic annotation and discovery of observational data sets described in the EML[6] metadata language. We intend to extend these tools to support the constructs and annotation approach presented here. We are also exploring summarization capabilities and the merging of multiple data sets via observational models. Finally, we are developing a number of domain-specific ecological ontologies to support the annotation of ecological data within our framework.

---

[6] http://knb.ecoinformatics.org/software/eml

References

1. Andelman, S., Bowles, C., Willig, M., Waide, R.: Understanding environmental complexity through a distributed knowledge network. BioSciences 54(3), 240–246 (2004)
2. Ellison, A., et al.: Analytic webs support the synthesis of ecological datasets. Ecology 87, 1345–1358 (2006)
3. Madin, J., Bowers, S., Schildhauer, M., Jones, M.: Advancing ecological research with ontologies. Trends Ecol. Evol. 23(3), 159–168 (2008)
4. Cox, S.: Observations and measurements. Technical Report 05-087r4, OGC (2006)
5. Tarboton, D., Horsburgh, J., Maidment, D.: CUAHSI community observations data model (ODM), version 1.0 (2007), http://water.usu.edu/cuahsi/odm/
6. Cushing, J., Nadkarni, N., Finch, M., Fiala, A., Murphy-Hill, E., Delcambre, L., Maier, D.: Component-based end-user database design for ecologists. J. Intell. Inf. Syst. 29(1), 7–24 (2007)
7. McGuinness, D., et al.: The virtual solar-terrestrial observatory: A deployed semantic web application case study for scientific research. In: AAAI (2007)
8. Williams, R., Martinez, N., Goldbeck, J.: Ontologies for ecoinformatics. J. of Web Semantics 4, 237–242 (2006)
9. Raskin, R.: Enabling semantic interoperability for earth science data (2004), http://sweet.jpl.nasa.gov
10. Madin, J., Bowers, S., Schildhauer, M., Krivov, S., Pennington, D., Villa, F.: An ontology for describing and synthesizing ecological observation data. Eco. Inf. 2, 279–296 (2006)
11. Tu, S., Wang, R.: Modeling data quality and context through extension of the ER model. In: Workshop on Information Technologies and Systems (1993)
12. Henricksen, K., Indulska, J., McFadden, T.: Modelling context information with ORM. In: OTM Workshops (2005)
13. Gregersen, H., Jensen, C.: Temporal entity-relationship models – a survey. TKDE 11, 464–497 (1999)
14. Stevens, S.: On the theory of scales of measurement. Science 103, 677–680 (1946)
15. Lenz, H., Shoshani, A.: Summarizability in OLAP and statistical data bases. In: SSDBM (1997)
16. McCarthy, J.: Notes on formalizing context. In: IJCAI (1993)
17. Beeri, C., Levy, A., Rousset, M.: Rewriting queries using views in description logics. In: PODS (1997)
18. Hurtado, C., Mendelzon, A.: OLAP dimension constraints. In: PODS (2002)
19. Guha, R., McCarthy, J.: Varieties of contexts. In: International and Interdisciplinary Conference on Modeling and Using Context (2003)
20. Analyti, A., Theodorakis, M., Spyratos, N., Constantopoulos, P.: Contextualization as an independent abstraction mechanism for conceptual modeling. Inf. Syst. 32(1), 24–60 (2007)
21. Petit, J., Toumani, F., Boulicaut, J., Kouloumdjian, J.: Towards the reverse engineering of denormalized relational databases. In: ICDE (1996)
22. Alhajj, R.: Extracting the extended entity-relationship model from a legacy relational database. Inf. Syst. 28(6), 597–618 (2003)
23. Davis, K., Aiken, P.: Data reverse engineering: A historical survey. In: WCRE (2000)
24. An, Y., Borgida, A., Mylopoulos, J.: Discovering the semantics of relational tables through mappings. J. Data Semantics VII, 1–32 (2006)

Towards a Compositional Semantic Account of Data Quality Attributes

Lei Jiang[1], Alex Borgida[1,2], and John Mylopoulos[1,3]

[1] University of Toronto
[2] Rutgers University
[3] University of Trento
{leijiang,jm}@cs.toronto.edu, borgida@cs.rutgers.edu

Abstract. We address the fundamental question: what does it mean for data in a database to be of high quality? We motivate our discussion with examples, where traditional views on data quality are found to be unsatisfactory. Our work is founded on the premise that data values are primarily linguistic signs that convey meaning from their producer to their user through senses and referents. In this setting, data quality issues arise when discrepancies occur during this communication. We sketch a theory of senses for individual values in a relational table based on its semantics expressed using some ontology. We use this to offer a compositional approach, where data quality is expressed in terms of a variety of primitive relationships among values and their senses. We evaluate our approach by accounting for quality attributes in other frameworks proposed in the literature. This exercise allows us to (i) reveal and differentiate multiple, sometimes conflicting, definitions of a quality attribute, (ii) accommodate competing views on how these attributes are related, and (iii) point to possible new definitions.

1 Introduction

The quality of any artifact is determined by the degree to which it fulfills its intended use ("fitness for purpose"). Arguably, for a database the purpose is answering questions about the application it models. Data quality (DQ), the fitness of data values for question-answering purposes, is widely accepted as a multi-dimensional and a hierarchical concept [23,13,3]. More than a dozen proposals have been made to characterize and define various aspects of DQ (also called *quality dimensions* or *quality attributes*) in terms of a classification scheme. Examples of such schemes include (i) accessibility, interpretability, usefulness and believability DQ [23] (ii) intrinsic, contextual, representational, and accessibility DQ [24], and (iii) mandatory vs. desirable, primary vs. secondary, and direct vs. indirect DQ [5].

Criticism of these approaches includes ambiguity, subjectiveness, and even circularity of definitions within a single classification [4], and inconsistency across multiple classifications [13]. As an example of circular definition, credibility in [23] is considered as a sub-attribute of believability, but it is itself defined as having sufficient evidence to be believed; as an example of inconsistent definition, in [24] completeness and believability belong to two disjoint categories, while they are related

Q. Li et al. (Eds.): ER 2008, LNCS 5231, pp. 55–68, 2008.

through a specialization link in [23]. This lack of precision and consistency in defining DQ attributes also prevents one from answering even the most basic questions about how DQ attributes relate. For example, does imprecision imply inaccuracy? Does our judgment of completeness presuppose the notion of relevance? Do concepts such as trust, believability and credibility refer to the same DQ attribute? If not, how do they differ?

The objective of this paper is to address these problems by offering a formal framework for DQ. In particular, we consider a DQ attribute as a complex expression, where the meaning of the attribute is captured in terms of the meaning of its constituents and the structure of the expression. Instead of defining each DQ attribute separately, we seek to answer the following questions: (i) what are the primitive constituents from which DQ attributes can be expressed and (ii) how can these constituents be combined in a meaningful way. The concept of "*sign*" provides such a primitive notion for the investigation of these questions. Data values in a database are above all linguistic signs that convey meaning from their producer to their user; DQ issues arise when discrepancies occur during this communication. Based on these observations, we propose a novel, compositional approach to understand and define DQ attributes in terms of a variety of primitive relationships between values and their senses. We evaluate our approach by accounting for DQ attributes in other frameworks proposed in the literature. This exercise allows us to (i) reveal and differentiate multiple, sometimes conflicting, definitions of a quality attribute; (ii) accommodate competing views on how these attributes should be related; and (iii) point to possible new definitions.

The rest of paper is structured as follows. We motivate our discussion with some examples where traditional views on DQ are unsatisfactory in determining whether data is defective (Section 2). We then describe our view of data quality based on a triadic model of signs (Section 3), and sketch a theory of senses for individual values in a relational table based on its semantics expressed using some ontology (Section 4). Next, we present the compositional approach to DQ and its evaluation (Section 5 and 6). Finally, we review related work (Section 7), and concluded and point to our future research plan (Section 8).

2 Motivating Examples

Consider a *Patient* table (Table 1) that records body temperatures for patients in a hospital. Suppose that each row shown here records the temperature of a particular patient at different time points (other rows are omitted). First, let us consider accuracy, one of the most studied DQ attributes. It has been defined as a measure of "*the closeness between a value v and a value v', considered as the correct representation of the real-life phenomenon v aims to represent*" [22,3]. For example, if the patient's real name is v' = *'Ben Cheung'*, but was recorded as v = *'Ben Franklin'* instead, we may conclude that v is inaccurate.

Example 1. In some cases, our judgment of accuracy does not rely on syntactic proximity of data values, but is affected instead by our interpretation of their meanings. For example, it would have been no less accurate to have *'98.6°F'* instead of *'37.0°C'* in the last row, as long as we understand that these two values represent the same temperature reading using different scales.

Table 1. The Patient table

Name	Temperature	Time
Ben Cheung	37.2°C	2007/11/05 13:05
Ben Cheung	38.5°C	2007/11/06 12:00
Ben Cheung	37.0°C	2007/11/07 11:55

Example 2. Moreover, whether a data value is considered accurate often depends on both its interpreted and intended meaning. For example, if there is no agreement on how the temperature should to be measured, we may interpret '37.2°C' in the first row as Ben's temperature measured under normal conditions, while it really represents his temperature after aspirin was administered. Inaccuracy caused by such a mismatch cause no less a problem than a typographical error (e.g., entering '36.2°C' instead of '37.2°C').

Example 3. Furthermore, accuracy cannot be considered in isolation: our judgment on accuracy of a value depends on the judgment of that of its related values. For example, consider '38.5°C' and '2007/11/06 12:00' in the second row. If we know that Ben's temperature was <u>39</u> degree Celsius on Nov. 6, 2007 at 12:00, we may want to conclude that '38.5°C' represents the real-world phenomenon (i.e., 39 degree Celsius) inaccurately. But, in doing so we have already made an assumption that '2007/11/06 12:00' is accurate! What if we instead know that Ben's temperature was 38.5 degree Celsius on Nov. 6, 2007 at <u>11:45</u>? In this case, are we willing to believe that it is the time not the temperature value that was inaccurately recorded?

Consider next completeness, another commonly studied DQ attribute, which has been defined as the percentage of all tuples satisfying the relational schema of a table (i.e., tuples in the true extension of the schema) which are actually presented in the table [3].

Example 4. Actually, it is impossible to talk about the "true" extension of a relational schema without knowing what the user's requirements are. Accordingly, the above data about Ben Cheung could be complete or incomplete depending on whether Ben's temperature is required to be measured only once or twice a day.

3 Nature of Data Quality

In this section, we describe our view of DQ, founded on the notion of signs [17]. Generally speaking, a *sign* is something that stands to someone for something else. Accordingly, we see values (together with their metadata) in databases as primarily linguistic signs standing for real world phenomena. Information processing is a form of communication realized by creating, passing and utilizing signs [12]; DQ issues arise when discrepancies occur during this communication.

In the *meaning triad* [12], a triadic sign model, a *symbol* (e.g., *'Ben Cheung'*) is connected to a *referent* (e.g., a particular person in the world), and a *sense* understood by its interpreter (e.g., the concept of that person in the interpreter's mind). The difference between the referent and sense of a symbol could be understood in analogy to that of the extensional and intensional definitions of a term. Moreover a symbol may have more than one "valid" sense (and referent), under different circumstances, according to different interpreters.

We find it useful to distinguish four kinds of senses/referents of a symbol:

- The *intended sense/referent* is the sense/referent of the symbol according to its *producer*. It is the meaning the producer intends to communicate, and is determined exclusively by the producer.
- The *interpreted sense/referent* is the sense/referent of the symbol according to its *user*. It is the meaning the user recognizes, and is determined exclusively by the user.
- The *supposed sense/referent* is the sense/referent, determined exclusively by the *requirements for production* of the symbol, such as conventions and regulations the producer has to comply with, ethical and social norms, etc.
- The *expected sense/referent* is the sense/referent, determined exclusively by the *conditions for use* of the symbol, such as the tasks, purposes and goals of the user.

To illustrate this distinction, consider the temperature value *'37.2°C'* in Table 1. Suppose Sudha, the doctor of Ben, needs to know his temperature, not lowered by an antipyretic, and measured around noon every day (because he is plotting a graph with X-axis points every 24 hours). She also expects the measurement to be taken using a thermometer in the mouth. A new nurse, Catherine, running late, measured Ben's temperature at 13:05, with a thermometer in the ear. Moreover, Catherine is unaware of the fact that Ben had taken an antipyretic at 12:40. As a result, by recording *'37.2°C'*, Catherine *intended* to say "Ben's temperature <u>without</u> antipyretic, measured <u>at 13:05</u> with a <u>tympanal</u> thermometer". If Catherine had been more careful, this value's *supposed* meaning would be "Ben's temperature <u>after</u> antipyretic, measured <u>at 13:05</u> with <u>some</u> thermometer". On the other hand, Sudha may *interpret* this value as "Ben's temperature <u>without</u> antipyretic, measured <u>at 13:05</u> (because he saw the time value in the table) with an <u>oral</u> thermometer", which is different from what he *expected*: "Ben's temperature <u>without</u> antipyretic, measured <u>around noon</u> with an <u>oral</u> thermometer".

Ideally, total data quality means that the four types of senses must match for each data value individually, and certain constraints must hold among the same types of senses for related values, especially ones in different fields of the same row. DQ issues arise when this does not hold. For example, when Sudha expects oral measurements, but this requirement is not specified explicitly, discrepancy is likely to exist between the expected and supposed senses. More generally, if some sources of variability (e.g., the type of thermometer used and patient conditions) are not captured in the data (or metadata), the communication between the producer and user will be ambiguous. Of course, whether or not such ambiguity is considered problematic depends on the purpose for which the data is to be used, and it is the role of the requirements specification to eliminate these problems.

4 Nature of Senses

Before using the preceding distinctions in a theory of DQ, it helps to flesh out a bit the notion of "sense" we have in mind. In this paper we concentrate on data values concerning object properties (e.g., length, temperature and color), rather than general relationships between objects. For this purpose, we follow the DOLCE ontology [14] in viewing the world as populated by entities, which include concrete physical objects (e.g., persons) as well as abstract regions (e.g., distance values); the latter can appear as the values of properties[1], called *qualia*, for objects. To help communication, entities have names that allow them to be uniquely identified within some more or less restricted context: 'Ben Cheung' is presumably sufficient to identify the patient currently in the hospital in the previous example. Naming qualia allows us, for example, to have the region named 'normal temperature' contain the region named '37°C', which in turn contains '37.2°C'. Qualia are associated with properties at specific times (which are also treated as qualia), allowing property values to change. In FOL, this might be written as ***temptrOf***('Ben Cheung', '2007/11/05 13:05') = '37.2°C'; intensional logics use other notations [7].

The fundamental premise of databases is that one can associate a semantics with a relational table such as *Patient(NM, TPTR, TM)* along the lines of "the unique person named *NM* has temperature property value *TPTR* at time *TM*", a semantics that must be shared by data producer and user for proper communication. Given a shared ontology, this might be written in FOL as

$$Patient(NM, TPTR, TM) \rightarrow$$
$$\exists!p: Person \;.\; hasName(p, NM) \wedge temptrOf(p, TM) = TPTR$$

where we simplify matters by omitting additional variables for qualia to be "named" by *TM* and *TPTR*.

Based on this, the interpreted senses of the values in *Patient('Ben Cheung', '37.2°C', '2007/11/05 13:05')* could be m = "*the unique person named Ben Cheung*", m' = "*the temperature quale for the unique person named Ben Cheung at time quale 2007/11/05 13:05*", and m'' = "*the time quale when the temperature quale 37.2°C was measured for the unique person named Ben Cheung*". Note that the senses of these values, and their derivation from the table semantics accounts for the situations we encountered in motivating examples in Section 2 (e.g., Example 3 concerns violation of the constraint that m' and m'' must refer to the same temperature and time quale).

The above account is idealized, since it is usually necessary to observe or measure properties. This introduces a process of measurement, which allows the semantic specification to capture additional requirements. For example, the following formula specifies the kind of instrument to measure the temperature with, and a constraint on the time when measurements are to be taken:

$$Patient(NM, TPTR, TM) \rightarrow$$
$$\exists!p: Person, instr: OralThermometer \;.\; hasName(p, NM)$$
$$\wedge measures(temptrOf(p, TM), TPTR, instr, TM) \wedge closeToNoon(TM)$$

---

[1] DOLCE calls properties "qualities", but we find this too confusing in our context, where we are talking about data quality. Also, DOLCE reifies properties into entities that "inhere" in objects -- a complication that is unnecessary in our context.

Moreover, measurements are almost never exact, so the precise semantics may need to talk about accuracy and precision errors for measurements or the instruments involved, the subject of metrology.

The above considerations allow us to see a basis for distinguishing different degrees of match between two senses m_1 and m_2 of a data value s, which will be important for our development of a theory of DQ. On the one hand, we have the ideal exact match $match_{exact}(m_1, m_2)$ when the senses are identical. At the other extreme, we have a total mismatch $match_{mismatch}(m_1, m_2)$ in cases such as when m_1 is a temperature quale while m_2 is a person. In between, we admit partial matches $match^{attr}_{partial}(m_1, m_2)$ where $attr$ is the attribute, of which s is a value; for example, the four senses of Ben's temperature value '37.2°C' discussed in the previous section would match partially. The precise details of partial match are under study, but are not important here; some of its properties include

- there is a reasoning process for deciding it, allowing for differing background knowledge (thus allowing one to discover that "37.0°C" and "98.6°F" refer to the same quale (or not));
- the arguments must agree on certain predicates and the identity of certain central entities (e.g., it is the same person's temperature that is being talked about);
- aspects concerning other predicates and entities (such as those dealing with measuring and its circumstances) are less crucial, and will lead to partial matches; the precise details of how these are to be weighted in a comparison are application goal-dependent;
- all other things being equal, the geometry of quale regions is used to compare similarity.

We also find useful a more precise variant of partial match, called $closer^{attr}(m, m_1, m_2)$, which indicates that m_1 is conceptually closer to m than m_2 is; it allows us to find that, all other things being equal, a 13:05 measurement of a particular property is closer to a noon one than a 14:30 measurement.

5   Defining Data Quality

We characterize data quality considering four *DQ aspects*, each of which contains a collection of *theoretical DQ predicates*. These predicates are defined in terms of the relationships among symbols and their senses from a single viewpoint, therefore providing primitive constituents from which DQ attributes can be expressed. A DQ attribute in practice (e.g., accuracy, completeness) normally correspond to predicates in more than one aspect. In what follows, we discuss a few important DQ predicates in each aspect. This is, however by no means an exhaustive list of possible predicates in these aspects.

5.1   Symbol Aspect

The first DQ aspect concerns the relationships involving symbols only, without explicitly mentioning their senses. Let S be a set of symbols of interest. First we may be interested in the membership of a symbol $s \in S$ in a subset S_{accept} of S. Let us denote this using the predicate $sym_{member}(s, S_{accept}) \Leftrightarrow s \in S_{accept}$. For example, $sym_{member}('50°C', S_{body\text{-}temp})$ does not hold, assuming $S_{body\text{-}temp}$ is the set of symbols representing the acceptable human body temperatures. For acceptable symbols, we may now consider a variety of relationships between them. The simplest such relationship is sameness: let $sym_{match}(s_1, s_2)$ hold whenever s_1 and s_2 have exactly the same syntactic form. When two symbols do not match exactly, we may consider which are closer syntactically, based on some distance function $distance_f$ (such as edit distance [3]). Let us write this using $sym_{closer}(s, s_1, s_2) \Leftrightarrow distance_f(s, s_1) < distance_f(s, s_2)$. For example, $sym_{closer}('Cheng', 'Cheung', 'Chiang')$ is true because changing from $'Cheng'$ to $'Cheung'$ requires fewer edits than to $'Chiang'$. Another interesting relationship, $sym_{more-detail}(s_1, s_2)$, concerns level of detail; for real numbers we might have $sym_{more-detail}('3.1415926', '3.14')$ indicating that, in normalized scientific notation, (i) the two arguments have the same exponent, (ii) the first argument has as least as many digits as the second one in the coefficient, and (iii) the coefficients agree in the digits presented.

5.2 The Meaning Aspect

This DQ aspect deals with the relationships involve the interpreted and intended senses of a symbol. According to H.P. Grice's classical account of speaker meaning, we rely on the *recognition* of our intention to communicate and we use that very recognition to get our message across [20]. In the context of data quality, this implies that in an ideal communication, there should be an exact match between intended and interpreted senses.

Let M be the set of senses to which the symbols in S *may* refer. First of all, we need to know whether for each symbol there is an interpreted (or intended) sense assigned to it by its user (or producer). Let us use $mea_{has-intp}(s, m)$ (respectively, $mea_{has-intd}(s, m)$) to indicate that a sense $m \in M$ is an interpreted (respectively, intended) sense of a symbol $s \in S$ [2]. For example, $\exists m \in M. mea_{has-intp}('37.2°C', m)$ probably does not hold for a physician who doesn't work in Ben's hospital, because she will not have a way to identify the person named Ben Cheung at that hospital.

Once we know that the interpreted and intended senses exist, we can then consider whether their existence is unique. Formally, let's define

$$mea_{has-uni-inp}(s) \Leftrightarrow \forall m_1, m_2 \in M. mea_{has-intp}(s, m_1) \wedge mea_{has-intp}(s, m_2) \rightarrow match_{exact}(m_1, m_2),$$

$$mea_{has-uni-int}(s) \Leftrightarrow \forall m_1, m_2 \in M. mea_{has-intd}(s, m_1) \wedge mea_{has-intd}(s, m_2) \rightarrow match_{exact}(m_1, m_2).$$

Conversely, we may also be interested in whether two symbols are synonyms from the user's or producer's perspective (i.e., sharing their interpreted or intended senses):

$$mea_{synonym-u}(s_1, s_2) \Leftrightarrow \exists m \in M. mea_{has-intp}(s_1, m) \wedge mea_{has-intp}(s_2, m) \wedge \neg sym_{match}(s_1, s_2)$$

$$mea_{synonym-p}(s_1, s_2) \Leftrightarrow \exists m \in M. mea_{has-intd}(s_1, m) \wedge mea_{has-intd}(s_2, m) \wedge \neg sym_{match}(s_1, s_2)$$

When a symbol has an interpreted and intended sense, we are mostly interested in whether there is a match between them. First we want to know if they match exactly

$$mea_{match}(s, m_1, m_2) \Leftrightarrow mea_{has-intp}(s, m_1) \wedge mea_{has-intd}(s, m_2) \wedge match_{exact}(m_1, m_2).$$

---

[2] Throughout the rest of the paper, when we mention symbol s, we mean a symbol token - its occurrence in a field of a particular table tuple. So $'37.2°C'$ is the occurrence of this symbol in row 1, column 2 of Table 1.

For example, $mea_{match}('37.2\,°C',\ m_1,\ m_2)$ does not hold when m_1 and m_2 are temperatures of a patient measured at different time points. In general, we may want to know, for partially matched senses, how closely they match. For example, when two symbols s_1 and s_2 share their intended senses (e.g., because people recorded the same value with different precision), we can state the fact that "the interpreted sense of s_1 is closer than that of s_2 to their shared intended sense" as

$$mea_{closer}(s_1,\ s_2,\ m,\ m_1,\ m_2) \Leftrightarrow mea_{has\text{-}intd}(s_1,\ m) \wedge mea_{has\text{-}intd}(s_2,\ m) \wedge mea_{has\text{-}intp}(s_1,$$
$$m_1) \wedge mea_{has\text{-}intp}(s_2,\ m_2) \wedge match^{attr}_{partial}(m_1,\ m) \wedge match^{attr}_{partial}(m_2,\ m) \wedge closer^{attr}(m,$$
$$m_1,\ m_2).$$

5.3 The Purpose Aspect

This DQ aspect deals with the relationships involve the interpreted and expected senses of a symbol from the user perspective. As we have mentioned, an ultimate criterion for data quality is fitness for purpose. In our framework, the intended use of data values is captured through their expected senses. Therefore, quality issues arise when the interpreted and expected senses of a data value do not match exactly.

We are interested in a variety of relationships involving expected senses. Predicates such as $pur_{match}(s,\ m_1,\ m_2)$, for indicating the interpreted sense m_1 and expected sense m_2 of the symbol s match exactly, and $pur_{closer}(s_1,\ s_2,\ m,\ m_1,\ m_2)$, for indicating the interpreted sense m_1 of s_1 is closer than the interpreted sense m_2 of s_2 to their shared intended sense m, are defined in a similar way to their counterparts in the meaning aspect. The existence of expected sense, however, deserves more discussion.

Unlike the interpreted sense which is determined by the user directly, the expected sense is determined by a particular application. If a doctor is only interested in studying the effect of psychotherapy on the temperature of the patient, we'll say that the blood pressure (or more obviously the number of chairs in the room) have no expected senses to that doctor. To formalize this, let M_e denote a subset of M, determined by the tasks and goals the user has to fulfill. In our example, M might have temperatures and blood pressures taken at any time, while M_e might only have temperatures taken around noon. We say $m \in M_e$ is an expected sense of a symbol s if m matches, at least partially, with the interpreted sense of s. This can be stated as

$$pur_{has\text{-}exp}(s,\ m) \Leftrightarrow m \in M_e \wedge \exists m' \in M.\ mea_{has\text{-}intp}(s,\ m') \wedge$$
$$(match^{attr}_{partial}(m,\ m') \vee match_{exact}(m,\ m')).$$

This also allows us to consider the existence of a symbol, given partial knowledge about its expected sense. For example, we cannot find a symbol s in Table 1 with the property $pur_{has\text{-}exp}(s,\ "Ben's\ cholesterol\ level\ on\ Nov.\ 5,\ 2007\ at\ 13{:}05")$.

When more than one expected sense exists, we may want to know if they are all comparable with respect to the interpreted sense of the symbol (so that later we can pick the closest one):

$$pur_{comparable\text{-}exp}(s) \Leftrightarrow \exists m \in M.\ mea_{has\text{-}intp}(s,\ m) \wedge \forall m_1,\ m_2 \in M_e.$$
$$pur_{has\text{-}exp}(s,\ m_1) \wedge pur_{has\text{-}exp}(s,\ m_2) \rightarrow closer^{attr}(m,\ m_1,\ m_2) \vee closer^{attr}(m,\ m_2,\ m_1)$$

For example, given a temperature value $'37.2\,°C'$ with its interpreted sense "the temperature quale of Ben measured at 13:05 with some thermometer", and two expected senses "temperature qualia of Ben measured at 13:05 with an oral/tympanal thermometer", then these two expected senses are probably not comparable, unless we have a theory on how different types of thermometers affect temperature measurement.

5.4 The Trust Aspect

This DQ aspect deals with the relationships involve the intended and supposed senses of a symbol from the producer perspective. According to [20], in order to establish audience trust, both the sincerity and authority conditions have to hold. In the context of our framework, this means the user has to believe that the producer is neither a liar (i.e., no discrepancy caused intentionally, e.g., due to falsification) nor a fool (i.e., no discrepancy caused unintentionally, e.g., due to observation bias). Trust issues arise therefore when there is discrepancy between intended and supposed sense. Predicates in the aspects, such as $tru_{has\text{-}sup}$, $tru_{comparable\text{-}sup}$ and tru_{match} are defined in the similar way as their counterparts in the purpose aspect. For lack of space, we do not elaborate them here.

6 Mapping Data Quality Attributes

We evaluate our approach by expressing quality attributes defined in the literature in our framework. One observation from this exercise will be that a single quality attribute often has multiple, sometimes conflicting, definitions. We differentiate these definitions by expressing them in terms of different (combinations of) theoretical quality predicates we have defined. This also allow us to accommodate competing views on how these attributes should be related, by making explicit the exact meaning of the attributes involved, and by distinguishing relationships that exist by definition and those that exist based on assumptions. Finally, this exercise also allows us to point out possibly new definitions.

6.1 Accuracy, Precision and Currency

Accuracy is normally understood as free of defects or correspondence to reality [24,13]. In [32], it is defined formally as the closeness between two representations s and s', where s' is the correct representation of the real-life phenomenon s *aims to* represent. If we accept that "correctness" here means "justified by some accepted standards or conventions", and make "closeness" be "identity" to get a Yes/No predicate, then this definition can be stated in terms of our symbol, meaning and trust aspects

$$accuracy_{symbol}(s) \Leftrightarrow \exists\, m \in M,\, s' \in S.\, mea_{has\text{-}intd}(s, m) \wedge tru_{has\text{-}sup}(s', m) \wedge sym_{match}(s, s').$$

According to this definition, we cannot have synonyms such as '37.0°C' and '98.6°F', which may have been desired. To accommodate this, we can change the perspective from a fixed phenomenon to a fixed representation [25]; it defines accuracy as the closeness between two real-life phenomena m and m', where m is what a symbol s aims to represent and m' is what s appears to represent. This view requires only the meaning aspect

$$accuracy_{meaning}(s) \Leftrightarrow \exists\, m_1, m_2 \in M.\, mea_{match}(s, m_1, m_2).$$

The fact that s_1 is more accurate than s_2 can then be represented in this view as

$$accuracy_{meaning\text{-}compare}(s_1, s_2) \Leftrightarrow \exists m, m_1, m_2 \in M. \, mea_{closer}(s_1, s_2, m, m_1, m_2).$$

A typical understanding of precision as a quality attribute is the degree of details data values exhibit. For example, precision of numeric values is often measured by the number of significant digits used [5]. A number (e.g., '3.1415926') is more precise than another one (e.g., '3.14'), assuming both represent the same phenomenon (e.g., the mathematical constant π), can be stated as

$$precision_{symbol}(s_1, s_2) \Leftrightarrow sym_{more\text{-}detail}(s_1, s_2) \wedge \exists m_1, m_2 \in M.$$
$$mea_{has\text{-}intd}(s_1, m_1) \wedge mea_{has\text{-}intd}(s_2, m_2) \wedge match_{exact}(m_1, m_2)$$

Precision is often considered in close relation to accuracy. A typical intuition is that low precision leads to inaccuracy [25,5], which however cannot be accommodated by $precision_{symbol}$ alone. This is because having greater degree of details doesn't guarantee a better interpretation towards the intended meaning. In order to support this intuition, we need a strengthened notion of precision

$$precision_{strengthened}(s_1, s_2) \Leftrightarrow precision_{symbol}(s_1, s_2) \wedge accuracy_{meaning\text{-}compare}(s_1, s_2).$$

From the opposite view, one considers accuracy as a prerequisite for precision: in order to say s_1 is a more precise than s_1, both have to be accurate (i.e., have matching intended and interpreted senses). This view can be defined as

$$precision_{meaning}(s_1, s_2) \Leftrightarrow sym_{more\text{-}detail}(s_1, s_2) \wedge \exists m_{11}, m_{12}, m_{21}, m_{22} \in M.$$
$$mea_{match}(s_1, m_{11}, m_{12}) \wedge mea_{match}(s_2, m_{21}, m_{22}) \wedge match_{exact}(m_{11}, m_{21}).$$

Now we really have a theorem $precision_{meaning}(s_1, s_2) \rightarrow accuracy_{meaning}(s_1) \wedge accuracy_{meaning}(s_2)$.

Currency as a DQ attribute is normally understood as the degree to which data are up to date [3,22]. As a first try, we could represent this understanding as:

$$currency_{naive}(s_1, s_2) \Leftrightarrow \exists m_1, m_2 \in M. \, mea_{has\text{-}intd}(s_1, m_1) \wedge mea_{has\text{-}intd}(s_2, m_2) \wedge t(m_1) > t(m_2)$$

where t returns the time component of a sense. One might notices that this definition allows us to compare the currency of the temperatures of different patients. When this is not desired, we can strengthen it using the notion of partial match

$$currency_{strengthened}(s_1, s_2) \Leftrightarrow \exists m_1, m_2 \in M. \, mea_{has\text{-}intd}(s_1, m_1)$$
$$\wedge mea_{has\text{-}intd}(s_2, m_2) \wedge match^{attr}_{partial}(m_1, m_2) \wedge t(m_1) > t(m_2)$$

Currency defined in this way is orthogonal to accuracy. As with precision, some authors consider a value s_1 is more current than another one s_2 only when both are accurate at a certain point in time [25]. This view can be captured by

$$currency_{meaning}(s_1, s_2) \Leftrightarrow \exists m_{11}, m_{12}, m_{21}, m_{22} \in M. \, mea_{match}(s_1, m_{11}, m_{12})$$
$$\wedge mea_{match}(s_2, m_{21}, m_{22}) \wedge match^{attr}_{partial}(m_{11}, m_{21}) \wedge t(m_{11}) > t(m_{21})$$

A further complication, which will be discussed below, relates currency to relevance [5].

6.2 Relevance, Completeness and Timeliness

Relevance considers how data fits its intended use [13]. In its simplest form, it can be defined on the purpose aspect alone (recall M_e is a subset of M, determined by the tasks, etc. the user of s has): $relevance_{purpose}(s) \Leftrightarrow \exists m \in M_e. \, pur_{has\text{-}exp}(s, m)$. This definition supports the view that relevance should evaluated before other quality attributes [5].

Intuitively, completeness concerns whether data is missing with respect to some reference set. In the simplest case, *value completeness* [3,19] refers to the existence of null values in a reference column, row or table. This definition can therefore be understood as $completeness_{symbol}(S_a) \Leftrightarrow \exists s \in S_a. \, sym_{match}(s, \text{"null"})$, where S_a is the set of data values of interest. In a more complicated situation, *population completeness* [19] of S_a is defined as the existence of missing values with respect to the reference set M_e: $completeness_{purpose}(S_a) \Leftrightarrow \forall m \in M_e \, \exists s \in S_a. \, pur_{has\text{-}exp}(s, m)$. While the notion of completeness concerns whether every relevant data value is presented, we may also consider whether every presented value is relevant (the closest terms proposed in the literature for this attribute are "appropriate amount of data" [13] and "conciseness"[25]):

$$completeness_{purpose\text{-}reverse}(S_a) \Leftrightarrow \forall s \in S_a \, \exists m \in M_e. \, pur_{has\text{-}exp}(s, m).$$

When both conditions need to be enforced, we can define:

$$completeness_{composite}(S_a) \Leftrightarrow completeness_{purpose}(S_a) \wedge completeness_{purpose\text{-}reverse}(S_a).$$

Some authors use timeliness to mean data is *sufficiently* up to date with respect to its intended use [3,21]. It can therefore be considered as another variant of currency [5]. The fact that a value s_1 is timelier than s_2 with respect to M_e can be stated as

$$currency_{purpose}(s_1, s_2) \Leftrightarrow currency_{meaning}(s_1, s_2) \wedge relevance_{purpose}(s_1) \wedge relevance_{purpose}(s_1).$$

6.3   Reliability and Believability

There is no generally accepted notion of reliability as a DQ attribute: some definitions overlap with that of accuracy [1], others are linked to dependability of the data producer [13], while still others are based on verifiability[16]. If we choose the last view -- that data is reliable if it can be verified (i.e., generated independently by different producers, possibly using different tools, methods, and etc.), we can define, given expect senses M_e

$$reliability_{trust}(s) \Leftrightarrow \exists m_1 \in M, m_2 \in M_e. \, tru_{match}(s, m_1, m_2).$$

This means what is intended to be represented by s matches exactly with what is supposed to be represented by it, according to the obligations the producer has. A violation of this condition may be caused by bias (i.e., lack of *objectivity* [3,24]) or intention (i.e., intentional *falsification* [13]) of the producer, or limitation of instrumentation, method, etc. Notice that reliability defined in this way is independent of accuracy. On the contrary, believability defined in [3,24] as "the extent to which data are accepted or regarded as true, real, and credible", clearly concerns both the meaning and trust aspects

$$believability_{meaning\text{-}trust}(s) \Leftrightarrow accuracy_{meaning}(s) \wedge reliability_{trust}(s).$$

7   Related Work

Some approaches to DQ share with ours the view that generic quality attributes (e.g., accuracy, completeness) may be understood in terms of more primitive quality constructs. In the Qurator project [15], such constructs (called *quality characterizations* or *QC*) are concrete, operational level quality attributes defined by scientists. For example, "accuracy" can be defined in terms of confidence *QC*, which can then be quantified using calculated number of experimental errors, or a function of the type of experimental equipment.

While the Qurator project provides a flexible way for specifying user-definable and domain-specific QCs in the context of e-Science, we are focusing on identifying primitive constructs that are reusable across domains. From a system-oriented view, [25] discusses various types of problematic correspondences (called of representation deficiencies) between a real world system (RW) and an information system (IS). For example, an incomplete representation means some RW phenomena are not (or cannot be) represented in IS, while an ambiguous representation means multiple RW phenomena have the same representation in IS. We also consider mismatches, but emphasize the role of producer and user, and mental representations (senses), abandoning the objectivist view of IS.

We are also not alone in considering DQ from a semiotics perspective. Thus, [21] proposes to understand and classify quality attributes in terms of syntactic (i.e., conformity to stored metadata), semantic (i.e., correspondence to external phenomena) and pragmatic (i.e., suitability for a given use) quality categories. Although these distinctions are embedded in our definitions of "senses" and "DQ aspects", they are only used in [21] to provide a conceptual framework to classify quality attributes. We also define quality attributes in terms of primitive constructs derived from these distinctions.

8   Conclusion

In this paper, we have proposed a novel, compositional framework for understanding and defining DQ attributes in a precise and comparable way, based on the notion of signs. We have also sketched a theory of senses for individual values in a relational table, based on its semantics expressed using some ontology. We have shown in our framework how multiple, sometimes conflicting, definitions of a DQ attribute could be differentiated, and how competing views on relating these attributes could be accommodated.

However, understanding DQ is just a means, not an end for us. Our ultimate goal in this quest is a methodology for "data quality by design". We have proposed a general goal-oriented quality design process for databases [10,11]. This process starts with application-specific goals where application data requirements are elicited and organized into an ordinary conceptual schema; then quality goals are modeled and operationalized to introduce new and modify existing data requirements in the initial schema. An important step during this process is to identify potential risks that may compromise quality of application data. The theory of senses provides exactly such machinery for a risk-based analysis. During schema design, one has to decide which components of the senses of application data values need to be modeled as schema elements (according to user's goals and assumptions); such decisions eventually affect the quality of the application data. For example, Doctor Sudha is able to understand correctly the temperature value '37.2°C' with respect to "when" it was measured, exactly because there is a "time" attribute in the *Patient* schema. However, the design decision to leave out other components (such as how it was measured, with what type of thermometer and by whom) contributes to Sudha's partially incorrect understanding of '37.2°C'. Our immediate next step is to refine the notion of senses and formalize partial match between senses, and use them to derive patterns of risk factors for database design.

References

1. Agmon, N., Ahituv, N.: Assessing Data Reliability in an Information Systems. Journal of Management Information Systems 4(2), 34–44 (1987)
2. An, Y., Borgida, A., Mylopoulos, J.: Discovering the Semantics of Relational Tables through Mappings. In: Spaccapietra, S. (ed.) Journal on Data Semantics VII. LNCS, vol. 4244, pp. 1–32. Springer, Heidelberg (2006)
3. Batini, C., Scannapieco, M.: Data Quality: Concepts, Methodologies and Techniques. Springer, Heidelberg (2006)
4. Bovee, M.: A Conceptual Framework and Belief-Function Approach to Assessing Overall Information Quality International. Journal of Intelligent Systems 18(1), 51–74 (2003)
5. Gackowski, Z.J.: Logical interdependence of data/information quality dimensions - A purpose focused view on IQ. In: Proc. of the 2004 International Conference on Information Quality (2004)
6. Calvanese, D., Giacomo, G.D., Lenzerini, M., Nardi, D., Rosati, R.: Data Integration in Data Warehousing. Journal of Cooperative Information Systems 10(3), 237–271 (2001)
7. Fitting, M.: Intensional Logic. In: Zalta, E.N. (ed.) The Stanford Encyclopedia of Philosophy (Spring 2007), http://plato.stanford.edu/archives/spr2007/entries/logic-intensional/
8. Grice, H.P.: Meaning. The Philosophical Review 66, 377–388 (1957)
9. Jeusfeld, M.A., Quix, C., Jarke, M.: Design and analysis of quality information for daa warehouses. In: Ling, T.-W., Ram, S., Li Lee, M. (eds.) ER 1998. LNCS, vol. 1507, pp. 349–362. Springer, Heidelberg (1998)
10. Jiang, L., Borgida, A., Topaloglou, T., Mylopoulos, J.: Data Quality by Design: A Goal-Oriented Approach. In: Proc. of the 12th International Conference on Information Quality (2007)
11. Jiang, L., Topaloglou, T., Borgida, A., Mylopoulos, J.: Goal-Oriented Conceptual Database Design. In: Proc. of the 15h IEEE Int. Requirements Engineering Conference, pp. 195–204 (2007)
12. Liu, K.: Semiotics in Information Systems Engineering. Cambridge University Press, Cambridge (2000)
13. Liu, L., Chi, L.N.: Evolutional Data Quality: A Theory-Specific View. In: Proc. of the 2002 International Conference on Information Quality (2002)
14. Masolo, C., Borgo, S., Gangemi, A., Guarino, N., Oltramari, A., Schneider, L.: Wonder-Web Deliverable D17 (2002)
15. Missier, P., Preece, A.D., Embury, S.M., Jin, B., Greenwood, M., Stead, D., Brown, A.: Managing Information Quality in e-Science: A Case Study in Proteomics. In: ER 2005 Workshops, pp. 423–432 (2005)

16. Naumann, F.: Do metadata models meet IQ requirements? In: Proc. of the 1999 International Conference on Information Quality, Cambridge, MA, pp. 99–114 (1999)
17. Peirce, C.S.: Collected Papers. In: Peirce, C.S., Hartshorne, C., Weiss, P., Burks, A. (eds.), vol. 8. Harvard University Press, Cambridge (1931–1958)
18. Pernici, B., Scannapieco, M.: Data Quality in Web Information Systems. In: Proc of the 21st int. Conference on Conceptual Modeling, pp. 397–413. Springer, London (2002)
19. Pipino, L.L., Lee, Y.W., Wang, R.: Data quality assessment. Comm. of ACM 45(4), 211–218 (2002)
20. Price, G.: On the communication of measurement results. Measurement 29, 293–305 (2001)
21. Price, R., Shanks, G.: A Semiotic Information Quality Framework. In: Proc. IFIP International Conference on Decision Support Systems, Prato (2004)
22. Redman, T.C.: Data Quality for the Information Age. Artech House, Boston (1996)
23. Wang, R.Y., Reddy, M.P., Kon, H.B.: Toward quality data: an attribute-based approach. Decision. Support Systems 13(3–4), 349–372 (1995)
24. Wang, R.Y., Strong, D.M.: Beyond accuracy: what data quality means to data consumers. Journal of Management Information Systems 12(4), 5–33 (1996)
25. Wand, Y., Wang, R.Y.: Anchoring data quality dimensions in ontological foundations. Communications of ACM 39(11), 86–95 (1996)

A Formal Model of Fuzzy Ontology with Property Hierarchy and Object Membership

Yi Cai and Ho-fung Leung

Department of Computer Science and Engineering
The Chinese University of Hong Kong
Shatin, Hong Kong, China
{ycai,lhf}@cse.cuhk.edu.hk

Abstract. In this paper, we propose a formal model of fuzzy ontology with property hierarchy by combining theories in cognitive psychology and fuzzy set theory. A formal mechanism used to determine object memberships in concepts is also proposed. In this mechanism, object membership is based on the defining properties of concepts and properties which objects possess. We show that our model is more reasonable in calculating object memberships and more powerful in concept representation than previous models by an example.

1 Introduction

With the development of the Semantic Web, ontologies play an important role in knowledge representation. Ontologies provide a way to describe and structure the information on the web. An ontology is generally defined as an 'explicit specification of conceptualization' and can be used to provide semantics to resources on the Semantic Web [1].

Traditional ontologies represent concepts as crisp sets of objects [2]. Objects are considered either to belong to or not to belong to a concept. However, there are many vague concepts in reality. These vague concepts have no clear boundaries. For example, 'hot water', 'red car' and so on. To extend the representation ability of ontologies to handle fuzzy concepts, some fuzzy ontologies are proposed based on fuzzy DLs (description logics) [3] [4] [5]. These fuzzy ontologies provide ways to represent the fuzziness of knowledge. However, object memberships are given by users manually or obtained by fuzzy functions defined by users in these fuzzy ontologies. While concepts, objects and properties are building blocks of ontologies, to our best knowledge, there lacks of a formal mechanism to determine memberships of objects in concepts automatically based on the defining properties of concepts and properties which objects possess. Thus, machine cannot obtain object memberships automatically while given defining properties of concepts and objects in ontologies. While properties are generally used in describing concepts and objects in ontology, we consider that it is desirable to formalize object membership in ontology based on properties of concepts and objects.

Au Yeung and Leung [6] consider that methods used by human beings in classification and categorization are useful in modeling a domain by ontology, while

Q. Li et al. (Eds.): ER 2008, LNCS 5231, pp. 69–82, 2008.

there is no such a consideration in previous ontology models. They propose a conceptual model of fuzzy ontology which is based on the theories in cognitive psychology. Nevertheless, their model can only represent the conjunction concepts (concepts defined by conjunction of properties). Furthermore, the Au Yeung-Leung model only can handle the concepts defined by independent properties. It requires to assume all properties in the ontology are independent (i.e., there is no relation between properties), and it lacks building blocks to handle the cases with dependent properties. Thus, we cannot infer some implicit knowledge based on the dependence of properties. For example, we cannot infer the property 'is a man' based on property 'is a tall man' because there is no relation between the two properties in the Au Yeung-Leung model.

To overcome the limitations of previous models of ontology, based on theories in cognitive psychology [7] [8], works in [9] and fuzzy set theory [10], we propose a novel formal model of fuzzy ontology with property hierarchy and object membership. Our model extends the expression and reasoning capability of ontologies in handling fuzzy concepts. It can handle the cases with dependent properties in ontology based on a property hierarchy, and represent conjunction concepts, disjunction concepts (concepts defined by disjunction of properties) and combination concepts (concepts defined by conjunction and disjunction of properties). Our model provides a more reasonable formal mechanism to determine object memberships in concepts than previous models. A main feature of this mechanism is that object membership is measured by the defining properties of concepts and properties which objects possess, which is based on the classical view in cognitive psychology.

The structure of this paper is as follows. Section 2 introduces the background and related work. We give a motivating example and state the limitations of the existing models in section 3. In section 4 we propose a novel formal model of fuzzy ontology with property hierarchy. A formal mechanism to determine the object memberships in concepts based on the defining properties of concepts and properties which objects possess is presented in section 5. We illustrate the use of our model by an example in section 6. Section 7 concludes the paper.

2   Background and Related Work

2.1   Classical View of Concept Representation in Cognitive Psychology

In cognitive psychology, how concepts are represented in the human memory is an important concern. It is generally accepted that concepts are characterized by properties [11]. One important model of concept representation based on properties is classical view. The classical view [7] [8] of concepts posits that each concept is defined by a set of properties which are individually necessary and collectively sufficient. Properties are atomic units which are the basic building blocks of concepts. Concepts are organized in a hierarchy and the defining properties of a more specific concept includes all the defining properties of its super-concepts. In classical view, there are clear-cut boundaries between members and non-members of the category. As a result, the classical view cannot handle the vague concepts.

2.2   Formal Models of Fuzzy Ontology

Currently, most ontologies are based on DLs (description logics) [12] and concepts are represented as crisp sets of objects (e.g., ontologies written in OWL DL) [1]. These ontologies cannot represent the fuzzy concepts. Several fuzzy DLs are proposed to handle the fuzzy concepts by combining fuzzy set theory [10] and description logics. For example, Straccia proposes a fuzzy $\mathcal{ALC}$ in [3] and a fuzzy $\mathcal{SHOIN}(\mathcal{D})$ in [4]. Stoilos et al. present a fuzzy $\mathcal{SHIN}$ in [5]. These fuzzy DLs vary in possessing different expressive power, complexity and reasoning capabilities. Some fuzzy ontologies are constructed based on fuzzy DLs or fuzzy logic [13] [14]. Besides, some works apply fuzzy ontologies for some applications. For instance, Cross and Voss [15] explore the potential that fuzzy mathematics and ontologies have for improving performance in multilingual document exploitation. These works can represent membership degrees of different objects in concepts. Nevertheless, in these models, object memberships are given by users manually or obtained by fuzzy functions defined by users. These works lack a formal mechanism to obtain the membership degrees of objects in concepts automatically based on the defining properties of concepts and properties which objects possess. Besides, there is no consideration of how people representing concepts in their mind.

Recently, Au Yeung and Leung [6] propose a formal model for fuzzy ontology by borrowing the idea of classical view. They have formalized the membership degrees of objects (they name the membership degree of objects as *likeliness*) in concepts by constructing several vectors in ontologies. They consider that a concept r can be defined by a single characteristic vector $\overrightarrow{c}_r$ of r which consists all the necessary properties of r. They assume relation among all properties is conjunction and all properties are independent. The value of each element in a characteristic vector is the minimal requirement of a corresponding property. An object a can be represented by a property vector $\overrightarrow{p}_a$, and each element in $\overrightarrow{p}_a$ corresponds to the degree to which the object possesses a property. The likeliness of an object in a concept is the degree to which the object satisfies the minimal requirements of defining properties of the concept.

3   Limitations of Previous Models

We use a motivating example to illustrate the limitations of previous models.

Example 1. Suppose an online-shop will select the top one hundred special customers to give them some discount. The concept 'special-customer' is a fuzzy concept and is defined as the union of two kinds of customers. One kind of special customer is defined by three properties A, B and C (properties of concepts 'special-customer' and 'customer' are given in table 1), i.e., this kind of special customers requires a customer must have bought at least five items (goods) belonging to 'expensive item' and possess average degree of all items that the customer has bought belonging to 'expensive item' as higher as possible. The other kind of special customers is defined by properties A, D, and E, i.e., it requires a customer must have bought at least one hundred items (not necessary expensive items) and there are at least one item that the customer has bought belonging to 'expensive item'. In this example, 'special-customer' is the sub-concept of 'customer' and 'expensive item' is the sub-concept of 'item'.

Table 1. Properties of concepts *'special-customer'* and *'customer'* in the motivating example

A	has customerID	B	buy at least five expensive items
C	possess average degree of all bought items belonging to expensive items	D	buy at least 100 items
E	buy at least one expensive items	F	buy at least one item

We suppose that the definition of the concept 'customer' denoted by C and that of the concept 'special-customer' denoted by SC are as following:

$$C : [A]_1 \ and \ [F]_1, \quad SC : ([A]_1 \ and \ [B]_1 \ and \ [C]_{0.6}) \ OR \ ([A]_1 \ and \ [D]_1 \ and \ [E]_{0.5})$$

where the subscript of each property is the minimal requirement of the property. Objects (e.g., all customers) satisfying all minimal requirements of defining properties of a concept (e.g., 'special-customer') belong to the concept to a degree 1. We want to calculate object memberships for there customers O_1, O_2 and O_3 in concept 'special-customer' and concept 'customer'. Table 2 are items bought by the three customers.

Table 2. Items bought by O_1, O_2 and O_3

O_1		O_2		O_3	
bought item	price	bought item	price	bought item	price
Furniture00002	1550	Book10032	120	Clothes02006	180
Eproduct00307	2500	Book20039	20	Clothes08001	80
...	...	...	...	...	...
Book07005	200	EletronicProduct70032	175	Book03102	140

For fuzzy ontologies based on fuzzy DLs or fuzzy logic (e.g., ontologies in [15]), they provide a model to represent the fuzziness of concepts, and object memberships in concepts are given by users previously or obtained by membership functions defined by users. However, there is no direct or principle of how to give object memberships or to define membership functions, so there may exist arbitrary assignments of object memberships or arbitrary definitions of membership functions. Moreover, while concepts, objects and properties are building blocks of these fuzzy ontologies, they lack a formal mechanism to give membership degrees to objects in concepts automatically based on the defining properties of concepts and properties which objects possess. Thus, for these fuzzy ontologies, machines cannot calculate the object memberships of O_1, O_2 and O_3 in concepts SC and C based on defining properties of the two concepts and properties the three objects possessing automatically.

If using the Au Yeung-Leung model which provides a formal mechanism for calculating object membership based on properties, we can obtain characteristic vectors for SC and C, property vectors of O_1, O_2 and O_3 as following:

$$SC : [A]_1, [B]_1, [C]_{0.6}, [D]_1, [E]_{0.5}, [F]_1; \quad C : [A]_1, [F]_1$$

$$O_1 : [A]_1, [B]_1, [C]_{0.8}, [D]_{0.2}, [E]_1, [F]_1; \quad O_2 : [A]_1, [B]_{0.2}, [C]_{0.1}, [D]_1, [E]_{0.8}, [F]_1$$

$$O_3 : [A]_1, [B]_1, [C]_{0.5}, [D]_{0.5}, [E]_1$$

The subscript of each property is the degree to which the object possessing the property. We calculate the customers' memberships of O_1, O_2 and O_3 in SC and C according to the axioms and equations in the Au Yeung-Leung model and get the results[1] as following: O_1 belongs to SC to a degree 0.2 and to C to a degree 1, O_2 belongs to SC to a degree 0.1 and to C to a degree1, O_3 belongs to both SC and to C to a degree 0. Such results are not reasonable. It is obvious that O_1 satisfies the minimal requirements of the first kind of special customers, while O_2 satisfies the minimal requirements of the second kind of special customers. Thus, O_1 and O_2 should belong to SC to a degree 1. For object O_3, it should be a member of C to a degree 1. The reason is that people can infer O_3 definitely has bought at least one items because O_3 has bought at least five expensive items. Thus it satisfies the minimal requirement of all properties of 'customer'.[2]

Thus, one limitation of the Au Yeung-Leung model is that a concept is represented by a set of properties and the relations among those properties are conjunction. Such a representation cannot represent disjunction concepts and combination concept, and may lead to unreasonable results. For example, concept 'special-customer' is a union of two kinds of customers. Another limitation is that all properties in the Au Yeung-Leung model are assumed to be independent while some of them should be dependent in reality. We cannot infer some properties based on their dependent properties in the Au Yeung-Leung model. For example, property 'buy at least five expensive items' definitely implies property 'buy at least one item'. Besides, there is no formal definition of property and no formal mechanism to obtain the degree to which an object possesses a property in the Au Yeung-Leung model. All degrees of an object possessing properties are given by user.

4   A Novel Formal Model of Fuzzy Ontology with Property Hierarchy

To overcome the limitations of previous models, we propose a novel formal model of fuzzy ontology by combining the classical view and fuzzy set theory. In our model, a concept is defined by properties, and some properties can be dependent within a property hierarchy specifying the subsumption relationships between properties. Membership degree of an object in a concept depends on the comparison of properties of the object and that of the concept.

4.1   A Conceptual Model of Fuzzy Ontology

We consider a fuzzy ontology O in a particular domain Δ as follows:

$$O_\Delta = (C, R, P, I)$$

where C is a set of fuzzy concepts, R is a set of fuzzy roles which are the relations between two objects, P is a set of fuzzy properties of concepts, and I is a set of objects.[3]

---

[1] Due to lack of space, we omit the details of calculation here.

[2] Because 'item' is the super-concept of 'expensive-item'.

[3] In the rest of this paper, all concepts, roles and properties are referred to fuzzy concepts, fuzzy roles and fuzzy properties respectively unless otherwise specified.

Fuzzy Concept. A fuzzy concept is a fuzzy set of objects. Objects are considered as members of a concept to some degrees. Such a degree is given by a fuzzy function.

Definition 1. *A fuzzy concept C is defined as following:*

$$C = \{a_1^{v1}, a_2^{v2}, ..., a_n^{vn}\}$$

where a_i is an object, vi is the membership degree of object i in concept C.

We say a_i is a member of C or a_i belongs to C to a degree vi. The degree of object a belongs to a fuzzy concept C is given by a fuzzy membership function:

$$\mu_C : A \rightarrow [0, 1]$$

where A is the set of objects. If there are objects whose membership degree in a concept C is greater than zero, and we name those objects as *members of concept C*.

According to classical view, concepts are organized as in a hierarchy. In our model, a *fuzzy concept hierarchy H_C* is a partial order on the set of all fuzzy concepts in the domain defining the subsumption relationship between fuzzy concepts.

Definition 2. *For two concepts X and Y, $X = \{a_1^{w1}, a_2^{w2}, ..., a_n^{wn}\}$ and $Y = \{a_1^{y1}, a_2^{y2}, ..., a_n^{yn}\}$, a_i is an object, w_i is the membership degree of a_i in fuzzy concept X and y_i is the membership degree of a_i in fuzzy concept Y. If $\forall a_i^{w_i} \in X, a_i^{y_i} \in Y, y_i >= w_i$ then X is subsumed by Y (or Y subsumes X) which is denoted as $X \subseteq Y$.*

Fuzzy Role. There may be some binary relations between objects in a domain, and we define them as follows.

Definition 3. *A fuzzy role R is a fuzzy set of binary relations between two objects in the domain. It is interpreted as a set of pairs of objects from the domain denoted by*

$$R = \{< a_1, b_1 >^{w_1}, < a_2, b_2 >^{w_2}, ..., < a_n, b_n >^{w_n}\}$$

where a_i and b_i are two objects, w_i is a real value between zero and one which representing the degree of strength of the relation between the two objects.

For example, we have a statement 'Bob extremely likes football'. There is a relation 'likes' between Bob and football, and the degree w_i of the strength of this relation is very high (extremely).

The degree of strength of the relation between two objects is given by a fuzzy membership function:

$$\mu_R : A \times B \rightarrow [0, 1]$$

where A and B are sets of objects. The set of objects A is named the *domain* of the role while the set of objects B is named the *range* of the role. If there are object pairs $< a_i, b_i >$ whose membership degree in a role R is greater than zero, and we name those object pairs as *members of fuzzy role R*.

In our model, roles are also organized in a hierarchy. A role hierarchy is a partial order on the set of all fuzzy roles in the domain defining the subsumption relationship between roles.

Definition 4. *For two fuzzy roles S and Q, $S = \{< a_1, b_1 >^{w_1}, < a_2, b_2 >^{w_2}, ..., < a_n, b_n >^{w_n}\}$ and $Q = \{< c_1, d_1 >^{y_1}, < c_2, d_2 >^{y_2}, ..., < c_n, d_n >^{y_n}\}$, if $\forall < a_i, b_i >^{w_i} \in S, < a_i, b_i >^{y_i} \in Q, y_i >= w_i$ then we say S is subsumed by Q (or Q subsumes S) denoted as $S \subseteq Q$. w_i is the degree of strength of $< a_i, b_i >$ in fuzzy role S and y_i is the degree of strength of $< a_i, b_i >$ in fuzzy role Q.*

Fuzzy Property. In our model, an object may have several roles with other objects. These roles with different ranges and the same domain (the same object) are considered as properties of the object.

Definition 5. *A fuzzy property P is defined as following:*

$$P = R.C$$

where R is a fuzzy role, C is a fuzzy concept which is the range of the fuzzy role R.

Concept C is a restriction on the range of the role R in property P, and it requires that all objects in the range of role R should be a member of concept C (i.e., $\mu_C(b_i) > 0$). P is interpreted as a fuzzy set of pairs of fuzzy role and fuzzy objects $(< a_i, b_i >, b_i)^{v_i}$. $< a_i, b_i >$ is a member of the fuzzy role R and b_i is a member of fuzzy concept C, and v_i is the degree of the object a_i possessing the property P.

The degree of objects possesses a property $P = R.C$ is given by a function:

$$\mu_P : R \times C \longrightarrow [0, 1]$$

where R is the set of fuzzy roles, C is the set of fuzzy concepts. If an object a has a fuzzy role (relation) $< a, b >$ with object b, $\mu_R(a, b) > 0$ and $\mu_C(b) > 0$, then we say a possesses a *property member* $(< a, b >, b)$ of property $P = R.C$ to a degree $\mu_P(< a, b >, b)$ where $1 \geq \mu_P(< a, b >, b) > 0$. Object a may possess more than one property members of P. All property members of a property belong to the property to a degree greater than zero. There are some axioms for function μ_P to observe.

Axiom 1. For an object a, a fuzzy property $P = R.C$, if $\mu_R(a, c) = 0$ or $\mu_C(c) = 0$ then $\mu_P(< a, c >, c) = 0$.

Axiom 2. For an object a, a fuzzy property $P = R.C$, if $\mu_R(a, c) = 1$ and $\mu_C(c) = 1$, then $\mu_P(< a, c >, c) = 1$.

Axiom 3. For an object a, a fuzzy property $P = R.C$, if $\mu_R(a, c) \geq \mu_R(a, d)$ and $\mu_C(c) \geq \mu_C(d)$, then $\mu_P(< a, c >, c) \geq \mu_P(< a, d >, d)$.

Axiom 4. For two objects a and b, a fuzzy property $P = R.C$, if $\mu_R(a, c) \geq \mu_R(b, d)$ and $\mu_C(c) \geq \mu_C(d)$, then $\mu_P(< a, c >, c) \geq \mu_P(< b, d >, d)$.

Axiom 5. For an object a, two fuzzy properties $P_1 = R.C$ and $P_2 = S.D$, if $\mu_R(a, e) \geq \mu_S(a, e)$, and $\mu_C(e) \geq \mu_D(e)$, then $\mu_{P_1}(< a, e >, e) \geq \mu_{P_2}(< a, e >, e)$.

Axioms 1 and 2 specify the boundary cases of calculating the degree of objects possessing properties. If $\mu_P(< a, c >, c) = 0$, it means $(< a, c >, c)$ is not a property member of P. If $\mu_P(< a, c >, c) = 1$, it means $(< a, c >, c)$ is definitely a member of

P. Axioms 3, 4 and 5 specify the influence of the membership degree of role and that of the range concept on the property memberships.[4]

There is a special kind of property named *fuzzy instance property*. For a property, it consists of some property members. If there is only one property member in the property, the property is so called a fuzzy instance property.

Analogously, a property hierarchy H_P is a partial order on the set of all properties in the domain defining the subsumption relationship between fuzzy properties.

Definition 6. *For two fuzzy properties P_1 and P_2,*

$$P_1 = \{(< a, c >, c)^{v_{1i}} \mid < a, c >^{w_{1i}} \in S, c^{y_{1i}} \in C\}$$

and

$$P_2 = \{(< a, c >, c)^{v_{2i}} \mid < a, c >^{w_{2i}} \in Q, c^{y_{2i}} \in D\}$$

*,if $\forall (< a, c >, c), (< a, c >, c)^{v_{1i}} \in P_1, (< a, c >, c)^{v_{2i}} \in P_2, v_{1i} \leq v_{2i}$, then P_1 is said to **be subsumed by** P_2 (or P_2 **subsumes** P_1), denoted by $P_1 \subseteq P_2$.*

Two theorems are obtained based on axioms and definitions introduced above.[5]

Theorem 1. *For two properties P_1 and P_2, if $P_1 = S.C, P_2 = Q.D, S \subseteq Q$, and $C \subseteq D$, then $P_1 \subseteq P_2$.*

Theorem 2. *For an object a and two properties P_1 and P_2, suppose a possesses P_1 to a degree $v^a_{P_1}$ and P_2 to a degree $v^a_{P_2}$. If $P_1 \subseteq P_2$, then $v^a_{P_1} \leq v^a_{P_2}$.*

For the example in section 3, we assume a customer O_c has a property 'buy.expensiveItem' and there is one property member 'buy.Eproduct00307' of 'buy.expensiveItem' ('Eproduct00307' is an item and 'buy.Eproduct00307' is also an instance property of O_c). According to theorem 1 and 2, we know that 'buy.expensiveItem' is a sub-property of 'buy.Item' ('expensiveItem' is a sub-concept of 'Item') and we can infer that O_c also possesses the property 'buy.Item' to a degree no less than that of 'buy.expensiveItem'.

Object Representation by Fuzzy Instance Properties. For the reason that an object a has several fuzzy relations (roles) with other objects, each specific member of a role and the object which is a member of the role's range concept can form an fuzzy instance property. Thus object a possesses a set of fuzzy instance properties and each of these properties has only one property member.

We consider an object in an ontology is represented by a set of fuzzy instance properties named *object property vector*. The relation among the fuzzy instance properties in the object property vector is conjunction.

$$\overrightarrow{P}_a = (p_{a,1}^{v_{a,1}}, p_{a,2}^{v_{a,2}}, ..., p_{a,n}^{v_{a,n}}), 1 \leq i \leq n$$

where $p_{a,i}$ is a fuzzy instance property a possessing, $v_{a,i}$ is the degree to which a possesses property $p_{a,i}$. For the reason that all properties in the object property vector are instance properties, thus $\forall i, v_{a,i} = 1$.

---

[4] For the interest of space, we omit all the verification of axioms in this paper.

[5] For the reason of space, we omit all proofs of theorems in this paper.

For the example in section 3, we assume a customer O_c has a customer id '20071202' and has bought two items 'Furniture00002' and 'Eproduct00307'. O_c is represented as

$$\overrightarrow{O}_c = (hasId.2001202 : 1, buy.Furniture00002 : 1, buy.Eproduct00307 : 1)$$

4.2   Two Kinds of Measurements of Objects Possessing Properties

In our model, the measure of the degree to which a possesses p_x is based on the property members of p_x which a possesses. There are two kinds of measurements on the set of property members which a possesses for a specific property p_x, which are named *quantitative measure* and *qualitative measure* for a possessing p_x.

N-property. The quantitative measure for a possessing p_x is a number restriction on property members of p_x which object a possessing. There are a set of quantifiers for modeling number restrictions on properties. We present six quantifiers used frequently here, which are $[\exists], [\forall], [\geq_n], [\leq_n], [>_n], [<_n]$ and n is an integer. We name a property with a quantifier as an *N-property*, e.g., $[\exists]p_x, [\forall]p_x$ and so on.[6]
   The degrees to which an object a possessing N-Properties presented above are given by fuzzy functions defined as following respectively:

$$\mu_{[\exists]P}(a, P) = max(\mu_{P_1^a}, ..., \mu_{P_m^a}), 1 \leq i \leq m \tag{1}$$

where $\mu_{P_i^a} = \mu_P(\mu_R(a, c_i), \mu_C(c_i))$ and c_i are objects in the domain.

$$\mu_{[\forall]P}(a, P) = min(\mu_{P_1^a}, ..., \mu_{P_m^a}), 1 \leq i \leq m \tag{2}$$

where $\mu_{P_i^a} = max(1 - \mu_R(a, c_i), \mu_C(c_i))$ and c_i are objects in the domain.

$$\mu_{[\geq_n]P}(a, P) = sup_{c_1,...,c_n \in \Delta^I}(min(\mu_{P_{c1}^a}, ..., \mu_{P_{cn}^a})) \tag{3}$$

where $\mu_{P_{ci}^a} = \mu_P(\mu_R(a, c_i), \mu_C(c_i))$ and c_i are objects in the domain.
   Furthermore, $\mu_{[>_n]P} = \mu_{[\geq_{n+1}]P}, \mu_{[<_n]P} = 1 - \mu_{[\geq_n]P}, \mu_{[\leq_n]P} = 1 - \mu_{[>_n]P}$, i.e., $[\leq_n]P = \neg([>_n]P), [<_n]P = \neg([\geq_n]P)$.
   For example, if a customer O_c has bought a set of items (e.g., 'Eproduct00307', 'Book07005' and so on). We can use the fuzzy functions defined above to calculate the degree of O_c possessing these N-properties. For instance, we can obtain that O_c possesses the property '$[\exists]$buy.Item' to a degree 1 according to equation 1. It means that O_c definitely buyers at least one item.

L-property. A qualitative measure of object a possessing a property P is a qualitative aggregation on the set of property members of P which object a possessing. We call a property with an aggregation function on property members as an *L-property*, which is in the form of $[\$]P$. $[\$]$ is a qualification aggregation on all property members, and we call it as a *qualifier*.

---

[6] We use the form of $[quantifier]P$ as syntax of N-property in order to distinguish from some concepts which are with quantifiers and without $[]$ in DLs, e.g., $\exists R.C$ is a concept in DLs.

There are several possible aggregation functions to aggregate all the property members [16]. One of the aggregation used frequently for qualitative measure is an average function for membership degrees of property members which objects possess in P and we present it here as following:

$$\mu_{[\$]P}(a, P) = \frac{\sum_{i=1}^{n} w_i^a}{n} \qquad (4)$$

where w_i^a is the membership degree of property member p_i of P object a possessing.

For example, suppose a customer O_c buys two items 'Eproduct00307' and 'Furniture00002' only. Both 'Eproduct00307' and 'Furniture00002' belong to 'expensiveItem' to a degree 1. Then we can obtain that O_c possesses '[\$]buy.expensiveItem' to a degree 1 according to equation 4. It means that O_c definitely buys expensive items.

Difference between Properties, L-properties and N-properties. L-Properties and N-properties are used to measure the degree an object possessing properties qualitatively and quantitatively, respectively. An L-property is a qualitative measurement of an object possessing a property based on aggregating all property members the object possessing for the property, while an N-property is a quantitative measurement of an object possessing a property based on a number restriction on all property members the object possessing for the property. To our best knowledge, there is no a formalization of qualitative measurement for the degree of an object possessing a property. These two measurements are frequently used measurements from two perspectives of people.

4.3 Concepts Represented by N-Properties and L-Properties

We combine the classical view and fuzzy set theory so that our model can handle the vague concepts. In our model, all members of a concept should possess all defining properties of the concept to some degrees. For the reason that N-properties and L-properties are quantitative measures and qualitative measures of properties an object possessing respectively, thus a concept can be defined by a set of N-properties and L-properties. Besides, there is a minimal requirement for each defining property of concepts. If an object possesses all defining properties of a concept to higher degrees, then it means that the object satisfies the minimal requirements of defining properties to higher degrees. Thus the object is given a higher membership degree in the concept.

Based on classical view and fuzzy set theory, we generalize the representation of a concept C as following:

$$\vec{C} = (\vec{S}_1, \vec{S}_2, ..., \vec{S}_m), 1 \leq i \leq m$$

and

$$\vec{S}_i = (p_{i,1}^{w_{i,1}}, p_{i,2}^{w_{i,2}}, ..., p_{i,n_i}^{w_{i,n_i}}), 1 \leq j \leq n_i$$

where n_i is the number of properties in $\vec{S}_i$. A $\vec{S}_i$ is named a *characteristic vector* of C which consists of a set of defining properties. The relation between characteristic vectors is union, and the relation between defining properties in a $\vec{S}_i$ is conjunction. $p_{i,j}$ is a defining property in a $\vec{S}_i$ and it can be either N-properties or L-properties. $w_{i,j}$ is considered as a minimal requirement of property $p_{i,j}$ and $w_{i,j} \in (0, 1]$.

5 Fuzzy Membership of Objects in Concepts

In our model, membership degree of an object a in concept C depends on the comparison of object property vector of a and characteristic vectors of C. If an object a possesses all the defining properties in one of characteristic vectors $\overrightarrow{S}_i$ of C to a degree greater than zero, then a is a member of C to some degree.[7] Besides, while object a possesses all the defining properties of any $\overrightarrow{S}_i$ of C to degrees which are greater than or equal to the minimal requirements of all defining properties of the specific $\overrightarrow{S}_i$ in C, the membership of a in concept C is equal to one. For the reason that concepts are represented by N-properties and L-properties while objects are represented by fuzzy instance properties, and properties in our model may be not independent, we need to do property alignment (aligning fuzzy instance properties of objects to defining properties of concepts) before measuring the membership of objects in concepts based on properties comparison.

5.1 Measuring Degrees of Objects Possessing Defining Properties of Concepts

For the reason that a concept is represented by a set of disjoint characteristic vectors, we need to align the property vector of object a to each characteristic vectors. We define a function for the alignment between object property vectors and characteristic vectors.

$$alignO : P_a \times S_x \rightarrow S_x^a$$

where P_a is the set of object property vectors, S_x is set of characteristic vectors and S_x^a is the set of aligned property vectors. The function $alignO(\overrightarrow{p}_a, \overrightarrow{S}_x)$ is used to align object property vector $\overrightarrow{p}_a$ to characteristic vector $\overrightarrow{S}_x$, the result of $alignO(\overrightarrow{p}_a, \overrightarrow{S}_x)$ is an aligned property vector $\overrightarrow{S}_x^a$ as following:

$$\overrightarrow{s}_x^a = (p_{x,1}^{w_{x,1}^a}, p_{x,2}^{w_{x,2}^a}, ..., p_{x,n}^{w_{x,n}^a}), 1 \le j \le n$$

where n is the number of properties of $\overrightarrow{S}_x$ and $w_{x,j}^a$ is the degree of object a possessing property $p_{x,j}$ in characteristic vector $\overrightarrow{S}_x$. In our model, we can obtain the degree of object a possessing each defining property $p_{x,j}$ ($p_{x,j}$ can be N-properties or L-properties) by the fuzzy membership function $\mu_{p_{x,j}}(\overrightarrow{p}_a, p_{x,j})$. The reason is that object a is represented by a vector of instance properties (i.e., a vector of property members) and measuring the degree of object a possessing an N-property or L-property is based on all property members of a possessing. Thus we can obtain $w_{x,j}^a = \mu_{p_{x,j}}(\overrightarrow{p}_a, p_{x,j})$ for each property $p_{x,j}$ where $\mu_{p_{x,y}}(\overrightarrow{p}_a, p_{x,j})$ is one of the membership functions of N-properties or L-properties defined in section 4.2 (e.g., equation 3 and 4).

5.2 Calculation of Object Fuzzy Memberships in Concepts

For a concept C and object a, we can align $\overrightarrow{p}_a$ to each characteristic vector $\overrightarrow{S}_x$ of C and get its aligned property vector $\overrightarrow{S}_x^a$. The degree of a property vector $\overrightarrow{p}_a$ satisfying

---

[7] If object a possesses all the defining properties of $\overrightarrow{S}_i$ of C to higher degrees, then its membership degree in C is higher.

the minimal requirements of a characteristic vector $\overrightarrow{S}_x$ is calculated by a comparison function of vectors.

$$\varphi : S_x^a \times S_x \to [0,1]$$

where S_x^a is the set of aligned property vectors and S_x is the set of characteristic vectors. There are some axioms for $\varphi(\overrightarrow{S}_x^a, \overrightarrow{S}_x)$ to observe.

Axiom 6. For a characteristic vector $\overrightarrow{S}_x$ of a concept and its aligned property vector $\overrightarrow{S}_x^a$, if for some properties $p_{x,i}$ in $\overrightarrow{S}_x^a$, we have $w_{x,i}^a = 0$, then $\varphi(\overrightarrow{S}_x^a, \overrightarrow{S}_x) = 0$.

Axiom 7. For a characteristic vector $\overrightarrow{S}_x$ of a concept and its aligned property vector $\overrightarrow{S}_x^a$, if for each properties $p_{x,i}$ in $\overrightarrow{S}_x^a$, we have $w_{x,i}^a \geq w_{x,i}$, then $\varphi(\overrightarrow{S}_x^a, \overrightarrow{S}_x) = 1$.

Axiom 8. For an object property vector $\overrightarrow{p}_a$, two characteristic vectors $\overrightarrow{S}_{x1}$ and $\overrightarrow{S}_{x2}$ of a concept, $\overrightarrow{S}_{x1}^a$ is the aligned property vector of $\overrightarrow{p}_a$ for $\overrightarrow{S}_{x1}$ and $\overrightarrow{S}_{x2}^a$ is the aligned property vector of $\overrightarrow{p}_a$ for $\overrightarrow{S}_{x2}$, if $w_{x1,i} \leq w_{x2,i}$ for some properties $p_{x,i}$, and $w_{x1,j} = w_{x2,j}$ for others properties $p_{x,j}$ where $i \neq j$, then $\varphi(\overrightarrow{S}_{x1}^a, \overrightarrow{S}_{x1}) \geq \varphi(\overrightarrow{S}_{x2}^a, \overrightarrow{S}_{x2})$.

Axiom 9. For a characteristic vector $\overrightarrow{S}_x$ of a concept, two aligned property vectors $\overrightarrow{S}_x^a$ and $\overrightarrow{S}_x^b$ for object a and b respectively, if $w_{x,i}^a \geq w_{x,i}^b$ for some properties $p_{x,i}$ and $w_{x,j}^a = w_{x,j}^b$ for others properties $p_{x,j}$ where $i \neq j$, then $\varphi(\overrightarrow{S}_x^a, \overrightarrow{S}_x) \geq \varphi(\overrightarrow{S}_x^b, \overrightarrow{S}_x)$.

Axioms 6 and 7 specify the boundary cases of objects satisfying the minimal requirements of properties of concepts. Axioms 8 and 9 concern how the degree of an object property vector satisfying the minimal requirement of a characteristic vector is varied.

Here, we present a possible function which satisfies axioms 6, 7, 8 and 9.

$$\varphi(\overrightarrow{S}_x^a, \overrightarrow{S}_x) = min(\tau_1, \tau_2, ..., \tau_n) \tag{5}$$

where

$$\tau_i = \begin{cases} \frac{w_{x,i}^a}{w_{x,i}} & w_{x,i}^a < w_{x,i} \\ 1 & w_{x,i}^a \geq w_{x,i} \end{cases} \tag{6}$$

where $w_{x,i}^a$ is the degree to which a possessing property $p_{x,i}$ and $w_{x,i}$ is the minimal requirement of property $p_{x,i}$ in $\overrightarrow{S}_x$.

Besides, we consider the fuzzy membership of an object a in fuzzy concept C depends on the following equation:

$$\mu_C(a) = max(\varphi(\overrightarrow{S}_1^a, \overrightarrow{S}_1), \varphi(\overrightarrow{S}_2^a, \overrightarrow{S}_2), ..., \varphi(\overrightarrow{S}_n^a, \overrightarrow{S}_n)) \tag{7}$$

One object may satisfy all the property minimal requirements of more than one characteristic vectors. We choose the maximal value of $\varphi(\overrightarrow{S}_i^a, \overrightarrow{S}_i)$ as the the membership of a in C because that the relation among $\overrightarrow{S}_i$ is disjunction. This is in line with fuzzy set theory.

6   An Illustrating Example

Let's revisit the example discussed in section 3. The concept 'special-customer' denoted by SC and the concept 'customer' denoted by C are defined as following using our model (Properties of SC and C formalized in our model are shown in table 3.):

Table 3. Properties of SC and C formalized in our model

A'	[∃]hasId.customerID	B'	[≥₅]buy.expensiveItem	C'	[$]buy.expensiveItem
D'	[≥₁₀₀]buy.Item	E'	[≥₁]buy.expensiveItem	F'	[∃]buy.Item

$$\vec{C} = (A' : 1, F' : 1), \quad \vec{SC} = \left(\begin{array}{l} \vec{SC}_1 = (A' : 1, B' : 1, C' : 0.6) \\ \vec{SC}_2 = (A' : 1, D' : 1, E' : 0.5) \end{array} \right)$$

For O_1, O_2 and O_3 in section 3, they are represented by fuzzy instance properties and items bought by the three customers are showed in table 2 in section 3. We align the property vectors of them to characteristic vectors of SC as following.

$$\vec{O_1} = (A' : 1, B' : 1, C' : 0.8) \cup (A' : 1, D' : 0.2, E' : 1)$$

$$\vec{O_2} = (A' : 1, B' : 0.2, C' : 0.1) \cup (A' : 1, D' : 1, E' : 0.8)$$

$$\vec{O_3} = (A' : 1, B' : 1, C' : 0.5) \cup (A' : 1, D' : 0.5, E' : 1)$$

The degrees of each object possessing defining properties (e.g., '[∃]buy.expensiveItem') is calculated based on all property members (e.g., 'buy.Furniture00002') possessed by the object for the corresponding property (e.g., 'buy.expensiveItem') using equations 1, 2, 3 and 4 in section 4.2.[8] For example, according to table 2, object O_1 has property members for property '[∃]buy.Item' such as O_1 possessing 'buy.Furniture00002', 'buy.Eproduct00307' and 'buy.Book07005', and these property members are belonged to '[∃]buy.Item' to degree 1. Then the degree of object O_1 possessing the property '[∃]buy.Item' is calculated using equation 1 as following:

$$\mu_{[\exists]buy.Item}(O_1, [\exists]buy.Item) = \max(1, 1, ...1) = 1$$

Then we can get the following result for SC by axioms 6, 7, 8, 9 and equations 5, 6, 7 introduced in section 5:

$$\mu_{SC}(O_1) = 1, \mu_{SC}(O_2) = 1, \mu_{SC}(O_3) = 0.83$$

Analogously, we can get the result for C as following:

$$\mu_C(O_1) = 1, \mu_C(O_2) = 1, \mu_C(O_3) = 1$$

Such results are more reasonable than that in previous models. For the reason that O_1 satisfies all minimal requirements of properties in $\vec{SC_1}$ while O_2 satisfies that in $\vec{SC_2}$ and O_3 satisfies a part of that in $\vec{SC_1}$, we obtain $\mu_{SC}(O_1) = 1, \mu_{SC}(O_2) = 1, \mu_{SC}(o_3) = 0.83$. Further more, according to theorem 1, we can obtain that 'buy.expensiveItem' is a sub-property of 'buy.Item'. Thus we can obtain $\mu_C(O_1) = 1, \mu_C(O_2) = 1, \mu_C(O_3) = 1$ without knowing the degree of each object possessing property F'.

---

[8] For the interest of space, we omit all the fuzzy functions of concepts and the calculation details here.

7   Conclusion

In this paper, we propose a novel formal model of fuzzy ontology with property hierarchy and object membership by combining the classical view and fuzzy set theory, and show that our model is more reasonable and powerful than previous models. Our model can handle the cases of representing concepts by dependent properties in ontology and represent all kinds of concepts (including conjunction concepts, disjunction concepts and combination concepts). Besides, our model also provides a formal mechanism to determine object memberships in concepts automatically based on the defining properties of concepts and properties which objects possess.

Acknowledgement

The work described in this paper was supported by a CUHK Research Committee Direct Grant for Research.

References

1. Antoniou, G., van Harmelen, F.: A Semantic Web Primer: Cooperative Information Systems. MIT Press, Cambridge (2004)
2. Staab, S., Studer, R.: Handbook on Ontologies. Springer, Heidelberg (2004)
3. Stracia, U.: A fuzzy description logic. In: AAAI 1998/IAAI 1998: Proceedings of the fifteenth national/tenth conference on Artificial intelligence/Innovative applications of artificial intelligence, pp. 594–599 (1998)
4. Straccia, U.: Towards a fuzzy description logic for the semantic web. In: Proceedings of the Second European Semantic Web Conference, pp. 167–181 (2005)
5. Stoilos, G., Stamou, G., Tzouvaras, V., Pan, J.Z., Horrocks, I.: The Fuzzy Description Logic f-SHIN. In: Proc. of the International Workshop on Uncertainty Reasoning for the Semantic Web (2005)
6. Au Yeung, C.M., Leung, H.F.: Ontology with likeliness and typicality of objects in concepts. In: Embley, D.W., Olivé, A., Ram, S. (eds.) ER 2006. LNCS, vol. 4215, pp. 98–111. Springer, Heidelberg (2006)
7. Murphy, G.L.: The big book of concepts. MIT Press, Cambridge (2002)
8. Galotti., K.M.: Cognitive Psychology In and Out of the Laboratory, 3rd edn. Wadsworth, Belmont (2004)
9. Parsons, J., Wand, Y.: Attribute-based semantic reconciliation of multiple data sources. Journal on Data Semantics 2800, 21–47 (2003)
10. Zadeh, L.A.: Fuzzy sets. Information and Control 8, 338–353 (1965)
11. Smith, E.E., Medin, D.L.: Categories and Concepts. Harvard University Press (1981)
12. Baader, F., Calvanese, D., McGuinness, D.L., Nardi, D., Patel-Schneider, P.F. (eds.): The description logic handbook: theory, implementation, and applications. Cambridge University Press, New York (2003)
13. Zadeh, L.A.: Fuzzy logic. Computer 21(4), 83–93 (1988)
14. Klir, G.J., Yuan, B.: Fuzzy sets and fuzzy logic:theory and applications. Prentice hall PTR, Englewood Cliffs (1995)
15. Cross, V., Voss, C.R.: Fuzzy ontologies for multilingual document exploitation. In: Proceedings of the 1999 conference of NAFIPS, pp. 392–397 (1999)
16. Yager, R.R.: On mean type aggregation. IEEE Transactions on Systems, Man and Cybernetics 26, 209–221 (1996)

What's in a Relationship: An Ontological Analysis

Giancarlo Guizzardi[1] and Gerd Wagner[2]

[1] Comp. Science Department, Federal University of Espírito Santo (UFES), Brazil
gguizzardi@inf.ufes.br
[2] Brandenburg University of Technology at Cottbus, Germany
wagnerg@tu-cottbus.de

Abstract. In a series of publications, we have proposed a foundational system of ontological categories which has been successfully used to evaluate and improve the quality of conceptual modeling grammars and models. In this article, we continue this work by using this foundational ontology to provide real-world semantics and sound modeling guidelines for one of the most fundamental (and yet one of the most problematic) constructs in conceptual modeling, namely, the *relationship type*. In addition, we systematically compare our approach with a classical ontological treatment of this construct in the literature, provided by the BWW framework.

1 Introduction

In recent years, there has been a growing interest in the application of *Foundational Ontologies*, i.e., formal ontological theories in the philosophical sense, for providing real-world semantics for conceptual modeling languages, and theoretically sound foundations and methodological guidelines for evaluating and improving the individual models produced using these languages.

For a number of years, we have been developing a foundational ontology named UFO (Unified Foundational Ontology) [1-3] by employing theories from Formal Ontology, Cognitive Psychology, Linguistics, Philosophy of Language and Philosophical Logics. In a series of publications, this reference ontology has been successfully applied to analyze a number of fundamental conceptual modeling constructs ranging from Roles, Types and Taxonomic Structures, Part-Whole Relations, Attributes, Weak Entities and Datatypes, among others. The system of ontological categories constituting UFO is presented in depth in [1], together with its empirical justifications and formal characterization.

In this article we continue this work by addressing one of the most fundamental (and yet one of the most problematic) constructs in conceptual modeling, namely, the *relationship type* (also named "association" or "relation"). Despite its importance, empirical evidence shows that the use of this construct is often problematical as a way of communicating meaning in an application domain [4]. In pace with [5], we believe that this is mainly due to the lack of consensus and imprecise definitions of its real-world semantics.

The remaining of this article is organized as follows. In section 2, we present the core categories of the UFO ontology, focusing on those aspects which are germane to

Q. Li et al. (Eds.): ER 2008, LNCS 5231, pp. 83–97, 2008.

the purpose of this article. In particular, in sections 2.4 and 2.5 we built on the work presented in [2] to propose an ontological theory of relations. In section 3, we employ the theory presented in section 2 to provide an ontological analysis of relationship types and well-founded guidelines for their representation in conceptual models. In section 4, we briefly compare the results of section 3 with a classical ontological treatment of this construct in the literature, provided by BWW framework. Section 5 presents some final considerations.

2 Background: The Unified Foundational Ontology (UFO)

The core of the UFO ontology is depicted in figure 1 below. A fundamental distinction in this ontology is between the categories of *Individual* and *Universal*. Individuals are entities that exist in reality possessing a unique identity. Universals, conversely, are space-time independent pattern of features, which can be realized in a number of different individuals. The core of this ontology exemplifies the so-called *Aristotelian ontological square* comprising the category pairs *Object-Object Universal*, *Trope-Trope Universal*. From a metaphysical point of view, this choice allows for the construction of a parsimonious ontology, based on the primitive and formally defined notion of *existential dependence* [1]: **Definition 1 (existential dependence):** Let the predicate ε denote existence. We have that an individual *x* is *existentially dependent* on another individual *y* (symbolized as *ed(x,y)*) iff, as a matter of necessity, *y* must exist whenever *x* exists, or formally **(1)**. $\mathbf{ed(x,y)} =_{\mathbf{def}} \square(\varepsilon(\mathbf{x}) \rightarrow \varepsilon(\mathbf{y}))$. In complementary manner, we define two individuals as independent from each other as: **(2)**. $\mathbf{indep(x,y)} =_{\mathbf{def}} \neg\mathbf{ed(x,y)} \wedge \neg\mathbf{ed(y,x)}$.

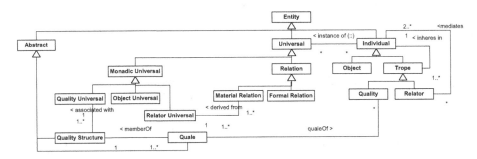

Fig. 1. Excerpt of the Foundational ontology UFO

2.1 Tropes and Objects

Intuitively, a trope is an instance of a property (i.e., the instance of an objectified property) of a specific entity: the redness of John's T-shirt is a trope that *inheres* to John's T-shirt (the host). Both John's T-shirt and the redness of John's T-shirt are individuals. However, they are individuals of very different natures. Tropes are individuals which can only exist in other individuals, i.e., they are *existentially dependent* on other individuals in the way, for instance, the color and the weight of an apple *a* depend on *a*, the electric charge of a conductor *c* depends on *c*, or John's headache depends on John. In contrast, individuals such as John, the apple *a*, and the conductor *c* do not inhere in other individuals and, hence, are not existentially dependent entities in this sense. In this article, we give the name *Object* to the latter type of individual.

As discussed in [1], there is solid evidence for tropes in the literature. On one hand, in the analysis of the content of perception, tropes are the immediate objects of everyday perception. On the other hand, the idea of tropes as *truthmakers* underlies a standard event-based approach to natural language semantics. The notion of tropes employed here comprises: (a) *Intrinsic Tropes* or *Qualities*: an individualized (objectified) color, temperature, or weight, a symptom, a skill, a belief, an intention, an electric charge; (b) *Relational Tropes* or *Relators*: a kiss, a handshake, a covalent bond, a medical treatment, but also *social objects* such as an enrollment, an employment, a purchase order and a commitment or claim.

Existential dependence can also be used to differentiate intrinsic and relational tropes: qualities are dependent on one single individual; relators depend on a plurality of individuals. More technically, a special type of existential dependence relation that holds between a trope *x* and the individual *y* of which *x* depends is the relation of *inherence* (*i*). Thus, for an individual *x* to be a trope of another individual *y*, the relation $i(x,y)$ must hold between the two. For example, inherence glues your smile to your face, or the charge in a specific conductor to the conductor itself. We then formally characterize a trope as an individual that inheres in (and, hence, is existentially dependent upon) another individual: **Definition 2 (Trope): (3). Trope(x)** $=_{\text{def}}$ **Individual(x)** $\wedge$ $\exists y\, i(x,y)$.

Inherence is irreflexive, asymmetric and intransitive relation. Moreover, in our framework, we adopt the so-called *non-migration* (or *non-transferability*) *principle*. This means that it is not possible for a trope *m* to inhere in two different individuals *a* and *b*: **(4).** $\forall x,y,z$ **(Trope(x)** $\wedge$ $i(x,y)$ $\wedge$ $i(x,z)$ $\rightarrow$ **y = z)**. The unique individual *y* that a tropes *x* inheres in is termed the *bearer* of *x* and is defined as follows: **Definition 3 (Bearer of a Trope)**[1]: **(5).** $\beta(x)$ $=_{\text{def}}$ $\iota y\, i(x,y)$. The bearer of a trope can itself be another trope. Examples include the individualized time extension, or the gravity of John's headache. The infinite regress in the inherence chain is prevented by the fact that there are individuals (namely *Objects*) that cannot inhere in other individuals.

2.2 Qualia and Quality Structures

The feature of tropes defined by the non-migration principle (formula 4) seems at first counterintuitive. For example, if we have two particulars *a* (a red apple) and *b* (a red car), and two tropes r_1 (particular redness of *a*) and r_2 (particular redness of *b*), we consider r_1 and r_2 to be different individuals, although perhaps qualitatively indistinguishable. What does it mean then to say that *a* and *b* have the *same* color? Due to (4), sameness here cannot refer to strict (numerical) identity, but only to a qualitative one (i.e., equivalence in a certain respect). We thus distinguish between the color of a particular apple (its quality) and its 'value' (e.g., a particular shade of red). The latter

---

[1] The iota operator (ι) used in a formula such as $\iota x\varphi$ was defined by Bertrand Russel and implies both the existence and the uniqueness of an individual *x* satisfying predicate φ.

is named *quale*, and describes a projection of an individual quality into a certain value space or measurement structure named a *quality structure* [1].

An attempt to model the relation between properties and their representation in human cognitive structures is presented in the theory of *conceptual spaces* introduced in [6]. The idea is that for several perceivable or conceivable quality universals there is an associated *quality structure* in human cognition. For example, height and mass are associated with one-dimensional structures with a zero point isomorphic to the half-line of nonnegative real numbers. Other properties such as color and taste are represented by multi-dimensional structures. Moreover, [6] defends that this notion should be understood literally, i.e., quality structures are endowed with certain geometrical properties (topological or ordering structures) that constrain the relations between its constituting dimensions. For example, both the dimensions of height and mass are totally ordered structures. For an in depth discussion on the topic of quality structures and their role in conceptual modeling one should refer to [1,2].

2.3 Relations and Relators

Relations are entities that glue together other entities. Every relation has a number of relata as arguments, which are connected or related by it. The number of a relation's arguments is called its arity. In the philosophical literature, two broad categories of relations are typically considered, namely, material and formal relations [7,8].

Formal relations hold between two or more entities directly, without any further intervening individual. In principle, it includes those relations that form the mathematical superstructure of our framework. Examples include existential dependence (*ed*), inherence (*i*), subtype-of, part-of, subset-of, instantiation(::), among many others not discussed here [1]. We name these relations here *basic formal relations* [7]. However, we also classify as formal those domain relations that exhibit similar characteristics, i.e., those relations of comparison such as is taller than, is older than, knows more Greek than. We name these relations *domain formal relations*. As pointed out in [8], the entities that are immediate relata of such relations are not objects but qualities. For instance, the relation heavier-than between two atoms is a formal relation that holds directly as soon as the relata (atoms) are given. The truth-value of a predicate representing this relation depends solely on the atomic number (a quality) of each atom and the material content of heavier-than is as it were distributed between the two relata. Moreover, to quote [8], "once the distribution has been effected, the two relata are seen to fall apart, in such a way that they no longer have anything specifically to do with each other but can serve equally as terms in a potentially infinite number of comparisons".

Material relations, conversely, have material structure on their own and include examples such as *working at*, *being enrolled at*, and *being connected to*. Whilst a formal relation such as the one between Paul and his knowledge x of Greek holds directly and as soon as Paul and x exist, for a material relation of *being treated in* between Paul and the medical unit MU_1 to exist, another entity must exist which *mediates* Paul and MU_1. We name these entities *relators*. Relators are individuals with the power of connecting entities. For example, a medical treatment connects a patient with a medical unit; an enrollment connects a student with an educational institution;

a covalent bond connects two atoms. The notion of relator (relational tropes) is supported by several works in the philosophical literature [7,8] and, the position advocated here is that they play an important role in answering questions of the sort: what does it mean to say that John is married to Mary? Why is it true to say that Bill works for Company X but not for Company Y?

An important notion for the characterization of relators (and, hence, for the characterization of material relations) is the notion of *foundation*. Foundation can be seen as a type of *historical dependence* [1], in the way that, for instance, an instance of *being kissed* is founded on an individual *kiss,* or an instance of *being punched by* is founded on an individual *punch,* an instance of *being connected to* between airports is founded on a particular flight connection.

Suppose that John *is married to* Mary. In this case, we can assume that there is an individual relator (relational trope) m_1 of type *marriage* that mediates John and Mary. The foundation of this relator can be, for instance, a wedding event or the signing of a social contract between the involved parties. In other words, for instance, a certain event e_1 in which John and Mary participate can create an individual marriage m_1 which existentially depends on John and Mary and which mediates them. The event e_1 in this case is the foundation of relator m_1.

Now, let us elaborate on the nature of the relator m_1. There are many qualities that John acquires by virtue of being married to Mary. For example, imagine all the legal responsibilities and rights that John has in the context of this relation. These newly acquired tropes are intrinsic qualities of John which, therefore, inhere and are existentially dependent on him. However, these qualities also depend on the existence of Mary. We name this type of qualities *externally dependent qualities*, i.e., externally dependent qualities are intrinsic tropes that inhere in a single individual but that are existentially dependent on (possibly a multitude of) other individuals: **Definition 4 (Externally Dependent Quality):** A quality x is externally dependent iff it is existentially dependent of an individual which is independent of its bearer. Fornally, **(6).** **ExtDepQuality(x) $=_{def}$ Quality(x) $\wedge \exists y$ indep(y,β(x)) $\wedge$ ed(x,y).**

In the same manner, there are also a number of individual qualities (e.g., rights and responsabilities) that Mary acquires by virtue of being married to John. Now, we can define an aggregate m_1 composed of all these externally dependent qualities that share the same foundation. In this example, m_1 is exactly the sum of all qualities (rights and responsabilities) acquired by John and Mary due to the same foundational event, i.e., m_1 is the instance of the relational property *marriage* that mediates John and Mary and that is the *truthmaker* of propositions such as "John is married to Mary", "Mary is married to John", "John is the husband of Mary", and "Mary is the wife of John".

A relator is said to mediate (or connect) the relata of a material relation (symbolized by $m(x,y)$). As discussed above, mediation is a special type of existential dependence relation or, more specifically, a sort of non-exclusive inherence (see [1] for formal details). Finally, we require that a relator mediates at least two distinct individuals, i.e., **(7). $\forall$x Relator(x) $\rightarrow \exists$y,w (y $\neq$ w $\wedge m(x,y) \wedge m(x,w)$).**

2.4 Universals

An *Object Universal* is a universal whose instances are objects (e.g., the universal Person or the universal Apple). A *Quality Universal* is a universal whose instances are individual qualities (e.g., the objectified color of this apple is an instance of the universal color, a particular headache is an instance of the universal Symptom), and a *Relator Universal* is one whose instances are individual relational tropes (e.g., the particular enrollment connecting John and a certain University is an instance of the universal Enrollment). Finally, a Relation is a universal whose instances are n-tuples or related elements (e.g., being older than, being married to, being the father of).

In general, conceptual specifications (such as UML class diagrams and ER specifications) represent conceptualizations only at the type level, i.e., only universals and relations among universals are typically represented. Thus, we define the formal relations of *Characterization* and *Mediation* as the counterparts at the type level of the relations *inheres in* and *mediates*, respectively. In these definitions, the symbol :: represents the formal relation of instantiation: **Definition 5 (Characterization)**: A universal U is characterized by a trope universal T iff every instance of U bears an instance of T. Formally, **(8). charac(U,T)** $=_{def}$ **Universal(U)** $\wedge$ **QualityUniversal(T)** $\wedge \forall x$ (x::U $\rightarrow \exists y$ y::T $\wedge i(y,x)$); **Definition 6 (Mediation)**: The mediation relation holds between a universal U and a relator universal U_R iff every instance of U is *mediated by* (*m*) an instance of U_R. Formally, **(9). mediation(U,U_R)** $=_{def}$ **Universal(U)** $\wedge$ **RelatorUniversal(U_R)** $\wedge \forall x$ (x::U $\rightarrow \exists r$ r::$U_R \wedge m(r,x)$).

Relator universals constitute the basis for defining material relations R whose instances are n-tuples of entities. In general, a material relation R can be defined by the following schema: **Definition 7 (Material and Formal Relations)**: Let $\phi(a_1,...,a_n)$ denote a condition on the individuals $a_1,...,a_n$

$$[a_1...a_n]::R(U_1...U_n) \leftrightarrow \bigwedge_{i \leq n} a_i::U_i \wedge \phi (a_1...a_n)$$

A relation is called *material* if there is a relator universal U_R such that the condition ϕ is obtained from U_R as follows: $\phi(a_1...a_n) \leftrightarrow \exists k$ (k::$U_R \wedge_{i \leq n} m(k,a_i)$)). In this case, we say that the relation R is derived from the relator universal U_R, or symbolically, *derivation(R,U_R)*. Otherwise, if such a relator universal U_R does not exists, R is termed a formal relation.

We can summarize this discussion as follows: (1) we make a fundamental distinction between formal and material relations. Whilst the former hold directly between two entities without any further intervening individual, the latter are induced by mediating entities called relators. Moreover, material relations are founded by material entities in reality, typically events, which are external to their relata. Domain formal relations, in contrast, are founded in qualities which are intrinsic to the their relata and, hence, can be reduced to relations between these qualities; (2) Relators are special types of (relational) tropes, i.e., particularized relational properties and are aggregations of externally dependent qualities; (3) Externally dependent qualities exemplify the properties that an individual has in the scope of a certain material relation; (4) We explicitly differentiate a relator universal from the material relations (classes of tuples) derived from that relator universal.

3   An Ontological Foundation for Conceptual Modeling Relations

In this section, we employ the set of ontological categories proposed is section 2 to analyze and provide foundations for conceptual modeling relationship types or relations.

These modeling concepts are represented in practically all conceptual modeling languages. Thus, the conclusions drawn in what follows can be extended to all these languages. However, with the sole purpose of exemplification, we shall refer in the sequel to these concepts as they are represented by UML's modeling primitives.

In most conceptual modeling languages, n-ary relationship types are taken to represent sets of n-tuples. In UML, the ER concept of a relationship type is called association: *"an association defines a semantic relationship that can occur between typed instances...An instance of an association is called a link...An association declares that there can be links between instances of the associated types. A link is a tuple with one value for each end of the association, where each value is an instance of the type of the end...An association describes a set of tuples whose values refer to typed instances."*[9, p.81]. The OMG UML Specification is somehow ambiguous in defining associations. An association is primarily considered to be a 'connection', but, in certain cases (whenever it has 'class-like properties'), an association may be a class: An association class is *"[a] model element that has both association and class properties. An AssociationClass can be seen as an association that also has class properties, or as a class that also has association properties. It not only connects a set of classifiers but also defines a set of features that belong to the relationship itself and not to any of the classifiers."*[9, p.118].

3.1   Representing Formal and Material Relations

An association A between the classes $C_1,...,C_n$ of a conceptual model can, in principle, be understood in our framework as a relation R between the corresponding universals $U_1,...,U_n$ whose extension consists of all tuples corresponding to the links of A. However, current conceptual modeling languages (including UML) do not distinguish between formal and material relations. In figure 2, an example of a formal relation is the relation of *temporal precedence* between Symptoms. In this model, the unstereotyped classes (Person, Patient and Medical Unit) represent object universals; the quality universal Symptom is represented by a class with the corresponding stereotype; Finally, the intrinsic property *start date* of a symptom (a universal whose instances are qualities of a quality) is not represented directly but instead by its associated quality structure, the tridimensional *DateDomain*. The representation rules used in this model amount to the modeling profile proposed in [1,2] and are discussed in depth there.

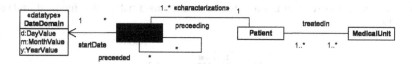

Fig. 2. Representing Objects, Qualities, Quality Structures and Relations

It is easy to see that the relation of *Precedence* in figure 2 is a domain formal relation since it is completely reducible to intrinsic qualities of the involved relata. It is common in conceptual modeling and knowledge representation languages that a number of formal meta-properties (e.g., reflexivity, symmetry, transitivity) are defined for relationships (e.g., OWL, F-LOGIC). In the specific case of *precedence*, these meta-properties are irreflexivity, anti-symmetry and transitivity and, hence, precedence is a strict *partial ordering* relation between symptoms that depends only on the starting date of each of them. Can we provide an explanation for these meta-properties?

As we have discussed in section 2, the immediate relata of domain formal relations are not objects but qualities. Take, for example, the relations of *taller than*, *heavier than* and *precedence*. All these relations can be reduced to relations between qualities: x is *taller than* y iff height(x) > height(y); x is *heavier than* y iff weight(x) > weight(y); x *preceeds* y iff startDate(x) < startDate(y), in which *height*, *weight* and *startDate* are attribute functions mapping the objects x and y to the corresponding qualia. All three quality structures involved in these expressions have a linear structure *ordered* by the < relation. By making this analysis explicit, it becomes evident that *precedence* is an ordered relation *because* the qualities founding this relation are associated with a *ordered* quality structure. In general, we can state that the meta-properties of a *formal relation* R_F can be derived from the meta-properties of the relations between qualia associated with the qualities founding this relation R_F.

Now, take for instance the relation *treatedIn* between Patient and Medical Unit in figure 2. This relation requires the existence of a third entity, namely an individual Treatment mediating a particular Patient and a particular Medical Unit in order for the relation to hold, i.e., it is an example of a material relation. There is a specific practical problem concerning the representation of *material relations* as standard associations as depicted in figure 2. This problem, mentioned in [10], is caused by the fact that the standard notation for associations collapses two different types of *multiplicity constraints*. In this particular example, the model represents that each Patient can be treated in *one-to-many* Medical Units and that each medical unit can treat *one-to-many* patients. However, this statement is ambiguous since many different interpretations can be given to it, including the following: (i) a patient is related to only one treatment in which possibly several medical units participate; (ii) a patient can be related to several treatments to which only one single medical unit participates; (iii) a patient can be related to several treatments to which possibly several medical units participate; (iv) several patients can be related to a treatment to which several medical units participate, and a single patient can be related to several treatments. The cardinality constraint that indicates how many patients (or medical units) can be related to one instance of Treatment is named *single-tuple* cardinality constraint. *Multiple-tuple* cardinality constraints restrict the number of treatments a patient (or medical unit) can be related to.

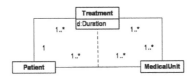

Fig. 3. Explicit representation of single-tuple and multiple-tuple cardinality constraints

How shall we represent a material relation in a conceptual modeling language such as UML such that the aforementioned problem could be addressed? Let us follow for now this (tentative) principle: a material relation R_M of the domain may be represented in a conceptual model by representing the relator universal associated with the relation as an association class. By applying this principle to the treatedIn relation aforementioned we obtain the model of figure 3. In this model, by modeling the relator universal *Treatment* as an association class one can explicitly represent both types of cardinality constraints.

The reader should notice that the aforementioned problem is not at all specific to this case. For another example of a situation where this problem arises see figure 4.a. In this case, the (material) relation statement is that: (a) a customer *purchases* one-to-many purchase items from one-to-many suppliers; (b) a supplier supplies one-to-many purchase items to one-to-many customers; (c) a purchase item can be bought by one-to-many customers from one-to-many suppliers. *PurchaseFrom* is a material relation induced by the relator universal *Purchase*, whose instances are individual purchases. Therefore, we have that $[a_1,a_2,a_3]::R_{purchFrom}$(**Customer, PurchaseItem, Supplier**) $\leftrightarrow a_1::$**Customer** $\wedge a_2::$**PurchaseItem** $\wedge a_3::$**Supplier** $\wedge \exists p$ (p::**Purchase** $\wedge m(p,a_1) \wedge m(p, a_2) \wedge m(p, a_3)$). In other words, for this relation to hold between a particular Customer, a particular PurchaseItem, and a particular Supplier, they must be mediated by the same Purchase instance.

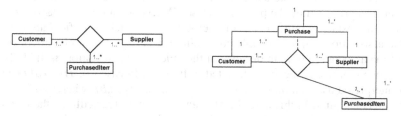

Fig. 4. Example of a material relation with ambiguous (a-left) and (b) with explicit representation of cardinality constraints

Once more, we can see that the specification in figure 4.a collapses single-tuple and multiple-tuple cardinality constraints. For this reason, thereare several possible ways of interpreting this model, including the following: (i) In a given purchase, a Customer participates by buying many items from many Suppliers and a customer can participate in several purchases; (ii) In a given purchase, many Customers participate by buying many items from many Suppliers, and a customer can participate in only one purchase; (iii) In given purchase, a Customer participates by buying many items from a Supplier, and a customer can participate in several purchases; (iv) In given purchase, many Customers participate by buying many items from a Supplier, and a customer can participate in several purchases. By depicting the Purchase universal explicitly (such as in figure 4.b), we can make explicit the intended interpretation of the material PurchaseFrom relation, namely, that in a given purchase, a Customer buys many items from a Supplier. Both customer and supplier can participate in several purchases. Although a purchase can include several items, each item in this model is a unique exemplar and, hence, can only be sold once.

Now it is important to emphasize that this problem is specific to material relations. Formal relations are represented by sets of tuples, i.e., an instance of the relation is itself a tuple with predefined arity. In formal relations, cardinality constraints are always unambiguously interpreted as being *multiple-tuple*, since there is no point in specifying single-tuple cardinality constraints for a relation with predefined arity. Hence, formal relations can be suitably represented as standard UML associations. One should notice that the relations between Patient and Treatment, and Medical Unit and Treatment are formal relations between universals (*mediation*). This is important to block the infinite regress that arises if material relations were required to relate these entities. The same holds for the pairwise associations between Customer, Supplier and PurchaseItem, on one hand, and Purchase on the other.

3.2   An Alternative to Association Classes

At first sight, it seems to be satisfactory to represent a material relation by using an association class to model a relator universal that induces this relation. Nonetheless, the interpretation of this construct in UML is quite ambiguous w.r.t. defining what exactly counts as instances of an association class. We claim that the association class construct in UML exemplifies a case of *construct overload* in the technical sense discussed in [11]. This is to say that there are two distinct ontological concepts that are represented by this construct.

To support this claim, we make use of the following (overloaded) semantic definition of the term as proposed by the pUML (precise UML) community: "an associaton class can have as instances either (a) a n-tuple of entities which classifiers are endpoints of the association; (b) a n+1-tuple containing the entities which classifiers are endpoints of the association plus an instance of the objectified association itself" [12]. Take as an illustration the association depicted in figure 3. In case (a), *TreatedIn* can be directly interpreted as a *relation*, whose instances are pairs *[a,b]*, whereas *a* is patient and *b* is medical unit. In this case, *[a,b]* is an instance of TreatedIn iff there is a relator Treatment connecting *a* and *b*. In interpretation (b), *TreatedIn* is what is named in [3] a *Factual Universal*. In short, if the relator r connects (mediates) the entities $a_1,...,a_n$ then this yields a new individual that is denoted by $\langle r: a_1,...,a_n \rangle$. Individuals of this latter sort are called *material facts*. For every relator universal R there is a set of facts, denoted by *facts(R)*, which is defined by the instances of R and their corresponding arguments. Therefore, an instance of *TreatedIn* in this case could be the material fact $\langle t_1: John, MedUnit_{\#1} \rangle$, whereas John is a Patient, $MedUnit_{\#1}$ is a Medical Unit and t_1 is a treatment relator.

As a trope, a relator can bear other tropes. For example, in figure 3 the temporal duration of a Treatment is a quality of the latter. Moreover, a relator can also be mediated by other relators such as, for instance, a relator universal *Payment* whose instances connect particular Treatments and Payers. For these reasons, between the two aforementioned interpretations for association classes, we claim that interpretation (b) should be favored, since it allows for the explicit representation of relators and their possible intrinsic and relational properties. However, there is still one problem with this representation in UML. Suppose that treatment t_1 mediates the individuals John, and the medical units $MedUnit_{\#1}$ and $MedUnit_{\#2}$. In this case, we have as instances of the association class Treatment both facts $\langle t_1: John, MedUnit_{\#1} \rangle$ and

$\langle t_1$: John, MedUnit$_{\#2}\rangle$. However, this cannot be represented in such a manner in UML. In UML, t_1 is supposed to function as an object identifier for a unique tuple. Thus, if the fact $\langle t_1$: John, MedUnit$_{\#1}\rangle$ holds then $\langle t_1$: John, MedUnit$_{\#2}\rangle$ does not, or alternatively, John and MedUnit$_{\#2}$ must be mediated by another relator. These are, nonetheless, unsatisfactory solutions, since it is the very same relator Treatment that connects one patient to a number of different medical units.

We therefore propose to represent relator universals explicitly as in figure 5. This model explicitly distinguishes the two entities: relator universals are represented by the stereotyped class «relator»; material relations are represented by a derived UML association stereotyped as «material». The dashed line between a material relation and a relator universal, represents that the former is derived from the latter (see *derived from* relation in section 2.5). To mark this difference to the similar graphic symbol in UML, we attach a black circle in the relator universal end of this relation. In this figure, a particular Treatment is existentially dependent on a single Patient and in a (immutable) group of medical units. This would mean in UML that for every association representing an existential dependency relation between a trope and the individual it depends on, the association end should have the *frozen* meta-attribute set to *true* on the side of the latter. This compound modeling construct should replace the ambiguous association class construct in UML. Unlike in figure 3, the entities representing a relator universal (the stereotyped class that replaces an association class), and the material relation (the association itself) are distinct entities. In fact, the latter is completely derived from the former (see definition 7). For instance, the relator universal Treatment and the material relation TreatedIn represent distinct entities and can possibly have different cardinalities, since the same relator t_1 can connect both the entities in [John, MedUnit$_{\#1}$] and [John, MedUnit$_{\#2}$]. Nonetheless, the cardinality constraints of TreatedIn can be completely deduced from the existential dependency relations (*mediation*) between Treatment and the universals whose instances are the relata of TreatedIn, namely, Patient and MedicalUnit.

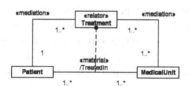

Fig. 5. Model with explicit representation of a Relator Universal, a Material Relation, and a (formal) derivation relation between the two

The benefits of this approach are even more evident in the case of n-ary relations with n > 2. Take the UML representation of a ternary relation in figure 4. In this specification, we are forced to represent the minimum cardinality of zero for all association ends. As explained in the UML specification [9, p.82]: *"For n-ary associations, the lower multiplicity of an end is typically 0. If the lower multiplicity for an end of an n-ary association of 1 (or more) implies that one link (or more) must exist for every possible combination of values for the other ends"*. As recognized by the

UML specification itself, n-ary associations in which there are tuples for every possible combination of the cross-product of the extension of the involved classes are atypical. Thus, in the majority of cases, the UML notation for n-ary associations completely looses the ability of representing real minimum cardinality constraints. Furthermore, as empirically demonstrated in [13], conceptual models without optional properties (minimum cardinality constraints of zero) lead to better performance in problem-solving tasks that require a deeper-level understanding of the represented domain.

The results of this section can be summarized in the following principle regarding the representation of formal and material relations in a conceptual model: In a conceptual model, any domain formal relation universal R_F may be directly represented as a standard association whose links represent the tuples in the extension of R_F. Conversely, a material relation R_M of the domain may be represented by a complex construct composed of: (i) *a class* stereotyped as «relator» representing the *relator universal*. The relator universal is associated to classes representing mediated entities via associations stereotyped as «mediation»; (ii) a standard association stereotyped as «material» representing a material relation whose links represent the tuples in the extension of R_M; (iii) a dashed line with a black circle in one of the ends representing the formal relation of derivation between R_M and the relator universal it derives from.

4   A Critical Comparison to the BWW Approach

The approach found in the literature that is closest to the one presented here is the so-called BWW approach presented in (e.g., [5,11,14]). In these articles, the authors report their results in mapping common constructs of conceptual modeling to an upper level ontology. Their approach is based on the BWW ontology, a framework created by Wand and Weber on the basis of the original metaphysical theory developed by Mario Bunge in [15].

In BWW, a property whose existence depends only on a single thing is called an *intrinsic property*. A property that depends on two or more things is called a *mutual property*. These concepts are analogous to our notions of *intrinsic* and *relational trope universals*. Nevertheless, in our approach properties are instantiated. Thus, our intrinsic properties can be better defined as universals whose instances inhere in a single individual, while relational properties are universals whose instances mediate multiple individuals. This marks an important distinction between the two approaches.

As demonstrated in [2], the ontological position behind the BWW approach (inherited from Bunge) is the *substance-attribute view*, whilst ours is a *trope-theoretical* one. Two consequences of their particular ontological choice are: (i) the denial of the existence of instances of properties; (ii) and the consequence denial of properties of properties (i.e., higher order properties). Thus, in BWW, only things (objects) possess properties. In particular, for the case of relational properties, this dictum leads to the following modeling principle: "Associations should not be modeled as classes" (rule 7 in [14]). This claim is not only perceived as counterintuitive by conceptual modeling practitioners (as shown by [16,17]), but, as discussed in depth [1,2], it is also controversial from a metaphysical point of view and puts BWW in a singular position among the foundational ontologies developed in the realm of computer science.

Moreover, even if both ontological choices were deemed equivalent, there are a number pragmatic reasons for defending the acceptance of property instances and, hence, in favor of accepting also the representation of non-object universals as conceptual modeling types [1,2]. Examples include the proper representation of weak entities and structured datatypes [2] and, to cite an example demonstrated here, the explicit representation of relator universals (relational properties), which allows for the disambiguation of single-tuple and multiple-tuple cardinality constraints in associations.

To provide one more example of the importance of relators in conceptual modeling, suppose the situation in which one wants to model that *students* are *enrolled* in *universities* starting on a certain date. Following the proscription of mutual properties being modeled as entity types, Wand and colleagues propose an alternative model for this situation depicted in Figure 6.a [5].

We claim that it is rather counterintuitive to think about a model of this situation in these terms. According to [5], relationships representing mutual properties are equivalent to n-ary attribute predicates. In this case, what is startDate supposed to stand for? Is it a binary predicate that holds, for example, for John and UFES, like in *startDate (John, UFES)*? This seems to be an absurd conclusion. Thus, startDate should at least be a ternary predicate applied to, for instance, *startDate (John, UFES, 14-2-2004)*. Now, suppose that there are many predicates like this one relating a student and a university. For example, the *start-date of writing the thesis*, the *start-date of receiving a research grant*, etc. We believe that, in this case, the authors would propose to differentiate the startDate depicted in figure 6.a by naming it *startDateofEnrollment*. But does not this move make it obvious that *startDate* is actually a property of the enrollment? In our approach, this can be explicitly modeled such as in figure 6.b. In contrast to figure 6.a, the model of 6.b makes an explicit distinction between a closed-linked relation between student and university and an indirect relation between student and start date.

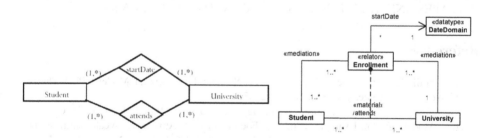

Fig. 6. (a-left) An alternative modeling of "properties of properties" in the BWW approach (from [5]); **(b)** The representation of "properties of properties" in our approach

5   Final Considerations

This article proposes an ontological theory of relations which makes a fundamental distinction between two different categories, namely, formal and material relations. This theory shows that only material relations stand for bonafide ontological relational properties (relational tropes or relators). Domain formal relations, in contrast, are simply useful logical constructions which do not stand for genuine properties of the things themselves but, instead, for the way we talk about these things. It is important to highlight that the theory presented here deals with domain relations as opposed to relations that form the meta-level structure of a modeling framework such as *parthood, generalization/specialization, participation* (in processes), *existential dependence*, among others. In our approach, these meta-relations have been formally treated elsewhere [1,3].

Making the aforementioned distinction explicit is important from an ontological point of view since the very nature of these categories is uncovered. However, this also bears important consequences from a modeling perspective. Deciding whether an n-ary term in the universe of discourse stands for a formal or material relation and, deciding which is the foundation of these relations, amounts to eliciting the very meaning of these terms. On one hand, uncovering the intrinsic tropes and associated quality structures underlying a domain formal relation can explain which are the formal meta-properties which should be described for that relation. On the other hand, recognizing and representing the relator universal underlying a material relation helps to disambiguate different sorts of cardinality constraints (a problem which is specific to material relations). Contrariwise, as demonstrated in [1], by not clearly representing relators and, due to the ambiguity of cardinality constraints, the standard notation for associations can collapse in a single representation, multiple relational properties with even contradictory semantics, which can be major source of interoperability problems. Furthermore, as discussed in depth in [18], the explicit representation of relator universals and their corresponding existential dependency relations provides a suitable mechanism for consistency preservation between static and dynamic conceptual models - an issue which we intend to give an ontological treatment in future works.

Acknowledgements. This research has been partially supported by the funding agencies FAPES (INFRA-MODELA project) and FACITEC (MODELA project).

References

1 Guizzardi, G.: Ontological Foundations for Structural Conceptual Models, PhD Thesis, University of Twente, The Netherlands (2005)

2 Guizzardi, G., Masolo, C., Borgo, S.: In Defense of a Trope-Based Ontology for Conceptual Modeling: An Example with the Foundations of Attributes, Weak Entities and Datatypes. In: Embley, D.W., Olivé, A., Ram, S. (eds.) ER 2006. LNCS, vol. 4215, pp. 112–125. Springer, Heidelberg (2006)

3 Guizzardi, G., Herre, H., Wagner, G.: On General Ontological Foundations of Conceptual Modeling. In: Spaccapietra, S., March, S.T., Kambayashi, Y. (eds.) ER 2002. LNCS, vol. 2503. Springer, Heidelberg (2002)

4 Batra, D., Hoffler, J.A., Bostrom, R.P.: Comparing representations with relational and EER models. Communications of the ACM 33(2), 126–139 (1990)

5 Wand, Y., Storey, V.C., Weber, R.: An ontological analysis of the relationship construct in conceptual modeling. ACM Trans. on Database Systems 24(4), 494–528 (1999)

6 Gärdenfors, P.: Conceptual Spaces: the Geometry of Thought. MIT Press, USA (2000)

7 Heller, B., Herre, H.: Ontological Categories in GOL. Axiomathes 14, 71–90 (2004)

8 Mulligan, K., Smith, B.: A Relational Theory of the Act. Topoi (5/2), 115–130 (1986)

9 OMG, UML 2.0 Infrastructure Specification, Doc.# ptc/03-09-15 (September 2003)

10 Bock, C., Odell, J.: A More Complete Model of Relations and Their Implementation: Relations as Object Types. Journal of Object-Oriented Programming 10(3) (June 1997)

11 Weber, R.: Ontological Foundations of Information Systems. Coopers & Lybrand, Melbourne (1997)

12 Breu, R., et al.: Towards a Formalization of the Unified Modeling Language. In: Proceedings fo the 11th ECOOP, Jyväskylä, Finland (1997)

13 Bodart, F., Patel, A., Sim, M., Weber, R.: Should Optional Properties Be Used in Conceptual Modelling? A Theory and Three Empirical Tests, Information Systems Research 12(4), 384–405 (2001)

14 Evermann, J., Wand, Y.: Towards ontologically based semantics for UML constructs. In: Kunii, H.S., Jajodia, S., Sølvberg, A. (eds.) ER 2001. LNCS, vol. 2224. Springer, Heidelberg (2001)

15 Bunge, M.: Treatise on Basic Philosophy. In: Ontology I. The Furniture of the World, vol. 3. D. Reidel Publishing, New York (1997)

16 Veres, C., Mansson, G.: Cognition and Modeling: Foundations for Research and Practice. Journal of Information Technology Theory and Application 7(1), 93–100 (2005)

17 Hitchman, S.: An interpretive study of how practitioners use entity-relationship modeling in a ternary relationship situation. Comm. Assoc. for Inf. Systems 11, 451–485 (2003)

18 Snoeck, M., Dedede, G.: Existential Dependency: The Key to semantic integrity between structural and behavioral aspects of object types. IEEE Transactions on Software Engineering 24(4) (April 1998)

An Upper Level Ontological Model for Engineering Design Performance Domain

Vadim Ermolayev[1], Natalya Keberle[1], and Wolf-Ekkehard Matzke[2]

[1] Department of IT, Zaporozhye National University, Zhukovskogo 66, 69063,
Zaporozhye, Ukraine
`vadim@ermolayev.com, kenga@zsu.zp.ua`
[2] Cadence Design Systems, GmbH, Mozartstr. 2 D-85622 Feldkirchen, Germany
`wolf@cadence.com`

Abstract. The paper presents our upper level lightweight descriptive model for the set of the Core ontologies of PSI[1] Suite. While PSI Suite of Ontologies is an interlinked modular library of ontologies describing the domain of engineering design performance in microelectronics, PSI upper level ontology is more domain-independent. It is a model of stateful creative dynamic processes, proactive agents, and objects situated in nested dynamic environments based on formal representation of time, events, and happenings. It may be used as an upper level theory for domain ontologies in different application domains having common features. PSI upper level ontology is designed as a semantic bridge facilitating to mapping PSI Domain ontologies to abstract ontological foundations and common sense. It is also used as semantic "glue" for bridging PSI ontologies with other theories, widely accepted in the domains where processes, states, and participating objects are the major entities. These mappings and semantic bridges are supposed to ease the commitment of potential users to PSI Suite. PSI upper level ontology is also used as a "proxy" for different kinds of evaluation of PSI ontologies in frame of our "shaker modeling" methodology for ontology refinement.

1 Introduction

PSI project develops the methodology and the toolset for assessing, predicting, and optimizing the performance of engineering design systems in microelectronics. Though design technology in this domain is well defined, many factors make design processes highly stochastic, non-deterministic, structurally ramified, time-bound – in a phrase, loosely defined and highly dynamic. The examples of such factors are: human factor, innovative character, the pace of technology change, the peculiarities of the market and customer requirements, etc. PSI uses simulation to observe and predict the course of a Dynamic Engineering Design Process (DEDP) with sufficient detail for making assessments grounded. Simulation allows playing "what-if" games to model the unpredictable character of the real business world of microelectronic design.

---

[1] Performance Simulation Initiative (PSI) is a research and development project of Cadence Design Systems, GmbH.

Q. Li et al. (Eds.): ER 2008, LNCS 5231, pp. 98–113, 2008.
© Springer-Verlag Berlin Heidelberg 2008

Finely grained and explicit knowledge of design processes and environments is an important intellectual asset which allows PSI methodology be convincing. This knowledge is formalized using the Suite of PSI ontologies. If someone imagines an arbitrary design flow, most certainly he or she will think in terms of: a goal – the state of affairs to be reached; an action which may bring the process closer to its goal; an object to apply actions to; a designer who acts and applies actions to objects; an instrument to be used by an actor to execute actions; and an environment in which the process occurs. All these interact in dynamics – depending on time and on events which manifest the changes in a design system which is the environment of a DEDP. The structure of the Suite of PSI Ontologies reflects this approach. It comprises six cross-linked Core ontologies: Time ontology; Environment, Event and Happening ontology; Actor ontology; Project ontology; Process and Process Pattern ontologies; and Design Artifact ontology. The "corolla" of this Core is formed by Extension ontologies collaboratively developed in PSI and PRODUKTIV+[2] projects. The most important Extensions are: Resource ontology with Tool package, Generic Negotiation ontology.

The ontology presented in this paper is the upper level part of PSI Suite of Ontologies. Its main purpose is putting the components of the Suite in line with the commonly accepted metaphysical and cognitive framework of the common sense represented by chosen reference ontologies. Additionally, we aim at providing semantic bridge to mainstream enterprise, business, and process modeling frameworks. Bridging PSI ontologies to these mainstream theories of process knowledge representation facilitates to easier commitment of engineering design domain professionals to the Suite. Upper level ontology also plays an integration and harmonization role in PSI Suite because it represents a rather domain-independent descriptive theory based on formal principles for harmonizing and integrating the underlying domain dependent modules with other relevant ontologies. In addition to being the semantic "glue" between the Suite and the outer world of knowledge representation presented ontology plays an important role in the methodology of knowledge engineering in PSI. It is the resource which is intensively used in the refinement and the evaluation of PSI Core Ontologies.

The rest of the paper is structured as follows. Section 2 outlines requirements and objectives which shaped out our upper level model. Section 3 puts PSI upper level ontology in the context of related work and presents our ontological choices. Section 4 outlines the taxonomy PSI upper level ontology and discusses the semantic contexts of its key concepts in detail. Section 5 sketches our ontology engineering methodology. Section 6 reports on the implementation and evaluation of the described ontology. Finally, concluding remarks are given and our plans for future work are outlined in Section 7.

2 Modeling Requirements

PSI project aims at developing models, methodologies, and software tools providing for rigorous engineering treatment of performance and performance management. PSI performance modeling and management approach focuses on performance as a pro-active action. A fine-grained dynamic model of a DEDP and a design system is

---

[2] PRODUKTIV+ is the R&D project funded by the German Bundesministerium für Bildung und Forschung (BMBF).

therefore developed. PSI approach considers that performance is embodied in its environment and is controlled by the associated performance management process.

A DEDP is a goal-directed process of transforming the representations of a design artifact in stateful nested environments. An environment comprises design artifact representations, resources, tools, and actors who perform actions to transform design artifacts using tools, consume resources. Actions are admissible in particular environment states and may be atomic or compound, state-transitive or iterative, dependent or independent on other actions. The components of an environment may generate internal events or may be influenced by external events. Events may have causal dependencies. A DEDP is a problem solving process which goals, partial goals, and environments may change dynamically. A decision taking procedure is associated with each state to allow environments adjust the process taking these changes into account. Decisions are taken by actors modeled by software agents.

PSI software tools are developed [1] for assisting project managers to make robust planning, monitoring, and management of their design projects aiming at reaching best possible performance. Grounded decisions in planning are based on the knowledge base of project logs accomplished in the past. These logs provide vast and finely grained records of the performance of accomplished projects and may be used for simulating the behavior of the design system in response to different influences. At project execution phase PSI software may be used for predicting the behavior of the design system in the future based on the record of the partially accomplished DEDP, the knowledge about its environment(s), and performance simulations.

Mentioned functionalities may only be implemented if a rich and expressive domain model is used. This model should be capable of facilitating agents reasoning about environments, events, and actions employed in decision taking procedures enacted at environmental states. These sorts of commonsense reasoning require ontological representations of time [2], environments, events and their subjective perceptions [3], processes, actions, actors, design artifacts, resources, tools [4, 5]. The models of these domain aspects form the Core and the Extensions of PSI Suite of Ontologies v.2.1 and v.2.2 [5].

3   Related Work and Modeling Choices

The main function of our upper level ontological model is putting the components of the Suite in line with the commonly accepted metaphysical and cognitive framework of the common sense. Common sense knowledge is captured by several foundational ontologies. Important examples are Suggested Upper Merged Ontology (SUMO) [6], Descriptive Ontology for Linguistic and Cognitive Engineering (DOLCE) [7], the upper level of OpenCYC [22], Basic Formal Ontology (BFO) [7]. Highly reputable linguistic resources like WordNet Linguistic Ontology (WordNet) [8] should also be considered. One more objective of introducing the upper level of the Suite is providing semantic bridges to mainstream enterprise, business, and process models like the Enterprise Ontology (EO) [9], Toronto Virtual Enterprise Ontology (TOVE) [10], Process Specification Language (PSL) [11].

In difference to the mentioned enterprise, business, and process modeling frameworks, which are, to a certain extent, domain independent (TOVE, PSL) or model manufacturing Domain (EO), PSI upper level ontology defines an abstract descriptive theory for the domain of engineering design processes and environments. As many foundational ontologies PSI upper level ontology has a clear cognitive orientation in the sense that it does not pretend being strictly and rigorously referential to the theories describing nature. Instead, it captures ontological categories and contexts based on human common sense reflecting socially dominant views on the Domain – characteristic at least to engineering design professionals. As such, the categories introduced in our ontology are not related to the intrinsic nature of the world but are rather thought of as "cognitive artifacts ultimately depending on human perception, cultural imprints and social conventions" [7]. Therefore, these categories assist in making already formed conceptualizations of PSI Suite of Ontologies explicit and referenced by the common sense. PSI upper level ontology also plays an integration and harmonization role of a foundational ontology [12] because it represents a rather domain-independent descriptive theory based on formal principles for harmonizing and integrating the underlying domain dependent modules with other relevant ontologies.

In contrast to foundational ontologies PSI upper level ontology is not foundational in the sense that it is not a profound and a complete theory in philosophical or, more precisely, cognitivistic sense. For example, it does not deal with many problems characteristic for foundational theories like: differences between abstract and concrete objects, particulars and universals; spatio-temporal co-localization of things; mereological axiomatization; etc. It also does not provide rich axiomatic sets for rigorously describing the semantics of the contained entities. Instead, other highly reputable foundational ontologies are used as reference sources for defining PSI upper level ontology components. The mappings of these components to those reference sources are explicitly specified. Choosing the most appropriate reference foundational ontologies among possible candidates is not an easy task because it requires ontological commitment to the chosen ontologies and their ontological choices. Typical ontological choices (also called meta-criteria) are: (i) Descriptivism vs. Revisionarism; (ii) Multiplicativism vs. Reductionism; (ii) Possibilism vs. Actualism; (iv) Endurantism vs. Perdurantism. A good comparative analysis of several well known foundational ontologies and their ontological choices has been undertaken in SmartWeb project [13]. Five most promising candidates among approximately a dozen available worldwide has been analyzed: BFO, DOLCE, Object-Centered High-level Reference Ontology (OCHRE) [7], OpenCYC, and SUMO. The results are given in Table 1. Typical ontological choices in line with modeling requirements of PSI project are discussed below. Based on this discussion our choice of reference foundational ontologies for the design of our upper level ontology is made.

Table 1. Foundational ontologies and their ontological choices [13]

Ontology Alternative	BFO	DOLCE	OCHRE	OpenCYC	SUMO
Descriptivism	-	+	-	+	+
Multiplicativism	-	+	unclear	unclear	+
Actualism	+	-	-	unclear	unclear
Perdurantism	+	+	-	unclear	+

Legend: + – the ontology supports the ontological choice; - – the ontology does not support the ontological choice; unclear – it is not clear if the ontology supports the ontological choice.

Descriptivism vs. Revisionarism. A descriptive ontology aims at describing the ontological assumptions based on the surface structure of natural language and human common sense. For example, a descriptive ontology distinguishes between physical and abstract objects based on the human common sense perception of these categories. It is common to consider that a physical object is a category of things which have tangible physical properties, can be sensed, are extended in space and time. On the contrary, an abstract object does not possess the abovementioned properties. A revisionary ontology is committed to capture the intrinsic nature of the world. As a consequence, such a commitment may impose that only entities extended in space and time exist. Though we refrain from modeling abstract things in PSI as much as possible[3], we still have to model immaterial things which are not made of matter, do not possess spatial properties, etc. Therefore, revisionarism would have been a wrong choice for PSI. PSI upper level ontology is a descriptive ontology and has to be based on a descriptive foundational ontology like DOLCE, OpenCYC, or SUMO.

Multiplicativism vs. Reductionism. A multiplicative ontology allows different entities to be co-localized in the same space-time. The difference of these entities means that they have different essential properties. For example, a silicon wafer of a chip (a material object) and a definite amount of silicon this wafer is made of (an amount of matter) are co-localized in space-time for the whole life of this particular chip. Reductionistic ontology postulates that each space-time location contains at most one object. Differences in essential properties are regarded as being linked to different points of view from which one can look at the same spatio-temporal entity. Reductionistic approach therefore extracts all essential properties different from spatio-temporal ones from entities and places them to the views on these entities. In PSI it is considered that an entity possesses all its essential properties and the views on an entity may reveal different subsets of these properties depending on the point of view. For example, an agent may be (i) a model of one physical person – a designer; (ii) a model of a group of designers working on one design project – a development team. PSI upper level ontology should therefore be a multiplicative ontology – like DOLCE or SUMO.

Possibilism vs. Actualism. An actualistic ontology postulates that everything that exists is actual. Things that are not actual and, therefore, do not exist may be withdrawn from consideration. Different forms of possibilism are based on different ways of the denial of this postulate. For example our beliefs, which are hypotheses based on incomplete, partial knowledge about the world, are very often roughly equally believed possible alternatives. Considering such alternatives is characteristic to human common sense and cognition. Committing to possibilism means being able to represent possibilia – possible alternative entities in a domain corresponding to different modalities in different possible worlds. Possibilism is particularly useful in reasoning about future courses of processes and about actions [14]. PSI upper level ontology has to be capable of modeling possibilia. For example, a design process depending on the future events in its environment may take one of the possible alternative courses. These alternative courses should all be considered and analyzed for choosing the best possible one to follow. Hence, we have to commit to possibilism of a foundational ontology like DOLCE or OCHRE.

---

[3] All concepts of PSI upper-level ontology are not abstract – Fig. 1.

Endurantism vs. Perdurantism. A fundamental ontological choice is the commitment to a way of modeling changes of things in time. Endurantism (also called 3D paradigm) postulates that all things do not change in time in the sense that all the proper parts of an entity (a whole) are present in this whole at any moment of the existence of this whole. Differently to that, perdurantism (also called 4D paradigm) assumes that entities may have different parts at different moments of their existence – meaning that entities have both spatial and temporal constituents. PSI upper level ontology needs to model both endurants and perdurants. Indeed, many of the concepts characteristic to engineering design always contain all their parts, but many other of them are composed of temporally different parts – like phases in a design process. Therefore, a reference foundational ontology for our ontology should be based on 4D paradigm, comprising 3D as a particular case. Such ontologies are BFO, DOLCE, and SUMO.

Hence, only DOLCE commits fully to all the ontological choices required by PSI. SUMO provides all the necessary features except possibilism. This is why we use the upper taxonomical level of DOLCE as our foundational framework. We also use SUMO extended by WordNet as a target for mapping the concepts of our upper level ontology and PSI Core Ontologies.

4 PSI Upper Level Ontology

The postulates, assumptions, objectives, and ontological choices of PSI modeling approach were presented in Sections 2 and 3. Here the semantic contexts of several key concepts of PSI upper level ontology[4] are discussed in detail: a Process, a State, an Object, an Agent, and a Rule. Fig. 1 pictures the taxonomy of PSI upper level ontology.

A Process (Fig. 2a) is a specialization of an Event [3] which is stateful and possesses pro-active character. A Process has its Environment – the part of the world which may influence the course of the Process or may be changed in the course of the Process. A Process is pro-actively directed by the Agent who manages it. Pro-activeness of the Agent is understood in the sense that the Agent pursues a particular Goal in the managed Process. This Goal is the State of the Environment which the Agent desires to make reached. It should also be mentioned that the change in the Environment is not produced by the Process, but by the entities who act in this process – those Agents who execute AtomicActions wrapped by the Process. In general, it is considered that changes may only be applied by Agents through execution of AtomicActions. For example, it is wrong to say that a multimedia controller layout has been designed by the process of logical design. In fact the appearance of the layout for the multimedia controller in a certain state of the Environment (the measurable change in the Environment [3]) has been achieved by the team of Agents who executed a particular sequence of AtomicActions. By that the Agents applied the sequence of particular changes to the Environment and guided the environment through the sequence of States towards the Goal. Processes in an engineering Environment

---

[4] Complete specification could be found at http://ermolayev.com/psi-public/PSI-META-v-2-2-Spec.pdf

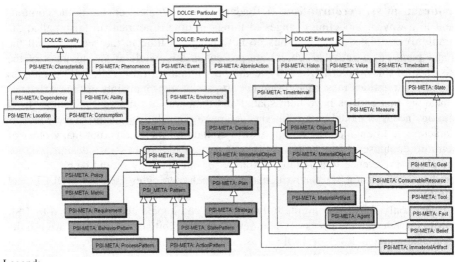

Legend:
(i) Concepts are colored reflecting classification by OntoClean property types (Section 6):
☐ - category, ☐ - type, ▨ - quasi-type, ☐ - material role, ▨ - mixin.
Categories, types, and quasi-types form the backbone taxonomy.
(ii) Semantic contexts of the concepts in rounded rectangles (⬭) are discussed in detail.

Fig. 1. The taxonomy of PSI upper-level ontology

can not connect any arbitrary State to any other arbitrary State because it is senseless with respect to the technology or the methodology. Some sequences of States may therefore be withdrawn from the engineering design routine and some other sequences of States may be suggested or prescribed by an industrial standard or a company policy. These prescriptions in terms of PSI upper level ontology are ProcessPatterns.

Any Process, as a pro-active stateful manifestation of a change in the Environment, is guided by its managing Agent to reach the State (Fig. 2b) of affairs in which the constituents of the Environment possess the properties partially or fully matching the Goal of that Agent. It is considered that a Process has reached its target State if such a state of affairs is reached. Otherwise the Process fails to reach its target State. A Goal, if complex, can be decomposed to simpler partial Goals as often done in problem solving. Such partial Goals are in fact the states of affairs that should be reached before the overall compound Goal can be attacked. States in upper level ontology are the configurations of the constituents of an Environment. It is considered that a State is reached when the constituents of the Environment have properties with Values in the ranges satisfactory matching the corresponding Goal or partial-Goal[5] of an Agent. In engineering design mentioned Goals are technologically controlled. For example, a technology of digital front-end design in microelectronics and integrated circuits prescribes that an overall Goal of a digital back-end design is the development of a

---

[5] In our agent-based software implementation such decomposition is the substantial part of work breakdown structure generation [1]. Goal decomposition is based on the ontological representation of design task and activity patterns provided by the Process Pattern Ontology of the Core of the PSI Suite.

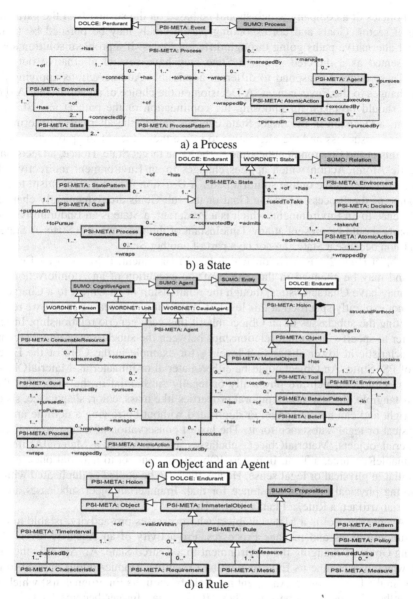

Fig. 2. Semantic contexts of the key concepts

design artifact in GDSII layout representation. At the same time the technology suggests that netlist, floorplan, placement and routing representations should be developed before the overall Goal can be reached. In these settings the States can be seen as technological milestones on the path through the problem solution space leading to the overall Goal. The requirements to the ranges of the property values of the constituents of the Environment are denoted by StatePatterns. StatePatterns are controlled by the Policies of a company which should be based on the standards of the particular industrial sector. Goals and corresponding partial Goals may be pursued by taking different alternative paths going through different States. If a problem solution space is represented as a directed graph, a State may have several alternative outgoing edges. These edges correspond to different admissible AtomicActions applying different changes to the Environment. A Decision on the choice of an admissible AtomicAction should be taken for choosing the continuation of the path at any State. In particular, a Decision in the target State chooses among the alternative to terminate the process in success and the alternative to refine the values of the properties of the constituents of the Environment heading to the same target State. Hence, a Decision is a specific AtomicAction which applies changes to an Environment indirectly – by choosing the alternative on the solution path. A Decision is also a mechanism to alter the course of the Process when the Goal or the sub-Goals are dynamically changed. In difference to an Environment, which is a Perdurant, a State is an Endurant because all its parts should be present at any TimeInstant of the presence of a State. A State is not a Holon because a State can not be a part of another State.

An Object (Fig. 2c) is a Holon which has Environment, belongs to an Environment, and may be changed in the course of the execution of an AtomicAction. An Object may have Characteristics, though the relationship of an Object to a Characteristic is not explicitly specified at this level of abstraction. The reason is that we refrain from letting the subclasses of an Object inherit this very generic relationship. Instead we prefer to specify individual relationships between the subclasses of an Object and a Characteristic at lower abstraction levels – for example in the Core or the Extensions of PSI Suite. An Object could be either material or immaterial. MaterialObjects are those Objects which are physically or legally substantial in the sense that they possess tangible physical non-temporal properties like mass, color, shape, size, speed, usage right and can not be copied or duplicated without borrowing a definite amount of physical or legal[6] substance for it. The law of conservation of matter is applicable to material objects. MaterialObject subclasses are an Agent, a MaterialArtifact, a ConsumableResource, a Tool. ImmaterialObjects in contract to material ones are not substantial in physical or legal sense. Hence, they can be copied or duplicated without consuming physical or legal substance for that. ImmaterialObject subclasses are an ImmaterialArtifact, a Rule, a Plan, a Fact, a Belief.

An Agent (Fig. 2c) is a MaterialObject who possesses pro-activity, is able to execute AtomicActions and manage Processes. Pro-activity of an Agent is revealed in pursuing Goals of changing the Environment to a desired State. An Agent is the only entity which can change its Environment by executing AtomicActions applied to the Objects in the Environment. An Agent has Beliefs about its Environment(s) which are the hypotheses believed to be true. These Beliefs may further become Facts if confirmed by the happenings [3] perceived by the Agents. Beliefs together with desires and intentions are important basic elements forming the behavior of an Agent. This behavior is regulated by BehaviorPatterns specified as Rules. An Agent is an abstract entity which is a generic model for an individual person (a manager, a designer), a

---

[6] By an odd term of "legal substance" we mean a legal permission to have an extra copy of an Object which is not a physical object in the sense of SUMO or DOLCE. A good example of such an Object is a software program with a license (legal substance).

group of persons or artificial agents acting on behalf of physical persons (a team or an organizational unit), or an external pro-active entity influencing the Environment of an observed Process in a definite way. These aspects of an Agent are specialized and refined at the lower abstraction levels by PSI Core ontologies.

A Rule (Fig. 2d) is an ImmaterialObject which is a principle, a condition, a procedure, a generic pattern, or a norm regulating possible process, action, behavior, or state of affairs. As far as a Rule subsumes to a Holon it inherits structural parthood relationship of a Holon. Hence, a Rule may be an atomic proposition or a more complex composition of other Rules. As far as a Rule is an Endurant no temporal parthood relationships are allowed for its proper parts – the composition of a rule can not be changed in time. A Rule itself still has a temporal property of validity – it is valid within a particular TimeInterval or several particular TimeIntervals. If a Rule is a principle or condition that customarily governs behavior then it subsumes to WordNet: Rule and further on to SUMO: Proposition. If a Rule is a generalization that describes recurring facts or events then it subsumes to WordNet: Law and further on to SUMO: Proposition. If a Rule is something regarded as a norm constraining possible action or behavior then it subsumes to WordNet: Regulation and further on to SUMO: Proposition.

5   Ontology Engineering Methodology

The methodology used in the design of PSI upper level ontology may be identified as "shaker modeling". It is the combination of bottom-up and top-down modeling techniques exercised in subsequent design iterations. The source for the top-down activity is PSI Theoretical Framework. The source for the bottom-up phase is domain knowledge acquired from subject experts and formalized in the Core of PSI Suite of Ontologies. Both kinds of sources are refined in iterations before performing the phases of upper level ontology design. The sources are also aligned to the foundational reference ontology and mapped to the common sense reference ontology using the upper level ontology as a semantic "glue" in the last two phases of every design iteration.

The most recent revision of the Theoretical Framework is used in the first phase – skeleton design of the upper level ontology. The outcome is represented as a UML class diagram. Skeleton design phase is a top-down activity because a more abstract theoretical framework is used as a source for the development of a more elaborated descriptive theory. In the refinement phase the harmonization of the skeleton of the upper level ontology with the previous stable revision of the Core Ontologies of PSI Suite is performed. The objectives of this harmonization activity are: (i) ensuring that the upper level model does not contain components which contradict to the core-level model in their semantics and (ii) ensuring that all core-level concepts are properly mapped to the upper level concepts. Previous stable revision of PSI Core Ontolgies is used to ensure upward compatibility of the revisions of the PSI Suite comprising the upper level ontology. The outcome of this phase is presented in the form of three separate UML class diagrams: (i) the taxonomical structure of the upper level ontology; (ii) the diagram of the "horizontal" relationships among the concepts of the upper level ontology; (iii) the mappings of the concepts of the Core Ontologies to the concepts of the upper level ontology. Refinement phase is a bottom-up activity because an upper level model is harmonized with the lower-level one – the core part of the domain theory. At the beginning of the alignment phase upper level ontology is checked for the conformance to the ontological choices of the reference foundational ontology and its taxonomical structure is formally evaluated. As DOLCE is chosen as a reference foundational ontology for PSI, the upper level model is checked for being descriptive, possibilistic, multiplicative, and perdurantistic. OntoClean [15] is used as a methodology for formal evaluation of the taxonomy. As result, the taxonomy is refined and formally evaluated. Further on, upper level ontology concepts are mapped to the reference ontology which has been chosen as a source of common sense semantics – SUMO+WordNet in our case. These mappings allow checking if our upper level theory is sound enough to adequately conform to human beliefs about what the world is. If the result of such verification is positive (all the mappings are easily built and their semantics is easily understood), then we may expect that PSI upper level ontology will be accepted by humans without major difficulties. These common sense mappings may also be used as "referees" at the subsequent bridging phase. Bridging phase is actually not the phase of ontology design. It is the activity in which upper level ontology is used as a semantic bridge to help evaluating the Core of PSI Suite against the other ontologies describing similar domain theories.

The iterations of PSI upper level ontology development are organized as shown in Fig. 3. The whole process is performed in two stages: (i) initial design and (ii) iterative refinement similarly to what is suggested by DILIGENT [16] methodology of collaborative ontology engineering. It may be stated that DILIGENT in our approach is used as the higher-level methodological framework organizing iterations in a needed way. DILIGENT is used because the development of our Suite of Ontologies is done in a distributed dynamic environment (several local groups of subject experts from different organizations in frame of PSI and PRODUKTIV+ projects take part).

The stage of the initial design is the preparatory activity at the very beginning of ontology design process. Its objective is to develop the initial revisions of the Theoretical Framework and the Core set of the domain ontologies. An initial revision of the upper level ontology is developed at the end of the initial design stage because it requires both as sources. Two revisions of the Theoretical Framework have been developed before starting the design of the upper level ontology. The second revision is the result of the refinement based on the user evaluation feedback on the first revision of the Core ontologies. Hence, even the first revision of the upper level ontology is designed with the account for the user evaluation of the domain theory. An iteration of the refinement stage also uses the latest revision of the Theoretical Framework developed in this iteration and the revision of the Core ontologies built in the previous iteration. Iteration starts with the development of the Core set of ontologies based on the upper level ontology revision of the previous iteration and ends by the development of the new revision of the upper level ontology.

Several kinds of ontology evaluation activities are undertaken in each design iteration (Fig. 3). The first one is user evaluation. The objective of the user evaluation is to find out if the Core set of ontologies fits the requirements of user teams and the requirements of the software development based on this set of ontologies. An external evaluation by independent experts may also be done at this stage to ensure that evaluation results are unbiased and of good quality. It has been found out [17] that for PSI Core ontologies probably the best fitting methodology is Pinto and Martens [18].

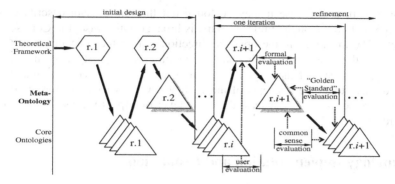

Fig. 3. Iterations of PSI upper level ontology design

The feedback of this iteration is taken into account in the refinement of the Theoretical Framework. The second kind of evaluation activity – formal evaluation, is undertaken at the Alignment phase after the newly developed revision of the upper level ontology has reached release candidate state. The objective of formal evaluation is to check the conformance of the taxonomy structure of the upper level ontology to metaproperties of rigidity, identity, and dependence [15]. The methodology for this kind of evaluation is OntoClean [15]. The results of the formal evaluation are used for the refinement of the release candidate of the upper level ontology. The third kind of evaluation activity is the evaluation of the Core set of ontologies versus the upper level ontology. Similarly to the formal evaluation it is performed at the Alignment phase. The conformance of the Core set to the common sense is now checked. The mappings of the Core ontologies to the reference common sense ontology (SUMO) are elaborated using the upper level ontology as the "glue", like for example in [19]. The result allows estimating how easily domain experts may (potentially) commit to the Suite of Ontologies. If the Core set maps well to the common sense reference ontology one may expect that the commitment of domain experts to it may be reached considerably easily. If the mapping is bad then the ontology is either a novel extension of the common sense conceptualization or, more probably, is badly designed. The feedback of this kind of evaluation is used in refining the Core ontologies and, later on, in refining the next revision of the upper level ontology. Finally, the fourth kind of evaluation is the comparison of the Core set of ontologies with the so called "Golden Standard" [20]. By "Golden Standard" we mean a highly reputable ontology describing the theory of the same or a similar domain which has already gained broad commitment by domain experts. The evidence of such a commitment may be that a "Golden Standard" ontology is the basics for a standard, a de-facto standard, or a standardization proposal. This kind of evaluation is performed at the Bridging phase. Similarly to the common sense evaluation the mappings of the Core set of ontologies to a "Golden Standard" are built. However, the objective of the evaluation is different. Completeness and expressiveness of the Core Ontologies are checked at this time. If all the concepts of a "Golden Standard" ontology are mapped by the concepts of the Core set then it may be estimated that the Core set covers the domain equally to or better than a "Golden Standard". Otherwise, the core set is less complete than the "Golden Standard". In the latter case the reasons of potential incompleteness should be analyzed. In a safe case it may be found out that the domain described by the "Golden Standard", though similar to ours, is broader. Otherwise, the Core set is incomplete. The mappings in the opposite direction – from the concepts of a "Golden Standard" to the concepts of evaluated Core ontologies, may help assessing the level of the expressiveness of the target. For example, if all the concepts of the "Golden Standard" map to single concepts of the evaluated Core set then it may be the case that the Core set possesses at least the same level of expressiveness at the "Golden Standard".

6 Ontology Implementation and Evaluation

PSI upper level ontology v.2.2 has been implemented in OWL-DL[7]. PSI Theoretical Framework v.2.0 [14] and Core ontologies of PSI Suite of Ontologies v.2.1 have been used as the knowledge sources. PSI Suite of Ontologies v.2.2 has been developed based on the elaborated upper level ontology v.2.2. Two different kinds of evaluation have been accomplished for the upper level ontology so far: formal evaluation and commonsense evaluation. Besides that, user evaluation of the set of the Core ontologies v.2.1 has been done before the beginning of the development of the upper level ontology v.2.2, as described in Section 5. "Golden Standard" evaluation is still in progress. User evaluation of the Core ontologies v.2.1 has been performed by the group of PSI software developers who used a goal-based evaluation routine to assess the appropriateness, the completeness, and the upward compatibility of the Suite of Ontologies. Appropriateness has been evaluated by checking if the Suite fulfils the requirements imposed by developed software. Completeness and upward compatibility with the previous revision has been checked by transferring the instances of the PSI knowledge base v.2.0 to v.2.1. User evaluation revealed minor problems which have been immediately resolved allowing us to fix v.2.1. Several issues have been listed as the ones for the future development. These issues have been taken into account in the revision of the Theoretical Framework v.2.0.

Formal evaluation of the taxonomy of PSI upper level ontology has been performed using OntoClean methodology [15]. The goal of taxonomy analysis is to verify if the structure of the taxonomy is formally correct. Other outcomes of this formal analysis are: (i) classifying taxonomy nodes according to OntoClean ontology of property types [21]; (ii) extracting the part of the analyzed taxonomy which is its backbone taxonomy [21]. In the course of this evaluation OntoClean meta-properties have been assigned to the concepts of the upper level ontology. After that OntoClean constraints have been applied to analyze if there are constraint violations in the taxonomy[8]. Applying OntoClean constraints to PSI upper level ontology subsumptions revealed no violations. Hence, the structure of the taxonomy is formally correct. Following [21], the concepts of PSI upper level ontology were classified according to

---

[7] Web Ontology Language, http://www.w3.org/TR/owl-guide/. OWL-DL implementation of PSI upper-level ontology is available at http://ermolayev.com/psi-public/psi-meta-v-2-2-draft.owl and its specification is at http://ermolayev.com/psi-public/PSI-META-v-2-2-Spec.pdf

[8] Detailed description of the results of this formal evaluation is given in PSI upper ontology specification.

OntoClean ontology of property types. As it has been found out, all its own concepts are Sortals. Non-sortal concepts are imported from DOLCE and are the categories forming the most upper part of the taxonomy. Among the sortals 16 are types and 17 are quasi-types. Categories, types and quasi-types form the backbone taxonomy of PSI upper level ontology. Among the remaining 6 concepts 5 are material roles and only 1 is a mixin. PSI upper level ontology does not contain phased sortals, formal roles and attributions. The backbone taxonomy and the parts of the ontology extending the backbone taxonomy are pictured in Fig. 1 using different shades of gray.

The objective of commonsense evaluation was to find out if the upper level ontology facilitates in mapping the Core ontologies to the reference foundational ontology. The mappings of the concepts of six PSI Core ontologies to WordNet+SUMO through PSI upper level ontology have been done using subsumptions. It has been found out that using upper level ontology as semantic "glue" made these mappings more precise and facilitated to defining the semantics of the concepts of the Core more explicitly. For example, looking up for a Project (the concept of PSI Project ontology) in WordNet+SUMO[9] reveals that a project is both: (i) "any piece of work that is undertaken or attempted" which subsumes to SUMO: IntentionalProcess and further to SUMO: Process; and (ii) "a planned undertaking" which subsumes to SUMO: Plan. The semantics of PROJECT: Project as specified in [5] reveals that a Project subsumes to PSI-META: Plan and consequently to SUMO: Plan. The mapping to SUMO: Process is therefore discarded as irrelevant. From the other hand, the analysis of the "hanging" concepts in the upper level ontology helps revealing the contexts in the Core which are still under-developed. For example, PSI-META: Goal does not subsume the concepts of the Core v.2.2. Therefore we may suspect that the aspects of goal-directed behavior in the Actor and Process Core ontologies v.2.2 still require refinement.

7 Concluding Remarks and Outlook

Presented ontology is the upper level descriptive theory for the Core set of PSI Suite of Ontologies. PSI Suite is an interlinked modular library of ontologies describing the domain of engineering design performance in microelectronics. PSI upper level ontology is more domain-independent. It formalizes an abstract theory of stateful creative dynamic processes, pro-active agents, and objects situated in nested dynamic environments based on the formal representation of time, events, and happenings. This upper level theory may be used as a higher-level framework for domain ontologies in different application domains having common features. PSI upper level ontology is designed as a semantic bridge formalizing the mappings of PSI Domain ontologies to abstract ontological foundations and common sense. It is also used as semantic "glue" for bridging PSI domain theory with other theories widely accepted in the domains where processes, states, and participating objects are the major entities. These mappings and semantic bridges are supposed to ease the commitment of potential users to PSI Suite. PSI upper level ontology is also used as a "proxy" for different kinds of evaluation of

---

[9] KSMSA Ontology Browser has been used: http://virtual.cvut.cz/ksmsaWeb/browser/title

PSI ontologies in frame of our "shaker modeling" methodology for ontology refinement. In its current revision presented ontology is still lightweight in the sense that it does not provide rich axiomatic definitions of domain semantics. The main reason is that in-depth domain axiomatization is done in the core of PSI Suite. However, some enrichment of the upper level theory with formal axioms for better describing bridges to common sense theories is planned for future work. One more direction of our future development is extending the sphere of influence of PSI upper level ontology to cover the Extensions of our Suite of Ontologies. We are also plan applying our upper level ontological framework in the domains adjacent to PSI and PRODUKTIV+. For example, it will be used in ACTIVE project[10] as one of the models for representing knowledge processes and their environments.

Bibliography

1. Sohnius, R., Jentzsch, E., Matzke, W.-E.: Holonic Simulation of a Design System for Performance Analysis. In: Mařík, V., Vyatkin, V., Colombo, A.W. (eds.) HoloMAS 2007. LNCS (LNAI), vol. 4659, pp. 447–454. Springer, Heidelberg (2007)
2. Ermolayev, V., Keberle, N., Matzke, W.-E., Sohnius, R.: Fuzzy Time Intervals for Simulating Actions. In: Kaschek, R., Kop, C., Steinberger, C., Fliedl, G. (eds.) UNISCON 2008. LNBIP, vol. 5, pp. 429–444. Springer, Heidelberg (2008)
3. Ermolayev, V., Keberle, N., Matzke, W.-E.: An Ontology of Environments, Events, and Happenings. In: Elci, A., Kone, M.T., Orgun, M.A. (eds.) Proc 3d Int. Workshop on Engineering Semantic Agent Systems. IEEE Computer Society CPS, Los Alamitos (2008)
4. Ermolayev, V., Jentzsch, E., Karsayev, O., Keberle, N., Matzke, W.-E., Samoylov, V., Sohnius, R.: An Agent-Oriented Model of a Dynamic Engineering Design Process. In: Kolp, M., Bresciani, P., Henderson-Sellers, B., Winikoff, M. (eds.) AOIS 2005. LNCS (LNAI), vol. 3529, pp. 168–183. Springer, Heidelberg (2006)
5. Ermolayev, V., Jentzsch, E., Keberle, N., Sohnius, R.: Performance Simulation Initiative. The Suite of Ontologies v.2.2. Reference Specification. Technical report PSI-ONTO-TR-2007-5, VCAD EMEA Cadence Design Systems, GmbH (2007)
6. Niles, I., Pease, A.: Towards a Standard Upper Ontology. In: Guarino, N., Smith, B., Welty, C. (eds.) Int. Conf. on Formal Ontologies in Inf. Systems, pp. 2–9. ACM Press, New York (2001)
7. Masolo, C., Borgo, S., Gangemi, A., Guarino, N., Oltramari, A.: WonderWeb Deliverable D18 Ontology Library (final), ICT Project 2001-33052 WonderWeb: Ontology Infrastructure for the Semantic Web (2003)
8. Fellbaum, C. (ed.): WordNet: An Electronic Lexical Database. MIT Press, Cambridge (1998)
9. Uschold, M., King, M., Moralee, S., Zorgios, Y.: The Enterprise Ontology. The Knowledge Engineering Review 13(1), 31–89 (1998)
10. Grüninger, M., Atefy, K., Fox, M.S.: Ontologies to Support Process Integration in Enterprise Engineering. Computational & Mathematical Organization Theory 6(4), 381–394 (2000)
11. Bock, C., Grüninger, M.: PSL: A Semantic Domain for Flow Models. Software Systems Modeling 4(2), 209–231 (2005)

---

[10] ACTIVE: Knowledge Powered Enterprise (http://www.active-project.eu/) is an Integrated Project funded by Framework Program 7 of European Union.

12. Mika, P., Oberle, D., Gangemi, A., Sabou, M.: Foundations for Service Ontologies: Aligning OWL-S to DOLCE. In: 13th Int. Conf. on WWW, pp. 563–572. ACM Press, New York (2004)
13. Oberle, D., et al.: DOLCE ergo SUMO: On foundational and domain models in the SmartWeb Integrated Ontology (SWIntO). J. Web Semantics 5(3), 156–174 (2007)
14. Ermolayev, V., Jentzsch, E., Matzke, W.-E., Pěchouček, M., Sohnius, R.: Performance Simulation Initiative. Theoretical Framework v.2.0. Technical report PSI-TF-TR-2007-1, VCAD EMEA Cadence Design Systems, GmbH (2007)
15. Guarino, N., Welty, C.: Supporting Ontological Analysis of Taxonomic Relationships. Data and Knowledge Engineering 39(1), 51–74 (2001)
16. Vrandečić, D., Pinto, S., Tempich, C., Sure, Y.: The DILIGENT Knowledge Processes. J. of Knowledge Management 9(5), 85–96 (2005)
17. Simperl, E.: Evaluation of the PSI Ontology Library. Technical report, DERI Innsbruck, Austria (2007)
18. Pinto, H.S., Martins, J.P.: A Methodology for Ontology Integration. In: Gil, Y., Musen, M., Shavlik, J. (eds.) 1st Int. Conf. on Knowledge Capture, pp. 131–138. ACM Press, New York (2001)
19. Keberle, N., Ermolayev, V., Matzke, W.-E.: Evaluating PSI Ontologies by Mapping to the Common Sense. In: Mayr, H.C., Karagiannis, D. (eds.) 6th Int. Conf. Information Systems Technology and its Applications, Gesellschaft für Informatik, Bonn. GI LNI, vol. 107, pp. 91–104 (2007)
20. Brank, J., Grobelnik, M., Mladenić, D.: A Survey of Ontology Evaluation Techniques. In: Grobelnik, M., Mladenić, D. (eds.) SiKDD 2005, pp. 166–169 (2005)
21. Guarino, N., Welty, C.A.: A Formal Ontology of Properties. In: Dieng, R., Corby, O. (eds.) EKAW 2000. LNCS (LNAI), vol. 1937, pp. 97–112. Springer, Heidelberg (2000)
22. Matuszek, C., Cabral, J., Witbrock, M., DeOliveira, J.: An Introduction to the Syntax and Content of Cyc. In: Proc. 2006 AAAI Spring Symp. on Formalizing and Compiling Background Knowledge and Its Applications to Knowledge Representation and Question Answering, Stanford, CA (2006)

A Multi-level Methodology for Developing UML Sequence Diagrams

Il-Yeol Song, Ritu Khare, Yuan An, and Margaret Hilsbos

The iSchool at Drexel, Drexel University,
3141, Chestnut Street, Philadelphia, PA 19104, USA
songiy@drexel.edu, rk84@drexel.edu, yan@ischool.drexel.edu,
mhilsbos@drexel.edu

Abstract. Although the importance of UML Sequence Diagrams is well recognized by the object-oriented community, they remain a very difficult UML artifact to develop. In this paper we present a multi-level methodology to develop UML Sequence Diagrams. Our methodology is significant in three aspects. First, it provides a multilevel procedure to facilitate ease of the development process. Second, it makes use of certain patterns to ensure the validity of SQDs. Third, it uses consistency checks with corresponding use-case and class diagrams. Throughout the steps of the method we present rules and patterns demonstrating correct and incorrect diagramming of common situations through examples. The purpose of this study is to serve as a reference guide for novice sequence diagram modelers. This methodology is particularly useful for novice practitioners who face challenges in learning the process of SQD development.

1 Introduction

Sequence Diagrams (SQDs) are one of the important dynamic modeling techniques in the UML. An SQD visualizes interactions among objects involved in a use case scenario. Although several methods have been proposed to develop an SQD, the development of SQDs remains a very difficult part of the object oriented development process. The development process is very intricate. As new objects and messages are identified, the diagram gets more packed and complicated. Also, at every step, multiple factors, such as which object to choose, which message to assign to what object, and what patterns to use for message passing, need to be taken care of simultaneously. As a result, the modeler very often ends up making mistakes in the diagram, and making an SQD which is inconsistent with other UML artifacts. Hence, we are motivated to develop an easy-to-use and practical method for SQD development.

In our earlier work, we presented a ten-step method (Song, 2001) for developing SQDs based on use case descriptions and a class diagram. In this paper, we extend our earlier work as follows: First, we re-organize the steps into three levels and each level is further divided into several stages so that we can focus on one issue at a time. Second, we add guidelines and patterns using correct and incorrect examples. Third, we provide consistency checks between an SQD and use case and class diagrams. This method brings forth the recommended visual patterns and warns against mistakes committed by SQD developers. The purpose of this study is to serve as a reference

Q. Li et al. (Eds.): ER 2008, LNCS 5231, pp. 114–127, 2008.

guide for novice SQD modelers. In this paper, we use UML 2.0 notation to present SQDs. For the notations of SQDs in UML 2, we refer Ambler (2008b) or Larman (2004).

The rest of the paper is organized as follows. Section 2 presents the research methods used and the related literature review. Section 3 describes the process of multi-level methodology to develop SQDs. Section 4 concludes our paper.

2   Research Setting and Related Literature Review

In this paper, we have come up with both correct and incorrect patterns of SQDs, as well as guidelines. The guidelines were tested and examples were collected for the past five years of teaching SQDs in a graduate class. Incorrect patterns have been found on the basis of our observation of the mistakes students make in SQD assignments to develop SQDs. Our subjects include students from different backgrounds including computer science, information science, psychology, biosciences, biomedical, and business. Students found our guidelines usable and effective.

There is a decent amount of research related to specification of semantics of the SQD. Xia and Kane (2003) present an attribute grammar based approach on defining the semantics of UML SQD to make it easily convertible to code. While both this paper and the work by Aredo (2000) prepare a framework for defining the semantics of an SQD to create a shared understanding across a design team, the problem of designing an SQD still remains unresolved especially for novices.

Baker et al. (2005) address the problem of automatically detecting and resolving the semantic errors that occur in SQD scenarios. The method proposed in this paper is claimed to be successful in detecting semantic inconsistencies in industrial case studies. Our method, however, takes a preventive action to deal with the semantic inconsistencies by basing itself on the commonly occurring valid patterns in SQD and avoiding the frequently committed mistakes by novices.

Li (2000) presents a parser that semi-automatically translates use case steps into message records that can be used to construct a sequence diagram. The work is based on syntactic structure of standardized sentences of use-case description. Although this work provides useful rules for novices, e.g. converting a use case to "message sends", it does not avoid common mistakes made by novices.

Other recent works on SQDs include use of SQDs for code generation, generation of SQDs through reverse engineering of code, and finding reusable SQDs from existing artifacts. Rountev and Connell (2005), and Merdes and Dorsch (2006) present reverse engineering techniques to extract an SQD from a program. Another interesting work 'REUSER' by Robinson and Woo (2004) automatically retrieves reusable SQDs from UML artifacts.

Our review shows that the research effort for developing an easy-to-use method for developing SQDs is still rare and far from satisfactory. Hence, the task of creating this artifact remains challenging to novices, and they continue to commit errors. We propose a multi-level methodology in order to develop the artifact in an incremental manner. We refer to the work by Bist, MacKinnon, and Murphy (2004) for guidelines in drawing SQDs.

3 A Multi Level SQD Development

An Overview

In this section we describe our proposed methodology to develop an SQD. The most significant portion of this work is that it offers a multi-level way to develop SQDs. Instead of considering multiple design issues at each step of SQD development, we propose focusing on one major issue at each level of the process to make best possible use of knowledge at every level. We begin designing in terms of the objects first which form the building blocks of an SQD. After the objects are well arranged, responsibilities are assigned to them in the next level. In the last level, the visual pattern of the SQD obtained from previous level is analyzed to make further modifications and produce the final version of the SQD. Furthermore, each level is divided into stages to focus on just one sub-issue at each stage, and to further simplify the overall development process. A multi-level development process also offers the following in a systematic manner:

- Maintenance of consistency with other UML artifacts (use-case and class diagrams).
- Correctness of the SQD by making use of certain rules and visual patterns.
- Warnings to stay away from frequently committed mistakes in drawing SQDs.

In this paper, we deal with the UML use-case descriptions that represent one main success scenario and zero or more included use cases. It is important to maintain consistency between the SQDs and other diagrams of the system model. The SQD depends on classes identified in the domain model. Therefore, before beginning to construct an SQD, the use cases should have been identified and use case descriptions generated for the use cases assigned to the current development iteration, and an analysis class diagram (domain model) constructed.

Fig. 1 shows the three-level development process. Table 1 summarizes the whole methodology. The three abstract levels are: the object framework level, the responsibility assignment level, and the visual pattern level. Each level comprises multiple stages.

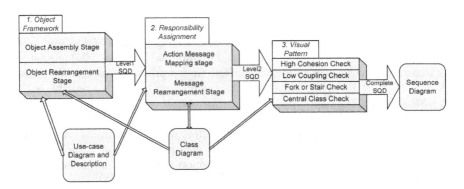

Fig. 1. A Component Diagram of Multi-level SQD Development

Table 1. The Steps of Multi-level SQD Development

(BO: Boundary object; CO: Control Object; EO: Entity Object)

---

1. Object Framework Level: Identify the building participants which constitute the basic framework of an SQD.

1.1 *Object Assembly Stage*: Identify the actor, primary BO, primary CO, secondary CO(s), secondary BO(s) for the SQD.

1.2 *Object Rearrangement Stage*: Rearrange the classes (and also the actor) in the following order: Actor, Primary BO, Primary CO, EOs (list in the order of access), and Secondary COs and Secondary BOs in the order of access.

2. Responsibility Assignment Level: Assign correct responsibilities to each object.

2.1 *Action-Message Mapping Stage*: Map every *automated* action in the use-case description to a message in the SQD. Each message would fall under one of the following categories: Instance creation and destruction, Association forming, Attribute modification, Attribute access, Input/Output/Interface, and Integrity-constraint checking.

2.2 *Message Re-arrangement Stage*: Perform arrangement checks such as: making sure that each message is traceable to the primary actor through activated objects, giving meaningful names to each message, checking consistency of SQD with class diagram, removing any unnecessary return messages, and checking for continuity of focus of control.

3. Visual Pattern Level: Apply final checks based on the visual patterns illustrated by the SQD.

3.1 *High Cohesion Check*: Make sure that the responsibilities assigned to a class are related, and there exists a high cohesion within a class.

3.2 *Low Coupling Check*: Re-arrange messages from one class to another class to reduce coupling.

3.3 *Fork or Stair Check*: Choose between the "fork" and the "stair" pattern depending on the relationship between classes, and taking into account the pros and cons of both patterns.

3.4 *Central Class Check*: It should be kept in mind that the class, which looks central in the class diagram, is likely to send most messages to other classes in the SQD.

3.1 The Object Framework Level

In this level, we identify the building blocks that constitute the framework of an SQD.

3.1.1 Object Assembly Stage: Following Are the Steps to Be Followed in This Stage

1. Select the initiating actor and initiating event from the use case description.
2. Identify the primary display screen needed for implementing the use case. Call it the p*rimary boundary object.*
3. Create a *primary control object* to handle communication between the primary boundary object and domain objects. It is not always necessary to have a *control object (CO)* between the *boundary object (BO)* and the *entity object (EO)*. A *BO* can directly pass message to an *EO*, if the message is simple and requires no manipulation.
4. If the use case involves any included or extended use case, create one *secondary CO* for each of them. UML 2.0 introduces specific notation for connecting sequence diagrams. The following method has previously been suggested, and may be simpler to apply, at least until modeling tools "catch up" to the UML 2 notation.

As shown in Fig. 2, use a separate CO for the supporting use case; show the supporting CO on the base use case SQD, with messages to and from indicating the flow of control (Song, 2001).

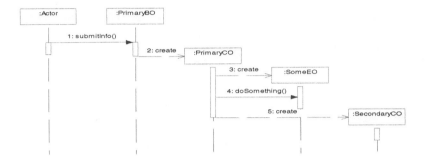

Fig. 2. The use of a Control Object for an Inclusion Use Case

5. Identify the number of major screens necessary to implement the use case. The following cases represent the situations that require creation of a new secondary BO:

   • A new window needs to be opened for user's input and the contents of the original window need to be kept visible
   • A new window only handles a sub-flow and the original window may proceed with the sequence regardless of the operations in the secondary window.

   Also, create a secondary CO for each of them.

6. From the class diagram, list all domain classes participating in the use case by reviewing the use case description. If any class identified from the use case description does not exist in the class diagram, add it to the class diagram. These classes become the EOs.

3.1.2 Object Rearrangement Stage

Use the classes just identified as participant names in the SQD. In a logical sequence of actions, tasks begin with an actor interacting with an interface (BO). The BO then passes control to a CO that has resources to carry the required actions, which then passes control to relevant EOs, and so on. Hence, list the actor and the classes in the following order: Actor, Primary BO, Primary CO, EOs (list in the order of access), Secondary BOs, and Secondary COs in the order of access.

3.2 Responsibility Assignment Level

Responsibility assignment refers to the determination of which class should implement a message, and which class should send the message. It is important to assign the correct set of responsibilities to each object because they become operations of corresponding objects in the design stage UML artifacts such as design-class diagrams. A message in an SQD is assigned to the class at the target of the message. For example, the message 4 *doSomething()* will be implemented as an operation in class

:SomeEO in Fig. 2. There are several guidelines that can be followed when assigning responsibility to classes. In this paper we follow the GRASP (General Responsibility Assignment Software Patterns) guidelines described by Larman (2004).

3.2.1 Action-Message Mapping Stage

Each action specified or implied in the use case description should have a corresponding message(s) in the SQD. Depending on the degree of completeness of the use-case description text, the author of the SQD may need to infer some of the operations. The messages are identified through the following procedure:

- Identify verbs from the use-case description.
- Remove verbs that describe the problem. Select verbs that solve the problem and call them *problem-solving verbs* (PSVs).
- From the PSVs, select the verbs that represent an *automatic* operation or a manual operation by the actor. We call these PSVs *problem-solving operations* (PSOs) and use them as messages in the SQD.

Larman (2004) uses three types of postconditions: *Instance creation and destruction, Association forming,* and *Attribute modification.* In this paper, we treat them as PSO categories. Here, we add three more PSO categories: *Attribute access, Input/Output/Interface,* and *Integrity-constraint checking. We use these six PSO categories to identify messages from a use case description. These six types of PSOs can also be used in identifying messages that are necessary but not explicit in the use case descriptions.*

A. Instance Creation and Destruction: The "Creator" pattern suggests rules for determining which object should send an object creation message (Larman, 2004). Class B should have the responsibility to send *create()* message to A in the following cases: B aggregates A objects; B records instances of A objects; B closely uses A objects; or B has the initializing data that will be passed to A when it is created. Often, the controller will have the initializing data, but an entity class will be assigned the responsibility when it is closely associated with the new object as in the first four cases. The UML 2 notation suggests that a created object should be placed at the creation height in the diagram, which Ambler (2008b) refers to as "direct creation".

Fig. 3 shows the correct SQD with the direct creation of object :SomeEO.

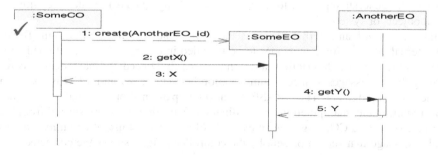

Fig. 3. Correct Object Creation at the Creation Height

B. Association Forming: If there is an association between two classes, then at least one of the SQDs must include a message that forms this association. If a depicted association is never supposed to be used at all, then there must be an error either in the class diagram or the SQD (Ambler, 2008b). Associations can be formed by creating the object with the appropriate parameters or by updating the appropriate parameter in the object. The association must be formed before other operations, which require visibility from the sender to the receiver, can be performed. Fig. 3 shows an example where the association is formed between :SomeEO and :AnotherEO by the parameter (AnotherEO_id) being passed to :SomeEO at creation. This makes the *getX()* message possible.

C. Attribute Modification (set/compute/convert): *For each postcondition that causes a state change, there should be a message. The messages change the value of attributes such as deposit_amount(), calc_subscription_charge(), and convert_cm_to_inch(). Any message that sets a value, computes a value, or converts one unit to another belongs to this message type.*

D. Attribute Access (get/find/compare/sort): This type of message reads values of attributes. Any message that gets a value, finds a value, compares values, and sorts values belongs to this message type.

A frequent mistake of novice developers is to try to update an attribute of a read-only class in the use case. We call such a class as a *reference class,* which refers to an entity class that just provides information to a use case, and that should not be updated by any interaction. Fig. 4 illustrates a case where the modeler did not understand the roles of the class :PricingPolicy. Fig. 4 is a portion of a sequence diagram submitted by a student for use case called "Add Paid Subscription" in a subscription automation system. This example is incorrect because :PricingPolicy is a class that stores the pricing rules. :PricingPolicy may be updated in a maintenance transaction, but not by a customer transaction of adding a new subscription. A tip-off is the class name. Any class name including "policy", "rule", or "template" is probably a reference class for any interaction except the use case to specifically update that class. This example also demonstrates the value of clear class names. Fig. 5 shows a correct depiction of the same interaction.

E. Input/Output/Interface: This type of messages is used (a) to input data, (b) to display output, generate report, or to save a data to a storage, and (c) to interface with external objects or systems.

Interaction with an external system is shown by a message from a CO to the BO of the external system. Some messages to be included in an SQD aren't mentioned anywhere in the use-case description; a designer of an SQD needs to make decisions regarding these messages. Entire communication between a BO and a CO is based on the designer's judgment. The GRASP "Controller" pattern stipulates that, for interactions requiring any manipulation or coordination, actor inputs are transferred from the interface (BO) to a CO. Fig. 6 is an example of an incorrect use of an entity class to send a message that should be sent by the controller. Fig. 7 shows the corrected version, sending a message from a CO to an external system.

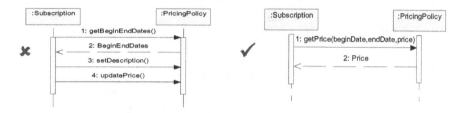

Fig. 4. Incorrect, updating a *reference* class

Fig. 5. Correct, getting information from a *reference* class

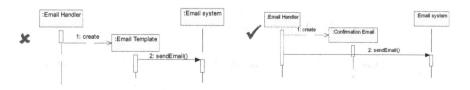

Fig. 6. Incorrect- Entity communicating with an external system

Fig. 7. Correct – Controller communicating with an external system

A common BO pattern is as follows. An actor creates a BO and enters some data. The BO creates a necessary CO and transfers data to it. After the CO completes whatever processing it is responsible for (which may include calling other COs), the CO returns some value to the calling BO. The BO displays some information for the actor. Fig. 8 shows an incorrect message sequence between an actor and the BO, and Fig. 9 shows an example of the correct use of a BO.

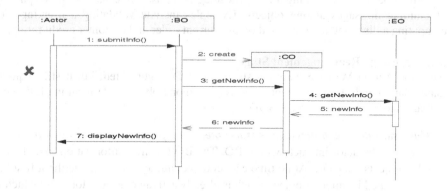

Fig. 8. An incorrect sequence of messages between a user and a window

It should be noted that a BO may access an EO directly, but this is only appropriate when the interaction is very simple, e.g. a retrieval of values from a single class, or an update to a single class with no calculations. Fig. 10 shows an example of this pattern.

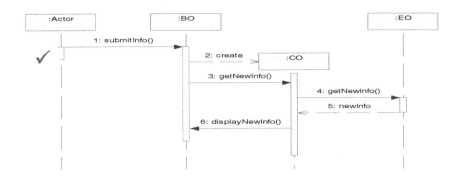

Fig. 9. A correct Sequence of messages

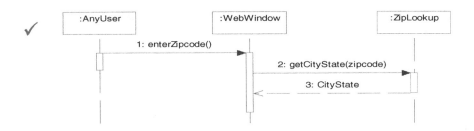

Fig. 10. An example of valid direct communication between BO and EO

F. Integrity-constraint (IC) Checking: Another message type in an SQD is an IC checking operation. Checking a complex integrity constraint usually requires passing of multiple messages among objects. Examples include validating a user input or computing a discount amount based on the current order and customer credit rating.

3.2.2 Message Rearrangement Stage

After the Action-Message mapping stage, an SQD is generated; but it still requires manipulation and re-arrangement of messages among objects. Perform the following to rearrange the messages in the SQD.

1. *Make sure that each message is traceable to the primary actor through activated objects.* The actor interacts with a BO. The BO transfers information to and from other objects via COs. At no time can an object initiate a message without first being activated by another object which is already activated, except for a BO which is activated by a message from the actor (Pooly and Steven, 1999). The exception to this is active objects, which are beyond the scope of this paper. Fig. 11 is an example of an invalid SQD, where the :PaymentHandler initiates a message without first being activated. Fig. 12 shows a correct version of the same diagram, where the :PaymentHandler is first activated by the :SubscriptionHandler.

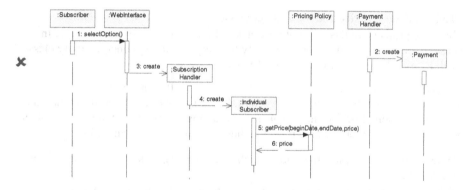

Fig. 11. Incorrect – Payment Handler was never activated

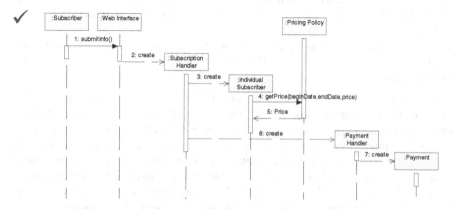

Fig. 12. Correct – Payment Handler is created

2. *Name each message with meaningful names.* Message names should clearly communicate what is being requested. For example, if a message to :Client is getting the
email address, the message *getEmailAddress()* is more descriptive than *getEmail()*.

Supply each message with optional parameters. The SQD will not necessarily show
all the relevant attributes as message arguments (Chonoles and Schardt, 2003). Some
parameters, however, should be shown, such as an object or parameter that is being
passed among multiple other objects. (Ambler 2008b; and Chonoles and Schardt,
2003). The items to verify with respect to message arguments are:

- Each depicted or implied argument represents either an input value or an attribute
of some class or a class in the class diagram. Specified parameters which represent
attributes or classes should match their depiction in the class diagram.
- The sender of the message containing the argument has visibility to the value or at-
tribute(s) used in the arguments.

3 Check the SQD for consistency with the Class Diagram. All entity classes used in
an SQD must appear in the class diagram. Conversely, if SQDs are completed for all
use cases within the project scope, all entity classes shown on the design class diagram must be used in at least one SQD, with the following caveats:

- This is not necessarily true for abstract classes.
- In many projects, SQDs will not be generated for the entire set of use cases. In that case, the modeler should mentally verify that any remaining concrete entity classes will be used by the yet-to-be-modeled SQDs.

4. *Check if return messages are implied or required.* It is not always necessary to show returns on SQDs (Arlow and Neustadt, 2002; Larman, 2004). Returns should be shown only when showing them makes the drawing more understandable (Ambler, 2008b; and Fowler 2000). Some rules that help to make this determination are:

- When a message implies the return, such as *getPrice()*, it is not necessary to show the return.
- When complex processing results in a new value that is returned to a calling routine, the return should be shown.
- Ambler(2008b) suggests "If you need to refer to a return value elsewhere in your SQD, typically as a parameter passed in another message, then indicate the return value on your diagram".
- Returns usually point from right to left, but not always; messages normally point from left to right, but not always. Therefore it is important to use the correct notation for clarity.

5. *Check for the correctness of focus of control.* The focus of control is also referred to as a method activation box (OMG 2003) or method-invocation box (Ambler, 2008a). The focus of control shows the time during which the object is active, or has control of the interaction. If an object receives a message (message no. 2 in Fig. 13) that needs to return a value to a calling class (:PaymentWindow), the focus of control for the calling class should be continuous as the object is just waiting for a response. The focus of control should remain active till a return message (message no. 3) is received from :PaymentHandler. Fig. 13 shows incorrect focus of control and a wrong return notation. A corresponding correct diagram is not shown due to limited space.

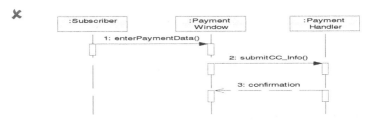

Fig. 13. Incorrect – broken focus of control; returns shown incorrectly

3.3 Visual Pattern Level

3.3.1 High Cohesion Check
"High Cohesion" stipulates that the responsibilities of a class should be closely related and should not be diverse. In Fig. 14, :PaidSubscriber is sending those messages to :Subscription that have nothing to do with the job of being a subscriber, i.e.

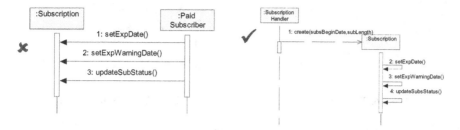

Fig. 14. An SQD with Low Cohesion   **Fig. 15.** An SQD with High Cohesion

:PaidSubscriber is handling the attributes which are irrelevant to its function, causing poor cohesion. A better solution is shown in Fig. 15, where the CO :SubscriptionHandler provides the data to :Subscription, which then calculates and sets the attributes itself.

3.3.2 Low Coupling Check

"Low Coupling" is a design goal to assign responsibilities such that coupling is reduced to the extent possible while observing "High Cohesion" and other guidelines. Use the following guidelines to achieve low coupling:

1. Ensure that the recipient object of a message and the parameter in a message is either part of the state of the sending object; passed as a parameter to the method sending the new message; or returned from a previous message sent within the current method (Law of Demeter; Rowlett, 2001).
2. To send a message, use a source class that is already coupled to the target class.
3. Introduce a CO if many messages are being passed between two classes. In this way, the CO can coordinate among multiple objects.
4. Make sure a parameter is not passed again and again in multiple messages.

3.3.3 Fork or Stair Check

Application of the aforementioned guidelines results in a visual pattern to the SQD, which is descriptively called a "fork" or "stair" pattern (Jacobson, 1992). Once constructed, a message sequence can have a very noticeable visual pattern resembling either a "fork" (Fig. 16) or a "stair" (Fig. 17). This effect is more than just appearance; it presents an overall indication of how responsibilities are assigned. An SQD will probably exhibit both patterns, depending on the relationships of the classes. A "fork" structure is recommended when messages could change the order of message sequences or when there is a central object that controls many messages as in the case of enforcing an integrity constraint. Interactions of control objects frequently show a "fork" pattern. This pattern helps in reuse, error recovery, and maintenance (Rowlett, 2001). A "stair" structure is recommended when there is no central object in the SQD or when messages have strong connections among objects based on relationships such as a temporal relationship (e.g, order – invoice – delivery – payment) or an aggregation hierarchy.

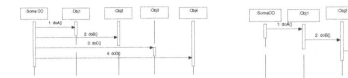

Fig. 16. The Fork Pattern   **Fig. 17.** The Stair Pattern

3.3.4 Central Class Check

Chonoles and Schardt (2003) presents the notion of "central class" concept. They suggest identifying a central class for a use case, and note that this class will probably do a large part of the work in the interaction. For example, if a use case involves the classes shown in Fig. 18, it can be seen that Obj2 is the central class – it has the shortest access route (least hops) to all the other classes in the interaction.   With this observation, if the modeler looks at the finished SQD (Fig. 19), he would notice a "fork" structure beginning from Obj5. It might be an indication that responsibilities are incorrectly assigned (Obj5 has the most difficult access to the other classes). On the other hand, a fork structure emanating from Obj2 would not be surprising.

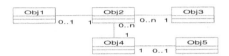

Fig. 18. Identifying the central class Obj2

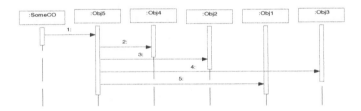

Fig. 19. Likely not a good pattern for the class diagram in Fig. 18

4 Conclusion

In this paper, we have presented a multi-level development methodology for developing SQDs in UML. Our research is motivated by the need of providing a practical method with easy-to-use guidelines for novice SQD developers. We have included guidelines and common visual patterns in SQDs, highlighting the frequently committed mistakes by novices. The guidelines were tested and examples were collected for the past five years of teaching SQDs in a graduate class. The students found our guidelines usable and effective. In future, we will perform a formal study to measure the number and nature of mistakes they make at each level of the methodology.

References

1. Ambler, S.W.: UML 2 Sequence Diagram Overview (2008a),
   http://www.agilemodeling.com/artifacts/sequenceDiagram.htm
2. Ambler, S.W.: UML Sequence Diagramming Guidelines (2008b),
   http://www.agilemodeling.com/style/sequenceDiagram.htm
3. Aredo, D.B.: Semantics of UML sequence diagrams in PVS. In: UML 2000 Workshop on Dynamic Behavior in UML Models, Semantic Questions, York, UK (2000)
4. Arlow, J., Neustadt, I.: UML and the Unified Process: Practical Object-Oriented Analysis and Design. Addison-Wesley Professional, Boston (2002)
5. Baker, P., Bristow, P., Jervis, C., King, D., Mitchell, B., Burton, S.: Detecting and resolving semantic pathologies in UML sequence diagrams. In: 10th European Software Engineering Conference, pp. 50–59. ACM, New York (2005)
6. Bist, G., MacKinnon, N., Murphy, S.: Sequence diagram presentation in technical documentation. In: 22nd Annual International Conference on Design of Communication: The Engineering of Quality Documentation, pp. 128–133. ACM, New York (2004)
7. Chonoles, M.J., Schardt, J.A.: UML 2 for Dummies. Wiley, Hoboken (2003)
8. Fowler, M.: UML Distilled: A Brief Guide to the Standard Object Modeling Language. Addison-Wesley Professional, Boston (2000)
9. Jacobson, I.: Object Oriented Software Engineering: A Use Case Driven Approach. Addison-Wesley Professional, Boston (1992)
10. Larman, C.: Applying UML and Patterns: An Introduction to Object-Oriented Analysis and Design and Iterative Development. Prentice Hall PTR, Upper Saddle River (2004)
11. Li, L.: Translating Use Cases to Sequence Diagrams. In: 15th IEEE International Conference on Automated Software Engineering, Washington, DC, pp. 293–296 (2000)
12. Merdes, M., Dorsch, D.: Experiences with the development of a reverse engineering tool for UML sequence diagrams: A case study in modern java development. In: 4th International Symposium on Principles and Practice of Programming in Java, pp. 125–134. ACM, New York (2006)
13. Object Management Group. UML 2.0 Superstructure Final Adopted specification (2003),
    http://www.omg.org/cgi-bin/doc?ptc/2003-08-02
14. Pooley, R., Stevens, P.: Using UML: Software Engineering with Objects and Components. Addison-Wesley, Harlow (1999)
15. Robinson, W.N., Woo, H.G.: Finding Reusable UML Sequence Diagrams Automatically. IEEE Software 21(5), 60–67 (2004)
16. Rountev, A., Connell, B.H.: Object naming analysis for reverse-engineered sequence diagrams. In: 27th International Conference on Software Engineering, pp. 254–263. ACM, New York (2005)
17. Rowlett, T.: The Object-Oriented Development Process: Developing and Managing a Robust Process for Object-Oriented Development. Prentice Hall, Upper Saddle River (2001)
18. Song, I.-Y.: Developing Sequence Diagrams in UML. In: 20th International Conference on Conceptual Modeling, pp. 368–382. Springer, London (2001)
19. Xia, F., Kane, G.S.: Defining the Semantics of UML Class and Sequence Diagrams for Ensuring the Consistency and Executability of OO Software Specification. In: 1st International Workshop on Automated Technology for Verification and Analysis, Taipei, Taiwan (2003)

Content Ontology Design Patterns as Practical Building Blocks for Web Ontologies

Valentina Presutti and Aldo Gangemi

ISTC-CNR, Semantic Technology Lab, Italy
{valentina.presutti,aldo.gangemi}@istc.cnr.it

Abstract. In this paper we present how to extract and describe emerging content ontology design patterns, and how to compose, specialize and expand them for ontology design, with particular focus on Semantic Web technologies. We exemplify the described techniques with respect to the extraction of two content ontology design patterns from the DOLCE+DnS Ultra Lite ontology, and by showing the design of a simplified ontology for the music industry domain.

1 Introduction

Computational ontologies in the context of information systems are artifacts that encode a description of some world (actual, possible, counterfactual, impossible, desired, etc.), for some purpose. They have a (primarily logical) structure, and must match both domain and task: they allow the description of entities whose attributes and relations are of concern because of their relevance in a domain for some purpose, e.g. query, search, integration, matching, explanation, etc.

Like any artifact, ontologies have a lifecycle: they are designed, implemented, evaluated, fixed, exploited, reused, etc. In this paper, we focus on patterns for ontology design [9,11].

Today, one of the most challenging and neglected areas of ontology design is *reusability*. The possible reasons include at least: *size* and *complexity* of the major reusable ontologies, *opacity* of design rationales in most ontologies, *lack of criteria* in the way existing knowledge resources (e.g. thesauri, database schemata, lexica) can be reengineered, and *brittleness* of tools that should assist ontology designers. On this situation, an average user that is trying to build or reuse an ontology, or an existing knowledge resource, is typically left with limited assistance in using unfriendly logical structures, some large, hardly comprehensible ontologies, and a bunch of good practices that must be discovered from the literature. On the other hand, the success of very simple and small ontologies like FOAF [5] and SKOS [18] shows the potential of really portable, or "sustainable" ontologies. The lesson learnt supports the new approach to ontology design, which is sketched here.

Under the assumption that there exist classes of problems that can be solved by applying common solutions (as it has been experienced in software engineering), we propose to support reusability on the design side specifically. We envision small ontologies with explicit documentation of design rationales, and best reengineering practices.

Q. Li et al. (Eds.): ER 2008, LNCS 5231, pp. 128–141, 2008.

These components need specific functionalities in order to be implemented in repositories, registries, catalogues, open discussion and evaluation forums, and ultimately in new-generation ontology design tools. In this paper, which is a result of the evolution of work described in [9], we describe small, motivated ontologies that can be used as practical *building blocks* in ontology design. A formal framework for (collaborative) ontology design that justifies the use of building blocks with explicit rationales is presented in [11].

We call the practical building blocks to be used in ontology design *Content Ontology Design Patterns* (CP, [9]). CPs encode *conceptual*, rather than *logical* design patterns. In other words, while Logical OPs [23] (like those investigated by [22]) solve design problems independently of a particular conceptualization, CPs propose patterns for solving design problems for the domain classes and properties that populate an ontology, therefore addressing *content* problems [9]. CPs exemplify Logical OPs (or compositions of Logical OPs), featuring a non-empty signature. Hence, they have an explicit non-logical vocabulary for a specific domain of interest (i.e. they are content-dependent). For example, a simple **participation** pattern (including objects taking part in events) emerges in domain ontologies as different as enterprise models [13], sofware management [20], and biochemical pathways [10]. Other, more complex patterns have also emerged in the same disparate domains.

CPs are strictly related to small use cases i.e., each of them is built out of a domain task that can be captured by means of competency questions [13]. A competency question is a typical query that an expert might want to submit to a knowledge base of its target domain, for a certain task. Moreover, CPs are transparent with respect to the rationales applied to the design of a certain ontology. They are therefore an additional tool to achieve tasks such as ontology evaluation, matching, modularization, etc.

For example, an ontology can be evaluated against the presence of certain patterns (which act as *unit tests* for ontologies, cf. [28]) that are typical of the tasks addressed by a designer. Furthermore, mapping and composition of patterns can facilitate ontology mapping: two ontologies drafted according to CPs can be mapped in an easier way: CP hierarchies will be more stable and well-maintained than local, partial, scattered ontologies. Finally, CPs can be also used in training and educational contexts for ontology engineers.

The paper is organized as follows: section 1.1 gives some background notions; section 2 defines the notion of CP, and briefly describes the online repository and Web portal; section 3 provides methodological guidelines for creating and reusing CPs, presents two of them, and an example of reuse. Finally, section 4 provides some conclusions and remarks.

1.1 Background

Ontology engineering literature has tackled the notion of design pattern at least since [6], while in the context of Semantic Web research and application, where ontology design patterns (OPs) are now a hot topic, the notion has been introduced by [10,24,26]. In particular, [10,26] take a foundational approach that anticipates that presented in [9]. Some work [4] has also attempted a learning approach (by using case-based reasoning) to derive and rank patterns with respect to user requirements. The research has also addressed domain-oriented patterns, e.g. for content objects and multimedia [2], software components [20], business modelling and interaction [12,15], relevance [17] etc.

Throughout experiences in ontology engineering projects[1] in our Laboratory, as well as in other ongoing international projects that have experimented with these ideas, typical conceptual patterns have emerged out of different domains, for different tasks, and while working with experts having heterogeneous backgrounds. For an historical perspective and a more detailed survey, the reader can refer to [1,9,12,14,16]

2   Content Ontology Design Patterns (CPs)

Content ontology design patterns (CPs) are reusable solutions to recurrent content modelling problems. In analogy to conceptual modeling (cf. the difference between class and use case diagrams in the Unified Modeling Language (UML) [21]) and knowledge engineering (cf. the distinction between domain and task ontologies in the Unified Problem-solving Method Development Language (UPML) [19]), these problems have two components: a domain and a use case (or task). A same domain can have many use cases (e.g. different scenarios in a clinical information context), and a same use case can be found in different domains (e.g. different domains with a same "competence finding" scenario). A typical way of capturing use cases is by means of *competency questions* [13]. A competency question is a typical query that an expert might want to submit to a knowledge base of its target domain, for a certain task. In principle, an accurate domain ontology should specify *all and only* the conceptualizations required in order to answer the competency questions formulated by, or acquired from, experts.

Based on the above assumptions, we define what a Content Ontology Design Pattern (CP) is:

> *CPs are distinguished ontologies. They address a specific set of competency questions, which represent the problem they provide a solution for. Furthermore, CPs show certain characteristics i.e., they are: computational, small and autonomous, hierarchical, cognitively relevant, linguistically relevant, and best practices.*

According to [9], such characteristics can be described as follows:

– *Computational components.* CPs are language-independent, and should be encoded in a higher-order representation language.[2] Nevertheless, their (sample) representation in OWL is needed in order to (re)use them as building blocks over the Semantic Web.
– *Small, autonomous components.* Regardless of the particular way a CP has been created (section 3.1 describes how to create a CP), it is a *small, autonomous* ontology.

---

[1] For example, in the projects *FOS*: http://www.fao.org/agris/aos/, *WonderWeb*: http://wonderweb.semanticweb.org, *Metokis*: http://metokis.salzburgresearch.at, and *NeOn*: http://www.neon-project.org

[2] Common Logic (see http://cl.tamu.edu/) is a good candidate because of its expressivity and computationally-sound syntax.

Smallness (typically two to ten classes with relations defined between them) and autonomy of CPs facilitate ontology designers. Smallness also allows diagrammatical visualizations that are aesthetically acceptable and easily memorizable.

- *Hierarchical components.* A CP can be an element in a partial order, where the ordering relation requires that at least one of the classes or properties in the pattern is specialized.
- *Inference-enabling components.* A CP allows some form of inference e.g. a taxonomy with two sibling disjoint classes, a property with explicit domain and range set, a property and a class with a universal restriction on that property, etc.
- *Cognitively relevant components.* CP visualization must be intuitive and compact, and should catch relevant, "core" notions of a domain. [9]
- *Linguistically relevant components.* Many CPs nicely match linguistic patterns called *frames*. A frame can be described as a lexically founded ontology design pattern; The richest repository of frames is FrameNet [3].
- *Best practice components* A CP should be used to describe a "best practice" of modelling. Best practices are intended here as *local*, thus derived from experts, emerging from real applications.

A Catalogue and Repository of CPs. The above definition provides ontology designers with the necessary means to identify CPs within existing ontologies. However, we believe it is important for reuse purpose, to have a repository of CPs and related services, where CPs can be added and retrieved, and to guarantee that published CPs have a high level of quality.

With the above principles in mind, we have set up the Ontology Design Patterns Web portal[3] (ODPWeb), where CPs are collected, classified, described with a specific template, and available for download. They respond to a common specification (which extends the above CP definition), and are described in terms of a template, which is inspired by the well known one used for Software Engineering design patterns [7]. The Web portal is open to contribution from any user, who is only required to register in order to have authoring rights. ODPWeb is intended as a space where ontology designers, practitioners, and Semantic Web users can discuss about web ontology design issues, find information about good practices, and download reusable components for building web ontologies. Moreover, the ODPWeb is associated with a lightweight (peer reviewing) workflow, which guarantees both quality of the published CPs and openness of the community.

3 CP Creation and Usage

Content Ontology Design Pattern (CP) creation and usage rely on a common set of operations.

- *import:* as with any ontology, it consists of including a CP in the ontology under development. This is the basic mechanism for CP reuse. Elements of a CP cannot be modified.

---

[3] http://www.ontologydesignpatterns.org.

- *clone:* consists of duplicating an ontology element i.e., a class and a property, which is used as a prototype[4]. We can distinguish among three kinds of clones:
    - *shallow clone*: consists of creating a new ontology element O' by duplicating an existing ontology element O. Axioms of O and O' will refer to the same ontology elements.
    - *deep clone*: consists of creating a new ontology element O' by duplicating an existing ontology element O, and by creating a new ontology element for each one that is referred in O's axiomatization, recursively.
    - *partial clone*: consists of deep cloning an ontology element, by keeping only a subset of its axioms.
- *specialization:* can be referred to ontology elements or to CPs. Specialization between ontology elements of a CP consists of creating sub-classes of some CP's class and/or sub-properties of some CP's properties. A CP c' is a specialization of a CP c, if at least one ontology element of c' specializes an ontology elements of c, and all ontology elements of c' are either a specialization of ontology elements of c, or clones of them.
- *generalization:* is the reverse of the specialization operation.
- *composition:* consists of associating classes (properties) of one CP with classes (properties) of other CPs by subsumption, by creating new owl restrictions, or by creating new properties.
- *expansion:* consists of enriching an ontology with ontology elements and axioms, which do not identify any CP or composition of them.

3.1   CP Creation

CPs mainly emerge either from ontologies (i.e., *foundational*, *core*, and *domain* ontologies)[5] or by reengineering other types of conceptual models (e.g. E-R models, UML models, linguistic frames, thesauri, etc.) to ontologies. CPs can be defined in four main ways:

- *Reengineering from other data models* A CP can be the result of a reengineering process applied to different conceptual modeling languages, primitives, and styles. [12] describes a reengineering approach for creating CPs starting from UML diagrams [21], workflow patterns [27], and data model patterns [16].
  Other knowledge resources that can be reengineered to produce candidate CPs are database schemas, knowledge organization systems (e.g. thesauri), and lexica for reengineering techniques on these resources). The reader can refer to [12] for more references.
- *Specialization/Composition of other CPs* A CP can be created either by composition of other CPs or by specialization of another CP, (both composition and specialization can be combined with expansion).
- *Extraction from reference ontologies* A CP can be *extracted from* an existing ontology, which acts as the "source" ontology. Extraction of a CP is a process consisting of (partial) cloning the ontology elements of interest from the source ontology.
- *Creation by combining the above techniques.*

---

[4] There is a strong analogy between the clone operation in OO software programming and the ontology element clone operation.

[5] see [9] for references.

Figure 1 shows the typical process that is performed by an ontology engineer for creating a CP by extraction from a reference ontology, possibly including specialization and expansion. The creation of a CP starts with the creation of a new ontology to which a suitable namespace is assigned. Each pattern has its own namespace that does not depend on that of the source ontology. The source ontology(ies) is(are) then imported. Elements of the source ontology must not be modified. Some tools allow designers to modify imported ontologies, when they are locally stored and writable. In such a case, it is a good practice to lock the imported ontologies in order to set access permissions to read-only.

The creation proceeds with the partial cloning of the ontology elements i.e., classes and properties, of interest. Some ontology design tools support the shallow clone operation [6], while deep clone and partial clone are not yet supported by any existing tool. Currently, in order to obtain a partial or deep clone of an ontology element we can either start from a shallow clone (when supported), or we can write a SPARQL CONSTRUCT query, and then manually update the results. For example, the SPARQL expression (1) allows us to extract the class DUL:Agent and its associated axioms from the source ontology, and to create the class Agent as a shallow clone of it. Within the results provided by the SPARQL engine, we can choose which axioms we want to keep. With this procedure, the selected axioms will still contain ontology elements from the source ontology. Therefore, we have to manually update such axioms in order to substitute those elements with new cloned ones.

$$CONSTRUCT\{:Agent\ ?r\ ?y\}$$
$$WHERE\{DUL:Agent\ ?r\ ?y\} \tag{1}$$

After all elements of interest have been cloned and updated, optional specialization and/or expansion is performed. At this point, possible disjointness axioms are introduced before launching the reasoner for consistency checking, and for inferences, some of which might be explicitly asserted. Finally, the imports are removed and the CP and its elements are annotated.

CPs that are published on ODPWeb are annotated by means of the *cp annotation schema*[7].

3.2   The Information Realization CP

In this section we describe a CP that is named **information realization**. It is created by extraction from the Dolce Ultra Lite ontology[8], and represents the relations between information objects like poems, songs, formulas, etc., and their physical realizations like printed books, registered tracks, physical files, etc.. We also show how it is extracted, and provide the main information according to that contained in its associated catalogue entry.

Figure 2 depicts some screenshots of the ontology editor while we extract the information realization CP. The arrows indicates the ontology element that we clone i.e.,

---

[6] e.g., TopBraid Composer available at http://www.topbraidcomposer.com/
[7] http://www.ontologydesignpatterns.org/schemas/cpannotationschema.owl
[8] http://www.loa-cnr.it/ontologies/DUL.owl

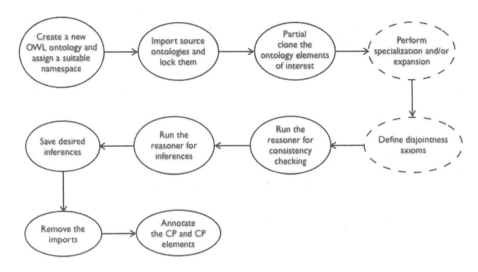

Fig. 1. The CP creation by extraction process. Circles with dashed lines indicates steps that can be skipped.

Fig. 2. The information realization CP extraction from Dolce+DnS Ultra Lite ontology. The arrows identify the class DUL:InformationObject, the result of its cloning, which is the class InformationObject, and the axiom kept and updated from the source class definition.

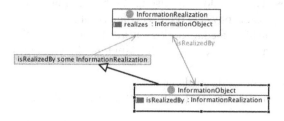

Fig. 3. The information realization CP UML graphical representation

`DUL:InformationObject`[9] The upper part of the picture depicts the axiomatization of `DUL:InformationObject`, in the bottom left part, the (shallow) clone functionality is applied to `DUL:InformationObject`. The clone operation result is a new class belonging to the information realization CP and namespace, named `InformationObject`. We also clone `DUL:InformationRealization` and create `InformationRealization`, and clone the two object properties `DUL:realizes`, and `DUL:isRealizedBy` and create `realizes`, and `isRealizedBy`, object properties. We remove the axioms we do not want to keep, and update the kept ones with the new ontology elements. In the bottom right of the picture is shown the resulting definition of `InformationObject`. It can be noticed that we keep the comment, and the restrictions on the `DUL:isRealizedBy` object property, and update the restricted property to the local cloned one i.e., `isRealizedBy`. We use the same approach for all the other ontology elements. Finally we remove the import and obtain the information realization CP. Figure 3 shows a UML diagram of the information realization CP. The **information realization CP** is associated with information according to the catalogue entry fields reported below:

- **Name:** Information Realization
- **Intent:** Which physical object realizes a certain information object? Which information object is realized by a certain physical object?
- **Extracted from:** The Dolce Ultra Lite ontology available at http://www.loa-cnr.it/ontologies/DUL.owl
- **Examples:** That CD is the recording of *The Dark Side of the Moon*
- **Diagram:** See Figure 3
- **Elements:**
    - `InformationObject`: A piece of information, such as a musical composition, a text, a word, a picture, independently from how it is concretely realized.
    - `InformationRealization`: A concrete realization of an InformationObject, e.g. the written document containing the text of a law.
    - `realizes`: A relation between an information realization and an information object, e.g. the paper copy of the Italian Constitution realizes the text of the Constitution.
    - `isRealizedBy`: A relation between an information object and an information realization, e.g. the text of the Constitution is realized by the paper copy of the Italian Constitution.

---

[9] DUL is the prefix for the Dolce+DnS Ultra Lite ontology namespace.

– **Consequences:** The CP allows to distinguish between information encoded in an object and the possible physical representations of it .
– **Known uses:** The Multimedia ontology, available at http://multimedia.sematicweb.org/COMM/multimedia-ontology.owl[10] used   this CP.
– **Building block:** The CP is available at http://wiki.loa-cnr.it/index.php/LoaWiki:informationrealization

With reference to the complete set of fields that compose the template, here we are missing: the **Also Known as** field, which provides alternative names for the CP; and the **Related CPs** field, which indicates other CPs (if any) that e.g., specialize, generalize, include, are components of, or are typically used with, etc. the CP.

3.3   The Time Indexed Person Role Pattern

The **time indexed person role** is a CP that represents time indexing for the relation between persons and roles they play. This CP is created by combining extraction and specialization. According to its associated catalogue entry, the main information associated with this CP are the following:

– **Name:** Time Indexed Person Role
– **Intent:** Who was playing a certain roles during a given time interval? When did a certain person play a specific role?
– **Extracted from:** The Dolce Ultra Lite ontology available at http://www.loa-cnr.it/ontologies/DUL.owl
– **Examples:** George W. Bush was the president of the United States in 2007.
– **Diagram:** See Figure 4, the elements which compose the CP are described in the **Elements** field.
– **Elements:**
  - `Entity`: Anything: real, possible, or imaginary, which some modeller wants to talk about for some purpose.
  - `Person`: Persons in commonsense intuition, i.e. either as physical agents (humans) or social persons.
  - `Role`: A Concept that classifies a Person
  - `TimeInterval`: Any region in a dimensional space that aims at representing time.
  - `TimeIndexedPersonRole`: A situation that expresses time indexing for the relation between persons and roles they play.
  - `hasRole`: A relation between a Role and an Entity, e.g. 'John is considered a typical rude man'; your last concert constitutes the achievement of a lifetime; '20-year-old means she's mature enough'.
  - `isRoleOf`: A relation between a Role and an Entity, e.g. the Role 'student' classifies a Person 'John'.

---

[10] Actually the multimedia ontology used a simplified version of Dolce Ultra Lite including classes and properties we have extracted (from the same source ontology) in order to define the CP.

- `isSettingFor`: A relation between time indexed role situations and related entities, e.g. 'I was the director between 2000 and 2005 ', i.e.: the situation in which I was a director is the setting for a the role of director, me, and the time interval.
  - `hasSetting`: The inverse relation of `isSettingFor`.
- **Consequences:** The CP allows to assign a time interval to roles played by people.
- **Building block:** The CP is available at
  http://wiki.loa-cnr.it/index.php/LoaWiki:timeindexedpersonrole

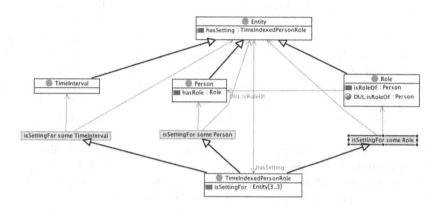

Fig. 4. The time indexed person role CP UML graphical representation

The **time indexed person role** CP is created by combining extraction, specialization, and expansion. The class `TimeIndexedPersonRole` is derived by specializing the Dolce Ultra Lite class `DUL:Classification` (pointed by the blue arrow), while the other elements are partially cloned with the same approach we use for classes and properties of the **information realization** CP.

3.4 CP Usage

Supporting reuse and alleviating difficulties in ontology design activities are the main goals of setting up a catalogue of CPs. In order to be able to reuse CPs, two main functionalities must be ensured: *selection* and *application*.

Selection of CPs corresponds to finding the most appropriate CP for the actual domain modeling problem. Hence, selection includes search and evaluation of available CPs. This task can be performed by applying typical procedures for ontology selection e.g., [25] and evaluation [8].

Informally, *intent* of the CP must match the actual local modeling problem. Once a CP has been selected, it has to be applied to the domain ontology. Typically, application is performed by means of import, specialization, composition, or expansion (see section 3). In realistic design projects, such operations are usually combined.

Several situations of matching between intent of CPs and local domain problem can occur, each associated with a different approach to using CPs. The following summary assumes a *manual* (re)use of CPs. An automatic support to CP selection and usage should take into account the principles informally explained in the summary below.

- *Precise or redundant matching.* The CP intent perfectly or redundantly matches the local domain problem. The CP is directly usable to describe the local domain problem: the CP only has to be *imported* in the domain ontology.
- *Broader matching.* The CP intent is more general than the local domain problem: the **Generalization Of** field of the CP's catalogue entry, may contain references to less general CPs that specialize it. If none of them is appropriate, the CP has firstly to be *imported*, then it has to be *specialized* in order to cover the domain part to be represented.
- *Narrower matching.* The CP intent matches is more specific than the local domain problem: the `odpschema:specializationOf`[11] property of the CP annotation schema may contain references i.e., URIs, to more general CPs it is the specialization of, the same information is reported in the **Specialization Of** field of the CP's catalogue entry. If none of them is appropriate, the selected CP has firstly to be *imported*, then it has to be *generalized* in order to cover the domain part to be represented.
- *Partial matching.* The CP intent partly matches the local domain problem: the **is Component Of** field of the CP's catalogue entry may contain CPs it is a component of. If none of such compound CPs is appropriate, the local domain problem has to be partitioned into smaller pieces. One of these pieces will be possibly covered by the selected CP. For the other pieces, other CPs have to be selected. All selected CPs have to be *imported* and *composed*. If the local domain problem is not too big, it is worth to propose a new entry to the catalogue of CPs for the resulting composed CP.

An example in the music domain As an example of usage we design a small fragment of an ontology for the music industry domain. The ontology fragment has to address the following competency questions:

- *Which recordings of a certain song do exist in our archive?*
- *Who did play a certain musician role in a given band during a certain period?*

The first competency question requires to distinguish between a song and its recording, while the second competency question highlights the issue of assigning a given musician role e.g., singer, guitar player, etc., to a person who is member of a certain band, at a given period of time. The intent of the **information realization** is related to the first competency question with a *broader matching*. The intent of the **time indexed person role** partially and broadly matches the second competency question. The second requirement also requires to represent membership relation between a person and a band[12]. Let's consider the case that we cannot find more specialized CPs for reusing. We proceed by following the above guidelines. Figure 5 shows a screenshot

---

[11] odpschema is a prefix for
  http://www.ontologydesignpatterns.org/schemas/cpannotationschema.owl
[12] The **collection entity** CP is about membership relations.

of the resulting ontology fragment. In the bottom part of the screenshot we find the import tab where the **information realization**[13] and **time indexed person role**[14] CPs are imported. Additionally, we import the **time interval** CP that allows us to assign a date to the time interval[15] In order to complete our ontology fragment we create: the class Song that specializes ir:InformationObject, the class Recording that specializes ir:InformationRealization, the class MusicianRole that specializes tipr:Role, the class Band, and the object property memberOf (and its inverse) with explicit domain i.e., tipr:Person, and range i.e., Band.

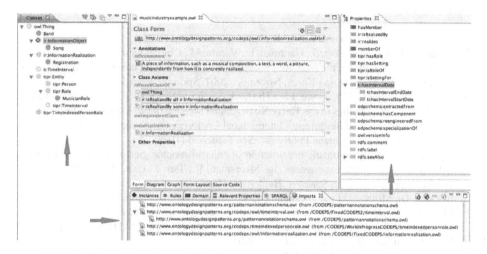

Fig. 5. The music industry example. The arrows indicate the imported CPs (bottom of the figure), and the ontology elements we have specialized (left and right side of the figure).

4   Conclusion and Remarks

Ontology design is a crucial research area for semantic technologies. Many bottlenecks in the wide adoption of semantic technologies depend on the difficulty of understanding ontologies and on the scarcity of tools supporting their lifecycle, from creation to adaptation, reuse, and management. The lessons learnt until now, either from the early adoption of semantic web solutions or from local, organizational applications, put a lot of emphasis on the need for simple, modular ontologies that are accessible and understandable by typical computer scientist and field experts, and on the dependability of these ontologies on existing knowledge resources.[16] In this paper, we have described content ontology design patterns, which are beneficial to ontology design in terms of

---

[13] We use the prefix ir for this CP.

[14] We use the prefix tipr for this CP.

[15] The **time interval** CP also defines two additional sub-properties of the hasIntervalDate for expressing a start and an end date to the time interval.

[16] References to review work of evaluation, selection and reuse methods in ontology engineering can be found in [12].

their relation to requirement analysis, definition, communication means, related work beyond ontology engineering, exemplification, creation, and usage principles.

We have shown how CPs can be created and reused, and presented two of them as sample entries from a larger catalogue, with an example in the design of a small ontology in the music domain. Finally, we have briefly described our ongoing work a Web portal where designers, practitioners, and users can discuss about, propose, and download content ontology design patterns.

References

1. Alexander, C.: The Timeless Way of Building. Oxford Press (1979)
2. Arndt, R., Troncy, R., Staab, S., Hardman, L., Vacura, M.: Comm: Designing a well-founded multimedia ontology for the web. In: Proceedings of the 4th European Semantic Web Conference (ISCW 2007), Busan Korea, November 2007. Springer, Heidelberg (2007)
3. Baker, C.F., Fillmore, C.J., Lowe, J.B.: The Berkeley FrameNet project. In: Boitet, C., White-lock, P. (eds.) Proceedings of the Thirty-Sixth Annual Meeting of the Association for Computational Linguistics and Seventeenth International Conference on Computational Linguistics, pp. 86–90. Morgan Kaufmann Publishers, San Francisco (1998)
4. Blomqvist, E.: Fully automatic construction of enterprise ontologies using design patterns: Initial method and first experiences. In: Meersman, R., Tari, Z. (eds.) OTM 2005. LNCS, vol. 3761, pp. 1314–1329. Springer, Heidelberg (2005)
5. Brickley, D., Miller, L.: Foaf vocabulary specification. Working draft (2005)
6. Clark, P., Thompson, J., Porter, B.: Knowledge patterns. In: Cohn, A.G., Giunchiglia, F., Selman, B. (eds.) KR2000: Principles of Knowledge Representation and Reasoning, pp. 591–600. Morgan Kaufmann, San Francisco (2000)
7. Gamma, E., Helm, R., Johnson, R.E., Vlissides, J.: Design Patterns. Elements of Reusable Object-Oriented Software. Addison-Wesley, Reading (1995)
8. Gangemi, A., Catenacci, C., Ciaramita, M., Lehmann, J.: Modelling Ontology Evaluation and Validation. In: Proceedings of the Third European Semantic Web Conference. Springer, Heidelberg (2006)
9. Gangemi, A.: Ontology Design Patterns for Semantic Web Content. In: Musen, M., et al. (eds.) Proceedings of the Fourth International Semantic Web Conference, Galway, Ireland. Springer, Heidelberg (2005)
10. Gangemi, A., Catenacci, C., Battaglia, M.: Inflammation ontology design pattern: an exercise in building a core biomedical ontology with descriptions and situations. In: Pisanelli, D.M. (ed.) Ontologies in Medicine. IOS Press, Amsterdam (2004)
11. Gangemi, A., Lehmann, J., Presutti, V., Nissim, M., Catenacci, C.: C-odo: an owl meta-model for collaborative ontology design. In: Alani, H., Noy, N., Stumme, G., Mika, P., Sure, Y., Vrandecic, D. (eds.) Workshop on Social and Collaborative Construction of Structured Knowledge (CKC 2007) at WWW 2007, Banff, Canada (2007)
12. Gangemi, A., Presutti, V.: Ontology design for interaction in a reasonable enterprise. In: Rittgen, P. (ed.) Handbook of Ontologies for Business Interaction, IGI Global, Hershey, PA (November 2007)
13. Gruninger, M., Fox, M.: The role of competency questions in enterprise engineering (1994)
14. Guizzardi, G.: Ontological foundations for structural conceptual models. PhD thesis, University of Twente, Enschede, The Netherlands, Enschede (October 2005)
15. Guizzardi, G., Wagner, G.: A unified foundational ontology and some applications of it in business modeling. In: CAiSE Workshops (3), pp. 129–143 (2004)
16. Hay, D.C.: Data Model Patterns. Dorset House Publishing (1996)

17. Gomez-Romero, J., Bobillo, F., Delgado, M.: An ontology design pattern for representing relevance in owl. In: Aberer, K., Choi, K.-S., Noy, N. (eds.) The 6th International Semantic Web Conference and the 2nd Asian Semantic Web Conference 2007, Busan, Korea (November 2007)

18. Miles, A., Brickley, D.: SKOS Core Vocabulary Specification. Technical report, World Wide Web Consortium (W3C) (November 2005),
http://www.w3.org/TR/2005/WD-swbp-skos-core-spec-20051102/

19. Motta, E., Lu, W.: A library of components for classification problem solving. ibrow project ist-1999-19005: An intelligent brokering service for knowledge-component reuse on the world- wide web. Technical report, KMI (2000)

20. Oberle, D.: Semantic Management of Middleware. The Semantic Web and Beyond, vol. I. Springer, New York (2006)

21. Object Management Group (OMG). Unified modeling language specification: Version 2, revised final adopted specification (ptc/04-10-02) (2004)

22. Semantic Web Best Practices and Deployment Working Group. Task force on ontology engineering patterns. description of work, archives, w3c notes and recommendations (2004),
http://www.w3.org/2001/sw/BestPractices/OEP/

23. Presutti, V., Gangemi, A., Gomez-Perez, A., Figueroa, M.-C.S.: Library of design patterns for collaborative development of networked ontologies. Deliverable D2.5.1, NeOn project (2007)

24. Rector, A., Rogers, J.: Patterns, properties and minimizing commitment: Reconstruction of the galen upper ontology in owl. In: Gangemi, A., Borgo, S. (eds.) Proceedings of the EKAW 2004 Workshop on Core Ontologies in Ontology Engineering. CEUR (2004)

25. Sabou, M., Lopez, V., Motta, E.: Ontology selection for the real semantic web: How to cover the queen's birthday dinner? In: Staab, S., Svátek, V. (eds.) EKAW 2006. LNCS (LNAI), vol. 4248, pp. 96–111. Springer, Heidelberg (2006)

26. Svatek, V.: Design patterns for semantic web ontologies: Motivation and discussion. In: Proceedings of the 7th Conference on Business Information Systems, Poznan (2004)

27. Van Der Aalst, W.M.P., Ter Hofstede, A.H.M., Kiepuszewski, B., Barros, A.P.: Workflow Patterns. Distributed and Parallel Databases 14, 5–51 (2003)

28. Vrandecic, D., Gangemi, A.: Unit tests for ontologies. In: Jarrar, M., Ostyn, C., Ceusters, W., Persidis, A. (eds.) Proceedings of the 1st International Workshop on Ontology content and evaluation in Enterprise, Montpellier, France, October 2006. LNCS, Springer, Heidelberg (2006)

Quality Patterns for Conceptual Modelling

Samira Si-Saïd Cherfi[1], Isabelle Comyn-Wattiau[2], and Jacky Akoka[3]

[1] CEDRIC-CNAM, 292 R Saint Martin, F-75141 Paris Cedex 03
sisaid@cnam.fr
[2] CEDRIC-CNAM and ESSEC Business School
wattiau@cnam.fr
[3] CEDRIC-CNAM and INT
akoka@cnam.fr

Abstract. Patterns have generated a large interest during last years. In software engineering, a pattern is a reusable solution based on the capitalization of well known and agreed practices. The role of a pattern is to speed up development process. The aim of this paper is twofold: it first proposes a concept of quality pattern. The latter is used to structure and to package predefined solutions for evaluation of conceptual modelling quality. The second contribution is related to the combination of two concepts, namely quality patterns and design patterns in a three-step process aiming at i) guiding the quality evaluation by the use of quality patterns, ii) helping designers improve conceptual models using design patterns, iii) evaluating the improvement by quality measurement.

Keywords: Conceptual model quality, quality patterns, design patterns, development process guidance, quality measurement.

1 Introduction

With increasing costs of software development and the growing centrality of information systems (IS) within organizations, building patterns is becoming widely recognized as an important activity. However, despite its importance, it is often ignored or carried out inefficiently. The reason lies within the complexity of the task related to the development of patterns. Building patterns, and more specifically quality patterns, is still considered as problematic. Moreover, choosing design patterns associated with specific quality patterns remains a difficult task. Although a number of patterns, especially design patterns, are available, none of them integrates quality evaluation. We argue that the accurate capture of quality factors and metrics plays a critical role in the elicitation of effective and usable quality patterns that could be used further to assist IS developers in the choice of the appropriate design patterns. The process of quality patterns engineering and the choice of the associated design patterns is still not well defined. In particular, the initial investigation and elicitation of the quality patterns relevant to the choice of design patterns is not supported by current development methods.

The work described in this paper takes the premise that adopting a three-phase engineering approach to conceptual modelling will offer a promise, especially for helping the activities of quality pattern-driven conceptual modelling. Our aims are threefold:

Q. Li et al. (Eds.): ER 2008, LNCS 5231, pp. 142–153, 2008.
© Springer-Verlag Berlin Heidelberg 2008

1. To draw upon information systems quality factors to develop a quality attributes specification, specifically incorporating i) quality goals relevant to conceptual modellers, ii) sufficient formality to allow the identification of quality attributes related to the quality goals.
2. To perform quality measurements leading to quality patterns.
3. To perform a design pattern-driven phase, based on quality patterns, and leading to conceptual model quality improvement.

In this paper, we propose a knowledge-based approach that helps in quality patterns-based development, combining quality and design patterns, leading to a better information system design.

The paper is organized as follows. Section 2 briefly reviews conceptual modelling quality and patterns research. Section 3 presents our knowledge-based approach including the underlying meta-model. Section 4 defines more precisely the content of quality patterns and design patterns. Section 5 illustrates our proposal for quality patterns driven in conceptual modelling. It combines quality goals, quality patterns, and design patterns in order to guide the conceptual modelling process. Finally, Section 6 presents the limitations and conclusions.

2 State of the Art

The issue of quality in conceptual modelling can be related at least to two problems: 1) quality evaluation, which includes quality definition and quality measurement, and 2) quality improvement. In this paper we propose to step forward by referring to a common concept: the pattern. This literature review is therefore composed of two main parts. First we summarize the findings in conceptual modelling quality. Then we synthesize the main results related to the application of patterns in information system design.

Quality in conceptual modelling has attracted much attention for more than ten years. [1] has laid the foundations allowing computer scientists i) to isolate the specificity of conceptual modelling quality vs. software quality, and ii) to clearly differentiate between quality goals and quality means. [2] provided a comprehensive state-of-the-art and argued that it is time to propose an international standard for evaluating the quality of conceptual modelling, in the same way as ISO/IEC 9126 has defined a framework for evaluating the quality of software products. We have proposed a framework enabling the evaluation of conceptual model quality according to three viewpoints: the designer, the user, and the developer. Each viewpoint is associated with a set of quality attributes which can be measured using several metrics [3]. These metrics have been validated through a survey to which have taken part 120 computer professionals [4]. Numerous meta-models have been presented to define quality concepts and to implement them [5,6].

Patterns originated as an architectural concept by Alexander [7]. In computer science, they have been applied to programming by [8]. However, we argue that their main impact has been achieved later with design patterns. Reuse of design patterns when building software is now admitted as a way to improve software reusability and maintainability [9]. A design pattern encapsulates a proven solution for a class of recurring design problems. Gamma distinguishes between creational, structural, and behavioural patterns. They respectively cope with class instantiation, class and object composition, and communication between objects. Research about patterns is orientated towards: i) the definition of patterns' catalogues (see for example [10,11]), ii) the use of patterns [12,13,14,15,16], and iii) the evaluation of patterns [17,18]. To the best of our knowledge, quality patterns are only introduced in [19]. In this paper, quality frames are proposed to capture experience in the context of quality improvement. These frame instantiations are called quality patterns. The latter inherit from the Goal/Question/Metric model: the goal expresses what should be investigated to measure quality and why, the questions are derived, and the related metrics define how to perform the investigation [20]. A quality pattern is divided into three major parts: i) the classification of the experience expressed through a number of attributes, ii) the description of the problem, its solution, and the context, iii) the explanation part.

In this paper, we propose to reconcile quality patterns and design patterns in the same approach where quality patterns encapsulate quality evaluation experience whereas design patterns tend to represent best practices in conceptual modelling. This approach is described in the next section.

3   The Quality Driven Approach

As it has been mentioned in Section 2, there are plenty of design patterns available in the literature. However, conceptual designers can be confused in the process of choosing the design patterns relevant to their problems. Some guidance is needed. Our approach aims at facilitating their choice by linking design patterns to quality patterns. Our knowledge base contains two types of information: knowledge about quality and knowledge related to design. Quality patterns are organized as trees whose roots are quality goals refined in quality attributes and, at the lower level, in quality metrics. Design patterns are those available in the literature. Our approach encompasses a quality pattern-driven process allowing the IS conceptual modeler to dynamically link quality patterns and design patterns (Figure 1). These dynamic links are represented by a meta-model described below.

The quality meta-model presented in Figure 2 describes the main concepts used in our approach and related to the evaluation of a modeling element, such as a UML class diagram, a use case, etc.. A *quality attribute* is a quality property to be achieved. It can be characterized by a set of sub characteristics that can be considered as refined quality attributes. Quality attributes could influence positively or negatively other quality attributes. For example, adding explicit knowledge in a conceptual schema generates new modeling elements. These elements will probably increase the expressiveness of the schema, but they will probably decrease its simplicity. Consequently, the "expressiveness" quality attribute influences another quality attribute, "simplicity" in this example.

A *quality goal* describes a high level intention regarding the quality of the specified system. This goal could be achieved by examining the specification at hand considering several quality attributes. For example, if we consider the following quality goal "*improve specification understandability*", we probably have to examine quality attributes such as readability, complexity, degree of documentation, etc.

A *quality metric* permits to measure the degree to which a conceptual model satisfies a quality goal. A quality attribute can be associated with several metrics. For example, the simplicity of a UML class diagram could be measured as the number of classes, the number of associations, the number of attributes, etc. More details on metrics are given in [21,3,22].

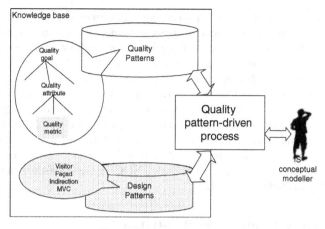

Fig. 1. The knowledge base

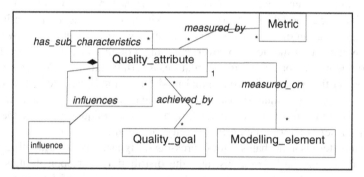

Fig. 2. The quality meta-model

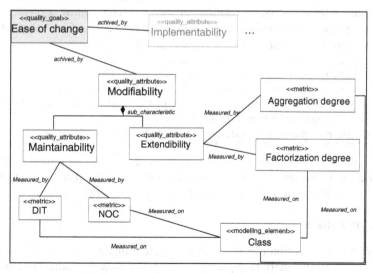

Fig. 3. Instantiation of the quality meta-model

A partial instantiation of the quality meta-model described above is presented in Figure 3. It illustrates the achievement refinement related to the quality goal "ease of change". The instantiation proposes two quality attributes allowing this achievement namely "Modifiability" and "Understandability". The "Modifiability" quality goal is decomposed into two sub characteristics, namely "maintainability" and "extendibility".

The objective of modifiability is to provide a system with a structure that can be adapted with a minimal effort to either maintain the current solutions improving their effectiveness ("maintainability") or to extend the system for future needs ("extendibility").

Several metrics related to the measure of maintainability are available in the literature. As an example, the DIT metric (Depth in Inheritance Tree) measures the position of a class in an inheritance tree, whereas the NOC metric measures the number of children directly related to a class [21].

4   Quality Patterns and Design Patterns

A pattern could be seen as a mean to package experience in order to reuse it in similar contexts. The meta-model presented in the previous section and its instantiation enable the capitalization of the knowledge about quality attributes and the way to measure them by the use of metrics. However, applying a quality oriented approach during the development of a conceptual model requires a certain expertise. Moreover, having information on the quality of a conceptual model is not sufficient to improve it. Our objective is to propose a quality pattern concept and structure to package the knowledge about i) the quality goals to achieve, ii) a set of techniques enabling the evaluation, and iii) a set of metrics supporting quality measurements.

A design pattern is a mechanism for expressing design structures. It identifies classes, instances, their roles, collaborations, and the distribution of responsibilities [23]. A pattern is supposed to capture the essential structure of a successful family of proven solutions to a recurring problem that arises within a certain context. Each pattern has a three-part rule, which expresses a relation between a certain context, a problem, and a solution. We propose to use the following outline that has become fairly standard within the software community to structure both quality and design patterns.

Name: a significant name summarizing the pattern objective.
Context: characterization of the situation in which the pattern applies.
Problem: description of the problem to solve or the challenge to be addressed.
Solution: the recommendation to solve the problem.
Related patterns: patterns that are closely related to the one described.

In the following section we will concentrate mainly on the description of the **solution** part as it is the essence of our contribution. For the other elements (**name**, **context** and **problem**) we suggest to use simple textual descriptions.

4.1   Quality Pattern

We describe in this section our proposal to structure quality patterns. The objective we assign to a quality pattern is to package an experience in the domain of conceptual modeling quality evaluation.

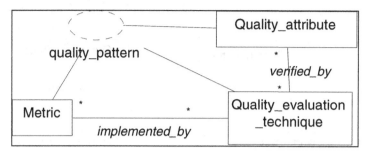

Fig. 4. The quality pattern: solution part structure

In order to define the concept of quality pattern, we need to define more precisely the solution part. The solution part should help in the evaluation of a specification according to a target quality attribute. As depicted in Figure 4, the solution involves three concepts: the quality attribute, the quality evaluation technique, and finally the metric.

The concepts of *quality attribute* and *metric* have been defined in the meta-model section. *A quality evaluation technique* also called *a means* is defined as *how* to achieve a quality goal [1]. For example, to verify whether a conceptual model is easy to maintain (maintainability quality attribute), we could use several evaluation techniques such as static analysis, dynamic analysis, data mining, etc.

Static analysis is a set of techniques for analyzing coupling in a given specification based on strictly structural criteria. These techniques as well as the ones related to dynamic coupling have been validated in several studies [24,25] as enabling to prove the impact of coupling on maintainability.

Dynamic analysis proposes to study coupling during run-time sessions [26].

Data mining techniques propose the usage of data mining to explore industrial software source code in order to understand it and to evaluate its maintainability [27].

We can therefore instantiate the quality pattern described in Figure 4 as follows:

Quality attribute: Maintainability
Quality evaluation techniques: static analysis, dynamic analysis, data mining,
Metrics: size evaluation (lines of code, number of classes, etc.), cohesion metrics, coupling metrics, etc.

4.2 Design Pattern

In this section, we propose to enrich the concept of design pattern to make its relationship with quality pattern more explicit.

The structure presented in Figure 5 suggests making more explicit the relationship between a design pattern and the underlying modelling principles. Indeed, it is largely agreed that design patterns are just object-oriented design principles [28] and that patterns lead to quality as they are based on good, agreed and proven principles.

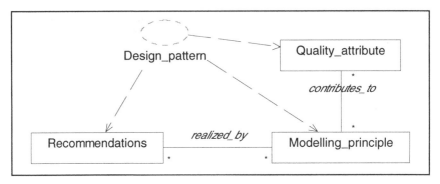

Fig. 5. The design pattern: solution part structure

The *recommendations* represent the proven solution captured in well known design patterns as objects, their collaborations and their responsibilities. The *modelling principle* explicitly represents the "good" modeling practice applied in the pattern. This principle contributes to the achievement of a given quality represented by some *quality attributes*.

For example, let's consider the "Indirection pattern" from [28]. The problem addressed by this pattern is the one of reducing direct coupling with objects which are subject to change. The solution proposes to use an intermediate object to mediate between other objects. We can find an application of this pattern in several cases, for example the use case control object, the controller object in the MVC framework, etc.

In reality, this pattern only supports well-known modelling principles such as modularity and low coupling. Moreover, we know that a modular system is easier to maintain, which means that finally, the "indirection pattern" could be a solution to be proposed problem if the value of a given specification regarding the "maintainability" quality attribute is evaluated as low.

5   Quality Pattern Driven Conceptual Modelling Process

In this section we detail the way we combine the knowledge contained in the quality meta-model, our quality patterns, and the design patterns extracted from the literature, in order to guide information systems designers and more precisely conceptual modellers.

Our approach is summarized in Figure 6. It consists of an iterative process containing three main phases respectively *quality attributes specification, quality measurement,* and *quality improvement* phases.

5.1   Quality Attributes Specification Phase

The objective of the first phase is to guide IS modellers formulating their quality goals in terms of quality attributes. This phase is composed of two activities: the definition by the modeller of the quality goal to be achieved and the identification of the quality attributes to be evaluated.

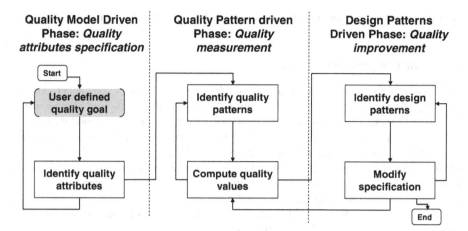

Fig. 6. The quality driven modelling process

For example, let's consider the following user defined quality goal: "obtain a schema easy to change". This goal is vague and must be converted to precise quality attributes, such as "modifiability" for example. This task could be performed by the mean of a set of questions or could be guided by providing the modeler with a list of predefined quality attributes. Each of the latter is accompanied by useful explanations helping in the selection of the suitable set of quality attributes to evaluate. The iteration proposed between the two activities of this phase allows the refinement and/or the redefinition of the quality goal according to the quality attributes suggested to the user.

5.2 Quality Measurement Phase

During this phase, our process helps matching the quality attributes, identified during the precedent phase, to a set of quality patterns. The IS modeller has the choice to select part or all of them. He/she is assisted during this choice by the description contained in each pattern (problem solved, context of application, summary of the solution supported, etc.).

Once the quality attribute has been identified, the quality driven process suggests defining it more precisely using the associated sub characteristics. The reason is due to the fact that patterns are defined at the lowest level of quality attributes refinement tree. At this last level, the objective is to associate metrics to those attributes.

For example, let's consider the *modifiability* quality attribute as the one selected during the first phase. The decomposition of this quality attribute into its sub characteristics suggests two more precise quality attributes that are "maintainability" and "extendibility" (see Figure 3).

If we suppose that the IS modeller is more interested in evaluating the maintainability of his/her specification, the knowledge encapsulated in this quality pattern provides him/her with a set of evaluation techniques enabling the measurement of a set of metrics relevant to maintainability. The instantiation of the pattern on the specification in hand will restrict the set of proposed alternative solutions. Indeed, each evaluation technique has a specific context in which it could be applied. For example, the dynamic analysis technique could be applied only if programming code is available.

5.3 Quality Improvement Phase

Let's consider again the maintainability quality attribute. One of the object oriented principles directly related to maintainability is "don't speak to strangers" also known as the law of Demeter [29]. This principle also supports encapsulation and modularity.

There are several design patterns based on these principles. The *indirection* pattern from [28], the *visitor,* or the *Façade* GoF patterns [23] are some examples. Of course, all these patterns are not suitable for all the situations nor they are applicable at each level of detail. The objective of our quality process is to include some guidelines to assist IS modellers choosing the right pattern to use.

Once the design pattern is selected, it will include in its solution part a set of advises on how to restructure the specification.

The quality process depicted in Figure 6 includes a potential iteration on the design pattern identification enabling a successive evaluation of several design patterns. It also gives the possibility to reevaluate the quality of the specification in order to verify whether it has been improved.

5.4 A quality Driven Scenario

As an illustration of our quality pattern-driven process, we present below a scenario.

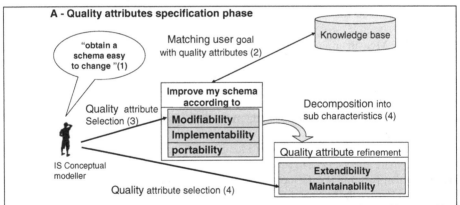

First of all, a conceptual modeller provides the following quality goal to achieve on his conceptual specification: "obtain a schema easy to change". We suppose that the word "change" in the goal expression leads the process to propose him/her a set of quality attributes related to change management: "modifiability", "implementability" and "portability". Each of these quality attributes is associated with an explanation helping the modeller to select the attribute corresponding to his/her needs.

The next step (corresponding to the curved arrow in phase A) results from the decomposition of the "modifiability" quality attribute into its sub-characteristics. The selection of the "maintainability" quality attribute corresponds to the end of this first phase.

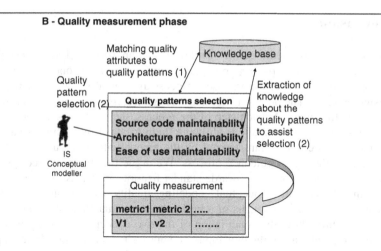

During this phase, the quality process allows us to match the "maintainability" quality attribute into three quality patterns extracted from the knowledge base, more specifically from the solution part of all quality patterns.

Let's suppose that the modeller selects the "architecture maintainability" quality pattern. The next step is the measurement of quality using the metrics defined in this pattern leading to a set of quality values provided to the modeller.

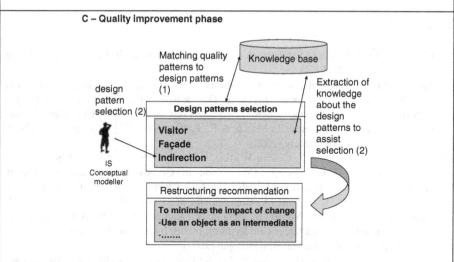

Finally, a set of design patterns corresponding to the quality pattern chosen and used during the precedent phase is proposed to the modeller. Let's suppose that he/she decides to choose the "indirection" pattern (based on the explanations available in the pattern). During the next step, restructuring recommendations are provided in order to improve the specification in hand.

At this stage, the modeller could either be satisfied by the result or decide to reevaluate the quality of his/her specification or decide to reject the recommendations provided by the process.

6 Conclusions

In this paper, we proposed a quality pattern-driven approach helping conceptual designers to choose design patterns potentially improving their conceptual models. In order to guide their choice, we propose a process dynamically linking quality patterns and design patterns. The quality is defined through a refinement process starting from high level quality goals. At each step of the process, the modellers are provided with explanations and recommendations allowing them to make their choices easily. Our main contribution can be characterized by the reconciliation of quality patterns and design patterns through a guidance process. We argue that the proposed quality pattern concept is a step forward towards standardization or at least a federation of efforts in the domain of conceptual modeling quality evaluation. Moreover, our approach proposes basic elements of a bridge between quality evaluation and quality improvement throughout the conciliation of the two concepts of quality patterns and design patterns into a single development approach. Our quality-driven approach allows conceptual modellers to take into account quality considerations very early in the IS life cycle and in an integrated manner.

Future directions of research include a concrete validation of the approach. It includes also the development of a more comprehensive set of quality patterns. Finally, there is a need to integrate this quality approach into a CASE environment to effectively exploit the contained knowledge and assistance.

References

1. Lindland, O.I., Sindre, G., Sølvberg, A.: Understanding Quality in Conceptual Modeling. IEEE Software 11(2) (1994)
2. Moody, D.L.: Theoretical and Practical Issues in Evaluating the Quality of Conceptual Models: Current State and Future Directions. Data & Knowledge Engineering 55 (2005)
3. Si-Saïd Cherfi, S., Akoka, J., Comyn-Wattiau, I.: From EER to UML Conceptual Modeling Quality. In: Spaccapietra, S., March, S.T., Kambayashi, Y. (eds.) ER 2002. LNCS, vol. 2503. Springer, Heidelberg (2002)
4. Si-Saïd Cherfi, S., Akoka, J., Comyn-Wattiau, I.: Perceived vs. Measured Quality of Conceptual Schemas: An Experimental Comparison. In: Grundy, J., Hartmann, S., Laender, A.H.F., Maciaszek, L., Roddick, J.F. (eds.) ER 2007. CRPIT, vol. 83, pp. 185–190 (2007)
5. Akoka, J., Berti, L., Boucelma, O., Bouzeghoub, M., Comyn-Wattiau, I., Cosquer, M., Goasdoue, V., Kedad, Z., Nugier, S., Peralta, V., Si-Saïd Cherfi, S.: A Framework for Quality Evaluation in Data Integration Systems. In: 9th International Conference on Enterprise Information Systems, Madeira, Portugal (2007)
6. Kolb, R., Bayer, J., Gross, H.-G., van Baelen, S.: Pattern-Based Architecture Analysis and Design of Embedded Software Product Lines. Empress Project Report D.2.1/D.2.2 (2003), http://www.empress-itea.org
7. Alexander, C., Ishikawa, S., Silverstein, M., Jacobson, M., Fiksdahl-King, I., Angel, S.: A Pattern Language: Towns, Buildings, Construction. Oxford University Press, New York (1977)
8. Beck, K., Cunningham, W.: Using Pattern Languages for Object-Oriented Programs. In: OOPSLA 1987 workshop on the Specification and Design for Object-Oriented Programming (1987)

9. Gamma, E., Helm, R., Johnson, R., Vlissides, J.: Design Patterns: Elements of Reusable Object-Oriented Software. Addison Wesley, Reading (1995)
10. Zdun, U., Avgeriou, P.: A Catalog of Architectural Primitives for Modeling Architectural Patterns. Information and Software Technology 50, 1003–1034 (2008)
11. Girardi, R., Marinho, L.B., Ribeiro de Oliveria, I.: A System of Agent-Based Software Patterns for User Modelling Based on Usage Mining. Interacting with Computers 17 (2005)
12. Kouskouras, K.G., Chatzigeorgiou, A., Stephanides, G.: Facilitating Software Extension with Design Patterns and Aspect-Oriented Programming. J. Systems and Software (2008)
13. Berdun, L., Pace, J.A.D., Amandi, A., Campo, M.: Assisting Novice Software Designers by an Expert Designer Agent. Expert Systems with Applications 34 (2005)
14. Tryfonas, T., Kearney, B.: Standardising Business Application Security Assessments with Pattern-Driven Audit Automations. Computer Standards & Interfaces 30 (2008)
15. Bass, L., John, B.E.: Linking Usability to Software Architecture Patterns through General Scenarios. J. Systems and Software 66 (2003)
16. Kim, D.K., El Khawand, C.: An Approach to Precisely Specifying the Problem Domain of Design Patterns. J. Visual Languages and Computing 18 (2007)
17. Hsueh, N.L., Chu, P.H., Chu, W.: A Quantitative Approach for Evaluating the Quality of Design Patterns. J. Systems and Software (2008)
18. Chatzigeorgiou, A., Tsantalis, N., Deligiannis, I.: An Empirical Study on Students' Ability to Comprehend Design Patterns. Computers & Education (2007)
19. Houdek, F., Kempter, H.: Quality Patterns – An Approach to Packaging Software Engineering Experience. ACM Software Engineering Notes 22 (1997)
20. Basili, V.R., Caldiera, G., Rombach, H.: Goal Question Metric Paradigm. In: Encyclopedia of Software Engineering, vol. 1. John Wiley & Sons, New York (1994)
21. Chidamber, S.R., Kemerer, C.F.: A Metrics Suite for Object Oriented Design. IEEE Trans. Softw. Eng. 20(6), 476–493 (1994)
22. Genero, M., Poels, G., Piattini, M.: Defining and Validating Metrics for Assessing the Understandability of Entity-Relationship Diagrams. Data Knowl. Eng. 64(3), 534–557 (2008)
23. Gamma, E., Helm, R., Johnson, R.E., Vlissides, J.M.: Design Patterns: Abstraction and Reuse of Object-Oriented Design. In: Nierstrasz, O. (ed.) ECOOP 1993. LNCS, vol. 707, pp. 406–431. Springer, Heidelberg (1993)
24. Li, W., Henry, S.: Object-Oriented Metrics that Predict Maintainability. J. Systems and Software 23(2), 111–122 (1993)
25. Basili, V.R., Briand, L.C., Melo, W.L.: A Validation of Object-Oriented Design Metrics as Quality Indicators. IEEE Trans. Software Engineering 22(10), 751–761 (1996)
26. Arisholm, E., Briand, L.C., Føyen, A.: Dynamic Coupling Measurement for Object-Oriented Software. IEEE Trans. Software Engineering 30(8), 491–506 (2004)
27. Kanellopoulos, Y., Dimopulos, T., Tjortjis, C., Makris, C.: Mining Source Code Elements for Comprehending Object-Oriented Systems and Evaluating their Maintainability. SIGKDD Explor. Newsl. 8(1) (2006)
28. Larman, C.: Applying UML and Patterns: an Introduction to Object-Oriented Analysis and Design and the Unified Process, 2nd edn. Prentice Hall, Englewood Cliffs (2001)
29. Lieberherr, K., Holland, H., Riel, A.: Object-Oriented Programming: an Objective Sense of Style. In: OOPSLA 1988 Proceedings (1988)

Automating the Extraction of Rights and Obligations for Regulatory Compliance

Nadzeya Kiyavitskaya[1], Nicola Zeni[1], Travis D. Breaux[2], Annie I. Antón[2],
James R. Cordy[4], Luisa Mich[3], and John Mylopoulos[1]

[1] Dept. of Information Engineering and Computer Science,
University of Trento, Italy
{nadzeya,nzeni,jm}@disi.unitn.it
[2] Dept. of Computer Science,
North Carolina State University, U.S.A.
{tdbreaux,aianton}@ncsu.edu
[3] Dept. of Computer and Management Sciences, University of Trento, Italy
luisa.mich@unitn.it
[4] School of Computing, Queens University, Kingston, Canada
cordy@cs.queensu.ca

Abstract. Government regulations are increasingly affecting the
security, privacy and governance of information systems in the United
States, Europe and elsewhere. Consequently, companies and software developers are required to ensure that their software systems comply with
relevant regulations, either through design or re-engineering. We previously proposed a methodology for extracting stakeholder requirements,
called rights and obligations, from regulations. In this paper, we examine
the challenges to developing tool support for this methodology using the
Cerno framework for textual semantic annotation. We present the results
from two empirical evaluations of a tool called "Gaius T." that is implemented using the Cerno framework and that extracts a conceptual model
from regulatory texts. The evaluation, carried out on the U.S. HIPAA
Privacy Rule and the Italian accessibility law, measures the quality of
the produced models and the tool's effectiveness in reducing the human
effort to derive requirements from regulations.

1 Introduction

In Canada, Europe and the United States, regulations set industry-wide rules for
organizational information practices [1]. Aligning information systems requirements with regulations constitutes a problem of major importance for organizations. These regulations are written in legal language, colloquially referred to
as *legalese*, which makes acquiring requirements a difficult task for software developers who lack proper training [2]. In this paper, we focus on the challenges
software engineers face in analyzing regulatory rules, called rights and obligations. If engineers misinterpret these sentences, for example by overlooking an
exception or condition in a regulatory rule, incorrect rights or obligations may be

Q. Li et al. (Eds.): ER 2008, LNCS 5231, pp. 154–168, 2008.

conferred to some stakeholders. Thus, extracting requirements from regulations is a major challenge in need of methodological aids and tools.

The tool-supported process that we envision for extracting requirements from regulations consists of three steps: (1) text is annotated to identify fragments describing actors, rights, obligations, etc.; (2) a semantic model is constructed from these annotations; and (3) the semantic model is transformed into a set of functional and nonfunctional requirements. The first two steps are currently supported by Breaux and Antón's systematic, manual methodology for acquiring legal requirements from regulations [3], [2], [4]. In this process, the requirements engineer marks the text using phrase heuristics and a frame-based model [5], [3] to identify rights or obligations, associated constraints, and condition keywords including natural language conjunctions [2]. These rights and obligations may be restated into restricted natural language statements [2], after which the rules can be modeled in Description Logic using the Semantic Parameterization process [4]. This Description Logic model can be queried and analyzed for ambiguities and conflicts [4]. Our work seeks to add tool support to this process to improve productivity, quality and consistency in the first step of the output. To achieve this goal, we adopt the Cerno framework [6] for semantic annotation. The framework initially requires the construction of linguistic markers to identify various concepts, on the basis of which it provides automated assistance to engineers.

The Cerno framework has been extended to deal with some of the complexities of regulatory text. The resulting extension is a new tool called *Gaius T.*[1] The contributions of this paper are to present Gaius T. with an empirical evaluation that compares performance of Gaius T. with the performance of human analysts using two regulatory documents written in different languages: the U.S. Health Insurance Portability and Accountability Act (HIPAA) Privacy Rule [7] and the Italian accessibility law (the Stanca Act) [8]. These contributions expand upon a short paper [9], in which we first outlined our preliminary research plan and first experiment with Gaius T.

The remainder of the paper is organized as follows. Section 2 discusses specific challenges that must be addressed by any tool supported process in the domain of regulations and policies, including Gaius T. In Section 3, we describe the Cerno annotation framework and introduce the new tool-supported process with Gaius T. Section 4 presents the design and evaluation through two case studies, with related work appearing in Section 5 and our conclusion in Section 6.

2   Complexity of Regulatory Texts

A number of challenges complicate the automated annotation of regulatory texts. For example, U.S. federal regulations are highly structured and written

---

[1] Named after Gaius Terentilius Harsa, a plebeian tribune who played an instrumental role in establishing the first formal code of laws through the Twelve Tablets in ancient Rome (462BC) (http://en.wikipedia.org/wiki/Terentilius)

in legalese. Despite this structure, the conventions of legalese are not always used consistently, there are intended and unintended ambiguities, and individual requirements are described across multiple sentences and paragraphs using cross-references. We now discuss several of these challenges.

Legalese written in different languages and by different legislatures introduce variability that must be addressed by automated tools. For example, the Italian language uses more accents and apostrophes than the English language, which affects how tools recognize important phrases. Similarly, Italian and English use different natural language grammars to express rights and obligations. In addition, the U.S. HIPAA Privacy Rule and the Italian Stanca Act use different document structures that affect the identification of rights and obligations. As a result, text processing tools that employ rules based on keywords, phrases and syntax cannot be naively adapted to other languages and jurisdictions without addressing these important issues.

In regulations, individual requirements can be elaborated in multiple sentences, intermixed into a single sentence or distributed across multiple paragraphs. For example, the HIPAA paragraph 164.528(a)(2)(ii) contains three sub-paragraphs (A), (B), and (C) in one sentence: "the covered entity must:(A)...;(B)...; and (C)...", in which each sub-paragraph describes a separate, obligated action. This hierarchical sub-paragraph structure presents several traceability challenges that our tool addresses by either identifying the subject from an encapsulating paragraph that relates to requirements stated in sub-paragraphs or by identifying which phrase fragments relate to a requirement in an encapsulating paragraph.

Cross-references to other regulations is further complicate matters. These cross-references elaborate [3], [2] and prioritize requirements [3] and may be difficult to disambiguate because cross-references can appear to be syntactically circular. For instance, HIPAA paragraph 164.528 (a)(2)(i) describes an obligation to suspend a right of an individual. This right is elaborated in a separate paragraph, denoted by the phrase "as provided in 164.512(d)". In paragraph 164.528(a)(2)(ii) that follows, the phrase "pursuant to paragraph (i)" refers back to the previous paragraph. Using Gaius T., each cross-reference in the document is annotated in such way that it can be browsed later using markup of the hierarchical document structure.

Finally, policies and regulations are *prescriptive* [10] rather than descriptive. Because stakeholders cannot afford to overlook regulatory requirements, a higher precision and recall for annotation or text-mining is required in this domain. We address this issue in the empirical evaluation described later in this paper.

3   Semantic Annotation Process

This section introduces the Cerno framework for semi-automatic semantic annotation and also presents the Gaius T. extension, intended specifically for the annotation of regulatory text [6].

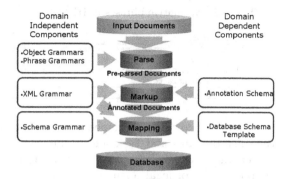

Fig. 1. Semantic annotation process in Cerno

3.1   The Cerno Framework

Cerno is based on a lightweight text analysis approach that is implemented using the structural transformation system TXL [11]. The architecture and the performance of the tool are described in detail in a previous paper [6]. To annotate input documents, Cerno uses context-free grammars to generate a parse tree before applying transformation rules, which generate output in a pre-specified format.

The process for generating semantic annotations in Cerno is based on a "design recovery" process borrowed from software reverse engineering [12]. As shown in Fig. 1, this process uses a series of successive transformation steps:

Step #1. The input document is parsed in accordance with the document structural grammar and a parse tree is produced. The parse result consists of structures such as "document", "paragraph", "phrase" and "word". The grammar is described as an ambiguous context-free TXL grammar using BNF-like notation (see an example in the next subsection in Fig. 2).

Step #2. Annotations are inferred using a domain-dependent annotation schema. This schema contains a list of tags for concepts to be identified, selected from the domain semantic model, and a vocabulary of indicators related to each concept. Cerno assumes that the annotation schema is constructed beforehand either automatically using some learning methods or manually in collaboration with domain experts. Indicator lists may include literal words (see further in Fig. 5) or names of parsed entities. They also can be *positive*, pointing to the presence of the given concept, or *negative*, pointing to the absence of this concept.

Step #3. Annotated text fragments are selected with respect to a predefined database schema template and stored in an external database. The database schema template embodies the desired output format. It is manually derived from the domain semantic model and represents fields of a target database.

Similar to Cerno, the methodology of Breaux and Antón uses a number of phrase heuristics that guide the process of identifying rights or obligations [2]. We

Table 1. Normative phrases in HIPAA

Concept type	Indicators

Right	`<actor>...</actor> may ; <actor>...</actor> can ;`
	`<actor>...</actor> could ; <policy>...</policy> permits ;`
	`<actor>...</actor> has a right to ; <actor>...</actor>`
	`should be able to`

Cross-Reference Constraint	`set by <cross-reference> ;...`

encode these heuristics into Cerno's domain-dependent components and enrich the framework with other domain- and task-specific knowledge. In this way, we can facilitate the generation of a requirements model. Moreover, we seek to formalize specific characteristics of legal documents and test the generality of our framework. The extensions to the Cerno framerwork for legal documents are further referred to as *Gaius T.*

3.2   Gaius T. for HIPAA

To evaluate Gaius T., we first annotate a fragment of the HIPAA Privacy Rule in order to identify instances of rights, obligations, and associated constraints, and then we evaluate the quality of the annotations obtained. The "objects of concern" that we annotate consist of: *right, obligation, exception*, and some types of *constraints* [2], in which a *right* is an action that a stakeholder is conditionally permitted to perform; an *obligation* is an action that a stakeholder is conditionally required to perform; a *constraint* is the part of a right or obligation that describes a single pre- or post-condition, and *exceptions* remove elements from consideration in a domain.

The manual analysis of the Privacy Rule yielded a list of normative phrases that identify many of these objects of concern [2], see examples in Table 1. All the normative phrases were employed as positive indicators in the domain-dependent indicators of Cerno's Markup step. Some of the indicators are complex patterns which combine both literal phrases and general concepts, thus assuming a preliminary recognition of several basic constructs: *cross-references* can be internal references that refer the reader of a regulation to another paragraph within the same regulation or external references, a citation of another regulation, act or law; *policy* is the name of the law, standard, act or other regulation document which establishes rights and obligations; and *actor* is an individual or an organization involved. To recognize these objects, we extended the parse step of Cerno with the corresponding object grammars.

Internal cross-references are consistently formatted throughout the Privacy Rule which results in consistent identification by the tool using a set of patterns shown in Fig. 2. However, due to the variety of reference styles used by different laws, it is necessary to extend these patterns when analyzing a new law, as we observed during our analysis of the Italian accessibility law.

To recognize instances of the actor and policy concepts, we exploit the fact that the Privacy Rule uses standard terms, called a *term-of-art*, consistently throughout the entire document. These terms are ritually defined in a separate definitions section, such as HIPAA section 160.103 titled "Definitions of HIPAA".

```
define citation
    '§ [opt space] [number] [repeat enumeration] | 'paragraph [space] [repeat enumeration]
    | 'paragraph [opt space] [decimalnumber] [repeat enumeration]
    |[decimalnumber][repeat enumeration]
end define
define enumeration
    '( [id] ') | '( [number] ')
end define
```

Fig. 2. The grammar for cross-reference object

```
Actor: ANSI, business associate(s), covered entit(y/ies), HCFA, HHS, <...>;
Policy: health information, designated record set(s), individually identifiable health
information, protected health information, psychotherapy notes; <...>;
```

Fig. 3. Indicators for basic entities

```
<Right>A <Actor>covered entity</Actor> may deny an <Actor>individual</Actor>'s
request for amendment,</Right> if it determines that the <Information>protected health
information</Information> or record that is the subject of the request:
<Index>(i)</Index> Was not created by the <Actor>covered entity</Actor>,
<Exception>unless the <Actor>individual</Actor> provides a reasonable basis to believe
that the originator of <Information>protected health information</Information> is no
longer available to <Policy>act</Policy> on the requested amendment </Exception> ...
```

Fig. 4. A fragment of the result generated by Gaius T. for HIPAA Sec.164.526

For example, it contains terms such as "policy", "business associate", "act", and "covered entity". Example indicators that are used to identify basic entities and that were derived from the definitions section are shown in Fig. 3.

In the sections that we analyzed, we found other terms that we could generalize into a common, abstract type, including event, date, and information. Thus, on the basis of the definition section, we derived a list of hyponyms for the basic entities: *actor* and *policy* as well as *event, date* and *information.*

The Gaius T. regulatory analysis process for the Privacy Rule is organized into three main phases: (1) Recognition of structural elements of the document: section boundaries, section attributes which are number and title, sentence boundaries (see [13]); (2) Identification of basic entities: actor, policy, event, date, information and cross-reference; (3) Deconstruction of a rule statement to identify its components and constraints. Fig. 4 illustrates an excerpt of annotated text from HIPAA section 164.526(a)(2) resulting from the application of Gaius T. Each embedded XML annotation is a candidate "object of concern." For instance, the "Index" annotation denotes the sub-paragraph index "(i)" and the Actor annotation denotes the "covered entity"; the latter appears twice in this excerpt.

3.3   Gaius T. for Italian Regulations

The Stanca Act [8] describes accessibility requirements governing web sites of the Italian Public Administration to ensure accessibility for the disabled. The Act includes technical requirements and general restrictions that web sites must

```
Obligation: dov[ere], è fatto obbligo, farla osservare, promuov[ere], comport[are],
costituiscono motivo di preferenza, defin[ire];
AntiObligation: non dov[ere], non sia, non si applica, non si possono stipulare, non
esprim[ere];
Right: po[sso|uoi|uò|ssiamo|tete|ssono|ssa];
AntiRight: non po[sso|uoi|uò|ssiamo|tete|ssono|ssa];
```

Fig. 5. A sample of the syntactic indicators used to identify categories in Stanca

```
Art. 10 (Regolamento di attuazione)
<Obligation>
1. <Constraint>Entro novanta giorni dalla data di entrata in vigore della presente
<Policy>legge</Policy></Constraint>, con <Policy>regolamento</Policy>emanato ai
sensi dell'articolo 17, comma 1, della <Policy>legge</Policy>23 agosto 1988, n. 400,
sono definiti:
a) i criteri e i principi operativi e organizzativi generali per l'accessibilità;
b) i <Resource>contenuti</Resource>di cui all'articolo 6, comma 2;
c) i controlli esercitabili sugli operatori privati che hanno reso nota l'accessibilità dei
propri siti e delle proprie <Resource>applicazioni</Resource>informatiche;
d) i controlli esercitabili sui <Actor>soggetti</Actor>di cui all'articolo 3, comma 1.
2. Il <Policy>regolamento</Policy>di cui al comma 1 è adottato previa consultazione
con le associazioni delle <Actor>persone disabili</Actor>maggiormente rappresentative,
con le associazioni di sviluppatori competenti in materia di accessibilità e di
produttori di <Resource>hardware</Resource>e <Resource>software</Resource>e
previa acquisizione del parere delle competenti Commissioni parlamentari,
<Constraint>che <Action>devono</Action>pronunciarsi entro quarantacinque giorni dalla
richiesta</Constraint>, e d'intesa con la Conferenza unificata di cui all'articolo 8 del
<Policy>decreto</Policy>legislativo 28 agosto 1997, n. 281.</Obligation>
```

Fig. 6. A fragment of the annotated accessibility law

respect. The annotation schema for the accessibility law contains *right, anti-right, obligation, anti-obligation, exception,* and some types of *constraints,* where *anti-rights* and *anti-obligations* state that a right or obligation is not conferred by a specific law, respectively [2].

For identification of actor instances in the Italian law, we adopted two solutions: (1) some instances were mined manually from the definition section "Definizioni"; (2) in order to acquire instances of actors not mentioned in the definitions, we exploited the results provided by a Part of Speech Tagger (POS) [14], i.e., all proper nouns we marked as actors. For resource instances, we followed only the first solution reusing the terms stated in the definition section.

In order to identify action verbs, we adopted the following heuristic: annotate all verbs in present tense, passive tense and impersonal tense. The verbs in the listed forms also refer to obligations, in accordance with the instructions for writing Italian legal documents [15]. Thus, the corresponding heuristic rule was adapted for identifying obligations.

For rights, obligations and their antitheses, it is more difficult to identify these statements in Italian than in English. For example, English modal verbs (must, may, etc.) are consistently used to state prescriptions, such as "the users must present their request," while Italian regulations use present active ("gli utenti presentano la domanda"), present passive ("la domanda è presentata") and impersonal tenses ("la domanda si presenta") of verbs to describe an obligation. The choice of the style highly depends on the individual lawmaker. Each of these styles is equally recommended by the law writing guidelines [15]. Therefore, in identification of rights and obligations, our strategy included: (1) translation of normative phrases identified for the HIPAA; (2) annotation of those sentences that contain verbs in the tenses that intrinsically express obligations as instances of obligation. A subset of the syntactic indicators for the Italian law is shown in Fig. 5 and a fragment of the annotated document in Fig. 6.

4   Empirical Evaluation

The proposed process for extracting rights and obligations was validated in a comparative evaluation that compared the number of automated annotations inferred by Gaius T. with the number of manually derived annotations. For the HIPAA Privacy Rule, we also evaluated the productivity effect of using the tool. The comparative evaluation was difficult to realize because in many cases manual and automated annotations are not comparable because the granularity of these annotations differed.

4.1   The HIPAA Document

After extending the framework as discussed in Section 3.2, we applied it to two sections of the HIPAA Privacy Rule [7]: 160 ("General Administrative Requirements") and 164 ("Security and Privacy"). Gaius T. parsed 33,788 words and required 2.79 seconds on a personal computer based upon an Intel Pentium 4, 3 GHz processor, RAM 2 Gb, running Suse Linux. This results include over 1800 basic entities and 140 rights and obligations.

Due to the lack of a gold standard (i.e., a reference annotated document to compare with), the annotation quality was evaluated manually by comparing results acquired from section 164.520 "Notice of privacy practices for protected health information". We chose this section because we can compare the Gaius T. results to the manual results reported by Breaux et al. [2]. The manual analysis by an expert analyst of the reported fragments, containing a total of 5,978 words or 17.8% of the Privacy Rule, took an average of 2.5 hours per section. The preliminary analysis of the resulting annotations for section 164.520 is summarized in Table 2. The number of rights, obligations, constraints and cross-references is reported for the manual process [2] and for Gaius T.

There are several notable distinctions that we can discuss at this stage of the analysis. Section 164.520 contains stakeholder rights whose description begins in one paragraph and continues into a sub-paragraph. The latter-half of these rights, and likewise for obligations, is called a *continuation*. Due to continuations,

Table 2. Comparative evaluation results for section 164.520 of HIPAA

	Rights	Obligations	Constraints	Cross-references
Gaius T.	12	15	5	31
Human	9	17	54	37

there are two false-positives in the number of rights and obligations reported. Furthermore, paragraphs 164.520(b)(1) and (b)(2) describe so-called "content requirements" that detail the content of privacy notices. and were not included in the number of stakeholder rights and obligations report by Breaux et al. [2]. Gaius T. identified four stakeholder rights in these two paragraphs. The total number of constraints was limited to those due to internal cross-references.

The tool correctly identified nearly all instances of the concepts actor, policy, event, information and date. It also correctly recognized section and subsection boundaries, titles and annotated paragraph indices. These annotations may be reused to manage cross-references and may provide useful input for the Semantic Parameterization process. Gaius T. largely reduces human effort and time spent for analysis by facilitating recognition of relevant text fragments.

In addition to the expert evaluation, we conducted an experiment inexperienced users using Gaius T. The goal of this study was to test the usefulness of the tool for non-experts in the regulatory text who may have to analyze such documents to generate requirements specifications for a new software system. The problem is that requirements engineers are not always supported by lawyers when designing new software. For this purpose, we selected section 164.520 of Privacy Rule for annotation by a different group of people, who are not working with rules and regulations directly. The experiment involved four junior researchers from the software engineering area, two of whom were not from the group working on the tool. We motivated the participants by paying a wage per hour of their work. All participants were non-native English speakers, received the same training in semantic annotation for one hour, but none of them had earlier participated in legal document analysis. A detailed explanation of the annotation process and examples of the concepts to be identified were available. Moreover, the participants were provided with a user-friendly interface to facilitate insertion and modification of tags in the input documents.

In this experiment, the participants were given two different parts of section 164.520 to annotate, one of which was original text and the other augmented with annotations generated by Gaius T. These parts were selected in such a way as to have an approximately equal number of statements and comprised 1,205 words and 1,057 words respectively. The annotators were asked to incrementally identify rule statements and their components in each of the two parts: first, inserting markups on the original page for the unannotated part, and second, modifying Gaius T.'s annotations in the part that was previously automatically annotated. We measured the time spent for annotation of both parts by each analyst and counted the number of different entities identified.

The quantitative results for this experiment are collected in Table 3 and include the number of entities collected by human annotators working with and without tool support. Observing this table, we notice that when annotators were assisted by Gaius T.: (a) the total number of entities identified was about 10 percent larger than when starting from the original document; however, t-test results do not allow us to claim that this improvement is statistically significant; (b) annotators were faster by about 12.3 per cent. The part of analysis that

Table 3. Number of extracted items for two fragments

	Fragment 1				Fragment 2			
	Without tool		With tool		Without tool		With tool	
	A1	A3	A2	A4	A2	A4	A1	A3
Obligations	10	2	13	13	9	12	10	13
Rights	3	9	0	2	6	4	2	1
Anti-Obligations	1	0	2	1	0	0	0	0
Anti-Rights	1	2	1	1	0	0	3	2
Constraints	36	23	18	16	36	32	41	19
Actors	45	14	56	19	22	11	17	50
Actions	25	14	27	18	28	22	24	44
Resources	32	34	29	14	22	14	31	27
Targets	1	5	4	0	9	10	11	5
Totals	154	103	150	84	132	105	139	161
Time in min	58	28	63	21	61	45	42	36

the annotators found the most complicated and time-consuming was relating constraints contained in a rule statement to their corresponding subjects.

The evaluation results obtained thus far look promising, but larger studies must be conducted to prove the observed improvement is statistically significance. Most important, unlike human annotations, automatic annotations are more consistent and much faster, and thus show promise as the technology improves. Nevertheless, as a result of our experimental study, we observed a number of current limitations of Gaius T. that should be addressed in future development of the tool:

- Additional types of constraints should be considered. The reason for missing some of constraints is that normative phrases for them are not explicitly provided by the manual methodology. Therefore the future development of the tool should involve revision of the annotation schema and indicators.
- Another problematic aspect in analyzing regulatory texts is that the concepts expressing constraints require correctly identifying the subject or object to which these constraints apply. This task is difficult for human analysts, especially if related fragments are scattered over a long statement. However, Gaius T. can facilitate their work by identifying a constraint phrase and subject candidates and then suggest to a human to connect the given constraint to the identified object that is most relevant.
- Identification of the subjects of conjunctions or disjunctions ("and", "or") must be completed for the Semantic Parameterization process. This task is problematic even for full-fledged linguistic analysis tools. In our case, we propose to extend the tool to highlight such cases and prompt a human analyst to resolve them manually.

4.2 The Italian Accessibility Law

After extending Gaius T. with features intended to support the analysis of Italian law, we applied it to the full text of the Stanca Act, containing a total of 6,185 words. The automatic annotation required only 61 milliseconds on a personal computer Intel Pentium 4, 3 GHz processor, RAM 2 Gb, running Suse Linux.

Table 4. Quantitative evaluation summary for the accessibility law

	Actors	Actions	Resources	Policies	Obligations	Anti-obli-gations	Rights	Anti-rights	Constraints
Gaius T.	241	77	279	86	26	2	7	1	12
Human	170	55	58	3	24	2	9	0	32

As a result, a total of 683 basic entities and 36 rights and obligations were identified.

Table 4 presents the results of this evaluation, consisting of the number of instances of the concepts of interest that the tool identified compared to a single human annotator. The tool outperformed the human annotator in identifying instances of the concepts actor, policy, action, and resource. As for complex concepts, the tool identified nearly all instances of rights and obligations, however the performance was essentially lower for the constraint concept.

There were difficulties in analyzing the Italian text for both the human annotator and the tool that emerged in this study. For example, the subject is frequently omitted, as in passive forms of verbs, or hidden by using impersonal expressions, thus making it difficult to correctly classify phrases in the regulatory fragment and find the bearer of a right or obligation. Surprisingly, the official English translation of the accessibility law in most cases explicitly states this information. Consider the use of verb phrases (in bold) to state the obligation in Italian and English versions of the same fragment, below:

Italian statement: *"Nelle procedure svolte dai soggetti di cui all'articolo 3, comma 1, per l'acquisto di beni e per la fornitura di servizi informatici, i requisiti di accessibilità stabiliti con il decreto di cui all'articolo 11* **costituiscono motivo di preferenza** *a parità di ogni altra condizione nella valutazione dell'offerta tecnica, tenuto conto della destinazione del bene o del servizio."*

English translation: *"The subjects mentioned in article 3, when carrying out procedures to buy goods and to deliver services,* **are obliged***, in the event that they are adjudicating bidders which all have submitted similar offers, to give preference to the bidder which offers the best compliance with the accessibility requirements provided for by the decree mentioned in article 11."*

Overall, the annotation results suggest that the Gaius T. process for regulation analysis is applicable to documents that are written in different languages. The effort required to adapt the framework for the new application was relatively small with respect to the implementation. This experiment also revealed several language differences that we were able to quantify using Gaius T. In our future work we plan to conduct a more extensive analysis that may remove other language effects independently from legislator effects.

5 Related Work

The idea of using contextual patterns or keywords to identify relevant information in prescriptive documents is not new. A number of methodologies based on similar techniques have been developed. However, tools to realize and synthesize these methods under a single framework are lacking. This review does not claim to be an exhaustive survey and we focus only on several works that are most related to our method with respect to the problem considered and our approach used.

The SACD system [16] relates well to our approach. The tool, implemented in Prolog, uses a combination of syntactic parsing and keyword-based rules, that rely on the regularity of prescriptive documents, to generate a knowledge base from the logical structure of regulatory text. Once the processing is completed, SACD requires attention of the human specialist in revising the results provided. Similar to Gaius T., SACD recognizes several layers in prescriptive texts: the structural layer, called *macrostructure*; the logical layer, called *microstructure*; and the *domain* layer describing domain-specific information.

Cleland-Huang et al. [17] suggested an algorithm for detection and classification of non-functional requirements (NFRs). In a pilot experiment, the indicator terms were mined from catalogs of operationalization methods for security and performance softgoal interdependency graphs and then used to identify NFRs in requirements specifications. Along similar lines, the EA-Miner [18] tool supports separation of aspectual and non-aspectual concerns and their relationships by applying natural language processing techniques to requirements documents. The identification criteria in EA-Miner is based on a domain specific lexicon that was built observing related words. Similarly to these methods, we use normative phrases to identify the presence of regulatory requirements. However, our tool further recognizes the paragraph structure of regulatory text, which is necessary to acquire complete requirements from across continuations. The challenge of continuations cannot be addressed by indicator terms alone. Antón proposed the Goal-Based Requirements Acquisition Methodology (GBRAM) to manually extract goals from natural language documents, including financial and healthcare privacy policies [19]. Additional analysis of these extracted goals led to new semantics for modeling goals [20], which distinguish rights and obligations, and new heuristics for extracting these artifacts from text [2]. These heuristics have been combined into a frame-based method for manually acquiring legal requirements and priorities from regulations [3]. As discussed in this paper, our tool incorporates several of these heuristics to identify rights and obligations.

Wilson et al. [21] performed a detailed analysis of NASA requirements documents to identify recommendations for writing clearer specifications. As a part of this work, the authors discovered that good requirements specifications use imperative verbs (shall, must, etc.) to explicitly state requirements, constraints or capabilities. They also introduced the notion of *continuances*, i.e., additional phrases that refine upon previously stated requirements. We observed similar findings in language regularities in prescriptive documents that were incorporated into our set of heuristics to detect requirements. We also operate with the notion of continuances, which we call continuations, across sub-paragraphs.

6   Conclusions

Regulations and policies constitute rich sources of requirements for software systems that must comply with these normative documents. In order to facilitate alignment of software system requirements and regulations, systematic methods and tools automating regulations analysis must be developed.

In [2], Breaux and Antón proposed a methodology for extracting stakeholder requirements from regulations. This paper presents a tool intended to provide automatic support for analyzing policy documents. The new tool-supported process - named Gaius T. - exploits the findings of our earlier work on requirements analysis, and exploits the Cerno framework to yield annotations marking instances of concepts found in regulation texts. These instances include rights and obligations that must be incorporated into software requirements to comply with the law. Our envisioned process fits into a broader context, in which a requirements engineer or other analyst must integrate requirements from multiple regulations that affect a single product, service or system. We reserve this broader integration challenge for future work and our current focus remains on the immediate challenge of correctly identifying requirements from regulations.

To verify to what extent the semantic annotation tool can be applied to the domain of regulatory texts, we devised two empirical studies, involving annotation of a fragment of the U.S. HIPAA regulations and the Italian accessibility law, and compared the performance of the tool with manual identification of instances of rights, obligations, and associated constraints. The results of this study are encouraging, and have also revealed a number of useful extensions for the tool and the tool-supported process. The phrase heuristics used are now extended for documents in English and Italian. We believe that our tool supported process can be re-used in regulations developed for different areas of human activity due to its modularity.

We are interested in developing reasoning facilities on the annotations using constraints of the domain meta-model, for instance, cardinality constraints. Apart from the regulation compliance problem, another potential application of this work may be in providing support to lawmakers in writing regulations in terms of improved consistency and reduced ambiguity for use by engineers. We believe that semi-automated tools such as the one proposed in this paper can be effectively used to improve the overall quality of rules and regulations at many levels.

Acknowledgments

This work has been funded, in part, by the EU Commission through the SERENITY project, the Natural Sciences and Engineering Research Council of Canada, Provincia Autonoma di Trento through the STAMPS project and the U.S. National Science Foundation ITR #032-5269.

References

1. Berghel, H.: The two sides of 'ROI': Return-on-investment vs. risk-of-incarceration. Communications of ACM 48(4), 15–20 (2005)
2. Breaux, T.D., Vail, M.W., Antón, A.I.: Towards regulatory compliance: Extracting rights and obligations to align requirements with regulations. In: Proc. of RE 2006, Washington, DC, USA, pp. 46–55. IEEE Computer Society Press, Los Alamitos (2006)
3. Breaux, T.D., Antón, A.I.: Analyzing regulatory rules for privacy and security requirements. IEEE Transactions on Software Engineering 34(1), 5–20 (2008)
4. Breaux, T.D., Antón, A.I., Doyle, J.: Semantic parameterization: A process for modeling domain descriptions. ACM Transactions on Software Engineering Methodology 18(2) (2009)
5. Breaux, T.D., Anton, A.I.: A systematic method for acquiring regulatory requirements: A frame-based approach. In: Proc. of RHAS-6, Pittsburgh, PA, USA, September 2007, Software Engineering Institute (SEI) (2007)
6. Kiyavitskaya, N., Zeni, N., Mich, L., Cordy, J.R., Mylopoulos, J.: Text mining through semi automatic semantic annotation. In: Reimer, U., Karagiannis, D. (eds.) PAKM 2006. LNCS (LNAI), vol. 4333, pp. 143–154. Springer, Heidelberg (2006)
7. U.S.A. Government: Standards for privacy of individually identifiable health information, 45 CFR part 160, Part 164 subpart E. In Federal Register 68(34), 8334–8381, February 20 (2003)
8. Italian Parliament: Stanca Act, Law no. 4, January 9, 2004: Provisions to support the access to information technologies for the disabled. Gazzetta Ufficiale 13, January 17 (2004)
9. Kiyavitskaya, N., Zeni, N., Breaux, T.D., Antón, A.I., Cordy, J.R., Mich, L., Mylopoulos, J.: Extracting rights and obligations from regulations: Toward a tool-supported process. In: Proc. of ASE 2007, pp. 429–432 (2007)
10. Moulin, B., Rousseau, D.: Knowledge acquisition from prescriptive texts. In: Proc. 3rd Int. Conf. on Industrial and engineering applications of artificial intelligence and expert systems, pp. 1112–1121. ACM Press, New York (1990)
11. Cordy, J.R.: The TXL source transformation language. Science of Computer Programming 61(3), 190–210 (2006)
12. Dean, T.R., Cordy, J.R., Schneider, K.A., Malton, A.J.: Using design recovery techniques to transform legacy systems. In: Proc. of ICSM 2001, November 2001, pp. 622–631 (2001)
13. Zeni, N., Kiyavitskaya, N., Mich, L., Mylopoulos, J., Cordy, J.R.: A lightweight approach to semantic annotation of research papers. In: Kedad, Z., Lammari, N., Métais, E., Meziane, F., Rezgui, Y. (eds.) NLDB 2007. LNCS, vol. 4592, pp. 61–72. Springer, Heidelberg (2007)
14. Schmid, H.: Probabilistic part-of-speech tagging using decision trees. In: Proc. of Int. Conf. on New Methods in Language Processing, Manchester, UK (1994)
15. Presidenza del Consiglio dei Ministri: Guida alla redazione dei testi normativi. Gazzetta Ufficiale 101(2), 105 (2001)
16. Moulin, B., Rousseau, D.: Automated knowledge acquisition from regulatory texts. IEEE Expert 7(5), 27–35 (1992)
17. Cleland-Huang, J., Settimi, R., Zou, X., Solc, P.: The detection and classification of non-functional requirements with application to early aspects. In: Proc. of RE 2006, Washington, DC, USA, pp. 36–45. IEEE Computer Society, Los Alamitos (2006)

18. Sampaio, A., Chitchyan, R., Rashid, A., Rayson, P.: EA-Miner: a tool for automating aspect-oriented requirements identification. In: Proc. of ASE 2005, pp. 352–355. ACM Press, New York (2005)

19. Antón, A.I., Earp, J.B., He, Q., Stufflebeam, W., Bolchini, D., Jensen, C.: Financial privacy policies and the need for standardization. IEEE Security and Privacy 2(2), 36–45 (2004)

20. Breaux, T.D., Antón, A.I.: Analyzing goal semantics for rights, permissions, and obligations. In: Proc. of RE 2005, pp. 177–186 (2005)

21. Wilson, W.M., Rosenberg, L.H., Hyatt, L.E.: Automated analysis of requirement specifications. In: Proc. of ICSE 1997, May 1997, pp. 161–171. ACM Press, New York (1997)

Location-Based Software Modeling and Analysis: Tropos-Based Approach

Raian Ali, Fabiano Dalpiaz, and Paolo Giorgini

University of Trento - DISI, 38100, Povo, Trento, Italy
{raian.ali,fabiano.dalpiaz,paolo.giorgini}@disi.unitn.it

Abstract. The continuous growth of interest in mobile applications makes the concept of location essential to design and develop software systems. Location-based software is supposed to be able to monitor the surrounding location and choose accordingly the most appropriate behavior. In this paper, we propose a novel conceptual framework to model and analyze location-based software. We mainly focus on the social facets of location adopting concepts such as actor, resource, and location-based behavior. Our approach is based on Tropos methodology and allows the analyst to elicit and model software requirements according to the different locations where the software will operate. We propose an extension of Tropos modeling and adapt its process to suit well with the development of location-based software. The proposed framework also includes automated analysis techniques to reason about the relation between location and location-based software.

1 Introduction

Advances in computing, sensing and communication technology have recently led to the growth of interest in software mobility. Mobility emphasizes several concerns (space, time, personality, society, environment, and so on) often not considered by the traditional desktop systems [1]. Besides computing ubiquity, the 21st century computing [2] is expected to have a core "mental" part: computing systems act on behalf of humans executing tasks without prompting them for and receiving their explicit requests, i.e. computing will realize the concept of agency. Advances in technology do not necessarily imply the easiness of exploiting it, rather more challenges are introduced. Software systems can be given more responsibility, and they can now actively support several decision making processes. Appropriate software development methods and models need to be developed, or adapted, to cope with the new achievable innovative requirements.

Location-based software is characterized by its ability to reason about the surrounding location, including the user, and adapt autonomously a behavior that complies with the location settings. Consequently, we need to model and analyze the variable locations that users can be part of, and define how location influences software. To adopt one behavior, the software needs to reason on what exists and what can be done, basing its choice on user preferences, cost, time, priority, and so on [3].

Q. Li et al. (Eds.): ER 2008, LNCS 5231, pp. 169–182, 2008.

In the area of context modeling, the relation between context and its use is not clearly considered (e.g. [4], [5] and [6]). We believe in the tight complementary relation between the variable behavior (both human and software ones) and context. When the relation between context and its use is omitted, we cannot answer questions like *"how do we decide the relevant context?"*, *"why do we need context?"* and *"how does context influence behavior adaptation?"*. Modeling context information has not to be a standalone activity, that is context has to be elicited in conjunction with the analysis we do for discovering alternative behaviors. Salifu et al. [7] investigate the use of problem frames to handle variability in context-aware software. In our work, we use goal analysis to elicit requirements without assuming that requirements are already recognized. We also integrate the goal and location models to enable useful automated analysis.

Software variability is a term commonly used to define a software provided with different behaviors, whose variants can be produced guaranteeing low costs, short time, and high quality [8]. Feature modeling is a well known modeling technique exploited by product line engineering to derive a tailored product from a family of possible products [9]. Location-based software is expected to select *autonomously* among the different alternatives it supports depending on the location settings. Lapouchnian et al. [10] propose techniques to design autonomic software based on an extended goal modeling framework, but the relation with the surrounding location is not focused on. A variant of this approach is proposed by the same authors in [11], where the emphasis is on variability modeling under the requirements engineering perspective, and on the classification of intentional variability when decomposing a goal. In our work, we focus on the variability of location, i.e. the unintentional variability, which influences the applicability and the efficiency of each goal satisfaction alternative.

Goal models, mainly adopted by KAOS [12] and Tropos [13,14] methodologies, represent a paradigmatic shift from object orientation. While goal-oriented analysis is more natural for the early stages of requirement analysis, the object-oriented analysis fits well to the later stages [15]. With goal models, we take a high level goal and start a top-down analysis to discover the more specific subgoals and tasks that are needed to satisfy that goal. Goal model allows for different alternatives to satisfy a goal, but it does not specify *where* each alternative can be adopted. Alternative behaviors and location variability are complementary. Supporting two alternative behaviors without specifying when to follow each of them rises the question *"why do we support two alternatives and not just one?"*. Conversely, considering location variability without supporting alternative behaviors rises the question *"what can we do if the location changes?"*.

In this paper, we introduce location-based Tropos as a variant of Tropos conceptual modeling framework [13,14], for developing location-based software. We deal with the social level of location, discuss how to model it and how it influences the adaptation of a location-based behavior. We discuss Tropos process for developing location-based software, and then suggest a new variant of it. We introduce three automated analysis on the proposed models to check software against location and vice versa.

The paper is structured as follows: Section 2 discusses location-based variability and a variety of conceptual modeling challenges introduced by it, and classifies the main features the location-based software in particular has to support. In Section 3, we study Tropos conceptual modeling framework for location-based software development. In Section 4, we introduce location-based Tropos, proposing modifications on Tropos at both modeling and process levels. In Section 5, we show several kinds of analysis on the new models, and in Section 6, we draw conclusions and present future work.

2 Location Variability and Location-Based Software

One main concern of software mobility is the ability to perceive the location where the user is, and then tailor a location-based bahavior to achieve user objectives. Location-based software has not only to perceive the technical details of computing environment (communication protocols, network roaming, data interoperability, and so on), but also the social environment the user is part of. The technical level will certainly be the base to handle the low level aspects of software interoperability, related to the machine level. On the other hand, the social level will be the base for tailoring human-oriented behaviors to achieve user goals. In this work, we focus on modeling the social variability of location and how it can be used to derive suitable behaviors for satisfying user goals.

Let us consider a passenger with the goal of buying a ticket in a railway station. Each specific railway station enables different ways to buy tickets (e.g., a passenger can buy a ticket through terminals, e-pay, offices, or through passenger assistance clerks when passenger needs help). Each of these different ways requires specific location properties. For example, buying through terminals requires that a free terminal exists, has one language in common with the passenger, and accept the money or the credit card the passenger has.

In order to satisfy user's needs and goals, location-based software is supposed to be able to select one appropriate behavior according to the location. The behavior has to be compliant with the current state of the location, considering the availability of resources and the existence of other users. Location may be characterized by different dimensions, such as the degree of expertise each user has (in using resources, and communicating with other users), the availability of resources, and the rules that have to be used to coordinate the use of resources, or regulate the interactions between users. In this vision, the conceptual modeling of software system needs to deal with a variety of challenges, such as:

1. *Location modeling constructs*: We need to find an appropriate set of modeling concepts that can capture efficiently a variable location.
2. *Location relevancy*: To build a location model, we need a systematic way to decide what has to be modeled, i.e. what is relevant in a location to the target software. E.g. when we model a railway station location, do we need to include passengers current position, or expertise in using PDAs, in the model? and how do we decide that?

3. *Location rules*: Location, as a system, will impose rules for the interaction among people and for the use of resources. Rules have to be integrated with the location model and modeled using location constructs. E.g. a railway station might impose the rule that only passengers who are foreigners or over a certain age can ask for assistance, and passenger assistant must help even if this implies stoping less priority activity the assistant is involved in.

4. *Location-based behavior*: To satisfy one of the user objectives, the current location allows a certain set of behaviors. Modeling the relation between the location and the corresponding possible behaviors is essential for location-based software. E.g. buying a ticket through e-payment can be done only if the station has a network and the passenger is allowed and able to access it.

5. *Hierarchial behaviors construction*: Modeling in a way to avoid *"one location, one behavior"* enumeration, to exploit commonality of both locations and behaviors fragments, and to enable a hierarchial construction of location-based behavior. E.g. getting passenger position automatically is a shared objective that needs an automatic positioning system in the station, and this objective is needed to satisfy other objectives like guiding passengers or listing the nearest terminals that in turn is needed for buying a ticket.

6. *Location-based behaviors evaluation*: Based on some payoff functions, each behavior in each location has to be evaluated. We need to model the criteria for evaluating alternative behaviors in variable locations. E.g. when a railway station provides both terminals and e-pay, the software has to decide which one to adopt, and consequently which tasks to do. We need modeling constructs for the criteria on which such kinds of decisions can be taken.

Location-based software is supposed to support mainly five features (hierarchically represented using feature model in Fig. 1):

- *Location identification*: Representing what exists, where the mobile user is, according to a pre-defined location model, i.e. instantiating the location model. E.g. software will receive railway station description and instantiate a railway station model that reflects the current station.
- *Location-based behavior adaptation*: Having an objective, and knowing the current location, the software will reason and select a possible, and even recommended, behavior through which the user objective can be achieved. Behaviors include operational tasks that are done by software, and non-operational ones the software assists, or simply asks, user to do. To tailor a location-based behavior, the software has to support features like:
- *Location-based information processing*:
    1. *Information request*: Software enables users to request location-based information explicitly, e.g. enabling passengers to ask for the train schedule in the current railway station. Other information requests are implicitly made when location changes, e.g. when train is not in the time, certain information has to be presented to passenger.
    2. *Relevant information extraction*: Filtering what is relevant, and composing useful information. E.g. when a train is late, but it is not the

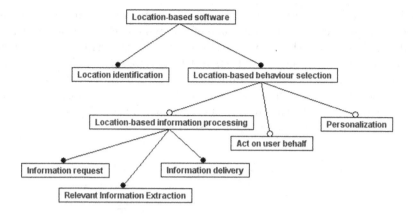

Fig. 1. Feature model for location-based software

passenger train, the warning has not to be shown. Also, when a passenger asks how to buy a ticket, and has only cash money that are not accepted by the railway station terminals, the location-based software will exclude terminals from the possible ways of buying a ticket.

3. *Information delivery*: Communicating information to the user in a right way. E.g. notifying the passenger assistant has not to be done by voice message when the assistant is using his/her PDA for a phone call. Also, a demo about using terminals should be interactive, only when the passenger has a good expertise in using PDAs.

– *Acting on behalf of user*: Location-based software will represent the user when interacting with other location actors, both in requesting and answering requests, and in using resources available in a location. E.g. when the passenger asks for a help, the help request will be prepared and sent on behalf of the passenger, including the information needed by the passenger assistant to decide how to accomplish the help.

– *Personalization*: Location-based software will behave differently with different users. Software considers user personality as one location mobility dimension. E.g. when both wireless and wired connections are available in a railway station, and the passenger prefers reliable connection, the software will lead passenger to wired connection terminal, and when passenger wants more easy connection, the software will configure wireless one.

3   Tropos for Location-Based Software

Our approach is based on Tropos methodology [13,14], which offers an agent-oriented conceptual framework for modeling both the social environment and the system-to-be. Tropos starts its software development life cycle with the *early requirements* phase. In this phase, the organization (location at the social level)

is modeled as a set of actors that strategically depend on each other for satisfying their objectives, then the rationale of satisfying each actor own objectives
is modeled. If we take the railway station scenario, the strategic dependency
between railway station actors with respect to the goal *Ticket is Issued* will be
as shown in Fig. 2. Tropos early requirement fits well to project the social structure of the location at a higher level as a set of actors and resources. Taking into
consideration a variable location, this phase will not be sufficient enough and we
will need to adapt it to deal with points such as:

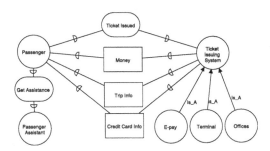

Fig. 2. A strategic dependency model for the railway station scenario

1. Tropos modeling supposes the existence of all modeled actors (terminal, e-
   pay, offices, passenger assistant), and this assumption will not hold when we
   consider a variable location, i.e. location structure is not static.
2. Tropos modeling has to consider actors and resources profiles to deal with
   several location modeling difficulties:
   (a) Tropos modeling is not able to differentiate between availability levels
       of actors and resources. In such modeling, all railway station terminals
       are equally available, but it is more useful to consider a terminal, that is
       close to the passenger, more available than a terminal which is far away.
   (b) Dependencies between actors are not required or achievable in every
       location, and we can not specify that using the rigid form of describing
       actors and resources in Tropos modeling. *Credit card info* can be required
       when *Ticket Issuing System* enables payment through credit cards, and
       when the passenger's credit card is compatible with the supported ones.
   (c) When more than one actor is available to satisfy one objective, there is
       no way to differentiate between them, and then to choose the best. If
       we consider *Terminal* and *E-Pay* as two *Ticket Issuing Systems* without
       considering their profiles and matching them with passenger profile, these
       two ticket issuing systems can not be differentiated.
3. Tropos proceeds, in the next step of early requirements phase, to analyze the
   rationale of *Ticket Issuing System* to satisfy *Ticket is Issued* goal, and that
   is not what we always need. *Ticket Issuing System* already exists, and we do
   not need to develop a software for it, rather for *Passenger* to deal with this
   already functioning system.

In Tropos *late requirements* phase, the system-to-be is introduced as a new actor that takes some responsibilities, already identified in the first phase, and provides an automated solution. The rational of the system-to-be actor is represented by a goal model, starting with a high level goal and finding alternative sets of behaviors that lead to the satisfaction of that goal. Considering location-based software, the rationale of the system-to-be actor is to find suitable behavior for each possible location. In our railway station scenario, the developed location-based software will be for passengers, and passenger assistants as mobile actors. It will work as an automated location expert that operates on the user's computing device, and knows both its user and its location social structure.

In a way different from Tropos late requirements, the system-to-be actor is not necessarily assigned an objective that is recognized in the first phase, and is mainly developed to assist users in the already functioning system that is modeled in the first phase. In our example, two system-to-be actors need to be introduced, one for *passenger* and another for *passengers assistant*. The rationale of these two location-based software actors is partially shown in Fig. 3. On this goal-oriented rationale model, that represents well the alternative behaviors of location-based software, we can also highlight several remarks:

1. The system-to-be has, in particular, two characteristics:
   (a) It is naturally decentralized, that is a location-based software will be assigned for each mobile actor that might also deal with another location-based software assigned to other actors. In our example, we need two location-based software actors, one for *Passengers*, and another for *Passenger Assistants*.
   (b) The responsibilities given to the system-to-be actors fall into the categories we have listed in Section 2, and the rationale analysis concerns how to assist the mobile users in an already functioning system. For example, passengers location-based software will choose the way that fits to them and to the station when they need to buy tickets, and it will interact with passengers assistants on behalf of the passengers for a help.
2. Tropos goal analysis supports different alternatives to satisfy the high level goals. What we need is a kind of location-based goal analysis, that adds location properties to each alternative specifying where it can be adopted. For example, in Tropos goal analysis shown in Fig.3, we do not specify where each of the possible alternatives for having a ticket can be adopted.
3. The contribution to softgoals can be location-based, and is not always static. The relation between the contribution and the location is omitted in the current Tropos goal model. For example, the goal *Wireless Connection* contributes better to the softgoal *Reliable Connection* when the passenger is close to wireless network access points, than it does when user is far from it.
4. The autonomous selection amongst alternatives, when more than one are available, needs to be specified based on some criteria. For example, in a railway station where offices are opened, terminals are available, and passenger has the ability to adopt each of these alternatives, we need to specify the decision to be taken.

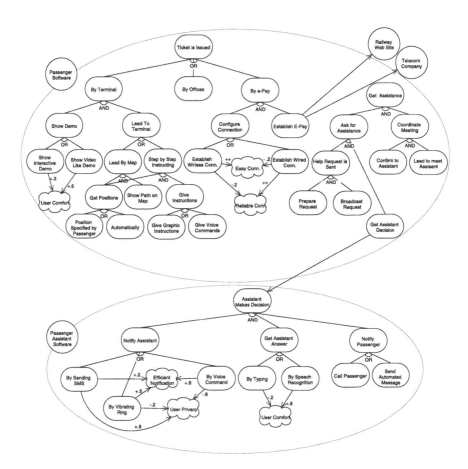

Fig. 3. System-to-be actors goal model for the railway station scenario

4   Location-Based Tropos

In the previous section we have addressed the potential and the limitation of
Tropos with regards to location-based software development. Early requirements
conceptualization, that concerns modeling location, is not sufficient enough to
model variable location and needs mainly to consider actors and resources profiles. We have shown the system-to-be, introduced in the late requirements, as
a set of location-based software actors that assist mobile actors to satisfy their
needs in a location. We have also addressed the gap between Tropos goal-oriented
rationale and location, since we need mainly to associate between the goal satisfaction alternatives and the locations where they can be adopted.

When the analyst builds the goal model shown in Fig. 3, a specific assumption
about the location, where each of the alternatives can be adopted, could be
thought about but was not explicitly represented in the model. Here we discuss

five variation points on Tropos goal model that might need location properties to take location-based decision:

1. *Location-based Or-decomposition*: Or-decomposition is the basic variability construct; in current Tropos the choice of a specific Or-alternative is left to the actor intention, without considering location properties that can inhibit some alternatives. E.g. the alternative *By Terminal* can be adopted when a terminal is free, has one language in common with the passenger, and supports the cash money -in both of the type (coins, papers) and the currency- or one credit card the passenger has. The alternative *E-Pay* can be adopted when there is a wireless network in the railway station and the passenger's PDA supports WiFi, or when there is a wired network with a cable-based connection terminals and the passenger's PDA has cable connectivity.
2. *Location-based contribution to softgoals*: The value of contributions to soft-goals can vary from one location to another. E.g. the goal *Interactive Demo* contributes positively to the softgoal *User Comfort* when the user has good expertise in using PDAs, and the used PDA has a touch screen, while the contribution is negative in the opposite case. Also, the goal *Wireless Connection* contribution to the softgoal *Reliable Connection* depends on the distance between passenger and WiFi access point to which passenger is connected.
3. *Location-based dependency*: In some locations, an actor might be unable to satisfy a goal using its own alternatives. In such case, the actor might delegate this goal to another actor that is able to satisfy it. E.g. delegation of the goal *Establish E-Pay* to the actor *Railway Website* can be done when that web site enables e-payment using one credit card in common with user's credit cards, and has a mobile device version.
4. *Location-based goal activation*: An actor, and depending on the location set-tings, might find necessary or possible triggering (or stopping) the desire of satisfying a goal. E.g. the goal *Assistant Makes Decision* is activated when the assistant is not doing any particular activity, has one language in com-mon with the requesting passenger, and close to that passenger.
5. *Location-based And-decomposition*: A sub-goal might (or might not) be needed in a certain location, that is some sub-goals are not always mandatory to fulfill the top-level goal in And-decomposition. E.g. The goal *Show Demo* has to be satisfied when the passenger is not familiar with using terminals.

The goal analysis of location-based Tropos associates location properties to each location-based variation point. In addition, this analysis helps to refine the initial location model represented in the first phase. If we consider the location properties in the above examples, we can identify how the location model of Fig.2 can be refined. The resulted location model of the railway station scenario, with respect to the location properties given in the examples above, is shown in Fig. 4. This model adds mainly actors and resources profiles, and also introduces new resources and actors that can influence tailoring location-based behavior.

There are two top-level classes in the location model: actors and resources (Res in the figure). The actor Passenger is characterized by some attributes:

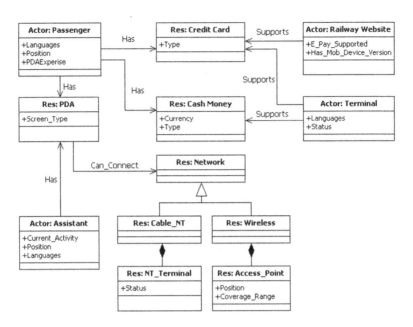

Fig. 4. Location model for the railway station scenario

spoken Languages (we put it as a single attribute to simplify the diagram), Position in the railway station, and Expertise in using PDAs. The passenger might have three relevant resources: PDA, Credit Card, and Cash Money. The resource PDA is characterized by an attribute Screen_Type, defining if the PDA has a touch screen or not, and it has a Can_Connect association to the Network it can connect to. A network can be specialized into Cable_NT and Wireless. Cable_NT stands for wired networks, and it is composed of a set of network terminals (NT_Terminals), characterized by a Status that can be free, busy, under maintenance, out of service, and so on. Wireless network is composed of several wireless access points (Access_Point); an Access_Point has the attributes Position and Coverage_Range, used together to compute if a customer is covered by an access point signal. The actor Assistant has a Current_Activity he/she is performing, a Position in the railway station, and spoken Languages. The assistant's relevant resources include only the assistant's used PDA. The actor Railway Website has the attributes E_Pay_Supported, to indicate if e-payments are supported, and Has_Mob_Device_Version, set to true when the website can be browsed by PDAs. The Credit_Card resource class represents the types of credit cards passenger might use, and terminals and railway station website might support. The actor Terminal might support multiple Languages, be in a variable Status, and support Credit Card or Cash Money payment.

We describe now our proposed *location-based Tropos process* that leads the production of our proposed models. We start by **(i)** modeling the social structure of a location class, before introducing the system to-be, using a strategic dependency diagram. In this step, we identify roughly the main location actors

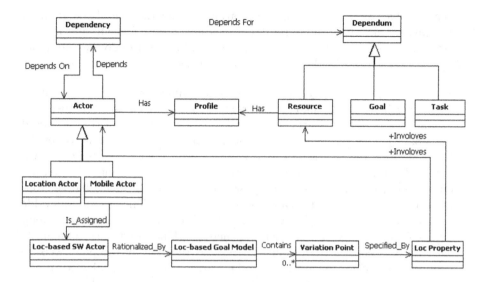

Fig. 5. A metamodel showing the proposed extension of Tropos

and the strategic dependencies between them. Then **(ii)**, this diagram is examined to determine a set of mobile actors, i.e. actors who need location-based software to assist them in the considered class of locations. The next step is to **(iii)** assign a system-to-be actor to each mobile actor, and to model the rationale of these system-to-be actors, using goal analysis. While doing the goal analysis, system analyst **(iv)** decides those location-based variation points, and specifies the location properties at each of them to help selecting between alternatives. Location properties refine the location model, that consists initially of the actors and resources recognized in the first step. System analyst **(v)** will extract new location model constructs (actors or resources properties and relations, new resources or actors) that each location property at each location-based variation point might contain, and keep updating the location model.

By following our proposed location-based Tropos process, we will have three models: the first is the classical Tropos strategic dependencies model, the second represents the location-based rationale of the system-to-be actors (Fig. 3 associated with location properties at the location-based variation points), and the third is the elicited location model (the model of Fig. 4). The metamodel of our proposed extension of Tropos modeling is shown in Fig.5.

5   Reasoning on Location-Based Models

We propose various types of analysis for examining location-based software against a specific location, and vice versa. A preliminary step consists of evaluating the validity of location properties at the variation points of the goal model on the current location instance. This step can be done automatically using an automated solver after formalizing the location and location-based goal models. In [16], we used class diagram to represent location, and we formalized it besides the location properties using Datalog¬. We used DLV solver to do the reasoning. Here we discuss several kinds of automated analysis on our proposed models:

- *Location-based goal satisfiability*: This kind of analysis is aimed to verify if a goal is achievable through one alternative in the current location instance. The analysis can be performed using the goal reasoning algorithm proposed by Giorgini et al. [17] on the goal model restricted by the evaluation of the location properties. A strategy for evaluating satisfiability follows a top-down approach: starting from a top-level goal, we should check that all (at least one) sub-goals in and- (or-) decompositions can be achieved, or that the top-level goal can be achieved via a *makes* (+1.0) contribution from an achievable goal. For example, in a railway station where there is no positioning system, offices are closed because of vacation, there is a kind of network compatible with the passenger's PDA connectivity, and the railway company website supports one of the passenger's credit cards for e-pay, the algorithm will mark the root goal *"Ticket is Issued"* as a satisfiable goal. The algorithm finds the alternative *E-Pay* satisfiable, because of the satisfiability of its two And-decomposition subgoals. The alternative *By Terminal* can not be satisfied due to the absence of any positioning system, and therefore the unsatisfiability of its and-decomposition subgoal *Lead to Terminal* that can not be satisfied by any of its alternatives in its turn. The alternative *By Offices* can not be adopted, because it requires a location property *Offices are working*, to be satisfied.

- *Location properties satisfiability*: This analysis checks if the current location structure is compliant with the software goals. It is exploited to identify what is missing in a particular location where some top-level goals have been identified as unsatisfiable by *location-based goal satisfiability* analysis. When a goal can not be satisfied, the analysis will identify the denying conditions and suggest ways for solving the problem. For example, in a railway station while passengers have PDAs with only wired connectivity feature, while railway station does not provide cable-based connection terminals, the previous analysis will mark *Configure Connection* as unsatisfiable goal. The reason is that location properties on each of the two connection modalities, wireless and wired, are not satisfied. Location properties satisfiability will reason on what is needed to satisfy the *Configure Connection* goal, i.e. what is needed to satisfy location properties on its alternative behaviors.

- *Preferences analysis*: This type of analysis requires the specification of preferences over alternatives. As shown in [18], preferences can be specified using softgoals. This analysis is useful in cases like:

  • When some locations allow for several alternatives to satisfy a goal: The selection will be based on the contributions (possibly location-based) to the preferred softgoals. For example, in a railway station where both *Wireless Connection* and *Wired Connection* can be satisfied, location-based software will adopt the one preferred by its users. User preferences can be specified over softgoals: when user gives more importance to *Reliable Connection* than *Easy Connection*, the *Wired Connection* alternative will be adopted, while *Wireless Connection* is adopted when user cares *Easy Connection* more than *Reliable Connection*.

• When a certain location does not allow for any alternative to satisfy a goal: The *location properties satisfiability* might provide several proposals about the needed location modifications. The adopted modifications are those that lead to satisfy more the preferences expressed over softgoals. For example, in one railway station where *Configure Connection* can not be satisfied due to the absence of wireless network, or cable based terminals, the railway adminstration has to decide between establishing wireless or wired network. When the railway station adminstration cares more *Reliable Connection*, a wired network terminals has to be installed over the station, while wireless access points will be installed when *Easy Connection* is more preferred.

6   Conclusions and Future Work

In this paper, we have shown the particularity and importance of modeling location variability for location-based software, and addressed some challenges the conceptual modeling faces with this regards. We classified several features location-based software in particular has to support. To develop location-based software we relied on Tropos methodology, and have shown its potential and limitation for developing such software. We have suggested to modify the conceptualization and the process of Tropos to fit well with location-based software development. We have shown three kinds of automated analysis on our proposed location-based models. In this work, we have considered the social level of a location class as a set of profiled actors and resources; our future work will be towards refining this modeling by finding a set of common concepts that can construct more specifically actors and resources profiles and relations. Consequently, we will also need a formal language that is expressive enough to represent the location-based models, and practical for the needed automated analysis.

Acknowledgement

This work has been partially funded by EU Commission, through the SERENITY project, by MIUR, through the MEnSA project (PRIN 2006), and by the Provincial Authority of Trentino, through the STAMPS project.

References

1. Krogstie, J., Lyytinen, K., Opdahl, A., Pernici, B., Siau, K., Smolander, K.: Research areas and challenges for mobile information systems. International Journal of Mobile Communications 2(3), 220–234 (2004)

2. Weiser, M.: The Computer for the Twenty-First Century. Scientific American 265(3), 94–104 (1991)
3. Ali, R., Dalpiaz, F., Giorgini, P.: Location-based variability for mobile information systems. In: Bellahsène, Z., Léonard, M. (eds.) CAiSE 2008. LNCS, vol. 5074, pp. 575–578. Springer, Heidelberg (2008)
4. Yau, S.S., Liu, J.: Hierarchical situation modeling and reasoning for pervasive computing. In: Proc. Fourth IEEE Workshop on Software Technologies for Future Embedded and Ubiquitous Systems (SEUS 2006), pp. 5–10 (2006)
5. Henricksen, K., Indulska, J.: A software engineering framework for context-aware pervasive computing. In: Proc. Second IEEE Intl. Conference on Pervasive Computing and Communications (PerCom 2004), p. 77 (2004)
6. Wang, X.H., Zhang, D.Q., Gu, T., Pung, H.K.: Ontology based context modeling and reasoning using owl. In: Proc. Second IEEE Annual Conference on Pervasive Computing and Communications Workshops, pp. 18–22 (2004)
7. Salifu, M., Yu, Y., Nuseibeh, B.: Specifying monitoring and switching problems in context. In: Proc. 15th Intl. Conference on Requirements Engineering (RE 2007), pp. 211–220 (2007)
8. Pohl, K., Böckle, G., van der Linden, F.: Software Product Line Engineering: Foundations, Principles, and Techniques. Springer, Heidelberg (2005)
9. Kang, K.C., Kim, S., Lee, J., Kim, K., Shin, E., Huh, M.: Form: A feature-oriented reuse method with domain-specific reference architectures. Ann. Softw. Eng. 5, 143–168 (1998)
10. Lapouchnian, A., Yu, Y., Liaskos, S., Mylopoulos, J.: Requirements-driven design of autonomic application software. In: Proc. 2006 conference of the Center for Advanced Studies on Collaborative research (CASCON 2006), p. 7. ACM, New York (2006)
11. Liaskos, S., Lapouchnian, A., Yu, Y., Yu, E., Mylopoulos, J.: On goal-based variability acquisition and analysis. In: Proc. 14th IEEE Intl. Requirements Engineering Conference (RE 2006), pp. 76–85 (2006)
12. Dardenne, A., van Lamsweerde, A., Fickas, S.: Goal-directed requirements acquisition. Sci. Comput. Program. 20(1-2), 3–50 (1993)
13. Bresciani, P., Perini, A., Giorgini, P., Giunchiglia, F., Mylopoulos, J.: Tropos: An agent-oriented software development methodology. Autonomous Agents and Multi-Agent Systems 8(3), 203–236 (2004)
14. Yu, E.: Modelling strategic relationships for process reengineering. Ph.D. Thesis, University of Toronto (1995)
15. Mylopoulos, J., Chung, L., Yu, E.: From object-oriented to goal-oriented requirements analysis. Commun. ACM 42(1), 31–37 (1999)
16. Ali, R., Dalpiaz, F., Giorgini, P.: Modeling and analyzing variability for mobile information systems. In: Gervasi, O., Murgante, B., Laganá, A., Taniar, D., Mun, Y., Gavrilova, M.L. (eds.) ICCSA 2008, Part II. LNCS, vol. 5073, pp. 291–306. Springer, Heidelberg (2008)
17. Giorgini, P., Mylopoulos, J., Nicchiarelli, E., Sebastiani, R.: Reasoning with goal models. In: Spaccapietra, S., March, S.T., Kambayashi, Y. (eds.) ER 2002. LNCS, vol. 2503, pp. 167–181. Springer, Heidelberg (2002)
18. Liaskos, S., McIlraith, S., Mylopoulos, J.: Representing and reasoning with preference requirements using goals. Technical report, Dept. of Computer Science, University of Toronto (2006), ftp://ftp.cs.toronto.edu/pub/reports/csrg/542

Risk Evaluation for Personal Identity Management Based on Privacy Attribute Ontology

Mizuho Iwaihara[1], Kohei Murakami[1], Gail-Joon Ahn[2],
and Masatoshi Yoshikawa[1]

[1] Department of Social Informatics, Kyoto University, Japan
kmurakami@db.soc.i.kyoto-u.ac.jp, iwaihara@i.kyoto-u.ac.jp,
yoshikawa@i.kyoto-u.ac.jp
[2] Department of Computer Science and Engineering, Arizona State University, USA
gahn@asu.edu

Abstract. Identity providers are becoming popular for distributed authentication and distributed identity management. Users' privacy attributes are stored at an identity provider and they are released to a service provider upon user's consent. Since a broad range of privacy information of different sensitiveness can be exchanged in advanced web services, it is necessary to assist users by presenting potential risk on financial and personality damage, before releasing privacy attributes. In this paper, we present a model of privacy attribute ontology and risk evaluation method on this ontology. Then we formalize several matching problems which optimize similarity scores of matching solutions under several different types of risk constraints. We show sophisticated polynomial-time algorithms for solving these optimization problems.

1 Introduction

A wide variety of new services are created on the web, by connecting existing web services. To carry out services and/or businesses with their customers, many of service providers (SP) require basic personal information of customers, such as name, address, phone number, as well as more critical information such as credit card number. Identity providers (IdPs) offer identity management functionalities, including user authentication and management of basic personal information. Since basic information such as name and email/postal addresses are frequently asked, provisioning of these information from IdP to SP through the user's one-click action can save the user's workload. Liberty Alliance[10], OpenID[11] and CardSpace[1] are proposed identity management standards which provide single sign-on and trust management. However, in these standards, users are still required to carefully examine requested attributes for sensitiveness and criticality. Then users select appropriate identities to be used for the request, where excessive exposure of identities and attributes should be avoided by users' discretion.

Web services are rapidly evolving to cover every kind of social activities among people, and categories of personal attributes are also growing beyond basic attributes. Social network services are offering exchange of very personal attributes such as such as age, ethnicity, religion, height and eye color. For example, orkut(www.orkut.com)

Q. Li et al. (Eds.): ER 2008, LNCS 5231, pp. 183–198, 2008.

has an registration form having 30 attributes for "social" page, 16 attributes for "professional" page, and 15 attributes for "personal" page. User-centric control of sharing of personal information is required for healthy support of social activities, and an identity provider of the near future should assist the user through categorization and evaluation of attributes from the point of criticality and sensitiveness.

In this paper, we propose the concept of *privacy attribute ontology* (PAO), built on the OWL web ontology language[12]. One of primal objectives of PAO is to provide a taxonomy of privacy attributes. Each class of PAO corresponds to a sensitive attribute or an identity, and an individual of the class corresponds to a value of the attribute. IdP manages a PAO as a shared ontology among users as well as a personal information database for each user. Also PAO provides risk evaluation functionality through financial and personality risk values defined on PAO classes. When a service provider presents a list of requested attributes, IdP matches the list with PAO classes, and then the risk values of the requested attributes are evaluated from matched classes. Here we have a number of issues to be solved. First, we need to design a matching algorithm that maximizes linguistic/structural similarities between PAO classes and requested attributes. Secondly, the algorithm also needs to consider risk constraints such that matched classes must not exceed given upper limits of risk values. The algorithm should select a low-risk combination of identities and attributes associated to these identities, covering requested attributes. In this optimization, we need to consider combination risks which arise if a certain combination of classes is selected for release.

The contribution of this paper is summarized as follows: (1) We present a model of privacy attribute ontology and risk evaluation method on this ontology. (2) We formalize matching problems which optimize similarity scores of matching solutions under three different types of risk constraints. (3) We show sophisticated polynomial-time algorithms for solving the optimization problems of (2).

P3P (Platform for Privacy Preferences Project) [14] is a standard for describing and exchanging privacy policies in XML format. While P3P is targeted at interpreting privacy practices of service providers, our research is focused on identity providers and users for managing linkages between privacy attributes and identities of different aspects.

Developing ontologies for privacy and trust management on the web has been discussed in the literature[4][5][7]. Our research is different in the way that we focus on risk evaluation for attribute disclosure and selecting disclosing attribute values (individuals) that have minimum risk values. Utilizing semantic web technologies for security and trust management on the web is discussed in [4], which covers authentication, delegation, and access control in a decentralized environment. But an ontology for assessing privacy risk values is not considered.

Matching and aligning ontologies have been extensively studied for integrating ontologies. As a linguistic approach, OntoGenie[13] uses WordNet[16] for extracting ontologies from web pages. Structural similarity is considered in [9] for neural network-based schema matching. Udrea et al.[15] combined data and structural matching as well as logical inference to improve quality. Our algorithms utilize these linguistic and structural approaches. But we need to deal with the new problem of considering risk values during matching. We have successfully solved ontology matching under various types of risk constraints.

The rest of the paper is organized as follows. In Section 2, we introduce an existing risk evaluation method for privacy information, and discuss automated risk evaluation based on privacy attribute ontology. In Section 3, we formalize privacy attribute ontology. In Section 4, we discuss matching requested attributes with PAO classes, and define optimization problems under certain risk constraints. In Section 5, we discuss several issues that need to be solved, and present polynomial-time algorithms for the optimization problems. Section 6 is a conclusion.

2   Risk Evaluation for Personal Identity Management

2.1   JNSA Privacy Risk Evaluation

Service providers holding customer's privacy data are having risk of privacy leakage. Several measures for evaluating risk of privacy leakage have been proposed. Japan Network Security Association (JNSA) published surveys on information security incidents[6]. The report also presents a method for estimating amount of compensation if a certain portion of privacy data are leaked. The JNSA model is based on classifying reported cases from court decisions and settlements, and the model was validated on these cases. Its evaluation proceeds as follows:

The value of leaked privacy data of an individuation is evaluated in terms of (a) economical loss and (b) emotional pain. The Simple-EP Diagram contains representative privacy attributes according to the dimensions of (a) and (b). Given an attribute, an integer from 1 to 3 is chosen as the value for each dimension. Let x (resp. y) be the value for (a) economical loss (resp. (b) emotional loss). Then the *sensitiveness factor* is defined as $EP = (10^{x-1} + 5^{y-1})$.

Given a collection of privacy attributes for an individual, we take maximum values for x and y from the Simple-EP Diagram. Suppose a record of an individual consists of the attributes: real name, address, birth date, sex, phone, medical diagnosis, bank account and password. Then by the Simple-EP Diagram, the value (x, y) is equal to $(1, 1)$ for real name, address, birth date, sex, and phone. On the other hand (x, y) is equal to $(2, 1)$ for medical diagnosis, and $(1, 3)$ for bank account and password. Since the maximum value for x is 2 and the maximum value for y is 3, we obtain $EP = 35$.

Let the *basic information value BIV* be 500 points, and let the *identifiability factor IF* be defined as: $IF = 6$ if the individual can be easily identified (for example, real name and address are included), $IF = 3$ if the individual can be identified by a certain effort (for example, real name is included, or address and phone are included), and $IF = 1$ otherwise (for the case identification is difficult). The leaked privacy information value $LPIV$ is computed by: $LPIV = BIV * EP * IF$. LPIV is designed to approximate the amount of compensation in Japanese yen paid to each leakage victim. The LPIV is further adjusted to reflect other factors such as the social status of the information holder and evaluation on the response after the incident. However, these factors are not directly related to our goal.

The JNSA risk evaluation model can be a basis of risk evaluation for risk-aware identity management, from the points that the model can capture the emotional and financial losses according to a classification of privacy attributes, and it enables quantitative comparison of the risks between attributes. However, the method requires human reasoning in determining values from the diagram.

2.2   Risk Evaluation at Identity Provider

The basic scenario of personal information management by an identity provider (IdP) utilizing PAO proceeds as follows:

1. IdP manages and holds personal information of the user.
2. The user requests execution of a service to the service provider (SP). SP sends to IdP *requested attributes* $\mathcal{RA}$ necessary for the service. $\mathcal{RA}$ includes basic identity information as well as privacy attributes of the user.
3. IdP matches attributes of $\mathcal{RA}$ with classes of PAO, to compute *releasing classes* $\mathcal{RC}$. In the matching process, IdP evaluates risks of releasing information held in $\mathcal{RC}$, and IdP tries to find $\mathcal{RC}$ which has maximum conceptual similarities with $\mathcal{RA}$, while $\mathcal{RC}$ satisfies a certain risk constraint imposed by the user.
4. $\mathcal{RC}$ is presented to the user. The user modifies and supplements $\mathcal{RC}$ if necessary. Some requested attributes A may not be included in $\mathcal{RC}$, because either A's risk is intolerable to the user or the user has declined release of of A. After SP and the user agree on $\mathcal{RC}$, the information on $\mathcal{RC}$ is sent from IdP to SP.

IdP manages a number of identities of the user, such as student ID, a number of email addresses, citizenship, net identities used for blogs and social network services. Some of these identities are anonymous, while others have solid identities. One identity is associated with a number of attributes, as well as other identities. In selecting $\mathcal{RC}$, IdP needs to find low-risk combination of attributes and avoid linking of identities if it is prohibited by the user.

2.3   Risk Evaluation Using Privacy Attribute Ontology

In the following, we summarize the basic notions of our risk evaluation method utilizing PAO.

Risk value is a numerical scale of 1 to 5 representing severity of the risk, where 1 is least severe and 5 is most severe. Risk values are categorized into financial and personality risk values. PAO holds risk values in its classes. However, some classes may not have risk values defined. If a risk value of C is undefined, then the risk value is inherited from C's super classes. If a class C is in the releasing class $\mathcal{RC}$, then the risk values of C become *effective*. The risk value of releasing classes $\mathcal{RC}$ is the maximum effective risk value in the classes of $\mathcal{RC}$.

Financial risk value (f-risk value for short) is a risk value for financial damage to the information subject (user). Credit card number, bank account number, and social security number should have high financial risk values. We use $r_f(\cdot)$ to denote the financial risk value function on various constructs such as class C and releasing classes $\mathcal{RC}$.

Personality risk value (p-risk value for short) is a risk value for personality damage to the user, including emotional pain, damage to social reputation, and generic damage caused by privacy breach. We use $r_p(\cdot)$ to denote the personality risk value function.

Combined risk value $r_c(\mathcal{RC})$ combines f-risk and p-risk values by the function $r_c(\mathcal{RC}) = cr(r_f(\mathcal{RC}), r_p(\mathcal{RC}))$ such that $cr(x, y) = c_1 \log(\mathcal{F}^x + \mathcal{P}^y) + c_2$, where the risk values x and y are converted into an exponential scale by the exponential functions of bases $\mathcal{F}$ and $\mathcal{P}$, and the average of these values are converted back to risk values by the logarithmic function. The bases $\mathcal{F}$ and $\mathcal{P}$ assign weights between the financial and personality risk values, and we can choose $\mathcal{F} = 10$ and $\mathcal{P} = 5$ following the JNSA model. Constants c_1 and c_2 shall be determined to let $cr(x, y)$ have a range between 1 and 5.

Combination risk is a risk arising from combination of attributes. Some privacy attributes, such as age and income, may be disclosed under an anonymous username, but combining these attributes with the real name raises the risk of privacy breach. Thus the user should be notified of such high risk combination. Also, the user holding a number of identities at IdP can choose one identity or a combination of identities to cover requested attributes. In this scenario, the user should be advised of the risk in linking several identities. For modeling combination risks, we need to introduce *combination risk classes* to PAO.

Risk limit is a given upper limit on f-risk, p-risk or combined risk values. If the user gives his/her tolerable risk limit, then disclosing attributes should not exceed the limit. Here exists an optimization problem for finding most-similar matching between the PAO classes and requested attributes, while satisfying the risk limit. Trustability of service providers can be reflected to risk limits, in a way that when dealing with a questionable service provider, the user can define a lower, more cautious risk limit. Detailed linkage between risk limits and existing trustability models is beyond the scope of the paper.

3 Modeling Privacy Attribute Ontology

In this section, we formalize privacy attribute ontology. We follow the definitions of OWL[12] as the underlying ontology model. A *class* represents a concept. A class is associated with zero or more *individuals* belonging to that class. An ontology can be represented as a directed graph, where nodes are labeled with a class name or an individual, and directed edges are labeled with link types. A link labeled `type` from an individual to a class represents the membership relation between the individual and the class. A link labeled `subClassOf` from class C_1 to class C_2 indicates that C_1 is a subclass of C_2 meaning that C_1 is a concept more specific than C_2 and an individual belonging to C_2 also belongs to C_1. A link labeled `partOf` from class C_1 to class C_2 indicates that C_2 is a *composite class* composed of a number of *component classes*, including C_1. Formally, if a class C_1 is connected to a class C_2 through a directed path of `partOf` and `subClassOf` links, then C_1 is a component class of C_2. `partOf` links are not allowed to form a directed cycle. We define *composite attributes* for requested attributes, similarly to composite classes.

PAO has two special link types named `financialRisk` and `personalityRisk`, representing the financial risk value $r_f(C)$ and and personality risk value $r_f(C)$ of a class

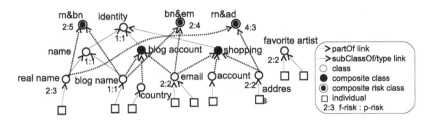

Fig. 1. Privacy attribute ontology

C, leading to individuals of real numbers in the range [1.0, 5.0]. An example of privacy attribute ontology is shown in Figure 1, where risk values are shown as numbers of the form $r_f : r_p$. Also, composite classes are depicted as black circles.

In PAO, we assume that each individual belongs to a single class. For an individual i belonging to multiple classes, we can insert a virtual class between i and these classes, to satisfy the single-class restriction. Thus this is not a tight restriction. Also, if some risk values need to be defined on particular individuals, we create a class for such an individual, and let all the risk values be defined on classes.

As discussed in Section 2.3, we introduce a *combination risk class*, which is a composite class connected by partOf links from its component classes. In Figure 1, combination risk classes are depicted as double circles. The risk value of a combination risk class is applied if all of its component classes are selected for release. For example, the class rn&bn represents that if real name and blog name are going to be released, then its risk values 2:5 will be applied. These values are higher than that of classes real name and blog name alone, indicating that combination of these classes increase the risk values, or it can be interpreted that the user is not allowing linking of these identities. Thus a combination risk class should have f-risk and p-risk values no less than that of its component classes.

PAO can be shared by a group of users so that the users' common knowledge on risks can be reflected. However, each user may have different views on privacy, and individuals in the ontology are also user-dependent. Thus personalization of PAO is necessary. Personalization of PAO can be done by the following ways: (a) overriding financial and/or personality risk values of a class, (b) adding individuals to a class, and (c) adding a class as a subclass of an existing class. Sharing and personalization of PAO is beyond the scope of this paper, so we do not elaborate on this direction any further.

4   Matching PAO and Requested Attributes

4.1   Matching Problems

Now we discuss evaluating risk of a set $\mathcal{RA}$ of requested attributes sent by a service provider, utilizing PAO. Then using the risk evaluation method, we consider optimization problems to find an optimum combination of releasing individuals that achieves given risk constraints.

For associating individuals of PAO and requested attributes $\mathcal{RA}$, we consider the following two-staged approach: First find a bipartite matching between classes of PAO and $\mathcal{RA}$, then choose an individual from each class selected by the matching. A bipartite matching finds a one-to-one mapping between classes and $\mathcal{RA}$. Since we assumed that each individual belongs to a single class, this process is straightforward.

We introduce *similarity score* $\sigma(C, A) \geq 0$ on a PAO class C and a requested attribute $A \in \mathcal{RA}$. When $\sigma(C, A) > \beta$ holds for a given lower threshold β, C and A are regarded as distinct concepts. We discuss construction of σ by linguistic similarities in Section 4.2. We construct a *matching graph* $G_{\sigma,\beta} = (\mathcal{C}, \mathcal{RA}, E)$ which is a bipartite graph such that $\mathcal{C}$ is the set of classes in PAO, $\mathcal{RA}$ is the set of requested attributes, and E is the set of edges (C_i, A_j) such that $C_j \in \mathcal{C}, A_j \in \mathcal{RA}$, and $\sigma(C, A) > \beta$ is true. We also use the similarity function σ for edge weights of the bipartite graph $G_{\sigma,\beta}(\mathcal{C}, \mathcal{RA}, E)$. The weighted bipartite matching problem can be solved in $O(N^3)$ time by the Hungarian method [8], where N is the number of nodes in $G_{\sigma,\beta}$. A *matching* M on bipartite graph $G_{\sigma,\beta} = (\mathcal{C}, \mathcal{RA}, E)$ is a bipartite subgraph $(\mathcal{C}_M, \mathcal{RA}_M, E_M)$ such that $CC_M \subseteq \mathcal{C}, \mathcal{RA} \subseteq \mathcal{RA}_M, E_M \subseteq E$, and no edge in E_M conflicts each other, that is, any two edges in E_M are not adjacent at either end. Let $\sigma(M)$ denote the sum of the edge weights of E_M. A matching M on $G_{\sigma,\beta}$ is a *maximum matching* if $\sigma(M) \geq \sigma(M')$ holds for any matching M' on $G_{\sigma,\beta}$.

Figure 2 shows an example of matching graphs. The nodes on the left are classes of PAO, and the nodes on the right are requested attributes. Here, '+' sign means a composite class or attribute, and '-' sign means a component class or attribute. Edge weights are not displayed in the graph. A matching is shown as bold edges in Figure 2. Notice that this matching includes edges (email, e-mail) and (address, address). These associations may appear reasonable, but unacceptable because structural integrity is ignored. The email class of PAO is a component of class blog account, while address of PAO is a component of class shopping. These composite classes represent distinct identities, and component classes should not be intermixed. Intuitively, a proper matching should preserve component-composite relationships. In Section 5.1, we discuss this component integrity and present a solution. We note that combination risk classes should be excluded from matching candidates, because they are just for internally defining combinational risk values.

Recall that the combined risk value is determined by maximum f-risk value r_f and p-risk value r_p found in releasing classes. In a matching $M = (\mathcal{C}_M, \mathcal{RA}_M, E_M)$, the set of matched classes $\mathcal{C}_M$ is the releasing classes. Let $r_f(M)$ and $r_p(M)$ be the maximum f-risk and p-risk values in M, respectively. Then the combined risk value $r_c(M)$ is computed by $cr(r_f(M), r_p(M))$.

Requested attributes $\mathcal{RA}$ may not have any matchable class in $\mathcal{C}$. Such a dangling attribute can be reported by the matching algorithm. In this case, the system needs to start a dialog with the user to create a new class in PAO for the attribute.

By using predefined parameters on risk limits and similarity score limits, a number of optimization problems can be defined:

1. **(similarity score maximization)** Tolerable upper risk limits m_f and m_p are given by the user, where $m_f > 0$ and $m_p > 0$ are *maximum f-risk value* and *maximum p-risk value*, respectively. The optimization problem is to find a matching M such that similarity score $\sigma(M)$ is maximum and $r_c(M) \leq cr(m_f, m_p)$ holds. The user may specify $m_f = \infty$ and/or $m_p = \infty$ if he/she does not restrict one or both of

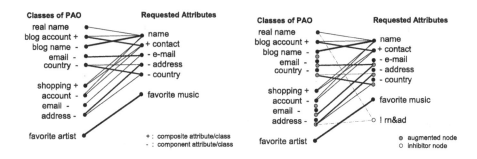

Fig. 2. Matching graph   **Fig. 3.** Augmented matching graph

the risk values. Another version of the problem is **similarity score maximization under combined-risk limit** m_c, which is to find a maximum matching under the constraint $r_c(M) \leq m_c$. In this case, we need to test varying combinations of m_f and m_p that satisfy $cr(m_f, m_p) \leq m_c$.

2. **(risk minimization)** This problem assumes that a lowerbound w_{min} for the total similarity score is given. The problem is to find a matching M such that $\sigma(M) > w_{min}$ and the combined risk value $r_c(M)$ is minimum.

3. **(combined score maximization)** Let $s_c(M)$ be *combined total score* defined by $s_c(M) = \sigma(M)/r_c(M)$. The problem is to find a matching M that maximizes $s_c(M)$. Unlike others, this problem does not have a predefined parameter.

Since specifying all the risk values is tedious, it is likely that some classes or individuals may not be given risk values in PAO. For this issue, we utilize subClassOf links of PAO for inferring risk values, based on the principle that a subclass inherits a missing property value from its parent. Here we also adopt the principle of taking the highest possible risk value, for conservative risk estimation.

(subClassOf rule) Let C be a class in PAO such that $r_f(C)$ is undefined. Let $C_1, \ldots, C_k$ be classes in PAO such that there is a path S_i of subClassOf links from C to each C_i and C_i is the only class in P_i where $r_f(C_i)$ is defined. Then let $r_f(C) := \max(r_f(C_1), \ldots, r_f(C_k))$. For the case $r_p(C)$ is undefined, simply replace r_f with r_p.

Applying the subClassOf rule to every class that has an undefined risk value gives us a unique PAO that has no undefined risk value, and this procedure can be done in linear time.

4.2 Linguistic Similarity

We use Jaro-Winkler score[2] for string similarity and WordNet similarity [16] for score on synonymity. Jaro-Winkler is effective for matching pairs having common substrings, such as between e-mail, email, Email and netmail. WordNet is a lexical dictionary, where words are ground into synonyms (synsets), each synset expressing a distinct concept. WordNet similarity is measured by conceptual-semantic and lexical relations between synsets. We use the sum of Jaro-Winkler score and WordNet score as the similarity score σ between PAO classes and $\mathcal{RA}$.

Table 1 shows an experimental result on matching names of PAO classes and attributes from web sign-up forms. We constructed a PAO containing 186 classes. The class names of this PAO are matched with two attribute sets from web sign-up forms of eBay and PayPal, using the above similarity score σ. Case 2 is matches detected by string similarity, which included pair "Primary telephone number" and "Primary telephone". Case 3 is matches detected by synonymity, which included pair "Secret Question" and "Security Question". Overall, the similarity score σ is showing enough accuracy for matching requested attributes with PAO.

Table 1. Linguistic matching result on PAO having 186 classes

case	total attributes	eBay	PayPal
	total attributes	17	23
1	string match with PAO classes	7	15
2	attributes matched by string similarity(Jaro-Winkler)	3/3	6/6
3	attributes matched by synonymity score (WordNet) (Excluding case 2)	3/5	1/2
4	attributes having no matching class in PAO	2	0

(detected matches)/(correct matches)

5   Matching Algorithms

5.1   Component Integrity and Two-Level Matching

First we formalize component integrity, and present a matching algorithm that achieves a certain type of component integrity while maximizing similarity score. At this moment, we assume that $m_f = \infty$ and $m_p = \infty$ hold, namely no constraint is given on risk values. We also assume that the PAO has no combination risk class. We extend the algorithm later in this section.

(**component integrity**) Let us consider a matching M between PAO classes $\mathcal{C}$ and requested attributes $\mathcal{RA}$. A matching M is said to satisfy *component integrity*, if the following holds: Let (C, A) and (D, B) be any pair of edges in M such that $C, D \in \mathcal{C}$ and $A, B \in \mathcal{RA}$. Then C is a component class of D if and only if A is a component attribute of B.

Note that PAO can have a multi-level component class, i.e., a composite class can be a component class of another class. PAO can also include a component class shared by multiple composite classes. In such a DAG-structured PAO, imposing the above component integrity becomes a hard problem:

Theorem 1. *Given a bipartite graph $G_{\sigma,\beta} = (\mathcal{C}, \mathcal{RA}, E)$ and a minimum weight w, deciding whether $G_{\sigma,\beta}$ has a matching M having weight $\sigma(M) > w$ and satisfying component integrity is NP-complete.*

Proof. (sketch) Transformation from SET PACKING[3].

Thus it is intractable to enforce the above composite integrity. Also this integrity does not consider link connectivities. In object-oriented modeling, link connectivities are often used to add different perspectives to a class. For example, consider the following subgraphs containing the class email in Figure 1: email → blog account, email → shopping, and email. Note that the last subgraph is a singleton node. These subgraphs represent e-mail of the blog account, email of the shopping identity, and emails of the person, respectively. Thus each subgraph is representing a different concept.

Now let us consider the following multi-level nesting of composite classes for matching: A class C is a *level-k component class* of D if (1) for $k = 1$, C is a component class of D, and (2) for $k > 1$, C is a component class of a level-$(k-1)$ component class of D.

We can adopt the interpretation such that for each different k, each path from a composite class to its level-k component class represents a distinct concept. To treat these paths as distinct concepts in matching, new nodes shall be created for each path for varying k. However, since PAO can have shared component classes, the number of such paths can be exponential to k. Thus considering all the paths to level-k component classes as matching candidates is impractical. In the following, we resrict level k to be 1, and augment the matching graph $G_{\sigma,\beta}$ with new nodes representing pairs of composite classes and their level-1 component classes. For each composite class D and component class C, we create a new node labeled with the concatenation $D.C$. Likewise, we create a new node labeled with the concatenation $B.A$ for composite attribute B and composite attribute A. Formally, let $G^a_{\sigma,\beta} = (\mathcal{C}^a, \mathcal{RA}^a, E^a)$ be the bipartite such that $\mathcal{C}^a = \mathcal{C} \cup \{D.C \mid D, C \in \mathcal{C}, C \text{ is a component class of } D\}$, $\mathcal{RA}^a = \mathcal{RA} \cup \{B.A \mid B, A \in \mathcal{RA}, A \text{ is a component attribute of } B\}$. The edge set E^a is obtained by adding edge $(D.C, B.A)$ to E for each new class $D.C$ and new attribute $B.A$ satisfying $\sigma(D.C, B.A) > \beta$, and removing edge (C, A) from E where C and A are component class and attributes, respectively. Here we remove the edge (C, A) because it will be represented by the new component-level edge $(D.C, B.A)$. We call $G^a_{\sigma,\beta}$ a *composite-augmented graph*. Also, we call a bipartite matching M^a on $G^a_{\sigma,\beta}$ an *augmented matching*.

For a class C shared by composite classes $D_1, \ldots, D_m$ in $G_{\sigma,\beta}$, $G^a_{\sigma,\beta}$ has duplicated nodes $C, D_1.C, \ldots, D_m.C$. Thus an augmented matching M^a can include one or more nodes from $C, D_1.C, \ldots, D_m.C$ in its edges. The following realizes integrity of level-1 component classes in augmented matching:

(**augmented component integrity**) An augmented matching M^a is said to satisfy *augmented component integrity*, if the following holds: Let $(D.C, B.A)$ and (D_1, B_1) be any pair of edges in M^a such that $D_1, C_1 \in \mathcal{C}$, $D.C \in \mathcal{C}^a$, $A, B \in \mathcal{RA}$, and $B.A \in \mathcal{RA}^a$. Then $D_1 = D$ holds if and only if $B_1 = B$ holds.

To satisfy augmented component integrity, we divide the matching of PAO and $\mathcal{RA}$ into two phases: First, we take each composite class D and each composite attribute B and solve matching between the component classes and attributes of D and C, and then augment the (linguistic) similarity score $\sigma(D, B)$ with the matching score (**component-level matching**). Secondly, we solve matching between the component classes and component attributes using the augmented scores (**composite-level matching**). The matching algorithm PAOMatch is shown in Figure 4.

---

1. For each class D in $\mathcal{C}$ and for each attribute B in $\mathcal{RA}$, compute augmented score $\sigma^a(D, B)$ as follows:

1.1 If either D or B is not a composite class/attribute, then let $\sigma^a(D, B) = \sigma(D, B)$ and goto Step 1.

1.2 /* Now D is a composite class and B is a composite attribute. */
Let C_i $(i = 1, \ldots, k)$ be the component classes of D. Let A_j $(j = 1, \ldots, m)$ be the component attributes of B.

1.3 Let G_{DB} be the bipartite graph such that its two node sets are $\{D.C_i\}$ and $\{B.A_j\}$, respectively, and each edge $(D.C_i, B.A_j)$ has augmented weight $\sigma^a(D.C_i, B.A_j)$. If $\sigma^a(D.C_i, B.A_j)$ is undefined for some i and j, then recursively apply Step 1.1-1.4 to obtain $\sigma^a(D.C_i, B.A_j)$.

1.4 Solve weighted bipartite matching on G_{DB} to obtain matching M_{DB} and its total maximum weight w_{DB}. Let $\sigma^a(D, B) = \sigma(D, B) + \lambda \cdot w_{DB}$. Here, $0 < \lambda < 1$ is a pre-defined damping factor.

2. /* Now $\sigma^a(D, B)$ is defined for each D and B. Note that $G_{\sigma^a,\beta}$ does not include augmented nodes. */
Solve weighted bipartite matching on $G_{\sigma^a,\beta}$, where edge weight σ is replaced by σ^a, and obtain matching M.

3. Construct solution matching M^a as follows: For each matching edge (D, B) in M, add the matching M_{DB} obtained at Step 1.3 to M.

Fig. 4. PAOMatch: Two-phased structural matching

Step 1 of PAOMatch computes maximum matching for each component class-attribute pair. Then the resulting weight w_{DB} is added to the linguistic similarity score $\sigma(D, B)$, to reflect structural similarity of the components of D and B (Step 1.4). Here, damping factor $0 < \lambda < 1$ is introduced to reflect the nesting level of component hierarchy. A component class or attribute far from its composite root will have a reduced influence to the score.

After solving maximum matching for each composite class and each composite attribute, the top-level matching is carried out (Step 2). Here, we use $G_{\sigma,\beta}^a$ to exclude component classes and component attributes, since component-level matching is already done at Step 1.

Figure 3 shows application of PAOMatch. Gray nodes are augmented nodes created for each component class/attribute at Step 1.3 of PAOMatch. At Step 1.4, Component-level matching is done between the augmented nodes of composite classes {blog account, shopping} and attribute {contact}. Using the scores of these matchings, composite-level matching is carried out (Step 2). In Figure 3, edge (blog account, contact) is chosen as one of the four composite-level edges. Thus edges (blog account.email, contact.e-mail) and (blog account.country, contact.country) are added at Step 3, as the result of component-level matching. On the hand, although component-level edges (shopping.email, contact.e-mail), (shopping.address, contact.address) are matched at component-level matching, they are eventually discarded because their parents shopping and contact are not matched. Notice that blog name is matched to name at the composite level, not as the composite class blog account.blog name.

Theorem 2. *For a matching graph $G_{\sigma,\beta} = (\mathcal{C}, \mathcal{RA}, E)$, let N be the number of nodes and E be the number of* partOf *links in $G_{\sigma,\beta}$. Then* PAOMatch *returns a maximum matching satisfying augmented component integrity in $O(N^3 + E^3)$ time.*

Proof. For augmented component integrity, suppose that augmented matching M^a includes edges $(D.C, B.A)$ and (D_1, B_1) such that $D_1, C_1 \in \mathcal{C}, D.C \in \mathcal{C}^a, A, B \in \mathcal{RA}$, and $B.A \in \mathcal{RA}^a$. Now, assume that $D_1 = D$ holds. Since $D.C$ is an augmented node, the edge $(D.C, B.A)$ must be added at Step 3 of PAOMatch as one of the edge in M_{DB}. Since matching at Step 2 guarantees that (D_1, B_1) is the only edge in M^a that is adjacent to $D_1 = D$, the composite attribute B of M_{DB} must be B_1. The only-if part can be shown by a symmetric argument.

For the time bound, first consider Step 1 of PAOMatch. Let $\mathcal{D}$ be the set of composite classes in $\mathcal{C}$, and let $\mathcal{B}$ be the set of composite attributes in $\mathcal{RA}$. Weighted bipartite matching is executed at Step 1.4 for each $D \in \mathcal{D}$ and for each $B \in \mathcal{B}$. Let $|D|$ (resp. $|B|$) denote the number of component classes of D (resp. component attributes of B). Then one execution of Step 1.4 takes $O((|D| + |B|)^3)$ time. The total time of Step 1.4 is bounded by $\sum_{D \in \mathcal{D}, B \in \mathcal{B}}(|D| + |B|)^3 \leq (\sum_{D \in \mathcal{D}} |D| + \sum_{B \in \mathcal{B}} |B|)^3 = E^3$. For Step 2, bipartite matching is performed on $G_{\sigma^a,\beta}$, which has N nodes. Thus Step 2 takes $O(N^3)$ time. Step 3 can be done in $O(N + E)$ time.   □

5.2 Combination Risk Class and Inhibitor

Now consider combination risk classes. A combination risk class D_r is a composite class having component classes $C_1, \ldots, C_k$, where C_i is a class in $\mathcal{C}$ or component-composite classes, and the risk values $r_f(D_r)$ and $r_p(D_r)$ are given. These risk values are applied when and only when all of D_r's component classes are selected in an augmented matching M^a. Thus combination risk classes can express high-risk combination of privacy attributes.

Let us consider similarity score maximization where tolerable maximum limits are imposed on f- and/or p-risk values, as we discussed in Section 4.1. If D_r exceeds the risk limit, selecting all the component classes of D_r should be prohibited in the matching. Now let $\mathcal{D}_r$ be the subset of combination risk classes such that $D_r \in \mathcal{D}_r$ exceeds a given risk limit. We need to design an algorithm that finds a maximum matching that avoids selecting all the component classes for each $D_r \in \mathcal{D}_r$. To solve this problem, we introduce a *combination inhibitor* $Inh(D_r)$, which is a supplementary graph constructed by the algorithm CombInhibitor, shown in Figure 5.

Let us reconsider the running example, and assume that p-risk limit $m_p = 4$ is given. Then rn&bn is the only combination risk class in Figure 1 that should be inhibited. CombInhibitor adds a component inhibitor for rn&bn to the augmented matching graph. In Figure 3, the inhibitor node is labeled as !rn&ad. The combination inhibitor works as follows: The dashed edges attached to the inhibitor node have the highest weight in the graph. Therefore, if both *real name* and shopping.address are selected in a matching M, we can always make another matching M' by replacing one of the matching edges, say, the one adjacent to real name, with (real name, !rn&ad). Then M' should have a score higher than M. Therefore maximum matching will give us a solution that avoids simultaneously selecting real name and

---

For each combination risk class $D_r \in \mathcal{D}_r$, do:

1. Add the following bipartite subgraph $Inh(D_r) = (V_h, U_h, E_h)$ to the augmented matching graph $G_{\sigma,\beta}^a(\mathcal{C}, \mathcal{RA}, E)$. Let $C_1, \ldots, C_k$ be the component classes of D_r.

1.1 The node set V_h equals the component classes $\{C_1, \ldots, C_k\}$, and the other node set U_h equals the singleton set $\{A_h\}$ containing a newly introduced *inhibitor node* A_h.

1.2 The edge set E_h consists of k edges $(C_1, A_h), \ldots, (C_k, A_h)$, where each edge has an equal weight w_h such that w_h is any fixed value higher than the maximum similarity score found in $G_{\sigma,\beta}(\mathcal{C}, \mathcal{RA}, E)$.

Fig. 5. CombInhibitor($\mathcal{D}_r, G_{\sigma,\beta}^a$): Adding combination inhibitors

`shopping.address`. Thus we have succeeded in preventing p-risk value from exceeding 4. Formally, we have the following property:

Theorem 3. *Suppose that a matching graph $G_{\sigma,\beta} = (\mathcal{C}, \mathcal{RA}, E)$ is augmented with the combination inhibitor $Inh(D_r)$ for each $D_r \in \mathcal{D}_r$, where $\mathcal{D}_r$ is a subset of combination risk classes of $G_{\sigma,\beta}$. Then a maximum matching M of $G_{\sigma,\beta}$ always includes an edge of $Inh(D_r)$ for any $D_r \in \mathcal{D}_r$. Thus there is no maximum matching that includes all the component classes of D_r.*

Proof. (omitted due to space limitation)

By the above theorem, just adding combination inhibitor $Inh(D_r)$ to the matching graph can prevent application of the exceeded risk values of D_r. The supplementary subgraphs introduced by combination inhibitors have a maximum total size equal to the size of combination risk classes. Thus adding combination inhibitors multiplies the graph size only by a constant factor. We also note that the total maximum weight includes the weight of inhibitor edges given by $w_{inh} =$ (the number of inhibitors)* w_h. Thus we need to subtract w_{inh} from the matching weight w_M to obtain the actual total similarity score.

5.3 Finding Optimum Matching

We use the following monotonicity in matching solutions for searching on risk values.

Lemma 1. *Let M_1^a be a matching of graph $G_{\sigma,\beta}$ such that M_1^a satisfies risk limits r_f and r_p. Then there is a matching M_2^a such that M_2^a satisfies risk limits $r_f' > r_f$ and $r_p' > r_p$, and $\sigma^a(M_1^a) \leq \sigma^a(M_2^a)$.*

Proof. It is obvious that M_1^a remains a matching under the weaker limits of r_f' and r_p'. Thus at least M_1^a satisfies the condition of M_2^a of the lemma. □

Let F (resp. P) be the number of distinct f-risk (resp. p-risk) values appearing in $G_{\sigma,\beta}^a$. If we are using 5-digit risk values, then we have $F \leq 5$ and $P \leq 5$. Figure 6 shows matching algorithms for the optimization problems defined in Section 4.1.

Algorithm MaxSim($G^a_{\sigma,\beta}, m_f, m_p$) /* Similarity score maximization under risk limit */

Input Augmented bipartite graph $G^a_{\sigma,\beta}$, maximum f-risk m_f, and maximum p-risk m_p, where m_f and/or m_f may be ∞. /*

Output Maximum augmented matching M^a of $G^a_{\sigma,\beta}$ such that $r_f(M^a) \le m_f$ and $r_p(M^a) \le m_p$.

1. Remove from $G^a_{\sigma,\beta}$ classes C such that $r_f(C) > m_f$ or $r_p(C) > m_p$.
2. Let $\mathcal{D}_r$ be the set of combination risk classes D_r such that $r_f(D_r) > m_f$ or $r_p(D_r) > m_p$ holds. Execute CombInhibitor($\mathcal{D}_r, G^a_{\sigma,\beta}$).
3. Apply PAOMatch to $G^a_{\sigma,\beta}$ to obtain M^a.

Algorithm MaxSimCombinedRisk($G^a_{\sigma,\beta}, m_c$) /* Similarity score maximization under combined-risk limit */

Input: Augmented bipartite graph $G^a_{\sigma,\beta}$, and maximum combined-risk m_c.

Output: Maximum augmented matching M^a of $G^a_{\sigma,\beta}$ such that $cr(r_f(M^a), r_p(M^a)) \le m_c$.

1. Assume that $F < P$. Otherwise in the following steps swap F with P, and swap m_f with m_p.
2. For each value r_f in F do:
2.1 Compute maximum r_p such that $cr(r_f, r_p) \le m_c$ holds.
2.2 Call MaxSim($G^a_{\sigma,\beta}, r_f, r_p$).
3. Report matching M^a that had maximum score at 2.2

Algorithm MinRisk($G^a_{\sigma,\beta}, w_{min}$) /* Risk minimization under minimum similarity score w_{min}. */

1. Assume that $F < P$. Otherwise in the following steps swap F with P, and swap m_f with m_p.
2. For each value r_f in F do:
2.1 Perform binary search on p-values to find minimum r_p such that result M^a of MaxSim($G^a_{\sigma,\beta}, r_f, r_p$) has score no smaller than w_{min}.
3. Report the matching found in Step 2.1 such that its combined risk r is minimum.

Algorithm MaxCombined($G^a_{\sigma,\beta}$) /* Combined score maximization. */
1. For each f-risk value p_f and for each p-risk value p_f, do:
1.1 Call MaxSim($G^a_{\sigma,\beta}, r_f, r_p$).
2. Report matching M^a that had maximum combined score $\sigma(M^a)/r_c(M^a)$ in Step 1.1.

Fig. 6. Algorithms for maximum matching under given risk constraints

Theorem 4. *Let F (resp. P) be the number of distinct f-risk (resp. p-risk) values appearing in augmented matching graph $G^a_{\sigma,\beta}$. Let R be $F + P$, and let N be the number of nodes and E be the number of* partOf *links in $G^a_{\sigma,\beta}$. The following holds:*

1. *MaxSim($G^a_{\sigma,\beta}, m_f, m_p$) solves similarity score maximization in $O(N^3 + E^3)$ time.*
2. *MaxSimCombinedRisk($G^a_{\sigma,\beta}, m_c$) solves similarity score maximization under combined-risk limit m_c in $O((N^3 + E^3)R)$ time.*
3. *MinRisk($G^a_{\sigma,\beta}, w_{min}$) solves risk minimization under minimum similarity score w_{min} in $O((N^3 + E^3)R \log R)$ time.*

4. $MaxCombined(G^a_{\sigma,\beta})$ *solves combined score maximization in* $O((N^3 + E^3)R^2)$ *time.*

Proof. 1. In Step 1 of $MaxSim(G^a_{\sigma,\beta}, m_f, m_p)$, classes C that violate the maximum limit m_f or m_p are removed. If these classes C are not removed, it is easy to construct a graph that has a maximum matching violating one of these limits. In Step 2, CombInhibitor introduces combination inhibitors so that by Theorem 3, any matching of $G^a_{\sigma,\beta}$ will not include a combination risk class that violates the limits. If CombInhibitor is not applied, it is easy to construct a graph that has a maximum matching that includes all the component classes of a combination risk class which violates the limits. Thus the matching obtained at Step 3 gives maximum score under the limits m_f and m_p. For the time bound, Step 1 and Step 2 can be done in linear time and increase the size of $G^a_{\sigma,\beta}$ by a factor of a constant. Thus by Theorem 2, Step 3 can be done in $O(N^3 + E^3)$ time.
2. For similarity score maximization under combined-risk limit m_c, testing maximum matching score among every combination of risk values r_f and r_p that satisfy the limit m_c guarantees that there will be no other matching that has a higher score while satisfying m_c. We do not need to test on combinations r'_f and r'_p which have combined risk values less than m_c, since by Lemma 1, matching score satisfying r'_f and r'_p does not exceed the score satisfying $r_f \geq r'_f$ and $r_p \geq r'_p$ such that $cr(r_f, r_p) \leq cr(r_f, r_p) \leq m_c$. For the time bound, $MaxSim(G^a_{\sigma,\beta}, r_f, r_p)$ is called $F \leq R$ times, which gives the bound $O((N^3 + E^3)R)$.
3. For risk minimization under minimum similarity score w_{min}, it is sufficient to test all the combinations of f-risk and p-risk values that have matching M^a such that $\sigma^a(M^a) \geq w_{min}$ holds. Again by Lemma 1, if a combination of r_f and r_p has a matching score greater than the minimum limit w_{min}, then all the combinations such that $r'_f \geq r_f$ and $r'_p \geq r_p$ also have matching score greater than w_{min}. This property allows us to perform binary search on r_f for each fixed r_p. Thus $MaxSim(G^a_{\sigma,\beta}, r_f, r_p)$ is called $O(R \log R)$ at Step 2.2 and we have the time bound.
4. For combined score maximization, again it is sufficient to test all the combinations of f-risk and p-risk values to find a matching M^a having maximum combined score $s_c(M^a) = \sigma(M^a)/r_c(M^a)$. Since the combined score $s_c = w/r$ does not have monotonicity, we try $MaxSim(G^a_{\sigma,\beta}, r_f, r_p)$ for $O(R^2)$ times. $\qquad\square$

6   Conclusion

In this paper, we proposed the concept of privacy attribute ontology for identity management involving complex attributes and identities. Our ontology model realizes risk evaluation of matching attributes, and the algorithms presented in this paper solve maximum similarity matching under various types of risk constraints.

Acknowledgment

This work is in part supported by the Grant-in-Aid for Scientific Research of JSPS (Japan Society for the Promotion of Science) (#18300031), and Strategic International Cooperative Program of JST (Japan Science and Technology Agency). The work of

Gail-J. Ahn was partially supported by the grants from US National Science Foundation (NSF-IIS-0242393) and the US Department of Energy Early Career Principal Investigator Award (DE-FG02-03ER25565).

References

1. Microsoft Developer Network (MSDN) CardSpace page,
   `http://msdn.microsoft.com/CardSpace`
2. Cohen, W., Ravikumar, P., Feinberg, S.: A Comparison of String Metrics for Matching Names and Records. In: Proc. KDD Workshop on Data Cleaning and Object Consolidation (2003)
3. Garey, M.R., Johnson, D.S.: Computers and Intractability - A Guide to the Theory of NP-Completeness. Freeman, New York (1979)
4. Kagal, L., Finin, T.W., Joshi, A.: A Policy Based Approach to Security for the Semantic Web. In: Fensel, D., Sycara, K.P., Mylopoulos, J. (eds.) ISWC 2003. LNCS, vol. 2870, pp. 402–418. Springer, Heidelberg (2003)
5. Jutla, D.N., Bodorik, P.: Sociotechnical Architecture for Online Privacy. IEEE Security & Privacy 3(2), 29–39 (2005)
6. Japan Network Security Association, Surveys on Information Security Incidents (in Japanese) (2006),
   `http://www.jnsa.org/result/2006/pol/insident/070720/`
7. Kolari, P., Li Ding, S., Ganjugunte, L., Kagal, A.J., Finin, T.: Enhancing Web Privacy Protection through Declarative Policies. In: Proc. IEEE Workshop on Policy for Distributed Systems and Networks(POLICY 2005) (June 2005)
8. Kuhn, H.W.: The Hungarian Method for the Assignment Problem. Naval Research Logistics Quarterly 2, 83–97 (1955)
9. Li, W.-S., Clifton, C.: SEMINT: a Tool for Identifying Attribute Correspondences in Heterogeneous Database Using Neural Networks. Data Knowledge Eng. 33(1), 49–84 (2000)
10. Liberty Alliance Project Homepage, `http://www.projectliberty.org/`
11. OpenID Foundation, `http://openid.net/`
12. OWL Web Ontology Language Overview, W3C Recommendation 10 (February 2004),
    `http://www.w3.org/TR/owl-features/`
13. Patel, C., Supekar, K., Lee, Y.: OntoGenie: Extracting Ontlogy Instances from WWW. In: Proc. Huaman Language Technology for the Semantic Web and Web Services, ISWC 2003 (2003)
14. The Platform for Privacy Preferences 1.1 (P3P1.1) Specification, W3C Working Group Note (November 13, 2006)
15. Udrea, O., Getoor, L., Miller, R.J.: Leveraging Data and Structure in Ontology Integration. In: Proc. ACM SIGMOD 2007, pp. 449–460 (2007)
16. WordNet — a Lexical Database for the English Language, Princeton University,
    `http://wordnet.princeton.edu/`

Beyond Control-Flow: Extending Business Process Configuration to Roles and Objects

M. La Rosa[1], M. Dumas[1,2], A.H.M. ter Hofstede[1], J. Mendling[1], and F. Gottschalk[3]

[1] Queensland University of Technology, Australia
{m.larosa,j.mendling,m.dumas,a.terhofstede}@qut.edu.au
[2] University of Tartu, Estonia
marlon.dumas@ut.ee
[3] Eindhoven University of Technology, The Netherlands
f.gottschalk@tm.tue.nl

Abstract. A configurable process model is an integrated representation of multiple variants of a business process. It is designed to be individualized to meet a particular set of requirements. As such, configurable process models promote systematic reuse of proven or common practices. Existing notations for configurable process modeling focus on capturing tasks and control-flow dependencies, neglecting equally important aspects of business processes such as data flow, material flow and resource management. This paper fills this gap by proposing an integrated meta-model for configurable processes with advanced features for capturing resources involved in the performance of tasks (through task-role associations) as well as flow of data and physical artifacts (through task-object associations). Although embodied as an extension of a popular process modeling notation, namely EPC, the meta-model is defined in an abstract and formal manner to make it applicable to other notations.

Keywords: Process model, configuration, resource, object flow.

1 Introduction

Reference process models such as the Supply Chain Operations Reference (SCOR) model [18] or the SAP Reference Model [5], capture recurrent business operations in their respective domains. They are packaged as libraries of models in several business process modeling tools and are used by analysts to derive process models for specific organizations or IT projects (a practice known as *individualization*) as an alternative to designing process models from scratch.

Reference process models in commercial use lack a representation of variation points and configuration decisions. As a result, analysts are given little guidance as to which model elements need to be removed, added or modified to address a given requirement. This shortcoming is addressed by the concept of *configurable process models* [15], which captures process variants in an integrated manner. This concept is a step forward towards systematic reuse of (reference) process models. However, existing configurable process modeling languages focus on the control-flow perspective and fail to capture resources, data and physical artifacts participating in the process.

Q. Li et al. (Eds.): ER 2008, LNCS 5231, pp. 199–215, 2008.

This paper extends a configurable process modeling notation, namely Configurable Event-driven Process Chains (C-EPCs), with notions of roles and objects. The proposed extension supports the representation of a range of variations in the way roles and objects are associated with tasks. We define a notion of valid configuration and an algorithm to individualize a configurable process model given a valid configuration. By construction, this algorithm ensures that the individualized process models are syntactically correct. The paper also explores interplays that occur across the control-flow, object flow and resource modeling perspectives during individualization. The proposal has been applied to a comprehensive case study in the film industry, which is used as an example throughout the paper.

The rest of the paper is structured as follows. Section 2 reviews previous work related to the modeling of object flow and resources in business processes and the notion of configurable process model. Section 3 introduces the working example and uses it to illustrate a meta-model that extends EPCs with resource and object flow modeling. Next, Section 4 explores the configuration of process models along the resource and object flow perspectives. Section 5 presents a formal model of a fully-featured C-EPC, which leads to the definition of an individualization algorithm. The paper concludes with a summary and an outlook on open issues.

2   Background and Related Work

2.1   Integrated Process Modeling

Business processes can be seen from a number of perspectives, including the control-flow, the data and the resource perspectives [9]. Control-flow is generally modeled in terms of activities and events related by control arcs and connectors. The resource perspective, on the other hand, is commonly modeled in terms of associations between activities and roles, where roles represent capabilities and/or organizational groups [1]. In UML Activity Diagrams (ADs) [6] and BPMN [19], this association is encoded by means of *swimlanes*. Each activity is associated with a swimlane representing a role or an organizational unit. UML ADs allow multiple swimlanes (or *partitions*) to be associated with an activity. In (extended) EPCs [17], symbols denoting roles or organizational units can be attached to tasks. In this paper, we define sophisticated role-based resource modeling features, which go beyond those found in UML ADs, BPMN and EPCs, and we layer configuration features on top of them. A notation-independent discussion of resource allocation for business processes is reported in [13,16].

The flow of data and physical artifacts is generally captured by associating objects with activities. UML ADs support the association of object nodes with activity nodes to denote inputs and outputs. One can associate multiple objects as input or as output of an activity. The execution of an activity consumes one object from each of the activity's input object nodes and produces one object in each of its output object nodes. Similar features are found in BPMN and extended EPCs. In this paper, we propose a more fine-grained approach to object flow modeling and mechanisms to capture variability in relation to tasks. Yet, we do not consider data mapping issues which are important for executable languages such as ADEPT$_{flex}$ [14], BPEL [3] or YAWL [2].

2.2   Configurable Process Modeling

Research on configurable business process models has focused on mechanisms for capturing variability along the control-flow perspective. Rosemann & van der Aalst [15] put forward the C-EPC notation where tasks can be switched on or off and routing connectors can be made configurable and linked through configuration requirements. Becker et al. [4] introduce an approach to hide element types in EPCs for configuration purposes. Although the emphasis is on tasks and control-flow connectors, this approach can also be used to show or hide resource or data types. However, this only affects the view on the EPC, not its underlying behavior. Also, this approach does not enable fine-grained configuration of task-role and task-object associations (beyond hiding). In previous work, we have investigated a set of process configuration operators based on skipping and blocking of tasks [7], and applied them to configure the control-flow of executable process modeling languages, such as YAWL and BPEL [8].

We use EPCs as a base notation to define variability mechanisms along the data and resource perspectives. Three reasons underpin this choice. First, EPCs are widely used for reference process modeling (cf. the SAP reference model). Secondly, EPCs provide basic features for associating data and roles to tasks, which we extend in this paper. Finally, this choice allows us to build on top of the existing definition of the C-EPC notation. Nonetheless, we define our extensions in an abstract manner so that they are applicable beyond the scope of EPCs.

3   Working Example

The working example in Fig. 1 is an extract of a reference process model on audio editing for screen post-production, which has been developed and validated in collaboration with subject-matter experts of the Australian Film Television & Radio School.[1] We chose this case study for the high level of creativity, and thus of variability, that characterizes the screen business. Indeed, the whole editing phase can radically change if the screen project aims to produce a documentary (usually without music) or a silent movie (without spoken dialogs). Below we describe the process as if it were non-configurable, to illustrate how we capture roles and objects participating in an EPC process. The configuration aspects will be addressed later on, so for now we ignore the meaning of the thick border of some elements in the picture.

EPC's main elements are events, functions, control-flow connectors, and arcs linking these elements. Events model triggers or conditions, functions correspond to tasks and connectors denote splits and joins of type AND, OR or XOR. We extend these concepts by associating roles and objects to functions, in an integrated EPC (iEPC). A role, depicted on a function's left hand, captures a class of organizational resources that is able to perform that function: e.g. the role Producer captures the set of all the persons with this role in a given screen project. A role is dynamically bound to one concrete resource at run-time (e.g. the Producer associated with function *Spotting session* will be bound to Michelle Portland). A resource can be human or non-human (e.g. an information system or a robot), but for simplicity, we only consider human resources in the example.

---

[1] The school's web-site can be accessed at www.aftrs.edu.au

An object, depicted on a function's right hand, captures a physical or software artifact of an enterprise, that is used (input object) or produced (output object) by a function. Each object in the process model is statically bound to a concrete artifact.

The first function is Spotting session, which starts once the shooting has completed. Roles and objects are linked to functions either directly or via a connector. For example, the OR-join between Composer and Sound Designer indicates that at least one of these roles is required to perform this activity. Composer is needed if the project features music, Sound Designer is needed if the project features sound, where sound consists of dialogs, effects (FX) and/or atmospheres (atmos). Based on the screening of the Picture cut, Composer and Sound Designer hold a Spotting session to decide what music or sound should be added at which point of time. This information is stored in the cues (e.g. Music cues for music). Picture cut is thus an input object, while the cues are output objects connected via an OR-split that indicates that at least one set of cues is produced, depending on the type of project. A spotting session may be supervised by at least two roles among Producer, Director and Assistant Director that have creative authority in the project. These roles are linked together by a *range* connector. This connector indicates the upper bound and lower bound for a number of elements (roles or objects) that are required (where k refers to the indegree for a join or to the outdegree for a split; in this case $k = 3$).

Once the cues are ready, the design of music and/or sound starts. In the former, the Composer records the project's Music tracks (an output) following the Music cues and using the Picture cut as a reference (an AND-join connects these two inputs). A Temp music file may also be produced at this stage. This object is linked to the function via a dashed arc, which indicates that an object, a role, or a combination thereof is optional, whereas a full arc indicates mandatoriness. Sound design is usually more complex as it involves the recording of the Dialog, FX and/or Atmos tracks, according to the respective cues on the Picture cut. The Editor or the Sound Designer are responsible for this task. Similarly to Music design, a Temp sound file may also be produced.

Afterwards, the Composer and/or the Sound Designer provide the Director and usually the Producer with an update on the work-in-progress. Producer is an optional role. At least one mandatory role is to be assigned to each function to ensure its execution. Temp files may be used by the Composer and by the Sound Designer as a guide for the Progress update (the OR-join between these two objects is thus optional). Generally, the result of this task is a set of notes describing the changes required; sometimes, however, the Composer or the Sound Designer may prefer not to take notes. If changes are needed, the Music and Sound design can be repeated as specified by the loop in the model. In this case, the notes can be used as input to these tasks.

Upon completion of the design phase, the Mixer and the Composer mix the Music tracks into a Music premix if the project has music, while the Mixer and the Sound Designer mix the Sound tracks into a Sound premix if the project has sound. The Producer may supervise both mixings. In Picture editing, the Picture cut is edited by an Editor, while a Negcutter is required if the cut is on Film. The cross below 'Picture cut' indicates that the object is consumed by the function and is no longer available afterwards. The process ends with Final mixing, where the Mixer with the Sound Designer and/or the Composer release a Final mix using the available Premixes. A Deliverable may also

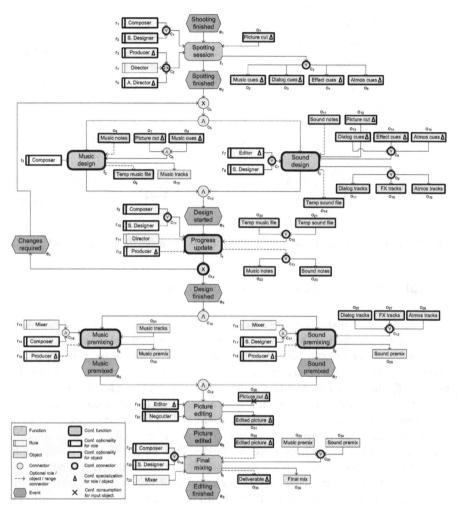

Fig. 1. The reference process model for audio editing

be released by overlaying the premixes onto the Edited picture, should a demo of the video with the integrated audio be required.

Beside the process model, we use a 'hierarchy model' to represent all the roles and objects referred to by the nodes of the process model. For example, in the editing process there are five nodes for the role Producer and four for the object Picture cut. A hierarchy model also captures the specializations that can be associated with a role or object, by means of a specialization relation. Fig. 2 shows the hierarchy models for the roles and objects of the editing process, where the specialization relation is depicted by an empty arrow linking a special role (object) to its generalization. Typically, for a role this relation represents a separation of tasks among its specializations (e.g., Executive Producer, Line Producer and Co-Producer share the Producer's duties). For an object, it represents a set of subtypes (e.g. 16mm and 35mm are two types of Film). The hierarchy models will be used later on in the configuration of the process model.

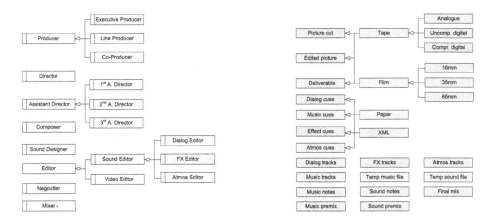

Fig. 2. The role-hierarchy model and the object-hierarchy model for the process of Fig. 1

4   Exploring Integrated Process Configuration

A reference process model provides a generic solution that needs to be individualized to fit a specific setting. For this reason, process configuration can be interpreted as a restriction of the reference process model's behavior [7,15]. Following this principle, we configure an integrated process model by restricting the behavior of a set of variation points (*configurable nodes*) identified in the reference process model. A variation point can be any active node of a process model (function, role, object or connector), and is represented via the use of a thick border. A configuration assigns each variation point a (set of) *configuration value(s)* to keep or restrict the node's behavior. Since arcs and events are not active elements of a process model, they are not directly configurable. However, as a result of configuring a variation point, neighboring events and arcs can be affected (e.g. an event can be dropped). The extended iEPC meta-model that captures these concepts is called Configurable iEPC (C-iEPC). In the following, we describe the characteristics of each variation point.

Configurable functions can be left 'activated' (ON), or restricted to 'excluded' (OFF) or 'optional' (OPT). The second value removes the function from the process model (i.e. the function is skipped from the process flow). The third value permits deferring this choice until run-time, so that the decision whether to execute or skip the function is made on an instance-by-instance basis. In the example, Music design is configurable: it can be set to OFF if the Director has planned not to have any music in the project, or to OPT to let the Director decide whether to have it or not, once the project has started.

Configurable control-flow connectors can be restricted to a less expressive connector type, or to a sequence of incoming control-flow nodes (in case of a join) or outgoing nodes (in case of a split). The last option is achieved by removing the connector altogether. An OR can be restricted to an XOR, to an AND or to a sequence. An XOR can only be restricted to a sequence. An AND cannot be restricted. For instance, if the project cannot afford the repetition of music and sound design, due to the costs involved, the configurable XOR-split (id. c_{14} of the example, can be set to the sequence starting with event Design finished, so as to exclude the loop after function Progress update. For further details on the configuration of the control-flow, we refer to [15].

Configurable roles and *objects* have two configuration dimensions: *optionality* and *specialization*, i.e. they can take a value for each dimension. If a configurable role (object) is 'optional' (OPT), it can be restricted to 'mandatory' (MND), or to 'excluded' to be removed from the process (OFF); if it is 'mandatory' it can only be restricted to 'excluded'. For example, if a project does not feature music, the participation of the Composer and the production of Music cues can be excluded from the Spotting session. Configurable roles and objects for which there exists a specialization in the hierarchy model, can be restricted to any of their specializations. As per the hierarchy model of Fig. 2, Picture cut can be specialized to Tape, if the project does not support an editing on Film. Also, the Producer associated with Progress update can be specialized to Line Producer and made mandatory, should the Director need creative support in this phase. The availability of a specialization for a role or object, is depicted with a small pyramid in the node's right-hand side.

Configurable input objects have a further configuration dimension – *usage*, such that those inputs that are 'consumed' (CNS) can be restricted to 'used' (USE). For instance, we can restrict Picture cut to *used* if its specialization is Tape, as only a Picture cut on Film is destroyed during the Picture editing.

Configurable range connectors have two configuration dimensions: *optionality* and *range restriction*. The same rules for roles and objects govern the possible changes of optionality values of a range connector. For example, the optional OR-join connecting the temp files in Progress update, can be made mandatory if the temp files are always used by this function. The range restriction is achieved by increasing the lower bound and decreasing the upper bound, or a choice can be made for a single node (role or object) to be associated with the function linked to the connector, effectively removing the connector altogether. This is allowed if the lower bound is 1 and the node is in the connector's preset (in case of a join), or in its postset (in case of a split). For example, the configurable range connector $(2 : k)$ associated with Spotting session, can be restricted to $(3 : k)$ – all the supervisors have to partake in the Spotting session, or to $(2 : 2)$ – exactly two of them have to partake. This is consistent with the configuration of the control-flow connectors, as the range connector subsumes any connector type. In fact, an OR is equivalent to a $(1 : k)$ range connector and can be restricted to an XOR $(1 : 1)$, to an AND $(k : k)$, to a single node, but also to any other reduced range (e.g. $2 : k$). An XOR can only be restricted to a single node. An AND $(k : k)$ cannot be restricted.

Under certain circumstances, a configuration node may not be allowed to be freely set, and this may depend on the configuration of other nodes. In fact, there can be an interplay between the configuration of functions and roles, or objects and functions, determined by the domain in which the reference process model has been constructed. For example, an Edited picture is needed in Final mixing only if a Delivery is produced, otherwise it must be excluded. *Configuration requirements* capture such restrictions in the form of logical predicates that govern the values of configurable nodes. In the following, we classify these requirements according to the type of interplay and support this classification with examples taken from the model of Fig. 1 (where M, S and U stand for the optionality, specialization and usage dimension, resp.):

Single Node requirements: constrain the configuration of a single node, i.e. no dependency exists on other nodes. For example, the Picture cut associated with the Spotting session cannot be excluded as this is the initial input object to the whole process [Req_1]. Another example constraining the specialization of roles is given by the Editor in Sound design, which cannot be specialized to Video Editor, due to the capabilities required by associated the function [Req_2]. Concerning the control-flow, the XOR-split (c_{14}) after Progress update cannot be set to the sequence starting with the event Changes required only, as this would lead to skip the whole premixing phase [Req_3].

Connector–Connector requirements: constrain the configuration of multiple connectors. For instance, the two OR-joins for the roles and the input objects of Progress update (id. c_{11} and c_{12}) must be restricted the same way [Req_4]. The configuration of the former join allows the restriction of the run-time choice of which role is to partake in Progress update, while the configuration of the latter allows the restriction of which temp files to be used. Although the second connector is optional (i.e. no temp file may be used), a configuration where, e.g., the first OR is restricted to AND and the second one is restricted to a mandatory XOR must be denied. The reason is that if temp files are available, these need to be linked to the roles Composer and Sound Designer that will actually use them: the Composer will use the Temp music files, while the Sound Designer will use the Temp sound files.

Function–Function requirements: constrain the configuration of multiple functions. For example, an editing project deals with the editing of music and/or sound, so at least one function between Music design and Sound design must be present [Req_5]. Another constraint exists, e.g., between Music premixing and Music design, as the former needs to be dropped if the latter is excluded from the model [Req_6].

Role–Role requirements: constrain the configuration of multiple roles. For example, the Producer in Music premixing must be specialized in the same way as the Producer in Sound premixing, since these roles are typically covered by the same person [Req_7 (on S)]. To run a Spotting session, at least one role between Composer and Sound Designer need to be present [Req_8 (on M)].

Object–Object requirements: constrain the configuration of multiple objects. For instance, all the occurrences of the objects Picture cut and Edited picture must have the same specialization as the object Deliverable, to ensure a consistent propagation of the picture medium throughout the process [Req_9 (on S)]. The Picture cut in Picture editing is consumed if it is specialized to Film [Req_{10} (on S, U)], as in this case the medium is physically cut (thus destroyed) and then spliced. Also, the exclusion of Dialog cues from Sound design implies the exclusion of Dialog tracks, since these are produced according to the cues [Req_{11} (on M)].

Connector–Node requirements: constrain the configuration of connectors and nodes. For example, the exclusion of function Progress update implies the restriction of the XOR-split (c_{14}) to the sequence starting with Design finished, as at run-time the repetition of the design phase depends on the result of Progress update [Req_{12}].

Function–Role requirements: constrain the configuration of functions and roles. For instance, Music design must be excluded if the Composer is excluded from this function. On the other hand, if Sound Designer is excluded from Sound Design, this function can still be performed by the Editor [Req_{13} (on M)].

Function–Object requirements: constrain the configuration of functions and objects. For example, function Progress update cannot be excluded if Temp music file in Music design or Temp sound file in Sound design are included, since the files are produced to be later used by this function. Otherwise, if Progress update is set to optional, the files cannot be made mandatory [Req_{14} (on M)].

Role–Object requirements: constrain the configuration of roles and objects. An example is given by the role Negcutter, which is only required if the project is edited and delivered on Film. Thus, if this role is mandatory, all the occurrences of Picture cut and Edited picture, and the Deliverable, must be specialized to Film. In this case the Picture cut in function Picture editing needs to be set to consumed [Req_{15} (on M, S, U)].

More complex requirements can be captured by combining requirements from the above classes. Fig. 3 shows the audio editing process that was followed by Bill Bennett to direct the feature film "Kiss or Kill".[2] This model is the result of configuring the reference process model of Fig. 1 for an editing on Tape without music. Here, for instance, Music premixing has been excluded and, as per Req_6, so has been Music design. Similarly, Progress update has been excluded, and thus, as per Req_{12}, the loop capturing the repetition of the design phase has also been removed. Moreover, the Editor in Picture editing has been specialized to a Video Editor (this complies with Req_2). Since the editing is on Tape, the Picture cut in input to Picture editing has been set to 'used' and specialized to Tape, and thus, as per Req_{15}, the Negcutter has been excluded from this function.

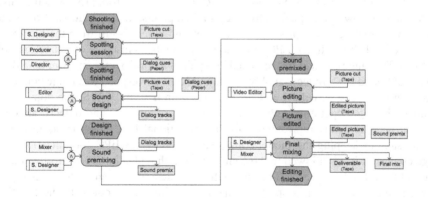

Fig. 3. The audio editing process model configured for a project without music

5   Correctness and Configuration of Integrated Process Models

This section presents an algorithm to generate an individualized iEPC from a C-iEPC with respect to a set of configuration values (i.e. a configuration). For example, this

---

[2] Kiss or Kill, 1997 (Australia), http://www.imdb.com/title/tt0119467

algorithm is able to generate the model shown in Fig. 3 from the model of Fig. 1 given a valid configuration. In doing so, the algorithm ensures the preservation of syntactic correctness, i.e. the individualized C-iEPC will be syntactically correct provided that the original C-iEPC was syntactically correct. To define this algorithm, we first need to define the notions of syntactically correct iEPC and valid configuration.

5.1 Integrated Business Process Model

In order to formally define the concepts of iEPC and correct iEPC, we first need to have a formal definition of role and object-hierarchies. A role (object) hierarchy is essentially a set of roles (objects) together with a specialization relation.

Definition 1 (Role-hierarchy Model). *A role-hierarchy model is a tuple $Rh = (R, \overset{R}{\leftarrow})$, where:*

- *R is a finite, non-empty set of* roles,
- *$\overset{R}{\leftarrow} \subseteq R \times R$ is the* specialization *relation on R ($\overset{R}{\leftarrow}$ is transitive, reflexive, acyclic[3]).*

Definition 2 (Object-hierarchy Model). *An object-hierarchy model is a tuple $Oh = (O, \overset{O}{\leftarrow})$, where:*

- *O is a finite, non-empty set of* objects, *i.e. physical or software artifacts,*
- *$\overset{O}{\leftarrow} \subseteq O \times O$ is the* specialization *relation on O ($\overset{O}{\leftarrow}$ is transitive, reflexive, acyclic).*

If $x_1 \overset{R/O}{\leftarrow} x_2$, we say x_1 is a *generalization* of x_2 and x_2 is a *specialization* of x_1 ($x_1 \neq x_2$). For example, Dialog Editor is a specialization of Editor.

The definition of iEPC given below extends that of EPCs from [15], which focuses on the control-flow only. Specifically, iEPCs add a precise representation of roles and objects participating in the process. These roles and objects stem from the hierarchy-models defined above. In an iEPC, each node represents an instance of a function, role or object. The range connector is modeled by a pair of natural numbers: lower bound (n) and upper bound (m). Indeed, an AND, OR and XOR correspond to a range connector resp. with $n = m = k$, with $n = 1, m = k$ and with $n = m = 1$. So we do not need to model the logic operators with separate connectors for roles and objects, although they can be graphically represented with the traditional EPC notation, as in Fig. 1. For the sake of keeping the model consistent with previous EPC formalizations, the range connector is not allowed in the control-flow, although a minimal effort would be required to add this construct. The optionality of roles, objects and range connectors, shown in the process as a property of the arc that links the node with the function, is modeled in iEPC as an attribute of the node. The consumption of input objects is modeled in the same way.

Definition 3 (iEPC). *Let F be a set of functions, $Rh = (R, \overset{R}{\leftarrow})$ be a role-hierarchy model and $Oh = (O, \overset{O}{\leftarrow})$ be an object-hierarchy model. An integrated EPC over F, Rh, Oh is a tuple $iEPC_{F,Rh,Oh} = (E, F_N, R_N, O_N, nm, C, A, L)$, where:*

---

[3] No cycles of length greater than one.

- E is a finite, non-empty set of events;
- F_N is a finite, non-empty set of function nodes for the process;
- R_N is a finite, non-empty set of role nodes for the process;
- O_N is a finite set of object nodes for the process;
- $nm = nf \cup nr \cup no$, where:
  - $nf \in F_N \to F$ assigns each function node to a function;
  - $nr \in R_N \to R$ assigns each role node to a role;
  - $no \in O_N \to O$ assigns each object node to an object;
- $C = C_{CF} \cup C_R \cup C_{IN} \cup C_{OUT}$ is a finite set of logical connectors, where:
  - C_{CF} is the set of control-flow connectors,
  - C_R is the set of range connectors for role nodes (role connectors),
  - C_{IN} is the set of range connectors for input nodes (input connectors),
  - C_{OUT} is the set of range connectors for output nodes (output connectors),
    where C_{CF}, C_R, C_{IN} and C_{OUT} are mutually disjoint;
- $A = A_{CF} \cup A_R \cup A_{IN} \cup A_{OUT}$ is a set of arcs, where:
  - $A_{CF} \subseteq (E \times F_N) \cup (F_N \times E) \cup (E \times C_{CF}) \cup (C_{CF} \times E) \cup (F_N \times C_{CF}) \cup (C_{CF} \times F_N) \cup (C_{CF} \times C_{CF})$ is the set of control-flow arcs,
  - $A_R \subseteq (R_N \times F_N) \cup (R_N \times C_R) \cup (C_R \times F_N)$ is the set of role arcs,
  - $A_{IN} \subseteq (O_N \times F_N) \cup (O_N \times C_{IN}) \cup (C_{IN} \times F_N)$ is the set of input arcs,
  - $A_{OUT} \subseteq (F_N \times O_N) \cup (F_N \times C_{OUT}) \cup (C_{OUT} \times O_N)$ is the set of output arcs,
    where A_R, A_{IN} and A_{OUT} are intransitive relations;
- $L = l_C^T \cup l_C^N \cup l_C^M \cup l_R^M \cup l_O^M \cup l_O^U$ is a set of label assignments, where:
  - $l_C^T \in C_{CF} \to \{AND, OR, XOR\}$ specifies the type of control-flow connector,
  - $l_C^N \in (C_R \cup C_{IN} \cup C_{OUT}) \to \mathbb{N} \times (\mathbb{N} \cup \{k\}) \cup \{(k,k)\}$, specifies lower bound and upper bound of the range connector,
  - $l_C^M \in (C_R \cup C_{IN} \cup C_{OUT}) \to \{MND, OPT\}$ specifies if a role connector, an input connector or an output connector is mandatory or optional,
  - $l_R^M \in R_N \to \{MND, OPT\}$ specifies if a role node is mandatory or optional;
  - $l_O^M \in O_N \to \{MND, OPT\}$ specifies if an object node is mandatory or optional;
  - $l_O^U \in O_N^{IN} \to \{USE, CNS\}$ specifies if an input object node is used or consumed, where $O_N^{IN} = dom(A_{IN}) \cap O_N$.

Given a connector c, let $l_C^N(c) = (n, m)$ for all $c \in C \setminus C_{CF}$. Then we use $lwb(c) = n$ and $upb(c) = m$ to refer to lower bound and upper bound of c. If F, Rh and Oh are clear from the context, we drop the subscript from $iEPC$. Also, we call all the function nodes, role nodes and object nodes simply as functions, roles and objects, wherever this does not lead to confusion.

We introduce the following notation to allow a more concise characterization of iEPCs.

Definition 4 (Auxiliary sets, functions and predicates). For an $iEPC$ we define the following subsets of its nodes, functions and predicates:

- $N_{CF} = E \cup F_N \cup C_{CF}$, as its set of control-flow nodes;
- $N_R = F_N \cup R_N \cup C_R$, as its set of role nodes;
- $N_{IN} = F_N \cup O_N^{IN} \cup C_{IN}$, as its set of input nodes;
- $N_{OUT} = F_N \cup O_N^{OUT} \cup C_{OUT}$, as its set of output nodes, where $O_N^{OUT} = dom(A_{OUT}) \cap O_N$;
- $N = N_{CF} \cup N_R \cup N_{IN} \cup N_{OUT}$, as its set of nodes;
- $\forall_{n \in N_\alpha} \overset{\alpha}{\bullet} n = \{x \in N_\alpha \mid (x, n) \in A_\alpha\}$, as the α-preset of n, $\alpha \in \{CF, R, IN, OUT\}$;
- $\forall_{n \in N_\alpha} n \overset{\alpha}{\bullet} = \{x \in N_\alpha \mid (n, x) \in A_\alpha\}$, as the α-postset of n, $\alpha \in \{CF, R, IN, OUT\}$;

- $E_s = \{e \in E \mid | \overset{CF}{\bullet} e| = 0 \wedge |e \overset{CF}{\bullet}| = 1\}$ *as the set of start events;*
- $E_e = \{e \in E \mid | \overset{CF}{\bullet} e| = 1 \wedge |e \overset{CF}{\bullet}| = 0\}$ *as the set of end events;*
- $C^S_{CF} = \{c \in C_{CF} \mid | \overset{CF}{\bullet} c| = 1 \wedge |c \overset{CF}{\bullet}| > 1\}$ *as the set of control-flow split connectors;*
- $C^J_{CF} = \{c \in C_{CF} \mid | \overset{CF}{\bullet} c| > 1 \wedge |c \overset{CF}{\bullet}| = 1\}$ *as the set of control-flow join connectors;*
- $link^\alpha(x, y) = \begin{cases} (y, x) \in A_R, \text{ if } \alpha = R, \text{ returns the role arc from } y \text{ to } x, \\ (y, x) \in A_{IN}, \text{ if } \alpha = IN, \text{ returns the input arc from } y \text{ to } x, \\ (x, y) \in A_{OUT}, \text{ if } \alpha = OUT, \text{ returns the output arc from } x \text{ to } y; \end{cases}$
- $degree(x) = \begin{cases} | \overset{R}{\bullet} x|, \text{ if } x \in C_R, \text{ returns the indegree of a role connector,} \\ | \overset{IN}{\bullet} x|, \text{ if } x \in C_{IN}, \text{ returns the indegree of an input connector,} \\ |x \overset{OUT}{\bullet}|, \text{ if } x \in C_{OUT}, \text{ returns the outdegree of an output connector;} \end{cases}$
- $p = \langle n_1, n_2, \ldots, n_k \rangle$ *is a control-flow path such that* $(n_i, n_{i+1}) \in A_{CF}$ *for* $1 \leq i \leq k - 1$. *For short, we indicate that p is a path from* n_1 *to* n_k *as* $p : n_1 \hookrightarrow n_k$. *Also,* $P(p) = \{n_1, \ldots, n_k\}$ *indicates the alphabet of p.*

We can now define a syntactically correct iEPC.

Definition 5 (Syntactically Correct iEPC). *An* $iEPC$ *is syntactically correct if it ful-fills the following requirements:*

1. *iEPC is a directed graph such that every control-flow node is on a control-flow path from a start to an end event: let* $e_s \in E_s$ *and* $e_e \in E_e$, *then* $\forall_{n \in N_{CF}} \exists_{p \in N^+_{CF}, p:e_s \hookrightarrow e_e} [n \in P(p)]$.
2. *There is at least one start event and one end event in iEPC:* $|E_s| > 0$ *and* $|E_e| > 0$.
3. *Events have at most one incoming and one outgoing control-flow arc:* $\forall_{e \in E} [| \overset{CF}{\bullet} e| \leq 1 \wedge |e \overset{CF}{\bullet}| \leq 1]$.
4. *Functions have exactly one incoming and one outgoing control-flow arc:* $\forall_{f \in F_N} [| \overset{CF}{\bullet} f| = |f \overset{CF}{\bullet}| = 1]$.
5. *Control-flow connectors have one incoming and multiple outgoing arcs or vice versa:* $\forall_{c \in C_{CF}} [(| \overset{CF}{\bullet} c| = 1 \wedge |c \overset{CF}{\bullet}| > 1) \vee (| \overset{CF}{\bullet} c| > 1 \wedge |c \overset{CF}{\bullet}| = 1)]$, *(split, join),* *Role connectors have multiple incoming arcs and exactly one outgoing arc:* $\forall_{c \in C_R} [| \overset{R}{\bullet} c| > 1 \wedge |c \overset{R}{\bullet}| = 1]$, *(join),* *Input connectors have multiple incoming arcs and exactly one outgoing arc:* $\forall_{c \in C_{IN}} [| \overset{IN}{\bullet} c| > 1 \wedge |c \overset{IN}{\bullet}| = 1]$, *(join),* *Output connectors have exactly one incoming arc and multiple outgoing arcs:* $\forall_{c \in C_{OUT}} [| \overset{OUT}{\bullet} c| = 1 \wedge |c \overset{OUT}{\bullet}| > 1]$, *(split).*
6. *Roles have exactly one outgoing arc:* $\forall_{r \in R_N} |r \overset{R}{\bullet}| = 1$.
7. *Objects have exactly one outgoing input arc or one incoming output arc:* $\forall_{o \in O_N} [(|o \overset{IN}{\bullet}| = 1 \wedge | \overset{OUT}{\bullet} o| = 0) \vee (|o \overset{IN}{\bullet}| = 0 \wedge | \overset{OUT}{\bullet} o| = 1)]$.
8. *Functions are linked to at least a mandatory role or a mandatory role connector:* $\forall_{f \in F_N} [\exists_{r \in \overset{R}{\bullet} f} [l^M_R(r) = MND] \vee \exists_{c \in \overset{R}{\bullet} f} [l^M_C(c) = MND]]$, *it follows that* $| \overset{R}{\bullet} f| > 0$.
9. *Roles and objects linked to connectors are mandatory:* $\forall_{r \in R_N} [r \in dom((R_N \times C_R) \cap A_R) \Rightarrow l^M_R(r) = MND]$, $\forall_{o \in O^{IN}_N} [o \in dom((O_N \times C_{IN}) \cap A_{IN}) \Rightarrow l^M_O(o) = MND]$, $\forall_{o \in O^{OUT}_N} [o \in dom((C_{OUT} \times O_N) \cap A_{OUT}) \Rightarrow l^M_O(o) = MND]$.
10. *Upper bound and lower bound of range connectors are restricted as follows:* $\forall_{c \in C_R \cup C_{IN} \cup C_{OUT}} [1 \leq lwb(c) \leq upb(c) \wedge (lwb(c) \leq degree(c) \vee upb(c) = k)]$, *where* $n \leq m$ *iff* $(n \leq m) \vee (m = k) \vee (n = m = k)$.

In the remainder, we assume an iEPC fulfills the above requirements. The editing process model of Fig. 1 is syntactically correct. However, Def. 5 does not prevent behavioral issues (e.g. deadlocks) that may occur at run-time. It is outside the scope of this paper to provide a formal definition of the dynamic behavior of iEPCs, as we only consider structural correctness in the context of configuration. Hence, here we briefly discuss its semantics for completeness, while for a formal definition we refer to a technical report [12].

The dynamic behavior of iEPC has to take into account the routing rules of the control-flow, the availability of the resources and the existence of the objects participating in the process. A state of the execution of an iEPC can be identified by a marking of tokens for the control-flow, plus a variable for each role indicating the availability of the relative resource, and a variable for each object, indicating their existence. A function is enabled and can fire if it receives control, if at least all its *mandatory* roles are available and all its *mandatory* input objects exist. The state of roles and objects is evaluated directly or via the respective range connectors. During a function's execution, the associated roles become unavailable and once the execution is concluded, the output objects are created (i.e. they become existent), and those ones that are indicated as *consumed*, are destroyed. Initial process objects, i.e. those ones that are used by a function that follows a start event (e.g. the Picture cut), exist before the execution starts. A function does not wait for an optional role to become available. However, if such a role is available before the function is executed, it is treated as a mandatory role.

5.2   Integrated Process Configuration

A C-iEPC is an extension of an iEPC where some nodes are identified as configurable, and a set of requirements is specified to constrain their values.

Definition 6 (Configurable iEPC). *A configurable iEPC is a tuple* $C\text{-}iEPC = (E, F_N, R_N, O_N, nm, C, A, L, F_N^c, R_N^c, O_N^c, C^c, RS^c)$, *where:*

- $E, F_N, R_N, O_N, nm, C, A, L$ *refer to the elements of a syntactically correct iEPC,*
- $F_N^c \subseteq F_N$ *is the set of* configurable functions,
- $R_N^c \subseteq R_N$ *is the set of* configurable roles,
- $O_N^c \subseteq O_N$ *is the set of* configurable objects,
- $C^c \subseteq C$ *is the set of* configurable connectors,
- RS^c *is the set of* configuration requirements.

All the auxiliary sets of Def. 4 are also defined for the configurable sets above. For example, $N^c = F_N^c \cup R_N^c \cup O_N^c \cup C^c$. A configuration assigns values to each configurable node, according to the node type.

Definition 7 (Configuration). *Let* $M = \{MND, OPT, OFF\}$ *be the set of optionality attributes,* $U = \{USE, CNS\}$ *the set of usage attributes,* $CT = \{AND, OR, XOR\}$ *the set of control-flow connector types and* $CTS_{CF} = \{SEQ_n \mid n \in N_{CF}\}$ *the set of sequence operators for control-flow. A* configuration *of* $C\text{-}iEPC$ *is defined as* $conf_{C-iEPC} = (conf_F, conf_R, conf_O, conf_C)$, *where:*

- $conf_F \in F_N^c \rightarrow \{ON, OPT, OFF\}$;
- $conf_R \in R_N^c \rightarrow M \times R$, *(M is used for optionality and R for role specialization)*;

- $conf_O = conf_{IN} \cup conf_{OUT}$, where:
  - $conf_{IN} \in O_N^{IN\,C} \to M \times O \times U$, ($O$ is used for object specialization and U for usage);
  - $conf_{OUT} \in O_N^{OUT\,C} \to M \times O$;
- $conf_C = conf_{C_{CF}} \cup conf_{C_R} \cup conf_{C_{IN}} \cup conf_{C_{OUT}}$, where:
  - $conf_{C_{CF}} \in C_{CF}^C \to CT \cup CTS_{CF}$, ($CT$ is used for the connector's type and CTS_{CF} to configure the connector to a sequence of nodes);
  - $conf_{C_R} \in C_R^C \to M \times ((\mathbb{N} \times \mathbb{N}) \cup R_N)$, ($\mathbb{N}$ and $\mathbb{N}$ are used for lower bound increment and upper bound decrement, R_N is used to configure a role connector to a single role);
  - $conf_{C_{IN}} \in C_{IN}^C \to M \times ((\mathbb{N} \times \mathbb{N}) \cup O_N^{IN})$, ($O_N^{IN}$ is used to configure an input connector to a single input object);
  - $conf_{C_{OUT}} \in C_{OUT}^C \to M \times ((\mathbb{N} \times \mathbb{N}) \cup O_N^{OUT})$, ($O_N^{OUT}$ is used to configure an output connector to a single output object).

We define the following projections over the codomain of $conf_{C-iEPC}$:
Let $x \in R_N^C \cup O_N^{OUT\,C}$, $\alpha \in \{R, OUT\}$ and $conf_\alpha(x) = (m, s)$, then $\pi^M(x) = m$ and $\pi^s(x) = s$. Let $x \in O_N^{IN\,C}$ and $conf_{IN}(x) = (m, s, u)$, then $\pi^M(x) = m$, $\pi^s(x) = s$ and $\pi^U(x) = u$; Let $x \in C_R^C \cup C_{IN}^C \cup C_{OUT}^C$ and $\alpha \in \{R, IN, OUT\}$, then if $conf_{C_\alpha}(x) = (m, (p, q))$, then $\pi^M(x) = m$, $\pi^i(x) = p$ and $\pi^d(x) = q$, otherwise if $conf_{C_\alpha}(x) = (m, y)$, then $\pi^M(x) = m$ and $\pi^N(x) = y$.

The restrictions on the values each configurable node can take, are captured by the following partial orders, which are used in the definition of a valid configuration. For example, the partial order on the optionality dimension, prevents a 'mandatory' node from being configured to 'optional', while it allows the contrary.

Definition 8 (Partial Orders for Configuration). *Let M, U, CT and CTS_{CF} as in Def. 7. The partial orders for configuration are defined as follows:*

- $\preceq^M = \{MND, OFF\} \times \{MND\} \cup M \times \{OPT\}$ *(on optionality)*,
- $\preceq^U = \{(n, n) \mid n \in U\} \cup \{(USE, CNS)\}$ *(on usage)*,
- $\preceq^{CF} = \{(n, n) \mid n \in CT\} \cup \{XOR, AND\} \times \{OR\} \cup CTS_{CF} \times \{XOR, OR\}$ *(on the type of control-flow connectors)*.

With these elements, we are now ready to define the notion of *valid configuration*.

Definition 9 (Valid Configuration). *A configuration $conf_{C-iEPC}$ is valid iff it fulfills the following requirements for any configurable node:*

1. *Roles and objects can be restricted to MND or OFF if they are OPT, or to OFF if they are MND ($\alpha \in \{R, O\}$):* $\forall_{x \in R_N^C \cup O_N^C} [\pi^M(x) \preceq^M l_\alpha^M(x)]$.
2. *Roles and objects can be restricted to any of their specialization:* $\forall_{x \in R_N^C \cup O_N^C} [\pi^s(x) \xleftarrow{\alpha} nm(x)]$.
3. *Input objects that are CNS can be restricted to USE:* $\forall_{x \in O_{IN}^C} [\pi^U(x) \preceq^U l_O^U(x)]$.
4. *Control-flow OR connectors can be restricted to XOR, AND or to SEQ_n; control-flow XOR connectors can be restricted to SEQ_n:*
   $\forall_{x \in C_{CF}^C, n \in N_{CF}} [conf_{C_{CF}}(x) \preceq^{CF} l_C^T(x) \wedge (conf_{C_{CF}}(x) = SEQ_n \Rightarrow ((x \in C_{CF}^S \wedge (x, n) \in A_{CF}) \vee (x \in C_{CF}^J \wedge (n, x) \in A_{CF})))]$ *(the sequence must be in the connector's postset in case of split or in its preset in case of join).*
   Also, the configuration to SEQ_n must allow at least one path from a start to an end event: let $e_s \in E_s$ and $e_e \in E_e$, then
   $\exists_{p \in N_{CF}^+, p: e_s \hookrightarrow e_e} \forall_{x \in C_{CF}^C \cap P(p)} [conf_{C_{CF}}(x) = SEQ_n \Rightarrow n \in P(p)].$

5. *Range connectors can be restricted to MND or OFF if they are OPT, or to OFF if they are MND:* $\forall_{x \in C_R^C \cup C_{IN}^C \cup C_{OUT}^C} [\pi^M(x) \preceq^M l_C^M(x)]$.

6. *Range connectors can be restricted to a smaller range or to a single node (role or object):*

   • Range: $\forall_{x \in C_R^C \cup C_{IN}^C \cup C_{OUT}^C}$:

       – $\pi^i(x) = \pi^d(x) = 0$, *if* $lwb(x) = upb(x) = k$ *(the AND case cannot be restricted),*

       – $lwb(x) + \pi^i(x) \leq \begin{cases} upb(x) - \pi^d(x), \text{ if } upb(x) \in \mathbb{N}, \\ degree(x) - \pi^d(x), \text{ if } lwb(x) \in \mathbb{N} \text{ and } upb(x) = k; \end{cases}$

   • Node $(\alpha \in \{R, IN, OUT\})$:

   $\forall_{x \in C_R^C \cup C_{IN}^C \cup C_{OUT}^C} [\pi^C(x) = y \Rightarrow (link^\alpha(x, y) \wedge lwb(x) = 1)]$ *(the node must be in the connector's postset in case of split or in its preset in case of join, and the lower bound be 1).*

Beside the structural requirements presented above, a configuration must fulfill the configuration requirements RS^c to be *domain-compliant*. We can express the configuration requirements of the editing process model using the notation in Def. 7. We refer to the nodes by their id., as shown in Fig. 1. For example, Req$_6$ is $conf_F(f_5) = ON \Rightarrow conf_F(f_2) = ON$, Req$_7$ is $\pi^s(r_{15}) = \pi^s(r_{18})$ and Req$_{10}$ is $\pi^U(o_{30}) = CNS \Leftrightarrow \pi^s(o_{30}) \overset{O}{\leftarrow} Film$.

The individualization algorithm applies a valid configuration to a syntactically correct C-iEPC, to generate a syntactically correct iEPC. The algorithm consists of a series of steps, each of which operates over a different type of element in a C-iEPC. The order of the steps in the algorithm has been chosen in such a way that no unnecessary operations are applied. For example, the control-flow connectors are configured first, as this operation may lead to skipping certain paths of the process model including connectors, events and functions. Then, all the roles, objects and range connectors that are

---

1. Apply control-flow connector configuration and remove arcs not involving sequences.
2. Remove nodes not on some path from an original start event to an original end event.
3. Replace functions switched off with an arc, and remove their roles, objects and connectors.
4. Remove range connectors switched off, together with their roles and objects.
5. Remove roles and objects switched off.
6. Remove range connectors no longer linked to roles and objects.
7. Replace all range connectors with a degree of one with arcs.
8. Increment lower bound and decrement upper bound of configured range connectors.
9. Align lower and upper bound of range connectors with potential change in degree.
10. Apply configuration of optionality dimension to roles, objects and range connectors; configuration of usage dimension to objects and configuration of specialization to roles and objects.
11. Remove functions without mandatory role assignment.
12. Replace one-input-one-output connectors with arcs.
13. Insert XOR-split, XOR-join and arcs to allow a bypass path for optional functions.

Fig. 4. Individualization algorithm

associated with functions no longer existing are removed as well. Finally, the remaining roles and objects are configured.

The formal definition of this algorithm can be found in a technical report [10]. In the report, we also prove that any iEPC yielded by the algorithm fulfils the properties of syntactical correctness presented in Def. 5.

6   Conclusion

This work has addressed a major shortcoming in existing configurable process notations: their lack of support for the data and resource perspectives. In doing so, we presented a rich meta-model for capturing role-task and object-task associations, that while embodied in the EPC notation, can be transposed to other notations. The study highlighted the intricacies that configurable process modeling across multiple perspectives brings. We identified interplays between perspectives. And while we define conditions to ensure syntactic correctness of individualized process models, we do not ensure semantic correctness.

In future work, we will investigate techniques for preventing inconsistencies in the individualized process models, such as object flow dependencies that contradict control flow dependencies. Also, while the proposal has been validated on a case study conducted with domain experts, further validation is required. The notion of configurable process model brings significant advantages, but concomitantly induces an overhead to the modeling lifecycle. In previous work [11] we have designed and implemented a tool, namely Quaestio, that provides a questionnaire-based interface to guide users through the individualization of configurable process models captured as C-EPCs. At present, we are extending this questionnaire-based framework to deal with C-iEPCs. The next step is to evaluate the framework by means of case studies in multiple domains and by conducting usability tests.

Acknowledgments. We thank Katherine Shortland and Mark Ward from the AFTRS for their valuable contribution to the design and validation of the reference models.

References

1. van der Aalst, W.M.P., van Hee, K.M.: Workflow Management: Models, Methods, and Systems. MIT press, Cambridge (2002)
2. van der Aalst, W.M.P., ter Hofstede, A.H.M.: YAWL: Yet Another Workflow Language. Information Systems 30(4), 245–275 (2005)
3. Alves, A., et al.: Web Services Business Process Execution Language (WS-BPEL) ver. 2.0, Committee Specification (January 31, 2007)
4. Becker, J., Delfmann, P., Dreiling, A., Knackstedt, R., Kuropka, D.: Configurative Process Modeling – Outlining an Approach to increased Business Process Model Usability. In: Proceedings of the 15th IRMA International Conference, New Orleans, Gabler (2004)
5. Curran, T., Keller, G.: SAP R/3 Business Blueprint: Understanding the Business Process Reference Model, Upper Saddle River (1997)
6. Engels, G., Förster, A., Heckel, R., Thöne, S.: Process Modeling Using UML. In: Dumas, M., van der Aalst, W.M.P., ter Hofstede, A.H.M. (eds.) Process-Aware Information Systems, pp. 85–117. Wiley, Chichester (2005)

7. Gottschalk, F., van der Aalst, W.M.P., Jansen-Vullers, M.H.: Configurable Process Models – A Foundational Approach. In: Reference Modeling. Efficient Information Systems Design Through Reuse of Information Models, pp. 59–78. Springer, Heidelberg (2007)

8. Gottschalk, F., van der Aalst, W.M.P., Jansen-Vullers, M.H., La Rosa, M.: Configurable Workflow Models. International Journal of Cooperative Information Systems 17(2), 177–221 (2008)

9. Jablonski, S., Bussler, C.: Workflow Management: Modeling Concepts, Architecture, and Implementation. International Thomson Computer Press, London (1996)

10. La Rosa, M., Dumas, M., ter Hofstede, A.H.M., Mendling, J., Gottschalk, F.: Beyond Control-flow: Extending Business Process Configuration to Resources and Objects (2007), Available at QUT ePrints, http://eprints.qut.edu.au/archive/00011240

11. La Rosa, M., Lux, J., Seidel, S., Dumas, M., ter Hofstede, A.H.M.: Questionnaire-driven Configuration of Reference Process Models. In: Krogstie, J., Opdahl, A., Sindre, G. (eds.) CAiSE 2007 and WES 2007. LNCS, vol. 4495, pp. 424–438. Springer, Heidelberg (2007)

12. Mendling, J., La Rosa, M., ter Hofstede, A.H.M.: Correctness of Business Process Models with Roles and Objects (2008), Available at QUT ePrints, http://eprints.qut.edu.au/archive/00013172

13. Mühlen, M.z.: Organizational Management in Workflow Applications - Issues and Perspectives. Information Technology and Management 5(3–4), 271–291 (2004)

14. Reichert, M., Dadam, P.: ADEPTflex: Supporting Dynamic Changes of Workflow without Loosing Control. Journal of Intelligent Information Systems 10(2), 93–129 (1998)

15. Rosemann, M., van der Aalst, W.M.P.: A Configurable Reference Modelling Language. Information Systems 32(1), 1–23 (2007)

16. Russell, N., van der Aalst, W.M.P., ter Hofstede, A.H.M., Edmond, D.: Workflow Resource Patterns: Identification, Representation and Tool Support. In: Pastor, Ó., Falcão e Cunha, J. (eds.) CAiSE 2005. LNCS, vol. 3520, pp. 216–232. Springer, Heidelberg (2005)

17. Scheer, A.W.: ARIS - Business Process Frameworks, 3rd edn. Springer, Berlin (1999)

18. Stephens, S.: The Supply Chain Council and the SCOR Reference Model. Supply Chain Management - An International Journal 1(1), 9–13 (2001)

19. White, S.A., et al.: Business Process Modeling Notation (BPMN), Version 1.0 (2004)

Value-Driven Coordination Process Design Using Physical Delivery Models*

Roel Wieringa[1], Vincent Pijpers[2], Lianne Bodenstaff[1], and Jaap Gordijn[2]

[1] University of Twente, Enschede, The Netherlands
{roelw,bodenstaffl}@ewi.utwente.nl
[2] Free University, Amsterdam, The Netherlands
{pijpersv,gordijn}@few.vu.nl

Abstract. Current e-business technology enables the execution of increasingly complex coordination processes that link IT services of different companies. Successful design of cross-organizational coordination processes requires the mutual alignment of the coordination process with a commercial business case. There is however a large conceptual gap between a commercial business case and a coordination process. The business case is stated in terms of commercial transactions, but the coordination process consists of sequences, choices and iterations of actions of people and machines that are absent from a business case model; also, the cardinality of the connections and the frequency and duration of activities are different in both models. This paper proposes a coordination process design method that focusses on the the shared physical world underlying the business case and coordination process. In this physical world, physical deliveries take place that realize commercial transactions and that must be coordinated by a coordination process. Physical delivery models allow us to identify the relevant cardinality, frequency and duration properties so that we can design the coordination process to respect these properties. In the case studies we have done so far, a physical delivery model is the greatest common denominator that we needed to verify consistency between a business case and a coordination process model.

1 Introduction

Current e-business technology enables the execution of increasingly complex cross-organizational business processes that link IT services provided by different companies. The complexity of these networks makes it important to make a business case that shows for each partner that it is economically sustainable to participate in the network, and to make this case before operational details of the coordination infrastructure are designed. A coordination process need be designed only if the business case is positive for each of the partners. But it is hard to design a coordination process based on a multi-party business case only, because the conceptual gap between the two is very large [1]. Where a

---

* Research supported by NWO project 638.003.407.

business case makes an estimation of numbers of commercial transactions and their monetary value over a period of time, a coordination process consist of operational activities performed at particular times satisfying specific cardinality, frequency and duration constraints. But despite this conceptual gap, the coordination process must be designed to be consistent with the business case, and this alignment must be maintained during the entire period of cooperation between the businesses.

Recent proposals to design coordination processes based on business case models [2,3,4] recommend that the process designer analyze a business case model to identify transfers of ownership before designing the coordination activities needed to implement a business case model. The reasoning is that the coordination process must realize the ownership transfers involved in commercial transactions, and that it therefore pays off to analyze ownership transfer first. However, the concept of ownership is very complex. Asking a process designer to analyze it before designing a coordination process does not simplify the process design task. Moreover, important process design information such as cardinality, frequency and duration properties of the coordination process are not uncovered this way. In this paper we take a less complex route, that nevertheless yields more information for the process designer. We start from the observation that the business case and coordination models are views on one shared physical world, where physical deliveries take place (section 5). Each commercial transaction is realized in physical deliveries, and the coordination process must coordinate these deliveries. Physical delivery modeling makes it easier to think about cardinality, frequency and duration properties of deliveries, and this in turn makes it relatively simple to design coordination processes that realize these deliveries (section 6). Our case studies provide support to the hypothesis that physical delivery models provide a shared semantic structure for proving mutual consistency between business case and coordination models (section 7).

In section 2 we describe our running example and in sections 3 and 6 we present a business case model and coordination model of this example, respectively. There are several notations for business case modeling, such as the e^3-*value* notation [5] used in this paper, REA [6] and BMO [7]. Our argument does not depend on the notation used as long as the business case model contains estimations of the value and number of commercial transactions between the business partners over a period of time. We explain the e^3-*value* notation in section 3. Well-known notations for coordination modeling are Petri Nets [8], BPMN [9] and UML activity diagrams. In this paper we use UML activity diagrams, because we want to show who is waiting for which activity, and which objects are passed around.

2   Running Example

Our running example concerns electricity distribution in the Netherlands: Electricity suppliers provide electricity to consumers by obtaining it from producers and having a distributor deliver it at the consumer's home. Consumers pay for electricity as well as for the use of the distribution network, and see this in their bill, where distribution is charged explicitly. However, they do all payments to the supplier, which then forwards payment for the distribution to the distributor. In the Netherlands there is one electricity distribution network per geographical region, but there are several suppliers and producers the consumer can choose from.

3   Value Modeling

An e^3-*value* model of a networked business case consists of a diagram, called a *value model,* that represents the businesses participating in the network for a period of time, what they exchange of value in this time, plus a set of estimations of the number and value of the exchanges, that allows us to calculate the net present value (NPV) (see e.g. [10] for an explanation of the NPV concept) of the revenue generated by these exchanges for each business. We call the time period represented by the value model the *time extent* of the model, or *extent* for short. The value model allows NPV estimations of revenue for the time extent of the model only. It is possible to consider a sequence of value models over subsequent time extents, where for example the first model represents initial investments and start-up and the second model represents exploitation of this initial investment.

Figure 1 shows a value model of electricity distribution. Rectangles represent *economic actors* that can have needs and can offer something in value in return, such as money, to meet those needs. Actors in a value model can be businesses or consumers. Stacked rectangles represent *market segments,* which are sets of economic actors with the same needs.

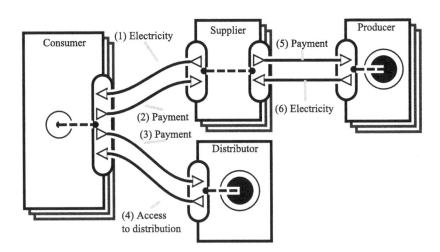

Fig. 1. Value model for electricity delivery. The value transfers have been numbered for ease of reference.

Actors are connected by *value transfers*. If the source or destination of a value transfer is a market segment, this means that all actors in this segment can produce or consume this transfer. Value transfers are transfers of so-called *value objects*. A value object can be a good, service, data, experience, or anything else of value to the receiver. What are value objects depends on the specific actors in case. Music may be of value to one actor and be a nuisance to another. The arrow may even be reversed in different value models involving the same value object. For example, a hotel may offer a wireless access provider the opportunity to provide wireless access to its guests—a captive market, which is of value to the access provider, who therefore pays the hotel for this. However, another hotel and another access provider, or the same two actors in another time period, may view this differently: The access provider takes care of a service regarded by all guests as normal infrastructure, and therefore the hotel pays the provider for this. What, in a given time extent, is of value to whom, is depends on the needs and desires of those actors in that time period.

Value transfers enter or leave an actor through a *value interface,* which is a unit of atomicity: In the time extent of the business case, when one transfer occurs, the other occurs too in that same period. e^3-*value* does not allow us to say *when* these transfers occur, only *that* they occur in the time extent of the business case. This is sufficient for the purpose of business case modeling, where we only need to estimate how often commercial transactions occur in the time extent of a business case, not when they occur.

Actors can have needs, represented by a dot placed inside the actor rectangle. An actor can have this need any number of times in the time extent of the model. When placed inside a market segment, the dot means that any actor in this segment can have this need. The commercial transactions required to meet a consumer need are linked by a dashed line called a *dependency path* to the consumer need. A bull's eye indicates the model boundary, i.e. further transactions such as those with suppliers down the value chain are not considered in this business case. This means that the business case developer does not view these transactions as having any impact on this business case. In general, a dependency path is an acyclic graph with and-or nodes. We will illustrate and-nodes in the health insurance example.

We believe that each conceptual model should have a single purpose and should contain all and only the information needed to fulfill this purpose. The purpose of an e^3-*value* model is to make a business case, and the graphical value model of figure 1 and the supporting computational techniques (not treated here) are exactly what is needed to do the NPV estimation of the revenue generated for each of the business actors in the case. The value model shows what is happening commercially, but does not tell us how this is done operationally. We use coordination models for that.

4   Cross-Organizational Case Coordination

In this section we use a variation of activity diagrams that retains the root of these diagrams in statecharts [11]. As pointed out earlier, we choose this statechart-like variation of activity diagrams because it makes explicit when an actor is performing activity and when it is waiting for someone else to do something. Figure 2 contains the legend.

Figure 3 shows a coordination process involving four named actors, a consumer c, supplier s, producer p and distributor d (in the lower half of the diagram). The process runs over a period of a year, i.e. the time extent of our business case. We indicated the parts of the coordination process that correspond to commercial transactions by dashed rounded rectangles. Payments 2 and 3 involve an monthly interaction between supplier and consumer and a further yearly interaction (one in this example) between the supplier and distributor. Payment 5 consists of a quarterly interaction between supplier and distributor. Delivery of electricity (value transfer (1)) and access to the distribution network (service provision(6)) are started in parallel to the payment procedures and stop at the end of the contract period (1 year). The case handled in this coordination process is the consumer need for electricity during one year.

The coordination model has no owner. No single actor is responsible for its execution. It is the joint responsibility of all actors that it is executed, and if each actor does what promised to do, then the coordination process occurs. The process in figure 3 makes the assumption that all actors are trustworthy, i.e. do what they should do. This is a simplifying assumption that we return to later. First, we turn to the central topic of this paper, which is how we can design a coordination process starting from a business case model.

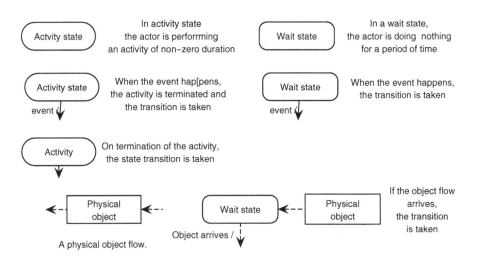

Fig. 2. Legend for the version of activity diagrams used in this paper

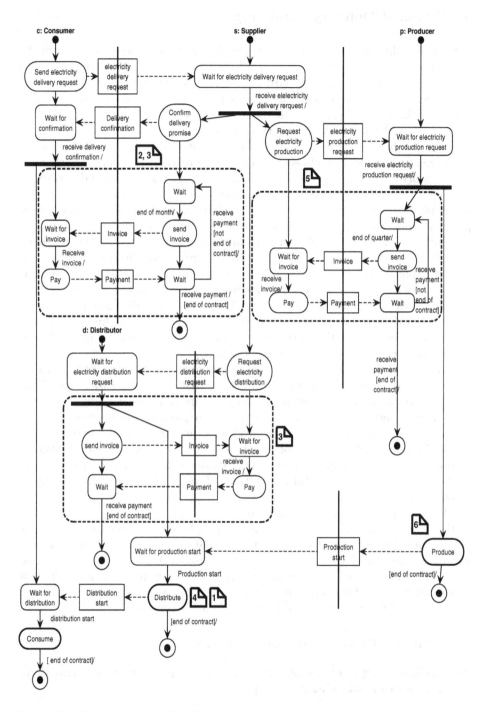

Fig. 3. Coordination process for the electricity delivery scenario of figure 4. The comment signs refer to value transfers.

5   Physical Delivery Modeling

We define a physical delivery model as a representation of the physical events by which business actors get access to a value object; a physical event is one that can be described using the standard physical measurements (meters, kilograms, Ampères, seconds). We will not use physical terms to describe physical objects ("rectangular piece of paper") but their socially defined names ("money"). But the objects and flows indicated by these names must be physical.

We claim that coordination modeling is facilitated by making a physical delivery model first, because the business case and coordination model are both views of a network of physical deliveries. Ultimately, every business case describes an economic view on the physical world, and every process model describes events in the physical world. Software is a state of hardware, and data is a state of the physical world too. Money is physical too, realized by means paper, metal, or computer hardware as digital money. Human services such as coaching, teaching, consultancy, providing help through a help desk, providing financial services, etc. consist of physical processes too, including people moving to places, advice being produced in the form of sounds, reports being written, and money being passed around or stored. Each of these processes has a physical realization, even though we usually talk about them as disembodied entities with certain financial, logical or semantic properties. But if there would be no physical events, none of these disembodied entities and events would exist.

Commercial transactions are usually accompanied by a system of legal rights and obligations, permissions and prohibitions that are treated by stakeholders as non-physical. However, creation of these norms must be done by a physical process (e.g. signing a document); we maintain physical evidence of the existence of these norms in the form of physical documents; and the norms govern physically observable behavior of people and goods in the real world, such as buying and selling, listening to music or watching a movie. The non-physicality of these legal norms is a useful fiction that allows us to abstract from complex physical processes.

Views such as a value model or a coordination process model represent part of the shared conceptual models by which people organize themselves. But to understand the relation between two models that are so fundamentally different, we must understand what each of these models means in terms of a shared physical world. We do this by means of physical delivery models, that will allow us to understand which physical activities realize commercial transactions and therefore need to be coordinated by a coordination process.

5.1   Physical Objects and Their Delivery

To help identifying the physical deliveries that realize commercial transactions, we distinguish the following kinds of physical objects.

- *Discrete goods* are identifyable entities that can form a set. Examples are physical products such as chairs and cars, but also inert physical entities such as houses and airport runways. The distinguishing feature is that when two physical goods are put together, they form a set of two elements.

- *Cumulative goods* do not preserve their distinctness when put together. When you add water to water, the result is still water. Ultimately, cumulative goods consist of atoms that form a set, but at the level of phenomena that interests us for physical delivery modeling, we will be talking about cumulative goods such as water or electricity. Where discrete goods can be measured by counting them, cumulative goods must be measured by choosing a measurement unit.

The distinction is not a metaphysical statement about the ultimate structure of the physical world but a hint what to look for when modeling physical deliveries. It is not important to allocate a physical object to exactly one of these two categories: What is important is to identify the physical objects to be coordinated in realizing commercial transactions. Cumulative goods can always be parceled into discrete units. For example, teaching is cumulative, but we usually parcel it into numbered lessons, which can be viewed as discrete goods.

Lexical objects are a particular kind of discrete goods, that have a meaning for stakeholders. Lexical objects are physical information carriers such as paper documents, states of a computer (digital documents), traffic signs, money coins, paper money, digital money, etc.

5.2   Delivery Scenarios

Figure 4 shows a delivery model for the business case of figure 1. Rectangles represent actors, which must be the same actors as those of the value model. We treat actor names as type names, and individuals can be represented by declaring proper names for them. So in figure 4 we represent four individuals named c, s, d and p. If there would have been, say, two producers p1 and p2, then we could have represented these as two distinct rectangles in the diagram, labeled by p1 and p2. And if we would have wanted to represent a set of producers of arbitrary size, then we could have represented the Producer type as a rectangle without a proper name for any individual producer.

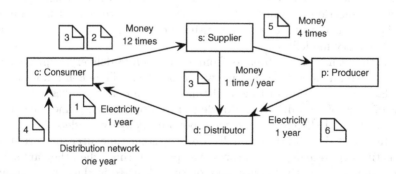

Fig. 4. Physical delivery scenario of an electricity consumer need. The numbers inside comment boxes refer to value exchanges in figure 1.

Figure 4 actually represents one delivery *scenario*. It shows what deliveries must occur to satisfy the need of consumer c in the time extent of the business case. This is the delivery scenario corresponding to the coordination scenario of figure 3, which shows how this consumer need is handled.

Another consumer could receive electricity from two producers, one producing "green" electricity and one producing "dirty" electricity, which would represented in that delivery scenario by means of two producer boxes. Alternatively, we could take the point of view of a particular supplier and show the network of deliveries that this supplier is involved in. In the Netherlands, this supplier would interact with many consumers and producers and with one distributor. Each of these scenarios has important consequences for the internal business processes performed by the actors.

In our delivery scenarios we will always take the point of one consumer, and more in particular of one consumer need, because the business network exists to satisfy this need. Our value and coordination models show the commercial and operational feasibility of meeting this need. The delivery scenario of a consumer need shows the deliveries in the network required to satisfy that need.

The delivery scenario abstracts from much of the infrastructure used to realize the business case. For example, banks used to make payments are not represented in figure 4. The reason is that a delivery model contains the same actors as a business case model; and the business case of this example ignores the payment infrastructure because the cost of using it does not impact the business case.

5.3   Types of Deliveries

Deliveries are represented by arrows pointing from provider to receiver. A physical delivery starts at the point in time when the receiver is able to physically handle the delivered object, which we will call *access*. This can happen in two ways: The physical object moves to the receiver, or the receiver moves to the physical object. The money and electricity transfers in figure 4 are of the first kind, because these are transported to the receiver. Delivery of the distribution network is of the second kind. The consumer probably obtained access to the electricity network because he/she moved into a house that is connected to the network. Connection of a network to a house and movement of the consumer into this house is out of scope of the business case and therefore out of scope of physical delivery modeling.

We distinguish *time-continuous* from *time-discrete* delivery, represented by double-headed and single-headed arrows, respectively. Time-continuous delivery takes place over a period of time and time-discrete delivery takes place at one instant of time of zero duration. All deliveries stop at some time, because our value models, and therefore their corresponding delivery models, have a finite time extent. But time-continuous deliveries stop some time after they are started, whereas time-discrete deliveries stop at the point in time when they are started. Labeling deliveries as time-continuous or time-discrete is choosing a granularity of time, because what is taken to be time-discrete at one level of granularity is a period at a lower level. The distinction is important because coordination for these two kinds of deliveries must guarantee different timing properties.

Deliveries are named after the physical entity that the receiver receives access to. This still leaves the modeler a choice what the physical entity received actually is: energy, electrons, atoms, metal, paper, coins, bank notes, money, a payment? All of these can be regarded as names of physical entities, albeit increasingly abstract names. Choosing an abstraction level is unavoidable in any modeling activity, but this is not an arbitrary choice. To choose a name, we first rule out names of which the meaning depends on the value or process models, because the delivery model should only represent basic information that is needed to understand these model. If we would now include in the delivery models information that can only be understood by first understanding a value- or process model, we would have introduced a vicious circularity. This rules out "payment" as a delivery name, for this is defined in terms of a commercial transaction in the value model.

Second, among the remaining possibilities we choose an abstraction that tells us what stakeholders want to be able to *observe* in any realization of the business case model. In all cases, energy, electrons and atoms are being delivered, but this is not what stakeholders want to observe. The supplier wants to observe a delivery of money from the consumer, and so this is the name of the delivery. In another case, such as one in which coin collectors are described, we could have selected "coins" as name for a delivery because this is what the collector wants to observe. They want to observe this because this is the physical event that they are willing to provide a reciprocal value object for, as indicated in the value model.

Because receivers are paying (in the form of some value object sacrificed by the receiver) for the delivery, they usually not only want to observe but also to measure the delivery. In the electricity example, the amounts of money transferred and of electricity delivered are what stakeholders want to measure when the value model is realized. They want to measure these phenomena because this is what the business case rests on; Participants can verify whether the business case is satisfied by observing these deliveries. The commercial transactions counted in the value model have a particular value that can then be observed at the delivery points in a delivery model, i.e. at the points where deliveries enter the receiver.

So the arrows in a delivery model represent observations, and possibly measurements, that stakeholders want to make in physical reality. Figure 4 tells us that in the time extent of the model, they expect to make 12 observations of money transfer from consumer c to supplier s, 1 year of electricity delivery of the distributor to the consumer, etc. The physical network is actually fitted with measurement instruments (electricity meters, information systems) that make and record these observations.

5.4   Frequency and Duration Properties

For one scenario, we can represent *frequency and duration* information. For time-discrete delivery we can state *how many times* delivery occurs in the time-extent of the business case, and for time-continuous delivery we can state *how long* a delivery takes place and *how many times* this takes place. Frequency and duration information provides us with an important guide for process design later. For example, the delivery scenario of figure 4 shows that the supplier collects consumer payments made monthly, and forwards them to the distributor 4 times a year. This requires therefore the distributor to maintain stores (databases) of information about payments and to execute a distributor process which processes batches of consumer payments.

5.5 Cardinality Properties

Instead of modeling a scenario from the point of view of one actor we can represent cardinality properties of deliveries in a viewpoint-independent model. Figure 5 shows a delivery model that does *not* take the point of view of any actor. All nodes represent types, except the distributor node because in our example there exists only one distributor. The diagram represents cardinality properties in the same way as is done in ER models [11]. The cardinalities in the diagram have the following meaning;

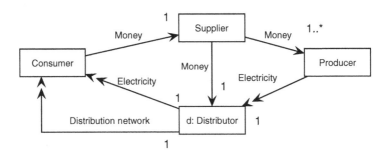

Fig. 5. Model of delivery cardinalities. See text for the semantics of cardinalities.

- Each consumer can transfer money to exactly one supplier. (Different consumers may transfer money to different suppliers.) Each supplier may receive money from any number of consumers.
- Each supplier can transfer money to at least one producer and each producer can receive money from any number of suppliers.
- Each consumer can receive electricity from exactly one distributor, each supplier can transfer money to exactly one distributor, and each producer supplies electricity to exactly one distributor. This is the meaning of the cardinality 1 at the distributor side of the connections to Distributor.
- Because we have named the distributor d, the model also says that all consumers receive electricity from the same distributor, all suppliers transfer money to the same distributor, that this is the same distributor that all consumers receive electricity from, etc.

5.6   Semantic Relation between Value–, Delivery– and Coordination Models

The physical delivery models provide a physical meaning to the commercial transactions identified in a value model and the activities represented in a coordination model. This is an informal meaning relation that the analyst can nevertheless make as precise as needed. The physical meanings of the commercial transactions in the electricity value model are listed in figure 6. These definitions do not follow from the models. Rather, the models allow the analyst to provide these definitions and use them to achieve a shared understanding with all stakeholders.

- In commercial transaction (1, 2) of figure 1 the supplier ensures that the consumer gets electricity and receives payment for this from the consumer. As shown in figures 3, 4 and 5, this is physically realized by the consumer transfering money to the supplier 12 times in the business case time extent (one year), and by the distributor delivering electricity to the consumer during this period.
- In commercial transaction (3, 4), the distributor makes available its distribution infrastructure to the consumer and the consumer pays for this. This is a time-continuous delivery of a discrete good, the distribution network. Payment by the consumer goes in two deliveries via the supplier. The supplier sends money to the distributor once a year.
- In commercial transaction (5, 6) the producer sells electricity to the supplier against a payment. Since the supplier only buys the electricity in order to provide it to the consumer, the producer delivers the electricity to the distributor, which can then pass it on to the consumer.

Fig. 6. Informal semantics of commercial transactions in terms of physical delivery models

6   Coordination Modeling

A coordination scenario is designed by first following the dependency path of a consumer need in the value model, and modeling the delivery scenario required to realize these transactions, including frequency and duration constraints. This in turn is then used to create a coordination scenario such as shown in figure 3, taking into account the meaning of each value transfer in terms of physical deliveries. The coordination model scenario gives more detailed, operational information than the delivery scenario and shows that commercial transactions occur according to well-known patterns, such as delivery of a service after a request for service, and payment after reception of an invoice. The coordination scenario operationalizes deliveries in terms of a number of objects that cross the boundaries between actors in figure 3, that realize the deliveries of the delivery scenario of figure 4. The coordination process satisfies the frequency and duration

- Each consumer needs to be able to pay one supplier (not necessarily the same supplier for all consumers) by transferring money 12 times. Scenario example: Consumer c must pay supplier s in 12 installments per year. Each consumer must be be able to access the distribution network and receive electricity from distributor d for a year.
- Each supplier must be able to receive money from any number of consumers as payment for electricity delivered and for the access to the distribution network, and forward the distribution fee to the distributor d. Scenario example: supplier s must be able to receive money payments from consumer c 12 times a year and forward the fee due to d once a year. Each supplier must also be able to pay for electricity bought from one or more producers. For example supplier s must pay producer p 4 times a year.
- Each producer must be able to receive money payments for electricity from any number of suppliers. Scenario example: Producer p must be able to receive payment for electricity 4 times a year. Each producer must also be able to provide electricity to distributor d. For example, producer p must be able to provide electricity to d for 1 year.
- The distributor must be able to supply electricity to any number of consumers through its distribution network, provided by any number of producers. It must be able to receive payments from suppliers for electricity delivered. Scenario example: It must be able to receive a yearly payment from supplier s for electricity delivered to a client of s.

Fig. 7. Coordination requirements for the business actors

requirements of the delivery scenario have been satisfied by loops (for payment in installments) and by start and stop actions (for time-continuous delivery).

As pointed out before, a coordination process is not owned by any actor; it is a joint responsibility to execute it, and it is actually executed by each actor performing its own business processes. Moreover, other scenarios may be needed to serve other consumers. A consumer who wants electricity from two producers (a "green" and a "dirty" one) will have a different delivery scenario and therefore a different coordination scenario, etc. Because these coordination scenarios are performed by every business actor performing its own business processes, the coordination scenarios are actually coordination *requirements* on these internal business processes. And the viewpoint-independent cardinality model of figure 5 imposes additional requirements, concerning the number of partners that an actor should be able to interface to. We summarize the coordination requirements requirements for each actor in figure 7, where the frequency and duration requirements of the delivery scenario are stated as examples. Note that the mismatches in cardinality of received and provided deliveries indicate a requirement to maintain buffers and do batch processing, for example for the supplier.

7   Discussion and Further Work

To summarize, we start from a situation where a business case has been made that is positive for each partner, for example in the form of an e^3-*value* model.

Before operationalizing this in terms of coordination scenarios, we propose modeling delivery scenarios first.

We have shown that delivery modeling can be used in the electricity delivery example, but can it be used in other examples? So far, we have done three other cases with delivery modeling: a health care insurance case, international trade with a bill of lading, and handling landing and docking at an international airport. These cases have a very diverse mix of commercial services and products exchanged among partners, and in all cases delivery modeling simplified coordination process design. Further case studies must indicate the limitations on applicability of delivery modeling.

Modeling physical flows is actually a very old idea, common in logistics, and used in earlier information system requirements methods such as ISAC and structured analysis in the 1970s [12]. Delivery modeling (and value modeling) are particular ways to do early requirements engineering, in which we identify business goals and needs to be supported by IT [13]. Current approaches to early requirements concentrate on transforming dependencies between business goals into system requirements and architectures and do not consider delivery coordination structures as we do [14].

There is some resemblance of delivery models to Jackson's problem frames [15]. Both kinds of models structure the world into domains (business actors in delivery models) that share phenomena at their interfaces (physically observable deliveries in delivery models). However, where problem frames are used to show how a machine inserted in a domain causes satisfaction of requirements, delivery models are used to show what observable deliveries must occur to satisfy a business case.

Zlatev, Wombacher [16] and Bodenstaff [17] defined reduced models as semantic structure in which to interpret e^3-value models and coordination models to prove that they are consistent. In the cases we have done so far, their reduced models turned out to be our physical delivery scenario models, without the cardinality, frequency and duration constraints. We think the reason for this is that reduced models represent the information shared by business case and coordination models, and that this shared information is exactly the physical deliveries that realize the value model and that must be coordinated by the coordination process. Further work is needed to show conclusively that reduced models are physical delivery models. In order to evaluate the usability of our approach, we plan to do an experimental evaluation of physical delivery modeling compared to other approaches that use legal concepts to arrive at a coordination process [2,4]. Although we emphasized the difference between physical and legal activities, it may turn out that for more complex models we may have to combine the two approaches, for example if we include physical ownership certificates. Even in this paper, some physical objects (coins, bills) are indicated by a legally defined name ("money").

In all our models we assume that all actors will do what they promise to do, e.g. will perform their business processes according to coordination requirements. In practice this is not a realistic assumption [18,19]. Actors may be unreliable because they intend to get a free ride from others, or because they lack the resources to live up to their promises. Either way, we must assess the risk of actors not satisfying the coordination requirements. The less trust we have in an actor, the higher we will assess the risk of doing business with this actor. For every trust assumption that we drop, we may have to add new business actors (e.g. trusted third parties) to the business case, or new activities (e.g. control mechanisms) to the coordination process, that will reduce the risk of the cooperation [20]. In our future research we will investigate what role delivery modeling can play in assessing trust assumptions and designing risk mitigation mechanisms.

Another very interesting further development is to identify different elements in a coordination process. In this paper we only introduced the parts of a coordination process that realize value object deliveries. There are many additional parts of a coordination process, such as activities to reduce the risk of fraud [20], handling exceptions, setting up and tearing down communication connections, setting up and tearing down membership of business networks, etc. [21].

Acknowledgment. We are grateful for the constructive comments of the referees on this paper.

References

1. Gordijn, J., Akkermans, J., Vliet, J.v.: Business modelling is not process modelling. In: Mayr, H.C., Liddle, S.W., Thalheim, B. (eds.) ER Workshops 2000. LNCS, vol. 1921, pp. 40–51. Springer, Heidelberg (2000)
2. Andersson, B., Bergholz, M., Grégoire, B., Johannesson, P., Schmitt, M., Zdravkovic, J.: From business to process models —a chaining methodology. In: Latour, T., Petit, M. (eds.) CAiSE 2006, pp. 211–218. Namur University Press (2006)
3. Pijpers, V., Gordijn, J.: Bridging business value models and process models in aviation value webs via possession rights. In: 40th Hawaii International International Conference on Systems Science (HICSS-40 2007), p. 175 (2007)
4. Weigand, H., Johannesson, P., Andersson, B., Bergholtz, M., Edirisuriya, A., Ilayperuma, T.: Value modeling and the transformation from value model to process model. In: Doumeingts, G., Muller, J., Morel, G., Vallespir, B. (eds.) Enterprise Interoperability: New Challenges and Approaches, pp. 1–10. Springer, Heidelberg (2007)
5. Gordijn, J., Akkermans, H.: Value-based requirements engineering: exploring innovative e-commerce ideas. Requirements Engineering 8, 114–134 (2003)
6. Geerts, G., McCarthy, W.E.: An accounting object infrastructure for knowledge-based enterprise models. IEEE Intelligent Systems and Their Applications, 89–94 (1999)
7. Osterwalder, A.: The Business Model Ontology - a proposition in a design science approach. PhD thesis, University of Lausanne, Lausanne, Switzerland (2004)
8. Jensen, K.: Coloured Petri Nets. Basic Concepts, Analysis Methods and Practical Use, 3 volumes. Springer, Heidelberg (1997)
9. OMG: Business Process Modeling Notation (BPMN) Specification (2006), www.bpmn.org

10. Horngren, C.T., Foster, G.: Cost Accounting: A Managerial Emphasis, 6th edn. Prentice-Hall, Englewood Cliffs (1987)
11. Wieringa, R.: Design Methods for Reactive Systems: Yourdon, Statemate and the UML. Morgan Kaufmann, San Francisco (2003)
12. Wieringa, R.: Requirements Engineering: Frameworks for Understanding. Wiley, Chichester (1996), http://www.cs.utwente/nl/~roelw/REFU/all.pdf
13. Mylopoulos, J., Fuxman, A., Giorgini, P.: From entities and relationships to social actors and dependencies. In: Laender, A.H.F., Liddle, S.W., Storey, V.C. (eds.) ER 2000. LNCS, vol. 1920, pp. 27–36. Springer, Heidelberg (2000)
14. Castro, J., Kolp, M., Mylopoulos, J.: Towards requirements-driven information systems engineering: the tropos project. Information systems 27(6), 365–389 (2002)
15. Jackson, M.: Problem Frames: Analysing and Structuring Software Development Problems. Addison-Wesley, Reading (2000)
16. Zlatev, Z., Wombacher, A.: Consistency between e3-value models and activity diagrams in a multi-perspective development method. In: Meersman, R., Tari, Z. (eds.) OTM 2005. LNCS, vol. 3760. Springer, Heidelberg (2005)
17. Bodenstaff, L., Wombacher, A., Reichert, M.U., Wieringa, R.J.: Monitoring collaboration from a value perspective. In: Chang, E., Hussain, F.K. (eds.) 2007 Inaugural IEEE International Conference on Digital Ecosystems and Technologies, Cairns, Australia, vol. 1, pp. 134–140. IEEE Computer Society Press, Los Alamitos (2007)
18. Bergholtz, M., Jayaweera, P., Johannesson, P., Wohed, P.: A pattern and dependency based approach to the design of process models. In: Atzeni, P., Chu, W., Lu, H., Zhou, S., Ling, T.-W. (eds.) ER 2004. LNCS, vol. 3288, pp. 724–739. Springer, Heidelberg (2004)
19. Wieringa, R., Gordijn, J.: Value-oriented design of correct service coordination processes: Correctness and trust. In: 20th ACM Symposium on Applied Computing, pp. 1320–1327. ACM Press, New York (2005)
20. Kartseva, V., Hulstijn, F., Gordijn, J., Tan, Y.H.: Modelling value-based interorganizational controls in healthcare regulations. In: Suomi, R., Cabral, R., Hampe, J.F., Heikkila, A., Jarvelainen, J., Koskivaara, E. (eds.) Proceedings of the 6th IFIP conference on e-Commerce, e-Business, and e-Government (I3E 2006). IFIP International Federation for Information Processing, pp. 278–291. Springer, Heidelberg (2006)
21. Gordijn, J., Eck, P.v., Wieringa, R.: Requirements engineering techniques for e-services. In: Georgakopoulos, D., Papazoglou, M. (eds.) Service-Oriented Computing, pp. 331–352 (2008)

Relaxed Compliance Notions in Adaptive Process Management Systems

Stefanie Rinderle-Ma[1], Manfred Reichert[1], and Barbara Weber[2]

[1] Ulm University, Germany
{stefanie.rinderle,manfred.reichert}@uni-ulm.de
[2] University of Innsbruck, Austria
Barbara.Weber@uibk.ac.at

Abstract. The capability to dynamically evolve process models over time and to migrate process instances to a modified model version are fundamental requirements for any process-aware information system. This has been recognized for a long time and different approaches for process schema evolution have emerged. Basically, the challenge is to correctly and efficiently migrate running instances to a modified process model. In addition, no process instance should be needlessly excluded from being migrated. While there has been significant research on correctness notions, existing approaches are still too restrictive regarding the set of migratable instances. This paper discusses fundamental requirements emerging in this context. We revisit the well-established compliance criterion for reasoning about the correct applicability of dynamic process changes, relax this criterion in different respects, and discuss the impact these relaxations have in practice. Furthermore, we investigate how to cope with non-compliant process instances to further increase the number of migratable ones. Respective considerations are fundamental for further maturation of adaptive process management technology.

1 Introduction

The ability to effectively deal with change has been identified as key functionality for any process-aware information systems (PAISs). Through the separation of process logic from application code, PAISs facilitate process changes significantly [1]. In the context of long-running processes (e.g., medical treatment processes [2]), PAISs must additionally allow for the propagation of respective changes to ongoing process instances. Regarding the support of such dynamic process changes, PAIS robustness is fundamental; i.e., dynamic changes must not violate soundness of the running process instances. This cannot be always ensured, for example, when "changing the past" of an instance. As example consider Fig. 1 where change Δ inserts two activities X and Y together with a data dependency between them. Applying Δ to instance I could lead to a situation where Y is invoked though its input data has not been written by X. Another challenge in the context of dynamic process changes concerns the treatment of the dynamic change bug [3]; i.e., the problem to correctly adapt process instance states (e.g., markings in a Petri Net) when performing a dynamic change.

Q. Li et al. (Eds.): ER 2008, LNCS 5231, pp. 232–247, 2008.

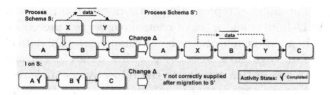

Fig. 1. Changing the Past

In response to these challenges adaptive PAISs have emerged, which allow for dynamic process changes at different levels [4,5,6,7,8,9,10]. Most approaches apply a specific correctness notion to ensure that only those process instances may migrate to a modified process schema for which soundness can be ensured afterwards. One of the most prominent criteria used in this context is *compliance* [4,11]. According to it, a process instance may migrate to schema S' if it is compliant with S'; i.e., the current instance trace can be produced on S' as well. Different techniques have been introduced to efficiently implement this compliance criterion [11,12]. Unfortunately, traditional compliance has turned out to be too restrictive, particularly in connection with loop structures or uncritical changes. Consequently, a large number of instances is excluded from being migrated to a modified schema, even if this does not violate soundness.

In this paper we relax the traditional compliance criterion in different respects, introduce new compliance classes and their properties, and discuss the impact the different relaxations have in practice. Orthogonally, data flow consistency in the context of compliance is discussed. Furthermore, we investigate how to cope with non-compliant process instances to further increase the number of migratable instances. In this context we extent existing approaches [11,8] based on traditional compliance. Altogether respective considerations are fundamental for further maturation of adaptive process management technology.

Section 2 introduces background information needed for the understanding of our work. In Section 3 we revisit the compliance criterion as introduced in [4,11], show how it can be relaxed in different ways to increase the number of migratable instances, and discuss the properties of the resulting compliance classes. Section 4 deals with the handling of non-compliant instances and presents different policies in this context. In Section 5 we extend our considerations to the data flow perspective. An example is given in Section 6. We discuss related work in Section 7 and conclude with a summary and outlook in Section 8.

2   Backgrounds

For each business process to be supported (e.g., handling a customer request or processing an insurance claim) a *process type* T represented by a *process schema* S has to be defined. For a particular type several process schemas may exist, representing the different *versions* and *evolution* of this type over time. In the following, a single process schema is represented as directed graph, which comprises a set of nodes – representing *activities* or *control connectors* (e.g., XOR-Split, AND-Join) – and a set of *control edges* (i.e., precedence relations) between them. In addition, a process schema comprises sets of data elements and data edges. A *data edge* links an activity with a *data element* and represents a read or write access of this activity to the respective data element. Based on process schema S at run-time new *process instances* can be created and executed. Start or completion events of the activities of such instances are recorded in *traces*. WIDE, for example, only records completion events [4], whereas ADEPT distinguishes between start and completion events of activities [11].

Definition 1 (Trace). *Let $\mathcal{PS}$ be the set of all process schemas and let $\mathcal{A}$ be the total set of activities (or more precisely activity labels) based on which process schemas $S \in \mathcal{PS}$ are specified (without loss of generality we assume unique labeling of activities). Let further $\mathcal{Q}_S$ denote the set of all possible traces producible on process schema $S \in \mathcal{PS}$. A particular trace $\sigma_I^S \in \mathcal{Q}_S$ of instance I on S is defined as $\sigma_I^S = <e_1, \ldots, e_k>$ (with $e_i \in \{Start(a), End(a)\}$, $a \in \mathcal{A}$, $i = 1, \ldots, k$, $k \in \mathbb{N}$) where the temporal order of e_i in σ_I^S reflects the order in which activities were started and/or completed over S.*[1]

Adaptive process management systems are characterized by their ability to correctly and efficiently deal with *(dynamic) process changes* [12]. Before discussing different levels of change, we give a definition on the topology of change.

Definition 2 (Process Change). *Let $\mathcal{PS}$ be the set of all process schemas and let S, $S' \in \mathcal{PS}$. Let further $\Delta = <op_1, \ldots, op_n>$ denote a process change which applies change operations op_i, $i=1,\ldots,n$ sequentially. Then:*

1. *$S[\Delta> S'$ if and only if Δ is correctly applicable to S and S' is the process schema resulting from the application of Δ to S (i.e., $S' \equiv S + \Delta$)*
2. *$S[\Delta>S'$ if and only if there are process schemas $S_1, S_2, \ldots, S_{n+1} \in \mathcal{PS}$ with $S = S1$, $S' = S_{n+1}$ and for $1 \leq i \leq n$: $S_i[\Delta_i>S_{i+1}$ with $\Delta_i = (op_i)$*

In general, we assume that change Δ is applied to a *sound* (i.e., *correct*) process schema S [13]; i.e., S obeys the correctness constraints set out by the particular process meta model (e.g., bipartite graph structure for Petri Nets). This is also called *structural soundness*. Furthermore, we claim that S' must obey *behavioral soundness* (i.e., any instance on S' must not run into deadlocks or livelocks). This can achieved in two ways: either Δ itself preserves soundness by formal pre-/post-conditions (e.g., in ADEPT [7]) or Δ is applied and soundness of S' is checked afterwards (e.g., by reachability analysis for Petri Nets).

Basically, changes can be triggered and performed at the process type and the process instance level. Changes to a process type T may become necessary to cover the evolution of real-world business processes captured by process schema of this type [9,11,10]. Generally, process engineers can accomplish process type changes by applying a set of change operations to the current schema version S of type T [14]. This results in a new schema version S' of T. Execution of future process instances is usually based on S'. In addition, for long-running instances it is often desired to migrate them to the new schema S' in a controlled and

---

[1] An entry of a particular activity can occur multiple times due to loopbacks.

efficient manner [11,12]. By contrast, changes of individual process instances are usually performed by end users. They become necessary to react to exceptional situations [7]. In particular, effects of such changes must be kept local, i.e., they must not affect other instances of same type. In both cases, structural and behavioral soundness have to be preserved. The former can be guaranteed since the underlying process schema has to be structurally correct again [11]. The latter, however, has to be explicitly checked. This is accomplished by certain correctness criteria which are subject to the following sections.

3   Revisiting Instance Compliance in Adaptive PAISs

Problems such as dynamic change bug (cf. Sect. 1) show that it is crucial to provide adequate correctness criteria in connection with dynamic process changes. Basically, the challenge is to correctly and efficiently migrate process instances to a modified schema. In particular, no instance should be unnecessarily excluded from such migration except this would lead to severe flaws (i.e., violation of soundness) later on. We first summarize fundamental requirements any correctness notion for dynamic process change should fulfill. Let S be the process schema which is transformed into another schema S' by change Δ; i.e., $S[\Delta > S'$.

Req. 1: Any criterion should guarantee correct execution of process instances on S after migrating them to S'; i.e., soundness has to be preserved; e.g., by ensuring correctly supplied inputs and correct instance states afterwards [12].
Req. 2: The criterion should be generally valid; i.e., it should be applicable independent of a particular process meta model.
Req. 3: The criterion should be implementable in an efficient way.[2]
Req. 4: The number of process instances running on S, which can correctly migrate to S', should be maximized.

Following considerations start with the *compliance criterion* which is a widely used correctness notion [4]. A detailed comparison of compliance and other correctness criteria can be found in [12]. In [12,15] it has been shown that this criterion guarantees Req. 1. Furthermore it presumes no specific process meta model, but is based on traces. Thus Req. 2 is fulfilled as well [11]. In addition, compliance can be checked for arbitrary change patterns [1,14], contrary to criteria which are only valid in connection with a restricted set of change patterns [9]. We have also demonstrated that it can be implemented efficiently [11,12] (cf. Req. 3). However, the traditional compliance criterion does not adequately deal with Req. 4; i.e., it needlessly excludes certain instances from being migrated, though this would be possible without affecting soundness. We relax this criterion by introducing different compliance classes to increase the number of migratable instances. Usually, one cannot decide on such relaxation automatically, but has to consider the particular application context as well. However,

---

[2] A discussion on the efficiency of correctness checks and a comparison of existing correctness criteria can be found in [12]. In the context of compliance, for example, it should be avoided to access whole trace information for each instance.

the possibility to choose between different compliance classes and to relax correctness constraints on demand enables us to provide advanced user support in connection with process schema evolution.

3.1   Compliance Class TC: Traditional Compliance

The essence of the following criteria is the notion of *compliance*:

Definition 3 (Compliance). *Let S, $S' \in \mathcal{PS}$ be two process schemas. Further let I be a process instance running on S with trace σ_I^S. Then: I is compliant with S' iff σ_I^S can be replayed on S'; i.e., all events logged in σ_I^S could also have been produced by an instance on S' in the same order as set out by σ_I^S.*

In the context of process change, compliance can be used as basis for the following correctness criterion:

Compliance Criterion 1 (Traditional Compliance TC). *Let S be a process schema and I be an instance on S with trace σ_I^S. Let further S be transformed into another schema S' by change Δ; i.e., $S[\Delta > S'$. Then: If I is compliant with S' (cf. Def. 3), this instance can correctly migrate to S'. Specifically, the instance state of I on S' can be logically obtained by replaying σ_I^S on S'. This state is correct again [12,15].*

Compliance Crit. 1 fulfills Req. 1–3 since it forbids changes not compliant with instance histories (reflected by their traces). In special cases, changes of already passed regions do not affect traces and are therefore not prohibited [11,12]. Assume, for example, that at process schema level activity X is inserted into a branch of an alternative branching. If this branch is skipped for a particular instance I at runtime, I will be compliant with the new schema even though its execution has passed the insertion point of X. Reason is that activities of the skipped branch and X do not write any entries into σ_I^S. Therefore trace σ_I^S can be replayed on S'; i.e., I is compliant with the modified schema.

Crit. 1 does not meet Req. 4 in a satisfactory way since it is too restrictive in several respects. Often instances are excluded from migration to the new schema version even though this would not lead to violation of soundness. Consider, for example, changes applied to loops. Even if an instance is compliant within the current loop iteration, according to Crit. 1 it will be considered as non-compliant, if at least one loop iteration took place. Thus, in the following we investigate how traditional compliance can be relaxed to allow for more migratable instances.

3.2   Compliance Class LTC: Loop-Tolerant Compliance

Crit. 1 will unnecessarily restrict the number of migratable instances if the intended process change affects loop constructs as the following example shows: *Example (Restrictiveness of Crit. 1 in conjunction with loops)* Consider process schema S from Fig. 2a and assume that activity X is inserted between activities A and B (situated within a loop construct). Assume that instance I has trace σ_I^S as shown in Fig. 2b. Following Crit. 1 change Δ cannot be propagated to I since

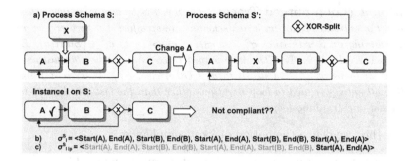

Fig. 2. Process Change Affecting Loop Construct

no trace entries for X have been written in the first two (already completed) iterations of the loop within σ_I^S. According to Crit. 1, therefore, I is considered as being non-compliant with new schema S' even though migration of I to S' would not violate soundness. Consequently, using Crit. 1 only instances which are in the first iteration of the loop construct might be compliant with S'.

In most practical cases it would be too restrictive to prohibit change propagation for in-progress or future loop iterations only because their previous execution is not compliant with the new schema. Think of, for example, medical treatment cycles running for months or years [2]. Any process management system which does not allow to propagate such schema changes (e.g., due to the development of a new medical drug) to already running instances (e.g., related to patients expecting an optimal treatment) would not be accepted by medical staff [2]. Therefore, we have to improve the representation of σ_I^S in order to exterminate its current restrictiveness in conjunction with loops. The key to solution is to differentiate between completed and future executions of loop iterations. From a formal point of view there are two possibilities. The first approach (*linearization*) is to logically treat loop structures as being equivalent to respective linear sequences. Doing so allows us to apply Crit. 1 (with full history information). However, this approach has an essential drawback – explosion of graph size. Thus we adopt another approach which works on a *projection on relevant trace information*, i.e., it maintains the loop construct, but restricts necessary evaluation to relevant parts of the trace. In this context, relevant information includes the actual state of a loop body, but excludes all data about previous loop iterations (cf. Fig. 2c). Note that the projection on relevant information does not physically delete the information about previous loop iterations, but logically hides them (i.e., traceability is not affected).

To realize the desired projection we logically discard all entries from the instance trace produced by a loop iteration other than the actual one (if the loop is still executed) or the last one (if the loop execution has been already finished). For the sake of simplicity we presume nested loops here. However, the described projection can be obtained for arbitrary loop structures as well. We denote this logical view on traces as the *loop-purged trace*.

Definition 4 (Loop-purged Trace). *Let $S \in \mathcal{PS}$ be a process type schema and $\mathcal{A}$ be the set of activities based on which schemas are specified. Let further I be a process instance running on S with trace $\sigma_I^S = < e_0, \ldots, e_k >$ (with $e_i \in \{Start(a), End(a)\}$, $a \in \mathcal{A}$, $i = 1, \ldots, k$, $k \in \mathbb{N}$). The loop-purged trace $\sigma_{I\ lp}^S$ can be obtained as follows: In absence of loops $\sigma_{I\ lp}^S$ is identical to σ_I^S. Otherwise, $\sigma_{I\ lp}^S$ is derived from σ_I^S by discarding all entries related to loop iterations other than the last one (completed loop) or the actual one (running loop).*

Based on this, we define the notion of *loop compliance*:

Compliance Criterion 2 (Loop-tolerant Compliance LTC). *Let S be a process schema and I be a process instance on S with trace σ_I^S. Let further S be transformed into another schema S' by change Δ; i.e., $S[\Delta > S']$. Then: We will denote I as loop-tolerant compliant with S' if the loop-purged trace $\sigma_{I\ lp}^S$ of I can be replayed on S'. If I is loop-compliant with S', it can correctly migrate to S'.*

As shown in [15], Crit. 2 fulfills Req. 1 – 3. In addition, it potentially increases the number of migratable instances when compared to Crit. 1. Thus it contributes to Req. 4. In Sect. 3.4 we measure the effects of switching from Compliance Class TC to Compliance Class LTC.

3.3   Compliance Class RLC: Relaxed Loop-Tolerant Compliance

Further relaxation of Compliance Class LTC (cf. Sect. 3.2) can be achieved when exploiting the semantics of the applied change. Specifically, certain changes (e.g., deleting activities) can be applied independently of the particular instance traces since their application does not affect behavorial soundness of instances. Contrary, inserting or moving activities within completed instance regions might affect behavorial soundness (e.g., causing deadlocks or livelocks). Consider Fig. 3a: Schema S is transformed into schema S' by applying change Δ. More precisely, Δ deletes two activities with a data dependency between them (in practice, for example, the first deleted activity could collect some customer data, while the second one just checks this data). Taking Crit. 1, instance I1 is compliant with S' whereas I2 is not; i.e., I2 is excluded from migration to S'. However, migrating I2 to S' would not result in any violation of soundness; i.e., the state of I2 on S' would be correct and no deadlocks or livelocks would occur.

How to reflect the deletion of already completed activities within instance traces? To preserve traceability, entries of such activities cannot be just physically deleted from traces. Instead, we logically discard them from traces (as for the loop-purged trace representation):

Definition 5 (Delete-purged Trace). *Let $S \in \mathcal{PS}$ be a process schema and $\mathcal{A}$ be the set of activities based on which schemas are specified. Let further I be an instance running on S with trace $\sigma_I^S = < e_0, \ldots, e_k >$ (with $e_i \in \{Start(a), End(a)\}$, $a \in \mathcal{A}$, $i = 1, \ldots, k$, $k \in \mathbb{N}$). Assume that a sound schema S is changed into another sound process schema S' by change Δ (i.e., $S[\Delta > S']$). The delete-purged trace $\sigma_{I\ dp}^S$ is obtained as follows: If Δ does not contain any delete operations $\sigma_{I\ dp}^S$ is identical to σ_I^S.*

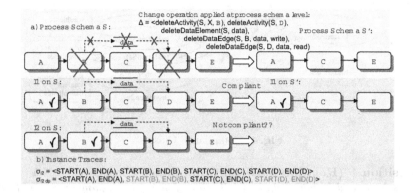

Fig. 3. Changing the Execution History of Process Instances – Example

Otherwise, $\sigma_{I\,dp}^{S}$ is derived from σ_{I}^{S} by (logically) discarding all trace entries related to activities deleted by Δ. Note that $\sigma_{I\,dp}^{S}$ can be produced on basis of loop-purged trace $\sigma_{I\,lp}^{S}$ as well (denoted by $\sigma_{I\,lp,dp}^{S}$).

Based on delete-purged and loop-purged traces, we define the notion of *relaxed (loop-tolerant) compliance*:

Compliance Criterion 3 (Relaxed Loop-tolerant Compliance RLC).

Let S be a schema and I be an instance on S with trace σ_{I}^{S}. Let further S be a sound schema which is transformed into another sound schema S' by change Δ; i.e., $S[\Delta > S'$. Then: We denote I as relaxed loop-tolerant compliant with S' if the loop-purged and delete-purged trace $\sigma_{I\,lp,dp}^{S}$ of I can be replayed on S'. If I is relaxed loop-tolerant compliant, it can correctly migrate to S'.

Traceability of delete operations can be realized using flags or time stamps as well. Consider the example depicted in Fig. 3b. Start/end events of the deleted activities are not physically deleted from σ_{I2} but logically discarded. Thus, it still can be seen from $\sigma_{I_{dp}}^{S}$ that activities B and C had been executed before, but then were deleted. This is a different semantics from rolling back activities since effects of the deleted activities are still present (no compensation activities are applied). Based on $\sigma_{I_{dp}}^{S}$, I2 becomes compliant with S'. Thus the number of compliant instances can be increased again (cf. Req. 4). Though Crit. 3 preserves soundness of affected instances, it depends on the particular application scenario whether it should be applied or not. In any case, based on the above considerations we are able to identify relaxed loop-compliant instances and report them accordingly. Final decision can be left to the process engineer.

3.4   Relation between Compliance Classes

Fig. 4 shows the different compliance classes discussed before. Obviously, the number of compliant instances increases the less restrictive the compliance criterion becomes. At the same time, the number of non-compliant process instances decreases. Formally:

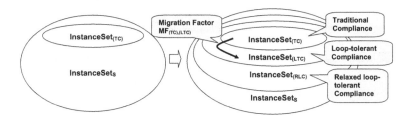

Fig. 4. Compliance Classes

Proposition 1 (Relation between Compliance Classes). *Let S be a sound process schema and InstanceSet$_S$ be a collection of instances running on S. Let further Δ be a change which transforms S into another sound process schema S'. We denote the set of instances which are compliant with S' based on compliance class CClass $\in$ {(TC), (LTC), (RLC)} as InstanceSet$_{CClass}$. Then:*

$$InstanceSet_{(TC)} \subseteq InstanceSet_{(LTC)} \subseteq InstanceSet_{(RLC)} \subseteq InstanceSet_S$$

To measure effects when relaxing a compliance class (e.g., TC to LTC), we use the following metrics:

Definition 6 (Migration Factor). *Assumptions as in Prop. 1. Then: The increase in number of instances which can migrate to S' when going from compliance class CClass1 to compliance class CClass2 ((CClass1, CClass2) $\in$ {(TC, LTC), (LTC, RLC), (TC, RLC)}) can be measured by the migration factor*

$$MF_{CClass1,CClass2} = \frac{||InstanceSet_{CClass1}| - |InstanceSet_{CClass2}||}{|InstanceSet_S|} \tag{1}$$

4   On Dealing with Non-compliant Process Instances

Even though it is possible to increase the number of compliant instances by switching to the next higher compliance class, the question remains how to deal with *non-compliant* instances. At minimum it is required that non-compliant instances may finish execution according to the schema they were started on or migrated to earlier. In many cases, however, it is desired to allow instances to migrate to the new process schema even though they are not compliant at first sight. For example, this can be crucial in the context of new legal regulations. Generally, it is desired to let as many instances as possible take benefit from future process schema changes. This refers to currently applied optimizations, but also to future ones (applied to the newly designed schema later on).

4.1   Relaxing Compliance

One possibility to deal with non-compliant instances is to relax the underlying compliance criterion. This means to move instances from a stricter compliance class to a relaxed one (cf. Fig. 5a). The effect of doing so can be measured by the migration factor (cf. Def. 6). If relaxation of the compliance class is not possible, non-compliant instances will have to be treated within their current compliance class (cf. Fig. 5b). We discuss different possibilities in the following.

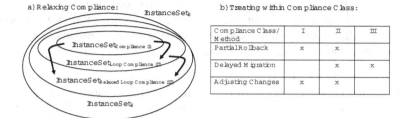

Fig. 5. Strategies for Treating Non-Compliant Instances

4.2 Treatment within One Compliance Class

We present different strategies for treating non-compliant instances within their particular compliance class; i.e., instances for which their execution "has proceeded too far". As illustrated in Fig. 5b, it depends on the kind of compliance class whether the application of a particular strategy makes sense. Furthermore, the applicability of the following strategies also depends on the semantics of the applied change operation. Altogether, based on the classification presented in Fig. 5b, the adaptive PAIS might suggest the following treatment strategies for non-compliant instances.

Partial Rollback. Several approaches from literature suggest restoring compliance of non-compliant instances by partially rolling them back in their execution [8,16]; i.e., applying this policy for instances which have progressed too far results in a compliant state. Thus a partial rollback is reasonable for compliance classes TC and LTC since both are based on instance states. Contrary, the essence of compliance class RLC is based on allowing changes of the past (specifically delete operations). Hence, rollback to earlier instance states does not make sense here. Generally, (partial) rollback of instances is connected with compensating activities [8] (e.g., if a flight has been booked, the compensating activity will be to cancel the booking). An obvious drawback is that it is not always possible to find compensating activities, i.e., to adequately rollback non-compliant instances. Furthermore, even if compensating activities can be found, this will be mostly connected with loss of work and thus will not be accepted by users.

Delayed Migration. An alternative approach to deal with a non-compliant instance is to wait until it becomes compliant again: Assume that process change Δ affects a loop construct[3] within schema S. Assume further that for instance I running on S this loop is currently being executed, but has proceeded too far to be compliant. However, instance I becomes a candidate for migration when the loop enters its next iteration; i.e., (relaxed) loop-tolerant compliance might be satisfied with delay (*delayed migration*). Such instances can be held as "pending to migration" until the loop condition is evaluated. As we have learned in ADEPT2, implementing delayed migration is not as trivial as it looks like at

---

[3] Thus delayed migration is applicable for compliance classes LTC and RLC.

first glance. At first, if an instance contained regularly or irregularly nested loops several events (loop backs) might exist to trigger the execution of a previously delayed migration. Furthermore, the interesting question remains how to deal with pending instances when further schema changes take place.

Adjusting Change Operations. The above strategies are based on the idea to reset non-compliant instances into a compliant state. Another approach is to adjust the intended change itself instead of the instance states. We illustrate this taking insert operations as example. However, this strategy can be also applied in the context of other change patterns (e.g., move). The idea is to exploit specific semantics of the insert operation [14]: When applying it, the user has to specify the position where to insert the new activities. Basically, this position depends on two kinds of constraints: first, *data dependencies* have to be fulfilled (e.g., an activity writing data element d has to be positioned before an activity reading d) and second, *semantic constraints* must be obeyed. Here we focus on handling data dependencies. Semantic constraints can be treated similarly.

Basically, adjusting changes can take place at the process type and the process instance level. Assume that a schema S is transformed into another process schema S' by change Δ. Let further I be an instance running on S which is not compliant with S'. If Δ is adjusted to Δ' at type level (transforming S into S''), all instances running on S will be checked for compliance with S'' afterwards (*global adjustment*). Alternatively, Δ can be adjusted specifically for I at instance level. The latter results in *bias* Δ_I; i.e., an instance-specific change which describes the difference between the process schema, I is linked to, and the instance-specific schema it is running on (*instance-specific adjustment*).

Global Adjustment: Consider Fig. 6 where change Δ_1 inserts activities X and Y with a data dependency between them into schema S. This results in schema S'. Instance I running on S is not compliant with S'. Reason is that X would be inserted before already completed activity B. As a consequence, if X is not executed, data will not be written and inputs of Y will not be supplied correctly in the sequel. However, aside any semantic constraints, activity X could be also inserted between activities B and C (Δ_2 transforming S into S''). Reason is that the writing activity (X) is still inserted before the reading one (Y). Thus all data dependencies are still fulfilled. When applying Δ_2, instance I will become compliant with S''.

Generally, more instances will become compliant with a changed process schema, if added activities are inserted "as late as possible". Most important, all data dependencies (or, additionally, semantics constraints) imposed by the process schema and the intended change must be fulfilled. For the given example this implies that activities X and Y can be inserted "later in the process schema" (i.e., as close to the process end as possible) as long as the data dependency between them is still fulfilled. Since a process schema might contain more than one process end node, the formalization of "later in a process schema" should not be based on structural properties; i.e., we aim at being independent of a particular process meta model. As for the compliance criterion, we use process traces in this context. Due to lack of space we omit a formalization here.

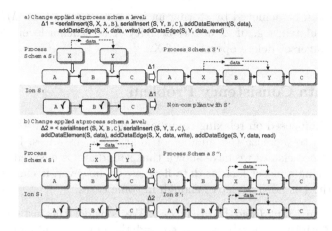

Fig. 6. Global Adjustment of Change Operations – Example

When inserting two or more data-dependent activities as depicted in Fig. 6, additional constraints must hold. More precisely, it cannot be allowed to move the insertion position of the writing activity "behind" the reading activity since the resulting schema would not be correct anymore.

Instance-specific Adjustment: Consider the example depicted in Fig. 7. Contrary to the above example, we do not adjust schema change Δ_1 but apply adjusted instance-specific change $\Delta_I(S)$ only to I at instance level. This results in instance-specific schema S_I. The bias between S_I and S' is captured within $\Delta_I(S')$ and reflects moving X to the position between B and Y.

Instance-specific adjustment can be generalized to make any non-compliant instance compliant with the changed process schema. The idea behind is the following: Let S be a process schema which is transformed into S' by change Δ. Let further I be an instance on S. So far, Δ is propagated to I when migrating I to S (i.e., I reflects Δ after its migration). However, if I is not compliant with S', Δ must not be applied to I. We still can migrate I to S' but without propagating

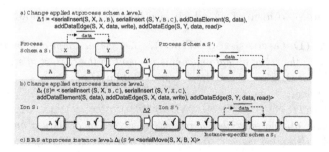

Fig. 7. Instance-Specific Adjustment of Change Operations – Example

Δ to I. This can be achieved by storing an instance-specific bias $\Delta_I(S')$ which has to be calculated; e.g., if Δ inserts activity X at schema level, $\Delta_I(S')$ will contain the "inverse" delete operation of X.

5   The Data Consistency Problem

So far, we have focused on relaxing compliance notions based on the underlying instance traces to increase the number of migratable instances. For three different compliance classes we have shown that soundness is ensured for affected instances. Having a closer look at data flow issues, however, it can be observed that even Crit. 1 is not restrictive enough in some cases.

Example (Inconsistent Read Data Access): We consider the instance depicted in Fig. 8a. Activity C has been started and therefore has already read data value 5 of data element d_1. Assume now that due to a modeling error read data edge $(C, d_1, read)$ is deleted and new read data edge $(C, d_2, read)$ is inserted afterwards. Consequently, C should have read data value 2 of data element d_2 (instead of data value 5). This inconsistent read behavior may lead to errors if, for example, the execution of this instance is aborted and therefore has to be rolled back. Using any representation of trace σ_I^S as introduced so far (i.e., σ_I^S or $\sigma_{I\ lp,dp}^S$), this erroneous case would not be detected. Consequently, this instance would be classified as compliant.

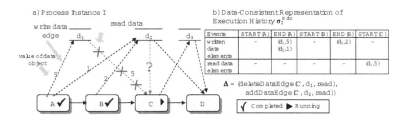

Fig. 8. Data Consistency Problem

We need an adapted form of σ_I^S which also incorporates data flow aspects.

Definition 7 (Data-consistent Trace). *Let the assumptions be as in Def. 1. Let further $\mathcal{D}_S$ be the set of all data elements relevant in the context of schema S. Then we denote $\sigma_I^{S\,dc}$ as data-consistent trace representation of σ_I^S*

with $\sigma_I^{S\,dc} = <e_1, \ldots, e_k>$:

$e_i \in \{START(a)^{(d_1,v_1),\ldots,(d_n,v_n)}\ END(a)^{(d_1,v_1),\ldots,(d_m,v_m)}\}$, $a \in \mathcal{A}$

where tuple (d_i, v_i) describes a read/write access of activity a on data element $d_i \in \mathcal{D}_S$ with associated value v_i $(i = 0, \ldots, k)$ if a is started/completed.

Using the data-consistent representation of σ_I^S the problem illutrated in Fig. 8a) is resolved as the following example shows [11,15]:

Example (Consistent Read Data Access Using $\sigma_I^{S^{dc}}$): Consider Fig. 8a. Assume that the data-consistent trace $\sigma_I^{S^{dc}}$ is used instead of σ_I^S. Then the intended data flow change Δ (deleting data edge $(C, d_1, read)$ and inserting data edge $(C, d_2, read)$ afterwards) cannot be correctly propagated to I since entry Start(C)$^{(d_1,5)}$ of $\sigma_I^{S^{dc}}$ cannot be reproduced on the changed schema.

The data-consistent representation $\sigma_I^{S^{dc}}$ can be used as basis for all other trace representations (cf. Def. 4 – 5). Thus data-consistent compliance works in combination with the other compliance classes TC, LTC, and RLC.

6   Example and Practical Impact

Consider the example depicted in Fig. 9. Schema S is transformed into schema S' by deleting activities B and D and the data dependency between them as well as by inserting activity X within the loop construct. Assume that instances I_k $(k = 1, \ldots, 1000)$ are clustered according to their state: For $k = 1, \ldots, 100$, at maximum, activities A, E, and F are completed (indicated by the grey milestone) whereas activities of the other parallel branch have not yet been executed. Particularly, the loop construct is within its first iteration. For $k = 101, \ldots, 200$, the loop has been executed more than once and activities B, C, and D have not yet been executed. For $k = 201, \ldots, 800$, activities of both branches have been executed, but the parallel branching has not completed yet (i.e., G is not activated). For $k = 801, \ldots, 1000$ (not depicted), G is either started or completed.

If Crit. 1 is applied to instances $I_1, \ldots, I_{1000}$, only $I_1, \ldots, I_{100}$ are considered as being compliant with S'. If relaxing to Compliance Crit. 2, additionally instances $I_{101}, \ldots, I_{200}$ become compliant. Thus a migration factor of $MF_{(I),(II)} = 0.1$ is achieved, i.e., 10 % more instances can migrate to S'. Finally, if we relax compliance to Crit. 3, additionally, $I_{201}, \ldots, I_{800}$ are considered as being compliant with S' and a migration factor $MF_{(II),(III)} = 0.6$ results; i.e., 80% of all process instances can migrate to S'. The remaining instances are non-compliant.

7   Related Work

There is a plethora of approaches dealing with correctness issues in adaptive PAISs [9,5,10,17,11,8]. The kind of applied correctness criterion often depends on the used process meta model. A discussion and comparison of the particular correctness criteria is given in [12]. Aside from the applied correctness criteria, mostly these approaches do neither address the question of how to increase the number of migratable instances nor how to deal with non-compliant instances. Most approaches which treat non-compliant instances are based on partial rollback [8,16] (cf. Sect. 4). An alternative approach supporting *delayed migrations* of non-compliant instances is offered by *Flow Nets* [5]. Even if instance I on S is not compliant with S' within the actual iteration of a loop, a delayed migration of I to the new change region is possible when another loop iteration takes place.

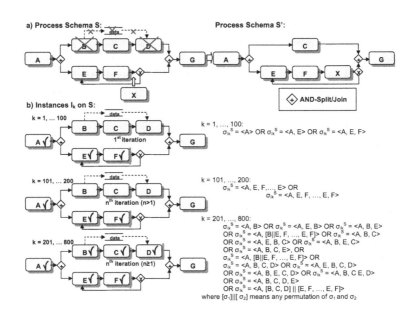

Fig. 9. Example

Frameworks for process flexibility have been presented in [18,14]. In [18], different paradigms for process flexibility and related technologies are described. [14] provides change patterns and evaluates different approaches based on them. However, [18,14] do not address relaxed soundness criteria for process changes.

8   Summary and Outlook

This paper addressed the question of how to increase the number of process instances which can migrate to a changed process schema. This is important in the context of new legal regulations or process optimizations. Thus, we revisited the notion of compliance – a widely-used correctness criterion in the context of process change – and introduced several classes of relaxed compliance. We also showed how the number of compliant instances can be increased by these relaxed notions. Furthermore, we discussed approaches dealing with non-compliant process instances and introduced new strategies in this context. In addition, we detected that traditional compliance is too relaxed in the context of data flow correctness and provided an adequate criterion for data-consistent compliance. Finally we presented a practical example. The concepts of loop-tolerant compliance and data consistency have been implemented in our ADEPT demonstrator [15]. Currently, the concepts are implemented within the full-blown adaptive PAIS ADEPT2. In future work we will investigate the relaxation of compliance more deeply: in addition to further relaxation classes, we will elaborate the strategy of using ad-hoc changes to migrate any non-compliant process instance (without instance-specific changes) to a changed process schema.

References

1. Weber, B., Rinderle, S., Reichert, M.: Change patterns and change support features in process-aware information systems. In: Krogstie, J., Opdahl, A., Sindre, G. (eds.) CAiSE 2007. LNCS, vol. 4495, pp. 574–588. Springer, Heidelberg (2007)
2. Lenz, R., Reichert, M.: IT support for healthcare processes – premises, challenges, perspectives. Data and Knowledge Eng. 61(1), 39–58 (2007)
3. van der Aalst, W.: Exterminating the dynamic change bug: A concrete approach to support worfklow change. Information Systems Frontiers 3, 297–317 (2001)
4. Casati, F., Ceri, S., Pernici, B., Pozzi, G.: Workflow evolution. Data and Knowledge Engineering 24, 211–238 (1998)
5. Ellis, C., Keddara, K., Rozenberg, G.: Dynamic change within workflow systems. In: COOCS 1995, pp. 10–21 (1995)
6. Kradolfer, M., Geppert, A.: Dynamic workflow schema evolution based on workflow type versioning and workflow migration. In: CoopIS 1999, pp. 104–114 (1999)
7. Reichert, M., Dadam, P.: ADEPT$_{flex}$ - supporting dynamic changes of workflows without losing control. J. of Intelligent Information Systems 10, 93–129 (1998)
8. Sadiq, S., Marjanovic, O., Orlowska, M.: Managing change and time in dynamic workflow processes. IJCIS 9, 93–116 (2000)
9. van der Aalst, W., Basten, T.: Inheritance of workflows: An approach to tackling problems related to change. Theoret. Comp. Science 270, 125–203 (2002)
10. Weske, M.: Formal foundation and conceptual design of dynamic adaptations in a workflow management system. In: HICSS-34 (2001)
11. Rinderle, S., Reichert, M., Dadam, P.: Flexible support of team processes by adaptive workflow systems. Distributed and Parallel Databases 16, 91–116 (2004)
12. Rinderle, S., Reichert, M., Dadam, P.: Correctness criteria for dynamic changes in workflow systems – a survey. Data and Knowledge Engineering. 50, 9–34 (2004)
13. Dehnert, J., Zimmermann, A.: On the suitability of correctness criteria for business process models. In: Bussler, C.J., Haller, A. (eds.) BPM 2005. LNCS, vol. 3812, pp. 386–391. Springer, Heidelberg (2006)
14. Weber, B., Reichert, M., Rinderle-Ma, S.: Change patterns and change support features - enhancing flexibility in process-aware information systems. Data and Knowledge Engineering (2008)
15. Rinderle, S.: Schema Evolution in Process Management Systems. PhD thesis, Ulm University (2004)
16. Reichert, M., Dadam, P., Bauer, T.: Dealing with forward and backward jumps in workflow management systems. Software and Syst. Modeling 2, 37–58 (2003)
17. Rinderle, S., Reichert, M., Dadam, P.: Evaluation of correctness criteria for dynamic workflow changes. In: van der Aalst, W.M.P., ter Hofstede, A.H.M., Weske, M. (eds.) BPM 2003. LNCS, vol. 2678, pp. 41–57. Springer, Heidelberg (2003)
18. Mulyar, N., Schonenberg, M., Mans, R., Russell, N., van der Aalst, W.: Towards a taxonomy of process flexibility (extended version). Technical Report BPM-07-11, Brisbane/Eindhoven: BPMcenter.org (2007)

On Measuring Process Model Similarity Based on High-Level Change Operations*

Chen Li[1], Manfred Reichert[2], and Andreas Wombacher[3]

[1] Information System group, University of Twente, The Netherlands
lic@cs.utwente.nl
[2] Institute of Databases and Information System, Ulm University, Germany
manfred.reichert@uni-ulm.de
[3] Database group, University of Twente, The Netherlands
a.wombacher@utwente.nl

Abstract. For various applications there is the need to compare the similarity between two process models. For example, given the as-is and to-be models of a particular business process, we would like to know how much they differ from each other and how we can efficiently transform the as-is to the to-be model; or given a running process instance and its original process schema, we might be interested in the deviations between them (e.g. due to ad-hoc changes at instance level). Respective considerations can be useful, for example, to minimize the efforts for propagating the schema changes to other process instances as well. All these scenarios require a method to measure the similarity or distance between two process models based on the efforts for transforming the one into the other. In this paper, we provide an approach using digital logic to evaluate the distance and similarity between two process models based on high-level change operations (e.g. to add, delete or move activities). In this way, we can not only guarantee that model transformation results in a sound process model, but also ensure that related efforts are minimized.

1 Introduction

Business world is getting increasingly dynamic, requiring from companies to continuously adapt business processes as well as supporting *Process-Aware Information Systems* (PAISs) [3] in order to cope with the frequent and unprecedented changes in their business environment [19]. Organizations and enterprises need to continuously Re-engineer their Business Processes (BPR), i.e. they need to be able to flexibly upgrade and optimize their business processes in order to stay competitive in their market. Furthermore, PAISs should allow for process flexibility, i.e., it must be possible for users to deviate from the pre-defined process model at the instance level if required.

The pivotal research on process flexibility over the last years [1,11] has provided the foundation for dynamic process change to reduce the cost of change

---

* Supported by the Netherlands Organization for Scientific Research (NWO) under contract number 612.066.512.

Q. Li et al. (Eds.): ER 2008, LNCS 5231, pp. 248–264, 2008.

in PAISs. Process flexibility denotes the capability to reflect externally triggered change by modifying only those aspects of a process that need to be changed, while keeping the other parts stable, i.e., the ability to change or evolve the process without completely replacing it [11]. To compare two process models is a fundamental task in this context. In particular, it becomes necessary to calculate the minimal difference between two process models based on high level changes. If we need to transform one model into another, for example, efforts can then be reduced and the transformation can go smoothly; i.e. we do not need to re-define the new process model from scratch, but only apply these high-level changes either at process type or process instance level. Several approaches like ADEPT [11], WASA [20] or TRAM [6], have emerged to enable process change support in PAIS (see [13] for an overview).

Based on the two assumptions that (1) process models are block-structured and (2) all activities in a process model have unique labels, this paper deals with the following fundamental research question:

Given two process models S and S′, how much do they differ from each other in terms of high-level change operations? And what is the minimal effort, i.e. the minimal number of change operations needed to transform S into S′?

Clearly, our focus is on minimizing the number of high-level change operations needed to transform process model S into process model $S′$. Soundness of the resulting process model should be also not sacrificed. We apply the high-level change operations as described in [11,19] in the given context. By considering high-level changes, we can distinguish our approach from traditional similarity measures like graph or sub-graph isomorphism [15]. Both only consider basic change primitives like insertion or deletion of single nodes and edges.

Answering the above research question will lead to better cost efficiency when performing BPR, since the efforts to implement the corresponding changes in the supporting PAIS are minimized. At process instance level, we can reduce the efforts to propagate process type changes to the running instances [13]. Finally the derived differences between original process model and its process instances can be used as a set of pure and concise logs for process mining [4].

In previous work, we have provided the technical foundation for users to flexibly change process models at both the process type and the process instance level. For example, users may dynamically *insert, delete* or *move* an activity at these two levels [11]. In addition, snapshot differential algorithms [7], known from database technology, can be used as a fast and secure method to detect the *change primitives* (e.g. to add or delete nodes and edges) needed to transform one process model into another.

Using this framework and snapshot differential algorithm, this paper applies Digital Logic in Boolean Algebra [14] to provide a new method to transform a process model into another one based on high-level change operations. This method does not only minimize the number of changes needed in this context, but also guarantees soundness of the changed process model, i.e. the process model remains correct when applying high-level change operations. We further provide two measures –*process distance* and *process similarity* –based on high-level change operations, which indicate how costly it is to transform process model S into model S', and how different S and S' are.

The remainder of this paper is organized as follows: Sec. 2 introduces backgrounds needed for the understanding of this paper. In Sec. 3 we discuss reasons and difficulties for deriving high-level change operations. Sec. 4 describes an approach to detect the difference between two process models. Sec. 5 discuss related work. The paper concludes with a summary and outlook in Sec. 6.

2   Backgrounds

Let $\mathcal{P}$ denote the set of all correct process models. A particular *process model* $S = (N, E, \ldots) \in \mathcal{P}$ is defined as a well-structured Activity Net [11]. N constitutes a set of activities a_i and E is a set of precedence relations (i.e. control edges) between them. To limit the scope, we assume Activity Nets to be block structured. Examples are depicted in Fig 1.

We assume that a process change (i.e. Activity Net Change) is accomplished by applying a sequence of high-level change operations to a given process model S over time [11]. Such change operations modify the initial process model by altering the set of activities and/or their order relations. Thus, each application of a change operation results in a new process model. We define *process change* as follows:

Definition 1 (Process Change). *Let $\mathcal{P}$ denote the set of possible process models and $\mathcal{C}$ the set of possible process changes. Let $S, S' \in \mathcal{P}$ be two process models, let $\Delta \in \mathcal{C}$ be a process change, and let $\sigma = \langle \Delta_1, \Delta_2, \ldots \Delta_n \rangle \in \mathcal{C}^*$ be a sequence of process changes performed on initial model S. Then:*

- *$S[\Delta\rangle S'$ iff Δ is applicable to S and S' is the process model resulting from the application of Δ to S.*
- *$S[\sigma\rangle S'$ iff $\exists\ S_1, S_2, \ldots S_{n+1} \in \mathcal{P}$ with $S = S_1$, $S' = S_{n+1}$, and $S_i[\Delta\rangle S_{i+1}$ for $i \in \{1, \ldots n\}$.*

Examples of high-level change operations and their effects on a process model are depicted in Table 1. Issues concerning the correct use of these operations and related pre-/post- conditions are described in [11]. If some additional constraints are met, the high-level change operations depicted in Table 1 will be also applicable at process instance level. Although the depicted change operations are discussed in relation to our ADEPT framework [11], they are generic in the sense that they can be easily transferred to other process meta models as well. For example, the change operations in Table 1 can be also expressed by the life-cycle inheritance rule as used in the context of Petri Nets [16]. We are referring to ADEPT in this paper since it covers by far most high-level change operations and change patterns respectively when compared to other approaches [19]. It further has served as basis for representing our method.

A trace t on process model S denotes a valid execution sequence $t \equiv <a_1, a_2, \ldots, a_k >$ of activities $a_i \in N$ on S according to the control flow defined by S. All traces process model S can produce are summarized in trace

Table 1. Examples of High-Level Change Operations

Change Operation Δ on S	opType	subject	paramList
insert(S, X, $\mathcal{A}, \mathcal{B}$, [sc])	insert	X	S, $\mathcal{A}, \mathcal{B}$, [sc]

Effects on S: inserts activity X between activity sets $\mathcal{A}$ and $\mathcal{B}$. It is a conditional insert if [sc] is specified (i.e. [sc] = XOR)

delete(S, X, [sc])	delete	X	S, [sc]

Effects on S: deletes activity X from S, i.e. X turns into a silent one. [sc] is specified ([sc] = XOR) when we block the branch with X, i.e. the branch which contains X will not be activated

move(S, X, $\mathcal{A}, \mathcal{B}$, [sc])	move	X	S, $\mathcal{A}, \mathcal{B}$, [sc]

Effects on S: moves activity X from its original position in S to another position between activity sets A and B. (it is a conditional insert if [sc] is specified)

replace(S, X, Y)	replace	X	Y

Effects on S: replaces activity X by activity Y

set $\mathcal{T}_S$. $t(a \prec b)$ is denoted as precedence relation between activities a and b in trace $t \equiv <a_1, a_2, \ldots, a_k>$ iff $\exists i < j : a_i = a \land a_j = b$. Here, we only consider traces composing 'real' activities, but no events related to silent activities i.e., activity nodes which contain no operation and exist only for control flow purpose, see Section 4.4. Finally, we will consider two process models as being the same if they are *trace equivalent*, i.e. $S \equiv S'$ iff $\mathcal{T}_S \equiv \mathcal{T}_{S'}$. The stronger notion of bi-similarity [5] is not required in our context.

3 High-Level Change Operations

3.1 Complementary Nature of Change and Execution Logs

Most PAISs support ad-hoc deviations at instance level and record them in *change logs*. Thus, they provide additional information when compared to traditional PAISs which only record *execution logs* (which typically document the start and/or end time of activities). Change logs and execution logs document different run-time information on adaptive process instances and are not interchangeable. Even if the original process model is given, it will be not possible to convert the change log of a process instance to its execution log or vice-verse. As example, take the original and simplified patient treatment process as depicted in Fig. 1a: a patient is *admitted* to a hospital, where he first *registers*, then *receives treatment*, and finally *pays*. Assume that, due to an emergency situation, for one

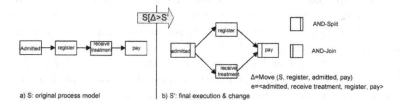

Fig. 1. Change Log and Execution Log are not Interchangeable

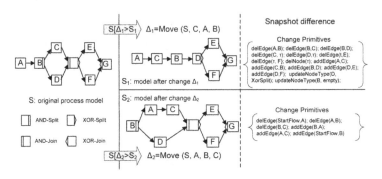

Fig. 2. High-level Change Operation and Corresponding change primitive

particular patient, we want to first start the treatment of this patient and allow him to register later during treatment. To represent this exceptional situation in the process model of the respective instance, the needed change would be to move activity *receive treatment* from its current position to a position parallel to activity *register*. This change leads to a new model S', i.e., $S[\sigma\rangle S'$ with $\sigma = <move(S,$ *reveive treatment, admitted, pay)* $>$. Meanwhile, the execution log e for this particular instance can be $e = <$ *admitted, receive treatment, register, pay* $>$ (cf. Fig. 1b). If we only have process model S and its execution log, it will be not possible to determine this change because the process model which can produce such execution log is not unique. For example, a process model with the four activities contained in four parallel branches could produce this execution log as well. On the contrary, it is generally not possible to derive the execution log from a change log, because execution behavior of S' is also not unique. For example, a trace $<$ *admitted, register, receive treatment, pay* $>$ is also producible on S' as well. Consequently, change logs provide additional information when compared to pure execution logs.

3.2   Why Do We Need High-Level Change Operations?

After showing the importance of change logs, we now discuss why we need high-level change operations rather than change primitives (i.e., low-level changes at edge and node level). Left side of Fig. 2 shows original process model S which consists of a parallel branching, a conditional branching, and a silent activity τ (depicted as empty node) connecting these two blocks. Assume that two different high-level change operations are applied to S resulting in models S_1 and S_2: Δ_1 moves activity C from its current location to the position between activities A and B, which leads to S_1 i.e., $S[\Delta_1\rangle S_1$ with $\Delta_1 = move(S,\text{C},\text{A},\text{B})$. Δ_2 moves A to the position between B and C, i.e. $S[\Delta_2\rangle S_2$ with $\Delta_2 = move(S,\text{A},\text{B},\text{C})$. Fig. 2 additionally depicts the change primitives representing snapshot differences between S and models S_1 and S_2, respectively. Using high-level change operations offers the following advantages:

1. High-level change operations guarantee soundness: i.e., application of a high-level change operation to a sound model S results in another sound model S' [11]. This also applies to our example from Fig. 2. By contrast, when applying one single change primitive (e.g., deleting an edge in S) soundness cannot be guaranteed anymore. Generally, if we delete any of the edges in S, the resulting process model will not be necessarily sound.
2. High-level change operations provide richer syntactical meanings than change primitives. Generally, a high-level change operation is built upon a set of change primitives which collectively represent a complex modification of a process model. As example take Δ_1 from Fig. 2. This high-level change operation requires *15* change primitives for its realization (deleting edges, adding edges, deleting the silent activity, and updating the node types).
3. An important aspect, not discussed so far, concerns the number of change operations needed to transform model S into target model S'. For example, we need only *one* move operation to transform S to either S_1 or S_2. However, when using change primitives, migrating S to S_1 necessitates *15* change primitives, while the second change Δ_2 can be realized based on *6* change primitives. This example also shows that change primitives do not provide an adequate means to determine the difference between two process models. Thus the required number of change primitives cannot represent the efforts for process model transformations.

3.3 The Challenge to Derive High-Level Change Operations

After sketching the benefits coming with high-level change operations, this section discusses challenges of deriving them. When comparing two process models, the change primitives needed for transforming one model into another can be easily determined by performing two snapshots and a delta analysis on them [7]. An algorithm to minimize the number of change primitives is given in [12]. However, when trying to derive the high-level change operations needed for model transformation, several challenges occur. As example consider Fig. 3:

1. When performing two delete operations on S (i.e., $\Delta_1 = delete(S, \text{B})$ and $\Delta_2 = delete(S, \text{C})$), we obtain a new model S'' (i.e., $S[\sigma\rangle S''$ with $\sigma =< \Delta_1, \Delta_2 >$), as well as an undetectable intermediate model S' with $S[\Delta_1\rangle S'$ and $S'[\Delta_2\rangle S''$. When examining the change primitives corresponding to each high-level change operation, we first need to add edge (A,C) after the first *delete* operation Δ_1, and remove this edge (A,C) when applying the second *delete* operation Δ_2. However, when performing a delta analysis for the original process model S and the resulting process model S'', the two change primitives (addEdge(A,C) introduced by the first *delete* operation and delEdge (A,C) introduced by the second one) jointly have no effect on the resulting process model S'', i.e., they cannot be detected by snapshot analysis. Consequently, deriving high-level change operations based on change primitives would be challenging because the change primitives required for every high-level change do not always appear in the snapshot differences between the original and resulting models. In Fig. 3, none of the two change

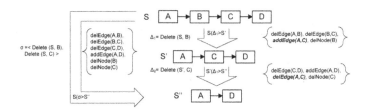

Fig. 3. Non-detectable Change Primitives

primitive sets associated with Δ_1 or Δ_2 constitute a sub-set of the change primitive set associated with σ.

2. Even if there is just one high-level change operation, it will remain difficult to derive it with delta algorithm. For example, in Fig. 3 the delta algorithm shows that *15* change primitives are needed to transform S into S_1. However, the depicted changes can be also realized by just applying one high level move operation to S.

4   Detecting the Minimal Number of High-Level Changes

In this section, we introduce our method to detect the minimal number of change operations needed to transform a given process model S into another model S'. As example, consider the process models S and S' in Fig. 4.

4.1   General Description of Our Method

As mentioned in Section 1, the key issue of our work is to minimize the number of change operations needed to transform a process model $S = (N, E, \ldots) \in \mathcal{P}$ into another model $S' = (N', E', \ldots) \in \mathcal{P}$. Generally, three steps are needed (cf. Fig. 4) to realize this minimal transformation:

1. $\forall a_i \in N \setminus N'$: *delete* all activities being present in S, but not in S'. This first step transforms S to S_{same} (cf. Fig. 4b).
2. $\forall a_i \in N \bigcap N'$: *move* all activities being present in both models to the locations as reflected by S'. Regarding our example, this second step transforms S_{same} to S'_{same} (cf. Fig. 4c).
3. $\forall a_i \in N' \setminus N$: *insert* those activities being present in S', but not in S. As depicted in Fig. 4, the third step transforms S'_{same} to S' (cf. Fig. 4d).

Insertions and deletions deal with changes of the set of activities. Here, we can hardly do anything to reduce efforts (i.e., the number of required insert/delete operations): New activities ($a_i \in N' \setminus N$) must be added and obsolete activities ($a_j \in N \setminus N'$) must be deleted.

The focus of minimality can therefore be shifted to the use of the *move* operation, which changes the structure of a process model, but not its set of activities.

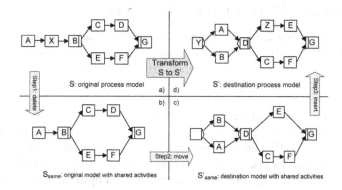

Fig. 4. Three Steps to Transform S into S'

Since a move operation logically corresponds to a delete followed by an insert operation, we can transform S_{same} to S'_{same} by maximally applying $n = |N \cap N'|$ move operations. Reason is that n move operations correspond to deleting all activities and then re-inserting them at their new positions. Correspondingly, n is the maximal number of change operations needed to transform one process model into another, both with same set of activities (S_{same} and S'_{same} in our example from Fig. 4). To measure the complete transformation from S to S', we formally define *process distance* and *process similarity* as follows:

Definition 2 (Process Distance and Process Similarity). *Let $S = (N, E, \ldots), S' = (N', E', \ldots) \in \mathcal{P}$ be two process models. Let further $\sigma = \langle \Delta_1, \Delta_2, \ldots \Delta_n \rangle \in \mathcal{C}^*$ be a sequence of change operations transforming S into S' (i.e. $S[\sigma\rangle S'$). Then the distance between S and S' is given by $d_{(S,S')} = min\{|\sigma| \mid \sigma \in \mathcal{C}^* \wedge S[\sigma\rangle S'\}$. Furthermore, process similarity between S and S' equals to $1 - \frac{d_{(S,S')}}{|N|+|N'|-|N \cap N'|}$, i.e., similarity equals to ((maximal number of changes - minimal number of changes) / maximal number of changes).*

4.2   Determining Required Activity Deletions and Insertions

To accomplish Step 1 and Step 3 of our method, we have to deal with the change of the activity set when transforming S into S'. It can be easily detected by applying existing snapshot algorithms [7] to both S and S'. As described in Section 4.1, as first step we need to *delete* all activities $a_i \in N \setminus N'$ contained in S, but not in S'. Regarding our example from Fig. 4, we can derive as our first high-level change operation $\Delta_1 = delete(S, \mathtt{X})$. Similarly, activities contained in S', but not in S, are inserted in Step 3, after having moved the shared activities to their respective position in S' (S'_{same} respectively). The parameters of the insert operation, i.e. the predecessors and successors of the inserted activity, are just like how they appear in S'. In this way, we obtain the last two change operations for our example: $Insert(S, \mathtt{Y}, \mathtt{StartFlow}, \{\mathtt{A}, \mathtt{B}\})$ and $Insert(S, \mathtt{Z}, \mathtt{D}, \mathtt{E})$.

4.3   Determining Required Move Operations

We now focus on Step 2 of our method; i.e., to transform two process models with same activity set using move operations. Here, we can ignore the activities not contained in both S and S' (cf. 4.2). Instead, we consider the two process models S_{same} and S'_{same} respectively, as depicted in Fig. 4.

Determine the Order Matrix of a Process Model. One key feature of our ADEPT change framework is to maintain the structure of the unchanged parts of a process model [11]. For example, if we delete an activity, this will neither influence the successors nor the predecessors of this activity, and also not their control relation. To incorporate this feature in our approach, rather than only looking at direct predecessor-successor relationships between two activities (i.e. control flow edges), we consider the transitive control dependencies between all pairs of activities; i.e., for every pair of activities $a_i, a_j \in N \bigcap N'$, $a_i \neq a_j$, their execution order compared to each other is examined. Logically, we check execution orders by considering all traces a process model can produce (cf. Sec. 2). Results can be formally described in a matrix $A_{n \times n}$ with $n = |N \bigcap N'|$. Four types of control relations can be identified (cf. Def. 3):

Definition 3 (Order matrix). *Let $S = (N, E, \dots) \in \mathcal{P}$ be a process model with $N = \{a_1, a_2, \dots, a_n\}$. Let further $\mathcal{T}_S$ denote the set of all traces producible on S. Then: Matrix $A_{n \times n}$ is called **order matrix** of S with A_{ij} representing the relation between different activities $a_i, a_j \in N$ iff:*

- $A_{ij} = \text{'1'}$ *iff* $(\forall t \in \mathcal{T}_S \text{ with } a_i, a_j \in t \Rightarrow t(a_i \prec a_j))$
  *If for all traces containing activities a_i and a_j, a_i always appears BEFORE a_j, we denote A_{ij} as '**1**', i.e., a_i is predecessor of a_j in the flow of control.*
- $A_{ij} = \text{'0'}$ *iff* $(\forall t \in \mathcal{T}_S \text{ with } a_i, a_j \in t \Rightarrow t(a_j \prec a_i))$
  *If for all traces containing activity a_i and a_j, a_i always appears AFTER a_j, then we denote A_{ij} as a '**0**', i.e. a_i is successor of a_j in the flow of control.*
- $A_{ij} = \text{'*'}$ *iff* $(\exists t_1 \in \mathcal{T}_S, \text{ with } a_i, a_j \in t_1 \land t_1(a_i \prec a_j)) \land (\exists t_2 \in \mathcal{T}_S, \text{ with } a_i, a_j \in t_2 \land t_2(a_j \prec a_i))$
  *If there exists at least one trace in which a_i appears before a_j and at least one other trace in which a_i appears after a_j, we denote A_{ij} as '*****', i.e. a_i and a_j are contained in different parallel branches.*
- $A_{ij} = \text{'-'}$ *iff* $(\neg \exists t \in \mathcal{T}_S : a_i \in t \land a_j \in t)$
  *If there is no trace containing both activity a_i and a_j, we denote A_{ij} as '**-**', i.e. a_i and a_j are contained in different branches of a conditional branching.*

We revisit our example from Fig. 4. The order matrices of S_{same} and S'_{same} are shown in Fig. 5. The main diagonal is empty since we do not compare an activity with itself. As one can see, elements A_{ij} and A_{ji} can be derived from each other. If activity a_i is a predecessor of activity a_j (i.e. $A_{ij} = 1$), we can always conclude that $A_{ji} = 0$ holds. Similarly, if $A_{ij} \in \{\text{'*'},\text{'-'}\}$, we will obtain $A_{ji} = A_{ij}$. As a consequence, we can simplify our problem by only considering the upper triangular matrix $A = (A_{ij})_{j>i}$.

Under certain constraints, an order matrix A can uniquely represent the process model, based on which it was built on. This is stated by Theorem 1. Before giving this theorem, we need to define the notion of *substring of trace*:

Definition 4 (Substring of trace). *Let t and t' be two traces. We define t is a sub-string of t' iff $[\forall a_i, a_j \in t, t(a_i \prec a_j) \Rightarrow a_i, a_j \in t' \wedge t'(a_i \prec a_j)]$ and $[\exists a_k \in N : a_k \notin t \wedge a_k \in t']$.*

Theorem 1. *Let $S, S' \in \mathcal{P}$ be two process models, with same set of activities $N = \{a_1, a_2, \ldots, a_n\}$. Let further $\mathcal{T}_S$, $\mathcal{T}_{S'}$ be the related trace sets and $A_{n \times n}$, $A'_{n \times n}$ be the order matrices of S and S'. Then $S \neq S' \Leftrightarrow A \neq A'$, if $(\neg \exists t_1, t'_1 \in \mathcal{T}_S : t_1$ is a substring of $t'_1)$ and $(\neg \exists t_2, t'_2 \in \mathcal{T}_{S'} : t_2$ is a substring of $t'_2)$.*

According to Theorem 1, there will be a one-to-one mapping between a process model S and its order matrix A, if the substring constraint is met. A proof of Theorem 1 can be found in [8]. A detailed discussion of the sub-string restriction is given in Section 4.4. Thus, when comparing two process models, it is sufficient to compare their order matrices (cf. Def. 3), since a order matrix can uniquely represent the process model. This also means that the *differences of two process models* can be related to the *differences of their order matrices*. If two activities have different execution order in two process models, we will define the notion of *conflict* as follows:

Definition 5 (Conflict). *Let $S, S' \in \mathcal{P}$ be two process models with same set of activities N. Let further A and A' be the order matrices for S and S' respectively. Then: Activities a_i and a_j are conflicting iff $A_{ij} \neq A'_{ij}$. We formally denote this as $C_{(a_i, a_j)}$. $\mathcal{CF} := \{C_{(a_i, a_j)} \mid A_{ij} \neq A'_{ij}\}$ then corresponds to the set of all existing conflicts.*

Fig. 5 marks up differences between the two order matrices in grey. The set of conflicts is as follows: $\mathcal{CF} = \{C_{(A,B)}, C_{(C,D)}, C_{(C,F)}, C_{(D,E)}, C_{(D,F)}, C_{(E,F)}\}$.

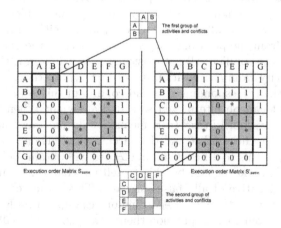

Fig. 5. Order Matrices of S_{same} and S'_{same} from Fig. 4

Optimizing the Conflicts. To come from S_{same} to S'_{same} (c.f. Fig. 4), we have to eliminate conflicts between these two models by applying *move* operations. Obviously, if there is no conflict for the two models, they will be identical. Every time we move an activity from its current position in S_{same} to the position it has in S'_{same}, we can eliminate the conflicts this activity has with other activities. For example, consider activity A in Fig. 4. If we move A from its position in S_{same} (preceding B) to its new position in S'_{same} (A and B are contained in two different branches of a conditional branching block), we can eliminate conflict $C_{(A,B)}$. As shown in the order matrices, moving A requires two steps. First, set the elements in the first row and first column of $A_{n \times n}$ (which corresponds to activity A) to empty, since A is moved away. Second, reset these elements according to the new order relation of A, when compared to the other activities from S'_{same}. So every time we move an activity, we are able to change the value of its corresponding row and column in the order matrices, i.e., we change these values corresponding to the original model to the values compliant with the target model. By doing this iteratively, we can change all the values and eliminate all the conflicts so that we finally achieve the transformation from S_{same} to S'_{same}.

A non-optimal solution would be to move all the activities involved in the conflicts as set out by $\mathcal{CF}$, from their positions in S_{same} to the positions they have in S'_{same}. Regarding our example from Fig. 5, to apply this straightforward method, we would need to move activities A, B, C, D, E and F from their positions in S_{same} to the ones in S'_{same}. However, this naive method is not in line with our goal to minimize the number of applied change operations. For example, after moving activity A from its current position in S_{same} to the position it has in S'_{same}, we do not need to move activity B anymore, because after applying this change operation, there are no activities with which activity B still has conflicts.

Digital logic in Boolean algebra [14] helps to solve this minimization problem. Digital logic constitutes the basis for digital electronic circuit design and optimization. In this field, engineers face the challenge to optimize the internal circuit design given the required input and output signals. To apply such technique in our context, we consider each process activity as an independent input signal and we want to design a circuit which can cover all conflicts defined by $\mathcal{CF}$ (cf. Def 5). If activity a_i conflicts to activity a_j, we can either move one of them or both of them from the positions they have in S_{same} to the ones they have in S'_{same}. Doing so, the conflict will not exist any more. Reason is that every time we move an activity from the position it has in S_{same} to the position it has in S'_{same}, we reset the corresponding row and column of this activity in the order matrix. A conflict can be interpreted as a digital signal: When the two input signals a_i and a_j are both "true"(this means we do not move activity a_i and a_j), we cannot solve the conflict and the 'circuit' shall give an output signal of "false". If we apply this to all conflicts in $\mathcal{CF}$, we will obtain all "false" signals. Meanwhile, the "circuit" should be able to tell us what will result in a "true" output (i.e., the negative of all "false" signals). This "true" output represents which activities we need to move. Regarding our example from Fig. 5, given the set of conflicts $\mathcal{CF}$, our logic expression then is: $\overline{AB + CD + CF + DE + DF + EF}$.

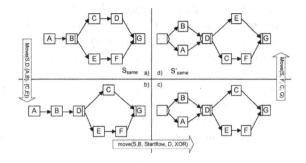

Fig. 6. Process Models After Every Move Operation

The complexity for optimizing the logic expression is NP-Hard [14]. Therefore it is advantageous to reduce the size of the problem. Concerning our example, we can cut down the optimization problem into two groups: one with activities A and B, and conflict $C_{(A,B)}$; another one with activities C, D, E and F, and the following set of conflicts $\{C_{(C,D)}, C_{(C,F)}, C_{(D,E)}, C_{(D,F)}, C_{(E,F)}\}$. Such a division can be achieved in $O(n)$ time in the following three steps. Step 1: List all conflicting activities, and set every activity as a group. Step 2: If conflicting activities a_i and a_j (i.e., $C_{(a_i,a_j)}$) are contained in two different groups, merge the two groups. Step 3: Repeat Step 2 for all conflicts in $\mathcal{CF}$. After these three steps, we can divide the activities as well as the associated conflicts into several groups. Regarding our example, the optimization problem can be divided into two sub-optimization problems: $\overline{AB}$ and $\overline{CD + CF + DE + DF + EF}$. We depict this by the two small matrices in Fig. 5.

Optimizing logic expressions has been intensively discussed in Discrete Mathematics. Therefore we omit details here and refer to Karnaugh map [14] and Quine-McCluskey algorithm [14]. We have implemented the latter in our proof-of-concept prototype. Regarding our example in Fig. 4, the two optimization results are $\overline{AB} = \overline{A} + \overline{B}$ for the first group and $\overline{CD + CF + DE + DF + EF} = \overline{D}\overline{F} + \overline{C}\overline{E}\overline{F} + \overline{C}\overline{D}\overline{E}$ for the second group. We can interpret this result as follows. For the second group, either we move activities D and F, or we move activities C, E and F, or we move activities C, D and E from their position in S_{same} to the positions they have in S'_{same}. Based on this we can transform S_{same} into S'_{same} since all conflicts are eliminated. As can be seen from the order matrices, if we change the value of the corresponding rows and columns of these activities in S_{same}, we can turn S_{same} into S'_{same}. Since we want to minimize the number of change operations, we can draw the conclusion that activities D and F must be moved. Same rule applies to the result of the first group. However, there is no difference whether to move either A or B since both operations count as one change operation. Here, we arbitrarily decide to move activity B.

So far we have determined the set of activities to be moved. The next step is to determine the positions where these activities need to be moved to. Operation $move(S, X, \mathcal{A}, \mathcal{B}, [sc])$ will be independent from other move operations (i.e., it does not matter in which order to move the respective activity) if its direct predecessors $\mathcal{A}$ and direct successors $\mathcal{B}$ do not belong to the set of activities to be moved. Regarding our example from Fig. 4, activity F satisfies this condition since its predecessor C and successor G are not moved. If this had not been the case, we would have to introduce silent activities to put the moved activity to its corresponding place in S'_{same}. For example, if we want to first move B to its position in S'_{same}, we will have to introduce a silent activity after B and before C and E. Only in this way, we can change the execution order of B to what it appears in S'_{same}. However, such silent activity will be not required if we first move activity D to the position it has in S'_{same}. A detailed discussion can be found in [11].

According to the position the moved activities have in S'_{same}, we can determine the parameters (i.e., the predecessors, successors and conditions) for every move operation. In S'_{same}, activity D has predecessors A and B, and successors E and C. So one move operations therefore is $move(S, \text{D}, \{\text{B}, \text{A}\}, \{\text{C}, \text{E}\})$. Similarly, we obtain the other two move operations: $move(S, \text{B}, \text{StartFlow}, \text{D}, XOR)$ and $move(S, \text{F}, \text{C}, \text{G})$. The intermediate process models resulting after every move operation are shown in Fig. 6. When comparing order matrices for each model in Fig. 6, it becomes clear that every move operation changes the values of the row and the column corresponding to the moved activity.

4.4   Coping with Silent Activities

A silent activity is an activity which does not contain any operation or action, and which only exists for control flow purpose. There are two reasons why we do not consider silent activities in our similarity measure:

1. The appearance of a silent activity can be random. We can add or remove silent activities without changing the behavior of a process model, e.g., we can replace a control flow edge in a process model by one silent activity or even a block of silent activities without influencing process model behavior.
2. The existence of a silent activity also depends on other activities and is subject to change as other activities change. As example consider Fig. 2. When applying change Δ_1 to S, the silent activity τ is automatically removed after activity C is moved away.

There is one exception for which we need to consider silent activities. Consider the two process models S_1 and S_2 in Fig. 7. If we ignore the silent activity τ (depicted as an empty node) in S_2, and derive the order matrix of S_2, it will be the same as the one of S_1. Obviously, the two process models are not equivalent since the trace sets producible by them are not identical. More precisely, $\mathcal{T}_{S_2}$ contains one additional trace when compared to $\mathcal{T}_{S_1}$. In general, if one process model can produce additional traces, which are the sub-string of other traces (cf. Def.4), there must be some silent activities we cannot ignore. Or if the direct predecessor and direct successor of one silent activity constitute an XORsplit and XORjoin, we can also not ignore this silent activity (cf. S_2 in Fig. 7).

Fig. 7 shows several process model transformations based on high-level change operations. Here we can identify the difference between the two types of deletion: $delete(S_4, \text{D})$ and $delete(S_4, \text{D}, XOR)$ (cf. Fig. 7). The former one turns an

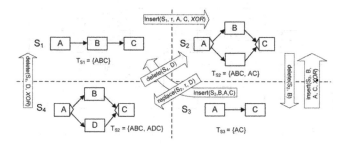

Fig. 7. The Influence of Silent Activity

activity into a silent one (transforming S_4 into S_2), while the latter one blocks the branch which contains activity D (transforming S_4 to S_1). When a branch is blocked, we do not allow the activities of the branch to become activated [16,11]. Since process models S_1 and S_2 have same order matrix, purely comparing order matrices (cf. Sect. 4) would not be sufficient in the given situation. Reason is that here the order matrix does not uniquely represent the process model, since the sub-string constraint (cf. Def.4) of Theorem 1 is violated. To extend our method such that it can uniquely represent a process model without the sub-string constraint, we must consider these special silent activities (i.e., a silent activity which is direct predecessor of an XORsplit and direct successor of an XORjoin) as well. They will appear in the order matrix and their execution orders compared with other activities will be documented.

However, the existence of a silent activity is still very much dependent on other activities, including the scenario described above. For example, if we delete B in S_2 as depicted in Fig. 7, we will transform S_2 into S_3, i.e., the silent activity will be simultaneously deleted when B is deleted. We can identify this situation by either examining the process model or the order matrix. In the process model, a silent activity τ can be automatically deleted if there is another silent activity τ' contained in the same block, but in another conditional branch (e.g., transforming S_2 to S_3). In the order matrix, we can automatically remove a silent activity τ if there is another silent activity τ' with same order relations to the rest of the activities as τ has.

In general, if a silent activity has an XORsplit as direct predecessor and an XORjoin as direct successor, we need to consider it when computing the order matrix of a process model. However, these silent activities can automatically be deleted when changing the process model. This requires us to perform additional checks on the process model or order matrix (as described above) after every change operation.

4.5 Summary

Taking our example from Fig. 4 (i.e., to transform S into S'), the following *six* change operations are required: $\sigma = \{delete(S, \mathbf{X}), move(S, \mathbf{F}, \mathbf{C}, \mathbf{G}), move(S, \mathbf{D}, \{\mathbf{A}, \mathbf{B}\}, \{\mathbf{C}; \mathbf{E}\}), \quad move(S, \mathbf{B}, \mathbf{StartFlow}, \mathbf{D}, XOR), \quad insert(S, \mathbf{Y}, \mathbf{StartFlow},$

		Figure 2			Figure 4			
		S	S_1	S_2	S	S_{same}	S'_{same}	S'
Figure 2	S	0 / 100%	1 / 86%	1 / 86%	4 / 50%	3 / 57%	3 / 57%	5 / 44%
	S_1		0 / 100%	2 / 71 %	4 / 50%	3 / 57%	3 / 57%	5 / 44%
	S_2			0 / 100%	5 / 38%	4 / 42%	3 / 57%	5 / 44%
Figure 4	S				0 / 100%	1 / 88%	4 / 50 %	6 / 40%
	S_{same}					0 / 100%	3 / 57%	5 / 44%
	S'_{same}						0 / 100%	2 / 78 %
	S'							0 / 100%

Fig. 8. Distances and Similarities of Different Process Models

$\{A,B\}$), and $insert(S,Z,D,E)$ }. Distance between the two models is *six* and similarity is *0.4* (cf. Def.2). To illustrate our method and these numbers in more detail, we compare the distances and similarities between the seven process models discussed so far: S, S_1 and S_2 from Fig. 2 and S, S_{same}, S'_{same} and S' from Fig. 4. Distance and similarity of two models are specified as *distance/similarity* in each corresponding cell in Fig. 8. As the transformation is commutative, we only fill in the upper triangle matrix. Taking Fig. 8, we can conclude:

1. Changing the activity set always leads to a modified distance. For example, $d_{(S_n,S'_{same})}$ always equals $d_{(S_n,S')} + 2$, where S_n stands for a process model other than S' or S'_{same} in Fig. 8. Reason is that S' contains two unique activities Y and Z when compared to S'_{same}, while the rest are identical.
2. If three process models S, S', and S'' have same activity sets, we will obtain $d_{(S,S'')} \leq d_{(S,S')} + d_{(S',S'')}$. It is easy to understand this because some activities could be moved twice when transforming S into S' and S' into S''.

5   Related Work

Various papers have studied the process similarity problem and provided useful results [17,16,21,2]. In graph theory, graph isomorphism[15] and sub-graph isomorphism [15] are used to measure similarity between two graphs. Unfortunately, these measures usually only examine edges and nodes and cannot catch the syntactical issues of a PAIS (e.g., guarantee soundness of a process model, differentiate AND-Split and XOR-Split, and handle silent activities). Algorithms for measuring tree edit distances [2] shows similar disadvantages, i.e., syntactical issues of a PAIS are missing. In the database field, the delta-algorithm [7] is used to measure the difference between the two models. It extends the above mentioned approaches by assigning attributes to edges and nodes [12]. Still, it can only catch change primitives, and will further run into problems when considering high-level change operations. Regarding Petri-nets and state automata, similarity based on change is difficult to measure since these formalisms are not very tolerant for changes. Inheritance rules [16] are one of the very few techniques showing the transformation of a process model described as Petri-net. Trace equivalence is commonly used to compare whether two process models are similar or identical [5]. In addition, bisimulation [16,18] extends trace equivalence by considering stronger notions. Also based on traces, [17] assign weights to each trace based on execution logs which reflect the importance of a certain trace. The edit distance [21] is also used to measure the difference between traces; the sum of them represents the differences of two models. Some similarity measures use two numbers (*precision* and *recall*) to evaluate the difference between process models S_1 and S_2 [17,10]. None of these approaches measures similarity by a unique and commutative number, based on the effort for process transformation.

6   Summary and Outlook

We have provided a method to quantitatively measure the distance and similarity between two process models based on the efforts for model transformation. High-level change operations are used to evaluate the similarity since they guarantee soundness and also provide more meaningful results. We further applied digital logic in boolean algebra so that the number of change operations required to transform process model S into process model S' becomes minimal. Respective distance and similarity measures have already been applied in the filed of process mining [9].

Additional work is needed to enrich our knowledge on process similarity. As a first step, we will extend our method so that it is able to measure the similarity between process models with additional constructs (e.g., loopbacks [11]) and data flows. The next step will be to enrich the model with semantic relations between activities and to give weight for each change operation, so that the similarity measure can be further applied to practice.

References

1. Balabko, P., Wegmann, A., Ruppen, A., Clément, N.: Capturing design rationale with functional decomposition of roles in business processes modeling. Software Process: Improvement and Practice 10(4), 379–392 (2005)
2. Bille, P.: A survey on tree edit distance and related problems. Theor. Comput. Sci. 337(1-3), 217–239 (2005)
3. Dumas, M., van der Aalst, W.M.P., ter Hofstede, A.H.M.: Process-Aware Information Systems. Wiley & Sons, Chichester (2005)
4. Günther, C.W., Rinderle, S., Reichert, M., van der Aalst, W.M.P.: Change mining in adaptive process management systems. In: Meersman, L., Zahir, T. (eds.) OTM 2006. LNCS, vol. 4275, pp. 309–326. Springer, Heidelberg (2006)
5. Hidders, J., Dumas, M., van der Aalst, W.M.P., ter Hofstede, A.H.M., Verelst, J.: When are two workflows the same? In: CATS 2005, Darlinghurst, Australia, pp. 3–11. Australian Computer Society, Inc. (2005)
6. Kradolfer, M., Geppert, A.: Dynamic workflow schema evolution based on workflow type versioning and workflow migration. In: COOPIS 1999, Washington, DC, USA, p. 104. IEEE Computer Society, Los Alamitos (1999)
7. Labio, W., Garcia-Molina, H.: Efficient snapshot differential algorithms for data warehousing. In: VLDB 1996, San Francisco, CA, USA, pp. 63–74 (1996)

8. Li, C., Reichert, M., Wombacher, A.: On measuring process model similarity based on high-level change operations. Technical Report TR-CTIT-07-89, University of Twente (2007)
9. Li, C., Reichert, M., Wombacher, A.: Discovering reference process models by mining process variants. In: ICWS 2008 (to appear, 2008)
10. Pinter, S.S., Golani, M.: Discovering workflow models from activities' lifespans. Comput. Ind. 53(3), 283–296 (2004)
11. Reichert, M., Dadam, P.: ADEPTflex -supporting dynamic changes of workflows without losing control. Journal of Intelligent Info. Sys. 10(2), 93–129 (1998)
12. Rinderle, S., Jurisch, M., Reichert, M.: On deriving net change information from change logs - the deltalayer-algorithm. In: BTW, pp. 364–381 (2007)
13. Rinderle, S., Reichert, M., Dadam, P.: Correctness criteria for dynamic changes in workflow systems: a survey. Data Knowl. Eng. 50(1), 9–34 (2004)
14. Brown, S., Vranesic, Z.: Fundamentals of Digital Logic with Verilog Design. McGraw-Hill, New York (2003)
15. Tan, P.N., Steinbach, M., Kumar, V.: Introduction to Data Mining. Addison-Wesley, Reading (2005)
16. van der Aalst, W.M.P., Basten, T.: Inheritance of workflows: an approach to tackling problems related to change. Theor. Comput. Sci. 270(1-2), 125–203 (January)
17. van der Aalst, W.M.P., de Medeiros, A.K.A., Weijters, A.J.M.M.: Process equivalence: Comparing two process models based on observed behavior. In: Dustdar, S., Fiadeiro, J.L., Sheth, A.P. (eds.) BPM 2006. LNCS, vol. 4102, pp. 129–144. Springer, Heidelberg (2006)
18. van Glabbeek, R.J., Weijland, W.P.: Branching time and abstraction in bisimulation semantics. J. ACM 43(3), 555–600 (1996)
19. Weber, B., Rinderle, S., Reichert, M.: Change patterns and change support features in process-aware information systems. In: Krogstie, J., Opdahl, A., Sindre, G. (eds.) CAiSE 2007. LNCS, vol. 4495, pp. 574–588. Springer, Heidelberg (2007)
20. Weske, M.: Formal foundation and conceptual design of dynamic adaptations in a workflow management system. In: HICSS 2001, Washington, DC, p. 7051 (2001)
21. Wombacher, A., Rozie, M.: Evaluation of workflow similarity measures in service discovery. In: Service Oriented Electronic Commerce, pp. 51–71 (2006)

Recommendation Based Process Modeling Support: Method and User Experience

Thomas Hornung[1], Agnes Koschmider[2], and Georg Lausen[1]

[1] Institute of Computer Science, Albert-Ludwigs University Freiburg, Germany
{hornungt,lausen}@informatik.uni-freiburg.de
[2] Institute of Applied Informatics and Formal Description Methods
Universität Karlsruhe (TH), Germany
koschmider@aifb.uni-karlsruhe.de

Abstract. Although most workflow management systems nowadays offer graphical editors for process modeling, the learning curve is still too steep for users who are unexperienced in process modeling. The efficiency of users may decrease when starting process modeling with minimal expertise and no obvious modeling support. This paper describes the first contribution towards a theoretically sound and empirically validated analysis of a recommender-based modeling support who is geared towards both novices and expert users. The idea is to interpret process descriptions as tags which describe the intention of the process. This leads us to the notion of virtual documents or signatures. Based on these signatures we provide a search interface to process models stored in a repository. Additionally the user can invoke a recommendation function during modeling time and the system automatically identifies and suggests relevant process fragments. By adding two additional criteria, the frequency of process reuse and structural correctness, we arrive at a full-fledged modeling support system, which provides an easy to use interface to the user while retaining a high fidelity to the user's modeling intentions. We validated our support system with a user experiment based on real-life process models and our prototype implementation.

1 Introduction

Although most workflow management systems nowadays offer graphical editors for process modeling, the learning curve is still too steep for users who are unexperienced in process modeling. Pure awareness of the modeling language syntax is often insufficient. Profound working knowledge of the user is required to apply a modeling language in practice. [1] argues that user's modeling expertise is one main success factor of process modeling. Therefore, the user efficiency may decrease when starting process modeling with minimal expertise and no obvious modeling support.

To ensure a certain degree of modeling support, several authors proposed the reuse of process models [2], [3] but yet with little impact on the modeling context and user intention. Clearly, a full-fledged modeling support system is required, which retains a high fidelity to the user's modeling intentions.

Q. Li et al. (Eds.): ER 2008, LNCS 5231, pp. 265–278, 2008.
© Springer-Verlag Berlin Heidelberg 2008

This paper describes the first contribution towards a theoretically sound and empirically validated analysis of a recommendation based modeling support, which assists the user twofold in modeling goal-oriented processes. Firstly, the user can search via a query interface for business processes or process parts (logically coherent groups of elements belonging together, e.g. approval, billing or assembly). The user can significantly save time in process modeling if a process matches the user request. Secondly, we use an automatic tagging mechanism in order to unveil the modeling objective of a user at process modeling time and to better fulfill the user's requirements. This feature of the modeling support system should be used if the user is not sure how to complete the process. In this case the results from the query can be unsatisfying due to the user's vague intention of the process model.

We validated our support system with an experiment using real-life process models and our prototype implementation. The evaluation confirmed that the modeling time and the number of operations of the reused processes can be reduced when using our process support tool. The evaluation results highlight which benefits users may have from our recommendation based modeling tool support:

- The system increases the efficiency of the user because users need less expertise to appropriately model processes,
- The tagging-based system increases the quality of the process models by highlighting the corresponding process parts that violate correctness criteria (e.g., structural deadlocks, which occur if an alternative flow initiated by an OR-split is synchronized by an AND-join),
- Our system overcomes the limitation of a controlled vocabulary for labeling process element names since the system considers process fragments with process vocabularies that are different from the one of the currently edited business process.

The remainder of the paper is structured as follows. Section 2 compares our approach with related work. Our tagging-based modeling support system will be explained in detail with a running example in Section 3. Section 4 presents our tagging algorithm and the creation of our process repository index. In Section 5 we will describe the business process search functionality and we will extend the search functionality in order to consider relevance. The cumulative ranking function and the complete recommendation algorithm is illustrated in Section 6. Initial evaluation results are presented in Section 7. Section 8 concludes the paper with an outlook on future research.

2   Related Work

Existing work in this area can be differentiated in four categories: (1) process reuse, (2) tagging, (3) process/service searching, and (4) research on ranking mechanisms.

To ensure a certain degree of modeling support, several authors proposed the reuse of process models [2], [3] but yet with little impact on the modeling context and user intention. All this contributions lack an extensive query interface and a recommendation function for process parts during process modeling. Additionally, the proposed ranking functions are theoretic without empirical validation.

Concerning the annotation of resources with tags the approach of [4] is relevant for our approach. This approach describes a method, which automatically generates personalized tags for Web pages. The method of [4] relies on the idea, that the personalized tags are generated based on the user's Desktop documents. In the current implementation we unveil the user intention during process modeling with the edited process elements. We plan to evaluate the idea of [4] in order to tag project documents, which also may help to reveal user requirements during process modeling. We omitted this idea for the current implementation as project documents are difficult to obtain.

Regarding the process searching area, the set of proposals found in the literature [5], [6], [7] and [8] do not provide adequate techniques for searching processes concerning the user intention while reusing processes. For instance, the approach of [6] extends a rudimental Web Service search by supporting more complex service description search capabilities. [6] indexes business processes for efficient matching in Web Service infrastructures where the input query is a business process that is modeled as an annotated finite state automaton. This approach does not focus on searching and indexing business processes but rather on searching for complex service descriptions of services such as process aspects (by searching for optional and mandatory requirements within the business processes).

Ranking functions have been defined for Semantic Web Service Discovery [9] or for Information Retrieval [10] where the ranking functions are based on an ontology structure or human interaction. As [11] argues that the effectiveness of tags classifying blog entries are for manual tags less effective content descriptors than automated ones we decided to disregard human interactions for the process ranking at the moment.

To summarize, there are some approaches which partially use related methods to implement a modeling support system but on a rather theoretical level without existing empirical validation. The aim of our work is to present a modeling support system including a comprehensive query interface, recommender and ranking function, which are theoretically sound and initially empirically validated.

3   Running Example

Our current implementation of the support system is described in Figure 1. The user wants to model a process describing the handling of order requests. Her intention is to model this process from the perspective of customers. Via a query interface the user searches for process parts concerning *customer requests*. The results from the query were displayed according to a ranking function where the user selected the appropriate recommendation due to her modeling intention and inserted the recommendation into her workspace via drag and drop.

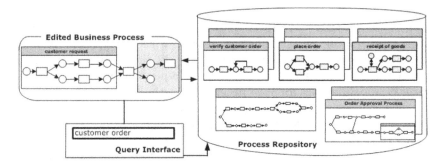

Fig. 1. Possible user interaction scenarios for finding an appropriate process part

Subsequently, the user continued to model the business process. At some point, she is not sure how to complete the process. Therefore she invokes the recommender system, which can be done in two ways. The user can either search via the query interface for fitting process parts (e.g., processes modeling *customer orders*) or invoke the recommender system by highlighting the corresponding elements for which the user wants to have a recommendation (in this figure the corresponding element group is highlighted with a gray rectangle). For the second alternative the recommender system automatically retrieves fitting process parts according to the user's modeling intention. The recommender component can only be invoked after modeling process elements (in contrast to the query interface, which is always accessible). Subsequently, the user can configure the process (part) suggestions in her workspace by inserting or deleting elements and save the modified process version in a process repository for further process reuse. In the initial development of our prototype we have populated our repository with 21 Petri net processes from real word projects and processes from the research literature concerning order and shipment procedures.

In the next two sections we present our process search algorithm.

4   Semantic Annotation of Business Process Models

Usually keyword extraction algorithms use as input documents and return a list of significant keywords, which outline the content of a document. The number of occurrences of each keyword implies a ranking in the sense that the keyword that appears most often is more relevant to the document than keywords that appear less often. We adopt the intention of keyword respectively tagging techniques to improve searching for fitting business processes. The tag extraction and scoring for business processes is inspired by the *Term and Document Frequency* measure, which is very fast to compute (cf. [12]). Each place and transition in a Petri net representation of a business process model is labeled with a description, which specifies the purpose of each activity or state respectively. Therefore, we can regard these words as tag candidates and thereby the whole Petri net as a virtual document. This allows us to use standard Information Retrieval (IR) techniques (cf. [13]) to build up an index over business process models. Here, we first remove common English words from the set of tag candidates because they appear so often in a typical natural language corpus that they do not convey any meaning specific to the business process. This phenomenon is often referred to as Zipf's law, which states that the frequency of any word is inversely proportional to its rank in the frequency table [14]. After stop word removal each keyword is assigned a tag score for this business process based on a modified version of the $tf * idf$ metric[1]:

$$\text{TagScore}(t_i) := \frac{\text{TF}(t_i)}{\Sigma_{j=1}^{N} t_j} * log(\frac{|P|}{|(p_j : t_i \in p_j)|})$$

Here, $\text{TF}(t_i)$ is the frequency of the tag t_i in transition or place labels, N is the total number of distinct tag candidates (after stop word removal), $|P|$ denotes the total number of indexed business processes and $|(p_j : t_i \in p_j)|$ is the number of business processes, where the tag t_i appears. The purpose of the idf part ($log(\frac{|P|}{|(p_j : t_i \in p_j)|})$) is to decrease the impact of words that are common over all business processes. In order to bridge the gap between different modeling vocabularies we determine for each keyword the set of synonyms via WordNet[2] and assign the same tag score to each word in the synonym set.

As mentioned above, the user can identify different distinct process fragments and assign a title to them (e.g., order approval, complaints handling, order receipt). To make these fragments searchable as well, we index them in the same way as if they were regular business processes and additionally store a pointer to the business process with which they are associated, e.g. for a business process which consists of three distinct process fragments, we would include four virtual documents in our index: the whole process, and each fragment as well.

In the next section we illustrate the supported retrieval possibilities for our annotated business processes and process fragments, whereas in Section 6 we describe the overall ranking algorithm used for recommending appropriate process fragments.

5   Searching for Process Fragments

The user has the possibility to use a tag based search functionality at each stage during the process modeling phase and can choose whether she wants to search for process parts, whole business processes or both. Since we used the open source Java search engine Lucene[3] as the underlying index and search framework, the scoring of the results is based on a mixture of the Vector Space Model (VSM) and the Boolean model. The key idea of the VSM is to represent each document, i.e. business process in our case, as a multi-dimensional vector, where the dimension is the total number of unique keywords that occur over the whole corpus, i.e. all indexed business processes. This vector constitutes the signature

---

[1] *Term frequency * inverse document frequency.*

[2] http://wordnet.princeton.edu/

[3] http://lucene.apache.org

of the process which is later used for retrieval. A query is interpreted as a vector in this space and the similarity of the query to documents is computed based on the cosine similarity $(cos(\theta) = \frac{v_{query} * v_{process}}{||v_{query}|| * ||v_{process}||})$ between the two vectors. More specifically, a business process b_j would be represented by the vector $b_j = [\text{TagScore}(t_1), \text{TagScore}(t_2), \ldots, \text{TagScore}(t_K)]$. Because we have enriched each tag with the additional synonym set, the dimension of the vector is not N, the total number of unique tags (except stop words), but $K = \Sigma_{i=1}^{N}|\text{SynSet}(t_i)|$, where $\text{SynSet}(t_i)$ denotes the set of all synonyms of t_i.

Continuing our example from Section 3 the user is searching for both process parts and entire business processes modeling *customer orders* (see Figure 2). The user activated WordNet in order to suggest processes, where process objects have been labeled with respect to a different vocabulary. The user can narrow down the number of recommendations by the criteria *First Element* and *Last Element* searching for a specific first or last element(s) in the process. An additional search criterion is the process property, where *cost* signifies a low cost process, *resource* indicates a process with full exploitation of resources, *fault* is a process with minimal fault rate and *standard* signifies a standard process. This four properties result from our practical process modeling experiences. If required, the user can introduce more annotation properties.

The recommender system found 10 results, which match the user's modeling intention and displays them ranked by their Lucene score. If the user is interested in a recommendation she can open a larger view of the process fragment by double clicking on the picture.

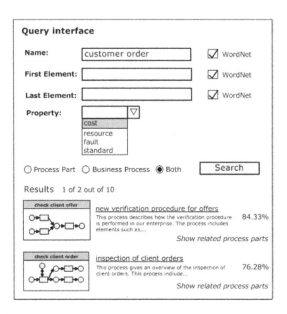

Fig. 2. Query for all process fragments that are related to *customer orders*

Besides the standard Boolean operators, such as AND, OR, and NOT the user can pose wildcard queries and perform fuzzy searches based on the Levenstein distance, or Edit distance algorithm [15].

Additionally, in Figure 2 the user can preview related process parts for each recommendation (see *Show related process parts*). The idea is that process parts that succeed or precede the part in question and were used in the same modeling domain the user is in at the moment (e.g. Manufacturing) can help to estimate the degree of fitness of a recommended part.

Therefore each business process model and thus each process part that occurs in this model is classified into a modeling domain before it is added to the process repository. We assume that the number of possible domains is usually fixed within a company and hence we can provide the user with an interface where she can choose to which domain the process belongs. Additionally, the process property can be provided in this stage. After a sufficient amount of process models are in the repository we could use automatic classification techniques such as a Naïve Bayes classifier [16] to automatically highlight a domain the process model is most likely to belong to, or the most likely process property respectively.

If the user now clicks on the *Show related process parts* button, the system shows two ranked lists of related processes, i.e. the preceding and the succeeding process parts.

6   Ranking of Recommendations

The process recommendations depicted in Figure 2 show results of a user query, which are ranked according to the Lucene score. If the user invoked the query search before starting modeling any node (and the suggested recommendations have never been selected by someone else), then the recommendations will exclusively be ranked as explained in Section 5. But the ranking mechanism changes if the user invokes the recommender function or the query interface once she already modeled process elements in her workspace. Then the ranking also depends on the modeling context (e.g., activities which were modeled and the control flow).

To completely rank fitting recommendations for the second scenario we extend the Lucene score, which was introduced in Section 5, with two additional criteria. Firstly, the frequency a user selected a specific process fragment in the past and secondly the number of structural errors. In our scenario a structural error can only occur in the interconnected process (to be composed of the edited business process and the recommended process).

An interconnected business process is considered *structurally correct* if it complies with the well-structuredness property [17]. This structural property for business processes is violated if for example an alternative flow initiated by an OR-split is synchronized by an AND-join. The benefit of this property is a good process modeling style, which makes understanding of the processes models easy and supports the detection of undesirable deadlocks[4]. The verification of structural properties is performed once for all process fragments that match the automatically generated Lucene query mentioned above. For instance, the interconnection of the edited business process (excluding the highlighted elements) with the first recommendation in Figure 2 would include a structural problem (an AND-split is synchronized by an OR-join, which is specified in the literature as a TP handle). Nevertheless, the user can insert this recommendation into her workspace. But, she needs to decide how to improve this business process. We assume, that the processes in the repository are already analyzed and thus we exclude (structural) deadlocks for them.

In Figure 1 the user highlighted three elements for which she wants to have a recommendation for both process fragments as well as whole business processes (see Figure 2). To determine relevant process parts, we extract the labels of each highlighted process object (place or transition) and remove common stop words, which yields the set t_{raw}. The remaining query tag candidates t_{raw} are then expanded with their related synonym sets, similarily as described in Section 5, resulting in the set t_{query}[5]. The initial process fragments are then determined by querying the Lucene index, where the query term is the concatenation of all tags in the set t_{query}. In the remainder of this chapter we present two additional criteria which are used to tweak the rank of the thus found process fragments.

As already mentioned previously we assume that users independently declare logically coherent process parts, which are stored with a title and optionally a description and a process property in the repository. This runs the risk that users store useless process parts in the repository because no consistency check is applied in order to evaluate the usefulness (a process part with one element may be regarded as useless). To remedy this we integrated the frequency a process fragment has been selected in the past into our ranking. If process fragments have been refreshed, respectively updated, the user will be informed about this with a remark. The updated processes are assigned the same frequency score as the old process version. If users decide against the updated process (and favor more often another recommendation) then the frequency score will automatically decrease over time.

To calculate the frequency a user selected a process we adapted the user count algorithm presented in [18]. Let U and P be the set of all users and processes, and p_{ij} is the number of selections of process j by the user i. The rating r_{uk_1} for the number of users u who have selected the process k is:

$$r_{uk_1} := \frac{\sum_{i \in U} t_{ik}}{|U|}$$

---

[4] An undesirable deadlock is a situation where a process instance is waiting for a progress, which cannot be performed because some task cannot be finished (a desirable deadlock is a situation where the process instance has finished its progress and the instance can not be reinvoked again).

[5] Note that $|t_{query}| = \Sigma_{i=1}^{N} |\text{SynSet}(t_{raw_i})|$, where $|t_{raw}| = N$.

where t_{ik} is calculated by the following equation:

$$t_{ik} := \left\{ \begin{array}{ll} 0 & (p_{ik} = 0) \\ 1 & (p_{ik} >= 1) \end{array} \right\}$$

t_{ik} is 0 if the user i has never selected the process k; otherwise it is 1.

The ranking r_{uk_2} for the number of selections of all users is calculated by:

$$r_{uk_2} := \frac{\sum_{i \in U} p_{ik}}{1 + \sum_{i \in U} \sum_{j \in P} p_{ij}}$$

The range of this value is $[0, 1)$. The score freqScr for a user u selecting a process p can then by determined as:

$$\text{freqScr} := \frac{r_{uk_1} + r_{uk_2}}{2}$$

Imagine the second process in Figure 2 has been selected more often than the first one (e.g., 5 vs. 3 times). After reranking (due to the frequency) the recommender system would list the process *check client order* higher than the process part *check client offer*.

The covered fitting recommendations are further reranked by the criterion of structural correctness [17]. Syntactically correct processes are ranked higher than process recommendations that will cause undesirable deadlocks in case of interconnection.

Due to capacity and resource restrictions we decided not to integrate a complete deadlock verification, which would be performed when searching for fitting processes and also whenever a user inserts a process fragment into her workspace. Instead, we favor only the verification of structural errors, which can easily be detected whenever the user inserts new nodes into her workspace. Structural errors are generally easy to find and correct. Generally, the score of the correctness degree depends on the relative number of structural errors where TP handles decrease the score less than PT handles (an OR-split is synchronized by an AND-join). A score of 1.0 for the correctness degree indicates a completely structurally correct recommendation. The penalty for structural conflicts is determined based on the frequency with which these conflicts occur for the considered process fragments. More formally:

$$\text{corrScr} := \left\{ \begin{array}{ll} 1 - 0.1 * \frac{N}{|PT| + |TP|} & \text{for PT handles} \\ 1 - 0.2 * \frac{N}{|PT| + |TP|} & \text{for TP handles} \end{array} \right\},$$

where N is the number of all recommended process fragments, $|PT|$ the number of recommended process fragments which would result in PT handles if the user would insert them into her workspace and $|TP|$ is defined similarly for TP handles. If the equation would result in a negative value for the structural correctness metric, i.e. corrScr < 0, we define corrScr to be 0. The intuition is that possible PT and TP handles are punished more severely if they occur rarely and less severely if almost every recommended process fragment would result in a TP or PT handle if inserted into the workspace.

The overall ranking for recommendations results from the following weighted equation:

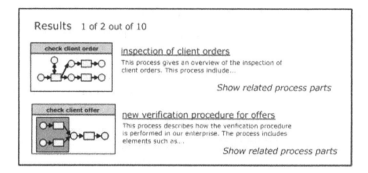

Fig. 3. New order of recommendations after reranking

$$R := w_1 * \mathrm{searchScr} + w_2 * \mathrm{corrScr} + w_3 * \mathrm{freqScr}$$

where $\Sigma_{i=1}^{n} w_i = 1$, and the Lucene score is assigned the greatest weight, i.e. the Lucene score has the most significant influence on the ranking.

The reranking of search results of Figure 2 gives the following final descending order as shown in Figure 3. Process elements, which cause (in case of interconnection) structural problems are highlighted with a gray rectangle. The choice for these ranking criteria is supported by our evaluation. The interviewed persons stated that element labels are the most important reason for choosing a recommendation followed by the process result and process structure. The user relevance feedback was unimportant. Instead the user appreciated the frequency score and the configuration window.

Furthermore, the standard process parts are element groups consisting of up to ten elements. From this point of view it makes no sense to consider the model size, the density of process elements or the average connector degree in the ranking, which have been identified by [19] as main factors for business process understandability.

7   Evaluation

To validate our modeling support system we conducted an evaluation. We completed our evaluation after the tenth person because the last four persons did not significantly change the recommendations. Instead they selected the processes edited by preceding interviewed persons. Among the ten interviewed persons were four beginners, two approved modelers and four advanced modelers. In the initial development of our prototype we have populated our repository with process models from real word projects concerning order and shipment processing. Additionally, we collected a set of process models from the research literature regarding the same application area. Before starting the evaluation the repository contained 21 process models including 15 process parts (which we manually declared from the 21 process models).

For these processes we build a questionnaire that should answer the following questions:

- Can the modeling time be reduced using the modeling support system?
- Can the number of operations (deletion, insertion) be reduced when reusing processes from the repository?

Mainly, the interviewed persons had experiences for improvement and documentation purposes and stated that the most influences on their process modeling are (modeling/enterprise) goals and requirements. All interviewees asked that they are modeling from left to right[6]. Finally, most persons declared that they are searching in the WWW or ask the corresponding persons for relevant information in order to model the business process. This statements confirmed our presumption that users spent some time to find relevant information. We therefore conclude, that a search capability is beneficial for process modeling.

Next, in the questionnaire we asked the users to model three business processes. For the first and the third process we provided detailed information about the process solution. The second process instruction was short: *model a business process for order approval.*

Except one person all interviewees started their process modeling tasks with the search interface. Subsequently, they inserted either all or only some elements of a recommendation or even several elements from different recommendations into their workspace. Then they finished their process modeling or continued their searching. Table 1 shows the average search results for the three business processes to be modeled. The average of searches performed for the first process model is almost two, for the second is one and for the third is the middle number. Next, the average of selected recommendations for the first and the third model converges to two and for the second model lies in the middle between 1 and 2.

Table 1. Overview of performed searches and requested recommendations

Average Number of...	1st Model	2nd Model	3rd Model
...searches performed	1.8	1.0	1.5
...recommendations proposed	38	26.77	37.5
...recommendations viewed to find fitting process	5.3	3.55	3.6
...recommendations selected	1.7	1.22	1.6

We determined for all three process tasks the Pearson correlation coefficients. None correlation coefficient is significant at a 95% confidence level (see Table 2). The only *demonstrative* correlation can be stated for the third process instruction. If we differentiate the number of searches performed according to the user's modeling experiences, then modeling beginners posed more queries than advanced users. One reason could be unsatisfying recommendation results or

---

[6] As mentioned previously, the current implementation supports both modeling techniques (starting at the modeling trigger or at the modeling output).

Table 2. Correlation parameters for the three modeling tasks in the questionnaire

task	corr. parameter	corr. coefficient	p-value
1	user exp. vs. # selected rec.	-0,0834	0,4093
	user exp. vs. # searches performed	0,0891	0,4033
2	user exp. vs. # selected recommendations	-0,2978	0,2017
	user exp. vs. # searches performed	0,0891	0,4033
3	user exp. vs. # selected recommendations	0,408	0,1208
	user exp. vs. # searches performed	0,5215	0,061

Table 3. Ranked process recommendations

#	Process Name	Score	Frequency	Operations
1	CheckOrder	95.02	5	15
...	...	...	...	...
10	Handle Customer Order	48.85	3	20

their uncertainty which process to choose. Advanced modelers mostly decided for one recommendation and customized it. But, the number of valid cases (interviewed persons) is too small in order to make any generalizable claims.

If the interviewees decided to use the query interface then the user could decide which recommendation to open. To realize this we prepended a table-based result list as depicted in Table 3 including the Lucene Score, the Frequency Score and the average number of operations (insertions and deletions) users have performed after adding the recommended process part into their workspace. To control the number of configurations we adopted the methods presented in [20] for version control of workflow process definition. This prepended representation of query results has two advantages. (1) Several users posed only *meaningless* queries such as searching for elements labeled *received order*, which is modeled in a variety of processes. Thus, this representation helps the user to find fitting processes (due to the process name) even when the query was non-declarative. (2) This representation is highly efficient compared to the view of recommendations (like in Figure 3), which requires a lot more time to load all models. With this prepended representation only the selected recommendations will be loaded in the graphical view.

Figure 4 shows our evaluation results concerning our initial questions to be answered by the questionnaire. The modeling time and the number of operations for the three modeling examples in the questionnaire decreases by the number of interviewee. The first person spent the most time to find a suitable process for reuse and customized the recommendations. The following interviewees reused the processes of the first person and edited them slightly. Subsequently, the last six interviewees adopted the processes of their predecessors with minimal modifications.

We determined the Pearson correlation coefficients for the correlation parameters time vs. number of processes and process parts in the repository and number of operations vs. number of processes and process parts in the repository. Both

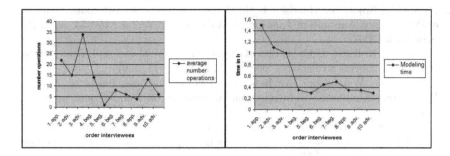

Fig. 4. Reduction of modeling time relative to interviewed persons

correlation parameters are significant at a 95 % confidence level (with a correlation coefficient of -0,82 and -0,6). Consequently, we conclude that our support system reduces modeling time and the number of operations, if suitable business processes are available in the repository.

8   Conclusion and Future Work

We presented a system for supporting users at modeling time which is focused on reducing both the modeling time and increasing the structural correctness at an early stage by providing a search functionality for process fragments stored in a repository. Additionally we proposed a novel recommendation algorithm which ranks process fragments based on three different criteria. First, a modified version of the Term and Document Frequency measure, which has been adapted for business processes. Second on the reuse of process fragments and third on the structural correctness of process parts. Our user evaluation suggests, that the recommender system reduces the number of required editing operations and of the modeling time.

For future work we plan to investigate a more elaborate multi-stage matching procedure, e.g. combining the Term and Document Frequency with the results of a Naïve Bayes classifier on process instances by using a voting prediction combiner (cf. [21]). Furthermore, as already mentioned in the related work section we plan to tag user guides or project documentations to additionally unveil user's requirements.

References

1. Bandara, W., Gable, G.G., Rosemann, M.: Critical Success Factors of Business Process Modeling. Technical report, Preprint series of Queensland University of Technology (2007)
2. Madhusudan, T., Zhao, J.L., Marshall, B.: A Case-based Reasoning Framework for Workflow Model Management. Data Knowl. Eng. 50, 87–115 (2004)
3. Kim, J.H., Suh, W., Lee, H.: Document-based Workflow Modeling: a Case-based Reasoning Approach. Expert Syst. Appl. 23, 77–93 (2002)

4. Paul, C.S., Nejdl, W., Handschuh, S.: P-TAG: Large Scale Automatic Generation of Personalized Annotation Tags for the Web. In: WWW, pp. 845–854. ACM Press, New York (2007)
5. Ghose, A., Koliadis, G.C.A.: Process Discovery from Model and Text Artefacts. In: IEEE Congress on Services, pp. 167–174 (July 9-13, 2007)
6. Mahleko, B., Wombacher, A.: Indexing Business Processes Based on Annotated Finite State Automata. In: International Conference on Web Services, pp. 303–311 (2006)
7. Shen, Z., Su, J.: Web service discovery based on behavior signatures. In: IEEE International Conference on Services Computing, pp. 279–286. IEEE Computer Society, Los Alamitos (2005)
8. Weijters, T., van der Aalst, W.: Process Mining: Discovering Workflow Models from Event Based Data. In: BNAIC, pp. 283–290 (2001)
9. Skoutas, D., Simitsis, A.S.T.: A Ranking Mechanism for Semantic Web Service Discovery. In: IEEE Congress on Services, pp. 41–48 (July 9-13, 2007)
10. Xu, J., Li, H.: AdaRank: a Boosting Algorithm for Information Retrieval. In: ACM SIGIR, pp. 391–398. ACM, New York (2007)
11. Brooks, C.H., Montanez, N.: Improved Annotation of the Blogopshere via Auto-tagging. In: WWW, Edinburgh, UK (2006)
12. Efthimiadis, E.N.: A User-centred Evaluation of Ranking Algorithms for Interactive Query Expansion. In: ACM SIGIR, pp. 146–159. ACM, New York (1993)
13. Salton, G., Mcgill, M.J.: Introduction to Modern Information Retrieval. McGraw-Hill, Inc., New York (1986)
14. Zipf, G.K.: Human Behaviour and the Principle of Least-Effort. Addison-Wesley, Cambridge (1949)
15. Cohen, W.W., Ravikumar, P., Fienberg, S.E.: A Comparison of String Distance Metrics for Name-Matching Tasks. In: Proceedings of IJCAI 2003 Workshop on Information Integration on the Web, pp. 73–78 (2003)
16. Mitchell, T.M.: Machine Learning. McGraw-Hill, New York (1997)
17. van der Aalst, W.M.: The Application of Petri Nets to Workflow Management. The Journal of Circuits, Systems and Computers, 21–66 (1998)
18. Ohsugi, N., Monden, A.M.K.: A Recommendation System for Software Function Discovery. In: APSEC, pp. 248–257 (2002)
19. Mendling, J., Reijers, H., Cardoso, J.: What Makes Process Models Understandable? In: Alonso, G., Dadam, P., Rosemann, M. (eds.) BPM 2007. LNCS, vol. 4714, pp. 48–63. Springer, Heidelberg (2007)
20. Zhao, X., Liu, C.: Version Management in the Business Process Change Context. In: Alonso, G., Dadam, P., Rosemann, M. (eds.) BPM 2007. LNCS, vol. 4714, pp. 198–213. Springer, Heidelberg (2007)
21. Bozovic, N., Vassalos, V.: Two-Phase Schema Matching in Real World Relational Databases. In: ICDE Workshops, pp. 290–296 (2008)

On the Formal Semantics of Change Patterns in Process-Aware Information Systems

Stefanie Rinderle-Ma[1], Manfred Reichert[1], and Barbara Weber[2]

[1] Ulm University, Germany
{stefanie.rinderle,manfred.reichert}@uni-ulm.de
[2] University of Innsbruck, Austria
Barbara.Weber@uibk.ac.at

Abstract. Due to a turbulent market enterprises should be able to adapt their business processes in a quick and flexible way. This requires adaptive process-aware information systems (PAISs) which are able to support changes at different levels and of different process aspects. As for process modeling languages, a multitude of approaches, paradigms, and systems for realizing adaptive processes have emerged. This variety makes it difficult for PAIS engineers to choose the adequate technology. Therefore we introduced a set of commonly used process change patterns which facilitate the comparison between different approaches and tools. In this paper, we provide the formal semantics of these change patterns to ground pattern implementation and pattern-based analysis of PAISs on a solid basis. As challenge, we want to describe the formal semantics of change patterns independent of a certain process meta model. Altogether, our formalization will enable unambiguous and systematic comparison of adaptive PAISs.

1 Introduction

For several reasons enterprises should provide flexible IT support for their business processes and be able to adapt them in a quick and flexible way. Process-aware information systems (PAISs) offer promising perspectives in this respect based on a strict separation of process logic and application code. The need for flexible and easily adaptable PAISs has been recognized for years and several competing paradigms for addressing process changes and flexibility have been developed (e.g., adaptive processes [1,2,3], case handling [4], declarative processes [5], and late modeling [1,6]). Still, there is a lack of methods for systematically comparing the change frameworks provided by existing process support systems. This, in turn, makes it difficult to assess the maturity and the change capabilities of those technologies, often resulting in wrong decisions and bad investments.

To make PAISs better comparable, *workflow patterns* have been introduced [7]. These patterns enable analyzing the expressiveness of process modeling tools and languages. Though workflow patterns enable building more flexible PAISs, an evaluation of a PAIS regarding its ability to deal with changes needs a broader view. In addition to the ability to pre-model flexible execution behavior based on

Q. Li et al. (Eds.): ER 2008, LNCS 5231, pp. 279–293, 2008.
© Springer-Verlag Berlin Heidelberg 2008

advanced workflow patterns), run-time flexibility has to be considered [2]. The latter is addressed by exception handling patterns [8], which describe different ways for coping with the exceptions that occur during process execution (e.g., activity failures). In many cases, changing the observable behavior of a running instance is not sufficient, but the process structure has to be adapted as well [9]. In addition, exception handling patterns cover changes at the *process instance level*, but are not applicable to *process schema changes*.

We extend existing workflow patterns by a set of patterns suitable for evaluating the run-time flexibility of PAISs. In [10,11] we have introduced 14 *change patterns*. Extensive case studies have shown that these change patterns are common and frequently applied in different domains [12]. Examples include the patterns *Insert*, *Move*, and *Replace*. Further, we have evaluated different approaches and tools with respect to their support of the different change patterns. As for workflow patterns, however, it is crucial to provide a *formal semantics* for change patterns; i.e., for each change pattern its effects must be precisely defined. Otherwise, ambiguities in the semantics of a change pattern (e.g., whether an activity is inserted in a serial or parallel manner) will hamper both their implementation and the comparison of existing change frameworks. Workflow patterns have been defined based on techniques with inherent formal semantics (e.g., Petri Nets [7] or Pi-Calculus [13]). However, such formalisms cannot be used to define change pattern semantics since we have to specify formal semantics of high-level change operations instead of workflow constructs. Further, since change patterns can be applied to different process meta models, their formal semantics should be described independent of a certain meta-model.

This paper provides a formal semantics for the change patterns presented in [10,12] to ground their implementation as well as pattern-based analysis of PAISs on a solid basis. First, we classify change patterns based on their semantics. To stay independent of a certain process meta model, we base change pattern semantics on execution traces (trace for short) of processes. Further, we illustrate it by examples and explanations. Together with workflow patterns, change patterns with precise and formal semantics will push the breakthrough of flexible PAISs in practice. Sect. 2 provides background information. In Sect. 3 we recall the change patterns presented in [10,11] and classify them based on their semantics. Sect. 4 provides the formal semantics for all 14 change patterns. Sect. 5 discusses related work and Sect. 6 concludes with a summary.

2   Backgrounds

This section introduces basic notions needed and recalls change patterns as presented in [10,11].

2.1   Basic Notions

Generally, for each business process to be supported (e.g., order handling), a *process type* represented by a *process schema* has to be defined. For one particular process type several process schemes may exist representing the different versions and evolution of this type over time. In the following, a process schema corresponds to a directed graph, which comprises a set of nodes representing process steps (i.e., activities) or control connectors (e.g, XOR-Split, AND-Join), and a set of control edges between them. The latter specify precedence relations. Activities can either be atomic or complex. While an atomic activity is associated with an invokable application service, a complex activity contains a reference to a sub process (schema). This enables the hierarchical decomposition of process schemes. Most of the patterns considered in this paper are not only applicable to atomic or complex activities, but also to sub process graphs with single entry and single exit node contained within the process schema (also denoted as hammocks [11]). In this paper, we use the term process fragment as a generalized concept covering atomic activities, complex activities (i.e., sub processes) and hammocks. If a pattern is denoted as being applicable to a process fragment, it can be applied to all these objects.

2.2   Process Changes and Adaptation Patterns

Changes of a process schema can be applied at the process type as well as the process instance level [2]. Process changes at the type level often necessitate change propagation to already running process instances. Ad-hoc changes of single process instances, in turn, are performed to deal with exceptional situations during runtime. In particular, ad-hoc changes result in an adapted instance-specific process schema [3]. The effects of such ad-hoc changes are usually instance-specific, and consequently do not affect any other ongoing process instance.

Change patterns (cf. Fig. 1) allow for the structural modification of a process schema at the type or instance level based on high-level change operations (e.g., to add an activity in parallel to another one). A high-level change operation, in turn, is based on a set of low-level change primitives (e.g., to add a single node or delete a single edge). Generally, change patterns can be applied to the whole process schema, i.e., the change region can be chosen dynamically. Therefore, change patterns are well suited for dealing with exceptions.

Design choices enable the parametrization of change patterns by keeping the number of distinct patterns manageable. For example, whether an atomic activity, a complex activity, or a hammock is deleted constitutes one design choice for the Delete Process Fragment pattern. Design choices which are not only relevant for a particular pattern, but for a set of patterns, are described only once for the entire pattern set. Typically, existing approaches only support a subset of the design choices in the context of a particular pattern. We denote the combination of design choices supported by a particular approach as a pattern variant. As discussed in [10,14], general design choices valid for all change patterns are

(A) the scope of the change pattern; i.e., whether it is possible to apply the pattern at process type or process instance level
(B) the level of granularity the change pattern operates on:
    atomic activity (1), sub process (2), and hammock (3).

AP1: Insert Process Fragment	**AP8**: Embed Process Fragment in Loop
AP2: Delete Process Fragment	**AP9**: Parallelize Activities
AP3: Move Process Fragment	**AP10**: Embed Process Fragment in Conditional Branch
AP4: Replace Process Fragment	**AP11**: Add Control Dependency
AP5: Swap Process Fragments	**AP12**: Remove Control Dependency
AP6: Extract Sub Process	**AP13**: Update Condition
AP7: Inline Sub Process	**AP14**: Copy Process Fragment

Fig. 1. Adaptation Patterns Overview

In this paper, we abstract from design choices (A) and (B) since they do not affect the formal semantics of change patterns as defined by us. Regarding Design Choice (A), for example, change pattern AP2 (Delete Process Fragment) could be implemented in a different way for the process type and the process instance level; e.g., replacing the activity to be deleted by a silent activity at the instance level, while physically deleting it at the type level. Furthermore, the applicability of change patterns at the instance level additionally depends on the state of the respective instances [2]. This, however, does not influence the formal semantics of pattern AP2 when defining it on basis of traces. Regarding Design Choice (B), we assume that sub processes as well as hammocks can be encapsulated within a complex activity. Then the formal semantics for applying change patterns to activities can be easily transferred to design choices B[2] and B[3] as well. Thus, in this paper, the definition of formal pattern semantics refers to activities instead of process fragments. Exceptions are patterns AP6 (Extract Sub Process), AP7 (Inline Sub Process), and AP8 (Embed Process Fragment in Loop), since AP6 and AP7 are applied to sub processes and AP8 to process fragments respectively (Design Choice (B)). Pattern-specific design choices, however, influence the formal semantics of these patterns. Take the insert pattern AP1 applied to an atomic activity as an example. To be able to exactly decide on its semantics, it is necessary to specify whether the activity is inserted in a serial, parallel, or conditional manner; i.e., the semantics of this change pattern is determined by taking the respective design choice into account. Thus, we consider design choices when formalizing patterns.

3   Semantics-Based Patterns Classification

To cluster formalization effects, we group change patterns according to their semantics; i.e., patterns with similar or related semantics (and therefore formalization) are summarized within one group.

Group 1 (Insertion patterns): Our first group consists of change patterns AP1 (Insert Activity), AP3 (Move Activity), and AP14 (Copy Activity) (cf. Fig. 2a).These patterns are more or less based on the insertion of an activity at a certain position. How this position is determined constitutes pattern-specific design choice (C); i.e., the activity can be inserted serially (C[1a]), in parallel

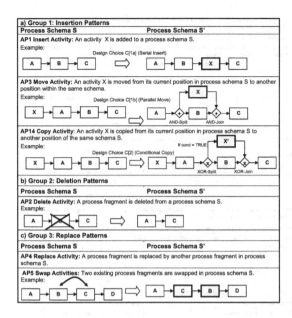

Fig. 2. Insertion, Deletion, and Replace Patterns (Groups 1 to 3) – Examples

(C[1b]), or conditionally (C[2]). As example consider Fig. 2a. On the left side source schemes are depicted to which AP1, AP3, and AP14 are applied assuming a particular design choice C. In this example a new activity is embedded between two single nodes. We generalize this later to activity sets as insertion patterns.

As can be seen from Fig. 2a, all patterns of Group 1 are based on the insertion of an activity. Obviously, this holds for AP1. For moving an activity (AP3), the respective activity is re-inserted after deleting it from its original position. Finally, when copying an activity X, it remains at its original position and a copy of X (with new label[1]) is inserted.

Group 2 (Deletion patterns): This group only contains one change pattern since its formalization does not directly relate to any other pattern. Fig. 2b shows the deletion of an activity from a process schema.

Group 3 (Replace patterns): Within the third group, we subsume change patterns AP4 (Replace Activity) and AP5 (Swap Activities). As example, consider Fig. 2c. Here activities B and C are swapped in schema S; i.e., activity B is (logically) replaced by activity C and vice versa.

Group 4 (Embedding patterns): There are two change patterns AP8 (Embed Process Fragment in Loop) and AP10 (Embed Process Fragment in Conditional Branch) which form Group 4. Note that for both patterns a process fragment is embraced by a new construct (i.e., a loop or conditional branching, cf. Fig. 3a). By applying one of these patterns, the respective process fragment is either

---

[1] We claim unique labelling of activities.

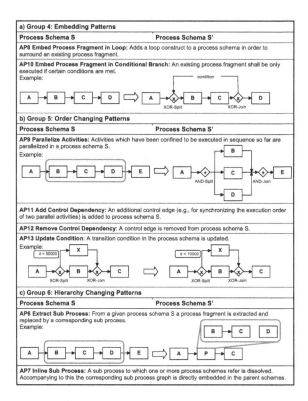

Fig. 3. Embedding, Order and Hierarchy Changing Patterns (Groups 4 to 6)

executed more often than before (AP8) or possibly not executed at all (AP10). Thus, a similar semantical description can be found for both patterns.

Group 5 (Order Changing / Update Patterns) comprises all patterns which either change the order of activities within a process schema or update transition conditions. As example, consider AP9 (Parallelize Activities) as depicted in Fig. 3b. AP9 changes the execution order for a selected set of activities, which are ordered in sequence before and parallelizes them within new schema S'; i.e., execution order of these activities is relaxed within the new schema. The same is achieved by removing control dependencies (AP12). Opposed to this, AP11 (Add Control Dependency) tightens the execution order of activities; e.g., two activities ordered in parallel before are executed in sequence when adding a control edge between them. Finally, AP13 (Update Condition) enables the modification of transition conditions. In Fig. 3b, for example, the transition condition of a particular branch is updated to "d < 10000" based on AP13.

Group 6 (Hierarchy Changing Patterns) comprises patterns which add or remove levels from a process schema and thus change its hierarchical structure. Pattern AP6 (Extract Sub Process) adds levels to a schema by extracting a selected sub process from schema S and nesting it "under" a new complex activity

P (cf. Fig. 3c). AP7 (Inline Sub Process) is the counter operation of AP6. It removes levels from the process hierarchy by dissolving complex activities and inlining the associated sub process schema into S.

4 Formalization of Adaptation Patterns

4.1 Basic Notions

First of all, we introduce basic notions needed for the following considerations. In workflow literature, for example, the formal description of control flow patterns has been based on Petri Nets [7] or Pi-Calculus [13]. Therefore these patterns have an inherent formal semantics. Regarding change patterns, we aim at a formal description independent of a particular process meta model. To achieve this, we base the formal description of change patterns on the behavioral semantics of the process schema before and after its change. One way to capture behavioral semantics is to use traces [15].

Definition 1 (Trace). *Let $\mathcal{PS}$ be the set of all process schemes and let $\mathcal{A}$ be the total set of activities (or more precisely activity labels) based on which process schemes $S \in \mathcal{PS}$ are specified (without loss of generality we assume unique labeling of activities in the given context). Let further $\mathcal{Q}_S$ denote the set of all possible traces producible on process schema $S \in \mathcal{PS}$. A particular trace $\sigma \in \mathcal{Q}_S$ is then defined as $\sigma = <a_1, \ldots, a_k>$ (with $a_i \in \mathcal{A}$, $i = 1, \ldots, k$, $k \in \mathbb{N}$) where the temporal order of a_i in σ reflects the order in which activities a_i were completed over S^2.*

Furthermore, we define the following two functions:

- *tracePred(S, a, σ) is a function which returns all activities within process schema S completed before the <u>first</u> occurence of activity a within trace σ. Formally: tracePred: $S \times \mathcal{A} \times \mathcal{Q}_S \mapsto 2^{\mathcal{A}}$ with*

$$tracePred(S, a, \sigma) = \begin{cases} \emptyset & \text{if } a \notin \{\sigma(i) \mid i \leq |\sigma|\} \\ & (\sigma(i) \text{ denotes the } i^{th} \text{ item in } \sigma, \text{ cf. Tab. 1}) \\ \{a_1, \ldots, a_k\} & \text{if } \sigma =< a_1, \ldots, a_k, a, a_{k+1}, \ldots, a_n > \\ & \wedge a_j \neq a \ \forall j = 1, ..., k \end{cases}$$

- *Analogously, traceSucc(S, a, σ) denotes a function which returns all activities within process schema S completed after the <u>last</u> occurence of activity a in trace σ. Formally: traceSucc: $S \times \mathcal{A} \times \mathcal{Q}_S \mapsto 2^{\mathcal{A}}$ with*

$$traceSucc(S, a, \sigma) = \begin{cases} \emptyset & \text{if } a \notin \{\sigma(i) \mid i \leq |\sigma|\} \\ \{a_{k+1}, \ldots, a_n\} & \text{if } \sigma =< a_1, \ldots, a_k, a, a_{k+1}, \ldots, a_n > \\ & \wedge a_j \neq a \ \forall j = k+1, ..., n \end{cases}$$

Function tracePred (traceSucc) determines the predecessors (successors) of the first (last) occurence of a certain activity within a trace; i.e., those activities which precede (succeed) the considered activity due to a loop back are not taken into account. Fig. 4 shows a schema with two loops, an example of a corresponding trace, and the sets resulting from the application of `tracePred` and `traceSucc` in different context.

---

^{2} A particular activity can occur multiple times within a trace due to loopbacks.

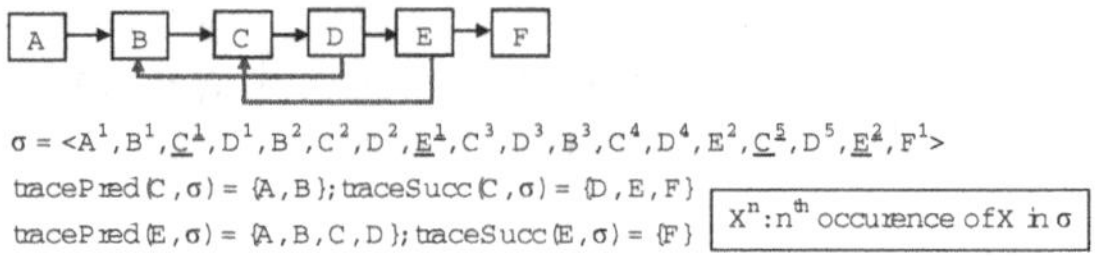

$\sigma = <A^1, B^1, \underline{C}^1, D^1, B^2, C^2, D^2, \underline{E}^1, C^3, D^3, B^3, C^4, D^4, E^2, \underline{C}^5, D^5, \underline{E}^2, F^1>$

$\text{tracePred}(C, \sigma) = \{A, B\}; \text{traceSucc}(C, \sigma) = \{D, E, F\}$

$\text{tracePred}(E, \sigma) = \{A, B, C, D\}; \text{traceSucc}(E, \sigma) = \{F\}$ | $X^n: n^{th}$ occurrence of X in σ

Fig. 4. Functions tracePred and traceSucc applied to trace

In addition to Def. 1, Table 1 contains useful notions which facilitate the formalization of the change patterns.

Table 1. Useful notions based on Def. 1

Let $\sigma = <a_1, \ldots, a_n> \in \mathcal{Q}_S$ be a trace on process schema S. Then:

$\lvert \sigma \rvert$: cardinality of σ
$\sigma(i) = a_i$: i^{th} item in trace σ
$x \in \sigma \iff \exists\, i \leq \lvert \sigma \rvert$ with $\sigma(i) = x$
$B \subseteq \sigma \iff \forall\, b \in B: b \in \sigma$
$\sigma_X^- \to$ discard all items from σ which belong to set X Example: $\sigma_{\{a_1, a_n\}}^- = <a_2, \ldots, a_{n-1}>$
$\sigma_X^+ \to$ discard all items from σ not belonging to set X example: $\sigma_{\{a_1, a_n\}}^+ = <a_1, a_n>$

4.2   Adaptation Pattern Semantics

Based on the meta model independent notions of Def. 1 and Tab. 1 we now describe formal semantics of the different change patterns introduced in Sect. 3 (cf. Fig. 2+3). The given formal specifications do not contain any constraints specific to a particular meta model. This has to be achieved separately by associating change operations with meta model-specific pre-/post-conditions. Our specifications contain generally valid pre-conditions where necessary; e.g., a node can only be deleted if it is present in the original schema. The post-conditions specify the effects of applying the respective change pattern (i.e., its semantics).

INSERTION PATTERNS (GROUP 1). The fundamental pattern of this group is AP1 (Insert Activity) since patterns AP3 (Move Activity) and AP14 (Copy Activity) are based on the insertion of an activity as well (cf. Fig. 2). Thus, we first present formal semantics for AP1. When formalizing the semantics of a change pattern we first specify necessary preconditions for its application. Then we describe the effects resulting from its application. To stay independent of a particular meta model, the latter is accomplished based on traces; i.e., we describe the relation between traces producible on original schema and modified schema.

Pattern Semantics 1 (Insert Activity, AP1). *AP1 corresponds to high-level operation* **op** = *Insert(S, x, A, B) $\mapsto$ S' where S and S' denote process schemes before*

and after change. Further A and B denote activity sets between which activity x shall be inserted. Then the semantics of AP1 is given as follows:
(1) S does not contain a node with label x. Further, S contains activity sets A and B.
(2) $\forall \mu \in \mathcal{Q}_{S'} : \exists \sigma \in \mathcal{Q}_S$ *with* $\mu_{\{x\}}^- = \sigma$ *and vice versa*
(3) Considered design choices: Serial Insert (C[1]) and Parallel Insert (C[2]):

$\forall \mu \in \mathcal{Q}_{S'}$ *with* $A \subseteq \mu$ *(i.e., all nodes of A contained in* μ*):*
$$\{\mu_{A \cup B \cup \{x\}}^+(i) \mid i = \nu, \ldots, \nu + |A| - 1\} = A \text{ for } \nu \in \mathbb{N}$$
$$\Longrightarrow$$
$$\mu_{A \cup B \cup \{x\}}^+(\nu + |A|) = x \wedge$$
$$\{\mu_{A \cup B \cup \{x\}}^+(i) \mid i = \nu + |A| + 1, \ldots, \nu + |A| + |B|\} = B$$

(1) formalizes generic pre-conditions for inserting an activity in schema S; e.g., the activity to be inserted must not yet be present in S. (2) defines the relation between traces on S and new schema S'. For each trace σ on S there exists a corresponding trace μ on S' for which $\mu_{\{x\}}^- = \sigma$ holds; i.e., when discarding newly inserted activity x from μ, this trace equals σ and vice versa. This expresses the close relation between traces producible on S and S'. It further indicates that traces on S' may additionally contain x whereas those on S do not.

Concerning AP1, we distinguish three design choices: Serial Insert (C[1a]), Parallel Insert (C[1b]), and Conditional Insert (C[2]) (see Fig. 2). Regarding design choices C[1a] and C[1b] the following conditions for newly inserted activity x in traces μ on S' hold (cf. *Pattern Semantics 1*): If all nodes of predecessor set A are contained in trace μ on S', then the entries of x and B will be present in μ as well. When projecting μ onto the entries of activity set $A \cup B \cup \{x\}$ (i.e., $\mu_{A \cup B \cup \{x\}}^+$), the entry of x is positioned directly after all entries of A and the entries of B directly succeed the entry of x within the respective trace. Note that the last condition (3) has to be modified in case of a conditional insert, since the presence of entries of A in μ on S' does not imply the presence of x.

Pattern Semantics 2 (Insert Activity, AP1 - Conditional Insert). *Let the preconditions be as in Pattern Semantics 1. Then*
(3') Considered design choice: Conditional Insert (C[2]):

$\forall \mu \in \mathcal{Q}_{S'}$ *with* $x \in \mu$*:*
$$\mu_{A \cup B \cup \{x\}}^+(\nu + |A|) = x$$
$$\Longrightarrow$$
$$\{\mu_{A \cup B \cup \{x\}}^+(i) \mid i = \nu, \ldots, \nu + |A| - 1\} = A \wedge$$
$$\{\mu_{A \cup B \cup \{x\}}^+(i) \mid i = \nu + |A| + 1, \ldots, \nu + |A| + |B|\} = B$$

Condition (3') implies that if x is present in μ on S' the entries of predecessor set A and successor set B will be contained in μ on S' as well. Furthermore, in the projection of μ onto the entries of activity set $A \cup B \cup \{x\}$ (i.e., $\mu_{A \cup B \cup \{x\}}^+$), the entries of A directly precede x and the entries of B directly succeed x.

Similarly, formal semantics for AP3 (Move Activity) can be defined. Conditions (3) and (3') which describe the position of x in μ (on S') are equal to the ones of AP1. However, there is a different pre-condition for AP3 (Move Activity): x must be present in S in order to be moved afterwards. The relation between traces on S and S' is also different from AP1 (Insert Activity). Formally:

$$\forall \sigma \in \mathcal{Q}_S: \exists \mu \in \mathcal{Q}_{S'} \text{ with } \sigma_{\{x\}}^- = \mu_{\{x\}}^- \text{ and vice versa}$$

Traces on S as well as traces on S' might contain x but at different positions. Therefore we claim that the projections of these traces (i.e., the traces where x will be discarded if present) have to be equal. Note that this reflects well the semantics of the Move change pattern.

Finally, AP14 (Copy Activity) is related to AP1 (Insert Activity) as well. Again the position of copied (and re-labelled) activity x' can be formalized by conditions (3) and (3') as for AP1 (Insert Activity). Similar to AP3 (Move Activity) the activity to be copied must be present in S (1). Additionally, labels of the activity to be copied and the copied activity itself must be different from each other and no activity with the new label must be already contained in S. Copying an activity x (with new label x') can be seen as inserting x' at the respective position. Therefore, the relation between traces on S and S' can be defined as for AP1, but based on x'; i.e., when discarding copied activity x' from μ (on S'), there exists an equal trace σ on S. Formally[3]:

$$\forall \mu \in \mathcal{Q}_{S'}: \exists \sigma \in \mathcal{Q}_S \text{ with } \mu_{\{x'\}}^- = \sigma \text{ and vice versa}$$

DELETION PATTERNS (GROUP 2). The semantics of AP2 (cf. Fig. 2) comprises preconditions and statements on the relation between traces on S and S':

Pattern Semantics 3 (Delete Activity, AP2). *AP2 corresponds to high-level operation* op $= Delete(S, x) \mapsto S'$ *where S and S' denote process schemes before and after its adaptation and x denotes the activity to be deleted. The semantics of AP2 is given as follows:*

(1) Process schema S contains a node with label x.
(2) $\forall \mu \in \mathcal{Q}_{S'}: x \notin \mu$
(3) $\forall \mu \in \mathcal{Q}_{S'}: \exists \sigma \in \mathcal{Q}_S \text{ with } \mu = \sigma_{\{x\}}^- \wedge$
    $\forall \sigma \in \mathcal{Q}_S: \exists \mu \in \mathcal{Q}_{S'} \text{ with } \sigma_{\{x\}}^- = \mu$

When deleting activity x, first of all, the process schema has to contain a node with label x. As an effect resulting from the application of AP2, all traces μ on S' must not contain x. Finally, for all projections of σ on S where x is discarded from σ we can find an equal trace on S' and vice versa.

REPLACE PATTERNS (GROUP 3). We illustrate AP5 (Swap Activities, cf. Fig. 2) since it "contains" the formalization for AP4 (Replace Activity). Note that swapping x and y can be (logically) seen as replacing x by y and y by x.

Pattern Semantics 4 (Swap Activities, AP5). *AP5 corresponds to high-level operation* op $= Swap(S, x, y) \mapsto S'$ *where S and S' denote process schemes before and after the adaptation. Further x and y denote the activities to be swapped. The semantics of AP5 is given as follows:*

(1) Process schema S contains one node with label x and one with label y.
(2) $\forall \sigma \in \mathcal{Q}_S: \exists \mu \in \mathcal{Q}_{S'} \text{ with } |\sigma| = |\mu| \wedge$

---

[3] A complete formalization of AP3 and AP14 can be found in a technical report [11].

$$\mu(i) = \begin{cases} \sigma(i) \ if \ \sigma(i) \ \notin \ \{x,y\} \\ x \quad if \ \sigma(i) \ = \ y \\ y \quad if \ \sigma(i) = x \end{cases}$$

and vice versa

Alternatively we can formulate (2) as follows:

(2') $\forall \ \sigma \ \in \ \mathcal{Q}_S$:

$\exists \ \mu \ \in \ \mathcal{Q}_{S'}$: *with* $|\sigma| \ = \ |\mu| \wedge \sigma^-_{\{x,y\}} \ = \ \mu^-_{\{x,y\}} \wedge (\sigma(k) \ = \ x \Longrightarrow \mu(k) \ = \ y)$

and vice versa

To be swapped, activities x and y must be both contained in schema S (1). The relation between trace σ on S and corresponding trace μ on S' can be formalized in two ways. In both cases, for all traces σ on S, there exists a corresponding trace μ on S' for which the cardinalities of σ and μ are equal. Regarding the positions of swapped activities x and y, we can explicitly state that for all traces σ on S, a trace μ on S' can be found such that all entries of μ are equal to entries of σ except at positions of x and y where the entries are swapped; i.e., at the position of x in σ, μ contains y and vice versa (2). Alternatively, for all traces σ on S there exists a corresponding trace μ on S' for which the projections of σ and μ resulting from discarding x and y are equal (2'). Further, μ contains the entry of y at the position of x in σ and vice versa.

EMBEDDING PATTERNS (GROUP 4). Formalization of pattern AP8 (Embed Process Fragment in Loop, cf. Fig. 3) is as follows:

Pattern Semantics 5 (Embed Process Fragment in Loop, AP8). *AP8 corresponds to high-level operation* op $=$ *Embed_in_Loop(S, P, cond)$\longmapsto$ S' where S and S' denote process schemes before and after its adaptation. Further P denotes the set of activities to be embedded into a loop and cond denotes the loop backward condition. Then the semantics of AP8 is given as follows:*

(1) *The sub graph on S induced by P has to be connected and must be a hammock, i.e., have single entry and single exit node.*

(2) $\mathcal{Q}_S \subset \mathcal{Q}_{S'}$

(3) $\forall \ \mu \ \in \ \mathcal{Q}_{S'}$: *Let μ' be the trace produced by discarding all entries of activities in P (if existing) from μ except the entries of one arbitrary loop iteration over P. Then $\mu' \in \mathcal{Q}_S$ holds.*

As a first characteristics, we formalize the relation between $\mathcal{Q}_S$ and $\mathcal{Q}_{S'}$. If the number of loop iterations is finite (i.e., the set of traces on a process schema containing loops is finite as well), $\mathcal{Q}_S \subset \mathcal{Q}_{S'}$ holds (1). Reason is that for all traces σ on S, a trace μ on S' can be found with $\sigma \ = \ \mu$ but not vice versa (due to the possibly iterative execution of the new loop).

To find a more specific characterization of the relation between $\mathcal{Q}_S$ and $\mathcal{Q}_{S'}$, for all traces μ on S' trace projection μ' is constructed as follows: All entries of activities from P (if existing) are discarded from μ except the entries of one arbitrary loop iteration; i.e., μ is projected onto a "loop-free" version of itself. Obviously, the resulting trace μ' is a trace on S as well (i.e., $\mu' \in \mathcal{Q}_S$).

For pattern AP10 (Embed Process Fragment in Conditional Branch), first of all, precondition (1) for AP8 must hold as well (cf. Pattern Semantics 5). Further, $Q_{S'} \subseteq Q_S$ holds. Due to the newly inserted conditional branch only a subset of traces might be generated on S' when compared to S. Finally, the relation between traces on S and traces on S' can be defined more precisely; i.e., for all traces σ on S, if we discard all entries of P from σ, the resulting projection is contained in the set of traces on S'. Formally:

$$\forall \sigma \in Q_S \colon \sigma_P^- \in Q_{S'} \ (\textit{if cond = FALSE is possible})$$

ORDER CHANGING / UPDATING PATTERNS (GROUP 5). This group comprises change patterns which change the execution order between activities or update transition conditions (cf. Fig. 3). We describe AP9 (Parallelize Activities), since AP12 (Remove Control Dependency) can be seen as special case of AP9. AP11 (Add Control Dependency) is the reverse operation to AP12. AP13 (Update Condition) is explained afterwards.

Pattern Semantics 6 (Parallelize Activities, AP9). *AP9 corresponds to high-level operation* op $= Parallelize(S, P) \mapsto S'$ *where S and S' denote process schemes before and after its adaptation. Further P denotes the set of activities to be parallelized. Then the semantics of AP9 is given as follows:*

(1) Within schema S, the sub graph induced by P constitutes a sequence with single entry and single exit node.

(2) $\forall \sigma \in Q_S \colon \exists \mu \in Q_{S'}$ with $\sigma = \mu$ (i.e., $Q_S \subset Q'_S$)

(3) $\forall p, p' \in P \colon \exists \mu_1, \mu_2 \in Q_{S'}$ with
   $(p \in tracePred(S', p', \mu_1) \wedge p' \in tracePred(S', p, \mu_2))$
   (assuming that the sequence defined by P can be enabled in S)

As a prerequisite of AP9, all activities to be parallelized must be ordered in sequence (1). As a basic characterization of AP9, the set of traces on S is a subset of the set of traces on S' (2) since traces on S' might contain entries reflecting a sequential order of P, too, but also any other execution order regarding activities from P (3). More precisely, every pair of activities contained in trace μ on S' is ordered in parallel in the new schema.

Regarding AP12 (Remove Ctrl Dependency), the formal semantics of AP9 is applied to exactly two activities. For AP11 (Add Control Dependency), the conditions of AP12 hold in reverse direction, i.e., execution order is made stricter on S' such that $Q_{S'}$ becomes a subset of Q_S.

A different semantics has to be defined for AP13 (Update Condition):

Pattern Semantics 7 (Update Condition, AP13). *AP13 corresponds to high-level operation* op $= Update\_Ctrl\_Dependeny(S, x, y, newCond) \mapsto S'$ *denote process schemes before and after its adaptation. Further oldCond (newCond) denotes the (transition) condition of control edge $x \rightarrow y$ in S' before (after) update. The semantics of AP13 is given as follows:*

(1) oldCond $\Longrightarrow$ newCond: $\forall \mu \in Q_{S'}$ for which transition condition newCond evaluates to TRUE: $\exists \sigma \in Q_S$ with $\mu = \sigma$

(2) *newCond* $\implies$ *oldCond*: $\forall\ \sigma\ \in \mathcal{Q}_S$ *for which transition condition oldCond evaluates to TRUE:* $\exists\ \mu\ \in\ \mathcal{Q}_{S'}$ *with* $\mu\ =\ \sigma$

(3) *Otherwise, for all traces* $\sigma\ \in\ \mathcal{Q}_S$ *there exists a trace* $\mu\ \in\ \mathcal{Q}_{S'}$ *for which the following holds: If we produce projections for* σ *and* μ *by discarding all entries belonging to the conditional branch with updated condition, these projections are equal.*

More precisely, we can derive a statement about the relation of traces between S and S' if we know the relation between old and updated condition ((1) or (2)). The projections of σ and μ as described in (3) can be easily accomplished based on, for example, block-structured process meta models.

PROCESS HIERARCHY CHANGING PATTERNS (GROUP 6). AP6 (Extract Sub Process) and AP7 (Inline Sub Process) are counterparts of each other (cf. Fig. 3). We illustrate AP6, the formal semantics of AP7 can be directly concluded. When formalizing AP6 a challenge is to specify the relation between traces μ on S' and traces σ on S. Note that the entries of P in μ might have to be inlined "instead of" the entry of x in σ. This becomes even more difficult in connection with loops since x is possibly executed multiple times.

Pattern Semantics 8 (Extract Sub Process (AP6)). *AP6 corresponds to high-level operation* op $=$ *Extract(S, P, x)* $\mapsto$ *S' where S and S' denote process schemes before and after its adaptation. Further P denotes the set of activities to be extracted and x denotes the label of the abstract activity which substitutes the sub graph induced by P (and refers to a corresponding sub process schema) on S'. Then the semantics of AP6 is given as follows:*

(1) *The sub graph on S induced by P has to be connected and must be a hammock, i.e., have single entry and single exit node.*

(2) $\forall\ \sigma\ \in\ \mathcal{Q}_S : \exists\ \mu\ \in\ \mathcal{Q}_{S'}$ *with* $\mu^-_{\{x\}}\ =\ \sigma^-_P\ \wedge$

$\forall\ \mu\ \in\ \mathcal{Q}_{S'} : \exists\ \sigma\ \in\ \mathcal{Q}_S : \sigma^-_P\ =\ \mu^-_{\{x\}}$

(3) *Let z denote the single exit node of the sub graph induced by P.*

Then: $\forall\ \sigma\ \in\ \mathcal{Q}_S$ *with* $\sigma^-_{P\backslash\{z\}}(k)\ =\ z : \exists\ \mu\ \in\ \mathcal{Q}_{S'}$ *with* $\mu(k)\ =\ x$

(4) *Let* $\mathcal{P}$ *denote the set of all traces over the sub graph induced by P and let further* $\pi\ \in\ \mathcal{P}$. *Then:*

$\forall\ \mu\ \in\ \mathcal{Q}_{S'}$ *with* $\mu(\nu_i)\ =\ x\ (i\ =\ 1,\ldots,n,\ \nu_i\ \in\ \mathbb{N}) : \exists\ \sigma\ \in\ \mathcal{Q}_S$ *with*

$$\sigma(k) = \begin{cases} = \mu(k) & k = 1,\ldots,\nu_1 - 1, \\ = \mu(k - j * |\pi| + j) & k = \nu_j + |\pi|,\ldots,\nu_{j+1} - 1\ \wedge \\ & k = \nu_n + |\pi|,\ldots,|\mu| + n * (|\pi| - 1) \\ = \pi(l) & k = \nu_i + l - 1 \end{cases}$$

where $j = 1,\ \ldots,\ n\text{-}1;\ l = 1,\ \ldots,\ |\pi|$.

The relation between traces on S and on S' can be formalized as follows: For all traces σ on S we can find a trace μ on S' for which the projections resulting from discarding all entries of sub process P from σ and discarding the entry of x from μ are equal (1). The interesting question is how to determine the position of x on S' when extracting P from S. For this, we build a projection of trace σ on S by discarding all entries of activities in P except the one of single exit entry z (2). Then we can find a trace μ on S' for which the position of z within the projection of σ determines the position of x in μ. The other direction (i.e., how to determine the positions of activities in P on S), which is also important in the context of AP7 (Inline Sub Process), is more challenging. We solve this by constructing a trace σ on S for all μ on S'. First the position(s) of x in μ is (are) determined $(\nu_1, ..., \nu_n)$. In the context of loops, this might be more than one position. Then the activities of P are inserted at this (these) position(s) within σ (3). The remaining part of σ can be constructed using the entries of μ, only the positions have to be shifted accordingly.

5   Related Work

Flexibility in PAISs has been addressed in different ways including declarative approaches [6], case-handling [4], and process changes at different levels [2,3,9]. Some approaches have additionally addressed instance-specific change and type-level change within one system [2]. All this work shows how crucial it is to provide sufficient solutions for flexible PAISs for applying them in practice. However, there is no common understanding of change operations or change patterns in all of these approaches such that for users it might be difficult to compare them with respect to their particular needs.

The general idea of using patterns to compare PAISs has been proposed by the workflow patterns project [7]. Based on respective patterns, the expressiveness of different process meta models and thus tools can be compared. Further patterns have been presented including data flow patterns [16], resource patterns [17], exception handling patterns [8], and service interaction patterns [18]. Most of them come along with a formal semantics, for example, based on languages such as Petri Nets [7] or Pi-Calculus [13].

For the first time, change patterns have been (informally) introduced in [10,11] and evaluated in [12]. However, no formal semantics of change patterns has been provided so far, even though this is crucial for implementing and comparing PAISs. This paper closes this gap.

6   Summary and Outlook

We have specified the formal semantics for process change patterns [10,11]. This provides the basis for implementing the patterns in PAISs as well as for comparing PAISs with respect to flexibility since ambiguities are discarded. We first classified the change patterns along similar semantics to facilitate the specification of their semantics. For each pattern its formal semantics has been specified based on traces to stay independent of a particular process meta model. Currently, we are formalizing the semantics of pre-defined change patterns [10,11] as well. Such patterns include, for example, the *Late Selection of Process Fragments* or the *Late Modeling of Process Fragments*. Our future work includes change patterns for aspects other than control flow (e.g., data or resources) and patterns for advanced change scenarios (e.g., adapting data flow when changing control flow). Further, we will provide a reference implementation and use the patterns for process refactoring [19].

References

1. Adams, M., ter Hofstede, A., Edmond, D., van der Aalst, W.: A Service-Oriented Implementation of Dynamic Flexibility in Workflows.. In: Proc. Coopis 2006 (2006)
2. Rinderle, S., Reichert, M., Dadam, P.: Flexible support of team processes by adaptive workflow systems. Distributed and Parallel Databases 16, 91–116 (2004)
3. Reichert, M., Dadam, P.: ADEPT$_{flex}$ – Supporting Dynamic Changes of Workflows Without Losing Control. JIIS 10, 93–129 (1998)
4. Van der Aalst, W., Weske, M., Grünbauer, D.: Case handling: A new paradigm for business process support. Data and Knowledge Engineering 53, 129–162 (2005)
5. Pesic, M., Schonenberg, M., Sidorova, N., van der Aalst, W.: Constraint-Based Workflow Models: Change Made Easy. In: CoopIS 2007, pp. 77–94 (2007)
6. Sadiq, S., Sadiq, W., Orlowska, M.: A Framework for Constraint Specification and Validation in Flexible Workflows. Information Systems 30, 349–378 (2005)
7. Van der Aalst, W., ter Hofstede, A., Kiepuszewski, B., Barros, A.: Workflow Patterns. Distributed and Parallel Databases 14, 5–51 (2003)
8. Russell, N., van der Aalst, W., ter Hofstede, A.: Exception Handling Patterns in Process-Aware Information Systems. In: Dubois, E., Pohl, K. (eds.) CAiSE 2006. LNCS, vol. 4001, pp. 288–302. Springer, Heidelberg (2006)
9. Rinderle, S., Reichert, M., Dadam, P.: Correctness Criteria for Dynamic Changes in Workflow Systems – A Survey. Data and Knowledge Engineering 50, 9–34 (2004)
10. Weber, B., Rinderle, S., Reichert, M.: Change patterns and change support features in process-aware information systems. In: Krogstie, J., Opdahl, A., Sindre, G. (eds.) CAiSE 2007. LNCS, vol. 4495, pp. 574–588. Springer, Heidelberg (2007)
11. Weber, B., Rinderle, S., Reichert, M.: Change Support in Process-Aware Information Systems - A Pattern-Based Analysis. Technical report, CTIT (2007)
12. Weber, B., Reichert, M., Rinderle-Ma, S.: Change patterns and change support features - enhancing flexibility in process-aware information systems. Data and Knowledge Engineering (2008)
13. Puhlmann, F., Weske, M.: Using the Pi-Calculus for Formalizing Workflow Patterns. In: van der Aalst, W.M.P., Benatallah, B., Casati, F., Curbera, F. (eds.) BPM 2005. LNCS, vol. 3649, pp. 153–168. Springer, Heidelberg (2005)
14. Zhang, F., D'Hollander, E.: Using Hammock Graphs to Structure Programs. IEEE Transactions on Software Engineering 30, 231–245 (2004)
15. Glabbeek, R.V., Goltz, U.: Refinement of actions and equivalence notions for concurrent systems. Acta Informatica 37, 229–327 (2001)
16. Russell, N., ter Hofstede, A., Edmond, D., van der Aalst, W.: Workflow data patterns. Technical Report FIT-TR-2004-01, Queensland Univ. of Techn. (2004)
17. Russell, N., ter Hofstede, A., Edmond, D., van der Aalst, W.: Workflow resource patterns. Technical Report WP 127, Eindhoven Univ. of Technology (2004)
18. Barros, A., Dumas, M., ter Hofstede, A.: Service Interaction Patterns. In: Bussler, C.J., Haller, A. (eds.) BPM 2005. LNCS, vol. 3812, pp. 302–318. Springer, Heidelberg (2006)
19. Weber, B., Reichert, M.: Refactoring process models in large process repositories. In: Bellahsène, Z., Léonard, M. (eds.) CAiSE 2008. LNCS, vol. 5074, pp. 124–139. Springer, Heidelberg (2008)

Modeling and Querying E-Commerce Data in Hybrid Relational-XML DBMSs

Lipyeow Lim, Haixun Wang, and Min Wang

IBM T. J. Watson Research Center
{liplim,haixun,min}@us.ibm.com

Abstract. Data in many industrial application systems are often neither completely structured nor unstructured. Consequently semi-structured data models such as XML have become popular as a lowest common denominator to manage such data. The problem is that although XML is adequate to represent the flexible portion of the data, it fails to exploit the highly structured portion of the data. XML normalization theory could be used to factor out the structured portion of the data at the schema level, however, queries written against the original schema no longer run on the normalized XML data. In this paper, we propose a new approach called eXtricate that stores XML documents in a space-efficient decomposed way while supporting efficient processing on the original queries. Our method exploits the fact that considerable amount of information is shared among similar XML documents, and by regarding each document as consisting of a shared framework and a small diff script, we can leverage the strengths of both the relational and XML data models at the same time to handle such data effectively. We prototyped our approach on top of DB2 9 pureXML (a commercial hybrid relational-XML DBMS). Our experiments validate the amount of redundancy in real e-catalog data and show the effectiveness of our method.

1 Introduction

Real data in industrial application systems are complex. Most data do not fit neatly into structured, semi-structured or unstructured data models. It is often the case that industrial data have elements from each of these data models. As an example consider managing product catalog data in E-Commerce systems. Commercial e-Commerce solutions such as IBM's Websphere Product Center (WPC) have traditionally used a vertical schema [1,2] in a relational DBMSs to manage the highly variable product catalog data. In addition to the vertical schema, the research community has proposed several strategies for managing data with schema variability using relational DBMSs. These include variations on the horizontal, the vertical, and the binary schema [3,4]. However, the relational data model remains ill-suited for storing and processing the highly flexible semi-structured e-catalog data efficiently. The flexibility of the XML data model, on the other hand, appears to be a good match for the required schema flexibility and Lim et al. [5] has proposed managing product catalog data using XML-enabled DBMS. However, the flexibility of XML in modeling semi-structured data usually comes with a big cost in terms of storage especially for XML documents that have a lot of information in common.

Q. Li et al. (Eds.): ER 2008, LNCS 5231, pp. 294–310, 2008.
© Springer-Verlag Berlin Heidelberg 2008

```
<ProductInfo>                            <ProductInfo>
  <Model>                                  <Model>
    <Brand>Panasonic</Brand>                 <Brand>Philips</Brand>
    <ModelID>TH-58PH10UK</ModelID>           <ModelID>42PFP5332D/37</ModelID>
  </Model>                                  </Model>
  <Display>                                <Display>
    <ScreenSize>58in</ScreenSize>            <ScreenSize>42in</ScreenSize>
    <AspectRatio>16:9</AspectRatio>          <AspectRatio>16:9</AspectRatio>
    <Resolution>1366 x 768</Resolution>      <Resolution>1024 x 768</Resolution>
    <Brightness>1200 cd/m2</Brightness>      <Brightness>1200 cd/m2</Brightness>
    <Contrast>10000:1</Contrast>             <Contrast>10000:1</Contrast>
    <PixelPitch>0.942mm</PixelPitch>         <ViewingAngle>160(H)/160(V)</ViewingAngle>
  </Display>                                </Display>
  ...                                      ...
</ProductInfo>                            </ProductInfo>
        (a) Panasonic Plasma HDTV                (b) Philips Plasma HDTV
```

Fig. 1. Two XML fragment of Plasma HDTV product info from on-line retailer newegg.com. Bold face denotes information that is unique to that XML document.

Example 1. Consider the XML fragments for the specifications of two plasma HDTV product on the www.newegg.com website. Not only do the two XML documents share many common structural elements (eg. "AspectRatio", "Resolution"), they also share many common values (eg. "16:9", "1200 cd/m2").

It is clear from Ex. 1 that XML descriptions of products in the same or similar category have many structural elements and values in common resulting in storage inefficiency. If minimizing storage were our only goal, XML compression methods (such as XMill [6] and XGrind [7]) could be used to eliminate most of the storage inefficiency at the expense of less efficient query processing due to the need for decompression. Another approach would be to apply XML normalization [8,9,10] on these XML documents assuming a super-root. Unfortunately, applying XML normalization poses two problems. First, XML normalization is a design-time process that requires both the schema and the functional dependencies of the XML data to be specified. In many real applications the functional dependencies are neither identified nor specified. In fact, some applications do not even require a schema to be specified. When a schema is specified, these schemas are typically part of industrial standards that do not admit any modification by a normalization process. Second, queries written against the original XML data no longer work against the normalized XML data[1]. This is a serious problem, because application developers typically write queries against the original XML data. The goal of our work is to exploit the redundancy in the XML data in order to support efficient storage of the data, efficient query processing over the data, and transparency to the user, i.e., the user need not re-design the schema of the XML data or rewrite the queries. In contrast to low-level compression methods and schema-based normalization methods, we explore structural as well as value similarities among a set of semi-structured data documents to create models that allow efficient storage and query processing. To our advantage, commercial DBMSs are rolling out native XML

---

[1] In theory, the queries on the original XML data could be transformed into queries on the normalized XML data. Unfortunately, there is no known query transformation algorithm for this purpose.

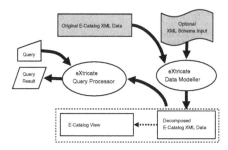

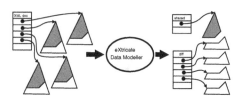

Fig. 2. Overview of our EXTRICATE system

Fig. 3. A collection of XML documents are decomposed into a shared XML tree and a collection of *diff* scripts. The shaded portion of the XML trees denote common information.

support [11,12], which provides a new option to managing data with high schema variability [5]. We leverage such systems to build a hybrid model for semi-structured data.

Our Approach. In this paper, we propose a new approach called EXTRICATE to manage data with high schema variability. Fig. 2 presents the EXTRICATE system on a high level. The EXTRICATE system consists of two main components: the EXTRICATE data modeler and the EXTRICATE query processor. The EXTRICATE data modeler takes as input the original XML collection, "extricates" a shared XML document (a *model*), stores the original documents as differences from the shared XML document, and generates a view of the decomposed data that has the same schema as the original data. The EXTRICATE query processor takes as input user queries written against the original data and transforms the query into a query processing plan for the decomposed data.

For concreteness, consider managing the electronic product catalog of an on-line retailer using a hybrid relational-XML DBMS. The product information can be stored in a table with an XML column using the following schema:

ecatalog(productID **INT**, categoryID **INT**, info **XML**).

Each product is uniquely identified by its productID. The categoryID encodes product category information like "Electronics > Plasma / LCD / DLP TV > Plasma TV > Panasonic" as a numerical identifier. The info field stores the detailed product information in XML form. These XML data can be queried, using embedded XPath expressions in SQL [11,13] or using XQuery. As motivated by Ex. 1, it is safe to argue that products in the same category usually exhibit considerable structural and value similarity. Conversely, products in different categories exhibit more differences both structurally as well as in terms of values. For instance, MP3 players have attributes such as *Storage Capacity*, *Supported Audio Formats*, etc., that HDTVs typically do not.

Using EXTRICATE, the ecatalog table will be decomposed internally into two tables, namely:

categoryInfo(categoryID **INT**, sharedinfo **XML**)

productInfo(productID **INT**, categoryID **INT**, diff **XML**)

The `categoryInfo` table stores the XML tree shared by all products in a particular category. The `productInfo` table encodes each of the original XML document in the `info` column as the *diff* or *edit transcript* from the shared XML tree of the associated category. Each XML document is therefore decomposed into a shared XML tree and its `diff` from the shared XML tree. Since the shared XML tree is stored once for all the XML documents in the category, significant storage savings can be obtained for highly redundant XML data.

From the perspective of the user of the e-catalog database, nothing has changed, because the e-catalog data is presented to the user as a view, which has the same schema as the original `ecatalog` table. Applications and queries on the `ecatalog` table require no change either: EXTRICATE's query processor will transform any query against the original `ecatalog` table into queries against the `categoryInfo` table, and if necessary, the `productInfo` table (some queries can be answered by accessing `categoryInfo` only). The query transformation is carried out by a rule-based query processor that is described in detail in Sect. 3.

Our Contributions. We summarize our contributions as follows:

- We propose a space-efficient and query-friendly model for storing semi-structured data that leverages commercial DBMSs with native XML support. We show that with the new model, we can dramatically reduce storage redundancy of XML data and improve query performance at the same time.
- We propose a query transformation algorithm to automatically rewrite user queries on the original data to queries on the data stored using our model without any user intervention. In many cases, the transformed queries can be answered much more efficiently than the original ones since they access much less amount of data.
- We show that our approach is friendly toward schema evolution, which occurs frequently in applications such as e-commerce data management.

Paper Organization. Sect. 2 presents EXTRICATE's data modeler. Query rewriting and processing is discussed in Sect. 3. We discuss data maintenance issues related to schema evolution in Sect. 5. Experimental results are presented in Sect. 6. We review related work in Sect. 6 and conclude in Sect. 7.

2   Data Modelling

Our EXTRICATE data modeler is inspired by the predictive compression paradigm, where the data is represented losslessly using a model that predicts the data approximately and the residue that is the difference between the predicted data and the true data. In an analogous fashion, EXTRICATE extracts a *shared* XML document from a set of XML documents and represents each of the original document using the shared document and the *diff* script. The shared XML document represents a "model" that predicts the XML documents in the collection. The *diff* script represents the "residue" that is a set of differences between the document and the shared document. Since the shared XML document is common to all the documents in the collection, we only need to

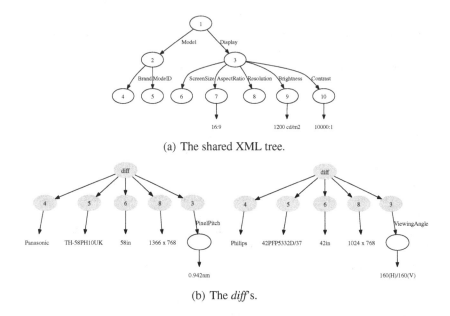

(a) The shared XML tree.

(b) The *diff*'s.

Fig. 4. The decomposed representation of the two HDTV XML documents in Fig. 1

store it once. Hence the entire collection of XML documents is stored as a single shared XML document and a collection of diff scripts, one diff script for each document in the collection (see Fig. 3).

Continuing with the e-catalog example, recall that the product information has been partitioned according to product categories and that the product information within the same category have both structural and value similarities. The product information are stored as XML documents and we will use a tree representation for XML documents in our discussion. Conceptually, the EXTRICATE data modeler first finds a *shared XML tree* for a collection of XML trees. The shared XML tree is the maximal sub-tree common to all the XML trees in the collection. The *diff* of each original XML tree from the shared XML tree can then be computed using known tree diff algorithms [14,15,16,17].

Example 2 (A Data Modelling Example). Consider the XML documents (represented as trees) of the two HDTV products shown in Fig. 1. The shared XML tree is shown in Fig. 4(a) and the differences are shown in Fig. 4(b).

Observe that the shared XML tree (1) is a single connected tree, (2) contains values in addition to structure. In practice, the shared tree may be further annotated with statistical information (e.g., the min, max values of, say, the listprice element).

Observe that each *diff* document represents a set of insertion operations onto the shared XML tree. Each of the two *diff* trees represents 4 insertions, as there are 4 child nodes under the root node. The name of these child nodes are node identifiers (NIDs), which identify the nodes or the location of insertion in the shared XML tree. These NIDs on the shared XML tree may be either implicitly maintained by the DBMS or explicitly annotated on the tree nodes.

It is clear that by inserting each sub-tree in the *diff* as the child of the node in the shared XML tree with the specified NID, the original XML document can be recovered.

A direct benefit of our decomposition is storage efficiency. Information common to all product documents within a category is "extricated" and stored once in the shared XML document, instead of being redundantly stored in every document. However, in contrast to XML compressors (such as XMill [6] and XGrind [7]) the goal of our method is not low-level compression: our decomposition method operates at the data model level with a focus on efficient query processing. In other words, the decomposition must be done in a query-friendly way, that is, we need to ensure queries on the original table can be mapped to queries on the decomposed tables and processed efficiently thereafter.

2.1 Finding the Shared XML Tree

In this section we discuss the first step of the decomposition process: finding the (largest) shared XML tree, given a set of XML documents having similar structures and values.

This problem is similar to the *maximal matching* problem [16] and is complementary to the problem of finding the smallest diff between two XML trees. Efficient algorithms exists for ordered trees [16]. For unordered trees, the problem is NP-hard [14], but polynomial time approximate algorithms [14,15] exist. However, our problem differs from the work mentioned above in that the the maximal matching need to be a connected tree. The goal of the above-mentioned related work is to find the maximal common fragments, i.e., a common forest among two XML trees in order to minimize the edit distance between the two XML trees. In contrast, our goal is to find a single rooted tree that is common to a collection of XML trees.

We discuss the case of finding shared XML documents for unordered trees, which is more difficult than for ordered trees. One difficulty in finding a single shared tree among a set of XML trees is that a set of unordered children nodes may have the same node name. The difficulty can be illustrated by the two XML documents shown in Fig. 5. The node B beneath A occurs twice in both documents. The largest shared document is not unique for these two documents. One alternative will contain all nodes except for node C, and the other all nodes except for node D. To find the largest shared document among a set of documents, we must store all such alternatives at every step, which makes the complexity of the entire procedure exponential.

In this work, we use a greedy approach. We find the shared document of two documents starting from their root nodes. Let n_1 and n_2 be the root nodes of two XML doc-

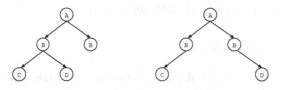

Fig. 5. A Shared XML document and the *diff*

Algorithm 1. MATCHTREE(n_1, n_2)

Input: n_1, n_2: root node of the two XML tree
Output: r: a shared subtree
1: **if** n_1 matches n_2 **then**
2:     $r \leftarrow$ new node
3:     copy n_1 to r
4: let $\mathcal{C}_1 = \{$child nodes of $n_1\}$
5: let $\mathcal{C}_2 = \{$child nodes of $n_2\}$
6: let $\mathcal{L} = \{$ node names common to $\mathcal{C}_1$ and $\mathcal{C}_2\}$
7: **for** each node name $l \in \mathcal{L}$ **do**
8:     let $\mathcal{C}_1(l) = \{$nodes from $\mathcal{C}_1$ with name $l\} = \{s_{11}, \cdots, s_{1m}\}$
9:     let $\mathcal{C}_2(l) = \{$nodes from $\mathcal{C}_2$ with name $l\} = \{s_{21}, \cdots, s_{2n}\}$
10:     **for** each $(s_{1i}, s_{2j}) \in \mathcal{C}_1(l) \times \mathcal{C}_2(l)$ **do**
11:         $r_{ij} \leftarrow$ MATCHTREE(s_{1i}, s_{2j})
12:     let $\mathcal{M} = \{r_{ij} : \forall i, j\}$
13:     **while** $\mathcal{M} \neq \emptyset$ **do**
14:         $r_{pq} \leftarrow \arg\max_{r_{ij} \in \mathcal{M}}$ SizeOf(r_{ij})
15:         add r_{pq} as a child node of r
16:         remove r_{pk} and r_{kq} from $\mathcal{M}, \forall k$
17: **return** r

Algorithm 2. Finding the shared XML document in a set of XML documents

---

Input: D: a set of XML documents (represented by their root nodes)
Output: r: a shared XML document
1: Assume $D = \{d_1, d_2, \cdots, d_n\}$
2: $s \leftarrow d_1$
3: **for** each document $d \in D$ **do**
4:     $s \leftarrow$ MATCHTREE(s, d)

---

uments. Two nodes are said to match if they have the same node type, and either they have same names (for element/attribute nodes) or they have the same values (for value nodes). If n_1 and n_2 do not match, then the shared document is an empty document. Otherwise, we recursively find matches for each of their child nodes. Special consideration is given to the case where several child nodes have the same name and the child nodes are unordered. Assume $\mathcal{C}_1(l) = \{s_{11}, \cdots, s_{1m}\}$ and $\mathcal{C}_2(l) = \{s_{21}, \cdots, s_{2n}\}$ are two sets of child nodes with the same name that we need to match. We find recursively the shared XML sub-tree for every pair (s_{1i}, s_{2j}) of the instances. Out of the $m \times n$ shared XML trees, we pick the shared XML sub-tree r_{pq} with the largest size and add r_{pq} as the child node of the current shared XML tree r. We remove all the shared trees associated with either s_{1p} or s_{2q} from the candidate set $\mathcal{M}$ so that they will not be chosen anymore. Then, we find the next largest in the remaining $(m-1)(n-1)$ candidate shared XML sub-trees. We repeat this process until no shared sub-trees can be found.

Algorithm 1 outlines the MATCHTREE procedure that finds a shared document between two XML documents. Based on the MATCHTREE procedure, Algorithm 2 finds the shared document among a set of XML documents.

2.2   Finding the Differences

After the shared XML tree is found, the difference between each document in the original collection and the shared XML tree can be found using existing tree diff algorithms [14,15,16,17]. In addition to finding the differences, we optionally annotate the

Algorithm 3. PROCESSQUERY(S, D, p)

Input: S shared trees, D diff's, p XPath
Output: R satisfying productIDs

```
 1: R ← ∅
 2: for all each shared tree s ∈ S do
 3:     let N be the set of NIDs of the maximal matching nodes
 4:     let p′ be the unmatched suffix of the XPath p
 5:     (N, p′) ← MaxMatchXPath( s, p )
 6:     if p′ = ε then
 7:        /* p completely matched */
 8:        R ← R ∪ fetchProductIDbyCat(catID(s))
 9:     else
10:        for each diff d ∈ D s.t. catID(d)=catID(s) do
11:           for each continuation node c ∈ fetch(N, d) do
12:              if MatchXPath (c, p′) then
13:                 R ← R ∪ fetchProductID(d)
14: return R
```

---

shared XML tree with statistics collected during the scan through each original document for finding the differences.

Difference model. We model the differences between an original document and the shared XML tree as a set of sub-tree insertions. In the most trivial case, a sub-tree can just be a single value. Each insertion is represented using an XML fragment consisting of a node specifying the node identifier (NID) that uniquely identifies the insertion point in the shared XML tree. The subtree rooted at that node is the subtree to be inserted. The fragments for all the insertions associated with a single original document are then collected under root node <diff>, forming the XML representation for the *diff* (see Fig. 4(b) for an example). A richer difference model may include deletions as well. However, we do not discuss this option in this paper.

Optional annotations. We annotate the shared XML tree with two types of additional information: node identifier (NID) annotation and value annotation. The NIDs are used by the difference representation to specify insertion location. As discussed in the example of Sect. 2, NIDs can be implicitly maintained by the DBMS or explicitly annotated as attributes in the shared XML tree. In Fig. 4(a), the node labels 7 and 9 denote the NIDs of the nodes AspectRatio, and Brightness respectively. These NID of these nodes are used in the *diff*s .

To facilitate efficient query processing, we may also optionally annotate nodes in the shared XML tree with some simple statistics about the values associated with those nodes. For example, consider the ScreenSize element in Fig. 4(a). Each of the two document has a different value for ScreenSize. We can annotate the ScreenSize element in the shared XML tree by the minimum and the maximum value (in this case 42in and 58in) so that query predicates such as /productInfo/Display [ScreenSize < 10] can be evaluated without accessing the *diff*s. These value annotations are collected while scanning the documents (for computing the *diff*) and added after the *diff*s are processed.

3   Query Processing

In this section, we show how queries against the original set of XML documents can be decomposed into queries against a set of shared trees and queries against their *diff*s. We

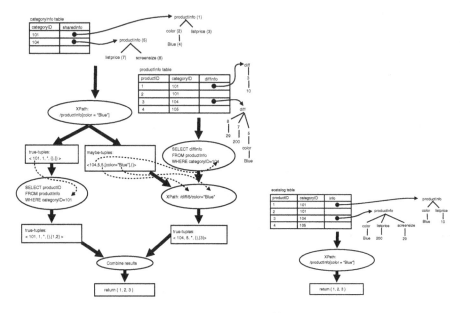

Fig. 6. Evaluating single constraint product search queries. The numbers in parenthesis beside the node labels denote the NIDs of the nodes.

Fig. 7. Evaluating single constraint product search queries on the original `ecatalog` table.

focus on filtering queries because these are the most common type of query on e-catalog data. A filtering query consists of a filtering condition specified in XPath on the XML column in the original table and fetches the tuples (or a projection thereof) that satisfy the filtering condition.

Algorithm 3 outlines the process of how filtering queries over documents of varied schemata are processed using sub-queries over the shared documents and the *diff*'s. The key idea is to first process the XPath filtering condition p on the shared trees S. For the shared trees that completely satisfy the filtering condition, the associated set of diff's need not be checked, instead all the associated tuples can be returned as satisfying the query. For the shared trees that contains partial matches to p, the associated diff's need to be consulted to complete the matching. The diff's that complete the matching of the remaining unmatched sub-path p' satisfy the query and the corresponding tuple can be returned. Note that in practice Algorithm 3 is implemented by leveraging SQL/XML queries over a hybrid relational-XML DBMS.

Example 3 (A single-constraint query). Suppose we want to find all products in the e-catalog that are blue in color. It is straightforward to ask such a query against the original `ecatalog` table using the following filtering query specified in the SQL/XML query language,

```
SELECT productID
FROM   ecatalog AS C
WHERE  XMLExists('$t/productInfo[color ="Blue"]'
```

```
PASSING BY REF C.info AS "t").
```

The query in Example 3 scans each row of the `ecatalog` table and evaluates the `XMLExists` predicate on the XML tree in the `info` field. If the predicate evaluates to true, the `productID` field of the row is returned. The SQL/XML function `XMLExists` returns true if a node matching the given XPath expression exists in the given XML tree.

Fig. 6 illustrates the process of evaluating the sample query (Example 3) against the two tables, `categoryInfo` and `productInfo`, in the e-catalog application. First, we evaluate the XPath expression against `categoryInfo` table. The result is a sequence of tuples that represent temporary matches. These temporary tuples fall into two types: true-tuples and maybe-tuples. **true-tuples** contain return nodes that satisfy the entire XPath expression. Since the predicate has been satisfied, the last matched node and the remaining XPath fields are empty. **maybe-tuples** contain return nodes that may satisfy the predicate when combined with the *diff* information.

For the true-tuples, all the documents in the category represented by the tuple satisfy the query. We therefore retrieve their document IDs from the *diff* table. The maybe-tuples, however, need to be further evaluated against the *diff* table in order to reject or accept them. To do this, we use the `categoryID` and the NID of the last matched node of each maybe-tuple to filter out irrelevant rows and nodes in the *diff* table. The remaining XPath expression of each maybe-tuple is then evaluated on the filtered node set from the the `diff` column. The maybe-tuples whose remaining XPath expression are satisfied by some `diff` are then returned as true-tuples.

Note that when the path expression contains the wildcard element '//', the above procedure may not work as described. To see this, let the path expression be in the form of "/a/b//c/d". If it is split into two path expressions at the position between "a" and "b" or between "c" and "d", then no change to the above procedure is necessary. There is, however, the possibility that the query dividing position occurs "inside" the '//' element. Thus, any node x under the path "/a/b" in a shared document will satisfy the prefix query. As a result, multiple queries in the form of "/x//c/d" will be issued against the *diff* table. In particular, if "/a/b" is empty, we will query the *diff* tables directly with the path expression "//c/d/". This represents the worst case, wherein the shared document table has no filtering power, and we need to process all of the *diff* tables for the query. In other words, we degenerate into the case of querying against the original table.

We focus on filtering queries, because they are arguably the most important type of queries on semi-structured data such as the e-catalog, which consists of documents of similar structures. In other applications, more complex types of queries may call for more sophisticated query transformation and processing techniques. As future work, we will study how to extend our simple algorithm to handle more query types and how to balance the load between the query transformation and the query execution processes.

Discussion: Query Performance. The query performance of EXTRICATE is dependent on the amount of redundancy in the XML documents. We briefly discuss this relationship by comparing the processing steps for querying the `categoryInfo` and `productInfo` tables to those for just querying the `ecatalog` table. For ease of exposition, we focus on single constraint queries, because, conceptually, multi-constraint queries are processed as multiple single constraint queries with an intersection operation at the end to combine the results.

Consider the high-level query processing plan for `categoryInfo` and `productInfo` in Fig. 6 and for the original `ecatalog` table in Fig. 7. The most expensive operator in terms of running time is the XPath operator. The XPath operator is a logical operator that retrieves nodes that satisfy a given XPath expression. In IBM's DB2 two physical operators [12,11] can be used to implement the XPath operator during runtime: (1) the XML navigation operator (XNav), which traverses a collection of XML trees in order to find nodes that match the given XPath expression, and (2) the XML index scan operator (XIScan), which retrieves all matching nodes from an XML index. In both cases, the running time of each physical operator is dependent on the following data characteristics: (1) the number of rows in the XML column, and (2) the size of the XML tree in each row. In our method, the data characteristics of the `categoryInfo` and `productInfo` tables depends on the level of redundancy in the product information of each category. In the following, we consider the worst case and the best case scenarios, and show how we can reap the most benefits from our scheme.

Worst Case: no data redundancy. In the worst case, there is no data redundancy: the shared XML document will be small, and all information stays with the *diff* documents. Most queries will have to go through the *diff* documents. Thus, our method will have no advantage over the method that processes the original `ecatalog` table directly. In this case, we should not apply our method at all.

Best Case: full data redundancy. In this extreme case, all the product information within a category is the same. The `diff` column of the `productInfo` table is empty and the `sharedinfo` column of the `categoryInfo` table contains all the information. However, the size of the `categoryInfo` table is much smaller than the size of the `ecatalog` table (note that the XML document size remains unchanged). In the processing plan for our method, the right branch (see Fig. 6) is never executed that is, no maybe-tuples will be produced, because the XPath can always be evaluated with certainty using the information in the `categoryInfo` table. Since the input size (`categoryInfo` table size) of the XPath operator in our method is significantly smaller than the input size (`ecatalog` table size) of the original method, our method will be significantly more efficient.

Most real life semi-structured data, including the e-catalog data used in our example, is likely to fall somewhere between the best and the worst case. We do not have control over data redundancy, however, the redundancy of the *diff* information within each category can be tuned by the data decomposition. In this paper, we assume that the data schema designer is responsible for data partitioning.

In general, the performance of our method highly depends upon the data redundancy level and the query workload. The higher the level of data redundancy level, the better our method will perform. Also, the more queries in the workload that can be answered by accessing the common documents only, the better our method will perform. As future work, we are exploring how to solve two problems within the data modeler: (1) How to measure the level of data redundancy when a data partition is given, (2) Given a query workload and a set of XML documents, how to form the best data partition so that our method will achieve the optimal performance. Note that if each original XML document is completely different from each other, no partitioning algorithm can produce partitions with high redundancy and our method is not suitable for such cases.

4 E-Catalog Maintenance

One of the challenges of managing data of varied schemata is maintaining the data when new objects, possibly of a different schema, are added. In our scheme, we need to address issues that arise when new data categories are added or old data categories are deleted. In this section, we show how to manage these tasks in our data model.

Deleting a category. Assume we want to remove an unwanted category whose categoryID is 102. Users will issue SQL delete statement on the original ecatalog view. Our EXTRICATE system will re-write the delete statement into corresponding delete statements on the decomposed tables, categoryInfo and productInfo.

Deleting individual documents. To delete an individual document, we simple remove a row that corresponds to the document in the productInfo table. Note that after many documents in a document category are deleted, the shared XML tree for that category may no longer be optimal (for instance, the remaining set of documents in the category may have more sharing). Hence a re-organization using the EXTRICATE data modeller may be necessary.

Adding individual documents of new category. When adding a collection of products belonging to a new category, we must identify the the shared document for the new category. We use the EXTRICATE data modeller to obtain the *diff*'s.

Adding an individual document of an existing category. Since the category of that document already exists, there must be at least one product in that category and there must be a shared XML tree for that category. When inserting a new document of that category, we compute a diff between the new document and the shared XML tree, and we store the diff output into the productInfo table. Because our difference model only supports insertions at this point, when the new document requires deletions in the shared document, we create new category for the new document. These documents can be re-integrated with the original category during re-organization. Extending our difference model to include deletions is part of our future work.

Adding a document with new product attributes. By new product attributes, we mean that the product attributes are new to the documents in the same category that are currently in the database. Note that the new product attribute may be encoded as an XML element or an XML attribute. Since the new product attribute does not occur in any other documents in the database, it will be stored as part of the diff in the productInfo table. No changes to the shared XML document is required. Note that XML (re-)validation and migration issues are beyond the scope of this paper. Our simple strategy for handling new attributes is therefore comparable to the vertical schema method in terms of cost-efficiency.

5   Experiments

We implemented a prototype of our method and investigated two issues in our experiments: (1) the amount of redundancy in real e-catalog data, and (2) the performance of EXTRICATE under different conditions. The EXTRICATE method exploits redundancy in the data; therefore, analyzing and understanding the amount of redundancy in real e-catalog data is essential. To investigate the performance of EXTRICATE, it is necessary to generate synthetic data that simulates different levels of redundancy in order to understand how our method performs under various conditions.

Redundancy in Real E-Catalog Data. We analyzed the product information of several categories of products at the on-line store, www.bestbuy.com and present the analysis on a representative subset of the data we collected.

In order to quantify the amount of redundancy in the data, we use the ratio of the data set size (in bytes) between the original data set and the decomposed data set,

$$redundancy = \frac{Size\ in\ bytes\ of\ original\ dataset}{Size\ in\ bytes\ of\ decomposed\ dataset}, \tag{1}$$

where the decomposed dataset is the size of all the shared XML document and the size of all the diff's produced by our method.

Table 1. Analysis of the redundancy in real e-catalog data

Source category	electronics/televisions/HDTVs
No. of products	90
Size of original XML	296,267 bytes
No. of shared XML	26
Size of shared XML	30,537 bytes
Size of diff XML	210,244 bytes
Redundancy	1.23

We use the EXTRICATE data modeler to decomposed the product information for all the HDTV products that we downloaded from www.bestbuy.com and measured the redundancy of the decomposed data with respect to the original data. The key statistics are tabulated in Table 1. We retained the website's categorization of the HDTV products into the "flat panel", "projection", and "up to 39 inches" sub-categories, and further partitioned the products in each of these sub-categories by their manufacturer Our results validate our assumption that e-catalog data contains significant amount of redundancy that can be exploited by EXTRICATE.

Performance of eXtricate. We investigate the performance characteristics of EXTRICATE over data with different characteristics as well as over different types of queries. Our goal is to understand how well our method performs on data and queries with different characteristics, and not so much on how well it performs on a single, specific set of real data and queries.

Data. We generated XML documents that are complete binary trees characterized by depth. A complete XML tree of depth d, will have $2^d - 1$ elements and 2^{d-1} leaf values. We simulate the amount of shared data between two XML documents by specifying the depth of the tree that is shared between them. For example, two XML trees of depth 6 with a shared depth of 4, will have common elements and structure up to a depth of 4. The sub-trees hanging off depth 4 will be different. The XML documents we used in our experiments have depth 6.

Each dataset consists of a number of XML documents from 4 categories. The amount of redundancy in each dataset is determined by (1) the number of documents in each category, and (2) the shared depth of the documents within each category.

Queries. We present our results for single constraint queries in this paper. We measure the performance of the same query on the original dataset (denoted in the plots by "query on original data") and on the decomposed dataset. For the decomposed dataset, we further measure the performance when the query requires both the shared documents and the diff's to answer the query (denoted in the plots by "query on shared + diff"), and when the query only requires accessing the shared document to answer the query (denoted in the plots by "query on shared". We run each query 1000 times on a multi-user machine running AIX unix and record the average elapsed time.

Performance vs Redundancy. We use the same approximate measure for redundancy as shown in Eq. 1 and measure the running time of the 3 different query types on different datasets with shared depth ranging from 2 to 5. The number of documents in each category, i.e., the number of documents sharing a single shared document, is set to 1000. We plot the running time against the redundancy of the data on Fig. 8(a). We observe that EXTRICATE provides significant improvement in query performance whether the diff's are used or not. When the query can be answered just by looking at the shared documents, the reduction in processing time is even more dramatic. Moreover, the performance improvements are not sensitive to the size of the shared XML tree among the documents in the same category.

Fig. 8(b) shows the same results in terms of speedup with respect to processing the query on the original, non-decomposed dataset. Observe that (1) the speedup for queries requiring access only to the shared document is much greater than the speedup for queries requiring access to the diff documents, (2) the speedups are decreasing slightly as the size of the shared tree increases. For queries requiring access only to the shared tree, increasing the size of the shared tree would logically lead to a smaller speedup and this is reflected in our experiments. For queries that require both the shared document and the diff's to answer, the decrease in speedup is mostly due to the increased processing time on the larger shared trees, and to a lesser extent on the number of sub-trees under the "⟨diff⟩" element in each diff document. The number of sub-trees under each "⟨diff⟩" element increases (even though each sub-tree is smaller) as the shared depth increases. When processing an XPath expression on the diff documents, this increases the number of sub-trees on which to match the XPath expression. For example if the shared depth is 5, the number of sub-trees in each diff document would be 2^4.

Performance vs Category Size. Another important factor affecting the amount of redundancy in the data is the number of documents sharing a single shared tree (this number is the same as the category size). We set the shared depth to 4 and vary the

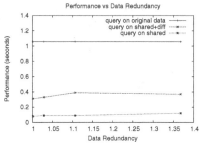
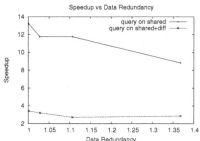

(a) Running time on single constraint queries over datasets with varying amount of shared data.

(b) Speedup of running the single-constraint queries on datasets with varying amount of shared data.

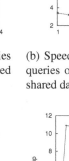
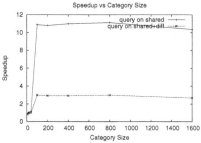

(c) Running time for single-constraint queries on datasets with varying number of documents sharing a single shared sub-tree.

(d) Speedup of running the single-constraint queries on datasets with varying number of documents sharing a single shared sub-tree.

Fig. 8. Performance of EXTRICATE over different conditions

number of documents within a category. The same queries were run and the elapsed time plotted in Fig. 8(d). Observe that the processing time remain constant for queries that only require access to the shared documents, because the table for shared documents is not affected by category size at all. When the category size is very small, the performance of EXTRICATE is almost comparable to running the query against the original data; however, when the category size becomes larger than 40, the speedup of our method becomes significant.

The speedups are plotted in Fig. 8(d). Our results match our intuition that as the number of documents sharing each shared document increases, the speedup increases.

6   Related Work

Managing e-catalog data using various relational DBMS strategies has been explored in [1,3,4,2]. The *horizontal schema* approach stores all the product information in a single table where the columns are the union of the attribute sets across all products and the rows represents the products. The *binary schema* [3,4] approach creates one table for each distinct attribute. Each table stores value-*OID* pairs. The *vertical schema* approach uses only one table with three columns: *OID*, *Attribute*, and *Value*. Each product is represented as a number of tuples in this table, one for each attribute-value combination. These approaches all have serious problems with data sparsity, schema evolution, usability, query processing complexity, difficulty in query optimization. Agrawal et al. proposed creating a horizontal view on top of a vertical schema [1] to ease the difficulty of writing queries on vertical schemata, but does not address the query performance problems. A middle-ware solution called *SAL*, Search Assistant Layer, has also been proposed in [2] to optimize queries written against vertical schemas. However, SAL is not able to leverage the full capability of the query optimizer, because it is not integrated with the DBMS engine.

On the XML front, a method using DBMS with native XML support to manage e-catalog data was proposed in [5]. The schema evolution problem is addressed using XML. Query performance is dependent on the XQuery/XPath processing engine inside the DBMS engine. Our paper builds upon their approach by decomposing the XML documents for storing product information in order to reduce storage redundancy and improve query performance.

Our decomposition-based storage model is also motivated by data compression techniques. While many XML compressors (such as XMill [6]) achieve higher compression rate, their goal is solely to minimize storage space. Query processing require decompression. In contrast, our goal is two pronged: reduce redundancy in storage and provide efficient query support. XGrind [7] is a query-friendly XML compressor that supports query processing in the compressed domain; however, XGrind is still a low level compressor relying on traditional encoding techniques (e.g., Huffman code) to encode strings in an XML document. Our EXTRICATE system does not perform string-level encoding, but models the redundancy in a collection of XML documents at a logical level.

XML normalization theory [8,9,10] also models the redundancy of XML data at the logical level. The fundamental difference between EXTRICATE and XML normalization is that XML normalization is a design-time process and requires the schema and the functional dependencies to be fully specified, whereas EXTRICATE makes no assumptions on the schema or the functional dependencies and is completely data-centric. Moreover XML normalization does not address transformation of queries to run on the normalized schema.

The problem of finding the intersection and diff of two XML trees is also a well studied problem. The survey article by Cobena et al. [17] provides a comprehensive description of all the techniques. In this paper, our focus is not on algorithms for find the intersection and diff, but on using these algorithms in a novel way to solve data management problems in E-commerce.

7 Conclusion

The native XML support in DBMSs promises to offer database users a new level of flexibility in managing semi-structured and unstructured data in relational DBMSs. However, this advantage may come with a significant cost in data storage and query processing if we do not use it wisely.

In this paper, we demonstrate how to combine the strengths of relational DBMSs and the flexibility of the XML support by a case study on managing E-commerce data.

We argue that while the e-catalog data appears to be lacking a unified structure, they do share common sub-structures and common values among different product descriptions, and the degree of such sharing could be very high for products in the same category. The extreme approach of storing each product description as a complete XML document without any schema constraint will thus result in huge overhead in terms of both storage and query processing. Handling the common parts and the differences separately leads to a natural approach: We only use the freedom when we really need it.

References

1. Agrawal, R., Somani, A., Xu, Y.: Storage and querying of e-commerce data. In: VLDB. Morgan Kaufmann, San Francisco (2001)
2. Wang, M., Chang, Y., Padmanabhan, S.: Supporting efficient parametric search of ecommerce data: A loosely-coupled solution. In: Chaudhri, A.B., Unland, R., Djeraba, C., Lindner, W. (eds.) EDBT 2002. LNCS, vol. 2490, pp. 409–426. Springer, Heidelberg (2002)
3. Copeland, G.P., Khoshafian, S.: A decomposition storage model. In: SIGMOD, pp. 268–279. ACM Press, New York (1985)
4. Khoshafian, S., Copeland, G.P., Jagodis, T., Boral, H., Valduriez, P.: A query processing strategy for the decomposed storage model. In: ICDE, pp. 636–643. IEEE, Los Alamitos (1987)
5. Lim, L., Wang, M.: Managing e-commerce catalogs in a DBMS with native XML support. In: ICEBE. IEEE, Los Alamitos (2005)
6. Liefke, H., Suciu, D.: XMill: An efficient compressor for XML data. In: Chen, W., Naughton, J.F., Bernstein, P.A. (eds.) SIGMOD, pp. 153–164 (2000)
7. Tolani, P., Haritsa, J.R.: XGrind: A query-friendly XML compressor. In: ICDE (2002)
8. Arenas, M., Libkin, L.: A normal form for XML documents. In: PODS, pp. 85–96 (2002)
9. Libkin, L.: Normalization theory for XML. In: Barbosa, D., Bonifati, A., Bellahsene, Z., Hunt, E., Unland, R. (eds.) XSym. LNCS, vol. 4704, pp. 1–13. Springer, Heidelberg (2007)
10. Arenas, M.: Normalization theory for XML. SIGMOD Rec. 35, 57–64 (2006)
11. Nicola, M., der Linden, B.V.: Native XML support in DB2 universal database. In: VLDB, pp. 1164–1174 (2005)
12. Ozcan, F., Cochrane, R., Pirahesh, H., Kleewein, J., Beyer, K., Josifovski, V., Zhang, C.: System RX: One part relational, one part XML. In: SIGMOD (2005)
13. Funderburk, J.E., Malaika, S., Reinwald, B.: XML programming with SQL/XML and XQuery. IBM Systems Journal 41 (2002)
14. Zhang, K.: A constrained edit distance between unordered labeled trees. Algorithmica 15, 205–222 (1996)
15. Wang, Y., DeWitt, D.J., yi Cai, J.: X-Diff: An effective change detection algorithm for XML documents. In: ICDE, pp. 519–530 (2003)
16. Chawathe, S.S., Rajaraman, A., Garcia-Molina, H., Widom, J.: Change detection in hierarchically structured information. In: SIGMOD, pp. 493–504. ACM Press, New York (1996)
17. Cobena, G., Abdessalem, T., Hinnach, Y.: A comparative study of XML diff tools (2002), http://www.deltaxml.com/pdf/is2004.pdf

Approximate Probabilistic Query Answering over Inconsistent Databases

Sergio Greco and Cristian Molinaro

DEIS, Univ. della Calabria, 87036 Rende, Italy
{greco,cmolinaro}@deis.unical.it

Abstract. The problem of managing and querying inconsistent databases has been deeply investigated in the last few years. Most of the approaches proposed so far rely on the notion of *repair* (a minimal set of delete/insert operations making the database consistent) and *consistent query answer* (the answer to a query is given by considering the set of 'repaired' databases). Since the problem of consistent query answering is hard in the general case, most of the proposed techniques have an exponential complexity, although for special classes of constraints and queries the problem becomes polynomial. A second problem with most of the proposed approaches is that repairs do not take into account update operations (they consider delete and insert operations only).

This paper presents a general framework where constraints consist of functional dependencies and queries may be expressed by positive relational algebra. The framework allows us to compute certain (i.e. tuples derivable from all or from none of the repaired databases) and uncertain query answers (i.e. tuples derivable from a proper not empty subset of the repaired databases). Each tuple in the answer is associated with a probability, which depends on the number of repaired databases from which the tuple can be derived. In the proposed framework, databases are repaired by means of update operations and repaired databases are stored by means of a "condensed" database, so that all the repaired databases can be derived by "expanding" the unique condensed database. A condensed database can be rewritten into a probabilistic database where each tuple is associated with an event (i.e. a boolean formula) and, thus, a probability value. The probabilistic query answer can be computed by querying the so obtained probabilistic database. As the complexity of querying probabilistic databases is $\#P$-complete, approximate probabilistic answers which are computable in polynomial time are considered.

1 Introduction

The problem of managing and querying inconsistent databases has been deeply investigated in the last few years. Most of the approaches proposed so far rely on the notion of *repair* (a minimal set of delete/insert operations making the database consistent) and *consistent query answer* (the answer to a query is given by considering the set of 'repaired' databases). Since the problem of consistent query answering is hard in the general case, most of the proposed techniques have an exponential complexity, although for special classes of constraints and queries (e.g., functional dependencies and queries consisting in checking if a tuple

Q. Li et al. (Eds.): ER 2008, LNCS 5231, pp. 311–325, 2008.

belongs to all the repaired databases) the problem becomes polynomial. Another problem with most of the proposed approaches is that repairs do not take into account update operations (they just consider delete and insert operations).

The next example shows how inconsistent databases are repaired and queried under the assumption that the only operations performed to repair the databases are insertion and deletion of tuples.

Example 1. Consider the relation schema *affiliation(Emp,Dept,City)* with the functional dependency $fd : Dept \rightarrow City$, stating that a department is located in a unique city. Consider now the following inconsistent relation *affiliation*:

affiliation

Emp	Dept	City
john	cs	rome
bob	cs	milan

According to most of the approaches proposed so far, the above database can be repaired by means of tuple deletions, thus the following repaired databases can be obtained:

$affiliation_1$ = { *affiliation(john, cs, rome)* }
$affiliation_2$ = { *affiliation(bob, cs, milan)*}

Consider the query $Q = \pi_{Emp}(\sigma_{Dept='cs'}affiliation)$ asking for the employees of the department *cs*. The consistent query answer [3,5,13] gives the employees *john* and *bob* as undefined, as *john* works for *cs* according to the first repaired database only, whereas *bob* works for *cs* according to the second repaired database only.   □

In the previous example, if we suppose that each tuple has an "unreliable" value only on the attribute $City$ and the remaining values are "reliable", then we would expect that the previous query gives both *john* and *bob* as certain, as the query does not regard the attribute $City$. Indeed, repairing inconsistent databases by means of tuple deletion eliminates useful information present in deleted tuples, e.g. information which is not involved in a constraint violation.

In order to cope with this problem, this paper presents a framework wherein inconsistent databases are repaired by means of tuple updates, as shown in the following example.

Example 2. Consider the inconsistent database *affiliation* of Example 1. It can be repaired by assigning the same value on the attribute $City$ to each tuple, that is we assign a unique city to the department *cs*. This value can be either *rome* or *milan*, as these values come from the source database. Thus, there exist two repaired databases, namely:

$affiliation_1$ = { *affiliation(john, cs, rome)*,   *affiliation(bob, cs, rome)* }
$affiliation_2$ = { *affiliation(john, cs, milan)*,   *affiliation(bob, cs, milan)* }

Consider the query Q of Example 1. By assuming the above repaired databases, Q gives the employees *john* and *bob* as certain, as they are derivable from all the repaired databases.   □

The technique presented in this paper allows us to compute certain (i.e. tuples derivable from all or from none of the repaired databases) and uncertain answers (i.e. tuples derivable from a proper not empty subset of the repaired databases). Moreover, each tuple in the answer is associated with a probability, which depends on the number of repaired databases from which the tuple can be derived (although the framework can be easily adapted so that the probabilities are determined by other criteria).

Example 3. Consider the following relation *emp*:

emp

Name	Dept
john	cs
john	math
bob	cs
bob	physics

which is inconsistent w.r.t. the functional dependency $fd : Name \rightarrow Dept$ and the query $Q = \pi_{Dept}(emp)$ asking for the departments of the employees. The intuition suggests that *cs* should be the most probable department as each employee could work for it, whereas *math* and *physics* should be less probable as only *john* could work for the former and only *bob* could work for the latter. The probabilistic answer gives $\{(cs, 3/4), (math, 2/4), (physics, 2/4)\}$ according to the previous consideration. Observe that, under the standard notion of consistent query answer, the departments *cs*, *math* and *physics* are undefined and there is no discrimination among them.   □

Thus, the proposed approach allow us to exploit better information in the source inconsistent database in two main aspects: (i) repairing by means of tuple updates, which is more fine-grained than the approaches based on tuple deletions, allows us to preserve useful information in the source database; (ii) probabilistic query answering allow us to discriminate among undefined tuples.

Related Work. Andritsos et al. [2] presented an approach for querying dirty databases containing duplicate tuples (i.e. inconsistent databases that violates a set of key constraints) where each duplicate is associated with a probability of being in the clean database. A technique for querying dirty databases is proposed. It consists in rewriting a query into an SQL query that computes each answer with the probability that the answer is in the clean database. The rewriting cannot be obtained in general as it is applicable only to a special class of select-project-join queries, called *rewritable queries*. The main difference between the approach presented in this paper and the one introduced in [2] is that we consider a more general framework, namely a special class of functional dependencies and positive relational algebra queries, and compute approximate probabilistic answers (i.e. answers whose associated probabilities are approximated), whereas the technique proposed by Andritsos et al. computes (exact) probabilistic answers for more restricted constraints and queries (key constraints and a subset of SPJ queries).

In [8] it has been shown that for every conjunctive query, the complexity of evaluating it on a probabilistic database is either PTIME or #P-complete, and an algorithm for deciding whether a given conjunctive query is PTIME or #P-complete is given. The problem of querying and managing probabilistic databases has been dealt with also in [7,9].

An approach for repairing inconsistent databases by means of tuple updates has been proposed in [17,4,18]. Specifically, [17] presents a notion of update-based repairing, and the construction of single databases, called *nuclei*, that can replace all (possibly infinitely many) repaired databases for the purpose of consistent query answering. The construction of nuclei for full dependencies and conjunctive queries is shown. Consistent query answering and constructing nuclei is generally intractable under update-based repairing. In [4] an approach for repairing inconsistent databases is proposed. In such a framework, a database which violates a set of functional and inclusion dependencies is repaired by modifying attribute values and by inserting new tuples. Each update operation has a cost. As finding a repaired database with minimum cost in this model is NP-complete, a heuristic approach is proposed.

Organization. The paper is organized as follows. Section 2 recalls some basic notions on querying and repairing inconsistent databases, and the probabilistic relational model presented in [12]. Section 3 presents our definition of repaired databases and a "condensed" form to represent the set of all repaired databases. Section 4 presents a notion of probabilistic query answering and shows how to compute an approximation of it in polynomial time. Finally, in Section 5 conclusions are drawn.

2 Preliminaries

It is assumed that the reader is familiar with relational databases and database queries [1,16]. This section first introduces preliminary notions on querying and repairing inconsistent databases, then presents the probabilistic relational model proposed in [12].

Querying and Repairing Inconsistent Databases. Database schemata contain knowledge on the structure of data, i.e. they give constraints on the form the data must have. The relationships among data are usually defined by constraints such as functional dependencies, inclusion dependencies and others. Generally, a database $\mathcal{DB}$ has an associated schema $\langle \mathcal{DS}, \mathcal{IC} \rangle$ defining the intentional properties of $\mathcal{DB}$: $\mathcal{DS}$ denotes the structure of the relations, while $\mathcal{IC}$ denotes the set of integrity constraints expressing semantic information over data. A database instance is inconsistent if it does not satisfy integrity constraints.

An id-repaired[1] database is a consistent instance minimally different from the original one. Thus, given a database $\mathcal{DB}$ and a set of integrity constraints $\mathcal{IC}$, $\mathcal{DB}'$ is an id-repaired database derived from $\mathcal{DB}$ if $\mathcal{DB}' \models \mathcal{IC}$ and the

---

[1] id-repaired database stands for repaired database obtained by means of insert and delete operations.

pair $(\mathcal{DB}' - \mathcal{DB}, \mathcal{DB} - \mathcal{DB}')$ is minimal, i.e. there is no database $\mathcal{DB}'' \neq \mathcal{DB}'$ such that $\mathcal{DB}'' \models \mathcal{IC}$ and both containements $\mathcal{DB}'' - \mathcal{DB} \subseteq \mathcal{DB}' - \mathcal{DB}$ and $\mathcal{DB} - \mathcal{DB}'' \subseteq \mathcal{DB} - \mathcal{DB}'$ hold. Thus, an id-repaired databases $\mathcal{DB}'$ is obtained from $\mathcal{DB}$ by means of a minimal set of insert and delete operations. Given a database $\mathcal{DB}$ and a set $\mathcal{IC}$ of integrity constraints, $\mathbf{DB_{id}}(\mathcal{DB}, \mathcal{IC})$ denotes the set of all the possible id-repaired databases for $\langle \mathcal{DB}, \mathcal{IC} \rangle$, that is the set of all repaired databases which are obtained by means of insert and delete operations.

A (relational) query Q is a pair $(g, \mathcal{P})$, where g is a predicate symbol denoting the output relation and $\mathcal{P}$ is the program (e.g. set of RA expressions) used to compute g. Given a database $\mathcal{DB}$, a set $\mathcal{IC}$ of integrity constraints and a relational query Q, the *consistent answer* [3] of Q over $\langle \mathcal{DB}, \mathcal{IC} \rangle$, denoted as $Q(\mathcal{DB}, \mathcal{IC})$, gives three sets, denoted as $Q(\mathcal{DB}, \mathcal{IC})^+$, $Q(\mathcal{DB}, \mathcal{IC})^-$ and $Q(\mathcal{DB}, \mathcal{IC})^u$. [4] These contain, respectively, the tuples which are *true* (i.e. belonging to [4] $\bigcap_{\mathcal{DB}_i \in \mathbf{DB_{id}}(\mathcal{DB}, \mathcal{IC})} Q(\mathcal{DB}_i)$), *false* (i.e. not belonging to $\bigcup_{\mathcal{DB}_i \in \mathbf{DB_{id}}(\mathcal{DB}, \mathcal{IC})} Q(\mathcal{DB}_i)$) and *undefined* (i.e. tuples which are neither true nor false).

In [13] it has been shown that given a database $\mathcal{DB}$, a set of integrity constraints $\mathcal{IC}$ and a query $Q = (g, \mathcal{P})$, then 1) checking if there exists a repair for $\mathcal{DB}$ such that the answer of Q is not empty is in Σ_2^P and $\mathcal{NP}$-hard, 2) checking whether the consistent answer of Q is not empty is in Π_2^P and $co\mathcal{NP}$-hard. In the same work it has been shown that when special constraints such as functional dependencies are considered, the problem of checking, for a given ground tuple t, whether (i) $t \in Q(\mathcal{DB}, \mathcal{IC})^+$ is $co\mathcal{NP}$-complete, (ii) $t \in Q(\mathcal{DB}, \mathcal{IC})^-$ is $co\mathcal{NP}$-complete, (iii) $t \in Q(\mathcal{DB}, \mathcal{IC})^u$ is $\mathcal{NP}$-complete. The problem becomes polynomial only when restricted functional dependencies and queries are considered (e.g. at most one functional dependency per relation and 'simple' conjunctive queries [6]).

Probabilistic Relational Model. We recall the probabilistic relational model presented in [12] (see also [9,10]). A *probabilistic relation* corresponds to an ordinary relation where the membership of a single tuple in the relation is affected by a probabilistic event. We distinguish between *basic* and *complex* events. Tuples of base relations are associated with basic events. Special events are the certain event $\top$, which is associated with deterministic tuples, and the impossible event $\bot$, which is associated with tuples that are not in the database. Each basic event e is associated with a (fixed) probability value denoted by $p(e)$; the probability of $\top$ is 1, whereas the probability of $\bot$ is 0. When new relations are derived by means of Probabilistic Relational Algebra (PRA) operators, each tuple in a derived relation depends on the tuples of the argument relation(s) from which it was derived. In order to express this relationship, we use complex events, which are Boolean combinations of events. Starting from the probabilities for the basic events, the probabilities of complex events can be computed by means of a function $\mathcal{P}$. The probability associated with a general event e is denoted by $Pr(e)$ and is equal to $p(e)$ if e is a basic event, whereas is equal to $\mathcal{P}(e)$ if e is a complex event. Observe that the function $\mathcal{P}$ takes into account the dependencies among basic events.

This model is based on an *intensional semantics*; this means that each tuple of a relation is associated with an event expression and the PRA operators also manipulate these expressions. The issue of associating probabilities with these expressions is dealt with separately. A probabilistic relational model based on an *extensional semantics* was proposed in [11]. In this model probabilities are attached to tuples; when applying an operator of the relational algebra, the probabilities of the result tuples are computed as a function of the tuple probabilities in the argument relation(s). This approach doesn't always work.

A probabilistic tuple t^p on a relation schema $R(W)$ is a pair $\langle t, e \rangle$, where t is a tuple over $R(W)$ and e is an event. A probabilistic relation on a relation schema $R(W)$ is a set of probabilistic tuples $t^p = \langle t, e \rangle$ such that t is defined over $R(W)$. A probabilistic database $\mathcal{DB}^p$ is a set of probabilistic relations plus a probabilistic function Pr. In the following, for a given probabilistic tuple t^p, t denotes the corresponding standard tuple; analogously, r and $\mathcal{DB}$ denote the (standard) relation and database corresponding to the probabilistic relation r^p and the probabilistic database $\mathcal{DB}^p$, respectively.

The PRA operators are defined as follows.

- *Selection.* Let r^p be a probabilistic relation

$$\sigma_\theta(r^p) = \{\langle t, e \rangle \mid \langle t, e \rangle \in r^p \wedge t \in \sigma_\theta(r)\}$$

- *Projection.* Let r^p be a probabilistic relation over $R(W)$ and A be a subset of W

$$\pi_A(r^p) = \{\langle t, e \rangle \mid t \in \pi_A r \wedge e = \bigvee_{\langle t', e' \rangle \in r^p \wedge\, t'[A]=t} e'\}$$

- *Cartesian product.* Let r^p and s^p be probabilistic relations

$$r^p \times s^p = \{\langle t_r.t_s, e_r \wedge e_s \rangle \mid \langle t_r, e_r \rangle \in r^p \wedge \langle t_s, e_s \rangle \in s^p\}$$

- *Union.* Let r^p be a probabilistic relation over $R(W)$ and s^p be a probabilistic relation over $S(W)$

$$r^p \cup s^p = \{\langle t, e \rangle \mid t \in r \cup s \wedge e = \bigvee_{\langle t, e' \rangle \in r^p \vee \langle t, e' \rangle \in s^p} e'\}$$

- *Difference.* Let r^p be a probabilistic relation over $R(W)$ and s^p be a probabilistic relation over $S(W)$

$$r^p - s^p = \{\langle t, e \rangle \mid \langle t, e \rangle \in r^p \wedge \not\exists \langle t, e' \rangle \in s^p\} \cup$$
$$\{\langle t, e_r \wedge \neg e_s \rangle \mid \langle t, e_r \rangle \in r^p \wedge \langle t, e_s \rangle \in s^p\}$$

Observe that the operators $\sigma, \pi, \times, \cup$ and $-$ are overloaded as we have used the same operators of standard relational algebra.

Example 4. Consider the probabilistic database $\mathcal{DB}^p$ consisting of the following probabilistic relations *emp* and *dept*:

emp

EName	Dept	
john	cs	e_1
john	math	e_2

dept

DName	City	
cs	rome	d_1
math	rome	d_2

Consider now the query:

$$Q = \pi_{City}(\sigma_{EName='john' \wedge Dept=DName}(emp \times dept))$$

asking for the cities where *john* works. In the evaluation of Q, firstly the cartesian products $emp \times dept$ is computed, giving the result below:

EName	Dept	DName	City	
john	cs	cs	rome	$e_1 \wedge d_1$
john	cs	math	rome	$e_1 \wedge d_2$
john	math	cs	rome	$e_2 \wedge d_1$
john	math	math	rome	$e_2 \wedge d_2$

Next, the selection operation $\sigma_{EName='john' \wedge Dept=DName}(emp \times dept)$ is computed and the following result is obtained:

EName	Dept	DName	City	
john	cs	cs	rome	$e_1 \wedge d_1$
john	math	math	rome	$e_2 \wedge d_2$

Finally, the projection operation $\pi_{City}(\sigma_{EName='john' \wedge Dept=DName}(emp \times dept))$ is computed, giving the result:

City	
rome	$(e_1 \wedge d_1) \vee (e_2 \wedge d_2)$

Thus, the answer contains *rome*, whose associated event is $(e_1 \wedge d_1) \vee (e_2 \wedge d_2)$; this means that *john* works in *rome* if either (i) he works for the department *cs* (event e_1) and *cs* is located in *rome* (event d_1), or (ii) he works for the department *math* (event e_2) and *math* is located in *rome* (event d_2).   □

We point out that, given a probabilistic database $\mathcal{DB}^p$ and a query Q, the probability associated with the tuples in $Q(\mathcal{DB}^p)$ is computed by means of the function Pr which takes into account the relations among basic events.

Example 5. Consider the probabilistic database $\mathcal{DB}^p$ and the query Q of Example 4. Given the probabilities for the basic events e_1, e_2, d_1, d_2 and assuming that all events are mutually independent $Q(\mathcal{DB}^p)$ gives the tuple *rome* along with its probability, namely $Pr((e_1 \wedge d_1) \vee (e_2 \wedge d_2)) = Pr(e_1) \times Pr(d_1) + Pr(e_2) \times Pr(d_2) - Pr(e_1) \times Pr(d_1) \times Pr(e_2) \times Pr(d_2)$.   □

3   Repairing

We assume two disjoint, infinite sets **dom** and **var** of *constants* and *variables* respectively. Each variable V has a domain $dom(V) \subseteq$ **dom** of possible values. A *symbol* is either a constant or a variable.

   A *condensed tuple ct* over a relation schema $R(W)$, where W is a set of attributes, is a total mapping from W to **dom** $\cup$ **var**; a *condensed relation* over $R(W)$ is a set of condensed tuples over the same schema $R(W)$, whereas a *condensed database* is a set of condensed relations. The value of ct on an attribute A in W is denoted $ct(A)$; this is extended so that for $Z \subseteq W$, $ct[Z]$ denotes the condensed tuple z over Z such that $ct(A) = z(A)$ for each $A \in Z$. The set of variables in ct is denoted by $var(ct)$, whereas the set of constants in ct is denoted by $const(ct)$. Analogously, for a given relation r (resp. database $\mathcal{DB}$), $var(r)$ and $const(r)$ (resp. $var(\mathcal{DB})$ and $const(\mathcal{DB})$) denote respectively the sets of variables and constants in r (resp. $\mathcal{DB}$). Moreover, ct (resp. r, $\mathcal{DB}$) is said to be *ground* if $var(ct) = \emptyset$ (resp. $var(r) = \emptyset$, $var(\mathcal{DB}) = \emptyset$). Ground condensed tuples (resp. relations, databases) are also called simply tuples (resp. relations, databases).

A *(ground) substitution* for a set of variables $\{V_1, \ldots, V_k\}$, $k \geq 0$, is a set of pairs $\{V_1/c_1, \ldots, V_k/c_k\}$ where $c_1, \ldots, c_k$ are constants such that $c_i \in dom(V_i)$ for $i = 1..k$. We also use the notation $\theta[1] = \{V \mid V/c \in \theta\}$ and $\theta[2] = \{c \mid V/c \in \theta\}$ to denote the sets of variables and constants in θ, respectively. $\theta(V) = c$ if there is a pair $V/c \in \theta$, otherwise $\theta(V) = V$.

The application of a substitution θ to a condensed tuple $ct = \langle p_1, \ldots, p_n \rangle$ is $\theta(ct) = \langle \theta(p_1), \ldots, \theta(p_n) \rangle$. Analogously, the application of a substitution θ to a condensed relation cr is $\theta(cr) = \{\theta(ct) \mid ct \in cr\}$, whereas the application of θ to a condensed database $\mathcal{DB}_c$ is $\theta(\mathcal{DB}_c) = \{\theta(cr) \mid cr \in \mathcal{DB}_c\}$.

Given a condensed relation cr (resp. database $\mathcal{DB}_c$), $\mathbf{G}(cr)$ (resp. $\mathbf{G}(\mathcal{DB}_c)$) denotes the set of all the (ground) relations (resp. databases) that can be obtained from cr (resp. $\mathcal{DB}_c$) by replacing all the variables in cr (resp. $\mathcal{DB}_c$) with constants belonging to the domains associated with variables.

Definition 1. *Canonical functional dependencies.* Let $R(W)$ be a relation schema and $\mathcal{FD}$ be a set of functional dependencies in standard form[2] over $R(W)$. $\mathcal{FD}$ is said to be in *canonical form* if $\forall X \to A \in \mathcal{FD}$ does not exist a functional dependency $Y \to B \in \mathcal{FD}$ such that $A \in Y$. $\qquad\square$

In the rest of the paper, we consider sets of functional dependencies in canonical form.

Let $R(W)$ be a relation schema, $\mathcal{FD}$ be a set of functional dependencies over $R(W)$ and r be an instance of $R(W)$. An *update operation* for r is a pair $u = (t, t')$ of tuples over $R(W)$ s.t. $t \in r \wedge t \neq t'$. The intuitive meaning of $u = (t, t')$ is that t is replaced by t', i.e. the updated relation obtained from r by applying u is $u(r) = r - \{t\} \cup \{t'\}$. Given a set of update operations $\mathcal{U}$, then we define the sets $\mathcal{U}^- = \{t \mid \exists (t, t') \in \mathcal{U}\}$ and $\mathcal{U}^+ = \{t' \mid \exists (t, t') \in \mathcal{U}\}$. We say that $\mathcal{U}$ is *coherent* if it does not contain two distinct update operations (t, t') and (t_1, t_2) such that either $t = t_1$ or $t = t_2$, that is (i) the same tuple t cannot be replaced by two distinct tuples t' and t_2, and (ii) a tuple t which is replaced by a tuple t' cannot be used to replace in turn a tuple t_1.

Given a set $\mathcal{U}$ of update operations for r, we denote by $\mathcal{U}(r)$ the updated relation obtained from r by applying all the update operations in $\mathcal{U}$, i.e. $\mathcal{U}(r) = r - \mathcal{U}^- \cup \mathcal{U}^+$. Moreover, we define the set $update(\mathcal{U}) = \{(t, A) \mid \exists (t, t') \in \mathcal{U}, A \in W \text{ s.t. } t(A) \neq t'(A)\}$. If a pair (t, A) is in $update(\mathcal{U})$, then we say that $\mathcal{U}$ *modifies the value of the tuple t on the attribute A.*

---

[2] We consider functional dependencies of the form $X \to A$, where X is a set of attributes whereas A is an attribute.

We say that the value of a tuple $t \in r$ on an attribute $A \in W$ is *uncertain* if there exists a tuple $t' \in r$ and a functional dependency $fd : X \to A \in \mathcal{FD}$ such that $\{t, t'\} \not\models fd$, that is $t[X] = t'[X]$ and $t(A) \neq t'(A)$. A set $\mathcal{U}$ of update operations for r is said to be *feasible* (w.r.t. r) if it modifies only uncertain values.

Definition 2. *Repair and repaired database.* Let $R(W)$ be a relation schema, $\mathcal{FD}$ be a set of functional dependencies over $R(W)$ and r be an instance of $R(W)$. A repair for $\langle r, \mathcal{FD} \rangle$ is a coherent and feasible set $\mathcal{U}$ of update operations for r such that (i) $\mathcal{U}(r) \models \mathcal{FD}$ and (ii) there is no set of update operations $\mathcal{U}'$ such that $update(\mathcal{U}') \subset update(\mathcal{U}) \wedge \mathcal{U}'(r) \models \mathcal{FD}$. The set of all the possible repaired relations for $\langle r, \mathcal{FD} \rangle$ is denoted as $\mathbf{DB_U}(r, \mathcal{FD})$. $\square$

Thus, a repair is a minimal set of attribute value modifications which makes a database consistent by modifying only uncertain values. Repaired relations are consistent relations derived from the source relation by means of repairs.

Given an inconsistent database $\mathcal{DB}$ and a set $\mathcal{FD}$ of functional dependencies, a repaired database is obtained by repairing each inconsistent relation in $\mathcal{DB}$. We denote by $\mathbf{DB_U}(\mathcal{DB}, \mathcal{FD})$ the set of all the repaired databases for $\langle \mathcal{DB}, \mathcal{FD} \rangle$.

Example 6. Consider the relation schema $emp(Name, Dept, City)$ with the functional dependencies $\mathcal{FD} = \{Name \to City, Dept \to City\}$. Consider now the following inconsistent relation r:

emp

Name	Dept	City
john	math	milan
john	cs	rome
bob	cs	venice
mary	physics	naples

Intuitively, in order to make the relation consistent the first three tuples should have the same value on the attribute $City$. There are three possible repairs for $\langle r, \mathcal{FD} \rangle$:

$$\mathcal{U}_1 = \{ (emp(john, cs, rome), \quad emp(john, cs, milan) \quad),$$
$$(emp(bob, cs, venice), \quad emp(bob, cs, milan) \quad) \}$$
$$\mathcal{U}_2 = \{ (emp(john, math, milan), emp(john, math, rome) \quad),$$
$$(emp(bob, cs, venice), \quad emp(bob, cs, rome) \quad) \}$$
$$\mathcal{U}_3 = \{ (emp(john, math, milan), emp(john, math, venice)),$$
$$(emp(john, cs, rome), \quad emp(john, cs, venice) \quad) \}$$

By applying the above repairs on r, the following repaired relations are obtained:

$$r_1 = \{ emp(john, math, milan), emp(john, cs, milan),$$
$$emp(bob, cs, milan), \quad emp(mary, physics, naples) \}$$
$$r_2 = \{ emp(john, math, rome), emp(john, cs, rome),$$
$$emp(bob, cs, rome), \quad emp(mary, physics, naples) \}$$
$$r_3 = \{ emp(john, math, venice), emp(john, cs, venice),$$
$$emp(bob, cs, venice), \quad emp(mary, physics, naples) \}$$

Therefore $\mathbf{DB_U}(r, \mathcal{FD}) = \{r_1, r_2, r_3\}$. $\square$

It is worth noting that, in the previous example, each repair updates the value of the attribute *City* so that all conflicting tuples have the same value for this attribute. The minimality guarantees that only values appearing in conflicting tuples are used. For instance, the following set of update actions

$$\mathcal{U} = \{ \ (\ emp(john, \ math,milan), \ emp(john, \ math, \ naples) \ ),$$
$$(\ emp(john, \ cs, \ rome), \quad emp(john, \ cs, \ naples) \quad),$$
$$(\ emp(bob, \ cs, \ venice), \quad emp(bob, \ cs, \ naples) \quad) \ \}$$

makes the database consistent, but as it is not minimal, it is not a repair.

Definition 3. *Condensed representation.* Let $R(W)$ be a relation schema, $\mathcal{FD}$ be a set of functional dependencies over $R(W)$ and r be an instance of $R(W)$. A condensed representation of all the repaired relations derivable from $\langle r, \mathcal{FD} \rangle$, denoted $r_{\mathcal{FD}}$, is a condensed relation s.t. $\mathbf{G}(r_{\mathcal{FD}}) = \mathbf{DB_U}(r, \mathcal{FD})$ and $var(r_{\mathcal{FD}})$ is minimal modulo renaming of variables. □

$\mathcal{DB}_{\mathcal{FD}}$ denotes the condensed database "representing" all the repaired databases derivable from $\langle \mathcal{DB}, \mathcal{FD} \rangle$, i.e. the condensed database such that $\mathbf{G}(\mathcal{DB}_{\mathcal{FD}}) = \mathbf{DB_U}(\mathcal{DB}, \mathcal{FD})$.

Example 7. Consider the inconsistent database r and the functional dependencies $\mathcal{FD}$ of Example 6. A condensed representation of all the possible repaired relations derivable from $\langle r, \mathcal{FD} \rangle$ is the following condensed relation $r_{\mathcal{FD}}$:

emp

Name	Dept	City
john	math	Y
john	cs	Y
bob	cs	Y
mary	physics	naples

$Y \in \{rome, milan, venice\}$

as $\mathbf{G}(r_{\mathcal{FD}}) = \mathbf{DB_U}(r, \mathcal{FD})$ and the set of variables introduced in $r_{\mathcal{FD}}$ is minimal. □

Theorem 1. *Given a database schema $\mathcal{DS}$, a set $\mathcal{FD}$ of functional dependencies over $\mathcal{DS}$ and an instance $\mathcal{DB}$ of $\mathcal{DS}$, then $\mathcal{DB}_{\mathcal{FD}}$ can be computed in polynomial time.* □

4   Querying

In this section we present a definition of probabilistic answer to queries over inconsistent databases. In particular, we first introduce the definition of probabilistic answer, where each tuple in the answer is associated with a probability (e.g., the fraction of repaired databases from which the tuple can be derived). Next, we show how to compute probabilistic query answer by querying a probabilistic database obtained from the condensed representation of all the repaired databases. Finally, we present how to compute an approximation of such an answer in polynomial time.

Definition 4. *Probabilistic query answer.* Given a database $\mathcal{DB}$, a set $\mathcal{FD}$ of functional dependencies and a relational query Q, the *probabilistic answer* of Q over $\langle \mathcal{DB}, \mathcal{FD} \rangle$, denoted as $Q^p(\mathcal{DB}, \mathcal{FD})$, is defined as follows

$$Q^p(\mathcal{DB}, \mathcal{FD}) = \{ (t, p_t) \mid \exists \mathcal{DB}_i \in \mathbf{DB_U}(\mathcal{DB}, \mathcal{FD}) \text{ s.t. } t \in Q(\mathcal{DB}_i),$$

$$p_t = \frac{|\{\mathcal{DB}_i | \mathcal{DB}_i \in \mathbf{DB_U}(\mathcal{DB}, \mathcal{FD}) \wedge t \in Q(\mathcal{DB}_i)\}|}{|\mathbf{DB_U}(\mathcal{DB}, \mathcal{FD})|} \}$$ ☐

The probabilistic answer gives a set of tuples along with their probabilities, where the probability of a tuple t is defined as the percentage of the repaired databases which give t by applying Q over them. It is worth noting that, unlike standard consistent answers, probabilistic answers allow us to discriminate among undefined tuples, giving them a measure of uncertainty. The tuples in a probabilistic answer can be ranked according to their probabilities, e.g. by decreasing probability.

Moreover, as the number of repaired databases can be exponential in the size of the database, the complexity of computing probabilistic answers using the formula of Definition 4 is also exponential. Next, we present a different method for computing probabilistic query answers over inconsistent databases.

Given two condensed tuples ct_1 and ct_2 and a substitution θ, we say that ct_1 subsumes ct_2 (or equivalently, ct_2 is an instance of ct_1) under θ, written as $ct_1 \sqsupseteq_\theta ct_2$, if $ct_2 = \theta(ct_1)$ and $\theta[1] \subseteq var(ct_1)$. Moreover, we say that $ct_1 \sqsupseteq_\theta ct_2$ if ct_2 is ground. Observe that for any two distinct tuples ct_1 and ct_2, $ct_1 \sqsupseteq_\theta ct_2$ implies that $ct_2 \not\sqsupseteq_\theta ct_1$.

The following definition introduces the concept of probabilistic relation derived from a (possibly inconsistent) relation.

Definition 5. *Derivation of probabilistic relations.* Let r be a relation and $\mathcal{FD}$ a set of functional dependencies over a relation schema $R(W)$. Let $r_{\mathcal{FD}}$ be the condensed representation for $\langle r, \mathcal{FD} \rangle$, then $r^p_{\mathcal{FD}}$ denotes the probabilistic relation derived from $r_{\mathcal{FD}}$ as follows:

$$r^p_{\mathcal{FD}} = \{ \langle t, e_t \rangle \mid \exists ct \in r_{\mathcal{FD}} \wedge \exists \theta \text{ s.t. } ct \sqsupseteq_\theta t \wedge e_t = \bigwedge_{X/c \in \theta} X/c \}$$

where $p(e_t) = p(\bigwedge_{X/c \in \theta} X/c)$ is computed by considering the standard probabilistic function and assuming that

- two events X/c_1 and X/c_2, where $c_1 \neq c_2$, are disjoint;
- two events X/c_1 and Y/c_2, with $X \neq Y$, are independent;
- $Pr(X/c) = \frac{1}{|dom(X)|}$.   ☐

Observe that, as said before, for deterministic tuples (i.e. probabilistic tuples $\langle t, e_t \rangle$ such that e_t is empty), it is assumed that $e_t = \top$ so that $Pr(\top) = 1$. We recall that a condensed representation $r_{\mathcal{FD}}$ of a set of repaired relations contains variables in place of uncertain values. In order to obtain a consistent repaired relation from $r_{\mathcal{FD}}$, for each variable we have to replace every occurrence of it with the same value (taken from its domain). This consideration is reflected by the first assumption in the previous definition. The second assumption states that values assigned to different variables are independent. As a variable V has

$n = |dom(V)|$ possible values, the probability of an event V/c (i.e. the value c is assigned to the variable V) is $\frac{1}{n}$, as stated by the last assumption in the above definition.

It is worth noting that the definition above does not take into account the number of occurrences of a value. In order to also consider the number of occurrences of values, the above probability function could be rewritten as $Pr(X/c) = \#c_X/\#X$, where $\#c_X$ is the number of occurrences of c in the source relation corresponding to X in the condensed relation and $\#X$ is the number of occurrence of X in the condensed relation. Clearly, if each value occurs once the probability function coincides with the one of Definition 5.

Example 8. Consider the database schema $r(A, B, C)$ with the functional dependency $fd = A \rightarrow B$ and the instance $R = \{r(a_1, b_1, c_1), r(a_1, b_2, c_2), r(a_1, b_1, c_3)\}$. The two repaired databases $R_1 = \{r(a_1, b_1, c_1), r(a_1, b_1, c_2), r(a_1, b_1, c_3)\}$ and $R_2 = \{r(a_1, b_2, c_1), r(a_1, b_2, c_2), r(a_1, b_2, c_3)\}$ are obtained by replacing, respectively, the unique occurrence of b_2 with b_1 and the two occurrences of b_1 with b_2. As the derived condensed relation is $R_{fd} = \{r(a_1, X, c_1), r(a_1, X, c_2), r(a_1, X, c_3)\}$ with $X \in \{b_1, b_2\}$, we have that $Pr(X/b_1) = 2/3$ and $Pr(X/b_2) = 1/3$. □

Given a probabilistic relation $r^p_{\mathcal{FD}}$, $r^b_{\mathcal{FD}}$ denotes the set of tuples $\{t|\langle t, e_t \rangle \in r^p_{\mathcal{FD}}\}$. Given a condensed representation $\mathcal{DB}_{\mathcal{FD}}$ of all the repaired databases for $\langle \mathcal{DB}, \mathcal{FD} \rangle$, the probabilistic database derived from $\mathcal{DB}_{\mathcal{FD}}$ will be denoted by $\mathcal{DB}^p_{\mathcal{FD}}$, whereas $\mathcal{DB}^b_{\mathcal{FD}}$ denotes the set of relations $\{r^b_{\mathcal{FD}}|r^p_{\mathcal{FD}} \in \mathcal{DB}^p_{\mathcal{FD}}\}$.

Example 9. Consider the inconsistent relation *affiliation* and the functional dependencies *fd* of Example 1. A condensed representation of all the repaired databases for $\langle affiliation, \{fd\} \rangle$ is as follows:

$affiliation_{fd}$

Emp	Dept	City
john	cs	X
bob	cs	X

$X \in \{rome, milan\}$

The above condensed relation can be "expanded" into the following probabilistic relation:

$affiliation^p_{fd}$

Emp	Dept	City	
john	cs	rome	X/rome
john	cs	milan	X/milan
bob	cs	rome	X/rome
bob	cs	milan	X/milan

where $X/rome$ and $X/milan$ are disjoint events and the probability of each of them is 0.5. The relation $affiliation^b_{fd}$ is equal to the projection of $affiliation^p_{fd}$ over the attributes $Emp, Dept$ and $City$. □

Theorem 2. *Given a database $\mathcal{DB}$ and a set of functional dependencies $\mathcal{FD}$,* $\mathbf{DB_U}(\mathcal{DB}, \mathcal{FD}) = \mathbf{DB_{id}}(\mathcal{DB}^b_{\mathcal{FD}}, \mathcal{FD})$. □

The previous theorem states that the repaired databases for $\langle \mathcal{DB}, \mathcal{FD} \rangle$ obtained by means of tuple updates, can be computed by repairing the database $\mathcal{DB}^b_{\mathcal{FD}}$ by means of insertion and deletion of tuples.

Theorem 3. *Given a database $\mathcal{DB}$, a set $\mathcal{FD}$ of functional dependencies and a relational query Q, then*

$$Q^p(\mathcal{DB}, \mathcal{FD}) = Q(\mathcal{DB}^p_{\mathcal{FD}})$$ □

The previous theorem states that given a database $\mathcal{DB}$, a set $\mathcal{FD}$ of functional dependencies and a relational query Q, the probabilistic query answer $Q^p(\mathcal{DB}, \mathcal{FD})$ can be computed as follows:

- firstly, a condensed representation of all the repaired databases for $\langle \mathcal{DB}, \mathcal{FD} \rangle$, namely $\mathcal{DB}_{\mathcal{FD}}$, is derived;
- next, $\mathcal{DB}_{\mathcal{FD}}$ is converted into a probabilistic database $\mathcal{DB}^p_{\mathcal{FD}}$;
- finally, the intensional evaluation of Q over $\mathcal{DB}^p_{\mathcal{FD}}$ is computed and probabilities to each tuple in the answer are assigned.

As computing the probability of an event e of an answer tuple is a #P-complete problem, next we present an approach for computing approximate probabilistic answers in polynomial time.

Approximate Probabilistic Query Answering. In this section we consider positive relational queries, that is queries using the relational operators σ, π, $\times$ and $\cup$. Moreover, we assume that PRA operators compute events written as DNF formulae, that is events are of the form $C_1 \vee \ldots \vee C_n$, where each C_i is a conjunction of events of the form X/c_X and events appearing more than one time in a conjunction are considered once.

Given an event $e = C_1 \vee \ldots \vee C_n$, its probability $Pr(e)$ can be computed by applying the well-known inclusion-exclusion formula, i.e.

$$Pr(e) = \sum_{k=1}^{n} (-1)^{k+1} \sum_{1 \leq i_1 < \ldots < i_k \leq n} Pr(C_{i_1} \wedge \ldots \wedge C_{i_k})$$

where the probability of a conjunction of events $C = e_1 \wedge \ldots \wedge e_k$ is equal to $Pr(e_1) \times \ldots \times Pr(e_k)$ if C does not contain two events X/c_1 and X/c_2 with $c_1 \neq c_2$, otherwise it is equal to 0.

The issue of approximating an inclusion-exclusion formula has been dealt with in [15,14]. In particular, a method to approximate an inclusion-exclusion formula in polynomial time has been proposed in [14]. Specifically, given an event $e = C_1 \vee \ldots \vee C_n$ and the probabilities of all the j-wise conjunctions of C_i for $j = 1..k$, $Pr(e)$ can be approximated with an error of $e^{-\Omega(\frac{k^2}{n \log n})}$. We denote by $Pr_k(e)$ the so obtained approximation of $Pr(e)$.

Definition 6. *Approximate probabilistic answer.* Given a database $\mathcal{DB}$, a set $\mathcal{FD}$ of functional dependencies and a relational query Q, the *k-approximate probabilistic answer* of Q over $\langle \mathcal{DB}, \mathcal{FD} \rangle$, denoted as $AQ_k(\mathcal{DB}, \mathcal{FD})$, is defined as follows

$$AQ_k(\mathcal{DB}, \mathcal{FD}) = \{\langle t, a_t \rangle \mid \exists \langle t, e_t \rangle \in Q(\mathcal{DB}^p_{\mathcal{FD}}) \text{ and } a_t = Pr_k(e_t)\} \qquad \square$$

Theorem 4. *Given a database $\mathcal{DB}$, a set $\mathcal{FD}$ of functional dependencies and a relational query Q, the k-approximate probabilistic answer of Q over $\langle \mathcal{DB}, \mathcal{FD} \rangle$ can be computed in polynomial time.* $\qquad \square$

5   Conclusions

This paper has presented a general framework for querying inconsistent databases where constraints consist of functional dependencies and queries may be expressed by positive relational algebra. The framework allows us to compute certain (i.e. tuples derivable from all or from none of the repaired databases) and uncertain query answers (i.e. tuples derivable from a proper not empty subset of the repaired databases). Each tuple in the answer is associated with a probability, which depends on the number of repaired databases from which the tuple can be derived. In our framework database are repaired by means of update operations and repaired databases are stored by means of a "condensed" database, so that all repaired databases can be derived by "expanding" the unique condensed database. A condensed database can be rewritten into a probabilistic database where each tuple is associated with an event (i.e. a boolean formula) and, thus, a probability value. The probabilistic query answer can be computed by querying the so obtained probabilistic database. As the complexity of querying probabilistic databases is $\#P$-complete, techniques computing approximate probabilistic answers in polynomial time have been used.

References

1. Abiteboul, S., Hull, R., Vianu, V.: Foundations of Databases. Addison-Wesley, Reading (1994)
2. Andritsos, P., Fuxman, A., Miller, R.J.: Clean Answers over Dirty Databases: A Probabilistic Approach. In: Proc. Int. Conf. on Data Engineering, vol. 30 (2006)
3. Arenas, M., Bertossi, L., Chomicki, J.: Consistent query answers in inconsistent databases. In: Proc. Symp. on Principles of Database Systems, pp. 68–79 (1999)
4. Bohannon, P., Flaster, M., Fan, W., Rastogi, R.: A Cost-Based Model and Effective Heuristic for Repairing Constraints by Value Modification. In: SIGMOD Conference, pp. 143–154 (2005)
5. Chomicki, J.: Consistent Query Answering: Five Easy Pieces. In: Proc. Int. Conf. on database Theory, pp. 1–17 (2007)
6. Chomicki, J., Marcinkowski, J.: Minimal-change integrity maintenance using tuple deletions. Information & Compututation 197(1-2), 90–121 (2005)
7. Dalvi, N., Suciu, D.: Management of Probabilistic Data Foundations and Challenges. In: Proc. ACM Symp. on Principles of Database Systems, pp. 1–12 (2007)

8. Dalvi, N., Suciu, D.: The Dichotomy of Conjunctive Queries on probabilistic Structures. In: Proc. ACM Symp. on Principles of Database Systems, pp. 293–302 (2007)
9. Dalvi, N., Suciu, D.: Efficient Query Evaluation on Probabilistic Databases. In: Proc. Int. Conf. on Very Large Data Bases, pp. 864–875 (2005)
10. Dey, D., Sarkar, S.: A Probabilistic Relational Model and Algebra. ACM Transanctions on Database Systems 21(3), 339–369 (1996)
11. Fuhr, N.: A Probabilistic Relational Model for the Integration of IR and Databases. In: Int. Conf. on Research and Development in Information Retrieval, pp. 309–317 (1993)
12. Fuhr, N., Rolleke, T.: A Probabilistic Relational Algebra for the Integration of Information Retrieval and Database Systems. ACM TODS 15(1), 32–66 (1997)
13. Greco, G., Greco, S., Zumpano, E.: A Logical Framework for Querying and Repairing Inconsistent Databases. IEEE TKDE 15(6), 1389–1408 (2003)
14. Kahn, J., Linial, N., Samorodnitsky, A.: Inclusion-Exclusion: Exact and Approximate. Combinatorica 16(4), 465–477 (1996)
15. Linial, N., Nisan, N.: Approximate Inclusion-Exclusion. In: Symposium on the Theory of Computing, pp. 260–270 (1990)
16. Ullman, J.K.: Principles of Data and Knowledge-Base Systems, vol. 1, 2. Computer Science Press, New York (1988)
17. Wijsen, J.: Database Repairing Using Updates. ACM Transactions on Database Systems 30(3), 722–768 (2005)
18. Wijsen, J.: Project-Join-Repair: An Approach to Consistent Query Answering Under Functional Dependencies. In: Proc. FQAS Conf., pp. 1–12 (2006)

Conjunctive Query Containment
under Access Limitations

Andrea Calì[1,3] and Davide Martinenghi[2]

[1] Oxford-Man Institute of Quantitative Finance
University of Oxford, UK
[2] Dip. di Elettronica e Informazione
Politecnico di Milano, Italy
[3] Computing Laboratory
University of Oxford, UK
andrea.cali@comlab.ox.ac.uk, martinen@elet.polimi.it

Abstract. Access limitations may occur when querying data sources over the web or heterogeneous data sources presented as relational tables: this happens, for instance, in Data Exchange and Integration, Data Warehousing, and Web Information Systems. Access limitations force certain attributes to be selected in order to access the tables. It is known that evaluating a conjunctive query under such access restrictions amounts to evaluating a possibly recursive Datalog program. We address the problem of checking containment of conjunctive queries under access limitations, which is highly relevant in query optimization. Checking containment in such a setting would amount to checking containment of recursive Datalog programs of a certain class, while, for general Datalog programs, this problem is undecidable. We propose a decision procedure for query containment based on the novel notion of crayfish-chase, showing that containment can be decided in co-NEXPTIME, which improves upon the known bound of 2EXPTIME. Moreover, by means of a direct proof, our technique provides a new insight into the structure of the problem.

1   Introduction

In Data Exchange and Integration [11,14,24], Data Warehousing, and Web Information Systems, querying heterogeneous data sources, possibly on the web, is a crucial issue. In this scenario, it is often the case that data sources impose *access limitations*, i.e., they require that the query that is executed on them has a special form. In particular, in the relational case, certain (fixed) attributes are required to be selected, i.e., associated to a constant. This is true, for instance, when the data source is accessible through a web form, that requires some fields to be filled in, or in some legacy databases.

The presence of access limitations significantly complicates query processing; in particular, as shown in [23,17,19], it requires the evaluation of a recursive query plan, which can be suitably expressed in Datalog.

Q. Li et al. (Eds.): ER 2008, LNCS 5231, pp. 326–340, 2008.

Example 1. Consider the following relational sources: $r_1(Title, City, Artist)$, representing information about concerts, with song title, city of performance, and artist name, and requiring the second attribute to be selected; $r_2(Artist, Nation, City)$, representing name, nationality and city of birth of artists, and requiring the first attribute to be selected. In this case, given the conjunctive query

$$q(A) \leftarrow r_2(A, italian, modena)$$

asking for names of Italian artists born in Modena, we notice that q cannot be immediately evaluated, since r_2 requires the first attribute to be bound to a constant (selected). However, the two attributes named *City* in r_1 and r_2 both represent city names, and similarly the attributes named *Artist* represent artist names.[1] In such a case, we can use names of artists extracted from r_1 to access r_2 and thus extract tuples that may contribute to the answer. More precisely, we start from the constant 'modena', present in the query, and access r_1; this will return tuples with new artist names; such constants (artist names) can be used to access r_2. In turn, new tuples from r_2 may provide new constants representing city names, that can be used to access r_1, and so on. Once this recursive process has terminated, we have retrieved all obtainable tuples that contribute to the answer.   □

Since accessing sources may be costly, especially on the web, an important issue is how to optimize query evaluation. Query containment [15,6] is a well-recognized problem in query evaluation and optimization, in particular in Data Integration and Exchange; containment between two queries q_1, q_2 holds if the result of q_1 is always a subset of the result of q_2, independently of the database on which the queries are evaluated.

In this paper we address the problem of checking containment of conjunctive queries in the presence of access limitations on the data sources. In particular:

1. We clearly state the problem in the case of access limitations, showing that it amounts to checking containment between two recursive Datalog programs (problem that is, in general, undecidable).
2. We introduce a novel formal tool to check containment of a conjunctive query into another under access limitations, namely the *crayfish-chase*, that is a set of databases that are representative of all databases that provide an answer to a query. The crayfish-chase is in general an infinite set.
3. We give a direct proof of the decidability of containment in this setting, by showing that, in order to check containment, it is sufficient to consider databases in the crayfish-chase whose size does not exceed a certain limit.
4. We provide an upper bound to the complexity of conjunctive query containment, showing that it can be decided in co-NEXPTIME, which improves the known bound of 2EXPTIME.

Finally, besides achieving a better worst-case complexity upper bound, the new technique provides an insight into the query containment problem, that paves

---
[1] In the following, this will be represented by the notion of *abstract domain*.

the way to the investigation of the containment problem under limitations for more expressive classes of queries, and under database dependencies.

2 Preliminaries

In this section we present the formal framework in which we address the problem of query containment.

We consider relations as sets of facts whose arguments are values belonging to given domains. Instead of using concrete domains, such as Integer or String, we deal with *abstract domains*, which have an underlying concrete domain, but represent information at a higher level of abstraction, which, referring to Example 1, distinguishes, e.g., strings representing artist names from strings representing song titles. Access limitations on a relation are constraints that impose that certain attributes must be *selected* (bound to a constant) for the relation to be accessed. More formally, a schema with access limitations is a pair $\langle \mathcal{R}, \Lambda \rangle$, where *(i)* $\mathcal{R}$ is a set of relational predicates, each with an associated *arity*; *(ii)* every attribute of a relational predicate $r \in \mathcal{R}$ has exactly one *abstract domain*; *(iii)* Λ is a set of access limitations, that specifies, for every attribute of every relational predicate, whether it is an *input* or an *output* attribute; in order to access a relation in a query, all input attributes must be selected. For convenience of notation, we indicate the access limitations of each relation as a sequence, of 'i' and 'o' symbols written as a superscript in the signature of the relation; an 'i' (resp., 'o') indicates that the corresponding argument is an input (resp., output) argument. A signature has the form $r^{\Lambda_r}(A_1, \ldots, A_n)$, where r is the relation name, n is the arity of r, Λ_r its access limitations, and each A_i is an abstract domain. A *relation* over such a signature is a set of facts of the form $r(c_1, \ldots, c_n)$ such that each c_i is a value belonging to abstract domain A_i. A *(database) instance* of a schema $\mathcal{S}$ is a union of relations, one over each signature in $\mathcal{S}$, i.e., it is a set of facts. In the following, we assume two fixed domains: a non-empty set Δ of constants and, for technical reasons, an infinite domain Δ_F of *fresh* constants. We call *concrete* those databases whose values belong to Δ and *virtual* those databases whose values belong to Δ_F; we also assume that constants in Δ_F cannot appear in queries. We sometimes indicate a sequence of terms (i.e., variables or constants) $t_1, \ldots, t_n$ as t, its length n as $|t|$, and similarly a tuple $\langle t_1, \ldots, t_n \rangle$ as $\langle t \rangle$, and its length n as $|\langle t \rangle|$. A *conjunctive query* (CQ) q of arity n over a schema $\mathcal{S}$ is written in the form

$$q(\boldsymbol{X}) \; \leftarrow \; conj(\boldsymbol{X}, \boldsymbol{Y})$$

where $|\boldsymbol{X}| = n$, $q(\boldsymbol{X})$ is called the *head* of q, $conj(\boldsymbol{X}, \boldsymbol{Y})$ is called the *body* of q and is a conjunction of atoms involving the variables in $\boldsymbol{X}$ and $\boldsymbol{Y}$ and possibly some constants, and the predicate symbols of the atoms are in $\mathcal{S}$; $\langle \boldsymbol{X} \rangle$ is denoted as head(q), the set of atoms in the body is denoted as body(q), and $|q|$ denotes $|\text{body}(q)|$. The set of constants appearing in q is denoted const(q), the set of variables var(q). A set of atoms $\mathcal{N}$ is *connected* if the non-directed graph $(\mathcal{N}, \mathcal{A})$ is connected, where $\mathcal{N}$ is the set of nodes, and $\mathcal{A}$ is the set containing exactly

$$\rho_1 : \qquad\qquad q(A) \leftarrow \hat{r}_2(A, \textit{italian}, \textit{modena})$$
$$\rho_2 : \qquad \hat{r}_1(T, C, A) \leftarrow r_1(T, C, A), dom_C(C)$$
$$\rho_3 : \qquad \hat{r}_2(A, N, C) \leftarrow r_2(A, N, C), dom_A(A)$$
$$\rho_4 : \qquad\quad dom_T(T) \leftarrow \hat{r}_1(T, C, A)$$
$$\rho_5 : \qquad\quad dom_C(C) \leftarrow \hat{r}_1(T, C, A)$$
$$\rho_6 : \qquad\quad dom_A(A) \leftarrow \hat{r}_1(T, C, A)$$
$$\rho_7 : \qquad\quad dom_A(A) \leftarrow \hat{r}_2(A, N, C)$$
$$\rho_8 : \qquad\quad dom_N(N) \leftarrow \hat{r}_2(A, N, C)$$
$$\rho_9 : \qquad\quad dom_C(C) \leftarrow \hat{r}_2(A, N, C)$$
$$\rho_{10} : \; dom_N(\textit{italian})$$
$$\rho_{11} : dom_C(\textit{modena})$$

Fig. 1. Datalog program for Example 2

all arcs between any two atoms in $\mathcal{N}$ that share a variable or a constant. A CQ q is *connected* if body(q) is. Every maximal subset of body(q) that is connected is called a *connected part* of q.

In the following we shall extensively use the notion of *mapping* from terms to terms, and typically we will map variables to terms, or fresh constants in Δ_F to constants in Δ. The term resulting from the application of such a mapping μ to a term t is written $\mu(t)$; note that μ also induces a mapping from a tuple $\theta = \langle t_1, \ldots, t_n \rangle$ to another tuple indicated $\mu(\theta) = \langle \mu(t_1), \ldots, \mu(t_n) \rangle$, from a fact $f = r(t_1, \ldots, t_n)$ to another fact indicated $\mu(f) = r(\mu(t_1), \ldots, \mu(t_n))$, and from a database $D = \{f_1, \ldots, f_m\}$ to another database indicated $\mu(D) = \{\mu(f_1), \ldots, \mu(f_m)\}$. A *substitution mapping* (or, simply, substitution) is a mapping from terms to terms that sends every constant into itself[2]; a substitution is *grounding* for a set of variables $\mathcal{V}$ if it sends each variable in $\mathcal{V}$ into a constant.

Given a database D, the *answer* $q(D)$ to a CQ q on D is the set of tuples $\langle c \rangle$ of constants, with $|c| = |\text{head}(q)|$, such that there is a substitution that sends body(q) to facts of D and head(q) to $\langle c \rangle$.

In the presence of access limitations on the sources, queries cannot be evaluated as in the traditional case, as will be shown in Example 2. Given a query over the data sources, an algorithm exists [17] that retrieves all the *obtainable* tuples in the answer to the query. Such an algorithm consists in the evaluation of a suitable Datalog program which extracts all obtainable tuples starting from a set of initial values, each with an associated abstract domain, as described in Example 1. The Datalog program, whose construction is sketched in Example 2, encodes the limitations on the sources that must be respected during evaluation of the query. The evaluation of the Datalog program is done as follows: starting from a set of initial values, that must include those appearing in the query, we access all the relations we can, according to their access limitations. With the new facts obtained (if any), we obtain new values with which we can repeat the process and access the relations again, until we have no way of making new accesses. The program extracts all facts obtainable while respecting the access limitations, but there may be facts in the sources that cannot be retrieved.

---

[2] Substitutions are sometimes written in postfix notation. Here we use infix notation.

Given a query q posed over a schema $\mathcal{S} = \langle \mathcal{R}, \Lambda \rangle$, a set of constants $I \subseteq \Delta$, and a database D for $\mathcal{S}$, we denote the answers obtained through the recursive evaluation described above as $\mathrm{ans}(q, \mathcal{S}, D, I)$. The tuples or facts extracted from D starting from I and respecting Λ are said to be Λ, I-*obtainable*. Notice that in general $\mathrm{ans}(q, \mathcal{S}, D, I) \subseteq q(D)$.

Example 2. Consider again Example 1, with $r_1^{oio}(T, C, A)$ and $r_2^{ioo}(A, N, C)$. The Datalog program generated by the algorithm of [17] for the query $q(A) \leftarrow r_2(A, italian, modena)$ is shown in Figure 1. The query is rewritten over the caches (rule ρ_1) defined in the cache rules ρ_2 and ρ_3; these also ensure that the facts that are stored in the caches are retrieved from the sources according to the access limitations. Rules $\rho_4 - \rho_9$ are the domain rules. Finally, ρ_{10}, ρ_{11} are facts assigning the right abstract domain to the initial constants. $\square$

We now come to the problem of containment. Since, in the presence of access limitations, the only way of accessing the sources to answer a query is to extract the facts recursively as described above, we will define the containment between two CQs by considering this query answering technique. As for the set of initial constants, in principle we may have additional constants with respect to those appearing in the two queries; therefore, as set of initial constants, we shall consider a superset of the union of the constants appearing in the two queries.

Definition 1. *Consider two CQs q_1, q_2 over a schema $\mathcal{S} = \langle \mathcal{R}, \Lambda \rangle$, and a set I such that $\mathrm{const}(q_1) \cup \mathrm{const}(q_2) \subseteq I \subseteq \Delta$; we say that q_1 is contained in q_2 under Λ with respect to I, denoted $q_1 \subseteq_{\Lambda, I} q_2$, if, for every database D for $\mathcal{R}$, we have $\mathrm{ans}(q_1, \mathcal{S}, D, I) \subseteq \mathrm{ans}(q_2, \mathcal{S}, D, I)$.*

From the previous definition, it follows that checking containment would amount to checking containment between two recursive Datalog programs, which in general is an undecidable problem [1]. However, in the following we will show that, due to the special form of the programs, checking containment under access limitations is indeed decidable.

3   Containment under Access Limitations

We start by observing that query containment under access limitations is essentially different from ordinary query containment, because, although the latter entails the former, the converse does not hold, as shown in Proposition 1.

Proposition 1. *Let q_1 and q_2 be two CQs over a schema $\langle \mathcal{R}, \Lambda \rangle$, and I a set of constants such that $I \supseteq \mathrm{const}(q_1) \cup \mathrm{const}(q_2)$. If $q_1 \subseteq q_2$ then $q_1 \subseteq_{\Lambda, I} q_2$, but the converse does not hold.*

Proof. Assume, w.l.o.g., that q_1 and q_2 have no variables in common. For each obtainable answer tuple $\langle t \rangle$ to q_1, there is a corresponding instance of $\mathrm{body}(q_1)$ whose facts are Λ, I-obtainable, i.e., there is a grounding substitution μ_t for $\mathrm{var}(q_1)$ such that the facts in $\mu_t(\mathrm{body}(q_1))$ are Λ, I-obtainable and

$\mu_t(\text{head}(q_1)) = \langle t \rangle$. Since containment is assumed, there exists a substitution λ such that $\lambda(\text{body}(q_2)) \subseteq \text{body}(q_1)$, and $\lambda(\text{head}(q_2)) = \text{head}(q_1)$. But then, for each answer tuple $\langle t \rangle$ to q_1 there is also an instance of $\text{body}(q_2)$ whose facts are Λ, I-obtainable that generates the same answer tuple $\langle t \rangle$. To see this, it suffices to note that the facts in $\mu_t(\lambda(\text{body}(q_2)))$ are Λ, I-obtainable since those in $\mu_t(\text{body}(q_1))$ are, and that $\langle t \rangle = \mu_t(\lambda(\text{head}(q_2)))$.

To see that the converse does not hold, consider a schema with two relations $r_1^{ii}(A, B)$ and $r_2^{oi}(B, C)$ and the queries $q_1(B) \leftarrow r_1(a, B)$ and $q_2(B) \leftarrow r_1(a, B), r_2(B, C)$. For every $I \supseteq \{a\}$ that does not contain any constant of abstract domain B, we have that $q_1 \subseteq_{\Lambda, I} q_2$. Indeed, when evaluating q_1, the only Λ, I-obtainable facts for r_1 are those whose second argument is some constant b that occurs as first argument in a fact for r_2, i.e., b is also an answer to q_2. However $q_1 \not\subseteq q_2$, since there is at least one database D such that $q_1(D) \not\subseteq q_2(D)$ (take, e.g., $D = \{r_1(a, b)\}$). ∎

We now present the foundations of our novel technique to check containment of CQs under access limitations. Similarly to what is done for containment of CQs under inclusion and functional dependencies [15], in order to check the containment of a query q_1 into another query q_2, we characterize the set of all databases that provide an answer tuple for q_1 by constructing, starting from q_1, a *set* of databases called *chase*. In our case, the chase is constructed according to the access limitations. With the chase at hand, we can evaluate q_2 over a finite set of databases in the chase of q_1 in order to check the existence of a counterexample to containment, i.e., a database D that provides an answer tuple to q_1 that is not in the answer to q_2 in D.

The chase of a CQ under access limitations is defined as follows. Each database of the chase starts from the *frozen* body of the query, i.e., the image of the body of the query according to some grounding substitution that sends variables to fresh constants. Then, according to the access limitations, we go back in the extraction process, adding facts that may lead to the extraction of the previous ones, and we continue to do that until all the facts we choose to add come from relations whose input arguments are filled in by initial values. Since we proceed somehow backwards, we call our chase *crayfish-chase*.

For convenience, we first need a preprocessing step (`constElim`) to eliminate constants in the query, as illustrated in Figure 2. The intuition is that a constant acts as a relation, called *artificial relation*, whose content is accessible and amounts only to the constant itself. Under this assumption, the constant-free query and the original one are equivalent, as specified in Proposition 2.

Proposition 2. *Let q be a CQ over a schema $\mathcal{S}$, I a set such that $\text{const}(q) \subseteq I \subseteq \Delta$, and $(\mathcal{S}', q') = \text{constElim}(\mathcal{S}, q, I)$. Let D be a database for $\mathcal{S}$ and let D' be as D plus one fact $\ell_c(c)$ for each artificial relation ℓ_c in $\mathcal{S}'$ with associated constant c. Then $q(D) = q'(D')$.*

Definition 2 (crayfish-chase). *Consider a CQ q over a schema $\mathcal{S} = \langle \mathcal{R}, \Lambda \rangle$ and a set I such that $\text{const}(q) \subseteq I \subseteq \Delta$. The crayfish-chase of q, denoted $\text{cchase}(q, \mathcal{S}, I)$, is the set of all finite databases that can be constructed as follows.*

INPUT: a schema $\mathcal{S}$, a CQ q over $\mathcal{S}$, and a set I such that $\text{const}(q) \subseteq I \subseteq \Delta$
OUTPUT: a schema $\mathcal{S}'$, a CQ q' over $\mathcal{S}'$

- Let $\mathcal{S}' := \mathcal{S}$, $q' := q$
- For each constant $a \in I$ with abstract domain A
  - Add signature $\ell_a^o(A)$ for the new artificial relation ℓ_a to $\mathcal{S}'$
  - Replace all occurrences of a in q', if any, with a fresh new variable X_a
  - If a occurs in q, add the conjunct $\ell_a(X_a)$ to the body of q'
- Return $(\mathcal{S}', q')$

Fig. 2. Algorithm `constElim` for elimination of constants

Each database $D \in \text{cchase}(q, \mathcal{S}, I)$ is represented as a forest, *the nodes of which are facts of D; each node n has a* level, *denoted $\text{level}(n)$, that is a non-negative integer. The set of nodes at level h in a database D will be called* level h *of D. The* depth *of D, denoted $\text{depth}(D)$, is the maximum level of nodes in D.*

1. *Let $(\mathcal{S}', q') = \text{constElim}(\mathcal{S}, q, I)$.*
2. *We fix a single injective substitution mapping μ for all databases of $\text{cchase}(q, \mathcal{S}, I)$ that sends each variable in $\text{var}(q')$ into a fresh new constant in Δ_F, and thus $\text{body}(q')$ into a set of facts; such facts will be level 0 of D. Each tree of the forest will be rooted at a node of level 0.*
3. *We call $\mu(\text{head}(q))$ the head of the crayfish-chase, denoted $\text{head}(\text{cchase}(q, \mathcal{S}, I))$.*
4. *For each fact $f = r(c_1, \ldots, c_n)$ at level k, and for each input attribute of r, say the i-th, there is exactly one fact $f' = r'(c'_1, \ldots, c'_m)$ such that $c_i = c'_j$, for some position j corresponding to an output attribute of r' having the same abstract domain as c_i's. If f is at level k, then f' must be at level $k+1$, and an arc (f, f') is in D. All other constants in f' must be fresh new constants in Δ_F, not appearing elsewhere in any of the levels less than or equal to $k+1$.*
5. *Each leaf of D is a fact of a (possibly artificial) relation without input arguments.*

The databases in the crayfish-chase of a query q, as stated in Lemma 1, are representative of all concrete databases that return an answer to q while respecting the access limitations, i.e., they are sufficient to retrieve all obtainable answers to q and yet do not add any other answer.

Definition 3. *A mapping λ from Δ_F to Δ is said to be* compatible *with a virtual database D (in short, D-compatible), if λ sends each constant ζ occurring in D in a fact $\ell_c(\zeta)$ of an artificial relation ℓ_c into the corresponding constant c.*

Lemma 1. *Let $\mathcal{S}$ be a schema, q a query over $\mathcal{S}$, and I a set of constants such that $\text{const}(q) \subseteq I \subseteq \Delta$. (a) For every concrete database D such that there exists a tuple $t \in \text{ans}(q, \mathcal{S}, D, I)$, there exists a database $D' \in \text{cchase}(q, \mathcal{S}, I)$ and a D'-compatible mapping λ from Δ_F to Δ such that $\lambda(D') \subseteq D$ and $t \in \text{ans}(q, \mathcal{S}, \lambda(D'), I)$.*

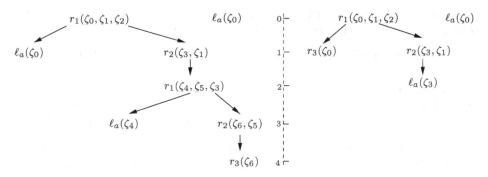

Fig. 3. Database forests in the crayfish-chase $\mathrm{cchase}(q, \mathcal{S}, I)$ of Example 3

(b) Conversely, for every database $D' \in \mathrm{cchase}(q, \mathcal{S}, I)$ and for every D'-compatible mapping λ from Δ_F to Δ such that $\lambda(D')$ is concrete, if there exists a tuple $t' \in \mathrm{ans}(q, \mathcal{S}, \lambda(D'), I)$, then there is a database D such that $t' \in \mathrm{ans}(q, \mathcal{S}, D, I)$.

Proof (sketch). (a) If t can be obtained in D, this means that there is a grounding substitution μ for $\mathrm{var}(q)$ such that $\mu(\mathrm{head}(q)) = t$ and all the facts in $\mu(\mathrm{body}(q))$ are obtainable and in D. Therefore, each fact in $\mu(\mathrm{body}(q))$ either has constants from I in all its input positions, or, inductively, for each constant c not from I in an input position there is some obtainable fact in D with c in an output position. But this models exactly a tree of a database of $\mathrm{cchase}(q, \mathcal{S}, I)$, with the only difference that here there may be more than one constant not from I in common in two facts, which can be captured by a mapping λ.
(b) This holds by construction: by applying λ to D' one obtains a database D with t' in the answer to q. ∎

Example 3. Assume we have a schema $\mathcal{S}$ with the following relations: $r_1^{iio}(A, B, A), r_2^{io}(A, B), r_3^o(A)$. Consider the query $q(X_2) \leftarrow r_1(a, X_1, X_2)$ and the set $I = \{a\}$. First of all, we transform the query by eliminating the constants: we get $q'(X_2) \leftarrow r_1(X_0, X_1, X_2), \ell_a(X_0)$, where ℓ_a is an auxiliary predicate with signature $\ell_a^o(A)$; no other auxiliary predicates are introduced. After freezing the query, we obtain two facts in the frozen body: $r_1(\zeta_0, \zeta_1, \zeta_2)$ and $\ell_a(\zeta_0)$; the head of $\mathrm{cchase}(q, \mathcal{S}, I)$ is $\langle \zeta_2 \rangle$. Every database in $\mathrm{cchase}(q, \mathcal{S}, I)$ is a forest of exactly two trees rooted at $r_1(\zeta_0, \zeta_1, \zeta_2)$ and $\ell_a(\zeta_0)$ respectively, since these two facts constitute the level 0 of every database in the chase; every tree rooted in $\ell_a(\zeta_0)$ will consist of only one node; two possible databases (forests) are depicted in Figure 3, separated by a dashed vertical line on which we have indicated the depth of the different levels. □

We now show that, when considering $q_1 \subseteq_{A, I} q_2$, once we have the crayfish-chase of q_1, the evaluation of q_2 over a database in the above chase can ignore the access limitations, as long as the same set of initial constants is used.

Lemma 2. *Consider two CQs q_1, q_2 over a schema $\mathcal{S} = \langle \mathcal{R}, \Lambda \rangle$, a set $I \subseteq \Delta$, and a database $D \in \text{cchase}(q_1, \mathcal{S}, I)$; then $\text{ans}(q_2, \mathcal{S}, D, I) = q_2(D)$.*

Proof. Straightforward, since all facts in D are, by construction, Λ, I-obtainable.∎

Lemma 3. *Consider two CQs q_1, q_2 over a schema $\mathcal{S} = \langle \mathcal{R}, \Lambda \rangle$, and a set I such that $\text{const}(q_1) \cup \text{const}(q_2) \subseteq I \subseteq \Delta$. Then $q_1 \subseteq_{\Lambda,I} q_2$ if and only if, for every database $D \in \text{cchase}(q_1, \mathcal{S}, I)$, $\text{head}(\text{cchase}(q_1, \mathcal{S}, I)) \in \text{ans}(q_2, D, \mathcal{S}, I)$.*

Proof (sketch). "$\Leftarrow$" Consider a generic concrete database B such that there exists a tuple t in $\text{ans}(q_1, \mathcal{S}, B, I)$; by Lemma 1, there exist a database $D \in \text{cchase}(q_1, \mathcal{S}, I)$ and a mapping λ from Δ_F to Δ compatible with D such that $\lambda(D) \subseteq B$ and $t \in \text{ans}(q_1, \mathcal{S}, \lambda(D), I)$. Now, by hypothesis, there exists a mapping μ that sends $\text{body}(q_2)$ to facts of D, and $\text{head}(q_2)$ to $\text{head}(\text{cchase}(q_1, \mathcal{S}, I))$; we have that $\lambda(\mu(\text{body}(q_2))) \subseteq B$ and $\lambda(\mu(\text{head}(q_2))) = t$. This proves that $t \in \text{ans}(q_2, \mathcal{S}, B, I)$ and thus that $q_1 \subseteq_{\Lambda,I} q_2$, since B was generic.
"$\Rightarrow$" Trivial, from the definition of containment under access limitations.   ∎

Now we come to the main result in this section, that follows trivially as a corollary of Lemma 2 and Lemma 3, stating that examining the databases of a crayfish-chase provides us with a necessary and sufficient condition to test containment of CQs under access limitations.

Theorem 1. *Consider two CQs q_1, q_2 over a schema $\mathcal{S} = \langle \mathcal{R}, \Lambda \rangle$, and a set I such that $\text{const}(q_1) \cup \text{const}(q_2) \subseteq I \subseteq \Delta$. Then, $q_1 \subseteq_{\Lambda,I} q_2$ if and only if, for every database $D \in \text{cchase}(q_1, \mathcal{S}, I)$, $\text{head}(\text{cchase}(q_1, \mathcal{S}, I)) \in q_2(D)$.*

Notice that the previous theorem does not provide any direct strategy for checking containment; indeed, given a CQ over a schema $\mathcal{S}$, and a set I of initial constants, the number of databases in $\text{cchase}(q_1, \mathcal{S}, I)$ may be infinite. Also, notice that, although all databases in $\text{cchase}(q_1, \mathcal{S}, I)$ are of finite size, there is in general no fixed bound on such size.

4   Decidability and Complexity

In this section we give a direct proof of decidability of checking containment between CQs under access limitations that exploits the notion of crayfish-chase. This will be done by showing that, while checking $q_1 \subseteq_{\Lambda,I} q_2$, when we look for a substitution that sends $\text{body}(q_2)$ to facts in some database $D \in \text{cchase}(q_1, \mathcal{S}, I)$ (and $\text{head}(q_2)$ to $\text{head}(\text{cchase}(q_1, \mathcal{S}, I))$), it is sufficient to consider databases in $\text{cchase}(q_1, \mathcal{S}, I)$ whose depth does not exceed a certain limit, depending on the schema and the queries. In particular, Lemma 5 states that in order to find a counterexample showing that $q_1 \not\subseteq_{\Lambda,I} q_2$, we need to consider only databases of the crayfish-chase of q_1 of limited depth. This allows us to provide an improved upper bound for the complexity of this problem, as shown in Theorem 2. This requires some preparatory lemmas and definitions.

We first show that two facts sharing a constant in a database of a crayfish-chase cannot be more than one level apart.

Lemma 4. *Consider a database D in a crayfish-chase. If two nodes n_1 and n_2 in D have a constant in common, then $|\text{level}(n_1) - \text{level}(n_2)| \leq 1$.*

Proof. If $n_1 = n_2$ the claim trivially holds. By construction of the crayfish-chase, the constants that appear at some level k of D cannot appear in any level greater than $k + 1$. In particular, all constants in output arguments are not propagated to the next level, while those in input arguments occur only in output fields in the next level, and therefore disappear after two levels. Therefore, either n_1 and n_2 are connected by an arc (and thus their levels are at a distance of 1), or each of them lies on a level less than 2 (not necessarily connected by an arc, since different nodes of level 0 may share constants).   ∎

As a consequence of Lemma 4, a connected part of n atoms of a query cannot be mapped on more than n contiguous levels.

Corollary 1. *Consider a CQ q over a schema $\mathcal{S} = \langle \mathcal{R}, \Lambda \rangle$, a set I such that $\text{const}(q) \subseteq I \subseteq \Lambda$, and a database $D \in \text{cchase}(q, \Lambda, I)$. Let $\mathcal{P}$ be any connected part of q', where $(\mathcal{S}', q') = \text{constElim}(\mathcal{S}, q, I)$; if there exists a substitution μ sending variables to constants in Λ_F that sends the atoms in $\mathcal{P}$ into facts of D, then $\max_{\{p_i, p_j\} \subseteq \mathcal{P}}(|\text{level}(\mu(p_i)) - \text{level}(\mu(p_j))|) \leq |\mathcal{P}|$, i.e., $\mu(\mathcal{P})$ lies onto at most $|\mathcal{P}|$ contiguous levels on D.*

Henceforth, we shall denote with subtree(c) the subtree (of a given tree) having node c as root, and containing *all* descendants of c; with k-subtree(c), k a positive integer, we denote the subtree rooted in c, and containing all descendants of c up to level $\text{level}(c) + k - 1$. Lemma 5, below, shows that if a query does not map onto a database of a crayfish-chase, then there is a (possibly different) database of the chase which has limited depth and onto which the query still cannot be mapped. To construct this database, we trim redundant parts by using the notion of subtree replacement.

Definition 4 (Subtree replacement). *Let D be a virtual database of a crayfish-chase, and consider two nodes $n_1 = r(c_1, \ldots, c_k)$ and $n_2 = r(d_1, \ldots, d_k)$ in D, such that n_2 is a descendant of n_1. Let μ be a mapping from Λ_F to Λ_F that sends d_i into c_i for $1 \leq i \leq k$ and every other constant into itself. Then, a replacement of subtree(n_1) with subtree(n_2) in D is the result of replacing subtree(n_1) with μ(subtree(n_2)).*

Lemma 5. *Consider two CQs q_1, q_2 over a schema $\mathcal{S} = \langle \mathcal{R}, \Lambda \rangle$, and a set I such that $\text{const}(q_1) \cup \text{const}(q_2) \subseteq I \subseteq \Lambda$; if there exists a database $D \in \text{cchase}(q_1, \mathcal{S}, I)$ such that $\text{head}(\text{cchase}(q_1, \mathcal{S}, I)) \notin q_2(D)$, then there exists a database $D' \in \text{cchase}(q, \mathcal{S}, I)$ such that $\text{head}(\text{cchase}(q_1, \mathcal{S}, I)) \notin q_2(D')$, and such that $\text{depth}(D') \leq 2 \cdot |\mathcal{R}| + |q_2| - 3$.*

Proof.
Case (1): q_2 is connected.

Subcase (1a). There is only one relation r among those in q_2 such that, for every database $B \in \text{cchase}(q_1, \mathcal{S}, I)$, if q_2 can be mapped onto facts of B, the

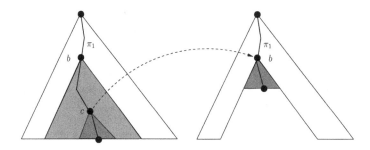

Fig. 4. Subtree replacement of subtree(b) with subtree(c) (Lemma 5)

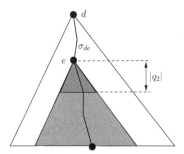

Fig. 5. Second phase of iterative subtree replacement (Lemma 5)

mapped fact f with smallest level has relation r and no mapped fact with a different relation has level equal to level(f).

Since q_2 is connected, if it is mapped onto a database, by Corollary 1, it will be mapped onto facts whose level is between level(f) and level(f) + $|q_2| - 1$.

Take now any path π_1 from a node at level 0 to a leaf of D. For simplicity, we say that a relation r occurs in a path π (and that π contains r), if a fact of the form $r(\zeta)$ occurs in it π. Since q_2 cannot be mapped onto D by hypothesis, a fortiori q_2 cannot be mapped onto any of the $|q_2|$-subtrees rooted in any of the occurrences of r in π_1. Let b be the node of π_1 with the occurrence (if any) of r with the smallest level (call a its parent if b is not at level 0) and let c be the one with the greatest level. We apply the replacement of subtree(b) with subtree(c), as shown in Figure 4. In the obtained database, q_2 continues to be not mappable, since *(i)* facts have been removed from D, and *(ii)* only one potential "join" has been added (that between c and a in D), which is irrelevant to q_2, since a's relation is certainly different from r, and r was assumed to be the only possible predicate at the smallest level of facts of the image of q_2 (and r does not occur above b in π_1). This step is repeated for every path in which r occurs. After this, in all paths from a node at level 0 to a leaf of the obtained database, r occurs at most once and q_2 is still not mappable.

To complete the transformation, we apply the following steps as long as possible to every path π_2 from a node at level 0 and a leaf.

- If π_2 does not contain r, we a apply subtree replacement, in the same way as was done for r above, for any relation occurring more than once in π_2; again, non-mappability of q_2 onto the database is preserved. At the end of the process, each such path will have at most length $|\mathcal{R}| - 1$.
- If π_2 contains r, let d be the node at level 0, and e the node with r; the segment σ_{de} of π_2 from d to e contains r only in e. If there is another relation s occurring more than once in σ_{de}, we apply the replacement of the subtree rooted at the occurrence of s in σ_{de} closest to d with the one with the occurrence in σ_{de} closest to e, as shown in Figure 5; again, non-mappability is preserved; besides, after all such replacements, σ_{de} has length at most $|\mathcal{R}|$. We apply in the same way all possible replacements to remove multiple occurrences of a relation in all subtrees rooted in a node of subtree(e) lying at level level$(e) + |q_2| - 1$. Thus, the $|q_2|$-subtree(e) (shaded in Figure 5) on which q_2 cannot be mapped is kept and the distance between e and the leaves will eventually be at most $(|q_2| - 1) + (|\mathcal{R}| - 1) = |q_2| + |\mathcal{R}| - 2$.

In total, the obtained database D' has depth at most $|\mathcal{R}|+(|q_2|+|\mathcal{R}|-2)-1 = 2 \cdot |\mathcal{R}| + |q_2| - 3$ and q_2 cannot be mapped onto D'.

Subcase (1b): There is more than one relation that can be on the smallest level of the mapped facts of q_2 in a crayfish-chase database; let call $\mathcal{F}$ the set of such relations. For each path in D from a node of level 0 to a leaf, consider the occurrence with smallest level among the relations in $\mathcal{F}$. For that relation, we apply the replacement of the first occurrence with the last occurrence on the path. Since it was the first occurrence of a relation in $\mathcal{F}$, the join added with the replacement will not introduce mappability of q_2. After all such replacements are applied, in each path from level 0 to a leaf, the relation, say r, of the occurrence, say a, with smallest level among the relations in $\mathcal{F}$ will occur only once. With this in mind, we proceed as in subcase 1a to eliminate all multiple occurrences of relations above a in the path, still preserving non-mappability, so that eventually level(a) will be at most $|\mathcal{R}| - 1$. Also, we safely apply all possible replacements to remove multiple occurrences of a relation in all subtrees rooted in a node of subtree(a) lying at level level$(a) + |q_2| - 1$, since in any such subtree r does not occur, and thus q_2 cannot be mapped onto (and we know that q_2 cannot be mapped onto the $|q_2|$-subtree(a), which is kept). In the end we still obtain a database D' with depth at most $2 \cdot |\mathcal{R}| + |q_2| - 3$ such that q_2 cannot be mapped onto D'.

Case (2): q_2 is not connected. We proceed as in the case of a connected query, and apply the same argument on one of the connected parts of q_2. Clearly, if a connected part of q_2 cannot be mapped, q_2 cannot be mapped either.   ∎

Finally, we characterize the computational complexity of our query containment problem, by providing an upper bound for it.

Theorem 2. *Containment of conjunctive queries under access limitations is decidable in co-NEXPTIME.*

Proof (sketch). By virtue of Theorem 1 and Lemma 5, in order to check containment, only databases of a limited depth need to be checked. There are only finitely many such databases that are different modulo isomorphism.

Let $q_1 \subseteq_{\Lambda,I} q_2$ be the containment to be decided for a schema $\mathcal{S} = \langle \mathcal{R}, \Lambda \rangle$. We use a nondeterministic algorithm that guesses a database $D \in \text{cchase}(q_1, \mathcal{S}, I)$ with maximum number of levels $\delta = 2 \cdot |\mathcal{R}| + |q_2| - 3$ that is a witness of non-containment; by Lemma 5, we know that we do not need to consider databases of bigger depth for this purpose. The guessed database has at most $O(W^\delta)$ nodes, where W is the maximum arity of the relations in $\mathcal{R}$; notice that each node has at most W children, each of which can be chosen in at most $|\mathcal{R}| \cdot W$ different ways. The database D can therefore be guessed in exponential time (w.r.t. δ) by a nondeterministic algorithm. After that, checking, on the same nondeterministic branch, whether $q_2(D)$ yields head($\text{cchase}(q, \mathcal{S}, I)$) can be done in polynomial time in the size of D, i.e., in exponential time w.r.t. δ. Therefore a witness for non-containment can be guessed in NEXPTIME, from which the thesis follows. ∎

5 Related Work

The issue of processing queries under access limitations has been widely investigated in the literature [23,17,19,18,12,10]; in particular, [12] considers the optimization of non-recursive plans, [10] addresses the problem in the case of query answering using views, and [23] presents a polynomial-time algorithm to decide whether a CQ can be answered in the presence of access limitations. Recursive query plans were introduced in [22,17]; in particular, [22] addresses the problem of query containment under access limitations.

The problem of checking containment of two CQs under access limitations was shown to be decidable in [22] in the setting of data integration systems using the local-as-view approach by reducing this problem to containment of a recursive Datalog program in a non-recursive one; the optimal complexity for this problem is 3EXPTIME [7]. In [18], the authors propose an encoding of CQs with access limitations into monadic Datalog programs; containment between monadic Datalog programs was shown to be decidable in 2EXPTIME in [8], which immediately provides a 2EXPTIME upper bound for containment of CQs under access limitations. The same upper bound is easily obtained by combining the results from Section 3 with the complexity of checking containment of a Datalog program in a CQ; such problem was shown to be decidable in 2EXPTIME (tight bound) in [7]. In this paper, we improve upon this upper bound by providing an algorithm that checks containment in co-NEXPTIME, as mentioned in the position paper [4] and informally presented in [3].

In [16], the author addresses the issue of *stability*, i.e., determining whether the *complete* answer to a query (the one that would be obtained with no access limitations) can always be computed despite the access limitations. [25] addresses the problem of ordering subgoals for non-recursive Datalog queries in oder to make the query executable from left to right complying with the access limitations. In [2], a run-time optimization technique, that exploits the information about database dependencies that hold on the sources, is presented; [5]

uses the structure of the query to minimize the accesses needed to retrieve all obtainable answers to a query. [9] solves the (quite general) problem of query answering using views [13] under integrity constraints and under access limitations by reducing it to the same problem under integrity constraints only; various extensions to the query languages are provided. In [20], the authors analyze the complexity of determining the *feasibility* of a query, i.e., determining whether there exists an equivalent query that is executable as is, while respecting the access limitations. [21] studies the complexity of the feasibility problem for CQs, UCQs, CQ$\bar{}$s and UCQ$\bar{}$s.

6 Conclusions

We have addressed the problem of containment of CQs in the case where access limitations are present on the relational schema. This problem is highly relevant in query optimization. In the presence of access limitations, the evaluation of a query is in general inherently recursive and can be encoded in a Datalog program. The problem of containment would then amount to checking containment between two Datalog programs, which is undecidable. However, in this particular case, containment checking is indeed decidable, and we have provided an improved upper bound to the complexity of the problem by exhibiting a nondeterministic algorithm that solves it.

With our crayfish-chase technique we have provided a direct proof of decidability that we plan to use for further investigations. In particular, we intend to extend our results to more general classes of queries, and to extend the problem by introducing integrity constraints on the schema. The combination of our crayfish-chase with the well-known chase based on inclusion and functional dependencies seems a promising direction of research. We also plan to extend the results presented in this paper by finding a lower complexity bound for the problem of query containment.

Acknowledgments. A. Calì was supported by the EPSRC project "Schema Mappings and Automated Services for Data Integration and Exchange" (EP/E010865/1). D. Martinenghi acknowledges support from Italian PRIN project "New technologies and tools for the integration of Web search services".

References

1. Abiteboul, S., Hull, R., Vianu, V.: Foundations of Databases. Addison Wesley Publ. Co., Reading (1995)
2. Calì, A., Calvanese, D.: Optimized querying of integrated data over the Web. In: Proc. of the IFIP WG8.1 Working Conference on Engineering Information Systems in the Internet Context (EISIC 2002), pp. 285–301. Kluwer Academic Publisher, Dordrecht (2002)
3. Calì, A., Calvanese, D.: Containment of conjunctive queries under access limitations (extended abstract). In: Proc. of SEBD 2006, pp. 131–138 (2006)

4. Calì, A., Calvanese, D.: Optimising query answering in the presence of access limitations (position paper). In: Proc. of the 2nd Workshop on Logical Aspects and Applications of Integrity Constraints (LAAIC 2006). IEEE Computer Society, Los Alamitos (2006)
5. Calì, A., Calvanese, D., Martinenghi, D.: Optimization of query plans in the presence of access limitations. In: Arenas, M., Hidders, J. (eds.) EROW 2007 (ICDT workshop), Informal proceedings, pp. 33–47 (2007)
6. Chandra, A.K., Merlin, P.M.: Optimal implementation of conjunctive queries in relational data bases. In: Proc. of STOC 1977, pp. 77–90 (1977)
7. Chaudhuri, S., Vardi, M.Y.: On the equivalence of recursive and nonrecursive datalog programs. J. of Computer and System Sciences 54(1), 61–78 (1997)
8. Cosmadakis, S.S., Gaifman, H., Kanellakis, P.C., Vardi, M.Y.: Decidable optimization problems for database logic programs. In: Proc. of STOC 1988, pp. 477–490 (1988)
9. Deutsch, A., Ludäscher, B., Nash, A.: Rewriting queries using views with access patterns under integrity constraints. In: Proc. of ICDT 2005, pp. 352–367 (2005)
10. Duschka, O.M., Levy, A.Y.: Recursive plans for information gathering. In: Proc. of IJCAI 1997, pp. 778–784 (1997)
11. Fagin, R., Kolaitis, P.G., Miller, R.J., Popa, L.: Data exchange: Semantics and query answering. Theor. Comp. Sci. 336(1), 89–124 (2005)
12. Florescu, D., Levy, A.Y., Manolescu, I., Suciu, D.: Query optimization in the presence of limited access patterns. In: Proc. of ACM SIGMOD, pp. 311–322 (1999)
13. Halevy, A.Y.: Answering queries using views: A survey. VLDB Journal 10(4), 270–294 (2001)
14. Hull, R.: Managing semantic heterogeneity in databases: A theoretical perspective. In: Proc. of PODS 1997, pp. 51–61 (1997)
15. Johnson, D.S., Klug, A.C.: Testing containment of conjunctive queries under functional and inclusion dependencies. J. of Computer and System Sciences 28(1), 167–189 (1984)
16. Li, C.: Computing complete answers to queries in the presence of limited access patterns. VLDB Journal 12(3), 211–227 (2003)
17. Li, C., Chang, E.: Query planning with limited source capabilities. In: Proc. of ICDE 2000, pp. 401–412 (2000)
18. Li, C., Chang, E.: Answering queries with useful bindings. ACM Trans. on Database Systems 26(3), 313–343 (2001)
19. Li, C., Chang, E.: On answering queries in the presence of limited access patterns. In: Van den Bussche, J., Vianu, V. (eds.) ICDT 2001. LNCS, vol. 1973, pp. 219–233. Springer, Heidelberg (2000)
20. Ludäscher, B., Nash, A.: Processing first-order queries under limited access patterns. In: Proc. of PODS 2004, pp. 307–318 (2004)
21. Ludäscher, B., Nash, A.: Processing union of conjunctive queries with negation under limited access patterns. In: Lindner, W., Mesiti, M., Türker, C., Tzitzikas, Y., Vakali, A.I. (eds.) EDBT 2004. LNCS, vol. 3268, pp. 422–440. Springer, Heidelberg (2004)
22. Millstein, T.D., Levy, A.Y., Friedman, M.: Query containment for data integration systems. In: Proc. of PODS 2000, pp. 67–75 (2000)
23. Rajaraman, A., Sagiv, Y., Ullman, J.D.: Answering queries using templates with binding patterns. In: Proc. of PODS 1995 (1995)
24. Ullman, J.D.: Information integration using logical views. In: Afrati, F.N., Kolaitis, P.G. (eds.) ICDT 1997. LNCS, vol. 1186, pp. 19–40. Springer, Heidelberg (1996)
25. Yang, G., Kifer, M., Chaudhri, V.K.: Efficiently ordering subgoals with access constraints

Automatic Extraction of Structurally Coherent Mini-Taxonomies

Khalid Saleem and Zohra Bellahsene

LIRMM - UMR 5506 CNRS University Montpellier 2,
161 Rue Ada, F-34392 Montpellier
{saleem,bella}@lirmm.fr

Abstract. Today, ontologies are being used to model a domain of knowledge in semantic web. OWL is considered to be the main language for developing such ontologies. It is based on the XML model, which inherently follows the hierarchical structure. In this paper we demonstrate an automatic approach for emergent semantics modeling of ontologies. We follow the collaborative ontology construction method without the direct interaction of domain users, engineers or developers. A very important characteristic of an ontology is its hierarchical structure of concepts. We consider large sets of domain specific hierarchical structures as trees and apply frequent sub-tree mining for extracting common hierarchical patterns. Our experiments show that these hierarchical patterns are good enough to represent and describe the concepts for the domain ontology. The technique further demonstrates the construction of the taxonomy of domain ontology. In this regard we consider the largest frequent tree or a tree created by merging the set of largest frequent sub-trees as the taxonomy. We argue in favour of the trustabilty for such a taxonomy and related concepts, since these have been extracted from the structures being used with in the specified domain.

Keywords: Ontology Learning, Mini-taxonomies, Collaborative Ontology Construction, Tree Mining, Large Scale.

1 Introduction

Semantic web provides a platform where machines can move one step further and understand the contextual meaning of the data. One of the most promising technique in this regard has been the ontology. Its utilisation has been demonstrated from simple schema matching for data integration [16] to large scale complex web services management [2] [1]. Ontologies are also making their way into social resource sharing systems, which evolve on user actions and interactions. Currently such environments use data structures like folksonomies [12], consisting of arbitrary keywords to resources by users, presenting a lightweight knowledge representation technique.

---

[1] Web Service Modeling Ontology - http://www.w3.org/Submission/WSMO/

Q. Li et al. (Eds.): ER 2008, LNCS 5231, pp. 341–354, 2008.
© Springer-Verlag Berlin Heidelberg 2008

There have been several works concerned with ontology engineering, elaborating manual and semi-automatic techniques. Ontologies have been build from scratch and from already available data content, in the form of text [3], web [6, 14,20], tables [19], relational schemas [13], XML schemas and documents [9]. In all these works the ontological constructs have been the same; terms, concepts, concept hierarchies, relations and rules or logic. These features of an ontology have been described in detail by Paul Buitelaar et al. [3] as an ontology learning layer cake. These ontology features have a direct relation to the layered approach of semantic web [1].

In this paper we propose a novel approach for finding domain ontology concepts as mini-taxonomies, using tree mining technique. The approach is further extended to build a base taxonomy for the domain ontology. Mining techniques extract frequent patterns from a large repository of data and growing frequent patterns mining predict possible extensions of these patterns. The function of tree mining is to find sub-tree patterns that are frequent in the given set of trees. A sub-tree pattern starts with one node and is incrementally augmented. There are different techniques [5] which mine rooted, labeled, embedded or induced, ordered or unordered sub-trees.

Contributions

Our approach presents a methodology for extracting mini-taxonomies, representing domain concepts, as frequent sub-trees from the given set of hierarchical structures. These hierarchical structures can be existing ontology taxonomies, XML schemas or some folksonomy having tree like data structure. For simplicity we use the word schema for these structures. The main features of our approach are as follows.

1. The approach is almost automatic, based on a tree mining technique supporting large scale scenarios. To support tree mining, we model input schemas as rooted ordered (depth-first) labelled trees.
2. The technique builds clusters of similar terms based upon labels similarity of input schemas' elements. The similarity is computed using label's syntactic, lexical and contextual (hierarchical) occurrence in the schema. Each cluster is represented by a single symbol i.e., the most frequent label in the input set of schemas, in each cluster.
3. It proposes ontology concepts as mini-taxonomies which are extracted using tree mining technique researched in [21].
4. It generates similar hierarchical patterns from extracted mini-taxonomies, in conjunction with similar terms clusters.
5. The approach automatically produces a trustable basic domain taxonomy from the given set of domain specific schemas, implying domain community consensus over it.
6. The approach was implemented as a prototype. We report on experiments using different real (COURSES [2]) and synthetic scenarios, demonstrating quality of generated mini-taxonomies using precision measure.

---

[2] http://www.cise.ufl.edu/research/dbintegrate/thalia/

The remainder of the paper is organized as follows. Section 2 presents the background of ontology engineering. In section 3 we discuss our work in relation to previous works in the domain of ontology learning and collaborative knowledge acquisition. In Section 4 we give detail of our approach, Automatic **Ex**traction of **S**tructurally Coherent Mini-**Tax**onomies (ExSTax). Section 5 demonstrates an example, using synthetic set of hierarchical structures to support our technique. Section 6 presents the experimental evaluation along with discussion on the results. Section 7 outlines future perspective and concludes.

2   Ontology Engineering Overview

Discussion on ontology building and utilisation has been around since early 90s. Ontology has been defined in [10] as an explicit, formal specification of a shared conceptualisation of a domain of interest. Formalization aspect highlights the machine readability of the ontology and shared conceptualization points toward its acceptance by the players of the domain. Initial ontology development endeavors resulted in the form of DAML[3] and OIL[4] languages. Today the features of the two languages have been extended to OWL[5], based on XML model.

Initial focus in ontology design has been the manual technique but with the passage of time more and more semi-automatic techniques have emerged, facilitated by ontology editing tools[6]. The semi-automatic approach is named as the ontology learning process.

Ontology learning is a combination of tasks organised as a layered approach, in the manner of increasing complexity. The tasks are enumerated by Paul Buitelaar et al. in [3] as term extraction, synonym and translation detection, concept formulation, concept hierarchies, relations, rule derivation and axiomatization.

Concept hierarchy, also called taxonomy (is-a relation), is a tree structure of classifications for a given set of ontological objects. It is considered to be the ontology backbone. At the top of this structure is a single classification, the root node, that applies to all objects. Nodes below this root are more specific classifications that apply to subsets of the total set of classified objects. So for instance, in common schemes of books, the root is called "Book" followed by nodes for the type: Art, Science, Fiction, Sports, etc. And each instance of "Book" concept can have properties like author, title, publisher etc. (Figure 1)

Our work is a step toward automatic conceptualisation of an ontology for a certain domain, already populated with large set of user defined hierarchical meta data structures for diverse applications. For example XML schemas, taxonomies etc. or entities from which hierarchical structures can be extracted, like web based query interface forms.

---

[3] DAML: Darpa Agent Markup Language - http://www.daml.org/

[4] OIL: Ontology Interface Layer - http://www.ontoknowledge.org/oil/

[5] OWL: Web Ontology Language - http://www.w3.org/TR/owl-features/

[6] Protege is a free, open source ontology editor and knowledge-base framework; http://protege.stanford.edu/

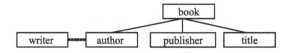

Fig. 1. Ontology taxonomy example

3   Related Work

One of the foremost technique applied for ontology learning has been *term extraction* from text. Similar terms are clustered together for further analysis and inception of inter term relations or taxonomy. These methods have their roots in natural language processing research [4]. Buitelaar et al. present their OntoLT approach as a plug-in for protege ontology editing tool. The authors define preconditions using XPATH expressions over the XML based linguistic annotations. The rules help in constructing or extending an ontology. The preconditions revolve around the linguistic constructs in a sentence. For example if the subject in the sentence corresponds to a certain morphological stem of a word.

Terms similarity computation has been researched in two ways. Primarily by using readily available lexical resources like Wordnet[7]. And secondly, by devising clustering algorithms based on the syntactic similarity of the terms. Information retrieval techniques [18] based on term indexing and data mining methods [11] provide the space for such algorithms.

There is no definite definition available for *concept formation*. Our approach follows the hierarchical representation of concepts [7] which can be extended, upon receiving further information about the concept. The extension idea has been pruned in [15] as binary relation extraction of terms and recommendations have been made for use of data mining co-occurrence algorithms. These methods can ultimately provide an incremental approach for ontology learning.

World wide web has also been extensively exploited in this regard. [20] describe a tool which prunes the web resources like Wikipedia, Wiktitionary, along with domain corpus for domain ontology learning. These resources are exploited against a set of candidates extracted from a set of ontology instances using the linguistic context. Another work by Maedche et al. [14] explains two algorithms, top-down and bottom-up approaches, for deducing taxonomic relations from the web based on heuristics. Our approach presents a similar top-down method, by applying tree-mining on the available hierarchical structures in a domain. In [9], the authors present the use of semi-structured schemata (XML and RDF based resources) for constructing a domain ontology, manually and semi-automatically.

Another interesting research for ontology generation is the use of tables extracted from web and other resources. Authors in [19] argue that the extraction of relational knowledge from tables is much easier than exploiting the text corpus. The research describes a comprehensive framework for assembling human created tables. The approach canonicalises each table information, generates a mini-ontology from it and then incrementally merges the mini-ontologies.

---

[7] http://wordnet.princeton.edu

Social collaborative networks present a new range of emerging semantics on the web. In such environments users set up lightweight conceptual structures, assigning arbitrary keywords, called tags, to resources. Such conceptual structures are also called folksonomies. Research work in [12] presents a data mining technique for discovering shared conceptualisations in folksonomies. The technique extends the data mining task of discovering all closed itemsets to frequent tri-concepts (user, tag and resource) extraction. With social networks gaining more ground, standards are also evolving for them. FOAF [8](Friend of a Friend) ontology standard is one such example, providing structural data model for the folksonomies. Thus paving the way for tree mining techniques in the social network environments.

4   Our Approach: ExSTax

In this section we present our approach, ExSTax, for detection of ontological concepts as mini-taxonomies, from the available domain specific hierarchical structures. We discuss the architecture, the related definitions and methods in length to clarify the novelty of our method.

4.1   Definitions

Following are the basic definitions supporting the implementation of our technique.

Definition 1 (Hierarchical Structure/Schema): A Hierarchical Structure $S = (V, E)$ is a rooted, labeled tree [21], consisting of nodes $V = \{0, 1, \ldots, n\}$, and edges $E = \{(x, y) \mid$ x,y $\in V\}$. One distinguished node $r \in V$ is called the root, and for all $x \in V$, there is a unique path from r to x. Further, lab:V $\rightarrow$ L is a labeling function mapping nodes to labels in $L = \{l_1, l_2, \ldots\}$.

In further text we will refer to hierarchical structure as tree. Tree nodes bear two kinds of information: the node label, and the node number allocated during depth-first traversal. Labels are linguistically compared to calculate label similarity (Definition 2, Label Semantics). Node number is used to calculate the node's tree context (Definition 3, Node Scope).

Definition 2 (Label Semantics): A label l is a composition of m strings, called tokens. We apply the tokenisation function tok which maps a label to a set of tokens $T_l=\{t_1, t_2, \ldots, t_m\}$. Tokenisation [8] helps in establishing similarity between two labels.
$tok : L \rightarrow \mathscr{P}(T)$, where $\mathscr{P}(T)$ is a power set over $T=\{t_1, t_2, \ldots\}$.

Example 1 (Label Equivalence): 'FirstName', tokenised as {first,name}, and 'NameFirst', tokenised as {name, first}, are equivalent, with 100 % similarity. •

---

[8] http://xmlns.com/foaf/0.1/

Label semantics correspond to the meaning of the label (irrespective of the node it is related to). It is the composition of meanings attached to the tokens making up the label. As shown by Examples 1 and 2, different labels can represent similar concepts. We denote the concept related to a label l as $C(l)$.

Example 2 (Synonymous Labels): 'WriterName', tokenised as {writer,name}, and 'AuthorName', tokenised as {author, name} are equivalent (they represent the same concept), since 'writer' is a synonym of 'author'. •

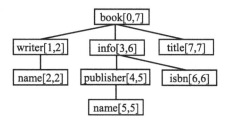

Fig. 2. Input hierarchical structure with scope

Definition 3 (Node Scope): In tree S each node $x \in V$ is numbered according to its order in the depth-first traversal of S (the root is numbered 0). Let $SubTree(x)$ denote the sub-tree rooted at x, and x be numbered X, and let y be the rightmost leaf (or highest numbered descendant) under x, numbered Y. Then the scope of x is $scope(x)=[X, Y]$. Intuitively, $scope(x)$ is the range of nodes under x, and includes x itself, see Figure 2. The count of nodes in $SubTree(x)$ is $Y - X + 1$.

4.2 Scope Properties

Scope properties describe the contextual placement of a node [21]. Property testing involves simple integer comparisons. We utilise these properties in frequent sub-tree detection.

Given x [X,Y], xd[Xd,Yd], xa[Xa,Ya], and xc[Xc,Yc]:

Property. 1: Descendant (x,xd), xd is a descendant of x: $Xd>X \land Yd\leq Y$

Property. 2: Ancestor (x,xa), complement of Property 1, xa is ancestor of x: $Xa<X \land Ya\geq Y$

Property. 3: Cousin (x,xc) with non-overlapping scope, xc is cousin of x: $Xc>Y$.

Example 3 (Scope Properties Use): Let us consider Figure 2. We perform the descendant node check on nodes [2,2] and [5,5] with respect to **writer**[1,2]. Node [2,2] is a descendant of [1,2], using Property 1, and node [5,5] is not a descendant of [1,2]. Conversely speaking **writer**[1,2] is an ancestor of node [2,2] and not of node [5,5] according to Property 2. Consider node **writer**[1,2] and node **publisher**[4,5]. The two nodes are cousin nodes since they satisfy the Property 3. •

4.3 Architecture

The architecture of our approach for ontology taxonomy learning through tree mining is shown in Figure 3. The approach is composed of five modules: (i) *Pre-Phase*, (ii) *Similar Terms Computation and Clustering*, (ii) *Concepts Formulation*, (iv) *Similar Mini-Taxonomies Generation* and (v) *Trustable Base Taxonomy Construction*, supported by a repository which houses oracles and concepts' taxonomies.

The system is fed a set of hierarchical structures (schemas). *Pre-Phase* module processes the input as trees, calculating the depth-first node number and scope (Definition 3) for each of the nodes in the input schema trees. At the same time, for each tree a listing of nodes is constructed, sorted in depth-first traversal order. As the trees are being processed, a sorted global list of distinct node labels, over the whole set of input, is created [17].

In *Similar Terms Computation and Clustering* module, similarity is derived for the tree nodes labels of the input trees. We tokenise the labels and expand the abbreviated tokens using an abbreviation oracle. Currently, we utilise a domain specific user defined abbreviation table. Further, token similarity is supported by a manually defined domain specific synonym table. Label comparison is based on similar token sets or similar synonym token sets. The architecture is flexible enough to employ additional abbreviation, synonym oracles or arbitrary string matching algorithms. To further refine the similarity, we employ the structural aspect also. Labels' instances at nodes in different trees are compared for ancestor level label instance similarity (Property 2). Any such existence helps in re-enforcing the similarity of current pair of labels and remove any ambiguity [17]. Based on the similarity, the terms are clustered together.

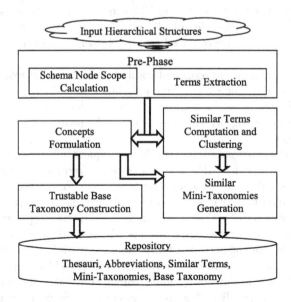

Fig. 3. Architecture for tree mining ontology concepts and taxonomy

In our approach concept is considered to be a small tree structure, referred as a mini-taxonomy and *Concepts Formulation* module discovers these mini-taxonomies. We utilise an extended version of frequent sub-tree mining approach described in [21] for this purpose. Once the set of mini-taxonomies have been extracted, the set is fed to the *Similar Mini-Taxonomies Generation* module. At this stage all possible similar mini-taxonomies are generated with the help of already computed similar labels clusters. The set of largest possible frequent sub-trees, from the output of concepts formulation module, acts as the input of *Trusted Base Taxonomy Construction* module. If there is just one tree, it is considered as the base taxonomy else all the sub-trees in the set are merged together to produce the base taxonomy.

The *Repository* is an indispensable part of the system. It houses oracles: thesauri and abbreviation lists. It also stores extracted terms, inter-term similarity, mini-taxonomies representing concepts and trustable base taxonomy. And it provides persistent support to the taxonomy learning process.

4.4   ExSTax Algorithm and Data Structures

The algorithm implemented for the *Concept Formulation* process acts as the kernel of our approach. It presents an iterative nature, extracting growing frequent sub-trees from a given set of trees. The sub-tree frequency support in the forest of trees is a user defined parameter. The algorithm takes as input the list of labels, with similar labels linked together to form a cluster (each cluster can have one or more labels). First task performed by the algorithm is to compute the frequency of each label in the forest of trees (Figure 5a). Next, with in each cluster, the label with the highest frequency in the forest of input trees is taken as the symbol representing the cluster. The frequency of the cluster symbol is computed by adding frequencies of all the labels in the cluster. Logically, all nodes labels in a cluster are replaced by the cluster symbol in the input set of trees (Figure 5b).

We consider symbol as the representation of a sub-tree. For example the symbol for a sub-tree with one node is the node label, and the symbol representing the tree S_1 in Figure 4 is "*book-author-name//publisher-name//title*" (- and / delimiters are used to signify the downward and upward traversal with in the tree, respectively).

From here on the process executes similar to frequent sub-tree mining algorithm given in [21]. In the first iteration, the process finds frequent sub-trees with size 1 (Figure 5b), and creates the vertical list data structure for further joining, referred to as join-list. Join-list entry is a composition of three elements; (i) tree number in which the sub-tree occur, (ii) the nodes numbers sequence representing the sub-tree which is the prefix of the rightmost node in the sub-tree, and (iii) scope of the right most node in the sub-tree. Only sub-trees with frequency equivalent or greater than the threshold are kept in the list. Threshold frequency is computed as '*support multiplied by number of input schemas divided by hundred*'.

In second pass, a new list of join-lists is created. Each frequent size 1 sub-tree is joined with every other size 1 sub-tree in the first join-list. The joining process first evaluates the similarity of element (i) and (ii) of the sub-tree join-list entries. If the pair passes the similarity test, it is subjected to Property 2 test. If the pair passes the Property 2 i.e., descendant test is true for the pair, a new symbol for the sub-tree of size 2 is created. If the sub-tree symbol does not exist in the second list, it is added to the list. The join-list entry of the symbol is added to its respective list. Like wise subsequent size 2 sub-trees are added to the list. At end of this iteration, frequency of each sub-tree is computed and only sub-trees with equivalent or higher frequency then threshold are kept in the list. The iterative process keeps executing till the sub-tree list does not have any frequent sub-tree. For joining sub-tree of size 2 or greater, Property 3 (cousin test) is also evaluated for computing a perspective candidate sub-tree symbol.

The last list of sub-trees contain either one or more sub-trees. This list acts as the input for computing the base taxonomy for the given set of hierarchical structures.

5   A Mini-Taxonomies Extraction Example

Figure 4 shows four trees after Pre-Phase. A list of labels created in this traversal is enumerated in Figure 5a with the similar labels clusters. Incremental execution of ExSTax algorithm is demonstrated in Figure 5b. There are six iterations before the algorithm stops, when it is not possible to generate much larger frequent sub-tree. The sub-tree generated in the last iteration can be considered as the base taxonomy for the given set of hierarchical structures. Figure 6 illustrates the taxonomy structure generated for the scenario.

The six iterations are presented in the six panels of Figure 5b. First iteration takes into account sub-trees of size one. Since there is no prefix sub-tree, the prefix data structure is empty. Each sub-tree symbol's vertical list entry is paired with other symbols' vertical list entries. The joining of vertical lists results in a structure of size two i.e., one sub-tree can only be descendant of the other in

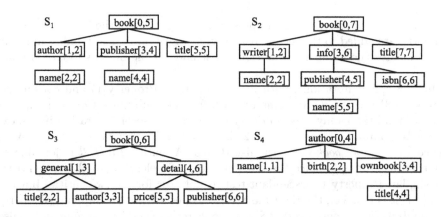

Fig. 4. Input set of 4 trees for learning base taxonomy using tree mining

a. Symbols List with frequency and
  Similar clusters (author, writer), (book, ownbook) and (detail, info)

author	book	birth	detail	general	info	isbn	name	ownbook	price	publisher	title	writer
2	3	1	1	1	1	1	5	1	1	3	4	2

b. Symbols representing sub-tree of size 1-6 with frequency greater then threshold and
  vertical join lists {tree number, prefix sub-tree, [number, scope (of right most node)]}

author	book	detail	name	publisher	title
1,,[1,2]	1,,[0,5]	2,,[3,6]	1,,[2,2]	1,,[3,4]	1,,[5,5]
2,,[1,2]	2,,[0,7]	3,,[4,6]	1,,[4,4]	2,,[4,5]	2,,[7,7]
3,,[3,3]	3,,[0,6]		2,,[2,2]	3,,[6,6]	3,,[2,2]
4,,[0,4]	4,,[3,4]		2,,[5,5]		4,,[4,4]
			4,,[1,1]		

* - indicates downwards move and / upwards move in the tree structure

author-name	book-author	book-detail	book-name	book-pub	book-title	detail-pub	pub-name
1,1,[2,2]	1,0,[1,2]	2,0,[3,6]	1,0,[2,2]	1,0,[3,4]	1,0,[5,5]	2,3,[4,5]	1,3,[4,4]
2,1,[2,2]	2,0,[1,2]	3,0,[4,6]	1,0,[4,4]	2,0,[4,5]	2,0,[7,7]	3,4,[6,6]	2,4,[5,5]
4,0,[1,1]	3,0,[3,3]		2,0,[2,2]	3,0,[6,6]	3,0,[2,2]		
			2,0,[5,5]		4,3,[4,4]		

book-author/detail, book-author-name, book-author/name, book-author/pub, book-author/title,
book-detail/pub, book-name/pub, book/name/title, book-pub-name, book-pub/title

book-author/detail-pub, book-author-name//name, book-author-name//pub,
book-author-name//title, book-author-name/title, book-author/pub-name, book-author/pub/title,
book-name/pub/title, book-pub-name//title

book-author-name//name/title, book-author-name//pub-name,
book-author-name//pub/title, book-author/pub-name//title

book-author-name//pub-name//title
1,01234,[5,5]   2,01245,[7,7]

Fig. 5. List of frequent sub-trees symbols, size 1 to 6 with 50% support in the input trees

this case. The sub-trees which are present in at least two of the input trees (50% support), are added to the second list. In vertical list entry, last number in prefix entry denotes the number of the right most node of the prefix sub-tree (Figure 5b).

In subsequent iterations, both descendant test (Property 1) and cousin test (Property 3) are applied to come up with frequent sub-trees. Consider the creation of mini-taxonomy "book-author/pub" from the second iteration in the example by joining subtrees of size 2. Let symbol "book-author" list, list A, is joined to symbol "book-pub" list, list B. List A, entity 1,0,[1,2] is joinable to list B entity 1,0,[3,4], since the schema and prefix elements of the two entities are similar. Property 1, descendant test, is not true for the two entities but the cousin test is true i.e., the right most node scopes are not overlapping (Property 3). Similarly list A, entity 3,0,[3,3] is joinable to list B entity 3,0,[6,6] and it also pass the Property 3. Thus supporting the 50 percent threshold frequency, and

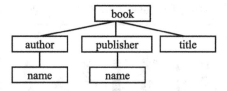

Fig. 6. Trusted extracted taxonomy

imply that the sub-tree with symbol "*book-author/pub*" is a frequent sub-tree of size 3.

Panels 3-5 present the symbols of extracted frequent sub-trees (mini-taxonomies) of sizes 3 to 5. The last panel of Figure 5b gives sub-tree with symbol composed of six labels. There are two vertical list elements, supporting the 50% support condition. The sub-tree (Figure 6)is present in input structures 1 and 2 (Figure 4).

6   Evaluation

The prototype implementation uses Java 5.0. A PC with Intel Xeon, 2.33 GHz processor and 2 GB RAM, running Windows XP was used. We have selected two data sets[9], BOOKS (synthetic) and COURSES (real), as the input hierarchical structures for our experiments.

Table 1. Characteristics of schema trees used in the experiments

Domain	BOOKS	COURSES
Number of Schemas	176	42
Average nodes per schema	8	8
Largest schema size	14	17
Smallest schema size	5	2
Schema Tree Depth	3	4

We examined the semantic quality of generated mini-taxonomies using the precision measure. Our target was to generate semantically meaningful taxonomic structures. Therefore, we manually scrutinized the generated tree patterns and computed the share of semantically applicable sub-trees among all found. With reference to Figure 4 structure S_1, a sub-tree structure "*book[0,5]-name[2,2]/name[4,4]*" is considered to be invalid, since it is semantically meaningless. Based on these considerations we show the precision measure computed from the experiments. Figure 7 shows the precision of 8 sets of input structures comprising of 8, 16, 50, 75, 100, 125, 150 and 176 sizes taken from BOOKS. The results are computed for three different tree mining support values 37, 50 and 75 percent.

---

[9] http://www.lirmm.fr/PORSCHE/TaxonomyLearning/

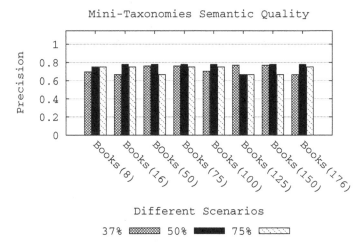

Fig. 7. Precision of ExSTax for eight sets of hierarchical structures from Books domain

In the other experiment performed on COURSES domain of XML schema instances, with support value set to 25 percent, we retrieved precision nearly equal to 1. And the base taxonomy generated in this experiment was Course-Title/Instructor/Room/Time.

Discussion
The experimental results show the precision measure for Books domain, to be between 0.65 and 0.8. Thus supporting the validity of our idea of mini-taxonomies extraction. The number of mini-taxonomies generated increased with decrease in the value of tree mining support parameter and vice versa. Therefore we selected the support values range (37-75), whose results could be verified manually. Secondly, it is quite difficult to estimate the recall measure in the experiments because of the large number of possible outputs. Devising a system for this purpose is out of the scope of current work. Another observation made during the execution is that ExSTax algorithm shows exponential scalability with respect to the size of input tree structures. Since we are concerned with the semantic validity of the output, we have not taken into account the time performance complexity of the algorithm.

7   Conclusion and Future Work

We have introduced a novel technique based on tree mining, for ontology taxonomy learning. The core idea behind this paper is to demonstrate the applicability of tree mining techniques for ontology taxonomy extraction in large scale scenario. The technique inherently supports the collaborative ontology learning by holistically exploiting the already available hierarchical structures in the domain.

We have investigated its scalability with respect to number of schemas. The experimental results demonstrate that our approach scales to hundreds of schemas.

The linguistic matching of node labels uses tokenisation, abbreviations and synonyms. Our method provides an almost automated solution to the large scale domain specific taxonomy learning problem.

Our results point to significant future research. Foremost, our work is directed for development of a mining solution for learning all aspects of domain ontology, comprising of term extraction, synonym and translation detection, concept formulation, concept hierarchies, relations, rule derivation and axiomatization. Further, we tend to do research for finding valid patterns missing from the generated set, to estimate the recall measure. We are also planning to investigate the application of our approach in P2P architectures and domain specific large scale social network environments. Another issue for the future is a benchmark for automatic ontology learning tools in a large scale scenario. To further benefit from tree mining, we are going to evaluate the advantage of the automatically extracted mini-taxonomies for the discovery of n:m complex mappings in context of research described in [7].

References

1. Antoniou, G., van Harmelen, F.: A Semantic Web Primer. MIT Press, Cambridge (2004)
2. Arpinar, I.B., Aleman-Meza, B., Zhang, R., Maduko, A.: Ontology-driven web services composition platform. In: IEEE CEC (2004)
3. Buitelaar, P., Cimiano, P., Magnini, B.: Ontology learning from text: An overview. In: Ontology Learning from Text: Methods, Evaluation and Applications Frontiers. IOS Press, Amsterdam (2005)
4. Buitelaar, P., Olejnik, D., Sintek, M.: A protege plug-in for ontology extraction from text based on linguistic analysis. In: Bussler, C.J., Davies, J., Fensel, D., Studer, R. (eds.) ESWS 2004. LNCS, vol. 3053. Springer, Heidelberg (2004)
5. Chi, Y., Muntz, R.R., Nijssen, S., Kok, J.N.: Frequent subtree mining - an overview. Fundamenta Informaticae 66(1-2), 161–198 (2005)
6. Cimiano, P., Pivk, A., Schmidt-Thieme, L., Staab, S.: Learning taxonomic relations from heterogeneous sources of evidence. In: ECAI WorkShop Ontology Learning and Population (2004)
7. Embley, D.W., Xu, L., Ding, Y.: Automatic direct and indirect schema mapping: Experiences and lessons learned. ACM SIGMOD Record 33(4), 14–19 (2004)
8. Giunchiglia, F., Shvaiko, P., Yatskevich, M.: S-match: an algorithm and an implementation of semantic matching. In: Bussler, C.J., Davies, J., Fensel, D., Studer, R. (eds.) ESWS 2004. LNCS, vol. 3053. Springer, Heidelberg (2004)
9. Gomez-Perez, A., Manzano-Macho, D.: Deliverable 1.5: A survey of ontology learning methods and techniques. Technical report, Universidad Politecnica de Madrid (2003)
10. Gruber, T.: Towards principles for the design of ontologies used for knowledge sharing. Human and computer Studies J. 43, 907–928 (1994)
11. He, B., Chang, K.C.-C., Han, J.: Discovering complex matchings across web query interfaces: a correlation mining approach. In: KDD, pp. 148–157 (2004)
12. Jasche, R., Hotho, A., Schmitz, C., Ganter, B., Stumme, G.: Discovering shared conceptualizations in folksonomies. Web Semantics: Science, Services and Agents on World Wide Web 6(1), 38–53 (2008)

13. Li, M., Du, X.-Y., Wang, S.: Learning ontology from relational database. In: IEEE ICMLC (2005)
14. Maedche, A., Pekar, V., Staab, S.: Ontology learning part one – on discovering taxonomic relations from the web. In: Web Intelligence (2002)
15. Maedche, A., Staab, S.: Ontology learning. In: Staab, S., Studer, R. (eds.) Handbook of Ontologies. Springer, Heidelberg (2004)
16. Noy, N.F.: Semantic integration: A survey of ontology-based approaches. ACM SIGMOD Record 33(4), 65–70 (2004)
17. Saleem, K., Bellahsene, Z., Hunt, E.: Porsche: Performance oriented schema mediation. Information Systems-Elsevier 33 (2008)
18. Schutze, H.: Word space. In: NIPS, pp. 895–902 (1993)
19. Tijerino, Y.A., Embley, D.W., Ding, Y., Nagy, G.: Towards ontology generation from tables. World Wide Web 8, 261–285 (2005)
20. Weber, N., Buitelaar, P.: Web-based ontology learning with isolde. In: ISWC WorkShops Web Content Mining with Human Language (2006)
21. Zaki, M.J.: Efficiently mining frequent embedded unordered trees. Fundamenta Informaticae 66(1-2), 33–52 (2005)

Analysis and Reuse of Plots Using Similarity and Analogy

Antonio L. Furtado, Marco A. Casanova,
Simone D.J. Barbosa, and Karin K. Breitman

Departamento de Informática – Pontifícia Universidade Católica do Rio de Janeiro
Rua Marquês de S. Vicente, 225 – Rio de Janeiro, Brasil – CEP 22451-900
{furtado,casanova,simone,karin}@inf.puc-rio.br

Abstract. A plot is a partially ordered set of events. Plot analysis is a relevant source of knowledge about the agents' behavior when accessing data stored in the database. It relies on logical logs which register the actions of individual agents. This paper proposes techniques to analyze and reuse plots based on the concepts of similarity and analogy, borrowed from cognitive science and linguistics. The concept of similarity is applied to organize plots as a library, and to explore the reuse of plots in the same domain. By contrast, the concept of analogy helps reuse plots across different domains. The techniques proposed in this paper find applications in areas such as computer games and emergency response information systems, as well as some traditional business applications.

Keywords: Temporal database, log, plot, narrative, similarity, analogy.

1 Introduction

Literary research addresses narratives at successive levels. The most basic level, the fabula, is defined as "a series of logically and chronologically related events that are caused or experienced by actors" [3]. A series of events is often called a *plot*, a notion that can be usefully transposed to the context of information systems. Intuitively, plots are the stories [25,26] that happen in the underlying mini-world and, as a result, produce state-changes in its database representation. More precisely, an event represents the result of the execution of some domain-oriented operation by an authorized agent, and a plot is a partially ordered set of events. What logically relates the events, and determines the precedence among them, is the interplay between the pre- and post-conditions in terms of which operations are defined. The pre- and post-conditions, in turn, reflect the integrity constraints and business rules prevailing in the application domain involved.

Plot analysis is a rich source of knowledge about the agents' behavior when accessing data stored in the database. It relies on (logical) database logs, also called audit trails, which register the actions of individual agents. A trivial example of a log is a bank account statement, which records the sequence of actions executed against the account. A second example comes from storytelling engines, such as **LOGTELL** [9,10], which model the world as a database and are based on a set of pre-defined actions and plots [10]. A log in this case is the trace of events generated by composing a story interactively. In the context of an emergency response information system

Q. Li et al. (Eds.): ER 2008, LNCS 5231, pp. 355–368, 2008.

[27], a log registers the actions taken when handling an emergency, or during a training exercise [8].

The thrust of this paper is to propose techniques to analyze and reuse plots applying the concepts of similarity and analogy, borrowed from cognitive science and linguistics [5,18]. We used these notions to explore database conceptual design techniques and query interfaces at previous stages of our research project [7,4]. In the present paper, we first discuss how to extract plots from logs. Then, we explore the concept of similarity to organize a plot library that helps reuse plots in the same domain. By contrast, we apply the concept of analogy to reuse plots across *different* domains.

Returning to our examples, we sometimes spend countless hours analyzing our bank account statement (our account log) to figure out recurrent similar groups (similar plots) of funds transfers, deposits, withdrawals and payments (the events in banking applications). Plots in this case are typically simple, say, a set of withdrawals and payments followed by a deposit or funds transfer to balance the account. For example, we may be overspending on certain weekends, which come after the (forgotten) due dates of a number of bills. If similar groups of events repeat month after month, i.e., similar plots reoccur every month, then we ought to change our spending pattern. Usually, such groups of events are not treated as plots because the relationships between the events are too simple: the withdrawals and payments merely precede the deposit or funds transfer. One may therefore use traditional data mining techniques to detect the pattern of recurring events.

As a second example, from the domain of digital storytelling, consider the **LOGTELL** engine which features a built-in planner that creates new plots from a library of pre-defined operations and plots. By analyzing plot similarities, the game designer may come out with recurrent patterns that he may reuse to generate new plots in other domains, by analogy. An entirely compatible approach has been proposed a long time ago in literary theory by the Russian researcher Vladimir Propp [24]. In order to specify the genre of fairy-tales, he described a set of 31 functions, comparable to what we are calling domain-oriented, or more appropriately here, genre-oriented operations, which he claimed to be enough to account for a large sample extracted from an anthology of fairy-tales compiled by Alekxandr Afanas'ev [1]. Propp's research in fact focused on finding analogous plots in different fairy-tales.

The third example comes from the domain of emergency response information systems, where logs are an essential resource [8]. A plot in this case is a set of interrelated actions that an emergency team must perform to mitigate a specific accident scenario during an emergency, such as to isolate and clean an area affected by the spill of a hazardous material. An analysis of the log of actions taken during the response to an accident may help settle legal disputes. Furthermore, if plots generated as responses to similar accident scenarios exhibit similar inappropriate sequences of mitigating actions, then the analysis is an indication that the emergency teams, equipment or procedures must be revised. Similarly, emergency response information systems are valuable tools to train emergency teams on how to react to accidents. In this case, the logs will be the result of simulated accidents. An analysis of the plots extracted from the logs will help assess how prepared the teams are, or else if some procedure is not appropriate, which is detected when the teams repeatedly generate similar inappropriate sequences of mitigating actions as a response to similar accidents. Plot analogy may also be a valuable pedagogical strategy to train the teams, i.e., if a team is trained in one type of accident, one might try to transpose, by analogy, the scenario and the plot mastered by the team to a different scenario and a different group of interrelated actions.

The practical relevance of the concepts of similarity and analogy, central to our work, has been amply recognized. Winston [29] is an early reference that describes a theory of analogy with applications to AI systems. Metaphors [18] have been used to improve human-computer interface design [5], in particular, and software design, in general [20]. The use of similarity and analogy in the context of database design has been explored in [7,4]. The plot extraction technique we adopt follows the AI tradition [15]. Our approach differs from research, such as [21], which focuses on the mining of rules from sequence databases, which are mostly based on statistical confidence levels. The notion of plot similarity we adopt also differs from the notion of process similarity introduced in [2], which computes a coefficient that indicates how dissimilar two processes are. Aalst et al. [28] describe an algorithm to extract a process model from such a log and represent it in terms of a Petri net. Their approach differs from ours in so far as the plot extraction technique, described in Section 2.3, is based on the semantics of the operations, expressed by pre- and post-conditions.

The paper is organized as follows. Section 2 introduces plots and related concepts, and outlines an algorithm to extract plots from logs. Section 3 discusses how to reuse plots in the same domain, employing the concept of similarity. Section 4 considers the reuse of plots across different domains, resorting to the notion of analogy. Section 5 contains the conclusion.

2   Basic Concepts and Techniques

2.1   Informal Characterization of the Basic Concepts

In this section, we informally introduce the basic concepts we use throughout the paper. Our notation is based on Prolog, from which we borrow variables, constants and literals [7,11]. Section 2.2 contains rigorous definitions for the main concepts.

Our database conceptual schema follows the usual conventions of the Entity-Relationship model [6]. In addition, the schema contains a repertoire of domain-oriented operations, defined through their pre- and post-conditions, as proposed in the STRIPS system [12]. In order to preserve the integrity constraints regulating the mini-world represented in the database, an operation can execute only if its pre-conditions currently hold, and the effect of its execution corresponds precisely to its post-conditions. A complementary requirement is that the state of the database may change only by executing an operation from the predefined repertoire.

To illustrate these concepts, we introduce a simple example schema in the domain of products and components:

entity classes:	`product, component`
attributes:	`pno` of `product`
	`cno, ctype, defective` of `component`
relationship:	`iscompof` associating `component` with `product`
operations:	`repair(pno,cno)`
	`order(ctype,cno)`
	`replace(pno,cno1,cno2)`

where instances of `product` are `identified` by pno, and instances of `component`, which is a *weak entity* [6], are identified via the `iscompof` relationship combined with the discriminating attribute cno. The value of attribute `ctype` indicates the type of a component, and the Boolean attribute `defective` exclusively qualifies those components that have been found to be defective.

Using the Prolog-based notation introduced in [7], the specification of the `Product` schema would be:

```
Schema: Product
Clauses --
    entity(product, pno)
    attribute(product, pno)
    entity(component, [pno/cno-iscompof-pno, cno])
    attribute(component, cno)
    attribute(component, ctype)
    attribute(component, defective)
    relationship(iscompof, component/n/total, product/1/total)
    operation(order, [ctype, cno])
    pre(order(A, B), [])
    post(order(A, B), [ctype(B, A), ¬defective(B)])
    operation(replace, [pno, cno, cno])
    pre(replace(A, B, C),
        [iscompof(B, A), ctype(B, D), ctype(C, D)])/diff(B, C)
    post(replace(A, B, C),
        [¬iscompof(B, A), iscompof(C,A)])/diff(B, C)
    operation(repair, [pno, cno])
    pre(repair(A, B), [defective(B)])
    post(repair(A, B), [¬defective(B)])
```

A database conceptual schema may also include *goal-inference rules* of the form $S \rightarrow G$, where S is a *situation* and G a *goal*, both of which are sets of literals. Such rules capture the motivation of an agent who, observing that a certain situation S holds, would be expected to execute the appropriate operations to reach a state where the goal G holds.

The conceptual schema we just introduced may include, for example, the goal-inference rule $S \rightarrow G$, where

```
S = [iscompof(X, Y), ctype(X, Z), defective(X)]
G = [iscompof(W, Y), ctype(W, Z), ¬defective(W)]
```

To conclude, we define events, logs and plots. An *event* is a statement of the form $o(p_1,...,p_n)$, where o is an operation name and $(p_1,...,p_n)$ is the parameter list of the operation, which is a list of (Prolog) terms. An event $o(p_1,...,p_n)$ is *ground* iff the parameter list does not contain variables.

A *log* is a sequence of ground events.

A *plot* is a pair $P=(E,D)$, where E is a set of events and $D \subseteq E \times E$ is a partial order over E. A plot $P=(E,D)$ is *ground* iff all events in E are ground.

The relation D defines a set of *precedence dependencies* over E and captures the idea that, if an event e_1 contributes, as a result of its post-conditions, to the pre-conditions of another event e_2, then e_1 must precede e_2 in the plot.

The precedence dependencies in a plot are denoted with the help of *tags*. More precisely, a plot is denoted as two lists: a list of expressions of the form t:e, where t is a constant, called a *tag*, and e is an event; and a list of expressions of the form t-u, where t and u are tags used in the first list. Tags are just a notational convenience, so that the plots P_1 and P_2 below are treated as *equivalent* plots:

$$P_1 = [[\texttt{f1: order(ct,c4), f2: replace(pr,c3,c4)],[f1-f2]]}$$
$$P_2 = [[\texttt{f7: replace(pr,c3,c4),f8: order(ct,c4)],[f8-f7]]}$$

As will be argued in the next sections, it is in general a useful practice to record a plot P together with an associated goal-inference rule. We therefore define an *indexed plot* as a triple (S,G,P), where P is a plot and $S{\rightarrow}G$ is a situation-goal rule, called the *circumstance* associated with P.

2.2   Formal Characterization of the Basic Concepts

In this section, we define the syntax and semantics of the basic concepts that support the Prolog implementation of the plot techniques described in this paper. For brevity, we use standard concepts from first-order languages without definition. We refer the reader to [10] for the details.

A *static ER language* $\mathcal{E}$ is a many-sorted first-order language whose alphabet contains a set $\mathcal{D}$ of *database symbols* to describe database conceptual objects.

A *substitution* is a function θ that maps variables of $\mathcal{E}$ into terms of $\mathcal{E}$ (of the same sort). A substitution θ is *ground* iff it maps variables of $\mathcal{E}$ into variable-free terms of $\mathcal{E}$. A substitution is *total* iff it is defined for all variables of $\mathcal{E}$; otherwise, it is *partial*. If otherwise indicated, we assume that a substitution is total.

An expression ϕ is a formula or a term of $\mathcal{E}$. Given a substitution θ, we use $\phi\theta$ to denote the expression obtained by applying θ to ϕ. A *(ground) instance* of ϕ is an expression obtained by applying a (ground) substitution to ϕ.

A *literal* is an expression of the form $p(t_1,...,t_n)$ or of the form $\neg p(t_1,...,t_n)$, where p is an n-ary predicate symbol of $\mathcal{E}$ and $t_1,...,t_n$ is a list of terms of $\mathcal{E}$. A *database literal* is a literal whose predicate symbol is in $\mathcal{D}$, and a *database fact* is a ground positive database literal.

A *structure* M for $\mathcal{E}$ assigns to each symbol s of $\mathcal{E}$ an *interpretation* s^M as for first-order languages. The notion that M *satisfies* a formula of $\mathcal{E}$ is also defined as usual. A *possible fact* of M is a database fact of $\mathcal{E}$ that is satisfied by M. A *possible database state* of M is a set of possible facts of M.

Let G be a conjunction (or a set) of ground database literals, K be a conjunction (or a set) of database literals, and s be a possible database state. Then,

- s *satisfies G for M*, denoted $s \vDash_M G$, iff $g\in s$, for each ground literal g that occurs in G

- s *satisfies K for M*, denoted $s \vDash_M K$, iff $s \vDash_M G$, for each ground instance G of K

A *static ER schema* is a pair $S{=}(\mathcal{E},\mathcal{C})$ such that $\mathcal{E}$ is a static ER language and $\mathcal{C}$ is a set of formulas of $\mathcal{E}$, called the *axioms* of S, that includes *ER constraints*, which capture ER concepts, and *domain constraints*, which capture properties of the application domain. A *model* of S is a structure of $\mathcal{E}$ that satisfies all axioms in $\mathcal{C}$.

A *dynamic ER language* $\mathcal{L}$ is a static ER language whose alphabet is extended to include a new set of symbols, the *operation names*, with an associated *arity*, and whose set of expressions is extended to include operation specifications, events, and situation-goal rules.

An *operation specification* for an n-ary operation name o is an expression O of the form $\{P\}o(x_1,...,x_n)\{Q\}$, where $x_1,...,x_n$ is a list of distinct variables, and P and Q are sets of database literals. We say that $o(x_1,...,x_n)$ is the *input declaration*, P is the *pre-condition* and Q is the *post-condition* of O.

A structure M for $\mathcal{L}$ is defined as for static ER languages, except that M assigns to each operation name o a set o^M of pairs of possible database states of M.

Let O be an operation specification for an n-ary operation name o and assume that O is of the form $\{P\}o(x_1,...,x_n)\{Q\}$. Let θ be a ground substitution of $\mathcal{L}$. Then, a pair (s,t) of possible database states in o^M *satisfies $O\theta$ for M* iff

- $s \vDash_M P\theta$ (the pre-conditions are satisfied in s for M)
- $t \vDash_M Q\theta$ (the post-conditions are satisfied in t for M)
- for every possible database fact f of M, if neither f nor $\neg f$ occur in $Q\theta$, then

  $t \vDash f$ iff $s \vDash f$ (which is the frame requirement: preservation of satisfaction from s to t for ground database literals that are neither established nor negated by the post-condition $Q\theta$, which is ground by assumption)

Furthermore, M *satisfies $O\theta$* iff every pair (s,t) of possible database states in o^M satisfies $O\theta$ for M. Finally, M *satisfies O* iff M satisfies every ground instance of O.

An *event* is an expression e of the form $o(t_1,...,t_n)$, where o is an n-ary operation name of $\mathcal{L}$ and $t_1,...,t_n$ is a list of terms of $\mathcal{L}$. The *parameter substitution* of e is the partial substitution θ_e that maps x_i into t_i, for $i \in [1,n]$, and is undefined for the other variables of $\mathcal{L}$. We define an interpretation in M for e as the set e^M consisting of all pairs (s,t) of possible database states in o^M such that (s,t) satisfies $O\rho$ for M, where $\rho = \theta_e \circ \varphi$, for some ground substitution φ.

Let e be an event of the form $o(t_1,...,t_n)$, O be the operation specification for o, and θ_e be the parameter substitution of e. Then, $O\theta_e$ is the *specification for e induced by O*. A structure M *satisfies $O\theta_e$ with respect to O* iff M satisfies every ground instance $O\rho$ of O, where $\rho = \theta_e \circ \varphi$, for some ground substitution φ.

A *temporal database* of a structure M is a sequence $S=(s_0,s_1,...)$ of possible database states of M.

A *situation-goal rule* is an expression of the form $S \rightarrow G$, where S and G are sets of database literals. A temporal database $S=(s_0,s_1,...)$ of M *satisfies* $S \rightarrow G$, denoted $S \vDash_M S \rightarrow G$, iff there are p and q, with $1 \le p \le q \le |S|$, such that $s_p \vDash_M S$ and $s_q \vDash_M G$.

A *dynamic ER schema* is a pair $\mathcal{D}=(\mathcal{L},\mathcal{A})$ such that $\mathcal{L}$ is a dynamic ER language and $\mathcal{A}$ is a set of formulas of $\mathcal{L}$, called the *axioms* of $\mathcal{T}$, that includes ER constraints, domain constraints, operation specifications and situation-goal rules, such that, for each operation name o of $\mathcal{L}$, there is exactly one operation specification for o in $\mathcal{A}$. A *model* of $\mathcal{D}$ is a structure for $\mathcal{L}$ that satisfies all axioms in $\mathcal{A}$.

Let e be an event of $\mathcal{L}$ and assume that e is of the form $o(t_1,...,t_n)$. One can prove that, if M is a model of $\mathcal{D}$, then M satisfies $o\theta_e$ with respect to the (unique) operation specification for o that occurs in $\mathcal{A}$.

We prefer to introduce logs and plots as meta-level concepts, rather than expressions of dynamic ER languages, to avoid complex syntactical structures. Let $\mathcal{L}$ be a dynamic ER language and M be a structure of $\mathcal{L}$ in what follows.

A *log* is a possibly empty finite sequence $E=(e_1,e_2,...,e_n)$ of ground events of $\mathcal{L}$. A temporal database $S=(s_0,s_1,...)$ of M *satisfies* $E=(e_1,e_2,...,e_n)$, denoted $S \vDash_M E$, iff $|S| > n$ and, for each $i \in [1,n]$, $(s_{i-1},s_i) \in e_i^M$ (i.e, e_i caused the transition from s_{i-1} to s_i).

A *plot* is a pair $P=(P_E,P_D)$, where P_E is a finite set of events and $P_D \subseteq P_E \times P_E$ is a partial order over P_E. A log $E=(e_1,e_2,...,e_n)$ is *consistent with* $P=(P_E,P_D)$ iff there is a ground substitution θ such that, for each event e in P_E, the ground instance $e\theta$ of e occurs in E and, for every $e_1,e_2 \in P_E$, if $(e_1,e_2) \in P_D$, then $e_1\theta$ precedes $e_2\theta$ in E.

A temporal database $S=(s_0,s_1,...)$ of M *satisfies* $P=(P_E,P_D)$, denoted $S\vDash_M P$, iff there is a log $E=(e_1,e_2,...,e_n)$ such that S satisfies E and E is consistent with P. Finally, a plot P is *consistent* with a set Π of situation-goal rules with respect to a structure M iff, for every temporal database S of M, if S satisfies P then S also satisfies Π.

2.3   Extracting Indexed Plots from a Log

In this section, we briefly introduce an algorithm to extract indexed plots from a log. The details of the algorithm can be found in [13].

The algorithm takes as input a goal-inference rule $S \rightarrow G$ and a log L, and outputs an indexed plot (S_P,G_P,P). The first step of the algorithm uses a simulation process that essentially recapitulates the evolution of the database while traversing the log. A subsequence M is extracted from the log L iff, prior to the execution of the first event in M, the situation S holds and, after the execution of the last event in M, a state is reached where G holds. This process may generate ground instances S_P and G_P of S and G, respectively. A plot P is obtained from M by a filtering process that keeps only the events whose post-conditions contribute to G_P and in addition, proceeding backwards recursively, those events that contribute to pre-conditions of events already included in P. The algorithm then outputs the indexed plot (S_P,G_P,P).

For example, consider the goal-inference rule $S \rightarrow G$, where

```
S = [iscompof(X, Y), ctype(X, Z), defective(X)]
G = [iscompof(W, Y), ctype(W, Z), ¬defective(W)]
```

and suppose that S and G are found to hold, respectively, before the first event, and immediately after the last event of the sub-sequence of the log shown below:

```
... order(ct,c4) ... replace(pr,c3,c4) ...
```

In view of the pre- and post-conditions of `order` and `replace`, defined in Section 2.1, the algorithm then outputs the indexed plot (S_P,G_P,P), where

```
S_p = [iscompof(c3, pr), ctype(c3, ct), defective(c3)]
G_p = [iscompof(c4, pr), ctype(c4, ct), ¬defective(c4)]
P   = [[f1: order(ct,c4), f2: replace(pr,c3,c4)],[f1-f2]]
```

3   Using Similarity to Organize and Reuse Plots

3.1   The Notion of Plot and Indexed Plot Similarity

A *similarity mapping* ρ is a bijective mapping between terms, that is, a set of pairs (u,v) of terms such that any two pairs are equal on the first component iff they are equal on the second component. Let K be a set of literals, e be an event, $P=(E,D)$ be a plot, and κ be a situation-goal rule of the form $S{\rightarrow}G$. Then, the expression $K\rho$ denotes the set $\{\ l\rho\ /\ l{\in}K\ \}$, the expression $e\rho$ denotes the event obtained by replacing each term u that occurs in e by v, if $(u,v){\in}\rho$, the expression $P\rho$ denotes the plot (F,G) such that $F=\{\ e\rho\ /\ e{\in}E\ \}$ and $G=\{\ (e\rho,f\rho)\ /\ (e,f){\in}D\ \}$, and the expression $\kappa\rho$ denotes the situation-goal rule $S\rho{\rightarrow}G\rho$.

Two plots P and P' are *similar* iff there is a similarity mapping ρ such that $P'=P\rho$. Likewise, two situation-goal rules $S{\rightarrow}G$ and $S'{\rightarrow}G'$ are *similar* iff there is a similarity mapping ρ such that $S'=S\rho$ and $G'=G\rho$. Given two indexed plots (S_1,G_1,P_1) and (S_2,G_2,P_2), we say that:

- (S_1,G_1,P_1) and (S_2,G_2,P_2) are *sgp-similar* iff there is a similarity mapping ρ such that $S_2=S_1\rho$, $G_2=G_1\rho$ and $P_2=P_1\rho$
- (S_1,G_1,P_1) and (S_2,G_2,P_2) are *sg-similar* iff $S_1{\rightarrow}G_1$ and $S_2{\rightarrow}G_2$ are similar situation-goal rules
- (S_1,G_1,P_1) and (S_2,G_2,P_2) are *p-similar* iff P_1 and P_2 are similar plots

For example, consider $I_1=(S_1,G_1,P_1)$, $I_2=(S_2,G_2,P_2)$ and $I_3=(S_3,G_3,P_3)$, where

```
S₁ = [iscompof(c3, pr), ctype(c3, ct), defective(c3)]
G₁ = [iscompof(c4, pr), ctype(c4, ct), ¬defective(c4)]
P₁ = [[f1: order(ct,c4), f2: replace(pr,c3,c4)],[f1-f2]]
S₂ = [iscompof(c1, pr), ctype(c1, ct), defective(c1)]
G₂ = [iscompof(c2, pr), ctype(c2, ct), ¬defective(c2)]
P₂ = [[f7: order(ct,c2), f8: replace(pr,c1,c2)],[f7-f8]]
S₃ = [iscompof(c3, pr), ctype(c3, ct), defective(c3)]
G₃ = [iscompof(c3, pr), ctype(c3, ct), ¬defective(c3)]
P₃ = [[f1: repair(pr,c3)], []]
```

Then, the plans P_1 and P_2 are similar. Indeed, $P_2 =P_1\rho$, where ρ is the similarity mapping that maps c4 into c2 and c3 into c1. To verify whether the precedence dependencies agree, it suffices to find a renaming of the tags of one of the plots that can render the sets of precedence dependencies of the two plots equal, as discussed in Section 2.1 (note that tags were not considered when introducing similarity mapping, since they are just a notational convenience and are not required to define plots). Likewise, the situation-goal rules $S_1{\rightarrow}G_1$ and $S_2{\rightarrow}G_2$ are similar, with ρ again as the similarity mapping. The indexed plots I_1 and I_2 are p-similar, sg-similar and sgp-similar. Moreover, I_3 is sg-similar to both I_1 and I_2, but not sgp-similar.

Finally, given two plots $P=(E,D)$ and $P'=(E',D')$, we say that a plot Q is a *most specific generalization (m.s.g.)* [13,16] of P and P' iff there are similarity mappings θ

and θ' such that $Q=P\theta=P'\theta'$, θ and θ' map terms into variables and θ and θ' are the least such similarity mappings. Note that Q is trivially similar to both P and P'.

For example, plot P_4 is an m.s.g. of plots P_1 and P_2 above, where

$$P_4 = [[\text{f1: order(ct,X), f2: replace(pr,X,Y)],[f1-f2]]}$$

Indeed, $P_4=P_1\theta=P_2\theta'$, where θ maps constants c4 and c3 into variables X and Y, respectively, and θ' maps constants c2 and c1 into variables X and Y, respectively (and tags f7 and f8 into f1 and f2, respectively).

The notion of m.s.g. extends to indexed plots by applying the similarity mappings also to the circumstances. Thus, $I_4=(S_4,G_4,P_4)$ is an m.s.g. of I_1 and I_2 above, where

$$S_4 = [\text{iscompof(X, pr), ctype(X, ct), defective(X)]}$$
$$G_4 = [\text{iscompof(Y, pr), ctype(Y, ct), ¬defective(Y)]}$$
$$P_4 = [[\text{f1: order(ct,Y), f2: replace(pr,X,Y)],[f1-f2]]}$$

3.2 Indexed Plot Libraries

The data administrator (DA) may apply the plot extraction algorithm of Section 2.3 to search the database log for a plot P responding to a goal-inference rule $S{\rightarrow}G$. The entire set of (S_p,G_p,P) indexed plots collected by the DA constitutes a *library of plots* (*LP*). Note that the *LP* will contain only ground indexed plots, extracted by the algorithm of Section 2.3. Furthermore, note that the *LP* may in fact contain similar plots, such as $I_1=(S_1,G_1,P_1)$, $I_2=(S_2,G_2,P_2)$ in the example of Section 3.1.

The DA may reduce such redundancy by replacing indexed plots which are sgp-similar by their most specific generalization, thereby constructing a *library of typical plots* (*LTP*). The DA may indeed directly construct the *LTP* as follows. As for the *LP*, suppose that the DA applies the plot extraction algorithm to search the log for an indexed plot (S_p,G_p,P) responding to a previously specified goal-inference rule $S{\rightarrow}G$. Before adding (S_p,G_p,P) to the *LTP*, the DA searches the *LTP* for an indexed plot (S_q,G_q,Q) which is sgp-similar to (S_p,G_p,P). If one such indexed plot is found, the DA replaces (S_q,G_q,Q) in the *LTP* by the most specific generalization of (S_p,G_p,P) and (S_q,G_q,Q).

If applied to the indexed plots $I_1=(S_1,G_1,P_1)$, $I_2=(S_2,G_2,P_2)$ and $I_3=(S_3,G_3,P_3)$, listed in Section 3.1, this strategy will keep $I_3=(S_3,G_3,P_3)$ and, since I_1 and I_2 are similar, will replace I_1 and I_2 by their m.s.g. $I_4=(S_4,G_4,P_4)$, also defined in Section 3.1.

To search the *LTP*, an interested agent supplies two lists, L_s and L_g. The library will return any indexed plot (S_p,G_p,P) such that (L_s,L_g) *matches* (S_p,G_p) in the sense that every literal in L_s unifies with some literal in S_p, and every literal in L_g unifies with some literal in G_p. As a consequence of unification, variables (not all, in some cases) in S_p and G_p – and consequently in P – will be consistently replaced by constants present in L_s or L_g. In other words, (L_s,L_g) is a more *concrete circumstance* which must fit in the more general (S_p,G_p) circumstance to justify the use of the associated plot P, which could then be used as an executable *plan*.

For example, assume that the *LTP* contains the indexed plots $I_3=(S_3,G_3,P_3)$ and $I_4=(S_4,G_4,P_4)$, defined above. Consider the pair of lists (L_s,L_g), where

$$L_s = [\texttt{iscompof(c3, pr), ctype(c3, ct)}]$$
$$L_g = [\texttt{iscompof(Z, pr), ¬defective(Z)}]$$

Searching the *LTP* with (L_s, L_g) yields $I_3=(S_3, G_3, P_3)$ and $I_4=(S_4, G_4, P_4)$.

However, note that P_3 and P_4, even though they were designed to operate the required transition to a state where G holds, are not equivalent with respect to their full effects. A wise precaution is to ascertain beforehand all that may be caused by running each plot, in view of possible undesired side-effects. This can be accomplished by simulating the execution of each plot, after supplying a *context*, defined as a set of literals, which captures aspects of the current state s_0. Simulation can employ a well-known recursive backward-chaining algorithm [13], which incidentally is the basis for simple plan-generators following STRIPS formalisms.

For example, consider the context C, where:

$$C = [\texttt{iscompof(c3, pr),ctype(c3, ct),defective(c3)}]$$

Then, the result of choosing to apply either P_3 or P_4 would be R_3 or R_4, where:

$$R_3 = [\texttt{¬defective(c3), ctype(c3, ct), iscompof(c3, pr)}]$$
$$R_4 = [\texttt{¬iscompof(c3, pr), ctype(c3, ct), ctype(Y, ct),}$$
$$\texttt{¬defective(Y), iscompof(Y, pr)}]$$

The fact that P_4 contains a variable Y, even after the simulated execution, and the fact that the variable figures in the result obtained certainly deserve attention. We can understand that, when placing the order, the foreman in charge of the product can only indicate the component type (the value of attribute ct). The value of the discriminating attribute cno will remain undetermined until the order is fulfilled, typically through the intermediacy of an agent involved with inventory management. Such problems can only be handled in multi-agent environments, a topic outside the scope of the present paper, wherein a plot would result from the combination of partial plots, each one including appropriate communicative acts [17], to be executed by different agents.

4 Plot Analogy

4.1 The Notion of Plot Analogy

The database schema introduced in Section 2.1 provides an example of weak entity. It has several typical features which recur in many other application domains. In [7], we argued that database conceptual design, especially if complex notions such as weak entities are involved, can be significantly facilitated by deriving new schemas from previously specified *analogous* schemas.

In this section, with the help of an example, we describe how to extend the analogy mapping introduced in [7] to cover domain-oriented operations, specified using pre- and post-conditions.

Given the schema of section 2.1, we first define a Weak Entity *schema pattern*, which a database designer may at any future time use to create new schemas:

```
Pattern: Weak Entity              operation(H, [F, D])
Example scheme: Product           pre(H, [I, J], [])
Clauses --                        post(H, [I, J],
                                       [[F, J, I], [¬G, J]])
   entity(A, B)                   operation(K, [B, D, D])
   attribute(A, B)                pre(K, [L, M, N],
   entity(C, [B/D-E-B, D])            [[E, M, L], [F, M, I],
   attribute(C, D)                    [F, N, I]])/diff(M, N)
   attribute(C, F)                post(K, [L, M, N],
   attribute(C, G)                    [[¬E, M, L], [E, N, L]])
   relationship(E,                    /diff(M, N)
      C/n/total, A/1/total)       operation(O, [B, D])
                                  pre(O, [L, J], [[G, J]])
                                  post(O, [L, J], [[¬G, J]])
Mappings --
   A:product                      G:defective
   B:pno                          E:iscompof
   C:component                    H:order
   D:cno                          K:replace
   F:ctype                        O:repair
```

Suppose that a database designer wants to build a Team schema, involving teams and their members, and recognizes (or is told) that the intuitive mental image of the prospective schema "looks very much like" what occurs in the Product schema: members of teams are like components of products, reflecting the well-known "an organization is a machine" metaphor [22]. This motivates the introduction of the *is-like analogy mapping*, a meta-level relationship. In this example, the declaration "Team is-like Product" establishes that Product can be taken as a *source schema* on which the definition of the *target schema* Team can be partly accomplished [14].

We developed an interactive prototype tool to experiment with these notions. It prompts the designer to answer questions of the form: "What corresponds to <name>?", where <name> figures in the supposedly known source schema. The tool will use the names that the designer types to instantiate the variables in the mapping component of the Weak Entity pattern.

In our example, the mapping correspondences, to be saved for future use, are:

```
product   → team            defective → unprepared
pno → tno                   iscompof  → ismembof
component → member          order → hire
cno → mno                   replace → reassign
ctype → spec                repair → train
```

Using these mappings, the tool will then create the Team schema:

```
Schema: Team

Clauses --
   entity(team, tno)
   attribute(team, tno)          relationship(ismembof,
                                      member/n/total,
entity(member,                        team/1/total)
   [tno/mno-ismembof-tno,
      mno])
   attribute(member, mno)
   attribute(member,spec)
   attribute(member,
      unprepared)
```

```
operation(hire, [spec, mno])        /diff(B, C)
 pre(hire(A, B),  [])               post(reassign(A, B, C),
 post(hire(A, B),                    [¬ismembof(B, A),
  [spec(B,A), ¬unprepared(B)])        ismembof(C,A)])/diff(B,C)
operation(reassign,                operation(train, [tno, mno])
   [tno, mno])                      pre(train(A, B)[unprepared(B)])
 pre(reassign(A, B, C),             post(train(A, B),
   [ismembof(B, A),                   [¬unprepared(B)])
    spec(B, D), spec(C, D)])
```

In general, analogy mappings are not total in either direction. For some elements of the source schema, the designer may reply that there is no corresponding element in the target schema. On the other hand, after closing the dialogue, the designer may declare additional elements that are specific to the target schema. Indeed, in more semantically rich cases, it is often convenient to proceed along successive dialogues, employing a series of source schemas, which can be interpreted as an attempt to cover different *aspects* by resorting to different metaphors [18].

Once it has been so derived, the Team schema (alone or as part of the design of a larger schema) is ready to be used, employing the terminology appropriate to its distinct application domain. One can imagine that project leaders will be among the agents, instead of the foremen of the source domain.

Analogy brings in the possibility to perform comparisons, queries, etc., that go across the two domains. For brevity, we shall consider just one example.

Imagine that a certain John, with a specialty designated as spec_s3, and who is currently a member of team Ta, is found to be unprepared. What can be done in this situation? This recalls the case of component c3 of product pr, when c3 was marked as defective. Can we transpose to John what was done to c3?

There are two possibilities for c3:

$$P_1 = [[f1:repair(pr, c3)], []]$$
$$P_2 = [[f1:order(ct,c4), f2:replace(pr,c3,c4)],[f1-f2]]$$

from which the analogous plots below can be readily derived:

$$P_1' = [f1:train(Ta, John)], []]$$
$$P_2' = [f1:hire(spec\_s3, Peter),$$
$$\qquad f2:reassign(Ta, John, Peter)], [f1-f2]]$$

In words, one can either submit the unprepared John for training, or look for someone else with the same specialization and perform a substitution. This kind of argument has a flavor of *case-based reasoning* [19,23,30], since it involves the adaptation of a previously used strategy to handle a different, but analogous problem.

4.2   Reusing Plots from the LTP across Domains by Analogy

We shall now see how analogy can play a helpful role in a multi-domain environment. If one is dealing simultaneously with more than one application domain, it is necessary to insert the name of the domain in question in the *LTP* entries.

For example, suppose the *LTP* only contains entries related to the Product schema, from which the new Team schema was derived. Recall that the mapping information indicating the correspondence between names in the two schemas, gathered in the course of the derivation process, is stored for future use.

Suppose that a team leader, an agent in the mini-world of the Team schema, tries to access the *LTP* using the pair of lists (L_s, L_g) as concrete circumstance, where

```
L_s = [ismembof(John, Ta), spec(John, spec_s3),
        unprepared(John)]
L_g = [ismembof(John, Ta), ¬unprepared(John),
        spec(John, spec_s3)]
```

A first direct attempt to perform a match inevitably fails, since there are still no entries for Team in the *LTP*. But since it has been declared that "Team is-like Product", and because the analogy mappings were kept, a search for analogous Product entries is automatically processed, producing the following two plots:

```
P_1 = [[f1:train(Ta, John)], []] ;
P_2 = [[f1:hire(spec_s3, X), f2:reassign(ta, John, X)],
        [f1-f2]]
```

5 Concluding Remarks

We argued that plots, indexed by the situation-goal circumstances that motivate their enactment, provide a compact representation for the real-life stories happening in the mini-world of management information systems. Using the concept of similarity, we first illustrated how to organize plots from the same domain in a library of typical plots, which are ready for reuse. Then, using the concept of analogy, we discussed how to reuse such plots across different domains.

Experiments with prototype implementations, based on logic programming, have been of much help to test our approach. We are developing more robust implementations that combine the techniques outlined in this paper with an emergency response information system that will establish a transition from such early prototype tools to practical applications. More research is also required for, among other objectives, defining more complex similarity criteria, and for developing efficient methods to handle multi-agent environments.

References

1. Afanas'ev, A.: Russian Fairy Tales. N. Guterman (trans.). Pantheon Books, New York (1945)
2. Bae, J., Caverlee, J., Liu, L., Rouse, W.B., Yan, H.: Process Mining by Measuring Process Block Similarity. In: Proc. Workshop on Business Process Intelligence (BPI at BPM), Vienna (2006)
3. Bal, M.: Narratology - Introduction to the Theory of Narrative. U. Toronto Press (2002)
4. Barbosa, S.D.J., Breitman, K.K., Furtado, A.L., Casanova, M.A.: Similarity and Analogy over Application Domains. In: Proc. XXII SBBD, João Pessoa, Brazil (October 2007)
5. Barbosa, S.D.J., de Souza, C.S.: Extending software through metaphors and metonymies. Knowledge-Based Systems 14 (2001)
6. Batini, C., Ceri, S., Navathe, S.: Conceptual Design – an Entity-Relationship Approach, Benjamin Cummings (1992)
7. Breitman, K.K., Barbosa, S.D.J., Casanova, M.A., Furtado, A.L.: Conceptual modeling by analogy and metaphor. In: Proc. CIKM 2007, Lisbon, Portugal (November 2007)

8. Carvalho, M.T., Freire, J., Casanova, M.A.: The Architecture of an Emergency Plan Deployment System. In: Proc. III Workshop Brasileiro de GeoInformática, Rio de Janeiro, Brasil, October 2001, pp. 19–26 (2001)
9. Ciarlini, A.E.M., Furtado, A.L.: Understanding and Simulating Narratives in the Context of Information Systems. In: Proc. 21st. International Conference on Conceptual Modeling, Tampere, Finland (October 2002)
10. Ciarlini, A.E.M., Veloso, P.A.S., Furtado, A.L.: A Formal Framework for Modelling at the Behavioral Level. In: Proc. 10th European-Japanese Conference on Information Modelling and Knowledge Bases (2000)
11. Fernandes, A., Ciarlini, A.E.M., Furtado, A.L., Hinchey, M.G., Breitman, K.K., Casanova, M.A.: Adding Flexibility to Workflows through Incremental Planning. Innovations in Systems and Software Engineering (2007)
12. Fikes, R.E., Nilsson, N.J.: STRIPS: A new approach to the application of theorem proving to problem solving. Artificial Intelligence 2(3-4) (1971)
13. Furtado, A.L., Ciarlini, A.E.M.: Constructing Libraries of Typical Plans. In: Proc. 13th Int. Conf. on Computer Advanced Information System Engineering (2001)
14. Holyoak, K., Thagard, P.: Mental Leaps. MIT Press, Cambridge (1996)
15. Kautz, H.A.: A Formal Theory of Plan Recognition and its Implementation. In: Allen, J.F., et al. (eds.) Reasoning about Plans. Morgan Kaufmann, San Francisco (1991)
16. Knight, K.: Unification: A Multidisciplinary Survey. ACM Comp. Surveys 21(1) (March 1989)
17. Labrou, Y., Finin, T.: History, State of the Art and Challenges for Agent Communication Languages. In: Informatik – Informatique, vol. 1 (2000)
18. Lakoff, G., Johnson, M.: Metaphors We Live By. U. Chicago Press (1980)
19. Leake, D.: Case-Based Reasoning. MIT Press, Cambridge (1996)
20. Lippert, M., Schmolitzky, A., Züllighoven, H.: Metaphor Design Spaces. In: Marchesi, M., Succi, G. (eds.) XP 2003. LNCS, vol. 2675. Springer, Heidelberg (2003)
21. Lo, D., Khoo, S.-C., Liu, C.: Efficient Mining of Recurrent Rules from a Sequence Database. In: Haritsa, J.R., Kotagiri, R., Pudi, V. (eds.) DASFAA 2008. LNCS, vol. 4947. Springer, Heidelberg (2008)
22. Morgan, G.: Images of organization. Sage Publications, Thousand Oaks (1998)
23. Muñoz-Avila, H., Cox, M.: Case-based plan adaptation: An analysis and review. IEEE Intelligent Systems (2007)
24. Propp, V.: Morphology of the Folktale. Laurence, S (trans.). U. Texas Press, Austin (1968)
25. Schank, R.: Tell me a Story. Northwestern University Press (1990)
26. Turner, M.: The Literary Mind. Oxford University Press, Oxford (1996)
27. Van de Walle, B., Turoff, M.: Emergency response information systems: emerging trends and technologies special section – Introduction. Comm. of the ACM 50(3), 29–31 (2007)
28. van der Aalst, W.M.P., Weijters, A.J.M.M., Maruster, L.: Workflow Mining: Discovering Process Models from Event Logs. IEEE Transactions on Knowledge and Data Engineering 47(2), 237–267 (2004)
29. Winston, P.H.: Learning and reasoning by analogy. Comm. of the ACM 23, 689–703
30. Yang, Q., Cheng, H.: Case Mining from Large Data Bases. In: Proc. 2003 Int. Conf. on Case-based Reasoning, Trondheim, Norway (2003)

Discovering Semantically Similar Associations (SeSA) for Complex Mappings between Conceptual Models

Yuan An and Il-Yeol Song

College of Information Science and Technology, Drexel University, USA
{yan,isong}@ischool.drexel.edu

Abstract. There is an increasing demand for discovering *meaningful* relationships, i.e., *mappings*, between conceptual models for interoperability. Current solutions have been focusing on the discovery of correspondences between elements in different conceptual models. However, a *complex* mapping associating a structure connecting a set of elements in one conceptual model with a structure connecting a set of elements in another conceptual model is required in many cases. In this paper, we propose a novel technique for discovering semantically similar associations (SeSA) for constructing complex mappings. Given a pair of conceptual models, we create a *mapping graph* by taking the cross product of the two conceptual model graphs. Each edge in the mapping graph is assigned a weight based on the semantic similarity of the two elements encoded by the edge. We then turn the problem of discovering semantically similar associations (SeSA) into the problem of finding shortest paths in the mapping graph. We experiment different combinations of values for element similarities according to the semantic types of the elements. By choosing the set of values that have the best performance on controlled mapping cases, we apply the algorithm on test conceptual models drawn from a variety of applications. The experimental results show that the proposed technique is effective in discovering semantically similar associations (SeSA).

1 Introduction

A mapping between two conceptual models specifies a *meaningful* relationship between the two conceptual models. Semantic mappings have been used increasingly in achieving interoperability [11], capturing data semantics [3], and enabling various operations in the generic model management framework [4]. A mapping can be a simple correspondence between two elements in different conceptual models. For example, if a concept C_1 in one ontology is "equivalent" to a concept C_2 in another ontology, then we could specify the mapping between C_1 and C_2 as $C_1 \leftrightsquigarrow C_2$, where we use the symbol "$\leftrightsquigarrow$" to indicate the correspondence. Moreover, a mapping can be a complex relationship between a structure/association connecting multiple elements in one model and a structure/association connecting multiple elements in another model. For example, the born_in association between the concept Person and the concept Country in one ontology somehow is "equivalent" to the composition of the association born_in between the concept Person and the concept City and the association located_in between the City and the concept Country in another ontology. A complex mapping relationship is often expressed in a declarative formula with precise semantics.

Q. Li et al. (Eds.): ER 2008, LNCS 5231, pp. 369–382, 2008.

Discovering mappings between models is a very difficult problem in both the database community [17] and the artificial intelligence community [1]. Nevertheless, great effort has been put into the problem of discovering correspondences between model elements, e.g., solutions for schema matching [16] and ontology mapping [10]. A few attempts take database schemas as their subjects and propose solutions for inferring *complex mappings* between database schemas [14,5]. There is little effort, however, for deriving *complex mappings* between conceptual models in the literature.

A conceptual model (abbreviated as CM) uses modeling constructs such as concepts, relationships, attributes, and constraints to describe a subject matter based on well-defined abstraction mechanisms. Example CMs include Entity-Relationship diagrams, UML class diagrams, and OWL ontologies. Many data-centric applications require solutions to the problem of discovering complex CM mappings to fulfill their goals, for example, data translation over the semantic web [8], data management in peer-to-peer systems [9], and deriving schema mappings using CMs [2]. Current solutions rely on humans to specify the complex CM mapping formulas when they are required - a time-consuming and error-prone task. With the increasing complexity of various CMs in many applications, it is desirable to automate the process. In this paper, we deal with the above discovery problem. We propose a solution to the problem of *discovering semantically similar associations (SeSA) between pairs of corresponding concepts*. Our method takes as input two CMs and a set of correspondences between concepts in the CMs, and generates pairs of semantically similar associations (SeSA). Each association is between a pair of concepts in a CM. The following example illustrates the need for a complex mapping and describes the input and output of our solution.

Example 1. Figure 1 shows two different CMs, CM_1 and CM_2, describing Person, City, and Country, where we use rectangles for concepts, circles for attributes, and lines for relationships. The CM_1 contains two relationships between two concepts Person and Country: a many-to-one (functional) relationship born_in and a many-to-many relationship worked_in, both indicated by the cardinality constraints. The concept Person has an attribute pName, and Country has an attribute countryName. On the other hand, CM_2 describes three relationships born_in, located_in, and hasBeenTo as well as three concepts Person, City, and Country. Some concepts have attributes.

Suppose that mappings between CM_1 and CM_2 are sought for information exchange (imagine that CM_1 is an ontology used by an information system wanting to load data from another system using ontology CM_2 or vice versa). The creation of complex

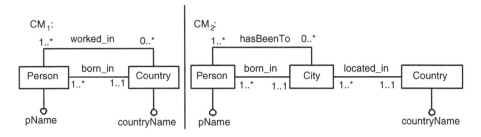

Fig. 1. Two Different CMs

mappings between two CMs is inherently difficult to automate. To alleviate the problem, we take a two-step approach: (1) specifying simple correspondences between elements in the two CMs; (2) inferring complex mappings between semantically similar structures.

In this paper, we assume that a user can specify correspondences between atomic elements in different CMs manually or using existing schema matching and ontology mapping tools [16,10]. In particular, we consider correspondences specified between concepts (which can be inferred from correspondences between attributes.) For instance, we assume that the following correspondences have been specified: CM_1: Person ⟿ CM_2:Person, CM_1:Country ⟿ CM_2:Country, where we use prefixes CM_1 and CM_2 to distinguish terms in different CMs. Given two pairs of corresponding concepts, our solution infers a list of pairs of associations. Each pair consists of an association between the pair of concepts in the first CM and an association between the corresponding pair of concepts in the second CM. For example, given the above correspondences, our solution is expected to produce the pair of associations

⟨
| CM_1:Person | `-- born_In ->-` | CM_1:Country |,

| CM_2:Person | `-- born_In ->-` | CM_2:City | `-- located_in ->-` | CM_2:Country |
⟩,

and the pair of associations

⟨
| CM_1:Person | `-- worked_in --` | CM_1:Country |,

| CM_2:Person | `-- hasBeenTo --` | CM_2:City | `--located_in->-` | CM_2:Country |
⟩,

where we use a notation "`-- born_In ->-` " to indicate that `born_in` is a many-to-one (functional) relationship, and a notation `-- hasBeenTo --` to indicate that `hasBeenTo` is a many-to-many relationship, and so on. In each pair, the two associations are "semantically similar" in terms of their cardinality constraints.

Furthermore, we can express a pair of SeSA as a mapping statement in a declarative language (see [3]) or an executable query in a particular query language (e.g., SPARQL [15]). ∎

Although in a wide range of applications discovering complex mappings between CMs is important and necessary, solutions to the problem are rare in the literature. This is due to many challenges involved including: how to determine the most likely associations between two concepts when there are multiple connections between them in a complex CM, how to *define* the "semantic similarity" between two associations in different CMs, how to efficiently discover "semantically similar" associations from complex CM graphs, and how to rank the mappings if there are many candidates returned by a solution. In this paper, we aim to discover an association δ_1 between a pair of concepts $\langle C_1, C_2 \rangle$ in a CM and an association δ_2 between a pair of concepts $\langle D_1, D_2 \rangle$ in another CM when given correspondences C_1 ⟿ D_1 and C_2 ⟿ D_2. We expect that δ_1 and δ_2 are "semantically similar". More complex associations connecting more than two concepts can be constructed by using the pair-wise associations so we leave it for the future work. In addition, we **do not** take the linguistic information encoded in the names of elements into consideration, which will be incorporated in the future work as well. Essentially, we seek for associations that are "semantically similar" in terms of the semantic types of relationships between concepts. For example, an ISA relationship is semantically similar to an ISA relationship, a partOf relationship is semantically similar to a partOf relationship, and so on. To effectively discover "semantically similar" associations from complex CMs, we create a mapping graph by taking the cross product of two CM graphs. We then turn the mapping discovery problem into a problem of finding some optimal structures in a graph, which can be solved by applying efficient graph-theoretic algorithms.

Our major contributions are: (1) we propose an innovative approach for discovering SeSA between CMs by using efficient graph-theoretic algorithms; and (2) we demonstrate the effectiveness of the proposed solutions through real world CMs. The rest of the paper is organized as follows. We contrast our approach with related work in Section 2. In Section 3 we present formal notations used later on. We describe the principles in Section 4 and the mapping discovery algorithm in Section 5. In Section 6 we report on experimental studies. Finally, we summarize the results of this work and conclude the paper in Section 7.

2   Related Work

A schema mapping tool infers meaningful relationships between a source and a target database schema from element correspondences. Typical schema mapping tools rely on integrity constraints, especially referential integrity constraints, to assemble "logically connected elements". These logical elements, together with the element correspondences, then give rise to mappings between the schemas. A representative schema mapping tool is Clio [14]. It is natural to ask whether we could utilize the mapping techniques developed in schema mapping tools by viewing the CMs as (relational) database schemas. Unfortunately, this approach does not work as illustrated below.

Let us view the CMs (consider CMs with only binary relationships for now) as relational schemas consisting of unary tables for concepts, binary tables for relationships and attributes. For example, in Example 1, the CM CM_1 could be viewed as a schema consisting of unary table CM_1:Person(x_1), binary tables such as CM_1:born_in(x_1,x_2) and CM_1:Country(x_2), and the obvious foreign key constraints from binary to unary tables; and the same view applies to the CM CM_2 thus creating various tables including CM_2:Person(y_1), CM_2:born_in(y_1, y_2) CM_2:City(y_2), CM_2:located_in(y_2, y_3), CM_2:Country(y_3) and again the obvious foreign key constraints. Suppose that element correspondences were given between the columns of unary tables Person and Country. Then one could in fact try to apply directly the schema mapping techniques to the problem. A desired mapping in Example 1 would not be produced due to the following reasons: (i) The schema mapping techniques (e.g., [14]) work by taking each table and using a chase-like algorithm to repeatedly extend it with columns that appear as foreign keys referencing other tables. Such "logical associations" in the source and target are then connected by queries. Specifically, for the CM CM_2 this would lead to logical relations such as CM_2:Person $\wedge$ CM_2:born_in $\wedge$ CM_2:City and CM_2:City

$\land$ CM_2:located_in $\land$ CM_2:Country, but not the entire connection from Person to Country through the intermediary concept City. (ii) The semantics that CM_1:born_in is many-to-one relationship leads us to prefer a many-to-one relationship/association between CM_2:Person and CM_2:Country in CM_2. The schema mapping techniques (e.g., [14]) do not use such semantics to pair up "logical associations".

The previous work [2] proposes a semantic approach for deriving schema mapping expressions by using the semantics of the modeling constructs in a CM. That work analyzes the graphical structures and the semantics of relationships (cardinalities, ISA, partOf, etc.,) of the CMs associated with input schemas to eliminate/downgrade *unreasonable* options that arise in mappings between database schemas. In this paper, we focus on the problem of discovering complex mappings between CMs and propose a novel technique which is different from the previous work.

Schema/ontology matching (e.g., [16,7,12,10]) identifies semantic relations between model elements based on their names, data types, constraints, and model structures. The primary goal is to find the one-to-one correspondences between model elements. We aim at the discovery of complex relationships between sets of model elements.

3   Conceptual Models (CMs) and Mappings between CMs

Conceptual Models. We consider in this paper the type of CMs, e.g., UML class diagrams, that are often used to describe static aspects of an application. However, we do not restrict ourselves to any particular language for describing CMs. Instead, we use a generic conceptual modeling language (CML), which contains many *common* aspects of most semantic data models (e.g., ER diagrams), UML class diagrams, ontology languages such as OWL, and description logics. Specifically, the language allows the representation of *entities/classes/concepts* (unary predicates over individuals), *object properties/relationships* (binary predicates relating individuals), and *datatype properties/ attributes* (binary predicates relating individuals with values such as integers and strings). Concepts are organized in the familiar ISA hierarchy. Relationships, and their inverses, are annotated with types such as partOf and subject to cardinality constraints, which here allow 1 as lower bounds (called *total* relationships), and 1 as upper bounds (called *functional* relationships). For n-ary relationships connecting more than two entities, and relationships with attributes, we represent them by *"reified relationships"* [6] concepts whose instances represent tuples, connected by so-called "roles" to the tuple elements.

A CM can be represented in a labeled graph called *CM graph*. We construct the CM graph from a CM as follows: We create a concept node labeled with C for each concept C, and an edge labeled with p from the concept node C_1 to the concept node C_2 for each binary relationship p linking C_1 to C_2; for each such p, we annotate it with type information such as partOf or reified role. For each subclass C_1 of a class C_2, create an edge labeled with ISA connecting C_1 to C_2 with cardinality 1..1 (a C_1 must be a C_2), and 0..1 on the inverse. Graphically, we use rectangles to represent concepts/classes and a line to represent relationships. Textually, a many-to-many relationship p between concepts C and D is written as $\boxed{C}$ ---p--- $\boxed{D}$, while a many-to-one (functional) relationship p is written as $\boxed{C}$ ---p->-- $\boxed{D}$.

In this paper, we assume that attributes are globally unique, simple, and single-valued (complex and multi-valued attributes can be transformed into concepts with simple and single-valued attributes.) We use circles to represent attributes. Each attribute is connected to the concept where the attribute belongs to. Since in this paper we focus on discovering associations between concepts, we will strip off attribute nodes in our illustrations in later sections.

CM Mappings. A declarative mapping statement over a pair of CMs $\langle CM_1, CM_2 \rangle$ is of the form $CM_1:E_1 \Leftrightarrow CM_2:E_2$, where E_1 and E_2 are expressions representing associations over CM_1 and CM_2, respectively. Since the symbol "$\Leftrightarrow$" can be interpreted as subset, superset, or equivalent operator according to the particular application, a more generic mapping statement is written as a two-tuple $\langle E_1, E_2 \rangle$. In the sequel, we will use associations directly in a mapping statement as $\langle \delta_1, \delta_2 \rangle$. The algorithm for translating an association into a conjunctive formula is provided in [3].

4   Principles for Mapping Discovery

We now turn to the task for discovering "semantically similar" associations between CMs. First, we present the principles underlying our approach.

The problem we are addressing is formulated as follows. Given two simple correspondences $v_1:C_1 \leadsto D_1$ and $v_2:C_2 \leadsto D_2$ linking two pairs of concepts $\langle C_1, C_2 \rangle$ and $\langle D_1, D_2 \rangle$ in conceptual models CM_1 and CM_2, respectively, find an association δ_1 between C_1 and C_2 and an association δ_2 between D_1 and D_2 such that δ_1 and δ_2 are "semantically similar." The problem is graphically described in Figure 2

A simple case is that both associations δ_1 and δ_2 are direct relationships, i.e., δ_1 is a relationship between $\langle C_1, C_2 \rangle$ and δ_2 is a relationship between $\langle D_1, D_2 \rangle$. To determine whether two relationships are semantically similar, we analyze the types of the relationships, e.g., partOf, and the cardinality con-

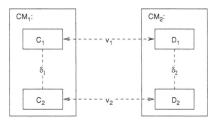

Fig. 2. The Mapping Discovery Problem

straints imposed on the corresponding concepts participating in the relationships. Our *first principle* is to use the semantic information encoded in the types of relationships and the cardinality constraints imposed on the relationships to discover semantically similar relationships.

However, for a complex CM, an association between two concepts may consist of a sequence of relationships through a set of intermediary concepts. Our goal is to discover SeSAs that are not just single relationships. For instance, each of the two pairs of associations discovered in Example 1 contains an association consisting two relationships that connect Person to Country in CM_2.

Our *second principle* is to analyze the semantic information encoded in the types of the relationships as well as the cardinality constraints imposed on the relationships to discover pairs of SeSAs. Given a CM graph $G_1 = (V_1, E_1)$, an association δ_1 in G_1 is an alternating sequence of different nodes and edges $\delta_1 = \langle v_1, \ell_1, v_2, \ell_2, v_3..., v_m, \ell_m, v_{m+1}\rangle$, where $v_i \in V_1$ and $\ell_i = (v_i, v_{i+1}) \in E_1$ for $i \in \{1, ..., m\}$. Likewise, for a CM graph $G_2 = (V_2, E_2)$, we can represent an association δ_2 as an alternating sequence of different nodes and edges as $\delta_2 = \langle u_1, \gamma_1, u_2, \gamma_2, u_3..., u_n, \gamma_n, u_{n+1}\rangle$, where $u_i \in V_2$ and $\gamma_i = (u_i, u_{i+1}) \in E_2$ for $i \in \{1, ..., n\}$. Intuitively, the following associations δ_1 and δ_2 are semantically similar:

1. $\delta_1=\langle v_1\rangle$, $\delta_2=\langle u_1\rangle$, and $v_1 \rightsquigarrow u_1$;
2. $\delta_1=\langle v_1\rangle$, $\delta_2=\langle u_1, \gamma_1, u_2\rangle$, $v_1 \rightsquigarrow u_1$, $v_1 \rightsquigarrow u_2$, and γ_1 is a functional or ISA relationships; or $\delta_1=\langle v_1, \ell_1, v_2\rangle$, $\delta_2=\langle u_1\rangle$, $v_1 \rightsquigarrow u_1$, $v_2 \leftrightsquigarrow u_1$, and ℓ_1 is a functional or ISA relationships;
3. $\delta_1=\langle v_1, \ell_1, v_2\rangle$, $\delta_2=\langle u_1, \gamma_1, u_2\rangle$, $v_1 \rightsquigarrow u_1$, $v_2 \rightsquigarrow u_2$, and ℓ_1 and γ_1 are two relationships that both are (i) the type of partOf relationships; (ii) ISA; (iii) many-to-one; or (iv) many-to-many;
4. $\delta_1=\langle v_1, \ell_1, v_2\rangle$, $\delta_2=\langle u_1, \gamma_1, u_2, ..., u_n, \gamma_n, u_{n+1}\rangle$, $v_1 \rightsquigarrow u_1$, $v_2 \rightsquigarrow u_{n+1}$, and $\gamma_i, i = \{1, .., n\}$ have the same semantic type as ℓ_1, e.g., $\gamma_i, i = \{1, .., n\}$ are all many-to-many relationships if ℓ_1 is many-to-many; or the symmetric case when δ_1 and δ_2 get exchanged.
5. $\delta_1=\langle v_1, \ell_1, v_2,..., v_m, \ell_m, v_{m+1}\rangle$, $\delta_2=\langle u_1, \gamma_1, u_2, ..., u_n, \gamma_n, u_{n+1}\rangle$, $v_1 \rightsquigarrow u_1$, $v_{m+1} \rightsquigarrow u_{n+1}$, and there is a partition of $\delta_1=\langle \delta_1^1, \delta_2^1, ..., \delta_k^1\rangle$ and a partition of $\delta_2=\langle \delta_1^2, \delta_2^2, ..., \delta_k^2\rangle$ such that δ_j^1 and $\delta_j^2, j = \{1, .., k\}$ are semantically similar.

The above conditions 1-4 describe several base cases for semantically similar associations (SeSA). Condition 5 states that two associations are considered semantically similar if they can be divided recursively into partitions in the same size, and the corresponding components of the partitions are semantically similar. The description provides guidelines for designing an algorithm; however, challenges are involved. First, what is the degree of similarity between two associations? Intuitively, the similarity between two "compatible" relationships should be greater than that between two paths with more than one relationships. Second, there are too many ways to enumerate associations between two concepts in a single CM graph. Which associations are the most likely ones in terms of mapping? Third, there are too many ways to enumerate the partitions of a single associations. How to divide an association into partitions? Can an edge/node be divided? How to efficiently decide whether two associations are semantically similar according to the condition 5?

To address these challenges, we turn to efficient graph-theoretic algorithms. The first step is to encode our mapping problem in terms of a single graph structure. We utilize the notion of cross product for two graphs which encodes certain relationships between the two graphs. We need to extend the notion of cross product to encode mapping relationships between two CM graphs.

5   Mapping Discovery Algorithm

In graph theory, the cross product $G = G_1 \times G_2$ of two graph $G_1 = (V_1, E_1)$ and $G_2 = (V_2, E_2)$ is the graph $G = (V, E)$, where $V = V_1 \times V_2$ and $t = (v_i u_i, v_j u_j) \in E$ for $v_i, v_j \in V_1$ and $u_i, u_j \in V_2$ if only if $e = (v_i, v_j) \in E_1$ and $r = (u_i, u_j) \in E_2$.

We extend the definition of the cross product of two graphs to *the notion of mapping graph* by allowing $t = (v_i u_i, v_j u_j) \in E$ if $v_i = v_j$ and $r = (u_i, u_j) \in E_2$, or $e = (v_i, v_j) \in E_1$ and $u_i = u_j$.

Definition 1 (Mapping Graph). *The mapping graph $M = G_1 \Leftrightarrow G_2$ of two graph $G_1 = (V_1, E_1)$ and $G_2 = (V_2, E_2)$ is the graph $M = (V, E)$, where $V = V_1 \times V_2$ and $t = (v_i u_i, v_j u_j) \in E$ for $v_i, v_j \in V_1$ and $u_i, u_j \in V_2$ if only if one of the following conditions is satisfied: (1) $e = (v_i, v_j) \in E_1$ and $r = (u_i, u_j) \in E_2$; (2) $v_i = v_j$ and $r = (u_i, u_j) \in E_2$; or (3) $e = (v_i, v_j) \in E_1$ and $u_i = u_j$.*

Example 2. Figure 3 (a) shows two graphs $G_1 = (V_1, E_1)$ and $G_2 = (V_2, E_2)$ that both are simple paths with three nodes. Figure 3 (b) shows the cross product of the two graphs $G = G_1 \times G_2$, while Figure 3 (c) shows the mapping graph of the two graph $M = G_1 \Leftrightarrow G_2$. ∎

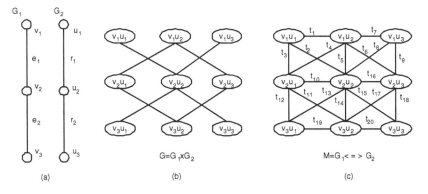

Fig. 3. Cross Product and Mapping Graph

An edge in the mapping graph $M = (V, E)$ encodes either a pair of edges or a node and an edge in the original graphs. For example, the edge $t_2 = (v_1 u_1, v_2 u_2) \in M$ in Figure 3 (c) encodes the edge $e_1 = (v_1, v_2) \in E_1$ and the edge $r_1 = (u_1, u_2) \in E_2$; the edge $t_1 = (v_1 u_1, v_1 u_2) \in M$ in Figure 3 (c) encodes the node $v_1 \in V_1$ and the edge $r_1 = (u_1, u_2) \in E_2$. Moreover, a path in the mapping graph encodes a way to map the source graph to the target graph. For example, the path $\langle (v_1 u_1, t_2, v_2 u_2, t_{15}, v_3 u_3) \rangle \in M$ in Figure 3 (c) maps in a "one-to-one" fashion the elements of the original path G_1 to the elements of the path G_2.

For two conceptual models CM_1 and CM_2, if we are given two pairs of concepts $\langle C_1, C_2 \rangle$ and $\langle D_1, D_2 \rangle$, then a path between the two nodes $\boxed{C_1 D_1}$ and $\boxed{C_2 D_2}$ in the mapping graph $M = \mathsf{CM}_1 \Leftrightarrow \mathsf{CM}_2$ gives rise to an association δ_1 between C_1 and C_2 and an association δ_2 between D_1 and D_2.

However, the mapping graph encodes all pairing ups between all possible associations connecting $\langle C_1, C_2 \rangle$ in CM_1 and all possible associations connecting $\langle D_1, D_2 \rangle$ in CM_2. In addition, the mapping graph also encodes pairing ups between possible partitions of an association and possible partitions of another association. For a very dense mapping graph, the number of paths between any pair of nodes is quite huge. Therefore, we need to address the problem of *discovering the paths in the mapping graph which probably encode those SeSA that are desirable.*

The solution is to assign weights to the edges of the mapping graph and discover an optimal structure such as shortest/longest/heaviest paths in the mapping graph. The weight of an edge in the mapping graph denotes the semantic similarity of the two elements encoded by the edge. We assign the similarity as a real number between 0 and 1. We use letter α for highest similarity, e.g., the similarity between two ISA edges, letter β for the similarity between an ISA edge and a functional relationship, letter λ for compatible similarity, e.g., the similarity between a node and a functional edge, and letter μ for the least similarity. Table 1 shows the categorization of pairs of elements and the similarity values that are assigned to the pairs.

Table 1. Assigning Similarity to Pair of Elements $\langle e_1, e_2 \rangle$ of two Conceptual Models CM_1 and CM_2

$\langle e_1, e_2 \rangle$, $e_1 \in CM_1$ $e_2 \in CM_2$	Similarity	$\langle e_1, e_2 \rangle$, $e_1 \in CM_1$ $e_2 \in CM_2$	Similarity
e_1=ISA edge e_2=ISA edge	$0 \leq \alpha \leq 1$	e_1=ISA edge e_2=functional edge	$0 \leq \beta \leq 1$
e_1=many-to-many edge e_2=many-to-many edge	$0 \leq \alpha \leq 1$	e_1=a node e_2=functional edge	$0 \leq \lambda \leq 1$
e_1=many-to-one edge e_2=many-to-one edge	$0 \leq \alpha \leq 1$	e_1=reified role edge e_2=reified role edge	$0 \leq \alpha \leq 1$
e_1=partOf edge e_2=partOf edge	$0 \leq \alpha \leq 1$	other	$0 \leq \mu \leq 1$

Example 3. Figure 4 (b) shows the mapping graph of the two graphs $G_1 = (V_1, E_1)$ and $G_2 = (V_2, E_2)$ in Figure 4 (a).

Both G_1 and G_2 contain a functional relationship edge which is indicated by an arrow, e.g., $e_1 = (v_1, v_2) \in E_1$, and a many-to-may relationship edge. Weights enclosed by parentheses are assigned to the edges of the mapping graph in Figure 4 (b). To reduce clumsiness, we only show two edge labels: t_2 and t_{15} in the Figure.

We compute the similarity between the two original paths by computing the weights of the paths that encode the two original paths. The weight of a path is the product of the weights of the edges along the path. The path $\langle (v_1 u_1, t_2, v_2 u_2, t_{15}, v_3 u_3) \rangle \in M$ has the heaviest weight α^2. By taking the weight of the heaviest paths, we obtain the similarity between the two original paths as α^2.   ∎

Equipped with the weighted mapping graph, we design the mapping discovery algorithm as to discover the heaviest paths between two given nodes, where the weight of a path is the product of the weights of the edges along the path. This is justified by our preference to the paths with fewer edges. Each edge has a greater weight/similary value. To compute the heaviest paths, we take the logarithm of the edge weights and negate the results. After this, the traditional algorithms for computing shortest paths in a graph, e.g., Dijkstra's algorithm, will produce the expected results. Figure 5 presents the procedure

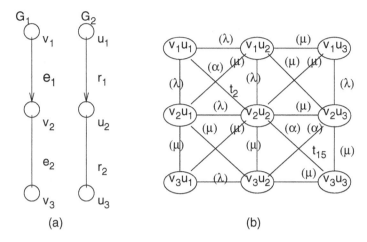

Fig. 4. Weight Assignments to a Mapping Graph

discSeSA(), which takes as input two CMs and two simple correspondences linking a pair of concepts in the first CM to a pair of concepts in the second CM. The results of the discSeSA() are pairs of desired associations. A resulted pair of associations are considered as "semantically similar" because they have the highest similarity based on the appropriate similarities assigned to the edges in the mapping graph.

6   Experimental Results

We now report our experimental results. The purpose of the experiments is three-fold: (1) selecting the values for the parameters α, β, λ, and μ which are presented in Table 1, (2) applying the proposed technique to various CMs in different applications, and (3) testing the efficiency and effectiveness of the proposed algorithm. The algorithm is implementated in JAVA and the experiments were conducted on a PC with an Intel Core 2 Duo processor and 2G memory.

Data Set. The test data sets (see Table 2) in our experiments were collected from a variety of applications. The CMs Sdb0, Sdb1, Sdb2, and Sdb3 are four versions of the conceptual model for describing a biological sample database extracted from the industrial GeneExpress Data Management (GXDM) project described in [13]. In this paper, we used controlled mapping cases based on these four CMs to empirically determine the values of the similarity parameters that would have the best performance. We experimented the mappings between Sdb0 and Sdb1, betwen Sdb1 and Sdb2, and between Sdb2 and Sdb3. The remaining three pairs of test CMs in our experiments were collected from our previous work in [2].

Table 2 shows the characteristics of the test CMs. For each pair, the table lists the numbers of nodes and the numbers of edges of the first and second CMs.

Selecting Values for the Similarity Parameters. The key to the proposed technique is to assign weights to the edges in the mapping graph. The value of a weight is based

---

Procedure: discSeSA(G_1, G_2, L)

Input: conceptual model graphs $G_1 = (V_1, E_1)$, $G_2 = (V_2, E_2)$, and simple correspondences $L=\{C_1 \leftrightsquigarrow D_1, C_2 \leftrightsquigarrow D_2 \mid C_1, C_2 \in V_1, D_1, D_2 \in V_2\}$

Output: $\{\langle \delta_1, \delta_2 \rangle \mid \delta_1$ is an association between C_1 and C_2, δ_2 is an association between D_1 and D_2, and δ_1 and δ_2 have the highest similarity$\}$

Steps:

1. Create the mapping graph $M = (V, E) = G_1 \Leftrightarrow G_2$ of the input CM graphs, where $V = V_1 \times V_2$ and E is the set of edges of the mapping graph;
2. **For** each edge $e = (v_i u_i, v_j u_j) \in E$, $v_i, v_j \in V_1$, $u_i, u_j \in V_2$
   (a) Assign a weight to e according to Table 1; the two elements encoded by the edge e are either two edges $(v_i, v_j) \in E_1$, $(u_i, u_j) \in E_2$, or a node and an edge, e.g., $v_i = v_j$.
3. **End for**
4. **For** each edge $e \in E$, let w be the weight of e
   (a) **Let** $w = -\lg w$
5. **End for**
6. **Let** $P = $ shorestPath(M)[a].
7. **Let** $A = $ makeAssociates(P)[b].
8. return A.

---

[a] shortestPath() computes the shortest paths of a weighted graph.
[b] makeAssociation(P) splits each path in P into two associations in the original graphs.

Fig. 5. discSeSA Procedure

Table 2. Characteristics of Test Data

First CM	# Nodes	# Edges	Second CM	# Nodes	# Edges	Time for Creating Mapping Graph (sec)	Avg. Time for Discovering SeSA (sec)
Sdb0	68	73	Sdb1	54	58	7.8	1.9
Sdb1	54	58	Sdb2	74	80	9.5	2.2
Sdb2	74	80	Sdb3	49	56	8.0	1.8
Bibliographic	75	80	DBLP	7	10	0.32	0.068
Amalgam1	7	14	Amalgam2	26	27	0.13	0.028
Factbook	52	112	Mondial	26	55	4.6	1.7

on the semantic similarity between two elements encoded by an edge. Table 1 presents the categorization of pairs of elements and the similarity values that are assigned. The values denoted by the letters α, β, λ, and μ are real numbers between 0 and 1. We hypothesized that different values assigned as element similarity might have different performance in terms of discovering SeSA. We conducted experiments to verify the hypothesis and hopefully to select the set of values that had the best performance on our controlled experiments. First, we assigned each parameter an array of possible values as follows. Let $\alpha = \{0.9, 0.8, 0.7, 0.6, 0.5\}$, $\beta = \{0.8, 0.6, 0.5, 0.4, 0.2\}$, $\lambda = \{0.8, 0.6, 0.5, 0.4, 0.2\}$, and $\mu = \{0.01\}$. Second, we chose a number of pairs of concepts in each of the following CMs: Sdb0, Sdb1, Sdb2, and Sdb3, and tested mappings between Sdb0 and Sdb1, between Sdb1 and Sdb2, and between Sdb2 and

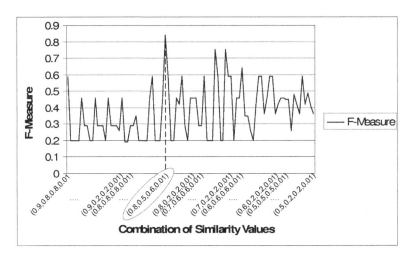

Fig. 6. Experimental Results for Selecting Similarity Values

Sdb3. Third, we combined the values from the four arrays under the constraints $\alpha \geq \beta$ and $\alpha \geq \lambda$, which indicate that the highest similarity value should not be less than other similarity values. Finally, for each combination of the values, we measure the performance of the algorithm using this set of values for assigning weights as described in the following.

To measure the performance of the algorithm, for each mapping case, we manually chose pairs of associations based on our understanding and expectation on the CMs. These selected pairs of associations acted as the "gold standard" when we compared the results generated by the algorithm using different similarity values. We were concerned with the following two questions: Did the algorithm generate all the expected pairs of associations? Did the algorithm generate pairs of associations that were not manually selected. The first concern is related to the traditional *recall* measure, while the second concern is about the *precision* measure. Specifically, let R be the set of "gold standard" pairs and let P be the set of pairs generated by the algorithm. The precision and recall measures are computed as: $precision = \frac{|P \cap R|}{|P|}$ and $recall = \frac{|P \cap R|}{|R|}$. To measure the overall performance, we take the harmonic mean of precision and recall which is called F-Measure, calculated as follows:

$$F \; measure = \frac{2}{\frac{1}{precision} + \frac{1}{recall}}.$$

Using the controlled mapping cases with expected results, we measure the performance of the algorithm with different similarity values in terms of the F-measures. Figure 6 shows the average F-meaures for all combinations of values over the controlled experiments. The x-axis lists the combinations of the values in the form of $(\alpha, \beta, \lambda, \mu)$. There were 91 combinations of values tested (the total number of combinations is 125 but some combinations were not considered due to the given constraints.) The highest peak of the average F-measure curve appears at the point on the x-axis which corresponds to the combination $\{\alpha = 0.8, \beta = 0.5, \lambda = 0.6, \mu = 0.01\}$. The ups and downs of the curve indicate that different values assigned as element similarity indeed had different performance.

Results of Applying the Algorithm. With the set of selected values for similarity, we applied the algorithm to the mapping pairs in our test data sets including SDB0,.., SDB3 again. The last two columns of Table 2 contain the times for creating mapping graphs and discovering SeSA for the test pairs. In terms of time complexity, it took several seconds to create a mapping graph for some pairs of CMs in our test set. However, the mapping graph of a certain pair only needs to be created once and can be reused many times. The process of discovering SeSA spent a couple of seconds to produce the final results. It employed the standard shortest path algorithm, e.g., Dijkstra's algorithm.

To evaluate the effectiveness of the algorithm, we continue to use the notion of *recall* and *precision*. This time, we conducted a post-inspection to measure the recall and precision. Specifically, for a mapping case, we inspected the pairs of associations generated by the algorithm against the CMs. For precision, we checked whether each pair in the result set indeed contained two "semantically similar" associations. For recall, we checked whether there were other "semantically similar" associations that were not returned by the algorithm. The inspection results showed that the algorithm is effective in discovering SeSA. In particular, precisions for all mapping cases were 100%, while the average recall over all mapping cases is about 90%. The imperfect recall is due to the algorithm's preference to heaviest (shortest) paths. For example, in the pair of CMs, CIA factbook and Mondial, both CMs contain a relationship $\boxed{\text{City}}$ `-- capital->-` $\boxed{\text{Country}}$ and a path $\boxed{\text{City}}$ `-- capital ->-` $\boxed{\text{Province}}$ `--located_in->-` $\boxed{\text{Country}}$. The algorithm generates the two relationships as a pair of SeSA excluding the two paths. A solution would be to set the similarity $\alpha = 1$; however, this setting would disable α as a damper factor for longer paths. We plan to extend the algorithm by using an additional parameter for controlling the content of the result set in our future work.

7   Conclusions

In this paper, we studied the problem of discovering semantically similar associations (SeSA) in two different conceptual models. Our method finds an association between a pair of concepts in one conceptual model and a "semantically similar" association between a pair of concepts in another conceptual model. We are motivated by the need of specifying complex semantic mappings between CMs for many applications that require interoperability such as data management over the semantic web and peer-to-peer systems. We proposed a novel technique for discovering desirable SeSA by using efficient graph-theoretic algorithms. Our solution is unique in that we turn the problem of discovering SeSA into a problem of finding shortest paths in a special graph called *mapping graph*. We create a mapping graph by taking the cross product of the two input CM graphs. Our contributions include experiments for evaluating the efficiency and effectiveness of the proposed algorithm. Experimental results showed that the technique was effective in discovering SeSA in our experiment setting. We plan to incorporate the linguistic information in the names of elements into the mapping discovery approach in the future work.

References

1. AAAI. AI Magazine, Special Issue on Semantic Integration 26(1) (2005)
2. An, Y., Borgida, A., Miller, R.J., Mylopoulos, J.: A Semantic Approach to Discovering Schema Mapping Expressions. In: Proceedings of International Conference on Data Engineering (ICDE), pp. 206–215 (2007)
3. An, Y., Borgida, A., Mylopoulos, J.: Discovering the Semantics of Relational Tables through Mappings. Journal on Data Semantics VII, 1–32 (2006)
4. Bernstein, P.: Applying Model Management to Classical Meta Data Problems. In: CIDR (2003)
5. Bonifati, A., Chang, E.Q., Ho, T., Lakshmanan, V.S., Pottinger, R.: HePToX: Marring XML and Heterogeneity in Your P2P Databases. In: Proceedings of International Conference on Very Large Data Bases (VLDB), pp. 1267–1270 (2005)
6. Dahchour, M., Pirotte, A.: The Semantics of Reifying n-ary Relationships as Classes. In: Information Systems Analysis and Specification, pp. 580–586 (2002)
7. Dhamankar, R., Lee, Y., Doan, A., Halevy, A., Domingos, P.: Imap: discovering complex semantic matches between database schemas. In: SIGMOD 2004: Proceedings of the 2004 ACM SIGMOD international conference on Management of data, pp. 383–394. ACM Press, New York (2004)
8. Halevy, A., Ives, Z.G., Mork, P., Tatarinov, I.: Piazza: data management infrastructure for semantic web application. In: Proceedings of International Conference on World Wide Web (WWW), pp. 556–567 (2003)
9. Halevy, A.Y., Ives, Z.G., Suciu, D., Tatarinov, I.: Schema Mediation in Peer Data Management Systems. In: Proceedings of the International Conference on Data Engineering (ICDE), pp. 505–516 (2003)
10. Kalfoglou, Y., Scholemmer, M.: Ontology Mapping: The State of the Art. The Knowledge Engineering Review 18(1), 1–31 (2003)
11. Lenzerini, M.: Data Integration: A Theoretical Perspective. In: Proceedings of the ACM Symposium on Principles of Database Systems (PODS), pp. 233–246 (2002)
12. Madhavan, J., Bernstein, P., Doan, A., Halevy, A.: Corpus-Based Schema Matching. In: Proceedings of the International Conference on Data Engineering (ICDE), pp. 57–68 (2005)
13. Markowitz, V., Topaloglou, T.: Applying Data Warehousing Concepts to Gene Expression Data Management. In: BIBE 2001, pp. 65–72 (2001)
14. Popa, L., Velegrakis, Y., Miller, R.J., Hernández, M.A., Fagin, R.: Translating web data. In: VLDB, pp. 598–609 (2002)
15. Prud'hommeaux, E., Seaborne, A.: SPARQL Query Language for RDF. W3C Working Draft 4 (2006), http://www.w3.org/TR/rdf-sparql-query
16. Rahm, E., Bernstein, P.A.: A Survey of Approaches to Automatic Schema Matching. VLDB Journal 10, 334–350 (2001)
17. SIGMOD. SIGMOD Record, Special Issue on Semantic Integration 33(4) (2004)

An Adverbial Approach for the Formal Specification of Topological Constraints Involving Regions with Broad Boundaries

Lotfi Bejaoui[1,2,3,4], François Pinet[3], Michel Schneider[3,4], and Yvan Bédard[1,2]

[1] Centre for Research in Geomatics (CRG), Laval University, Quebec (QC) Canada
`lotfi.bejaoui.1@ulaval.ca`
[2] Industrial Research Chair in Geospatial Databases for Decision Support, Laval University, Quebec (QC), Canada
`yvan.bedard@scg.ulaval.ca`
[3] Cemagref-Clermont-Ferrand, France
`francois.pinet@cemagref.fr`
[4] Dept. Computer Sciences, Blaise-Pascal University, Clermont-Ferrand, France
`michel.schneider@isima.fr`

Abstract. Topological integrity constraints control the topological properties of spatial objects and the validity of their topological relationships in spatial databases. These constraints can be specified by using formal languages such as the spatial extension of the *Object Constraint Language* (OCL). Spatial OCL allows the expression of topological constraints involving crisp spatial objects. However, topological constraints involving spatial objects with vague shapes (e.g., *regions with broad boundaries*) are not supported by this language. Shape vagueness requires using appropriate topological operators (e.g., *strongly Disjoint, fairly Meet*) to specify valid relations between these objects; otherwise, the constraints cannot be respected. This paper addresses the problem of the lack of terminology to express topological constraints involving regions with broad boundaries. We propose an extension of *Spatial OCL* based on a geometric model for objects with vague shapes and an adverbial approach for topological relations between regions with broad boundaries. This extension of *Spatial OCL* is then tested on an agricultural database.

1 Introduction

Internal spatial data quality is judged by several components, including completeness and logical consistency [14, 24]. Logical consistency is defined as the number of features, relationships, or attributes that have been correctly encoded in accordance with the integrity constraints [7, 19, 21] for the feature data specification [14]. Integrity constraints are defined at the conceptual level through specific tools [1]. In spatial databases, additional integrity constraints are required to control topological properties of geometries (e.g., *line simplicity*), semantic aspects (e.g., *a house has one level at least*), and topological relations (e.g., *agricultural spread parcels should be disjoint or adjacent)* in addition to basic constraints (e.g., *domain constraints*) [13, 22]. In this paper, we are interested in integrity constraints involving topological relations in transactional databases.

Q. Li et al. (Eds.): ER 2008, LNCS 5231, pp. 383–396, 2008.
© Springer-Verlag Berlin Heidelberg 2008

Formal specification of topological integrity constraints requires using an unambiguous formal language adapted to spatial databases. A spatial database-oriented language should allow the specification of both alphanumeric and spatial constraints [10, 16]. Currently, an extension of the Object Constraint Language (OCL) called Spatial OCL [10, 16] allows formal expression of spatial integrity constraints. Spatial OCL is based on the 9-Intersection model [11]. OCL provides a framework to define integrity constraints on classes' attributes or to differentiate between classes by using the *navigation* concept. This language has several advantages. First, it is easier to write an OCL constraint than its corresponding SQL query. Second, it is considered a subset of UML and based on the object-oriented paradigm commonly used in the software engineering domain. However, Spatial OCL cannot define topological constraints involving objects with vague shapes such as regions with broad boundaries [3, 4, 6, 8, 9, 17, 23]. These objects cannot be presented through crisp shapes [25] and therefore their topological relations cannot be identified by applying a spatial model for crisp objects such as the 9-Intersection model [11] or the CBM method [5]. For example, an integrity constraint may state that "a pollution zone *A* should not *overlap* a pollution zone *B*." The topological operator *overlap* cannot have the same definition as in the 9-Intersection model [11], because pollution zones can be viewed as regions with broad boundaries. They are not composed of the same topological invariants as crisp regions (they have broad boundaries instead linear ones) [18, 26]. Then, these regions with broad boundaries can overlap each other with different strengths: *weakly, fairly, strongly,* or *completely.* A classification of integrity constraints involving objects with vague shapes has been proposed in [2]. In this paper, we address the problem of the lack of terminology in Spatial OCL [10, 16] to express topological constraints involving objects with vague shapes. The main objective of this paper is to extend Spatial OCL in order to support topological constraints for regions with broad boundaries. We aim to extend the meta-model of Spatial OCL by proposing new types for objects with vague shapes and new topological operators adapted to regions with broad boundaries.

The paper is organized as follows. In section 2, we briefly review the notion of objects with vague shapes. Then, we present a spatial model for regions with broad boundaries and qualitative identification of their topological relations according to the *Qualitative Min-Max (QMM)* model presented in [3]. In section 3, we review related works on the specification of topological constraints, especially the approach using Spatial OCL [10, 16]. In section 4, we present our extension of Spatial OCL in order to formally express topological relations between regions with broad boundaries by using the QMM model [3]. Section 5 presents an example of a spatial database storing information about agricultural spreading activities. Some spatial objects stored in this database such as spread parcels have vague shapes, and therefore their topological constraints are expressed by using the extension of Spatial OCL. Section 6 presents the conclusions of this work.

2   Objects with Vague Shapes

2.1   Categorization of Spatial Objects with Vague Shapes

According to [12, 15], *shape vagueness* refers to the difficulty of distinguishing the shape of one object from its neighborhood. It is an intrinsic property of an object that has a spatial extent in a known position but does not have a well-defined shape (e.g., a pollution zone, a lake, a forest stand, etc.) [12]. We distinguish three basic types of *spatial objects with vague shapes*: *broad points, lines with vague shapes* (i.e., *lines with broad boundaries, lines with broad interiors* or *broad lines*), and *regions with broad boundaries*. Figure 1 shows an example of each one of these types of objects. A region has a vague shape when it is surrounded by a broad boundary instead of a sharp one (Figure 1c); we refer to these as *regions with broad boundaries* (e.g., a pollution zone). A line has a vague shape when its boundary (endpoints) and/or its interior are broad (Figure 1b; e.g., the itinerary of an historic explorer). For lines, we make a distinction between *broad interior* and *broad boundary* as we consider them specializations of *linear shape vagueness*. This distinction is also useful for points because a point does not have a boundary; it is only composed of an interior. A point's shape corresponds to the elementary space portion, which refers to its interior (Figure 1a). A broad point arises when there is a difficulty to distinguish the punctual object from its neighborhood (e.g., a mountain peak).

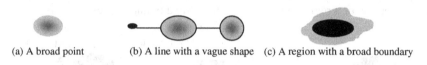

(a) A broad point   (b) A line with a vague shape   (c) A region with a broad boundary

Fig. 1. Examples of objects with vague shapes

Figure 2 shows our general categorization of objects with vague shapes. Three types of objects with vague shapes are specified: region with a broad boundary, line with a vague shape and broad point. Shape vagueness for lines can be a property of their boundaries (endpoints) and/or interiors. A line has a broad boundary when one of the endpoints at least is broad. A line with a vague shape can also correspond to a line where the interior is partially or completely broad; we speak about lines with broad interiors. The constraint *Overlap* means that a line may combine different types of shape vagueness. A line can have a broad boundary and a broad interior at the same time. Finally, a line can be completely broad when there is a difficulty to distinguish each point of the line from its neighborhood.

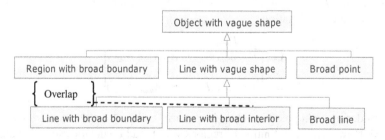

Fig. 2. Categorization of objects with vague shapes

2.2 Regions with Broad Boundaries and Their Topological Relations

In this paper, we define a region with a broad boundary according to the *QMM* model [3]. A region with a broad boundary is then composed by two crisp subregions: (1) *a maximal extent A_{max}* (i.e., the representation of the region when the boundary is considered as far as possible) and (2) *a minimal extent A_{min}* (i.e., the representation of the region when the boundary is considered as close as possible). These two extents should are related by one of the following topological relations: $Equal^1(A_{min}, A_{max})$ or $Contains(A_{min}, A_{max})$ or $Covers(A_{min}, A_{max})$ (Figure 3). The broad boundary refers to the difference between these two extents. This difference may include area everywhere around the minimal extent (i.e., regions with completely broad boundaries), may include area in some locations but not others around the minimal extent (i.e., regions with partially broad boundaries) or empty everywhere around the minimal extent (i.e., regions with no broad boundaries, or crisp regions). In Figure 3b, we present an example of a region with a partially broad boundary. The boundary is partially broad because the difference between the maximal extent and the minimal one is empty in some locations. Figures 3a and 3c, represent an example of a crisp region and another one of a region with a completely broad boundary, respectively.

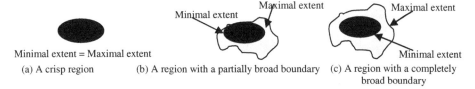

(a) A crisp region   (b) A region with a partially broad boundary   (c) A region with a completely broad boundary

Fig. 3. Regions with broad boundaries

In order to specify topological relations between two regions with broad boundaries, we apply the 9-Intersection model [11] to identify the subrelations between the minimal and maximal extents of regions involved [3]. These subrelations are described through a 4-Intersection matrix including the values $R_1(A_{min}, B_{min})$, $R_2(A_{min}, B_{max})$, $R_3(A_{max}, B_{min})$, and $R_4(A_{max}, B_{max})$, where A and B are two regions with broad boundaries. Each cell of the 4-Intersection matrix receives one of the eight possible topological relations between two simple crisp regions (i.e., *Disjoint, Overlap, Meet, Equal, Contains, Inside, Covers, Covered by*). The 4-Intersection matrix corresponds to the following representation:

$$\begin{array}{c} \\ A_{min} \\ \\ A_{max} \end{array} \begin{array}{c} B_{min} \qquad\qquad B_{max} \\ \left[\begin{array}{cc} R_1(A_{min}, B_{min}) & R_2(A_{min}, B_{max}) \\ R_3(A_{max}, B_{min}) & R_4(A_{max}, B_{max}) \end{array} \right] \end{array}$$

By considering eight possible values in a matrix' cells, $8^4 = 4096$ matrices can be distinguished. However, the definition of regions with broad boundaries specifies that only

---

[1] The spatial relations (i.e., *Equal, Contains, Covers*) used in this definition are those defined in (Egenhofer and Herring, 1990).

three relations between minimal and maximal extents are possible: $Equal(A_{max}, A_{min})$, $Contains(A_{max}, A_{min})$, or $Covers(A_{max}, A_{min})$. Thus, the contents of the matrix's cells are not mutually independent. For example, if the maximal extents are disjointed, it is inconsistent to have an *Overlap* relation between the minimal extents. By studying the possible consistency of matrices describing topological relations, we deducted that only 242 topological relations are possible between two simple regions with broad boundaries [3]. With regards to the content of a matrix, a topological relation can be classified into different clusters. Since eight values are possible in each cell of the 4-Intersection matrix, eight basic clusters can be distinguished: *DISJOINT, CONTAINS, COVERS, COVEREDBY, INSIDE, MEET, OVERLAP,* and *EQUAL.* In [3], we used four adverbs in order to qualify the membership of one relation to the clusters involved: *weakly* (only one of the matrix's cells has the same name as the cluster), *fairly* (two of the matrix's cells have the same name as the cluster), *strongly* (three of the matrix's cells have the same name as the cluster), and *completely* (all of the matrix's cells have the same value). Then, we distinguish for each basic cluster four subclusters which refer to the four levels of membership specified above: *weakly, fairly, strongly* and *completely.* Figure 4 presents some relations which belong to different subclusters of *CONTAINS* and *DISJOINT* clusters according to the contents of their respective matrices.

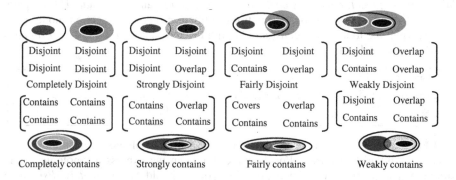

Fig. 4. Qualification of a topological relation between two regions with broad boundaries

In Figure 4, the fourth topological relation of the first line belongs with different strengths to the following clusters: *weakly* to *DISJOINT cluster, weakly* to *CONTAINS cluster,* and *fairly* to *OVERLAP cluster.* Hereafter, we integrate this adverbial approach into the object constraint language Spatial OCL.

3   Specification of Topological Constraints in Spatial Databases

3.1   Integrity Constraints in Spatial Databases

In spatial databases, additional integrity constraints are required to insure consistency of spatial objects [7, 21, 22]. In this paper, we are interested in topological constraints. These constraints control the validity of topological relations between spatial objects. We study formal expression of these constraints for regions with broad boundaries by using an extension of Spatial OCL.

3.2   OCL and Spatial OCL

OCL is a formal language that can be used to model invariants on UML models [16, 20]. These invariants can correspond to the integrity constraints of a database. Integrity constraints are defined in an UML class diagram. They correspond to conditions that must be satisfied for all instances of a class at any time. The class ruled by the constraint is called *context*. The principle of *navigation* consists in specifying integrity constraints which involve objects of different classes by using their associations. The following constraint specifies that the distance of an agricultural spread parcel from the closest lake must be greater than 100 meters:

```
Context Spreading_Parcel inv:
self.distance_lake > 100
```

In order to define spatial integrity constraints, Duboisset et al. [10] and Pinet et al. [16] proposed an extension of OCL's meta–model. This extension consists in adding geographic basic types (i.e., *point*, *line*, and *region*) to the meta-model of OCL (Figure 5). Moreover, topological relations can be expressed through Spatial OCL by using eight new topological operators added to the language: *overlaps*, *contains*, *is inside*, *are adjacent*, *covers*, *is covered by*, *are disjoint*, and *are equal*. These operators correspond to the topological relations defined in the 9-Intersection model [11]. For example, the topological constraint "buildings and roads *should not overlap each other*" is specified as follows:

```
Context road inv:
Building.allInstances→forAll(b|Self.geometry→aredisjoint(b)or
self.geometry→areAdjacent(b))
```

Additional OCL extensions are required to deal with topological constraints for regions with broad boundaries. For example, how can we express a topological constraint which specifies that "two pollution zones should be *completely disjoint* or *fairly meet* each other"? We need more tolerant topological operators than those currently used in Spatial OCL. Hereafter, we propose an extension of the Spatial OCL in order to support the formal expression of topological constraints between regions with broad boundaries. We call this extension Adverbial Spatial OCL for *Objects with vague shapes* (AOCL$_{OVS}$ for short). AOCL$_{OVS}$ is based on the *QMM* spatial model [3] and It consists of integrating a set of keywords of Spatial OCL in order to express the strength of topological relations specified in a constraint.

4   Adverbial Spatial OCL for Objects with Vague Shapes (AOCL$_{OVS}$)

In Spatial OCL [10, 16], geometric types are generalized through an abstract type called *BasicGeoType*. *BasicGeoType* allows definition of constraints on spatial attributes called *geometry*. Each value of *geometry* attribute value is a bag of elements; the type of each element is *BasicGeoType*. In order to consider vague shapes, we propose two abstract subclasses of geometries generalized by *BasicGeoType*: a type for *Objects with vague shapes* (*OVSType*) and another one for *Objects with Crisp Shapes* (*OCSType*). *OVSType* is a generalization of three basic types of objects with vague shapes: *broad point, line with a vague shape* and *region with a broad boundary*. A region with a broad boundary is composed by two crisp polygons (i.e., this relation is expressed through an aggregation between the type *Region with a broad boundary* and the type *Polygon*), which represent the minimal extent and maximal extent of the object, respectively. Figure 5 shows a general extension that covers three basic types of objects with vague shapes. In this paper, we focus on the topological constraints only for regions with broad boundaries.

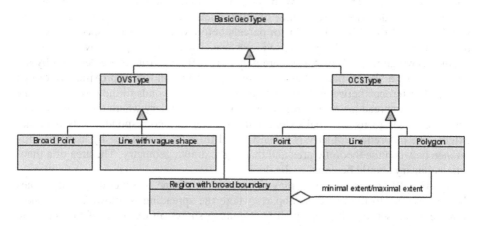

Fig. 5. Extension of the meta–model of Spatial OCL

The qualitative approach proposed in the *QMM* model [3] distinguishes 40 clusters (eight basic clusters and 32 subclusters) of topological relations between regions with broad boundaries (Section 2.2). Consequently, the proposed Spatial OCL extension introduces forty new topological operators adapted to regions with broad boundaries. These operators provide a qualitative evaluation of the strength of a topological relation. These operators can appear in OCL expressions when objects have the *OVSType* (Object with Vague Shape Type) and more precisely *Region with a broad boundary* type. A region with a broad boundary is considered valid when it verifies the next conditions:

1. Each one of the minimal extent and maximal extent verifies the closeness and connectedness conditions of a simple crisp region.
2. The minimal and maximal extents of a region with a broad boundary are related by one of the following topological relations: *Contains* (*max, min*), *Covers* (*max, min*), or *Equal* (*max, min*) (cf. section 2.2).

These last conditions are the *invariants* of the spatial model. We call these invariants *meta-constraints*, which control the validity of a region declared as a *Region with a broad boundary* (*RBB*).

5 Example in Agricultural Spreading Activities

Agricultural spreading activities consist of putting an organic substance *on* or *into* the soil in order to improve its agricultural productivity. In France, this activity is strictly controlled by public organizations, because substances used in spreading can be dangerous for ecological systems if they are not reasonably applied. The quantities and types of these substances depend on several criteria such as the parcel emplacement and soil type. For that, farmers should declare the areas to be spread and their references (i.e., they declare an *outline for the area to be spread*). Then, data about spreading activities are stored into a national spatial database. This database is accessed by a GIS-based tool available on the Web. The GIS-Based tool allows retrieving and updating of data describing spreading outlines declared by farmers. Farmers use the GIS-based tool to declare the areas of parcels before drawing their respective geometries on the screen through a GIS-based interface. The areas computed by the GIS tool for the drawn geometries of parcels are generally different from those declared by the farmer. Thus, a spread parcel has a theoretic geometry and an approximately drawn one. The difference between these two geometries corresponds to the broad boundary of a parcel. A spread parcel is a region with a broad boundary where the inner geometry corresponds to its minimal extent and the outer one corresponds to its maximal extent. The theoretic geometry is reconstructed from the drawn one by using the difference between the theoretic area and that of the drawn geometry. The area of a theoretic geometry should be equal to the drawn area.

Additionally, a spread parcel may be composed of one or several capacity zones that correspond to the parcel's subparts where the spreading is allowed with conditions (e.g., preserving the soil quality). Figure 6 shows an example of the theoretic geometry of a spread parcel (P_{Theo}), the drawn geometry of the same spread parcel (P_{Dr}), the theoretic geometry of a capacity zone Z1 ($Z1_{PTheoc}$), and the drawn geometry of a capacity zone Z1 ($Z1_{PDr}$). In this paper, we present a part of the conceptual schema of our spatial database (Figure 7). The class *Parcel* refers to an agricultural parcel contained by a spreading perimeter. A parcel is described by an identifier, a declared area, an area computed from the drawn geometry (*Draw_area*), and geometry with a vague shape composed by the drawn geometry and the theoretic one. Capacity zones are also defined as regions with broad boundaries. Finally, a spreading perimeter is a global area containing one or several spread parcels. Figure 7 presents a part of the class diagram of the spatial database storing data about agricultural spreading activities.

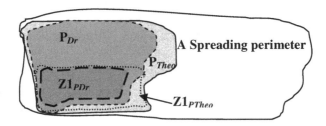

Fig. 6. An example of spatial data stored in the spreading agricultural database

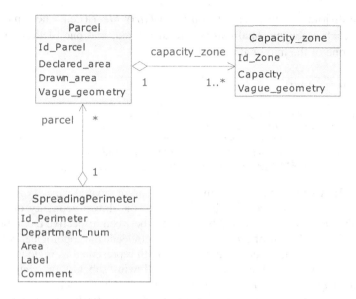

Fig. 7. Class diagram of the agricultural spreading database

5.1   Formal Expression of Constraints

The constraints presented below are expressed by using the AOCL$_{OVS}$ and they principally concern the spread parcels and their capacity zones. In this section, the *maximal extent* of one spread parcel refers to the theoretic geometry whether it covers or contains the drawn area, which is the minimal extent of the region in this case. In the same way, the drawn geometry refers to the maximal extent whether it covers or contains the theoretic geometry, which refers to the minimal extent in this second case. The minimal extent refers to the intersection of the theoretic geometry and the drawn one if they overlap each other. In this last case, the maximal extent refers to the union of the theoretic geometry and the drawn one.

Constraint 1: In a spreading outline, the parcels declared by farmers should be disjointed or meet each other. In the same way, the drawn geometries of these parcels, which have been manually drawn through a GIS-based tool, should also verify one of the topological relations: *Disjoint* or *Meet*. In our database, a parcel is an object with a vague shape, because a broad boundary results from the difference between the theoretic and drawn geometry. The topological relation between two parcels is valid when it belongs to one of the following subclusters: *completely Disjoint* (i.e., when both minimal and maximal extents are disjointed), *completely Meet* (i.e., when both minimal and maximal extents meet each other), *strongly Disjoint* and *weakly Meet* (i.e., when maximal extents meet each other but minimal extents are disjointed), or *fairly Disjoint* and *fairly Meet* (i.e., when maximal extents meet each other, minimal extents are disjointed, and one of the minimal extents meets one of the maximal extents):

```
Context Parcel inv:
Parcel.allInstances → forAll (b| self<>b implies
self.vague_geo→completely Meet(b.vague_geo) or
self.vague_geo→completely Disjoint(b.vague_geo) or
(self.vague_geo→strongly Disjoint(b.vague_) and self.vague_geo→weakly
Meet(b.vague_geo)) or (self.vague_geo→fairly Disjoint(b.vague_geo) and
self.vague_geo→fairly Meet(b.vague_geo)))
```

Constraint 2: A spread parcel is composed by one or several capacity zones. A capacity zone is inside, and covered by or equal to the drawn geometry of the parcel involved. The same relations should be respected between respective theoretic geometries of a parcel and each of its capacity zones. Indeed, the topological relation between a parcel and each of its capacity zones (both represented as regions with broad boundaries) is valid if it belongs to one of the following subclusters: *completely Contains, completely Covers, strongly Contains* and *weakly Covers, strongly Contains* and *weakly Overlap, fairly Contains* and *fairly Covers, fairly Contains* and *weakly Covers* and *weakly Overlap, strongly Covers* and *weakly Contains, fairly Contains* and *fairly Covers,* or *strongly Covers* and *weakly Overlap*:

```
Context Parcel inv:
self.vague_geo→ forAll (b| self.capacity_zone.vague_geo→ exists(d|
(b.vague_geo→completely Contains(d.vague_geo)) or
(b.vague_geo→completely Covers(d.vague_geo)) or (b.vague_geo→strongly
Contains(d.vague_geo) and b.vague_geo→weakly Covers(d.vague_geo)) or
(b.vague_geo→strongly Contains(d.vague_geo) and b.vague_geo→weakly
Overlap(d.vague_geo)) or (b.vague_geo→fairly Contains(d.vague_geo) and
b.vague_geo→fairly Covers(d.vague_geo)) or (b.vague_geo→fairly
Contains(d.vague_geo) and b.vague_geo→weakly Covers(d.vague_geo) and
b.vague_geo→weakly Overlap(d. vague_geo)) or (b.vague_geo→strongly
Covers(d.vague_geo) and b.vague_geo→weakly Contains(d.vague_geo)) or
(b.vague_geo→fairly Contains(d.vague_geo) and b.vague_geo→fairly
Covers(d.vague_geo)) or (b.vague_geo→strongly Covers(d.vague_geo) and
b.vague_geo→weakly Overlap(d.vague_geo))))
```

Constraint 3: Inside one spread parcel, two different capacity zones should verify one of the following specifications: *completely Disjoint, completely Meet, (strongly Disjoint and weakly Meet)* or *(fairly Disjoint and fairly Meet)*.

```
Context Capacity_zone inv:
self.allInstances → forAll (a,b| a<>b and a.parcel=b.parcel implies a.
vague_geo→completely Meet(b.vague_geo) or a.vague_geo→completely
Disjoint(b.vague_geo) or (a.vague_geo→strongly Disjoint(b.vague_geo)
and a.vague_geo→weakly Meet(b.vague_geo)) or (a.vague_geo →fairly
Disjoint(b.vague_geo) and a.vague_geo→fairly Meet(b.vague_geo)));
```

Constraint 4: *P* is a spreading perimeter composed by *N* spread parcels. The sum of areas of minimal extents of spread parcels is less than or equal to the area of *P*. However, the sum of areas of maximal extents of spread parcels is greater than or equal to the declared area of *P*. The expression "*self.parcel.vague_geo.minimal_extent.area→sum()*" provides the sum of areas of minimal extents of parcels belonging to the spreading perimeter involved. In other words, this function makes the same thing for maximal extents of capacity zones in one spread parcel.

```
Context SpreadingPerimeter inv:

self.parcel.vague_geo.minimal_extent.area→sum() ≤ self.area and
self.parcel.vague_geo.maximal_extent.area→sum() ≥ self.area
```

5.2   Implementation of AOCL$_{OVS}$

In this work, OCL expressions can be automatically translated into SQL code by using a constraint editor called OCL2SQL initially developed by Tudresden University before to be extended by [10, 16], first for topological constraints for crisp regions and next, in the present paper, for regions with broad boundaries. Figure 8 shows the architecture of OCL2SQL application. It is a Java application in which constraints are defined in an UML class diagram stored in an *xmi* file. The constraints are written by using AOCL$_{OVS}$ specifications to be verified according the class diagram involved. OCL2SQL editor translates these constraints in SQL language, wherein new topological operators are defined as PL/SQL functions managed by the DBMS (Database Management System) Oracle. For example, the next constraint specifies that two pollution zones should be strongly disjointed. For this constraint we give the correspondent SQL code. The SQL script generated by OCL2SQL is then executed on the data stored in an Oracle spatial database in order to retrieve possible inconsistencies.

Constraint 5:

```
Context Pollution_zones inv:

Parcel.allInstances→forAll (b| self<>b implies self.vague_geo→
strongly Disjoint(b.vague_geo)
```

Oracle Spatial SQL:
select * from OV_Pollution_Zone SELF
where not (not exists ((select PK6 from OV_ Pollution_Zone) minus
    select PK6 from OV_ Pollution_Zone SELF2 where (SELF.PK6 = SELF2.PK6) OR
      stronglyDisjoint((select PK4 from OV_VAGUE_GEO
        where PK4 in (select GEOMETRY_PK4 from
                    OV_ Pollution_Zone where PK6 = SELF2.PK6)),
                  (select PK4 from OV_VAGUE_GEO where PK4 in
                  (select GEOMETRY_PK4 from OV_ Pollution_Zone
            where PK6 = SELF2.PK6)) , OV_VAGUE_GEO)=0));

Figure 8 schematizes the architecture of the extension of OCL2SQL, which covers topological constraints involving regions with broad boundaries. This figure is adapted from [10].

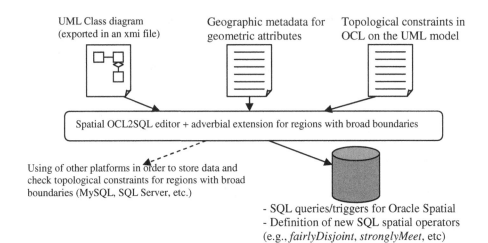

UML Class diagram   Geographic metadata for   Topological constraints in
(exported in an xmi file)   geometric attributes   OCL on the UML model

Spatial OCL2SQL editor + adverbial extension for regions with broad boundaries

Using of other platforms in order to store data and
check topological constraints for regions with broad
boundaries (MySQL, SQL Server, etc.)

- SQL queries/triggers for Oracle Spatial
- Definition of new SQL spatial operators
(e.g., *fairlyDisjoint*, *stronglyMeet*, etc)

Fig. 8. Architecture of the application used to check the OCL constraints (this figure is adapted from [10])

6 Conclusion

Respecting topological constraints is an important aspect of internal spatial data quality. Topological constraints can be expressed through Spatial OCL [10, 16], which integrates the 9-Intersection model to specify topological relations. However, Spatial OCL lacks syntactical tools to express topological constraints for objects with vague shapes. In this paper, we addressed the problem of formal specification of topological constraints for objects with vague shapes and especially regions with broad boundaries. For that, we presented a spatial model for regions with broad boundaries, where topological relations are identified according to subrelations between their minimal and maximal extents [3]. Then, topological relations are qualitatively classified by exploring similarity between subrelations identified. Four adverbs are used to describe the strength of a topological relation between two regions with broad boundaries: *weakly*, *fairly*, *strongly*, or *completely*.

This paper makes three main contributions. First, the meta-model of Spatial OCL has been extended in order to consider new data types covering spatial objects with vague shapes. We proposed a new abstract type called *OVSType* (*Object with Vague Shape Type*), which can be specialized into *broad point*, *line with a vague shape*, and *region with a broad boundary*. Second, our adverbial approach for topological relations between regions with broad boundaries has been integrated into Spatial OCL. Forty new topological operators have been proposed as additional keywords of Spatial OCL in order to deal with topological constraints involving regions with broad boundaries. We have called this extension *Adverbial spatial OCL for Objects with Vague Shapes* ($AOCL_{OVS}$ for short). Third, $AOCL_{OVS}$ has been integrated into the constraint editor OCL2SQL, which automatically generates Oracle Spatial SQL code of the topological constraints from their $AOCL_{OVS}$ expressions. This framework has been tested using a spatial database storing data about agricultural spreading activities. Some constraints have been specified for this database. These constraints principally involve spread parcels and their capacity zones presented as regions with broad boundaries.

In the future, we aim to extend this approach in two main directions. First, we will generalize our framework in order to specify topological relations involving different objects with vague shapes (i.e., *broad points*, *lines with vague shapes*, and *regions with broad boundaries*). Second, we will study the specification of topological constraints involving regions with vague complex shapes (e.g., regions with several kernels, regions composed by several subregions with broad boundaries).

References

1. Bédard, Y., Larrivée, S., Proulx, M.J., Nadeau, M.: Modeling Geospatial Databases with Plug-Ins for Visual Languages: A Pragmatic Approach and the Impacts of 16 Years of Research and Experimentations on Perceptory. In: Wang, S., et al. (eds.) ER Workshops 2004. LNCS, vol. 3289, pp. 17–30. Springer, Heidelberg (2004)
2. Bejaoui, L., Bédard, Y., Pinet, F., Salehi, M., Schneider, M.: Logical consistency for vague spatiotemporal objects and relations. In: The 5th International Symposium on Spatial Data Quality (ISSDQ 2007), Enschede, Netherlands (June 2007)
3. Bejaoui, L., Bédard, Y., Pinet, F., Schneider, M.: Qualified topological relations between objects with possibly vague shape. International Journal of Geographical Information Sciences (to appear, 2008)
4. Burrough, P.A., Frank, A.U.: Geographic Objects with Indeterminate Boundaries. Taylor & Francis, London (1996)
5. Clementini, E., Di Felice, P.: A Comparison of Methods for Representing Topological Relationships. Information Sciences 3, 149–178 (1995)
6. Clementini, E., Di Felici, P.: Approximate topological relations. International Journal of Approximate Reasoning 16, 173–204 (1997)
7. Cockcroft, S.: A Taxonomy of Spatial Data Integrity Constraints. Geoinformatica 1(4), 327–343 (1997)
8. Cohn, A.G., Gotts, N.M.: The 'egg-yolk' representation of regions with indeterminate boundaries. In: Burrough, P., Frank, A. (eds.) Proceedings of the GISDATA Specialist Meeting on Spatial Objects with Undetermined Boundaries, pp. 171–187. Taylor & Francis, Abington (1996)
9. Dilo, A.: Representation of and reasoning with vagueness in spatial information: A system for handling vague objects. PhD thesis, ITC, Netherlands, p. 187 (2006)
10. Duboisset, M., Pinet, F., Kang, M.A., Schneider, M.: Precise modeling and verification of topological integrity constraints in spatial databases: from an expressive power study to code generation principles. In: Delcambre, L.M.L., Kop, C., Mayr, H.C., Mylopoulos, J., Pastor, Ó. (eds.) ER 2005. LNCS, vol. 3716, pp. 465–482. Springer, Heidelberg (2005)
11. Egenhofer, M., Herring, J.: A mathematical framework for the definition of topological relations. In: Brassel, K., Kishimoto, H. (eds.) Proceedings of the Fourth International Symposium on Spatial Data Handling, Zurich, Switzerland, pp. 803–813 (1990)
12. Erwig, M., Schneider, M.: Vague regions. In: Scholl, M.O., Voisard, A. (eds.) SSD 1997. LNCS, vol. 1262, pp. 298–320. Springer, Heidelberg (1997)
13. Frank, A.U.: Tiers of ontology and consistency constraints in geographical information systems. Int. J. of Geographical Information Science 15(7), 667–678 (2001)

14. Guptill, S.C., Morrison, J.L.: Spatial data quality. In: Guptill, S.C., Morrison, J.L. (eds.) Elements of spatial data quality, Elsevier Science Inc., New York (1995)

15. Hazarika, S.M., Cohn, A.G.: A taxonomy for spatial vagueness, an alternative egg-yolk interpretation. In: Montello, D.R. (ed.) COSIT 2001. LNCS, vol. 2205, pp. 92–107. Springer, Heidelberg (2001)

16. Pinet, F., Duboisset, M., Soulignac, V.: Using UML and OCL to maintain the consistency of spatial data in environmental information systems. Environmental modelling & software 22(8), 1217–1220 (2007)

17. Reis, R., Egenhofer, M.J., Matos, J.: Topological relations using two models of uncertainty for lines. In: Proceeding of the 7th international Symposium on Spatial Accuracy Assessment in Natural Resources and Environmental Sciences, Lisbon, Portugal, 5 - 7 July, pp. 286–295 (2006)

18. Rodriguez, A.: Inconsistency Issues in Spatial Databases. In: Bertossi, L., Hunter, A., Schaub, T. (eds.) Inconsistency Tolerance. LNCS, vol. 3300, pp. 237–269. Springer, Heidelberg (2005)

19. Salehi, M., Bédard, Y., Mir, A.M., Brodeur, J.: Classification of integrity constraints in spatiotemporal databases: toward building an integrity constraint specification language. International Journal of Geographical Information Science (submitted, 2007)

20. Schmid, B., Warmer, J., Clark, T.: Object Modeling with the OCL: the Relational Behind the Object Constraint Language, p. 281. Springer, Heidelberg (2002)

21. Servigne, S., Ubeda, T., Puricelli, A., Laurini, R.: A Methodology for Spatial Consistency Improvement of Geographic Databases. GeoInformatica 4(1), 7–34 (2000)

22. Souris, M.: Contraintes d'intégrité spatiales. In: Devillers, R., Jeansoulin, R. (eds.) Qualité de l'information géographique, Lavoisier, pp. 100–123 (2006)

23. Tang, T.: Spatial object modeling in fuzzy topological spaces: with applications to land cover change. PhD thesis, University of Twente (2004) ISBN 90-6164-220-5

24. Van Oort, P.: Spatial data quality: from description to application. In: Publication on Geodesy 60, Delft, December 2006, Geodetic Commission, Netherlands (2006)

25. Yazici, A., Zhu, Q., Sun, N.: Semantic data modeling of spatiotemporal database applications. Int. J. Intell. Syst., 881–904 (2001)

26. Zhan, F.B., Lin, H.: Overlay of Two Simple Polygons with Indeterminate Boundaries. Transactions in GIS 7(1), 67–81 (2003)

Capturing Temporal Constraints
in Temporal ER Models

Carlo Combi[1], Sara Degani[1], and Christian S. Jensen[2]

[1] Department of Computer Science - University of Verona
Strada le Grazie 15, 37134 Verona, Italy
{carlo.combi,sara.degani}@univr.it
[2] Department of Computer Science - Aalborg University
Selma Lagerlöfs Vej 300, DK-9220 Aalborg Øst, Denmark
csj@cs.aau.dk

Abstract. A wide range of database applications manage information
that varies over time. The conceptual modeling of databases is frequently
based on one of the several versions of the ER model. As this model does
not provide built-in means for capturing temporal aspects of data, the
resulting diagrams are unnecessarily obscure and inadequate for documentation purposes. The TIMEER model extends the ER model with
suitable constructs for modeling time-varying information, easing the
design process, and leading to easy-to-understand diagrams. In a temporal ER model, support for the specification of advanced temporal constraints would be desirable, allowing the designer to specify, e.g., that
the value of an attribute must not change over time. This paper extends
the TIMEER model by introducing the notation, and the associated semantics, for the specification of new temporal constraints.

Keywords: Conceptual modeling, database design, entity-relationship
models, temporal databases, temporal data models, temporal constraints.

1 Introduction

A wide range of database applications manage information that varies over time:
travel applications such as airline, train, and hotel reservations; record-keeping
applications such as medical records; and financial applications like banking
account management are some examples. Frequently, in the database design process for such applications, traditional data models are used; one of the several
versions of the Entity-Relationship (ER) model is a common choice [1,3]. The
ER model is easy to understand and use, and it allows one to define database
schemata by means of easy-to-comprehend diagrams. Nevertheless, it does not
explicitly support the management of time-varying information, and it is mainly
left to the application designers and developers to discover and implement the
temporal concepts meaningful for the application itself; this makes the design
process more complex and leads to difficult-to-understand database diagrams.
For this reason, a wide range of temporal extensions of the ER model have been

Q. Li et al. (Eds.): ER 2008, LNCS 5231, pp. 397–411, 2008.

developed by the research community over the years [6]. These extensions allow a more natural and elegant design of temporal databases, providing means for capturing the temporal aspects of the recorded data. Existing temporal ER extensions, however, do not consider some advanced temporal aspects in data modeling, such as, for example, specifying that an attribute cannot change over time, or that an entity identifier cannot be re-used for different entities in different times. In this paper, we extend the temporal data model TimeER [3,7], introducing new notations for the specification of advanced temporal constraints, thus enhancing the expressiveness and temporal support of the model. In particular, we propose some extensions to the notion of key constraint; we apply the concept of time-invariance to attributes and relationships; finally we introduce new temporal superclass/subclass relationship constraints. We are not aware of any other temporal ER model that supports the temporal constraints defined in this paper.

The paper is structured as follows. Section 2 introduces the TimeER model and a temporal relational model that we will use to define the semantics of the new temporal constraints; in Sect. 3, we describe a motivating example taken from a clinical scenario; in Sect. 4, we define new advanced temporal constraints for the TimeER model; Section 5 describes the semantics of the temporal key constraint defined in Sect. 4; finally, Sect. 6 offers concluding remarks and identifies directions for future research.

2   Background

In the following, we describe the main aspects of the TimeER model; furthermore, we present a temporal relational data model that will be used for the definition of the semantics of the new temporal constraints.

2.1   The TimeER Model

The Time Extended ER (TimeER) model [3,7] extends the EER model described by Elmasri and Navathe [1]. Existing ER constructs with their usual semantics are retained, and new notation providing implicit temporal support is added. More specifically, built-in temporal support is included for entities, relationships, and attributes. Four types of temporal aspects of information can be captured in a TimeER diagram, namely *valid time*, *transaction time*, *lifespan*, and *user-defined time* [8]. Table 1 indicates which aspects of time may be associated with each database concept. Note that TimeER offers support for both lifespan and valid time for relationships, as a relationship can be perceived as an entity that exists in its own right, or as a "complex attribute" of the involved entities. Temporal aspects are captured adding annotations to the modeling constructs: LS indicates lifespan support, VT indicates valid-time support, TT indicates transaction-time support, LT indicates lifespan and transaction time support, and finally BT indicates both valid and transaction time support. In Sect. 3, we describe an example that illustrates how temporal information is represented in a TimeER diagram.

Table 1. Association of aspects of time to TIMEER database concepts

	Entity types	Relationship types	Super/subclass relationships	Attributes
Lifespan	Yes	Yes (entity view)	No	No
Valid time	No	Yes (attribute view)	No	Yes
Transaction time	Yes	Yes	No	Yes

2.2 The Surrogate-Based Relational Model

In the following, we describe the surrogate-based relational model. A mapping from TIMEER modeling constructs to the surrogate-based relational model is defined in [4].

Domains of Attributes. The surrogate-based relational model supports the lexical domains of the standard relational model: $\mathcal{D}_D = \{D_1, \ldots, D_n\}$. Further, it supports a domain of surrogates, termed the *E-domain*, and three time domains, D_{LS} (lifespan domain), D_{VT} (valid time domain) and D_{TT} (transaction time domain).

Surrogates are system-generated unique internal identifiers; their values cannot be modified by the users of the model. Attributes defined over the E-domain are called *E-attributes*, and attributes defined over the time domains are termed *time attributes*. As a convention, the names of E-attributes end with the character ø; the names of time attributes are LS_s, LS_e, VT_s, VT_e, TT_s, TT_e, where s and e indicates start and end of the considered temporal dimension, respectively.

Relations. The surrogate-based relational model has two types of relations, *E-relations* and *A-relations*. E-relations are used to represent TIMEER entity types and also relationship types that are considered to exist in their own right. An *E-relation* has a single *E-attribute* and a number of time attributes, depending on the time support specified for the corresponding entity type. *A-relations* represent entity or relationship attributes. An A-relation references, through a surrogate, the E-relation corresponding to the entity type the represented attributes belong to. If the represented attribute is temporal, the A-relation has also a number of time attributes.

Keys and Constraints. In traditional relational models, a primary key normally serves two roles: it is a lexical identifier, and it models existence. In the surrogate-based data model, lexical identification and existence are separated: E-relations only have a primary key, as the term "primary key" is used to exclusively model existence; A-relations have a unique identifier termed "key" [4]. At any point in time, null-values are not allowed in E-relations (Entity Integrity Constraint), and all surrogates referenced from an A-relation must exist in the corresponding E-relation (Referential Integrity Constraint). Pairs of time attributes are used to record the starting and the ending chronons of time intervals. The semantics of temporal aspects is enforced through the definition of a number of constraints on the database. For example, the valid time of any tuple of an A-relation must be included in the lifespan of the referenced tuple of the corresponding E-relation. These constraints are not enforced automatically by the data model, but must be enforced by explicit specifications, e.g., using assertions.

3   Motivating Example

We proceed to briefly introduce a motivating example taken from the clinical context. The TIMEER diagram in Fig. 1 models a clinical database that stores information about patients, their admission into the hospital, drugs, and physicians. A patient is identified by an SSN (Social Security Number) and is characterized by name, address, and birth place; it must be considered that the SSN of a patient could change over time if, e.g., the patient changes name for some reasons. Information about changes of patients' addresses are recorded, too. The hospital records the patients' hospitalization history, and when this information is current in the database. Each hospital admission is characterized by a code and by the admission reason. Three different kinds of hospital admission are possible: emergency admission, regular admission, and day-hospital admission. For each emergency admission, the database stores information about the assigned bed number and the emergency level, and about possible changes of bed; for each regular admission, information about the assigned bed number (and possible changes to it) and the reservation number are recorded. Moreover, for each day-hospital admission the database stores information about the reservation number.

The hospital mantains data about drugs and about each single drug package. Each drug is identified by its National Drug Code (NDC) and is characterized by a name and by the drug class (prescription drug or over-the-counter drug); the NDC of a drug can neither vary over time, nor be re-assigned to a different drug. For each drug package, the tracking code is recorded; the tracking code of a drug package cannot vary over time; moreover, it cannot be re-assigned to other drug packages before six years from its assignement. Information about patient allergies to drugs are stored too; it must be considered that once a drug allergy is recognized, it cannot disappear.

Physicians make diagnoses on patients; each physician is identified by a code and is characterized by a name. The hospital keeps track of diagnosis histories, and also of when this information is recorded in the database. Physicians can be either hospital physicians or general practitioners; the basic information of a physician needs to remain in the database even in the case the physician decides to resign.

The TIMEER model allows one to represent several temporal aspects of the above example. First of all, changes of the address of a patient are captured through the VT annotation for the attribute *address* of the entity *Patient*. Changes of bed of a patient are modeled similarly. Moreover, the TIMEER model

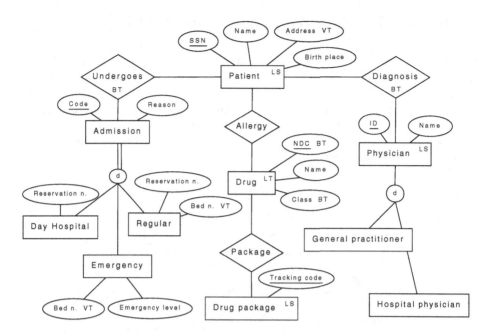

Fig. 1. A TimeER diagram modeling a clinical database

allows one to keep track of the hospitalization history of a patient, and of when that information is available in the database, through the BT annotation for the relationship *Undergoes*. Similarly, the *Diagnosis* relationship is annotated with BT to record patient diagnosis history and the time during which the information is available in the database. The existence-times of entities *Patient*, *Physician*, and *Drug package* are recorded by the LS annotation for the respective entities; moreover, for the entity *Drug* existence-time and time of occurence in the database are stored by the LT annotation.

Nevertheless, we can observe that some of the database requirements cannot be properly expressed by TimeER constructs. First of all, TimeER keys have a snapshot-reducible semantics [7], as it is ensured that any key at any point in time uniquely identifies an entity; this notion, however, is not sufficient to constrain a key value to be time-invariant, as is required for the *Tracking code* attribute of the entity *Drug package*; moreover, it does not allow one to express the fact that a key value cannot be assigned to two different entities at two different points in time, as is required for the *NDC* attribute of the entity *Drug*. The notion of time-invariance cannot be expressed for regular attributes either; this would be desirable for the attribute *Birth place* of the entity *Patient*, as the birth place of a person does not change over time; moreover, TimeER does not provide means to express the fact that a drug allergy of a patient cannot disappear over time. Finally, TimeER superclass/subclass relationship constraints do not allow one to express, for example, that the kind of admission of a patient cannot change over time.

4   Introducing New Temporalities in TIMEER

In this section we introduce the main contribution of the paper, namely the definition of advanced temporal constraints for TIMEER diagrams. First, we consider the key constraint, and we define different versions of it, considering its temporal aspects. Then we apply the notion of time invariance to attributes and relationships. Finally, we define new temporal constraints over superclass/subclass relationships. Figure 2 shows how the diagram in Fig. 1 can be modified to also capture the new constraints.

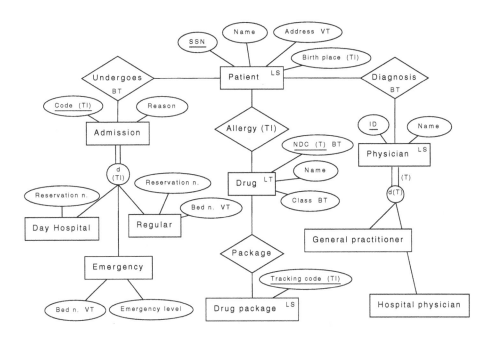

Fig. 2. The TIMEER diagram modeling the clinical database with the new constraints

4.1   Key Constraints

As the traditional ER model, the TIMEER model allows one to indicate that a set of attributes represents the key of an entity type. TIMEER keys have a snapshot-reducible semantics. In a temporal ER model, however, it may be desiderable to have the possibility of specifying different kinds of key constraints, considering the relationship between key attributes and time. In the following, we first describe the notion of snapshot-reducible key as defined in the TIMEER model. Therefore, we define and compare two advanced notions of key constraint, namely the *time-invariant key constraint* and the *temporal key constraint*.

Definition 1 (Snapshot-Reducible Key). *An entity snapshot-reducible key (or simply entity key) is a group of the entity's attributes that has to satisfy the following constraint: at any point in time, the mapping from the entity set to the corresponding set composed of groups of values for the key attributes is one-to-one.*

Definition 1 states that a snapshot-reducible key, at any point in time, uniquely identifies an entity. The concept of snapshot-reducible key is defined in terms of conventional keys and snapshot reducibility: snapshot reducibility ensures, for example, that at any point in the valid time domain, a single-valued attribute, for which valid time is captured, has only one value for an entity; combining this with the conventional key constraint, we have that any key attribute at any point in time uniquely identifies an entity.

An example scenario describing the application of the snapshot-reducible key constraint is represented by the entity *Patient* in Fig. 2. The Social Security Number of a patient can be updated over time; for example, a foreigner moving to Italy could change his surname on the basis of the Italian surname attribution rules, which are different from those of the patient's original country; as a consequence, the Social Security Number, too, has to be modified. Then, the *SSN* key attribute has a snapshot-reducible semantics, as its value for a specific entity has to be unique at each single point in time, but it may vary over time.

For a snapshot-reducible key, it is ensured that at any point in time, each entity has a different value for the key attribute; however, for two different points in time, the same key value could identify two different entities, or an entity could be identified by two different values of the key. Considering this aspect, we introduce in the TimeER model the possibility of specifying two more restrictive kinds of key. We call the first one *time-invariant key*, and it is defined as follows.

Definition 2 (Time-Invariant Key). *An entity time-invariant key is a group of the entity's attributes with the following properties: it is a snapshot-reducible key, and the values of the key attributes of an entity do not change over time in the valid-time domain.*

The second point in Definition 2 states that an entity is identified by the same time-invariant key value for all times in the valid-time domain: if we fix a single point in the transaction-time domain (if required) and then consider two different points in the valid-time domain, the same entity cannot have two different values for the key attribute. In other words, two entities identified by different time-invariant key values are different entities.

An example of application of time-invariant key is represented by the *Tracking code* key attribute of the entity *Drug package* in Fig. 2. The tracking code is a unique number associated with each drug package that cannot be repeated for at least six years. This means that two drug packages identified by different tracking codes are different packages, but the same tracking code could identify two different drug packages at two different valid-time instants. It follows that the *Tracking code* key has a time-invariant semantics.

If an entity key is defined as time-invariant, it cannot have two different values for the key attributes at two different valid-time points, but the key value can be reassigned to different entities over time. We introduce a third kind of key constraint in TIMEER that is even more restrictive than the time-invariant key, as it also prevents the reassignement of key values over time. It is defined as follows.

Definition 3 (Temporal Key). *An entity temporal key is a group of the entity's attributes with the following properties: it is a time-invariant key, and the values of the key attributes of an entity cannot be reassigned to a different entity in the valid-time domain.*

The first and the second point of Definition 3 imply that two entities identified by different time-invariant key values are different entities; the third point implies that two entities identified by the same time-invariant key value are the same entity. The *NDC* attribute of the entity *Drug* in Fig. 2 is an example of a temporal key. Indeed, the National Drug Code is a number unique to every drug type that can neither vary over time for a specific drug type, nor be reassigned to a different drug.

The graphical notation for the three kinds of key is the following. To indicate that an entity attribute is a snapshot-reducible key, the key attribute name is underlined. For a time-invariant key, the label (TI) is placed to the right of the attribute name, and it is underlined together with the attribute name; for a temporal key, a (T) is used in the same way.

For all the three kinds of keys it is possible to specify, besides valid time, transaction time, too. Specifying the valid time for a time-invariant or a temporal key does not serve the purpose of keeping track of changes of the key value in the valid-time domain; however, even though a temporal key value cannot vary over time, specifying its valid time can be useful, as it enables the capture of the starting and the ending instants of validity of the value. Moreover, the specification of transaction time for time-invariant key attributes allows one to view previously current database states.

4.2   Time-Invariant Attributes

Similarly to how we applied the notion of time-invariance to entity keys, we can apply this notion to simple attributes.

Definition 4 (Time-Invariant Attribute). *A time-invariant attribute is an attribute whose value does not change over time in the valid-time domain.*

This means that, (possibly) given a fixed point in the transaction-time domain, a time-invariant attribute of a given entity cannot have two different values for two different points in the valid-time domain. Time-invariant attributes model entity and relationship properties that do not vary over time. A simple example is the attribute *Birth place* of the entity *Patient* in Fig. 2. As the birth place of a person does not change over time, the attribute is specified as time-invariant.

As we can see in the figure, the graphical notation for time-invariant attributes is the label (TI) placed to the right of the attribute name. Valid and/or transaction time can be specified also for time-invariant attributes.

4.3   Time-Invariant Relationships

The notion of time-invariance can be applied to entity relationships, too.

Definition 5 (Time-Invariant Relationship). *A relationship between two entities is time-invariant if, once it has been established, it holds as long as both involved entities exist in the mini-world.*

Definition 5 implies that a time-invariant relationship can start at any point during the existence of the involved entities, but that, after the starting instant, it has to hold for all the time during which the involved entities exist in the modeled reality.

In Fig. 2, the entity *Patient* is related to the entity *Drug* by means of the relationship *Allergy*. It can be observed that once a drug allergy is recognized, it cannot disappear; therefore, each instance of the relationship *Allergy* holds as long as the involved *Patient* and *Drug* instances exist in the modeled reality. It follows that the relationship *Allergy* is time-invariant.

A time-invariant relationship R is represented by placing the label (TI) in the right corner of the diamond representing R. Temporal support can be specified also for time-invariant relationships.

4.4   Superclass/Subclass Participation Constraints

The TIMEER model allows one to specify snapshot totality and disjointness constraints over superclass/subclass relationships, which state that the traditional totality and disjointness constraints, respectively, must hold at each single point in time. In many situations, however, the notions of snapshot totality and disjointness constraints are not adequate to express the actual semantics of the superclass/subclass relationship. We therefore define the advanced notions of *temporal totality constraint, temporal disjointness constraint,* and *time-invariant superclass/subclass relationship.*

Definition 6 (Temporally-Total Superclass/Subclass Relationship).
Let E and $E_1, \ldots, E_n$ be TIMEER entities such that E is a superclass and $E_1, \ldots, E_n$ are subclasses of E. If the superclass/subclass relationship is temporally total, then each member of the superclass is a member of at least one of the subclasses for at least one time instant in its lifespan.

A temporally total superclass/subclass relationship is represented by placing the label (T) near the double line that represents the total participation constraint.

A situation, in which the temporal totality constraint is necessary to express the actual semantics of a superclass/subclass relationship, is represented by the superclass *Physician* and its subclasses in Fig. 2. The modeled database keeps track of hospital physicians and general practitioners; suppose that the hospital inserts data about a physician through occurrences of either entity *General practitioner* or entity *Hospital physician*. If a physician resigns, for example to start working privately, the basic information about the entity still needs to remain in the database; therefore, from the instant of the physician's resignation, the entity becomes an instance of the superclass only. It follows that each physician recorded in the database must be a general practitioner or a hospital physician for at least one time instant in its lifespan. This condition can be expressed by means of the temporal totality constraint.

Definition 7 (Temporally-Disjoint Superclass/Subclass Relationship).
Let E and $E_1, \ldots, E_n$ be TimeER *entities such that E is a superclass and $E_1, \ldots, E_n$ are subclasses of E. If the superclass/subclass relationship is temporally disjoint then an instance e of E is a member of at most one of the subclasses for all times in its lifespan.*

A temporally disjoint superclass/subclass relationship is represented by placing the label (T) in the circle containing the specification of the disjointness constraint.

As an example, consider the superclass/subclass relationship given by the entity *Physician* and its subclasses in Fig. 2. Suppose that the considered hospital does not allows a hospital physician to become a general practitioner, and vice–versa. In this case, the superclass/subclass relationship is temporally disjoint, as for all its lifespan, an instance of *Physician* can be a member of at most one of the two subclasses *General practitioner* and *Hospital physician*.

Definition 8 (Time-Invariant Superclass/Subclass Relationship). *A superclass/subclass relationship is time-invariant if each member of the superclass that belongs to one or more subclasses is a member of those subclasses for all of its lifespan.*

From the definition, it follows that the existence time of each instance of the subclasses is equal to the existence time of the corresponding instance of the superclass.

An example of time-invariant relationship is shown in Fig. 2, by the superclass *Admission* and its subclasses. A patient admission can only be an emergency admission, a regular admission, or a day hospital admission at a time, and the kind of admission cannot change over time. Therefore, an instance of the entity *Admission* is an instance of one of its subclasses *Emergency admission, Regular admission,* or *Day hospital* for all its lifespan; it follows that the superclass/subclass relationship is time-invariant. A time-invariant superclass/subclass relationship is represented by placing the label (TI) in the circle representing the superclass/subclass relationships.

5   Semantics

The semantics of the TimeER constraints defined in Sect. 4 can be expressed by means of their mapping to the surrogate-based relational model, presented in Sect. 2.2. In the following, we give the semantics for the temporal key constraint.

5.1   Semantics of the Temporal Key Constraint

In order to define the semantics of the temporal key constraint through its mapping to the target relational model, we first recall how entity types and their attributes are mapped to relations of the surrogate-based relational model [4]. For a temporal entity type, an E-relation is created as the union of the E-attribute and the time attributes corresponding to the temporal support specified for the entity type. Moreover, for each temporal attribute, an A-relation is created as the union of the E-attribute, the attribute itself, and the associated time attributes.

Some constraints apply to the relations created by the mapping [4]. First of all, it must be enforced that the information recorded by the A-relation is snapshot reducible: for A-relations recording valid time only, this means that no two tuples of the A-relation containing the same E-attribute can have overlapping valid-time intervals; similar constraints apply for A-relations recording transaction time only or both valid time and transaction time.

A temporal constraint must hold to ensure that attributes of temporal entities cannot be associated with time intervals for which the entities do not exist or are not registered in the database. For example, if the tuples in an A-relation representing temporal attributes record valid-time only, then the valid-time intervals have to be included in the lifespan interval recorded by the tuple of the E-relation with the same value of the E-attribute. Similar constraints apply for all the combinations of temporal support for the A-relation and the E-relation.

As an example, Table 2 represents the result of the mapping of the entity *Drug* in Fig. 2 and of its attributes. The attributes that are overlined in the relations indicate the primary keys of the relations, while attributes that are underlined constitute keys of the relations. The term *primary key* exclusively indicates existence; consequently, only E-relations have primary keys. The unique identifier of an A-relation is simply termed a *key*. In the example, the primary key of the E-relation *Drug* includes the LS_s timestamp attribute; the reason is that the surrogate-based relational model allows an entity to reborn in the database. It is worth noting that (possibly non temporally continuous) histories of entities and their attribues can be suitably derived through joins between the E-relation and the A-relations representing the considered entity. The attributes that the user may have specified as a key for an entity type in the diagram are indicated by the symbol "u.k." in a relation. Foreign keys of relations are indicated by the symbol "f.k." following the attribute names.

A further constraint must be enforced to ensure that, for each instant of validity of the value of an entity attribute, a corresponding value exists in the A-relation representing the user-defined key. Constraint 1 ensures this in the case where the user-defined key is a temporal key.

Table 2. The result of the mapping of the entity *Drug* in Figure 2

Drug		
drugø	LS$_s$	LS$_e$

Drug_NDC						
drugø f.k.	NDC u.k.	VT$_s$	VT$_e$	TT$_s$	TT$_e$

Drug_name	
drugø f.k.	name

Drug_class					
drugø f.k.	class	VT$_s$	VT$_e$	TT$_s$	TT$_e$

Constraint 1. *Let E be a* TimeER *entity with a temporal key for which valid time only is captured. Let R be the A-relation storing the temporal key of E, and let r_i be a tuple variable over R. Let S be an A-relation representing an attribute of E, and let s_i be a tuple variable over S. Let $R\emptyset$ and $S\emptyset$ be the foreign key of R and S, respectively, referring to the surrogate attribute of the E-relation representing E. Then:*

$$\forall s_i \in S \; \exists r_i \in R(s_i.S\emptyset = r_i.R\emptyset \wedge [s_i.VT_s, s_i.VT_e] \subseteq [r_i.VT_s, r_i.VT_e])$$

Constraint 1 can be straightforwardly defined for the cases in which transaction time also is captured for the A-relation recording the entity attribute and/or for the A-relation recording the temporal key.

We therefore define the mapping of the temporal key constraint as Constraint 2 and Constraint 3; these constraints apply to the relation representing the temporal key attribute. Constraint 2 applies in the case where valid time only is captured for the temporal key attribute, and Constraint 3 applies when both valid time and transaction time are captured.

Constraint 2. *Let E be a* TimeER *entity with a temporal key for which valid time only is captured. Let R be the A-relation storing the temporal key of E, and let r_i, r_j be tuple variables over R. Let X be the group of attributes of R that represents the temporal key of E. Let $R\emptyset$ be the foreign key of R referring to the surrogate attribute of the E-relation representing E. Then:*

$$\forall r_i, r_j \in R \; ((r_i.R\emptyset = r_j.R\emptyset \; \Leftrightarrow r_i.X = r_j.X) \wedge$$
$$((r_i.X = r_j.X \wedge [r_i.VT_s, r_i.VT_e] \cap [r_j.VT_s, r_j.VT_e] \neq \emptyset) \Rightarrow r_i = r_j)).$$

Constraint 3. *Let E be a* TimeER *entity with a temporal key for which both valid and transaction time are captured. Let R be the A-relation storing the temporal key of E, and let r_i, r_j be tuple variables over R. Let X be the group of attributes of R that represents the temporal key of E. Let $R\emptyset$ be the foreign key of R referring to the surrogate attribute of the E-relation representing E. Then:*

$$\forall r_i, r_j \in R \; (((r_i.R\emptyset = r_j.R\emptyset \wedge$$
$$[r_i.TT_s, r_i.TT_e] \cap [r_j.TT_s, r_j.TT_e] \neq \emptyset) \Leftrightarrow r_i.X = r_j.X) \wedge$$
$$((r_i.X = r_j.X \wedge [r_i.VT_s, r_i.VT_e] \cap [r_j.VT_s, r_j.VT_e] \neq \emptyset \wedge$$
$$[r_i.TT_s, r_i.TT_e] \cap [r_j.TT_s, r_j.TT_e] \neq \emptyset) \Rightarrow r_i = r_j))$$

As an example, Table 3 shows an instance of the relation $Drug\_NDC$ of Table 2 that satisfies Constraint 3. Indeed, for each single point in the transaction-time domain, the mapping from the set of the NDC attribute values to the $Drug$ entity set is one-to-one. Table 4, on the contrary, shows an instance that violates Constraint 3, as the key value of the entity with surrogate-value ø1 varies over time; moreover, the key value 00002-7597-01 that, during the valid-time interval [1, 20], is assigned to the entity with surrogate value ø2, is the value for the key attribute of the entity identified by the surrogate value ø3 during the valid-time interval [21, NOW].

Table 3. An example of satisfaction of temporal key constraint

$Drug\_NDC$

drugø f.k.	NDC u.k.	VT_s	VT_e	TT_s	TT_e
ø1	50242-0040-62	1	NOW	1	10
ø1	60575-4112-01	1	NOW	11	UC
ø2	00002-7597-01	1	NOW	1	UC

Table 4. An example of violation of temporal key constraint

$Drug\_NDC$

drugø f.k.	NDC u.k.	VT_s	VT_e	TT_s	TT_e
ø1	50242-0040-62	1	10	1	UC
ø1	60575-4112-01	11	NOW	11	UC
ø2	00002-7597-01	1	20	1	UC
ø3	00002-7597-01	21	NOW	21	UC

The notion of temporal key constraint can be defined by means of suitable temporal functional dependencies derived from those proposed in the literature [9] for a bitemporal data model, and by introducing the *temporal natural join* operator.

Intuitively, if X and Y are sets of non-timestamp attributes of a relation schema S, a *temporal functional dependency* $X \xrightarrow{\text{T}} Y$ exists on S if, considering an instance of S as a collection of snapshot relations, the corresponding conventional functional dependency $X \longrightarrow Y$ holds on each such snapshot in isolation. Moreover, a *strong temporal functional dependency* $X \xrightarrow{\text{Str}} Y$ exists on S if, (possibly) fixed a transaction time instant, if the value of X does not vary in two different valid time instants, then the value of Y does not vary as well. Finally, a *strong temporal equivalence* $X \xleftrightarrow{\text{Str}} Y$ exists on S if $X \xrightarrow{\text{Str}} Y$ and $Y \xrightarrow{\text{Str}} X$.

Table 5a shows an instance of the $Drug\_class$ relation with the schema described in Table 2, and an instance of the $Drug\_NDC$ relation that satisfies the temporal key constraint; Table 6b shows the result of a temporal natural join over these two instances. A temporal natural join is a binary operator that generalizes the snapshot natural join to incorporate one or more time dimensions. Tuples in a temporal natural join are merged if their explicit join attribute values match, and they are temporally coincident in the given time dimensions. We can notice that the following temporal functional dependencies hold for the S relation: $Drug\emptyset \xleftrightarrow{Str} NDC$ and $NDC \xrightarrow{T} S$, where S is the set of all the attributes of relation S.

Table 5.

$Drug\_NDC$

drug∅ f.k.	NDC u.k.	VT_s	VT_e	TT_s	TT_e
∅1	50242-0040-62	1	NOW	1	10
∅1	60575-4112-01	1	NOW	11	UC
∅2	00002-7597-01	1	NOW	1	UC

$Drug\_class$

drug∅ f.k.	class	VT_s	VT_e	TT_s	TT_e
∅1	Prescription	1	NOW	1	10
∅1	Over-the-counter	1	NOW	11	UC
∅2	Prescription	1	NOW	1	UC

(a) Satisfaction of temporal key constraint

$S = Drug\_NDC \bowtie^T Drug\_class$

drug∅ f.k.	NDC u.k	class	VT_s	VT_e	TT_s	TT_e
∅1	50242-0040-62	Prescription	1	NOW	1	10
∅1	60575-4112-01	Over-the-counter	1	NOW	11	UC
∅2	00002-7597-01	Prescription	1	NOW	1	UC

(b) The temporal natural join over the relations in Table 6a

The temporal key constraint can therefore be defined as follows.

Definition 9. *Let E be an entity, and let $A_1, \ldots, A_n$ be the A-relation schema that represent the attributes of E. Let $E\emptyset$ be the surrogate attribute of E, and let X be the set of attributes representing the key of E. Let S be the relation schema derived from the temporal natural join of $A_1, \ldots, A_n$. Then X is termed temporal key if $E\emptyset \xleftrightarrow{Str} X$ and $X \xrightarrow{T} S$.*

6   Summary and Research Directions

In this paper we extended the expressiveness of the TIMEER model [3,7] with new constructs for specifying advanced temporal constraints. More specifically, we focused on enabling the expression of different temporal semantics of attributes and relationships, for keys, and for superclass/subclass relationships.

Furthermore, we demonstrated how it is possible to define the semantics of the temporal constraints by means of a surrogate-based relational model.

As for future work, we will focus on the completeness of the proposed extension of TimeER with respect to the requirements of database designers. Moreover, we will evaluate our proposal with respect to real-world conceptual design tasks, through the use of a prototype implementing the described constraints.

References

1. Elmasri, R., Navathe, S.B.: Fundamentals of Database Systems, 2nd edn., Benjamin/Cummings (1994)
2. Gregersen, H.: TimeERplus: A Temporal EER Model Supporting Schema Changes. In: Jackson, M., Nelson, D., Stirk, S. (eds.) BNCOD 2005. LNCS, vol. 3567, pp. 41–59. Springer, Heidelberg (2005)
3. Gregersen, H.: The Formal Semantics of the TimeER model. In: 3rd Asia-Pacific Conference on Conceptual Modelling, vol. 53, pp. 35–44. Australian Computer Society, Hobart (2006)
4. Gregersen, H., Mark, L., Jensen, C.S.: Mapping Temporal ER Diagrams to Relational Schemas. Technical report TR–39, TimeCenter (1998)
5. Gregersen, H., Jensen, C.S.: On the Ontological Expressiveness of Temporal Extensions to the Entity-Relationship Model. In: 1st International Workshop on Evolution and Change in Data Management, pp. 110–121. Springer, Paris (1999)
6. Gregersen, H., Jensen., C.S.: Temporal Entity Relationship Models - a Survey. IEEE Trans. Knowl. Data Eng. 11, 464–497 (1999)
7. Gregersen, H., Jensen, C.S.: Conceptual Modeling of Time-Varying Information. In: 2nd International Conference on Computing, Communications and Control Technologies, Austin, pp. 248–255 (2004)
8. Jensen, C.S., Dyreson, C.E. (eds.): Dagstuhl Seminar 1997. LNCS, vol. 1399, pp. 367–405. Springer, Heidelberg (1998)
9. Jensen, C.S., Snodgrass, R.T.: Temporally Enhanced Database Design. In: Advances in Object-Oriented Data Modeling, pp. 163–193. MIT Press, Cambridge (2000)

Temporal Constraints in Non-temporal Data Modelling Languages

Peter McBrien

Dept. Computing, Imperial College London, London SW7 2AZ
pjm@doc.ic.ac.uk

Abstract. It is common to find that the definition or common usage of a data modelling language causes there to be restrictions placed on the evolution of data values that are associated with schemas expressed in that modelling language. This paper terms these restrictions *temporal constraints*, and defines three types of temporal constraint which are argued to be useful modelling concepts, capturing important real-world semantics about objects and their relationships. By reviewing how these temporal constraints are implied by either the definition or usage of UML and the relational modelling languages, this paper will use the temporal constraints to give precise definitions of modelling concepts that to date have been left only vaguely and partially understood. It will also consider the implementation of these constraints in SQL.

Keywords: Data modelling, dynamic behaviour, conceptual modelling, temporal constraints.

1   Introduction

This paper reviews what will be termed the **temporal constraints** (which are also known as **dynamic constraints**) of data modelling languages, which we define to mean the restrictions that are placed on the evolution of the extent of a schema expressed in a data modelling language. In particular, this paper describes constraints on the evolution of the extent in **transaction time** [1] which may be implemented without the necessity of keeping a transaction time database. Hence we are considering temporal constraints which may be applied in a non-temporal data modelling language.

To illustrate the concept of temporal constraints in non-temporal data modelling languages, consider the UML schema in Fig. 1. A normal interpretation of this schema is that once an instance x has been created of the passenger class, then it will not be possible that later the same x appears as an instance of cargo class. More generally, the normal interpretation of object oriented modelling languages is that an object identifier cannot be associated with two different classes and refer to the same thing. However, this interpretation is not to be found in the definition of the UML modelling language [2], and indeed some research work has been conducted into programming languages which remove this restriction [3]. Another example is found in the UML **association** construct, where the definition of UML makes it unclear if a instance tyre could exist after the deletion of aircraft, and if is does, whether it could then be assigned to another aircraft.

Q. Li et al. (Eds.): ER 2008, LNCS 5231, pp. 412–425, 2008.

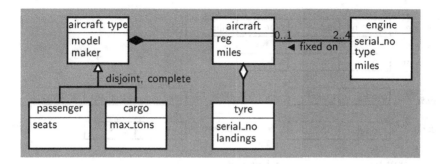

class: ⟨⟨aircraft_type⟩⟩
attribute: ⟨⟨aircraft_type, model⟩⟩
attribute: ⟨⟨aircraft_type, maker⟩⟩
class: ⟨⟨passenger⟩⟩
attribute: ⟨⟨passenger, seats⟩⟩
class: ⟨⟨cargo⟩⟩
attribute: ⟨⟨cargo, max_tons⟩⟩
generalisation: ⟨⟨aircraft_type, {disjoint, complete}, passenger, cargo⟩⟩
class: ⟨⟨aircraft⟩⟩
attribute: ⟨⟨aircraft, reg⟩⟩
attribute: ⟨⟨aircraft, miles⟩⟩

composition: ⟨⟨_, aircraft_type, aircraft, 1..1, 0..N⟩⟩
class: ⟨⟨tyre⟩⟩
attribute: ⟨⟨tyre, serial_no⟩⟩
attribute: ⟨⟨tyre, landings⟩⟩
aggregation: ⟨⟨_, aircraft, tyre, 0..1, 0..N⟩⟩
class: ⟨⟨engine⟩⟩
attribute: ⟨⟨engine, serial_no⟩⟩
attribute: ⟨⟨engine, type⟩⟩
attribute: ⟨⟨engine, miles⟩⟩
association: ⟨⟨fixed_on, aircraft, engine, 0..1, 2..4⟩⟩

Fig. 1. S^{uml}: A UML schema for a database of a aircraft fleet, together with its description as a set of schema objects

Related work will be considered in detail at the end of the paper in Section 4. One contribution of this paper is to define in Section 3 a set of temporal constraints that restrict the evolution of instances of a schema expressed (and stored as) a non-temporal data modelling language. The definitions are made in a manner that allows them to be defined on any data modelling language that fits a certain structure that this paper reviews in Section 2, which has already been shown [4,5] to be sufficient to support the relational, UML, ER, ORM and XML modelling languages. A second contribution of the paper is to discuss the extent to which these temporal constraints are (sometimes rather vaguely) already implied by the definitions of data modelling languages, by discussing in depth how the temporal constraints can be applied to UML and the relational data model.

An advantage gained in defining precisely the temporal modelling constraints and identifying temporal constraints in schemas is that it reveals where there is the possibility of inconsistencies when data is transferred between the schemas of information systems that have been built around different data modelling languages. For example, the relational schema in Fig. 2 would be regarded as equivalent to the UML schema in Fig. 1 under conventional UML to relational mapping approaches [6]. Indeed, at any one time, it will be possible to map instances of one schema into instances of the other schema. However, there are evolutions of the instances of the relational schema that would not be permitted in the instances when mapped into the UML schema. For example, in the relational schema it would be possible to delete an entry x from the

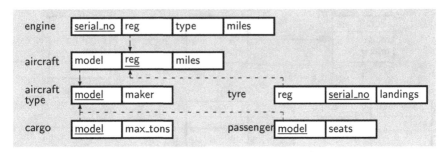

table: $\langle\langle$ aircraft_type$\rangle\rangle$
column: $\langle\langle$ aircraft_type, model$\rangle\rangle$
column: $\langle\langle$ aircraft_type, maker$\rangle\rangle$
table: $\langle\langle$ passenger$\rangle\rangle$
column: $\langle\langle$ passenger, model$\rangle\rangle$
column: $\langle\langle$ passenger, seats$\rangle\rangle$
table: $\langle\langle$ cargo$\rangle\rangle$
column: $\langle\langle$ cargo, model$\rangle\rangle$
column: $\langle\langle$ cargo, max_tons$\rangle\rangle$
table: $\langle\langle$ aircraft$\rangle\rangle$
column: $\langle\langle$ aircraft, model$\rangle\rangle$
column: $\langle\langle$ aircraft, reg$\rangle\rangle$
column: $\langle\langle$ aircraft, miles$\rangle\rangle$
table: $\langle\langle$ tyre$\rangle\rangle$
column: $\langle\langle$ tyre, reg$\rangle\rangle$
column: $\langle\langle$ tyre, serial_no$\rangle\rangle$
column: $\langle\langle$ tyre, landings$\rangle\rangle$

table: $\langle\langle$ engine$\rangle\rangle$
column: $\langle\langle$ engine, serial_no$\rangle\rangle$
column: $\langle\langle$ engine, reg$\rangle\rangle$
column: $\langle\langle$ engine, type$\rangle\rangle$
column: $\langle\langle$ engine, miles$\rangle\rangle$
primary_key: $\langle\langle$ engine, serial_no$\rangle\rangle$
primary_key: $\langle\langle$ aircraft, reg$\rangle\rangle$
primary_key: $\langle\langle$ aircraft_type, model$\rangle\rangle$
primary_key: $\langle\langle$ cargo, model$\rangle\rangle$
primary_key: $\langle\langle$ passenger, model$\rangle\rangle$
primary_key: $\langle\langle$ tyre, serial_no$\rangle\rangle$
foreign_key: $\langle\langle\langle\langle$ aircraft, model$\rangle\rangle$, $\langle\langle$ aircraft_type, model$\rangle\rangle\rangle\rangle$
foreign_key: $\langle\langle\langle\langle$ passenger, model$\rangle\rangle$, $\langle\langle$ aircraft_type, model$\rangle\rangle\rangle\rangle$
foreign_key: $\langle\langle\langle\langle$ cargo, model$\rangle\rangle$, $\langle\langle$ aircraft_type, model$\rangle\rangle\rangle\rangle$
foreign_key: $\langle\langle\langle\langle$ tyre, reg$\rangle\rangle$, $\langle\langle$ aircraft, reg$\rangle\rangle\rangle\rangle$
foreign_key: $\langle\langle\langle\langle$ engine, reg$\rangle\rangle$, $\langle\langle$ aircraft, reg$\rangle\rangle\rangle\rangle$

Fig. 2. S_1^{rel}: A relational schema for a database of a aircraft fleet, together with its description as a set of schema objects

passenger table, and insert it into the cargo table, whilst leaving the instance x unchanged in aircraft_type, and hence have the *same* instance of an aircraft type change from passenger to cargo types. As already discussed, this is normally not permitted in object-oriented models.

2 Models and Schemas

Using the notation of AutoMed [7], a modelling language, or **model**, m contains a set of modelling constructs, where each **construct** c is used to represent some class of data structure that holds set, bag or list of data values, and/or constraints on sets, bags or lists of data values. A **schema** s comprises of a set of schema objects, where each **schema object** o is typed to some construct c. To date, almost without exception, researchers have considered that any given information system uses a single modelling language. Such single modelling language schemas can then be described by
$s^m = \{c_1 : \langle\langle o_1 \rangle\rangle, c_1 : \langle\langle o_2 \rangle\rangle, \ldots, c_n : \langle\langle o_{m-1} \rangle\rangle, c_n : \langle\langle o_m \rangle\rangle\}$.

When a schema object has some collection of data associated with it, we call the data the **extent** of the schema object. The data associated with such **extensional** schema objects o can be returned by the function $Ext(o)$. Using the classification of modelling constructs in [8], there are three classes of construct for which schema objects carry an extent:

- **nodal** constructs may be used to define schema objects that are present in a schema independently of other schema objects. For example, a UML class is a nodal construct, since schema objects such as class:$\langle\langle\text{aircraft\_type}\rangle\rangle$ and class:$\langle\langle\text{aircraft}\rangle\rangle$ in S^{uml} may exist without any other classes in the UML schema. A relational table is also a nodal construct, since schema objects such as table:$\langle\langle\text{aircraft\_type}\rangle\rangle$ and table:$\langle\langle\text{aircraft}\rangle\rangle$ may exist without any other tables in the relational schema.

  Typically, the instances of a UML class are identified using object identifies, so we might find that

  $Ext(\text{class:}\langle\langle\text{aircraft}\rangle\rangle) = \{\langle 100\rangle, \langle 101\rangle, \dots\}$

  $Ext(\text{class:}\langle\langle\text{aircraft\_type}\rangle\rangle) = \{\langle 200\rangle, \langle 201\rangle, \dots\}$

  In predicate logic, these extents would cause the term class:$\langle\langle\text{aircraft}\rangle\rangle(X)$ to bind X to first 100, then 101, etc.

  Relational tables are typically identified using **natural keys** [10] (*i.e.* keys made up of attributes which have a meaning in the real-world, such a post codes, peoples names, tax numbers, *etc*), so we might find

  $Ext(\text{table:}\langle\langle\text{aircraft}\rangle\rangle) = \{\langle\text{G-CWQS}\rangle, \langle\text{G-FDWC}\rangle, \dots\}$,

  i.e. the registration codes of the aircraft.

- **link-nodal** constructs are used to define schema objects that can only exist when connected to other schema objects, but contain data that is not present in the schema objects they are connected to. For example, in UML attribute:$\langle\langle\text{aircraft, miles}\rangle\rangle$ is a link-nodal construct, since it can only exist when connected to class:$\langle\langle\text{aircraft}\rangle\rangle$. A relational column such as column:$\langle\langle\text{aircraft, miles}\rangle\rangle$ is also link nodal since it can only exist when connected to table:$\langle\langle\text{aircraft}\rangle\rangle$. The definition of link-nodal constructs implies that the following rule about the extent of link-nodal schema objects is always true:

  $\text{link-nodal:}\langle\langle E, A\rangle\rangle(X, Y) \rightarrow \text{nodal:}\langle\langle E\rangle\rangle(X)$

  Hence, given the extent of class:$\langle\langle\text{aircraft}\rangle\rangle$ and the above rule, we might find that $Ext(\text{attribute:}\langle\langle\text{aircraft, miles}\rangle\rangle) = \{\langle 100, 2945321\rangle, \langle 101, 506834\rangle, \dots\}$, and give the extent of table:$\langle\langle\text{aircraft}\rangle\rangle$ and the above rule we might find that

  $Ext(\text{column:}\langle\langle\text{aircraft, miles}\rangle\rangle) = \{\langle\text{G-CWQS}, 2945321\rangle, \langle\text{G-FDWC}, 506834\rangle, \dots\}$

  Note that a peculiarity of the natural key based modelling languages is that the link-nodal schema object used to define the key will contain duplicates, so we might find

  $Ext(\text{column:}\langle\langle\text{aircraft, reg}\rangle\rangle) = \{\langle\text{G-CWQS}, \text{G-CWQS}\rangle, \langle\text{G-FDWC}, \text{G-FDWC}\rangle, \dots\}$.

- **link** constructs are used to define schema objects that can only exist when connected to two or more other schema objects, and contain data that is also present in the schema objects they are connected to. For example, the UML schema object association:$\langle\langle\text{fixed\_on, aircraft, engine}\rangle\rangle$ is a link construct, since it has to be connected to class:$\langle\langle\text{aircraft}\rangle\rangle$ and class:$\langle\langle\text{engine}\rangle\rangle$. The definition of link-nodal constructs implies that the following rule about the extent of link-nodal schema objects is always true:

$link: \langle\langle R, E_1, E_2 \rangle\rangle (X, Y) \rightarrow nodal: \langle\langle E_1 \rangle\rangle (X) \wedge nodal: \langle\langle E_2 \rangle\rangle (Y))$

Hence, given the extent of class: $\langle\langle$aircraft$\rangle\rangle$ and class: $\langle\langle$aircraft_type$\rangle\rangle$ above, we might find

Ext(composition: $\langle\langle$_, aircraft_type, aircraft$\rangle\rangle$) = $\{\langle 200, 100 \rangle, \langle 200, 101 \rangle, \ldots \}$.

Note that there are no examples of link constructs found in the relational model.

A fourth type of construct is used to define **constraint** schema objects that have no associated extent, but place restrictions on the extents of the schema objects that appear within the constraint schema object. Figs. 1 and 2 illustrate the representation of a UML schema and a relational schema as a set of schemes. The UML schema includes a generalisation constraint schema object, and the relational schema includes primary_key and foreign_key schema objects, but null/notnull constraints have been omitted from the schema for brevity, since they are not used in this paper.

3   Temporal Constraints

We will identify in the following subsections three temporal constraints that have to some extent already implicitly been used in data modelling languages, but to date have not been explicitly identified as general modelling concepts in their own right that may be applied to any non-temporal data modelling language, though as we will see, sometimes have been made available for specific modelling constructs in specific modelling languages.

To accurately characterise the concepts, we will use discrete linear **temporal logic** [11] to define when certain properties hold. In the discrete linear model of time, we view the state of the information system passing through a (possibly infinite) series of states, where each state has one successor (next time) state, and one predecessor (previous time) state. In the terminology of temporal databases, we are modelling the **transaction time** [1] of the information system (but note that in this paper, we do *not* assume that we keep a transaction time history of the states of the information system).

The temporal logic we use in this paper is first order predicate logic with the addition of two binary operators, Until and Since, and hence is often referred to as **US-Logic**. The statement A Until B means that A holds at every time up to and including the time when B holds. From this operator, a number of derived unary and binary operators can be defined (where $\top$ represents truth, and holds in every state):

$\bigcirc A \equiv A$ Until $\top$
A While $B \equiv A$ Until $\neg \bigcirc B$
$\Diamond A \equiv \top$ Until A
$\Box A \equiv A$ While $\top$

which we illustrate with the following examples:

1. $\bigcirc \langle\langle A \rangle\rangle (X)$ means that in the next time there is an instance X of schema object $\langle\langle A \rangle\rangle$. Hence the formula $\langle\langle A \rangle\rangle (X) \rightarrow \bigcirc \langle\langle A \rangle\rangle (X)$ means that if X is an instance of $\langle\langle A \rangle\rangle$ at any time, then it will be an instance of $\langle\langle A \rangle\rangle$ at the next time, and $\langle\langle A \rangle\rangle (X) \rightarrow \neg \bigcirc \langle\langle A \rangle\rangle (X)$ means that if X is an instance of $\langle\langle A \rangle\rangle$ at any time, then it will not be an instance of $\langle\langle A \rangle\rangle$ at the next time.

2. $\langle\langle A\rangle\rangle(X)$ While $\langle\langle B\rangle\rangle(X)$ holds if X is an instance of $\langle\langle A\rangle\rangle$ for the entire period that X continues to be an instance of $\langle\langle B\rangle\rangle$.

3. $\Diamond\langle\langle A\rangle\rangle(X)$ means that in some future time there is an instance X of schema object $\langle\langle A\rangle\rangle$. Hence the formula $\langle\langle A\rangle\rangle(X) \rightarrow \Diamond\langle\langle A\rangle\rangle(X)$ means that if X is an instance of $\langle\langle A\rangle\rangle$ at any time, then X will be an instance of $\langle\langle A\rangle\rangle$ at some future time, and $\langle\langle A\rangle\rangle(X) \rightarrow \neg\Diamond\langle\langle A\rangle\rangle(X)$ means that if X is an instance of $\langle\langle A\rangle\rangle$ at any time, then it will never be an instance of $\langle\langle A\rangle\rangle$ again.

4. $\Box\langle\langle A\rangle\rangle(X)$ means that in all future times there is an instance X of schema object $\langle\langle A\rangle\rangle$. Hence the formula $\langle\langle A\rangle\rangle(X) \rightarrow \Box\langle\langle A\rangle\rangle(X)$ means that if X is an instance of $\langle\langle A\rangle\rangle$ at any time, then it will so for ever more, and $\langle\langle A\rangle\rangle(X) \rightarrow \neg\Box\langle\langle A\rangle\rangle(X)$ means that if X is an instance of $\langle\langle A\rangle\rangle$ at any time, there will be some time in the future when it is not an instance.

3.1 Monogamy and Lifetime Monogamy

In general, the concept of **monogamy** involves something being related to just one other thing at any one time. In data modelling, this concept is captured using optional or mandatory cardinality constraints — *i.e.* cardinality constraints with an upper bound of one. For example, association:$\langle\langle\text{fixedon}, \text{aircraft}, \text{engine}\rangle\rangle$ in Fig. 1 makes class:$\langle\langle\text{engine}\rangle\rangle$ have a monogamous relationship with class:$\langle\langle\text{aircraft}\rangle\rangle$, meaning each engine can only be fixed on one aircraft at a time. In our representation of data modelling, we can say that an instance of a nodal schema object appearing in some link-nodal or link schema object is monogamous for that schema object if one of the following rules hold, which in essence state that there cannot be two instances of the link-nodal or link schema object for the same monogamous schema object instance.

$monogamous(nodal:\langle\langle E_1\rangle\rangle, link:\langle\langle R,E_1,E_2\rangle\rangle) \overset{\text{def}}{=}$
$\quad link:\langle\langle R,E_1,E_2\rangle\rangle(X,Y) \rightarrow \neg\exists Z.link:\langle\langle R,E_1,E_2\rangle\rangle(X,Z) \wedge Y \neq Z$

$monogamous(nodal:\langle\langle E_2\rangle\rangle, link:\langle\langle R,E_1,E_2\rangle\rangle) \overset{\text{def}}{=}$
$\quad link:\langle\langle R,E_1,E_2\rangle\rangle(X,Y) \rightarrow \neg\exists Z.link:\langle\langle R,E_1,E_2\rangle\rangle(Z,Y) \wedge Y \neq Z$

$monogamous(nodal:\langle\langle E\rangle\rangle, link\text{-}nodal:\langle\langle E,A\rangle\rangle) \overset{\text{def}}{=}$
$\quad link\text{-}nodal:\langle\langle E,A\rangle\rangle(X,Y) \rightarrow \neg\exists Z.link\text{-}nodal:\langle\langle E,A\rangle\rangle(X,Z) \wedge Y \neq Z$

Hence for Fig. 1, we can state:
$\quad monogamous(class:\langle\langle\text{engine}\rangle\rangle, association:\langle\langle\text{fixedon}, \text{aircraft}, \text{engine}\rangle\rangle)$
$\quad monogamous(class:\langle\langle\text{tyre}\rangle\rangle, aggregation:\langle\langle\_, \text{aircraft}, \text{tyre}\rangle\rangle)$
$\quad monogamous(class:\langle\langle\text{aircraft}\rangle\rangle, composition:\langle\langle\_, \text{aircraft\_type}, \text{aircraft}\rangle\rangle)$

Note that this definition of monogamy does not prevent **serial monogamy**, *i.e.* an instance of the nodal class being monogamous at any one time, but changing its relationships over time. For UML **associations**, this definition is intuitively correct. For example, it would allow a class:$\langle\langle\text{engine}\rangle\rangle$ instance to be moved from one class:$\langle\langle\text{aircraft}\rangle\rangle$ to another. However, the definition of UML **aggregation** and **composition** are defined to usually imply that members of the aggregation are not allowed to change from one group to another [2]. Here we suggest that this 'usually' be strengthened to a **lifetime monogamous** temporal constraint, that prevents serial monogamy. Once a certain value Y has been associated with a schema object in its connection with a particular instance X of some other schema object, then during one period of existence of X there may not be some different value Z used instead of Y. Specifically:

$\text{lifetime\_monogamous}(nodal\!:\!\langle\!\langle E_1\rangle\!\rangle, link\!:\!\langle\!\langle R,E_1,E_2\rangle\!\rangle)\stackrel{\text{def}}{=}$
  $link\!:\!\langle\!\langle R,E_1,E_2\rangle\!\rangle(X,Y)\rightarrow$
    $(\neg\exists Z.link\!:\!\langle\!\langle R,E_1,E_2\rangle\!\rangle(X,Z)\wedge Y\neq Z)\,\text{While}\,nodal\!:\!\langle\!\langle E_1\rangle\!\rangle(X)$

$\text{lifetime\_monogamous}(nodal\!:\!\langle\!\langle E_2\rangle\!\rangle, link\!:\!\langle\!\langle R,E_1,E_2\rangle\!\rangle)\stackrel{\text{def}}{=}$
  $link\!:\!\langle\!\langle R,E_1,E_2\rangle\!\rangle(X,Y)\rightarrow$
    $(\neg\exists Z.link\!:\!\langle\!\langle R,E_1,E_2\rangle\!\rangle(Z,Y)\wedge X\neq Z)\,\text{While}\,nodal\!:\!\langle\!\langle E_2\rangle\!\rangle(Y)$

$\text{lifetime\_monogamous}(link\text{-}nodal\!:\!\langle\!\langle E,A\rangle\!\rangle)\stackrel{\text{def}}{=}$
  $link\!:\!\langle\!\langle E,A\rangle\!\rangle(X,Y)\rightarrow$
    $(\neg\exists Z.link\!:\!\langle\!\langle E,A\rangle\!\rangle(X,Z)\wedge Y\neq Z)\,\text{While}\,nodal\!:\!\langle\!\langle E\rangle\!\rangle(X)$

i.e. lifetime monogamy for a nodal schema object in a link or link-nodal schema object implies monogamy for the duration of a single lifespan of the nodal schema object. We will interpret the semantics of UML modelling to imply for Fig. 1:

  $\text{lifetime\_monogamous}(\text{class}\!:\!\langle\!\langle\text{tyre}\rangle\!\rangle,\text{aggregation}\!:\!\langle\!\langle\_,\text{tyre},\text{aircraft}\rangle\!\rangle)$
  $\text{lifetime\_monogamous}(\text{class}\!:\!\langle\!\langle\text{aircraft}\rangle\!\rangle,\text{composition}\!:\!\langle\!\langle\_,\text{aircraft\_type},\text{aircraft}\rangle\!\rangle)$

The first line above means that an instance of class:$\langle\!\langle\text{tyre}\rangle\!\rangle$ can only ever be associated with one class:$\langle\!\langle\text{aircraft}\rangle\!\rangle$ during one period of existence of a tyre, *i.e.* a tyre can only be used on one aircraft, but there is no constraint of which of the tyre or the aircraft existed first, and the tyre can be taken off the aircraft without destroying either the tyre or the aircraft. The second line means that an instance of class:$\langle\!\langle\text{aircraft}\rangle\!\rangle$ can only ever be associated with one class:$\langle\!\langle\text{aircraft\_type}\rangle\!\rangle$.

Note that the UML concept of **readOnly** implies that a value must be set during object initialisation, and hence implies a mandatory cardinality constraint in combination with a lifetime monogamous temporal constraint. Note that the relational model has no constructs that imply the lifetime monogamous constraint on link schema objects or link-nodal schema objects, and UML does not provide the constraint in conjunction with optional cardinality constraints. However, this does not mean the it would not be useful to introduce a specific lifetime monogamous temporal constraint to these models. For example, if attribute:$\langle\!\langle\text{aircraft},\text{reg}\rangle\!\rangle$ were lifetime monogamous, one could build a plane without a registration code, register it, and later cancel the registration code before scraping the aircraft, but ensure that one never assigns a different registration code to the aircraft. This would also be readily implemented in SQL using triggers to control the updating of a column, such that a state column was set to true when a data column was set to null, prohibiting any further setting of data column value.

3.2   One-Off

The **oneoff** temporal constraint means that once a schema object instance is deleted, the same instance cannot exist again. For nodal schema objects, this constraint is easily characterised as

$\text{oneoff}(nodal\!:\!\langle\!\langle E\rangle\!\rangle)\stackrel{\text{def}}{=}$
  $nodal\!:\!\langle\!\langle E\rangle\!\rangle(X)\wedge\neg\bigcirc nodal\!:\!\langle\!\langle E\rangle\!\rangle(X)\rightarrow\neg\Diamond nodal\!:\!\langle\!\langle E\rangle\!\rangle(X)$

stating that if X is an instance of $nodal\!:\!\langle\!\langle E\rangle\!\rangle$ at any time, and at the next time it is not an instance of $nodal\!:\!\langle\!\langle E\rangle\!\rangle$, then there will be no future time when X is an instance of $nodal\!:\!\langle\!\langle\text{E}\rangle\!\rangle$. The oneoff temporal constraint is often associated with nodal schema objects in object-oriented models, where once a class instance has been deleted, the same class instance cannot be restored. For example, once instance $\langle 100\rangle$ has been deleted of class: $\langle\langle aircraft \rangle\rangle$, there would not in the future be an instance $\langle 100 \rangle$ of class: $\langle\langle aircraft \rangle\rangle$. By contrast, models such as the relational models when based **natural keys** do not support the oneoff temporal constraint. This is because a relational database has no mechanism to stop a natural key being reinserted into the database after it has previously been deleted.

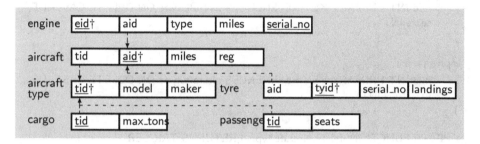

Fig. 3. S_2^{rel}: A variant of S_1^{rel} using auto-increment keys, marked with a † in the diagram. Note that cargo and passenger do not have auto-increment keys, since they inherit the value of the key from aircraft_type)

If the relational system uses **auto-increment** keys, then the behaviour would be more similar to that of the object oriented system. Fig. 3 presents a version of Fig. 2 where auto-increment keys have been used (and Fig. 4 the SQL definitions of some of the tables), and then we can state

oneoff(table: $\langle\langle aircraft \rangle\rangle$)
oneoff(table: $\langle\langle aircraft\_type \rangle\rangle$)
oneoff(table: $\langle\langle engine \rangle\rangle$)
oneoff(table: $\langle\langle tyre \rangle\rangle$)

since once a key value has been generated for an auto-increment key, the value will not be generated again in the future. A problem remains with the tables implementing the subclasses passenger and cargo, which are unable to use auto-increment keys. We can solve this problem with our implementation of the final temporal constraint presented in the next subsection.

Definition of oneoff for link-nodal and link schema object takes a similar form to that for nodal schema objects:

oneoff($link$-$nodal$: $\langle\langle E,A \rangle\rangle$) $\overset{\text{def}}{=}$
    $link$-$nodal$: $\langle\langle E,A \rangle\rangle(X,Y) \wedge \neg \bigcirc link$-$nodal$: $\langle\langle E,A \rangle\rangle(X,Y) \rightarrow$
        $\neg link$-$nodal$: $\langle\langle E,A \rangle\rangle(X,Y)$ While $nodal$: $\langle\langle E \rangle\rangle(X)$

oneoff($link$: $\langle\langle R,E_1,E_2 \rangle\rangle$) $\overset{\text{def}}{=}$
    $link$: $\langle\langle R,E_1,E_2 \rangle\rangle(X,Y) \wedge \neg \bigcirc link$: $\langle\langle R,E_1,E_2 \rangle\rangle(X,Y) \rightarrow$
        $\neg link$: $\langle\langle R,E_1,E_2 \rangle\rangle(X,Y)$ While $nodal$: $\langle\langle E_1 \rangle\rangle(X) \wedge nodal$: $\langle\langle E_2 \rangle\rangle(Y)$

Neither UML nor the relational models have constructs that imply oneoff to link-nodal or link schema objects, and the semantics of such a constraint would only be of use in relatively few circumstances. For example, if we added to the UML schema in

```
CREATE TABLE aircraft_type
(    mid INT PRIMARY KEY,
     maker VARCHAR(20)
)

CREATE TABLE passenger
(    mid INT PRIMARY KEY REFERENCES aircraft_type ON DELETE CASCADE,
     seats INT
)

CREATE TABLE cargo
(    mid INT PRIMARY KEY REFERENCES aircraft_type ON DELETE CASCADE,
     max_tons INT
)

CREATE FUNCTION delete_aircraft_type() RETURNS TRIGGER
AS 'BEGIN
     DELETE FROM aircraft_type WHERE aircraft_type.tid=OLD.tid;
     RETURN NULL;
     END' LANGUAGE plpgsql;

CREATE TRIGGER passenger_subclass_aircraft_type AFTER DELETE ON passenger
FOR EACH ROW EXECUTE PROCEDURE delete_aircraft_type();

CREATE TRIGGER cargo_subclass_aircraft_type AFTER DELETE ON cargo
FOR EACH ROW EXECUTE PROCEDURE delete_aircraft_type();
```

Fig. 4. Definition using the Postgres RDBMS SQL language of triggers being used to implement the final temporal constraints

Fig. 1 oneoff(attribute:$\langle\langle$aircraft, reg$\rangle\rangle$), then an aircraft could change its registration number, but not revert to a previously used registration number. It should be noted that the general implementation of oneoff is costly in storage terms, since it requires a transaction time history be kept a schema object declared as one-off so that a check can be made each time a new instance is created that the instance had not been present at some time in the past. The specific case of oneoff being applied to object identifiers and auto-increment keys is not costly in storage terms since only a single variable incrementing new values need be kept in order to ensure unique values over time.

3.3 Final

The **final** temporal constraint means that once a instance of a schema object has been created, then that instance will remain until one of the instances of the schema objects it is dependent upon is deleted. Specifically, for nodal schema objects, we state:

final($nodal$:$\langle\langle E_1\rangle\rangle$, $nodal$:$\langle\langle E_2\rangle\rangle$) $\stackrel{\text{def}}{=}$
    $nodal$:$\langle\langle E_2\rangle\rangle(X) \rightarrow nodal$:$\langle\langle E_2\rangle\rangle(X)$ While $nodal$:$\langle\langle E_1\rangle\rangle(X)$

meaning that once a instance exists in *nodal*:$\langle\langle E_2\rangle\rangle$, it must continue to exist whilst the same values exists in *nodal*:$\langle\langle E_1\rangle\rangle$. UML **generalisations** imply the final temporal constraint between the child and parent nodes. For the schema in Fig. 1 we can state:

final(class:$\langle\langle$aircraft_type$\rangle\rangle$,class:$\langle\langle$passenger$\rangle\rangle$)

final(class:$\langle\langle$passenger$\rangle\rangle$,class:$\langle\langle$aircraft_type$\rangle\rangle$)

final(class:$\langle\langle$aircraft_type$\rangle\rangle$,class:$\langle\langle$cargo$\rangle\rangle$)

final(class:$\langle\langle$cargo$\rangle\rangle$,class:$\langle\langle$aircraft_type$\rangle\rangle$)

Hence, when an instance of class:$\langle\langle$passenger$\rangle\rangle$ is deleted, then so must the instance of class:$\langle\langle$aircraft_type$\rangle\rangle$, and *vice versa*.

There is no modelling construct in the relational model that directly implies final on its schema objects, but there is some limited support for implementing the final constraint. Firstly, if we added the SQL constraint ON DELETE CASCADE to primary keys of table:$\langle\langle$passenger$\rangle\rangle$ and table:$\langle\langle$cargo$\rangle\rangle$, as illustrated by the table definitions in Fig. 4, then we would be able to state:

final(table:$\langle\langle$aircraft_type$\rangle\rangle$,table:$\langle\langle$passenger$\rangle\rangle$)

final(table:$\langle\langle$aircraft_type$\rangle\rangle$,table:$\langle\langle$cargo$\rangle\rangle$)

since deleting a row from table:$\langle\langle$aircraft_type$\rangle\rangle$ will cause the cascading of a delete on table:$\langle\langle$passenger$\rangle\rangle$ or table:$\langle\langle$cargo$\rangle\rangle$. Secondly, if we added the SQL trigger for each of the passenger and cargo table, as illustrated by the trigger definitions in Fig. 4, which executes a function that deletes the same identifier from the parent aircraft_type table, then a deletion of either table:$\langle\langle$passenger$\rangle\rangle$ or table:$\langle\langle$cargo$\rangle\rangle$ would trigger a deletion of table:$\langle\langle$aircraft_type$\rangle\rangle$. The presence of such a trigger then allows us to state:

final(table:$\langle\langle$passenger$\rangle\rangle$,table:$\langle\langle$aircraft_type$\rangle\rangle$)

final(table:$\langle\langle$cargo$\rangle\rangle$,table:$\langle\langle$aircraft_type$\rangle\rangle$)

In defining the final constraint for link-nodal constructs, there are two cases to consider. Applying the first rule below to a UML attribute or a relational column would mean that once a value was assigned to the attribute/column it could not be changed. For example final(attribute:$\langle\langle$aircraft, reg$\rangle\rangle$) would mean that a registration number of a aircraft could not be changed. Interestingly, this modelling concept is absent from the UML[1] and relational languages, but is present in some object oriented programming languages which UML targets (for example the final keyword in Java and readonly keyword in C#).

final(*link-nodal*:$\langle\langle E,A\rangle\rangle$) $\overset{\text{def}}{=}$

link-nodal:$\langle\langle E,A\rangle\rangle(X,Y) \rightarrow$ *link-nodal*:$\langle\langle E,A\rangle\rangle(X,Y)$ While *nodal*:$\langle\langle E\rangle\rangle(X)$

final(*link-nodal*:$\langle\langle E_1,A_1\rangle\rangle$,*link-nodal*:$\langle\langle E_2,A_2\rangle\rangle$) $\overset{\text{def}}{=}$

link-nodal:$\langle\langle E_1,A_1\rangle\rangle(X,Y) \wedge$ *link-nodal*:$\langle\langle E_2,A_2\rangle\rangle(Z,Y) \rightarrow$

link-nodal:$\langle\langle E_2,A_2\rangle\rangle(Z,Y)$ While *link-nodal*:$\langle\langle E_1,A_1\rangle\rangle(X,Y)$

The second rule causes a value appearing in one link-nodal that is also appearing in a second link-nodal to cause the same second value to continue to exist whilst the first continues to exist. For example, if we stated on S_2^{rel}

final(column:$\langle\langle$aircraft, tid$\rangle\rangle$,column:$\langle\langle$aircraft_type, tid$\rangle\rangle$)

---

[1] It is interesting to note that the semantics of final would appear to match the semantics of the addOnly property of link nodal and link constructs available in some versions of UML prior to UML 2.0. Also removed in UML v2.0 was the concept of **createOnly**, which stated that values could be added once but no more to a property. Both addOnly and createOnly forbid changes.

then we would have the same semantics present in the relational model as we gave to the UML composition construct above, and aircrafts would not be able to change aircraft types.

For link constructs, there again two types of final constraint. Applied to a UML association, the first rule below says that once an instance of the association has been created it remains in existence whilst both of the classes it associates exist. The second two rules strengthen the rule to say that the instance of the association will continue in existence until just one of the classes it associates is deleted.

$$\text{final}(link:\langle\langle R, E_1, E_2\rangle\rangle) \stackrel{\text{def}}{=}$$
$$link:\langle\langle R, E_1, E_2\rangle\rangle(X, Y) \rightarrow$$
$$\quad link:\langle\langle R, E_1, E_2\rangle\rangle(X, Y) \text{ While } (nodal:\langle\langle E_1\rangle\rangle(X) \wedge nodal:\langle\langle E_2\rangle\rangle(Y))$$
$$\text{final}(nodal:\langle\langle E_1\rangle\rangle, link:\langle\langle R, E_1, E_2\rangle\rangle) \stackrel{\text{def}}{=}$$
$$\quad link:\langle\langle R, E_1, E_2\rangle\rangle(X, Y) \rightarrow link:\langle\langle R, E_1, E_2\rangle\rangle(X, Y) \text{ While } nodal:\langle\langle E_1\rangle\rangle(X)$$
$$\text{final}(nodal:\langle\langle E_2\rangle\rangle, link:\langle\langle R, E_1, E_2\rangle\rangle) \stackrel{\text{def}}{=}$$
$$\quad link:\langle\langle R, E_1, E_2\rangle\rangle(X, Y) \rightarrow link:\langle\langle R, E_1, E_2\rangle\rangle(X, Y) \text{ While } nodal:\langle\langle E_2\rangle\rangle(Y)$$

In UML, the **composition** construct often implies a coincidence in lifetimes of the classes in the composition. We propose to restrict this definition to stating that the member class of a composition is final in the composition. In Fig. 1, this means we can state:

$$\text{final}(class:\langle\langle aircraft\rangle\rangle, composition:\langle\langle \_, aircraft\_type, aircraft\rangle\rangle)$$

meaning that once an aircraft has been assigned to an aircraft type, it cannot be changed to another aircraft type. We would not want to associate the final temporal constraint with UML **aggregations**. For example, if $\text{final}(aggregation:\langle\langle \_, aircraft, tyre\rangle\rangle)$ was declared for the UML schema, then once $\langle 100,107\rangle$ has been added as an instance, it would remain until the tyre $\langle 107\rangle$ was deleted from $class:\langle\langle tyre\rangle\rangle$, preventing us from removing instances from aggregations.

4   Related Work

There has been a considerable amount of work conducted into the modelling of temporal constraints in temporal data models (for example [12,13,14,15,16]). By contrast, this paper considers temporal constraints that may be used, or are already implied, in existing non-temporal data models.

In the field of data modelling, the most comprehensive previous treatment can be found in [17,18], which deal with the temporal behaviours of nodal and link-nodal constructs, but not of link constructs. Also, [17,18] do not explicitly relate their definitions to specific modelling languages, though the relationship with ER and UML modelling is clear. In [17], for nodal constructs, the concept of **permanent** constraint is defined where an object, once it exists, must stay in existence whilst the information system remains in operation.

$$\text{permanent}(nodal:\langle\langle E\rangle\rangle) \stackrel{\text{def}}{=}$$
$$\quad link:\langle\langle E\rangle\rangle(X) \rightarrow \square nodal:\langle\langle E\rangle\rangle(X)$$

This is similar to the final constraint, with the difference that the final constraint is always defined relative to some other object. We argue that this is more intuitive, since is corresponds to the real world concept of something entering its final state, yet not necessarily continuing to exist forever.

In [17], there is the concept of **frequency** being **single** or **multiple**. Applied to entities the concept of single corresponds to exactly to the definition of one-off in this paper. However, applied to attributes, it differs from one-off in allowing an attribute to change value and then return to value during its single existence (where the definition of one-off states that a particular value may be used only once). The authors also introduce concept of **durability**, which may be **durable** or **instantaneous**, where instantaneous means that an object only exists for one chronon in the temporal model. This is a common distinction in temporal data models, since it allows instantaneous schema objects to be stored with one time value per instance (the time of the instance occurred at), whilst durable schema objects require a pair of time values representing the interval the instance exists for (or set of such pairs if there is set of intervals).

In [18], there was a discussion of how generalisations could be classified into **static** if sub-class memberships could not evolve over time, or **dynamic** if they could. In [19], the concept of **temporal behaviour** of UML associations is defined, and characterised as **static** or **dynamic** depending on whether the values on the association for a particular class may be changed. There is also consideration to the definition of delete propagations across associations.

Work on the temporal constraints on nodal objects has also been conducted in the field of ontologies. In [20,21] a classification of unary predicates (equivalent to our nodal constructs) into **rigid**, **anti-rigid**, and **non-rigid** was introduced. The rigid constraint takes the same definition as the permanent constraint in [17]:

$$rigid(nodal{:}\langle\langle E_1 \rangle\rangle) \overset{\text{def}}{=}$$
$$nodal{:}\langle\langle E_1 \rangle\rangle(X) \rightarrow \Box(nodal{:}\langle\langle E_1 \rangle\rangle(X))$$

Recently, it has been proposed that ORM be extended to include this distinction [22]. The definition of rigid shares the flaw we discussed in relationship to the permanent constraint from [17]. This flaw was recognised in [23], which proposed **existential rigidity**, where a value appearing in $nodal{:}\langle\langle E_1 \rangle\rangle$ forces the value to also appear in some related $nodal{:}\langle\langle E_2 \rangle\rangle$:

$$existential\_rigid(nodal{:}\langle\langle E_1 \rangle\rangle, nodal{:}\langle\langle E_2 \rangle\rangle) \overset{\text{def}}{=}$$
$$nodal{:}\langle\langle E_1 \rangle\rangle(X) \rightarrow \Box(nodal{:}\langle\langle E_1 \rangle\rangle(X) \rightarrow nodal{:}\langle\langle E_2 \rangle\rangle(X))$$

If we applied this to our relational model as:

existential_rigid(table:$\langle\langle$aircraft_type$\rangle\rangle$,table:$\langle\langle$passenger$\rangle\rangle$
existential_rigid(table:$\langle\langle$aircraft_type$\rangle\rangle$,table:$\langle\langle$cargo$\rangle\rangle$)

then we would have to implement a temporal history of data instance from tables table:$\langle\langle$passenger$\rangle\rangle$ and table:$\langle\langle$cargo$\rangle\rangle$ (which are the relational tables implementing the subclasses of table:$\langle\langle$aircraft_type$\rangle\rangle$), since if a value where to be deleted and reinserted into table:$\langle\langle$aircraft_type$\rangle\rangle$ then we would need to ensure that if also appeared in the correct subclass table.

From the above discussion, it can be seen that the definitions in this paper are the first to be made across all types of modelling construct, and also the first to be defined in a manner that is implementable without the necessity of maintaining a full transaction time history of data.

5   Summary and Conclusions

In this paper, we defined three temporal constraints called lifetime monogamy, oneoff, and final, that may be used to model the changes that are permitted to the extents associated with schema objects in static non-temporal data modelling languages. Loosely speaking, (i) lifetime monogamy models the concept that mandatory or optional relationships are restricted further to disallow serial monogamy, (ii) oneoff models the concept that things cannot be reincarnated, and (iii) final models the concept that once a value has been assigned, it cannot be changed.

We have given precise definitions of these three constraints in linear temporal logic, and have discussed how some of these constraints are already fully or partially implied by constructs found in the UML and relational languages. Our definitions are made in terms of very general modelling concepts of nodal, link-nodal and link modelling constructs, and this approach has previously been shown to be capable of representing a wide variety of modelling languages [8,4].

The precise definitions of temporal constraints serve to give two advantages. First, the modelling constructs of UML and the relational model are better understood, leading to a more accurate modelling of the real world when using these languages. Secondly, the definitions serve to expose the differences that exist between modelling languages, and allow action to be taken to overcome these differences. We illustrated this second advantage by describing how SQL CASCADE and TRIGGER constructs can be used to implement the temporal constraints, and hence make a relational based system be capable of holding a schema that corresponds more exactly with a UML schema than is the case in current approaches to UML to relational mapping.

To shorten the presentation, we have restricted the class of modelling languages discussed to those with binary link schema objects and with link and link-nodal schema objects that only connect with nodal schema objects. However the extension of the work to remove those restrictions is straightforward.

References

1. Jensen, C., et al.: A consensus glossary of temporal database concepts. SIGMOD Record 23(1), 52–64 (1994)
2. Group, O.M.: Unified Modeling Language: Superstructure 2.1.1. Technical report, OMG (2007)
3. Drossopoulou, S., Damiani, F., Dezani-Ciancaglini, M., Giannini, P.: More Dynamic Object Re-classification: FickleII. ACM Transactions On Programming Languages and Systems 24(2), 153–191 (2002)
4. Boyd, M., McBrien, P.: Comparing and transforming between data models via an intermediate hypergraph data model. Journal on Data Semantics IV, 69–109 (2005)
5. McBrien, P., Poulovassilis, A.: A semantic approach to integrating XML and structured data sources. In: Dittrich, K.R., Geppert, A., Norrie, M.C. (eds.) CAiSE 2001. LNCS, vol. 2068, pp. 330–345. Springer, Heidelberg (2001)
6. Cabibbo, L., Carosi, A.: Managing inheritance hierarchies in object/relational mapping tools. In: Pastor, Ó., Falcão e Cunha, J. (eds.) CAiSE 2005. LNCS, vol. 3520, pp. 135–150. Springer, Heidelberg (2005)

7. Boyd, M., Kittivoravitkul, S., Lanzanitis, C., McBrien, P., Rizopoulos, N.: AutoMed: A BAV data integration system for heterogeneous data sources. In: Persson, A., Stirna, J. (eds.) CAiSE 2004. LNCS, vol. 3084, pp. 82–97. Springer, Heidelberg (2004)

8. McBrien, P., Poulovassilis, A.: A uniform approach to inter-model transformations. In: Jarke, M., Oberweis, A. (eds.) CAiSE 1999. LNCS, vol. 1626, pp. 333–348. Springer, Heidelberg (1999)

9. Date, C., Darwen, H., McGoveran, D.: Relational Database: Selected Writings 1994–1997. Addison-Wesley, Reading (1998)

10. Date, C.: Object identifiers vs. relational keys. In: [9], ch. 12, pp. 457–476

11. Fisher, M., Gabbay, D., Vila, L. (eds.): Handbook of Temporal Reasoning in Artificial Intelligence. Elsevier, Amsterdam (2005)

12. Artale, A., Parent, C., Spaccapietra, S.: Modeling the evolution of objects in temporal information systems. In: Dix, J., Hegner, S.J. (eds.) FoIKS 2006. LNCS, vol. 3861, pp. 22–42. Springer, Heidelberg (2006)

13. Finger, M., McBrien, P.: Temporal conceptual-level databases. In: Temporal Logics: Mathematical Foundations and Computational Aspects, vol. 2, pp. 409–435. OUP (2000)

14. Gregersen, H., Jensen, C.: Temporal entity-relationship models: a survey. IEEE Trans. KDE 11(3), 464–497 (1999)

15. Spaccapietra, S., Parent, C., Zimanyi, E.: Modeling time from a conceptual perspective. In: Proc. CIKM, pp. 432–440 (1998)

16. McBrien, P., Seltveit, A., Wangler, B.: An entity-relationship model extended to describe historical information. In: Proceedings of CISMOD 1992, Bangalore, India, pp. 244–260 (1992)

17. Costal, D., Olivé, A., Sancho, M.R.: Temporal features of class populations and attributes in conceptual models. In: Embley, D.W. (ed.) ER 1997. LNCS, vol. 1331, pp. 57–70. Springer, Heidelberg (1997)

18. Olivé, A., Costal, D., Sancho, M.R.: Entity evolition in IsA hierarchies. In: Akoka, J., Bouzeghoub, M., Comyn-Wattiau, I., Métais, E. (eds.) ER 1999. LNCS, vol. 1728, pp. 62–80. Springer, Heidelberg (1999)

19. Albert, M., Pelechano, V., Fons, J., Ruiz, M., Pastor, O.: Implementing UML association, aggregation, and composition. A particular interpretation based on a multidimensional. In: Eder, J., Missikoff, M. (eds.) CAiSE 2003. LNCS, vol. 2681, pp. 143–158. Springer, Heidelberg (2003)

20. Guarino, N., Carrara, M., Giaretta, P.: An ontology of meta-level categories. In: Proc. of 4th KR, pp. 270–280 (1994)

21. Guarino, N., Welty, C.: Ontological analysis of taxonomic relationships. In: Laender, A.H.F., Liddle, S.W., Storey, V.C. (eds.) ER 2000. LNCS, vol. 1920, pp. 210–224. Springer, Heidelberg (2000)

22. Halpin, T.: Subtyping revisited. In: Proper, H., Halpin, T., Krogstie, J. (eds.) Proc. EMMSAD 2007, pp. 128–138 (2007)

23. Anderson, W., Menzel, C.: Modal rigidity in the ontoclean methodology. In: Proc. FOIS, pp. 119–127 (2004)

Integrated Model-Driven Development of Goal-Oriented Data Warehouses and Data Marts

Jesús Pardillo and Juan Trujillo

Lucentia Research Group,
Department of Software and Computing Systems,
University of Alicante, Spain
{jesuspv,jtrujillo}@dlsi.ua.es

Abstract. A *corporate data warehouse* is a repository that provides decision makers with a large amount of historical data concerning the overall enterprise strategy. In order to customize the data warehouse, many organizations develop concrete *data marts* focused on a particular department or business process. However, their integrated development is still an open problem for many organizations due to the technical and organizational challenges involved during the design of these repositories as a complete solution. Therefore, we present here a design approach in order to build both the corporate data warehouse and data marts from user's requirements in an integrated way. Our approach consists on linking information requirements to specific data marts elicited by using the *goal-oriented requirement engineering*, which are automatically translated into the implementation of the corresponding data repositories by means of *model-driven engineering* techniques. Its great advantage is that user's requirements are captured since the very-early development stages of a data-warehousing project in order to automatically translate them into the entire data-warehousing platform.

Keywords: data warehouse, data mart, customization, model-driven engineering, goal-oriented requirement engineering, conceptual modeling.

1 Introduction

A data-warehousing architecture defines a set of data repositories and their relationships to support the decision-making process in a given organization. Several architectural options [1,2,3,4,5] and methodologies [6,7,8,9,10] have been proposed to develop these repositories. Specifically, there are two foundational data-warehousing alternatives that have been broadly discussed [11]: the *top-down* approach originally stated by Inmon [12] and the *bottom-up* stated by Kimball [13]. The basis of these approaches consists on which data repositories should be developed first: a *corporate data warehouse* where organization's data are stored and integrated in a single repository (top-down) or *departmental data marts* where data are aggregated and customized for particular information needs (bottom-up). Although the first one is considered the most elegant solution

Q. Li et al. (Eds.): ER 2008, LNCS 5231, pp. 426–439, 2008.

from a theoretical point of view, it is usually hard to implement since the project scope involves the whole organization [1], and thus, the second approach is more suitable for agile developments despite the problems that arise during data-mart integration [1,14]. Both approaches fail when they try to derive the second data repositories (*i.e.*, data marts or corporate data warehouse, respectively) due to the inherent high cost or the technical problems. In order to overcome these limitations, Kimball [13] also proposed a bus architecture articulated by *conformed dimensions*. These dimensions mean 90 percent of the integration efforts spent in order to tie data marts together [13]. They are obtained by agreement of the whole organization, hence, supporting truly cross-departmental decision-making processes. Despite it all, this proposal is designed at the logical level (*i.e.*, by using relational schemata), therefore, it does not provide suitable mechanisms to drive complex developments such as methodologies [6,7,8,9,15,16] based on conceptual modeling [17,18,19,20] can actually do.

However, we claim that the surrounding architectural debate [11] has been overlooked by the current development approaches mainly based on conceptual modeling. These approaches have focused on capturing information requirements by means of the *multidimensional modeling* [13,14] that organize data in terms of *facts* and *dimensions* of analysis, but without specifying how data repositories (*i.e.*, corporate data warehouse and their dependent data marts) are built from them. For instance, departmental data marts can be built from different development teams in isolation. Thus, they lack in incorporating conformity issues to solve the integrated development of data marts and corporate data warehouses. In order to assure cross-departmental information needs such as the answered by *drill-across* operations during the "on-line analytical processing" (OLAP) [14].

In this paper, we present an approach based on *goal-oriented requirement engineering* [21] and *model-driven engineering* [22] technologies to solve the architectural debate [11] by supporting the Kimball's insights [13] at the conceptual level. This proposal is based on our previous works [23,9,15,16,17] in order to propose a modeling framework, in terms of goals that the data warehouse should achieve together with the required information for conforming analysis dimensions; and also, a transformation architecture based on the "model-driven architecture" (MDA) [24] approach to automatically derive both the corporate data warehouse and its dependent data marts in an integrated way. Thus, we enable decision makers to response their cross-departmental information needs.

The remaining text is organized as follows: the next section introduces the motivating example in order to illustrate common conformity problems. Section 3 presents our goal-oriented model-driven approach for the integrated development of data warehouses. The related development platform and our example-scenario implementation is outlined in Section 4. Then, Section 5 discusses the related work. The last section expounds conclusions and outlines future work.

2 Background

Current development approaches [6,7,8,9,10] lack for specifying organizational concerns of the data warehousing with regards to the architectural debate [11]. Their practitioners design several schemata for each data mart that are not aligned by any criteria, *i.e.*, they are developed in isolation. As a result, developers obtain schemata where data structures are ill-defined due to non-unified data representations such as in the example scenario of Fig. 1. These schemata[1] show the multidimensional models of two independent data marts to support decision making on inventory and sales business processes. It illustrates a common situation that occurs when developers do not deal with integration issues.

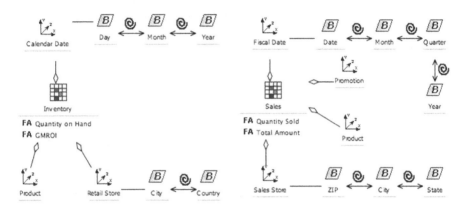

Fig. 1. Data models of independent data marts: retail inventory and sales example

The multidimensional modeling is the foundation of data warehouses [13,14] where data under analysis are arranged in facts (represented as ▦ in Fig. 1) and dimensions (⊿) around analysts can describe them, resembling the well-known star-like structures [13]. Both facts and dimensions are also represented by means of measures (**FA**) and aggregation hierarchies (◉) based on different aggregation levels (/B/), respectively. Despite both facts are described by similar dimensions (*i.e.*, by date, product, and store), decision makers cannot drill across them to fulfill their cross-departmental information needs since they are not integrated.

Regarding date and store dimensions (explicitly shown in Fig. 1), several misconceptions arise. On the one hand, (i) calendar-day and fiscal-date aggregation levels compromise the same concept but they are specified by different attributes[2], (ii) (calendar) years and (fiscal) years are different but they are equally named, and (iii) fiscal dates also need to be aggregated into quarters. On the other hand, (iv) stores are described at different granularities [13] in each data mart (*i.e.*, ZIP aggregation level in inventory and the city level in the sales fact), and (v) cities are aggregated into different levels in each model

---

[1] The multidimensional models herein are based on the UML profile presented in [17].

[2] By convention, concepts are equally named only if they have the same representation.

(*i.e.*, countries for retail stores and states for sales stores). Hence, in the current approaches, drilling across these dimensions is not possible [13,25].

Kimball in [13] proposes the conformity of dimensions by agreement between every data-mart development team, later providing a foundational definition of conformed dimensions: "two dimensions are *conformed* if the fields that you use as common row headers have the same domain" [26]. However, this definition is oriented at the logical level [19], where name matching of logical structures (*i.e.*, tables, columns, and rows) is necessary to enable drill-across operations by sorting and merging relational database structures. For this reason, some authors [25,27] generalize the conformity constraints at the conceptual level. For example, [25] supports conformity by finding functional dependencies between dimensions instances. On the other hand, other authors [28] in the literature establish more general schema equivalences in terms of their information capacity.

In the sake of simplicity, we assume an adaptation of the definition in [26] for the conceptual level: sharing dimensions between conceptual multidimensional models implies that we can reuse them through data marts in order to enable cross-departmental decision-making processes. Therefore, our approach is based on discovering by agreement the information needs through data marts and combine them into a master conformed template that fulfills all these needs. Even more, with our approach we can also provide the integrated development of the corporate data-warehouse that populates the data marts; and thus, reducing the expensive efforts involved in data integration [29].

3   Integrated Development of Model-Driven Goal-Oriented Corporate Data Warehouses and Data Marts

In this section, we present a development approach for data warehouses based on: (i) discovering information needs for each data mart by applying goal-oriented requirement engineering techniques [21], (ii) conforming the obtained dimension-related requirements by using a conformity authority that assures agreement and commitment between every data-mart stakeholder, (iii) providing a conceptual framework to model the underlying data repositories, and (iii) automatically translating the information requirements obtained since the very-early stages of development to the final implementation by using a model-driven engineering approach [22], specifically the well-known MDA proposal [24] that has been successfully employed in our previous work [23,9,15,16].

3.1   Goal-Oriented Reasoning for Conforming Data Marts

Kimball [13] advocates a "dimension authority" as the responsible stakeholder for managing conformed dimensions by defining, maintaining, and publishing them to each data mart; hence, conformity means an organizational commitment instead of meaning only a technical decision. Nevertheless, this author does not provide any mechanisms to support it. Therefore, we propose to enrich

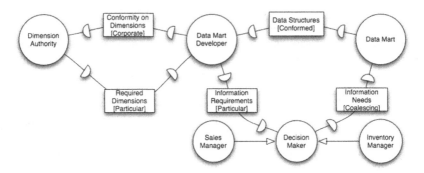

Fig. 2. Stakeholders and their resource dependencies in a data-mart development

the organizational modeling in goal-oriented approaches [9,7,8] by also taking into account conformity issues by explicitly establishing a dimension authority. It is worth mentioning that we can response data-mart needs, but also integrate them into the strategic policies of the whole organization.

Fig. 2 sketches the general overview of the involved stakeholders in a data-mart development after including a dimension authority[3]. The process starts with the elicitation of the information requirements for a particular decision maker in the department (*e.g.*, a sales or inventory manager in Fig. 2). By using goal-modeling terminology [21], a data-mart developer *intentionally depends* (represented as –D–) on other organizational *actors* (◯), *i.e.*, decision makers, in order to obtain the *resource* (☐) of their particular information requirements. These dependencies are modeled by means of strategic-dependency diagrams like the shown in Fig. 2. Then, a data-mart developer depends on the dimension authority to conform dimensions as a result of the corporate agreement. On the other hand, for this aim, the dimension authority needs the dimensions to be conformed for the different data-mart teams. Hence, data marts can deploy data structures already conformed that enable decision makers to fulfill their information needs. Due to the achieved conformity, data-mart coalescing queries [27] can be employed during cross-departmental decision-making processes.

As we stated, conformity issues require mechanisms to manage the involved rationale about which decisions are taken to obtain conformed dimensions. Following our previous work [9], every stakeholder has a rationale in order to accomplish their strategic dependencies in the organization. Thus, we can apply the same principles for also modeling the rationale of the dimension authority by means of strategic-rationale diagrams [21]. Fig. 3 illustrates a rationale for our running example (see Fig. 1). In [9], we describe how to derive data-warehouse information requirements by hierarchically reasoning from strategic goals to decisional ones, and then, to informational goals.

We employ our goal-modeling framework for data warehouses to discover dimensions in each data mart such as calendar or fiscal dates (see Fig. 3). For each dimension, a data-mart developer conforms the discovered dimensions to the

---

[3] These goal diagrams are based on i^* notation [21] which we adapt to UML in [9].

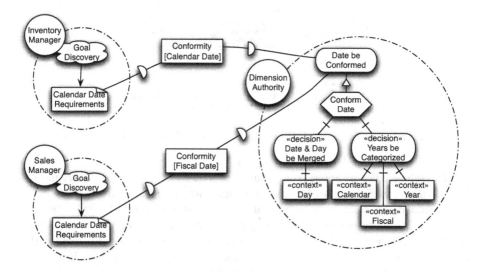

Fig. 3. Example dimension authority's rationale to conform date dimensions

project's dimension authority. For this aim, resource dependencies (*e.g.*, conformity on calendar date) are modeled in the strategic-dependency diagram. Then, dimension authority's rationale (represented as ⦂⦂) is employed to conform the date dimensions of both data marts. The related date conformities depend on the same *goal* (◯) actually being that date be conformed. Then, the *means* for achieving this *end* (─▷) is the *task* itself (◇) to conform date, which is *decomposed* (─+) in two additional goals in our scenario.

On the one hand, date and day aggregation levels (see Fig. 1) mean the same entity but with different representations; and thus, the dimension authority decides (*«decision »* goal[4]) that these levels be merged resulting the new conformed day context (*«context »* resource)[5]. On the other hand, calendar and fiscal years are identically represented but they really have different occurrences (*e.g.*, a fiscal year usually covers two calendar years), therefore, the dimension authority decides to conform them by specifying a general year context that is specialized in calendar or fiscal years regarding which occurrence is stored.

3.2   Conceptual Modeling of the Data-Warehousing Architecture

In this section, we enrich our conceptual modeling framework for data warehouses [17] in order to tailor the represented schemata for specific data repositories, *i.e.*, data marts or the corporate data warehouse itself. First, we extend the previous three-layer packaging architecture [17] by also including the deploying data repositories (*i.e.*, data marts and corporate data warehouse). Fig. 4 shows the relationships between the different packages. The entire model of a corporate

---

[4] These stereotyped elements belong to our *i**-based [21] modeling framework [9].

[5] Contexts [9] are translated later into the dimension's aggregation hierarchies.

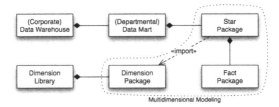

Fig. 4. Packaging architecture to model an integrated data-warehousing solution

data warehouse is composed (represented as ◆ [24]) of all the data-mart models. Furthermore, each model of a departmental data mart is composed of several *star packages* (a conceptualization of a logical *star schema* [13,30]), and each one is additionally composed of several *fact packages*[6]. Moreover, we define a *dimension library* as a catalog for publishing master conformed dimensions that can be obtained from the dimension authority's rationale (explained in the next section) and reused in each data-mart model. Hence, it is composed of several *dimension packages* containing the project's conformed dimensions that are imported («*import*» dependency relationships [24]) by the star packages in order to describe the contained facts.

Specifically, Fig. 5 shows the library of master conformed dimensions obtained from the dimension authority's rationale of our running example. It is worth noting that the dimension library is the foundation to automatically derive the dependent data-mart schemata later in an integrated way. For instance, the required date dimensions (*i.e.*, calendar and fiscal) are combined into the conformed date dimension that allows describing inventory and sales facts by the commitment of every particular information requirements: by merging day and date aggregation levels, and categorizing years. On the other hand, conformity on store dimensions is achieved by means of the <*ZIP, city, state, and country*> aggregation hierarchy.

In addition to the dimension library, we have defined an extension of the well-known "unified modeling language" (UML) [24] to specify the modeling elements exposed in our packaging architecture (Fig. 4). This extension is defined as a UML profile [24] where we specify *stereotypes* such as «*DataMart*» or «*CorporateDW*» to represent the multidimensional models of data marts and corporate data warehouse, respectively[7]. Complementarily, these stereotypes have *tag definitions* to describe their particular properties, *e.g.*, {*dependent*} data marts or {*conformed*} dimensions[8]. The proposed packaging architecture is applied to our example scenario and shown in Fig. 6. Inventory and sales data marts are modeled as packages (properly stereotyped) which depend («*import*» dependencies) on the corresponding {*conformed*} dimensions (properly tagged) that are contained in the retail dimension library. Even more, the retail

---

[6] See [17] for further references about the packaging mechanisms sketched herein.

[7] Stereotype icons are hidden in order to highlight only their semantics.

[8] Due to the space constraints, we omit a formal description of this modeling extension.

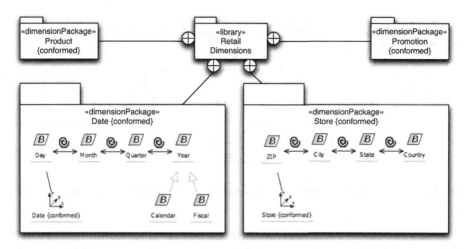

Fig. 5. Dimension library for modeling conformed dimensions of the retail data marts

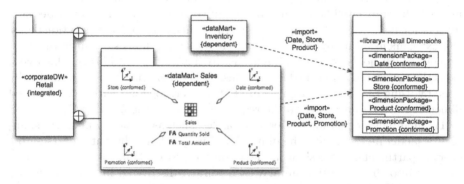

Fig. 6. Integrated data-warehousing model for retail inventory and sales analysis

corporate data warehouse is modeled as a package containing every data mart (□ with ─⊕ relationships) in the data-warehousing architecture. With the provided conceptual modeling framework, we can translate the previously exposed goal reasoning into multidimensional models. They conceptualize data structures required not only to deploy data marts but also the entire corporate repository.

3.3   Conceptual Modeling Mapping: From Goals to Data Structures

Any of the presented models (*i.e.*, goal-based or multidimensional ones) can be mapped in order to automatically derive data structures for both corporate data warehouse and its dependent data marts. Fig. 7 shows the model-transformation architecture to this aim. The transformation chain begins from *i** diagrams [21] to our conceptual modeling framework. Their mappings are based on our previous work [9], where every «*measure*» and «*context*» resources discovered during the goal-oriented reasoning are automatically translated into fact measures and dimensions, respectively, contained in a unique multidimensional model.

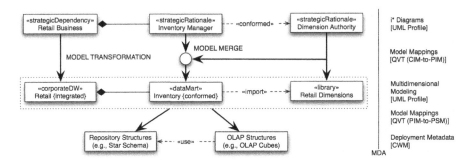

Fig. 7. Model-driven architecture for data warehousing based on conformed dimensions

In this paper, we decompose the transformation process into *measure–fact* and *context–dimension* mappings. Whereas the mappings presented in [9] are oriented to generate a single data repository in isolation, information requirements to be translated herein are spread on: (i) rationales of data-mart decision makers for measure–fact mappings, and (ii) dimension authority's rationale for context–dimension mappings. Thus, we translate the dimension authority's rationale, which holds contexts of analysis, to the conceptual library which contains the translated conformed dimensions. This transformation is automatically done by using the model mappings of [9]. However, together with each obtained dimension, we also map it into the required package structure (see Fig. 4).

The mapping of decision maker's rationales, such as inventory manager's, implies a model merging with the dimension library (shared by data marts across every department). As we show in Fig. 6, since conformed dimensions are already mapped into the dimension library, each context discovered in these rationales (conformed by the dimension authority) is translated into an «*import*» dependency from the related fact to the conformed dimension. Thus, it is assured that facts in each data mart can be drilled across the conformed dimensions. Moreover, the model of entire (corporate) data warehouse that contains every data mart is also automatically derived from the whole strategic-dependency model (Fig. 2). Once again, the packaging scaffolding (Fig. 4) is also taken into account for deriving the models of data marts and the corporate data warehouse.

On the other hand, from the conceptual modeling of data repositories, we also automatically derive the deployment metadata that implement them. These transformations are carried out by model mappings adapted from [23,15,16]. Essentially, the involved mappings match every multidimensional concept with both data structures of the data repository and client metadata to query it following a multidimensional view. Specifically, facts and dimensions, together with their measures and aggregation hierarchies, are mapped at the logical level [19] into the corresponding tables and columns of a star schema [13,30] concerning the relational model. Given the model of the corporate data warehouse that collects all the dependent data marts, by applying the mappings in [15,16], we obtain the data structures which implements the corporate repository. Given a data-mart model, we obtain the corresponding aggregated and customized version of the entire repository. It is worth noting that these data structures are conformed by their dimensions, therefore, we can automatically obtain their deployment counterparts in an integrated way. Even more, based on our previous work [23], we also automatically generate the required metadata to query them by using OLAP applications [14]. With this mapping, we overcome the tedious process of manually define client metadata from the deployed databases. Therefore, decision making processes involving the whole organization can be effectively done. Due to the space constraints, we omit a formal description of the presented mappings based on our previous works [23,9,15,16].

4   Development Platform and Implementation

Our proposal is based on the best-known initiative for model-driven engineering [22], namely the "model-driven architecture" (MDA) [24]. The related standards that we employ are also shown in Fig. 7. On the one hand, for goal-oriented requirement engineering, we employ i^* diagrams [21] supported by our UML profile presented in [9]. With regards to multidimensional modeling of data warehouses, we use the UML profile presented in [17] enriched for their architectural modeling as we have previously described. In addition, the "common warehouse metamodel" (CWM) [24] is employed to represent the deployed data structures for both the underlying databases and OLAP applications [14] in a vendor-independent manner. On the other hand, model transformations are specified in the "query/view/transformation" (QVT) [24] language that contains a declarative part for enabling us to easily design the required model mappings. Our transformation chain, speaking in the QVT terminology, is divided into three stages concerning each modeling framework: "computer-independent model" (CIM), "platform-independent model" (PIM), and "platform-specific model" (PSM). Hence, they allow us to smoothly isolate the deployment platform by means of different abstraction levels, tackling complex projects such as data warehousing.

All the modeling frameworks and model transformations concerning our proposal have been implemented in the Eclipse[9] development platform. Specifically, we employ several of its plugins implementing the MDA standards: for instance, the "model development tools" (MDT) for supporting UML and UML profiles, the "eclipse modeling framework" (EMF) for specifying CWM metadata representations in a vendor-independent manner, medini QVT and SmartQVT in order to specify and launch model-to-model QVT mappings with its declarative or imperative part, respectively, or MOFScript to design model-to-code Mof2Text [24] mappings to automatically implement the final data-warehousing solution. We have combined them to provide an "integrated development environment" (IDE) to manage data-warehousing projects based on model-driven engineering. By using this tool, we have implemented the running example as a proof of concept of our approach (see Fig. 8). Specifically, in the left-hand side of the figure, the inventory data mart is modeled, in this case, in order to

---

[9] URL: http://www.eclipse.org (March 2008)

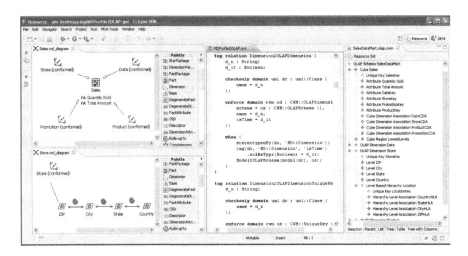

Fig. 8. Our IDE based on the Eclipse platform for model-driven data warehousing

automatically transform it into the deployment OLAP metadata (shown as the right-hand side), by means of applying the QVT mapping at the center of Fig. 8.

5   Related Work

We can divide the development approaches for data warehouses that appear in the literature into those that present methods or guidelines to capture information requirements such as [6,7,8,9] and those that present modeling frameworks for data structures that response these requirements [17,18,19,20]. Specifically, only few authors [7,8,9] have investigated goal-oriented approaches like the presented herein. However, none of them try to capture conformity issues between decision maker's requirements or derive multidimensional data models for every involved data repository in an entire data-warehousing architecture. Thus, researchers have investigated the conceptual modeling of data warehouses mainly focused on *intraschema* properties such as additivity [31] and aggregation hierarchies [32].

However, research community has made great efforts to the related issues of data integration and view materialization [29]. For instance, [30] recognizes three kinds of multi-star data models (*i.e.*, constellation, galaxy, and star cluster), however they are focused on the logical structures. Thus, real conformity mechanisms or data-repository deployments are not established. At the conceptual level, the best efforts for modeling *interschema* properties have been done by [20,25,27]. In [25], several kinds of relationships between facts and dimensions to drill across different schemata are discussed. Nevertheless, this model is oriented to complex data relationships that decision makers do not usually require [33]. Once again, there are not mechanisms in order to achieve agreement and commitment between data-mart stakeholders. In addition, [27] proposes the "dimension compatibility" notion to drill across data marts; nevertheless, it is not oriented to the integrated development of the involved data repositories.

Finally, the proposed library of conformed dimensions is a similar conception to the design pattern approach that has been investigated by [34] in order to propose dimensional patterns for data warehouses. However, these patterns act as design guidelines, and they do not mean suitable conformity mechanisms to enable integrated architectural deployments. It is worth noting that other authors such as [35] also propose automatic mechanisms to generate OLAP schemata, however these mechanisms are not conceived for solving the conformity among dimensions neither driving an entire data-warehousing architecture.

6 Conclusion

With this work, we present an approach to design a whole architecture for data warehousing in an integrated way since the very-early stages of development. The great benefits of our proposal are the following:

- We capture information requirements at the early development stages, hence, we can anticipate risks at the very beginning of every project.
- The proposal is based on goal-oriented requirement engineering [21] that allows developers to align particular information needs with the strategic policies of the whole organization.
- We coordinate the agreement and commitment between distributed data-mart stakeholders to conform their multidimensional models, also providing artifacts to document these conformity agreements.
- The usage of models can drive complex developments [22] such as data-warehousing architectures since their inception to the final deployment.
- Developing a data-warehousing architecture without paying attention to the underlying software platforms, delegating this knowledge to the scaffolding model-transformation architecture.
- Providing reusable assets for multidimensional models by means of a catalog of conformed dimensions enabling the design of modular systems.
- The automatic deployment of both corporate data warehouse and dependent data marts in an integrated way. It means a practical solution to the architectural debate [11].
- Enabling cross-departmental queries by automatically generating the OLAP metadata supported by conformed dimensions for each involved data mart.

Further investigations can be carried out in order to enrich the proposed approach, for instance, providing semantics-aware frameworks for conformity reasoning and information-requirement discovery, or suitability metrics to compare the ideal dimensions obtained from the data-mart requirements with the master conformed dimensions that we design. We plan to formalize the specification of the underlying methodology in a process-oriented modeling language, accompanied by the appropriate empirical validation.

Acknowledgements

This work has been supported by the ESPIA (TIN2007-67078) project from the Spanish Ministry of Education and Science, and by the QUASIMODO (PAC08-0157-0668) project from the Castilla-La Mancha Ministry of Education and Science (Spain). Jesús Pardillo is funded by the Spanish Ministry of Education and Science under FPU grant AP2006-00332.

References

1. Watson, H.J., Annino, D.A., Wixom, B.H., Avery, K.L., Rutherford, M.: Current Practices in Data Warehousing. Inf. Syst. Manage. 18(1), 1–9 (2001)
2. Jukic, N.: Modeling Strategies and Alternatives for Data Warehousing Projects. Commun. ACM 49(4), 83–88 (2006)
3. Cabibbo, L., Torlone, R.: An Architecture for Data Warehousing Supporting Data Independence and Interoperability. Int. J. Cooperative Inf. Syst. 10(3), 377–397 (2001)
4. Jarke, M., Jeusfeld, M.A., Quix, C., Vassiliadis, P.: Architecture and Quality in Data Warehouses: An Extended Repository Approach. Inf. Syst. 24(3), 229–253 (1999)
5. Samos, J., Saltor, F., Sistac, J., Bardés, A.: Database Architecture for Data Warehousing: An Evolutionary Approach. In: Quirchmayr, G., Bench-Capon, T.J.M., Schweighofer, E. (eds.) DEXA 1998. LNCS, vol. 1460, pp. 746–756. Springer, Heidelberg (1998)
6. Luján-Mora, S., Trujillo, J.: Applying the UML and the Unified Process to the design of Data Warehouses. J. Comput. Inform. Syst. 17(2), 12–42 (2006)
7. Giorgini, P., Rizzi, S., Garzetti, M.: Goal-oriented requirement analysis for data warehouse design. In: DOLAP, pp. 47–56 (2005)
8. Bonifati, A., Cattaneo, F., Ceri, S., Fuggetta, A., Paraboschi, S.: Designing Data Marts for Data Warehouses. ACM Trans. Softw. Eng. Methodol. 10(4), 452–483 (2001)
9. Mazón, J.N., Pardillo, J., Trujillo, J.: A Model-Driven Goal-Oriented Requirement Engineering Approach for Data Warehouses. In: ER Workshops, pp. 255–264 (2007)
10. Sen, A., Sinha, A.P.: A Comparison of Data Warehousing Methodologies. Commun. ACM 48(3), 79–84 (2005)
11. Breslin, M.: Data Warehousing Battle of the Giants: Comparing the Basics of the Kimball and Inmon Models. Bus. Intel. J. 9(1), 6–20 (2004)
12. Inmon, W.H.: Building the Data Warehouse. Wiley, Chichester (2005)
13. Kimball, R., Ross, M.: The Data Warehouse Toolkit: The Complete Guide to Dimensional Modeling. Wiley, Chichester (2002)
14. Chaudhuri, S., Dayal, U.: An Overview of Data Warehousing and OLAP Technology. SIGMOD Record 26(1), 65–74 (1997)
15. Mazón, J.N., Pardillo, J., Trujillo, J.: Applying Transformations to Model Driven Data Warehouses. In: Tjoa, A.M., Trujillo, J. (eds.) DaWaK 2006. LNCS, vol. 4081, pp. 13–22. Springer, Heidelberg (2006)
16. Mazón, J.N., Trujillo, J.: An MDA approach for the development of data warehouses. Dec. Support Syst. (in press, 2007)
17. Luján-Mora, S., Trujillo, J., Song, I.Y.: A UML profile for multidimensional modeling in data warehouses. Data Knowl. Eng. 59(3), 725–769 (2006)

18. Golfarelli, M., Maio, D., Rizzi, S.: The Dimensional Fact Model: A Conceptual Model for Data Warehouses. Int. J. Cooperative Inf. Syst. 7(2-3), 215–247 (1998)
19. Hüsemann, B., Lechtenbörger, J., Vossen, G.: Conceptual data warehouse modeling. In: DMDW, p. 6 (2000)
20. Abelló, A., Samos, J., Saltor, F.: YAM^2: a multidimensional conceptual model extending UML. Inf. Syst. 31(6), 541–567 (2006)
21. Yu, E.S.K., Mylopoulos, J.: Understanding "Why" in Software Process Modelling, Analysis, and Design. In: ICSE, pp. 159–168 (1994)
22. Bézivin, J.: Model Driven Engineering: An Emerging Technical Space. In: GTTSE, pp. 36–64 (2006)
23. Pardillo, J., Mazón, J.N., Trujillo, J.: Model-driven OLAP Metadata for Data Warehouses. In: BNCOD (in press, 2008)
24. Object Management Group: Model Driven Architecture (MDA), Unified Modeling Language (UML), Common Warehouse Metamodel (CWM), Query/View/Transformation Language (QVT), MOF Model to Text Transformation Language (Mof2Text) (March 2008), http://www.omg.org
25. Abelló, A., Samos, J., Saltor, F.: On relationships offering new drill-across possibilities. In: DOLAP, pp. 7–13 (2002)
26. Kimball, R.: The Soul of the Data Warehouse, Part Two: Drilling Across. Intel. Enterprise Mag. (April 2003)
27. Cabibbo, L., Torlone, R.: On the Integration of Autonomous Data Marts. In: SSDBM, pp. 223–231 (2004)
28. Hurtado, C.A., Mendelzon, A.O., Vaisman, A.A.: Updating OLAP Dimensions. In: DOLAP, pp. 60–66 (1999)
29. Vassiliadis, P.: Gulliver in the land of data warehousing: practical experiences and observations of a researcher. In: DMDW, pp. 12–1 (2000)
30. Moody, D.L., Kortink, M.A.R.: From enterprise models to dimensional models: a methodology for data warehouse and data mart design. In: DMDW, p. 5 (2000)
31. Horner, J., Song, I.Y., Chen, P.P.: An analysis of additivity in OLAP systems. In: DOLAP, pp. 83–91 (2004)
32. Malinowski, E., Zimányi, E.: Hierarchies in a multidimensional model: From conceptual modeling to logical representation. Data Knowl. Eng. 59(2), 348–377 (2006)
33. Pedersen, T.B.: How Is BI Used in Industry?: Report from a Knowledge Exchange Network. In: Kambayashi, Y., Mohania, M., Wöß, W. (eds.) DaWaK 2004. LNCS, vol. 3181, pp. 179–188. Springer, Heidelberg (2004)
34. Jones, M.E., Song, I.Y.: Dimensional modeling: Identification, classification, and evaluation of patterns. Dec. Support Syst (in press, 2007)
35. Niemi, T., Nummenmaa, J., Thanisch, P.: Constructing OLAP Cubes Based on Queries. In: DOLAP (2001)

Design Metrics for Data Warehouse Evolution

George Papastefanatos[1], Panos Vassiliadis[2], Alkis Simitsis[3], and Yannis Vassiliou[1]

[1] National Technical University of Athens, Athens, Hellas
{gpapas,yv}@dbnet.ece.ntua.gr
[2] University of Ioannina, Ioannina, Hellas
pvassil@cs.uoi.gr
[3] Stanford University and HP Labs, California, USA
alkis@{db.stanford.edu,hp.com}

Abstract. During data warehouse design, the designer frequently encounters the problem of choosing among different alternatives for the same design construct. The behavior of the chosen design in the presence of evolution events is an important parameter for this choice. This paper proposes metrics to assess the quality of the warehouse design from the viewpoint of evolution. We employ a graph-based model to uniformly abstract relations and software modules, like queries, views, reports, and ETL activities. We annotate the warehouse graph with policies for the management of evolution events. The proposed metrics are based on graph-theoretic properties of the warehouse graph to assess the sensitivity of the graph to a set of possible events. We evaluate our metrics with experiments over alternative configurations of the same warehouse schema.

1 Introduction

How good is the design of a data warehouse? What makes the design of a data warehouse good or bad? Typically, such questions are answered by a set of empirical rules, such as 'are your dimensions aligned?', 'is the warehouse following a typical design pattern, such as star or snowflake?', 'are the partitions and indexes of the warehouse built appropriately?', and so on. All these recipes are based on practical observations of the past, as well as rules of thumb that have been established by expert practitioners and although valuable, they simply transfer the lessons learned the hard way in the "craft" of data warehouse design.

At the same time, the scientific community is not in possession of a fundamentally established theory for the evaluation of the quality of a data warehouse. So far, the researchers have dealt with metrics that evaluate the design quality of the database schema with respect to high level goals, such as completeness, understandability, etc. both at the conceptual [16] and the logical level [3, 9]. Although structural properties of the database or the warehouse (e.g., number of dimensions or foreign keys) are considered, the employed approaches restrict themselves to constructs internal to the database without taking into account the incorporation of constructs surrounding the database into their models, nor the fact that a software construct, and especially an information system, evolves over time. Since software maintenance makes up for at least 50% of all resources spent in a project, maintainability is an important factor for

Q. Li et al. (Eds.): ER 2008, LNCS 5231, pp. 440–454, 2008.

the determination of the quality of a design. The problem is quite hard, since changes in the schema of a database-centric system (and thus, a data warehouse) affect both its internals but also, the surrounding deployed applications. Thus, the minimal interdependence of these software modules results in higher tolerance to subsequent changes and should be measured with a principled theory. Related work for view redefinition [5, 8, 10] and data warehouse evolution [2, 4, 6, 7] has provided rewriting techniques and theoretical cost models; yet, a well founded model that captures all the environment of a warehouse and objectively assess its vulnerability to changes is missing.

In this paper, we propose a set of metrics with two major characteristics. Firstly, they act as predictors for the vulnerability of a software module of a data warehouse (either internal, e.g., a dimension table, or external, e.g., an aggregated measure in a user's report) to future changes to the structure of the warehouse. Secondly, they facilitate the assessment of the quality of alternative designs of the warehouse with a particular viewpoint on the evolution of the data warehouse.

To achieve the abovementioned goal, we base our approach on two pillars.

First, we model the whole environment of the warehouse as a graph. We do not restrict the modeling to fact and dimension tables along with their interrelationships and any available views, but we extend the modeling to incorporate all the elements of an information system. To this end, *we add queries as integral parts of the configuration of a data warehouse.* In practice, a typical database is surrounded by forms, reports, web pages, stored procedures, and triggers deployed on the database server. Each of these software artifacts hides a list of queries via which it communicates with the database and exchanges queries and data with it. In addition, a data warehouse comprises a set of extract-transform-load (ETL) scripts, necessary for its population and refreshment with fresh source data. Queries constitute a convenient abstraction that captures the "skeleton" of all these applications w.r.t. their interrelationship to the database. We model the whole environment as a graph, with relations, attributes, constraints, queries, and query operands being the nodes of the graph, while the part-of or querying relationships are modeled as the edges connecting these nodes.

Second, our treatment for the evolution of the warehouse over time is based on events such as 'rename measure', 'add dimension attribute', 'delete dimension table', and so on. All these events are applied over the corresponding node and propagated over the appropriate subset of the graph. This way, given an evolution event, we can detect all the affected nodes. Moreover, we can define policies to regulate how a node will react to the possible change; e.g., a node can block -veto- an event, state the deletion of a dimension table, and isolate subsequent software modules that depend upon it from the effects of the change. We have built a what-if analysis tool that assesses potential evolution scenarios based on the above principles.

Based on these two pillars (detailed in Sections 2 and 3, respectively), in this paper, we provide a set of metrics for the assessment of the vulnerability of all the design structures in a data warehouse environment (Section 4). We exploit the graph and provide metrics like the *degrees* (in, out, and total) *of a node*, the *transitive degrees of a node* (standing for the extent to which other nodes transitively depend upon it), and the *degrees of a summarized variant of a module* (e.g., a view) that abstract the internal semantics of the module and focus on its coupling to the rest of the environment. We also provide an information theoretic definition of a *module's entropy* that simulates the extent to which the vulnerability of a node is surprising. Finally, we extensively experiment with various configurations in the setup of a reference warehouse (Section 5) and assess both the effectiveness of the proposed metrics (i.e., how well do they actually predict the impact of evolution events to a design construct) and how different design alternatives for the same schema behave w.r.t. evolution.

2   Graph Based Modeling for Data Warehouses

In this section, we summarize our graph modeling technique that uniformly covers relational tables, views, ETL activities, database constraints, and SQL queries as first class citizens. The proposed modeling technique represents all the aforementioned database parts as a directed graph $G=(V,E)$. The nodes represent the entities of our model and the edges represent the relationships among these entities. Originally, the model was introduced in [12] and here, we provide only a short summary.

Each **relation** R($\Omega_1, \Omega_2, ..., \Omega_n$) in the database schema is represented as a directed graph, which comprises: (a) a *relation node*, R, representing the relation schema; (b) n *attribute nodes*, $\Omega_i \in \Omega$, i=1..n, one for each of the attributes; and (c) n *schema relationships*, $\mathbf{E_s}$, directing from the relation node towards the attribute nodes, indicating that the attribute belongs to the relation.

The graph representation of a Select - Project - Join - Group By (SPJG) **query** involves a new node representing the query, named *query node*, and *attribute nodes* corresponding to the schema of the query. The query graph is a directed graph connecting the query node with all its schema attributes, via *schema relationships*. In order to represent the relationship between the query graph and the underlying relations, we resolve the query into its essential parts: SELECT, FROM, WHERE, GROUP BY, HAVING, and ORDER BY, each of which is eventually mapped to a subgraph. The edges connected the involved attribute and operand nodes are annotated as *map-select, from*, and *where relationships*. Aliases in the FROM clause (mostly needed in self-joins for our modeling) are annotated with *alias* edges. The direction of the edges is from the query node to the attribute nodes. WHERE and HAVING clauses are modeled via a left-deep tree of logical operands to represent the selection formulae; all the involved edges are annotated as *where* and *having relationships*, respectively. Nested queries are part of this modeling, too.

For the representation of aggregate queries, we employ two special purpose nodes: (a) a new node denoted as GB∈**GB**, to capture the set of attributes acting as the aggregators; and (b) one node per aggregate function labeled with the name of the employed aggregate function; e.g., COUNT, SUM, MIN. For the aggregators, we use edges directing from the query node towards the GB node that are labeled <group-by>, indicating *group-by relationships*, $\mathbf{E_G}$. Then, the GB node is connected with each of the aggregators through an edge tagged also as <group-by>, directing from the GB node towards the respective attributes. These edges are additionally tagged according to the order of the aggregators; we use an identifier i to represent the i-th aggregator. Moreover, for every aggregated attribute in the query schema, there exists an edge directing from this attribute towards the aggregate function node as well as an edge from the function node towards the respective relation attribute.

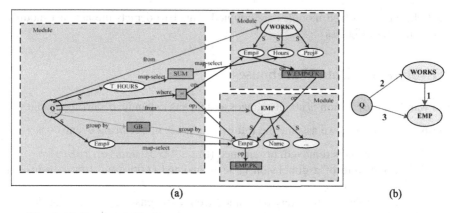

Fig. 1. (a) Graph and (b) abstract representation of an example aggregate query [12]

Both edges are labeled <map-select> and belong to $\mathbf{E_M}$, as these relationships indicate the mapping of the query attribute to the corresponding relation attribute through the aggregate function node. The representation of the ORDER BY clause of the query is performed similarly.

Functions used in queries are denoted as a special purpose node $F_i \in \mathbf{F}$ having the name of the function. Each function has an input parameter list comprising attributes, constants, expressions, and nested functions, and one (or more) output parameter(s). **Views** are considered either as queries or relations (materialized views). An **ETL activity** is modeled as a sequence of SQL views. *DML statements* are denoted as queries. Fig. 1 depicts the proposed graph representation for the following query:

```
Q: SELECT EMP.Emp# as Emp#, Sum(WORKS.Hours) as T_Hours
   FROM EMP,WORKS WHERE EMP.Emp#=WORKS.Emp# GROUP BY EMP.Emp#
```

Modules. A module is a sub-graph of the overall graph in one of the following patterns: (a) a relation with its attributes and all its constraints, (b) a view with its attributes, functions and operands, and (c) a query with all its attributes, functions and operands. Modules are disjoint with each other and connected through edges concerning foreign keys, map-select and so on. Within a module, we distinguish *top-level* and *low-level* nodes. Top level nodes are used to signify the identity of the module; for that purpose, query, relation and view nodes are used as top-level nodes. Low-level nodes comprise the rest of the module. Edges are classified into *provider* and *part-of* relationships. Provider edges are intermodule relationships (e.g., $\mathbf{E_M}$, $\mathbf{E_F}$), whereas part-of edges are intramodule relationships (e.g., $\mathbf{E_S}$, $\mathbf{E_W}$). In Fig. 1, the graph comprises 3 modules corresponding to the query and the relations subgraphs.

Zoom in/out. Abstracting the graph into a modular representation at a coarser level of detail (zoom-out) involves the following steps: (a) for each query, view or relation module, all low-level nodes and intramodule edges are suppressed and only the respective top-level node is retained, and, (b) all inter-module edges apart from *from* and *foreign key* edges are dropped. A surviving edge between two modules is annotated with a weight corresponding to the number of the edges that originally connected the two modules. We call this weight the *strength* of the edge as it assesses how tightly the involved modules are coupled. Fig. 1(b) depicts the abstract modular representation of Fig. 1(a).

3 Evolution in Data Warehouses

Data warehouse evolution is about changes and means to handle occurring changes.

Events. In our setting, we assume the following classes of occurring events:

- C1. A dimension is removed, or renamed (DEL, UPD Dimension Table)
- C2. The structure of a dimension table is updated (ADD, DEL, UPD Dimension Attribute)
- C3. A fact table is completely decoupled from a dimension (DEL FK), or decoupled from one dimension and coupled to another (UPD FK)
- C4. The measures of a fact table change (ADD, DEL, UPD measure)

An update can signify a change of data types or a renaming of a construct (our practical experience [12] indicates that it mostly refers to the latter.) We do not check for additions of fact or dimension tables, because such events do not result in a direct impact to any other logical warehouse construct per se. Given these changes that can occur to a data warehouse, their basic impact is that all software modules that use these database structures must be rewritten. The impact can be both syntactic (in the sense that all views and queries using a deleted attribute will crash) and semantic (in the sense that a new attribute in a relation or a modified condition in a view might require a rewriting of all the queries that use it). Assume for example that an attribute *FullName* is split to attributes *FirstName* and *LastName* or a view condition '*Year* = *2007*' is altered to '*Year* > 2006'. The former change has syntactic impacts to all the queries using the attribute and the latter has semantic impact, since some of the queries using the view require exactly values of 2007, whereas some others will serve the purpose with any value greater than 2006.

Handling of events. Given an event posed to one of the warehouse constructs (or, equivalently, to one of the nodes of the graph of the warehouse that we have introduced), the impact involves the possible rewriting of the constructs that depend upon the affected construct either directly, or transitively. In a non-automated way, the administrator has to check all of these constructs and restructure the ones he finds appropriate. This process can be semi-automated by using our graph-based modelling and annotating the nodes and the edges of the graph appropriately with policies in the event of change. Assume for example, that the administrator guarantees to an application developer that a view with the sum of sales for the last year will always be given. Even if the structure of the view changes, the queries over this view should remain unaffected to the extent that its SELECT clause does not change. On the contrary, if a query depends upon a view with semantics '*Year* = *2007*' and the view is altered to '*Year* > 2006', then the query must be rewritten.

The main idea in our approach involves annotating the graph constructs (relations, attributes, and conditions) sustaining evolution changes (addition, deletion, and modification) with policies that dictate the way they will regulate the change. Three kinds of policies are defined: (a) *propagate* the change, meaning that the graph must be reshaped to adjust to the new semantics incurred by the event; (b) *block* the change, meaning that we want to retain the old semantics of the graph and the hypothetical event must be vetoed or, at least, constrained, through some rewriting that preserves the old semantics; and (c) *prompt* the administrator to interactively decide what will eventually happen. In [13] we have proposed a language that greatly alleviates the designer from annotating each node separately and allows the specification of default behaviors at different levels of granularity with overriding priorities. Assume that a default behavior for the deletion of view attributes is specified via the language of [13]. This policy can later be overridden with a directive for the behavior of the attributes of view V (again via the same language). Again, this policy can in turn be overridden with a specification for the behavior of attribute $V.A$.

Given the annotation of the graph, there is also a simple mechanism that (a) determines the status of a potentially affected node on the basis of its policy, (b) depending on the node's status, the node's neighbors are appropriately notified for the event. Thus, the event is propagated throughout the entire graph and affected nodes are notified appropriately. The STATUS values characterize whether (a) a node or one of its children (for the case of top-level nodes) is going to be deleted or added (e.g., TO-BE-DELETED, CHILD-TO-BE-ADDED) or (b) the semantics of a view have changed, or (c) whether a node blocks the further propagation of the event (e.g., ADDITION-BLOCKED).

4 Metric Suite

Various approaches exist in the area of database metrics. Most of them attempt to define a complete set of database metrics and map them to abstract quality factors, such as maintainability, good database design, and so on. In this section, we introduce a metric set based on the properties of the warehouse graph for measuring and evaluating the design quality of a data warehouse with respect to its ability to sustain changes. Metrics are based on properties of the aforementioned graph model.

4.1 Degree-Related Metrics

The first family of metrics comprises simple properties of each node in the graph. The main idea lies in the understanding that the in-degree, out-degree and total degree of a node v demonstrate in absolute numbers the extent to which (a) other nodes depend upon v, (b) the dependence of v to other nodes and (c) v is interacting with other nodes in the graph, respectively. Specifically, these metrics are:

- *In-degree*, $D^I(v)$, *Out-degree*, $D^O(v)$, *Degree*, $D(v)$, of a node v, with the simple semantics that have already been mentioned. These metrics have been introduced in [15] and assess the dependence and the responsibility of each node.
- *In Transitive, Out Transitive, Transitive degree.* The simple degree metrics of a node v are good measures for finding the nodes that are directly dependent on v or on which v directly depends on, but they cannot detect the transitive dependencies between nodes. Thus, if we consider the graph $G(V,E)$, the transitive degrees of a node $v \in V$ with respect to all nodes $y_i \in V$ are given by the following formulae:

$$TD^I(v) = \sum_{y_i \in V} \sum_{p \in paths(y_i,v)} count(e_p), \text{ for all distinct edges } e_p \in paths \text{ of the form } (y_i,v)$$

$$TD^O(v) = \sum_{y_i \in V} \sum_{p \in paths(v,y_i)} count(e_p), \text{ for all distinct edges } e_p \in paths \text{ of the form } (v,y_i)$$

$$TD(v) = TD^I(v) + TD^O(v)$$

- *Zoomed-out degree.* Assuming the degrees of the detailed graph can be computed, one can measure the degrees of the nodes of the zoomed-out graph. As already mentioned in section 2, zooming-out annotates edges with strengths, so the following formulae can be defined:

$$D^{Is}(v) = \sum_i strength(e_i), \text{ for all edges } e_i \text{ of the form } (y,v)$$

$$D^{Os}(v) = \sum_i strength(e_i), \text{ for all edges } e_i \text{ of the form } (v,y)$$

$$D^s(v) = D^{Is}(v) + D^{Os}(v)$$

- *Zoomed-out transitive degree*: Similarly to above, we may extend the transitive degrees to the zoomed-out graph, so the following formulae can be defined:

$$TD^{Is}(v) = \sum_{y_i \in V} \sum_{p \in paths(y_i,v)} strength(e_p), \text{ for } e_p \in paths \text{ of the form } (y_i,v)$$

$$TD^{Os}(v) = \sum_{y_i \in V} \sum_{p \in paths(v,y_i)} strength(e_p), \text{ for } e_p \in paths \text{ of the form } (v,y_i)$$

$$TD^s(v) = TD^{Is}(v) + TD^{Os}(v)$$

There are several other variants of these graph-based measures that we do not explore here. We can define *Category-constrained degrees*, which constrain degrees by edge categories. For example, we might be interested only in the number of part-of outgoing edges of a relation. We can also measure the importance of modules (e.g., using the frequency of a query's execution) and obtain *weighted variants* of the aforementioned metrics.

4.2 Entropy – Based Metrics

Entropy is used to evaluate the extent to which a part of a system is less likely to be affected by an evolution event than other parts [1]. Given a set of events $A=[A_1,..., A_n]$ with probability distribution $P=\{p_1,...,p_q\}$, respectively, entropy is defined as the average information obtained from a single sample from A:

$$H(A) = -\sum_{i=1}^{n} p_i \log_2 p_i$$

Assume a node v in our graph $G(V,E)$. We define the probability that $v \in V$ is affected by an arbitrary evolution event e over a node $y_k \in V$ as the number of paths from v towards y_k divided by the total paths from v towards all nodes in the graph, i.e.,

$$P(v|y_k) = \frac{paths(v, y_k)}{\sum\limits_{y_i \in V} paths(v, y_i)} \text{ , for all nodes } y_i \in V.$$

The information we gain when a node v is affected by an event occurred on node y_k is $I(P(v \mid y_k)) = \log_2 \frac{1}{P(v \mid y_k)}$ and the entropy of node v wrt the whole graph is then:

$$H(v) = -\sum\limits_{y_i \in V} P(v \mid y_i) \log_2 P(v \mid y_i), \text{ for all nodes } y_i \in V.$$

The above quantity expresses the average information we gain, or equivalently the amount of "surprise" conveyed, if node v is affected by an arbitrary evolution event on the graph. Observe that high entropy values correspond to nodes with a higher dependence with the rest of the graph. For instance, a query defined over only one relation has an entropy value of 0, whereas a query defined over a view which in turns accesses two relations has an entropy value of $\log_2 3$.

Moreover, we can apply the exact same technique to the zoomed out-graph $G^s(V^s, E^s)$, by defining the probability of a node $v \in V^s$ to be affected by an evolution event over a node $y_k \in V^s$ as:

$$P^s(v|y_k) = \frac{\sum\limits_{p \in paths(v,y_k)} strength(e_p)}{\sum\limits_{y_i \in V^s} \sum\limits_{p \in paths(v,y_i)} strength(e_p)} \text{ , for all nodes } y_i \in V^s.$$

with $e_p \in E^s$ being the edges of all the paths of the zoomed out graph stemming from v towards y_k. Similarly, the entropy of node $v \in V^s$ is:

$$H^s(v) = -\sum\limits_{y_i \in V^s} P^s(v \mid y_i) \log_2 P^s(v \mid y_i), \text{ for all nodes } y_i \in V^s.$$

5 Evaluation – Experiments

Goals. There are two major goals in our experiments. First, we have investigated the extent to which the proposed metrics good indicators for the prediction of the effect evolution events have on the warehouse. A clear desideratum in this context is the determination of the most suitable metric for this prediction under different circumstances. A second goal involves the comparison of alternative design techniques with respect to their tolerance to evolution events.

Experimental setup for the first goal. To achieve the goal of determining the fittest prediction metric, we need to fix the following parameters: (a) a data warehouse schema surrounded by a set of queries and possibly views, (b) a set of events that alter the above configuration, (c) a set of administrator profiles that simulate the intention of the administrating team for the management of evolution events, and (d) a baseline method that will stand as an accurate estimate of the actual effort needed to maintain the warehouse environment.

We have employed the TPC-DS [14] schema as the testbed for our experiments. TPC-DS is a benchmark that involves six star schemas (with a large overlap of shared dimensions) standing for Sales and Returns of items purchased via a Store, a Catalog and the Web. We have used the Web Sales schema that comprises one fact table and thirteen dimension tables. The structure of the Web Sales schema is interesting in the sense that it is neither a pure star, nor a pure snowflake schema. In fact, the dimensions are denormalized, with a different table for each level; nevertheless, the fact table has foreign keys to all the dimension tables of interest (resulting in fast joins with the appropriate dimension level whenever necessary). Apart from this "starified" schema, we have also employed two other variants in our experiments: the first involves a set of views defined on top of the TPC-DS schema and the second involves the merging of all the different tables of the Customer dimension into one. We have isolated the queries that involve only this subschema of TPC-DS as the surrounding query set of the warehouse. The views for the second variant of the schema were determined by picking the most popular atomic formulae at the WHERE clause of the surrounding queries. In other words, the aim was to provide the best possible reuse of common expressions in the queries.

We created two workloads of events to test different contexts for the warehouse evolution. The first workload of 52 events simulates the percentage of events observed in a real world case study in an agency of the Greek public sector. The second workload simulates a sequence of 68 events that are necessary for the migration of the current TPC-DS Web sales schema to a pure star schema. The main idea with both workloads is to simulate a set of events over a reasonable amount of time. Neither the internal sequence of events per se, nor the exact background for deriving the events is important; but rather, the focus is on the events' generation that statistically capture a context under which administration and development is performed (i.e., maintenance of the same schema in the first case, and significant restructuring of a schema in the latter case). The distribution of events is shown in Table 1.

We have used an experimental prototype, HECATAEUS [11], for the identification of the impact of hypothetical evolution events. We have annotated the graph with policies, in order to allow the management of evolution events. We have used three annotation "profiles", specifically: (a) *propagate all*, meaning that every change will be flooded to all the nodes that should be notified about it, (b) *block all*, meaning that a view/query is inherently set to deny any possible changes, and (c) *mixture*, consisting of 80% of the nodes with propagate policies and 20% with blocking. The first policy practically refers to a situation without any annotation. The second policy simulates a highly regulatory administration team that uses HECATAEUS to capture an evolution event as soon as it leaves its source of origin; the tool highlights the node where the event was blocked. The third policy simulates a rather liberal environment, where most events are allowed to spread over the graph, so that their full impact can be observed; yet, 20% of critical nodes are equipped with blocking policies to simulate the case of nodes that should be handled with special care.

Summarizing, the configuration of an experiment involves fixing a schema, a set of policies and a workload. We have experimented with all possible combinations of values. The measured metrics in each experiment involve the execution of the workload of evolution events in the specified configurations and the measurement of the

Table 1. Distribution of events

Operation	Distribution 1	Distribution 2
Rename Measure	29% (15)	0% (0)
Add Measure	25% (13)	0% (0)
Rename Dimension Attribute	21% (11)	0% (0)
Add Dimension Attribute	15% (8)	37% (25)
Delete Measure	6% (3)	0% (0)
Delete Dimension Attribute	4% (2)	44% (30)
Delete FKs	0%	13% (9)
Delete Dimension Table	0%	6% (4)

affected nodes. Specifically, each node of the graph is monitored and we get analytic results on how many times each node was affected by an event. This measurement constitutes the baseline measurement that simulates what would actually happen in practice. This baseline measurement is compared to all the metrics reported in Section 4, being evolution-agnostic or not.

Experimental Setup for the second goal. The second goal of our experiments is to compare alternative designs of the warehouse with each other – i.e., we want to find which design method (pure star, TPC-DS with or without views) is the best for a given designer profile (which is expressed by the policies for the management of evolution). Thus, the comparison involves the compilation of the baseline measurements, grouped per policy profile and alternative schema. We measure the total number of times each node was affected and we sum all these events. The intention is to come up with a rough estimation of the number of rewritings that need to be done by the administrators and the application developers (in this setting, it is possible that a query or view is modified in more than one of its clauses). A second measurement involves only the query part: we are particularly interested in the effort required by the application developers (which are affected by the decisions of the administration team), so we narrow our focus to the effect inflicted to the queries only.

5.1 Effectiveness of the Proposed Metrics

In this experiment, we evaluate the effectiveness of the proposed metrics using the first distribution of events. We have constructed the following nine configurations by fixing each time a value for the schema and the policy. The schema takes one of the values {Web Sales (*WS*), Web Sales extended with views (*WS-views*), star variant of Web Sales (*WS-star*)} and the policy takes one of the values {*Block-All*, *Propagate-All*, *Mixture*}. In the rest, we discuss our findings organized in the following categories: (a) Fact Tables, (b) Dimension Tables, (c) Views, and (d) Queries.

Facts. Our experiments involved a single fact table. We observed that the number of events that occurred to the fact table does not change with the overall architecture. The presence of more or less dimensions or views did not affect the behavior of the fact table; on the contrary, it appears that the main reasons for the events that end up to the fact table, are its attributes. Therefore, the main predictor for the behavior of the evolution of the fact table is its out-degree, which is mostly due to the part-of relationships with its attributes.

Dimension Tables. Evolution on dimension tables can also be predicted by observing their out-degree, since this property practically involves the relationship of the dimension with its attributes as well as its relationship via foreign keys with other dimensions. Figure 2 depicts this case for the original web sales schema and its star variant, for which all customer-related dimensions have been merged into one dimension. Our baseline (depicted as a solid line with triangles) involves the actual number of times a node belonging to a dimension table was affected.

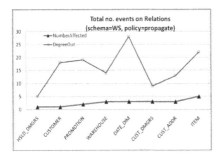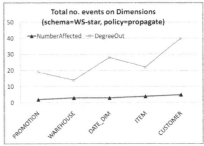

Fig. 2. Events affecting dimensions: (a) WS schema, (b) WS-star schema

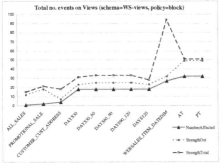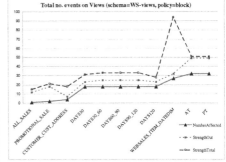

Fig. 3. Events affecting views: (a) WS-star and WS schema, (b) WS-views schema

Despite the spikes at the heavily correlated date dimension, out-degree is a predictor, keeping in mind that it is the actual trend that matters and not the values themselves.

Views. Views behave practically uniformly for all configurations, independently of schema or policy. Observe Fig. 3 where we depict our findings concerning views. It is clear that strength of out-degree (strength-out) and total strength are the best predictors for the evolution of views with the former being an interestingly accurate predictor in all occasions. Figure 3(a) is a representative of all the six configurations for the original web sales schema and its star variant. The policy makes no difference and all six experiments have resulted in exactly the same behavior. The rest of the metrics miss the overall trend and are depicted for completeness. Fig. 3(b) shows a representative graphical representation of the metrics, showing that the strength of the out-degree is consistently effective, whereas the total strength shows some spikes (mainly due to views that are highly connected to the sources, although these sources did not generate too much traffic of evolution events after all). The rest of the metrics behave similarly with Fig. 3(a).

Queries. Queries are typically dependent upon their coupling to the underlying DBMS layer. As a general guideline, the most characteristic measure of the vulnerability of queries to evolution events is their transitive dependence. A second possible metric suitable for a prediction is the entropy; however, it is not too accurate. Other metrics do not seem to offer good prediction qualities; the best of them, out-degree, does not exceed 70%. Recall that the baseline for our experiment is the actual number of events that reached a query (depicted as a solid line decorated with triangles in Fig. 4 and 5). Finally, we stress that the trend makes a metric successful and not the precise values.

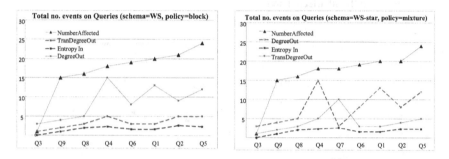

Fig. 4. Events affecting queries: (a) WS schema, (b) WS-star schema

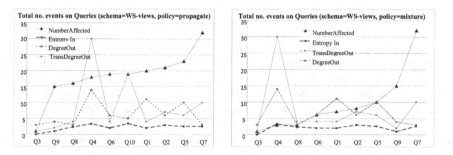

Fig. 5. Total number of events affecting queries: (a) Behavior for the WS-views with propagate policy; (b) Behavior for the WS-views schema with mixture policy

Fig. 4 shows two characteristic plots for the original web sales schema and its star variant. Each plot is a representative of the other plots concerning the same schema, with the trends following quite similar behavior. In all cases, transitive dependence gives a quite successful prediction, with around 80% accuracy. It is noteworthy that in the case of the 20% of failures, though, the metric identifies a query as highly vulnerable and in practice, the query escapes with few events. Fortunately, the opposite does not happen, so a query is never underestimated with respect to its vulnerability. Entropy is the second best metric and due to its smoothness, although it follows transitive dependence's behavior, it misses the large errors of transitive dependence, although it also misses the scaling of events, for the same reason.

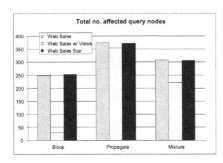
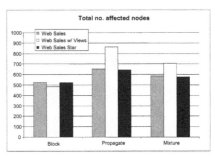

Fig. 6. Comparison of *WS, WS-views, WS-star* design configurations for distribution 1: (a) only affected queries and (b) all affected nodes

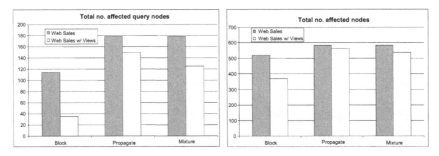

Fig. 7. Comparison of *WS, WS-views* design configurations for distribution 2: (a) only affected queries; (b) all affected nodes

Queries are quite dependent on the policy and schema: views seem to block the propagation of events to the queries. Fig. 5(b) shows a significant drop for the values of affected queries when the policy is a mixture of propagation and blocking policies. The propagate-all policy depicted in Fig. 5(a) presents the flooding of the events, which involves more than double the number of occurrences as compared to the numbers of Fig. 5(b) for 80% of the cases. A block-all policy involved only 3 of the 10 queries and it is not depicted for lack of space). Interestingly, the transitive degree has a success ratio of 80%, as opposed to the rather unsuccessful out-degree.

5.2   Comparison of Alternative Design Configurations

We compared the three alternative design configurations of our system in order to come up with an estimation of the number of rewritings that need to be done by the administrators and the application developers, and to assess the effect that a different schema configuration has on the system. Thus, we measured the number of affected nodes and specifically, the number of affected query nodes for the nine different configurations of policy sets and schemata. The first distribution of events was applied to all schemas, whereas the second was applied only to *WS* and *WS-views*.

Fig. 6 describes the effect that a design alternative has on how affected system constructs are in the case of evolution. A star schema has less maintenance effort than the other variants due to its reduced size. Clearly, the presence of views augments the effort needed by the administration team to maintain them (shown in the increased number of affected nodes of Fig. 6b), which is because nodes belonging to views are extensively affected. Still, the interference of views between the warehouse and the queries serves as a "shield" for absorbing schema changes and not propagating them to queries. The drop in query maintenance due to the presence of views is impressive: *whatever we pay in administration effort, we gain in development effort*, since the cost of rewritings in terms of human effort mainly burdens application developers, who are obliged to adapt affected queries to occurred schema changes. The case of schema migration strengthens this observation (Fig. 7). As for the different policy sets, we observe that blocking of events decreases the number of affected nodes in all configurations and saves significant human effort. It is, however, too conservative, constraining even the necessary readjustments that must be actually made on queries and views. On the other hand, propagate and mixture policy sets have an additional overhead, which is balanced by the automatic readjustments that are held on the system.

6 Conclusions

In this paper, we have proposed a set of metrics for the evaluation of the vulnerability warehouse modules to future changes and for the assessment of the quality of alternative designs of the warehouse. We have learned that out-degrees help as predictors for the fact and the dimension tables of the warehouse; the strength of out-degree (strength-out) and total strength are very good predictors for the evolution of views; the transitive dependence and entropy are good predictors for the vulnerability of queries. As far as warehouse design is concerned, we have an elegant theory to characterize the trade-offs between administration and development costs that result from the choice of adding views or "starifying" the schema of a warehouse.

Further experimentation and novel metrics along with theoretical validation of the proposed ones are clear topics for future work.

References

1. Allen, E.B.: Measuring Graph Abstractions of Software: An Information-Theory Approach. In: METRICS (2002)
2. Bellahsene, Z.: Schema evolution in data warehouses. Knowl. and Inf. Syst. 4(2) (2002)
3. Berenguer, G., et al.: A Set of Quality Indicators and their Corresponding Metrics for Conceptual Models of Data Warehouses. In: Tjoa, A.M., Trujillo, J. (eds.) DaWaK 2005. LNCS, vol. 3589. Springer, Heidelberg (2005)
4. Blaschka, M., Sapia, C., Höfling, G.: On Schema Evolution in Multidimensional Databases. In: Mohania, M., Tjoa, A.M. (eds.) DaWaK 1999. LNCS, vol. 1676. Springer, Heidelberg (1999)
5. Fan, H., Poulovassilis, A.: Schema Evolution in Data Warehousing Environments - A Schema Transformation-Based Approach. In: Atzeni, P., Chu, W., Lu, H., Zhou, S., Ling, T.-W. (eds.) ER 2004. LNCS, vol. 3288. Springer, Heidelberg (2004)
6. Favre, C., Bentayeb, F., Boussaid, O.: Evolution of Data Warehouses' Optimization: A Workload Perspective. In: Song, I.-Y., Eder, J., Nguyen, T.M. (eds.) DaWaK 2007. LNCS, vol. 4654. Springer, Heidelberg (2007)

7. Golfarelli, M., Lechtenbörger, J., Rizzi, S., Vossen, G.: Schema versioning in data ware-houses: Enabling cross-version querying via schema augmentation. Data Knowl. Eng. 59(2), 435–459 (2006)

8. Gupta, A., Mumick, I.S., Rao, J., Ross, K.: Adapting materialized views after redefinitions: Techniques and a performance study. Information Systems (26) (2001)

9. Levene, M., Loizou, G.: Why is the snowflake schema a good data warehouse design? Information Systems Journal 28(3), 225–240 (2003)

10. Nica, A., Lee, A.J., Rundensteiner, E.A.: The CSV algorithm for view synchronization in evolvable large-scale information systems. In: Schek, H.-J., Saltor, F., Ramos, I., Alonso, G. (eds.) EDBT 1998. LNCS, vol. 1377. Springer, Heidelberg (1998)

11. Papastefanatos, G., Anagnostou, F., Vassiliadis, P., Vassiliou, Y.: Hecataeus: A What-If Analysis Tool for Database Schema Evolution. In: CSMR (2008)

12. Papastefanatos, G., Vassiliadis, P., Simitsis, A., Vassiliou, Y.: What-if Analysis for Data Warehouse Evolution. In: Song, I.-Y., Eder, J., Nguyen, T.M. (eds.) DaWaK 2007. LNCS, vol. 4654. Springer, Heidelberg (2007)

13. Papastefanatos, G., et al.: Language Extensions for the Automation of Database Schema Evolution. In: ICEIS (2008)

14. The TPC BENCHMARK^{TM} DS (April 2007),
    http://www.tpc.org/tpcds/spec/tpcds1.0.0.d.pdf

15. Vassiliadis, P., Simitsis, A., Skiadopoulos, S.: Modeling ETL activities as graphs. In: DMDW (2002)

16. Wedemeijer, L.: Defining Metrics for Conceptual Schema Evolution. In: FMLDO (2000)

A Domain Engineering Approach for Situational Method Engineering

Anat Aharoni and Iris Reinhartz-Berger

Department of Management Information Systems,
University of Haifa, Haifa 31905, Israel
anatah@mis.haifa.ac.il, iris@mis.haifa.ac.il

Abstract. Methodologies are one of the most significant key factors to the success of project development. Since there is no single methodology that can be uniquely pointed as "the best", the discipline of situational method engineering (SME) promotes the idea of creating method components, rather than complete methodologies, and tailoring them to specific situations at hand. In this paper we present a holistic approach, called ADOM-SME, for representing method components and tailoring them into situational methodologies. This approach, whose roots are in the area of domain engineering (also known as product line engineering), supports specifying the five main methodological aspects (products, work units, stages, producers, and model units), as well as instantiating them into endeavour concepts, using a single frame of reference. Furthermore, the proposed approach enriches the standard metamodel for development methodologies, ISO/IEC 24744, by supporting the creation of valid situational methodologies and guiding their tailoring.

Keywords: Method Engineering, Situational Method Engineering, Metamodeling, ISO/IEC 24744, Domain Engineering, Product Line Engineering.

1 Introduction

The need for effective, appropriate, and flexible software development processes has increased as the complexity and variety of computer-based systems rose. Furthermore, the need to make method engineering more adaptable and flexible, taking into consideration organizational, technical, and human-related constraints and requirements, became important. The situational method engineering (SME) discipline [11, 15, 23] promotes the idea of creating method components rather than complete methodologies and tailoring them to specific situations at hand. Recently, efforts have been made for standardizing the area of (situational) method engineering, yielding the OPEN Process Framework (OPF) [21, 32], OMG's Software Process Engineering Metamodel (SPEM) [18], and ISO/IEC 24744 [5, 13]. ISO/IEC 24744, which is the most recent work and incorporates experience from earlier SME approaches, defines a metamodel for development methodologies. This standard refers to both methodologies and their instances (in the form of endeavours), as well as to five aspects of the modeled method components or methodologies: work units (the process aspect), work products (the artifact aspect), producers (the people aspect), stages (the temporal

Q. Li et al. (Eds.): ER 2008, LNCS 5231, pp. 455–468, 2008.

aspect), and model units (the language aspect). All these aspects are described and specified using an object-oriented terminology, concentrating on the methodology structural aspects and paying less attention to the behavioral aspects. A designated graphical notation for ISO/IEC 24744 was proposed in [7]. This notation covers all concepts described by ISO/IEC 24744, but does not support the endeavour activities.

This paper introduces an approach for representing methodologies and method components that also supports the integration and tailoring of method components into complete methodologies that best suit specific situations. This approach does not violate ISO/IEC 24744, but rather enriches it in order to support the creation of valid situational methodologies and guide their tailoring. It adapts a domain engineering approach, called Application-based DOmain Modeling (ADOM) [25, 30], to the special needs of the SME field. ADOM-SME is based on a three layered framework: application, domain, and language. The application layer includes the SME metamodel, which is a variation of that presented in ISO/IEC 24744. The domain layer includes the different method components and the developed situational methodologies. Finally, the language layer includes any modeling language that can be used for both describing metamodels and method component models. We chose to use Object-Process Methodology (OPM) [3] as the underlying language in this paper due to its balance treatment of structure and behavior specification, its formality (expressed through a metamodel [24]), and its accessibility to different types of users. OPM combines ideas from object-oriented and process-oriented approaches into a single frame of reference, enabling expression of mutual relationships and effects between objects and processes. Thus, ADOM-SME enables specifying in a single model work units, work products, producers, stages, and model units, as well as the structural and procedural relationships among them.

The rest of the paper is organized as follow. Section 2 reviews recent works in the area of situational method engineering. Section 3 briefly describes ADOM and OPM, while Section 4 introduces and exemplifies the ADOM-SME approach and explains how it supports the different SME activities. Finally, Section 5 concludes and refers to future research plans.

2 Literature Review

Situational Method Engineering (SME) [15, 23] deals with customizing and tailoring methodologies to specific situations. For this purpose, SME approaches treat methodologies as composed of method components, which are stored along with their usage features in method bases. Method engineers are responsible for searching, retrieving, and tailoring method components from those method bases according to the situations that they are facing. A situation in this context can be defined as a vector of characteristics that relate to the organization, the project, the developing team, the customer, etc.

Two main aspects of method components and methodologies are structural (product-related) and behavioral (process-related). Most of the current software development methodologies and a significant part of SME approaches focus on just a single aspect. The software process improvement community, centered on standards such as SPICE [12] and CMM [29], believes that these aspects are not completely separated and the quality of software products, for example, can be improved by improving the quality of the processes that yield them [12]. Other approaches believe that complex systems cannot be viewed as predictable processes and, hence, they suggest concentrating on the products, which are changed less often. Gonzalez-Perez and Henderson-Sellers [6] further claim that products are more people-oriented and better at dynamically reorganizing the work to be done.

Recently, more works have recognized the need to model both process and product aspects of methodologies. Some of them offer connection points for "plugging in" the complementary components, while others refer to the process and product aspects as elementary constituents of the approach. OMG's Software Process Engineering Metamodel (SPEM) [18], for example, is used for describing a concrete software development process or a family of related software development processes. Process enactment, i.e., planning and executing projects, is outside the scope of SPEM, although some examples of enactment are included for explanatory purposes. The OPEN Process Framework (OPF) [21, 32] is a free, public domain, industry-standard approach for the production of endeavor-specific development methods. It consists of a repository of reusable method components documented as hierarchical linked Web pages, including construction and usage guidelines. Its metamodel describes the organizational structure of the repository and includes six types of method components: Endeavor, Language, Producer, Stage, Work Product, and Work Unit. However, OPF mainly concentrates on the methodology layer at the expense of the endeavour layer and its relationships to the methodology layer. Recently, OPF's metamodel was reorganized to fit ISO/IEC 24744. OOSPICE [19] is an expansion of the Software Process Improvement and Capability dEtermination (SPICE) approach that covers Component-based Development (CBD). OOSPICE refers only to the methodology layer and focuses on the processes, technology and quality concerns in component-based software development, neglecting the specification of structural and product aspects of methodologies. Its metamodel is directed at supporting the need for methodologies to be generated at various capability levels [8].

Incorporating experience from different works in the field, ISO/IEC 24744 [5, 13] defines a metamodel for development methodologies that refers to three modeling layers: metamodel, methodology, and endeavour. While the methodology layer is relevant to method engineers and includes models that are constrained and directed by the chosen metamodel, the endeavour layer is relevant to developers and includes models that are constrained and directed by the method in use. Instantiation relations (specified as belonging to the "powertype" class) are defined between these layers, such that an element in the endeavour (methodology) layer is a "powertype" instance of an element in the methodology (metamodel) layer. In particular, methodology elements are specialized into resources, which can be used as they are at the endeavour layer, and templates, which need to be instantiated at the endeavour layer. Five classes of templates and correspondingly five classes of endeavour elements are defined for representing work units, work products, producers, stages, and model units. All these concepts, including the behavioral ones such as work units and stages, are expressed via class diagrams (in UML 1.4.2 notation), text tables, and a natural language, hurting the (semi-) formality of the methodology procedural aspects representation. The designated graphical notation for ISO/IEC 24744 that is proposed in [7] associates for each methodological concept a different symbol. Pre-conditions and post-conditions of actions are expressed as free textual expressions that are linked to the corresponding action symbols. A methodology may be specified in this notation via several diagram types: lifecycle diagrams, which represent the overall structure of a method; enactment, which represent a specific enactment of a method and its relationship to the method specification; process diagrams, which describe the details of the processes used in a method; and action diagrams, which describe the usage interactions between tasks and work products. The notation specification does not explicitly refer to consistency issues between these types of diagrams. In particular, the same element can appear in several diagram types, playing different roles and exhibiting various (contradicting) features.

Mirbel [16] divided SME approaches into three categories according to the different objectives they aim to achieve. The first category focuses on documenting the methodologies and their components (e.g., [22]). The second category deals with retrieving method components and evaluating their similitude (e.g., [2]). The focus of the third category is defining guidelines for reusing, tailoring, and customizing the different method components in daily developer tasks (e.g., [14]). Most SME approaches focus just on one activity, hence, belonging to a single SME category. OPF and SPEM, for example, mainly focus on the representation of method components. ISO/IEC 24744 also concentrates on the representation of method components, but provides implicit mechanisms for retrieving method components and basically tailoring them (e.g., the classes element kind, conglomerate, reference, and source).

To summarize, the main shortcomings of existing SME approaches are: (1) supporting mainly the methodology layer, partially neglecting the endeavour layer which is needed for the developers who use situational methodologies, (2) using an object-oriented modeling language, specifying procedural aspects structurally, (3) applying multi-view approaches, potentially rising consistency problems, and (4) concentrating on just a single SME activity, making other activities more difficult and decreasing the ability for smooth transition between the different SME activities. The purpose of this paper is to present a holistic approach which overcomes these shortcomings without violating the ISO/IEC 24744 standard.

3 ADOM and OPM

The Application-based DOmain Modeling (ADOM) approach [25, 30] aims at handling both reuse and validation of application models according to the domain knowledge. Its framework includes three layers: application, domain, and language. The application layer consists of models of particular applications, including their structure and behavior. The intermediate domain layer consists of specifications of various domains, i.e., families of applications that share common features as well as exhibit variability. Examples of domains that can be included in the domain layer are web applications, multi agent systems, and process control systems. The domain specifications capture the knowledge gained in specific domains in the form of concepts, features, and constraints. Finally, the language layer includes meta-models of modeling languages, such as UML. ADOM is a quite general approach and can be applied to different modeling languages. However, when applying ADOM to a specific modeling language, this language is used in both domain and application layers, easing the inter-layer tasks by employing the same terminology in both layers.

In the context of SME, development methodologies and processes can be considered as a domain. Thus, the application layer, which corresponds to the endeavour layer in ISO/IEC 24744, includes the different method components and the developed situational methodologies, while the domain layer, which corresponds to the methodology layer in ISO/IEC 24744, includes the SME metamodel.

ADOM's reuse process is mainly done by configuration and specialization, such that the constraints enforced by the domain layer provide guidance to the reuse process and the development of models in the application layer. Configuration is the selection of a subset of existing elements from a domain model for the purpose of specifying a lawful specific application model. ISO/IEC 24744 refers to this type of operations through resources, which are methodology elements. Specialization, on the other hand, is the result of applying general knowledge derived from a domain model into a specific application model. In [28] five possible specialization operations are identified: refinement, sub-typing, contextual adoption, omission, and inclusion. ISO/IEC 24744 refers to this type of operations through templates, which are also methodology elements that are "powertype" instantiated by endeavour elements. The ADOM approach also explicitly enforces constraints among the different layers: the domain layer enforces constraints on the application layer, while the language layer enforces constraints on both the application and domain layers. Furthermore, as opposed to ISO/IEC 24744, the ADOM approach explicitly refers to validation issues and, in particular, whether an application model is considered as a valid instantiation of a domain model. More on this issue can be found at [25].

As noted, ADOM can be used with various modeling languages in order to support different development tasks, such as business modeling, requirement elicitation, and analysis and design. Indeed, the only requirement of ADOM from the associated modeling language is to have a classification mechanism that enables categorizing elements according to other elements (UML stereotypes are an example for such mechanism). However, ADOM promotes using the same modeling languages, techniques, and methods in both domain and application layers. The reasons for this are: (1) treating domain models similarly to application models utilizes to the fullest the expressiveness of the modeling language. In particular, it extends the ability to specify behavioral constraints or templates with respect to several domain analysis methods, and (2) using the same terminology in both layers makes the inter-layer tasks easier. In particular, the creation and validation of application models according to domain models in ADOM is quite straight-forward, consequently resulting in a more accessible approach for the developers and a simpler approach for tool developers.

In this work we choose to use Object-Process Methodology (OPM) which supports the coexistence of structural and behavioral specifications in the same model, in order to support handling the five main methodological aspects presented by ISO/IEC 24744: product, process, producer, stage, and model unit. OPM [3] is a holistic approach to the modeling, study, development, and evolution of systems, supported by a CASE tool called OPCAT [20]. The main elements in OPM are entities and links. *Entities* generalize objects, processes, and states. *Objects* are things that exist, while *processes* are things that transform objects by creating or destroying them, or by changing their states. Two main features of OPM entities are *affiliation*, which determines whether the entity is systemic or external (environmental), and *essence*, which determines whether the entity is physical or informational. *Links*, which connect entities (objects, processes, or states), can be structural or procedural. *Structural links* express static, structural relations between pairs of objects or processes. Aggregation, generalization, characterization, and instantiation are the four fundamental structural relations in OPM. General structural relations can take on any semantics, which is expressed textually by their user-defined tags. The behavior of a system is manifested in OPM in three major ways: (1) processes can transform (generate, consume, or change the state of) objects, (2) objects can enable processes without being transformed by them, and (3) objects can trigger events that (at least potentially, if preconditions are met) invoke processes. For each such way, different *procedural links* are defined.

The complexity of an OPM model is controlled through three refinement/ abstraction processes, which enable the user to recursively specify and refine the system under development to any desired level of detail without losing legibility and comprehension of the complete system: in-zooming/out-zooming concentrates on behavioral and procedural refinement/abstraction, unfolding/folding focuses on structural refinement/abstraction, and state expressing/suppressing shows/hides the possible states of an object. These mechanisms enable smooth transition between the different development stages. Furthermore, a set of rules guarantees that the various diagrams in the same model are consistent with each other (these rules are enforced by OP-CAT). Soffer et al. [27] proved that OPM is ontologically complete according to the Bunge-Wand-Weber (BWW) evaluation framework, which aims to be a theoretical foundation for understanding the modeling of information systems.

In OPM, each entity exhibits two additional features: role and multiplicity indicator. Like UML stereotypes, a *role* is a model entity whose information content and form are the same as those of the basic model entity, but its meaning and usage are different. Roles are used within an application model in order to associate an entity to its domain counterpart. They are recorded in the upper left corner of the entity frame.

A special kind of role, called *tailoring info*, may appear in a domain model, indicating the tailoring information of the corresponding elements. As will be explained in Section 4, the tailoring info should get values in the application model rather than be specialized or configured and is used for retrieval purposes. As the number of tailoring info attributes may be very large, separate XML or SGML files can be maintained instead (or in addition to) the visual representation of the tailoring info in the domain models. The exact lists of features that characterize the different types of method components is derived from works that were done in the area of SME, such as [16, 17], from practitioners, and from the element kinds in ISO/IEC 24744.

A *multiplicity indicator*, specified in the domain model, constrains the number of application elements that can be configured or specialized from the same domain element in any application in the domain. The multiplicity indicators of OPM entities (objects, processes, and states) are recorded in the lower right corner of their frame and is optionally many (0..m) by default, i.e., when not explicitly appear. The multiplicity indicators of links are specified closely to the link ends, similarly to cardinalities in application models, and they are mandatory single (1..1) by default, in order to preserve cardinality conventions from the application layer. Note that while link cardinality refers to the number of instantiations of a certain *application concept* in the data layer, multiplicity indicators of links refer to the number of instantiations of a certain *domain concept* (i.e., type) in the application layer.

4 ADOM-SME and Its Supported Activities

In this section, we explain how the different SME activities are supported in the ADOM-SME approach. Section 4.1 refers to the domain (methodology) layer, while Section 4.2 refers to the creation and representation of method components in the application (endeavour) layer. Finally, the retrieval and tailoring activities are the focus of Section 4.3.

4.1 The Methodology Layer in ADOM-SME

Fig. 1 is the top-level diagram in the domain (methodology) layer of ADOM-SME. It includes the five methodological aspects mentioned in ISO/IEC 24744. However, as opposed to ISO/IEC 24744 where all these concepts are represented by object classes, work units and stages are represented in the proposed approach as process classes, emphasizing their procedural and behavioral nature. Due to the OPM ability to characterize objects by processes and processes by objects, one can specify the behavior of objects and associate informational features to processes. Furthermore, as opposed to work products and model units that are systemic (internal) and informational objects, producers are environmental (external) and physical objects that represent human stakeholders or groups of such. Similarly to the "actionType" class in ISO/IEC 24744, ADOM-SME has means for expressing the relationships between processes and products: if a process creates a product than a result link connects them, if a process modifies a product than an effect link connects them, and if a process only reads a product than an instrument link connects them. However, the expressive of ADOM-SME goes beyond that of ISO/IEC 24744 in representing other relationships between the different concepts: a process can consume (destroy) a product, a product or a producer can trigger a process, and a process (product) can consist of other processes (products). Pre-conditions and post-conditions are expressed as objects (possibly in specific states) that are linked via in-coming or out-going links to processes.

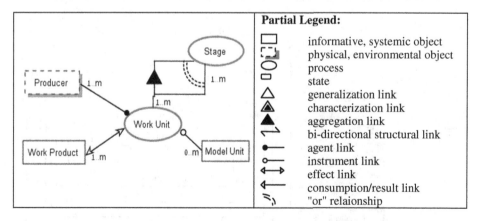

Fig. 1. The top level domain (methodology) model in ADOM-SME

Due to space limitations, we concentrate here on the procedural aspects of the methodology which ADOM-SME uniquely treats, namely work units and stages. A work unit may be triggered by producers and use model units in order to affect (create, destroy, or modify) work products. Unfolding the work unit concept, Fig. 2 shows three specializations of work units: process, task, and technique. A *process* is a large-grained work unit operating within a given area of expertise. Tasks and techniques are small-grained work units: *tasks* focus on *what* must be done in order to achieve given purposes, and *techniques* refer to *how* to achieve these purposes. A process consists of (sub-) processes or tasks, and a technique may be mandatory, recommended, discourage, forbidden, or optional for a certain task [9]. Each work unit may need to save different types of statuses and periods. This is modeled in the domain (methodology) layer as two (mandatory many) attributes that a work unit should exhibit. In addition, work units exhibit four tailoring info attributes: *Min Capability Level*, which refers to the minimal requirements for the maturity of the organization regarding the performance of a given work unit; *Unit Source*, which indicates the methodologies from which the work unit is derived, *Project Duration*, which specifies the duration of projects to which the given work unit is suitable; and *Flexibility to Changes*, which specifies the forgivingness of the given work unit to frequent client changes. For clarity purposes, the tailoring info attributes are grayed, separating them from "regular" attributes in the methodology layer.

In ISO/IEC 24744, stages are used for specifying the temporal aspect of methodologies and method components. Stages are divided into stages with duration, which are managed intervals of time within endeavours, and instantaneous stages, which are managed points in time within endeavours. We extend this usage in order to support tailoring of several work units into more meaningful method components. In other words, stages include different work units and guide their execution. Four common ways to tailor work units are sequentially, concurrently, incrementally, and iteratively. Fig. 3 exemplifies concurrent stages, in which the work units are executed independently and/or in parallel, and iterative stages, in which single work units are executed several times in order to improve the created work products. Both stages are

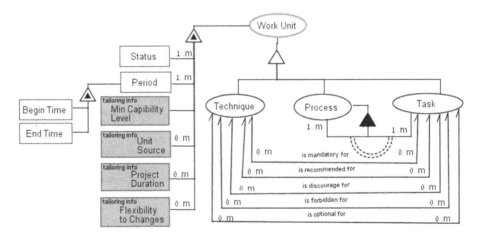

Fig. 2. Unfolding the work unit concept in the domain (methodology) layer of ADOM-SME

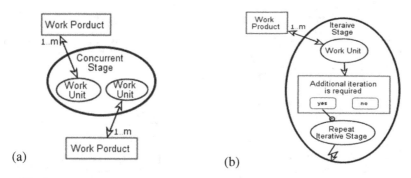

Fig. 3. (a) Zooming into a concurrent stage. (b) Zooming into an iterative stage.

specializations of the Stage concept. Note that in OPM the vertical axis within an in-zoomed process defines the execution order: the sub-processes of a sequential process are depicted in the in-zoomed frame of the process stacked on top of each other with the earlier process on top of a later one, while sub-processes of a parallel process appear side by side, at the same height.

4.2   The Endeavour Layer in ADOM-SME

In the application layer of ADOM-SME, the different (specific) method components and situational methodologies are specified, using the domain model terminology, rules, and constraints. For this purpose, each element in an application (endeavour) model is associated with domain (methodology) elements as its roles, such that an application element has to fulfill all the constraints induced by its associated roles (domain elements) in the domain layer. Furthermore, all the tailoring info attributes of a domain element have to get values (in the form of states) in the corresponding instantiated application elements.

Fig. 4 demonstrates an endeavour method component taken from RUP [26]. All the roles of systemic, informational objects in these figures are specializations of work products as specified in the methodology layer. Fig. 4 (a) zooms into the "Requirement Extraction" process, modeling its conventions, documents, required participants, and the main tasks. Fig. 4 (b) unfolds the task called "obtain an understanding of the domain" to show its recommended and optional techniques. Finally, Fig. 4(c) specifies the situations to which the requirement extraction process is suitable: the organization capability level is at least 2, the project duration is at least one year, and the flexibility to changes is low. The unit source of this component is RUP.

4.3   Retrieving and Tailoring Method Components in ADOM-SME

As noted, in the domain layer of ADOM-SME, the different methodological concepts exhibit tailoring info attributes which are instantiated in the application (endeavour) layer, specifying the exact situations (or ranges of situations) to which a given method component suits. The requirement extraction process from Fig. 4, for example, is suitable for CMMI requirements for Maturity Level of at least 2 [10], for customers who do not impose changes frequently, and for projects that are planned to be developed more than one year.

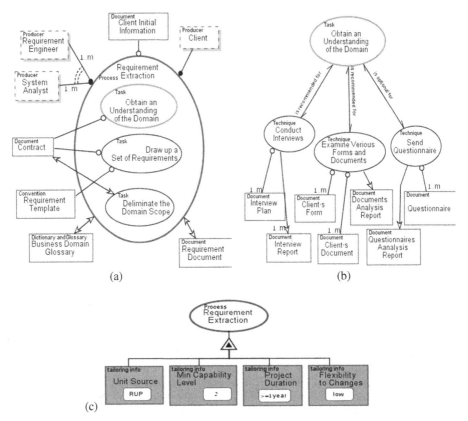

Fig. 4. (a) The "Requirement Extraction" process in-zoomed. (b) The "Obtain an Understanding of the Domain" task unfolded, showing its recommended and optional techniques. (c) The "Requirement Extraction" process unfolded, showing its tailoring info.

For carrying out the retrieval and tailoring activities, we treat the different method components as semantic Web services. Their inputs, outputs, pre- and post-conditions, and triggers are automatically translated to OWL-S [1], while the methodology layer serves as their ontology. Current semantic web services discovery solutions were developed in the context of automatic service composition. Thus, the "client" of the discovery procedure is an automated computer program rather than a human, with little tolerance, if any, to inexact results. However, in our case, method components which might be semantically distanced from each other can be manually glued by method engineers. Hence, we chose to use a semantic approach to approximate service retrieval, called OPOSSUM [31]. OPOSSUM's model relies on a simple and extensible keyword-based query language, and enables efficient retrieval of approximate results, including approximate service compositions. In order to retrieve compositions that contain method components from different methodologies, dependencies between method components are to be inferred. OPOSSUM treats two types of inferring dependencies between Web services (method components in our case): flow and empirical. Two method components q and p are flow-dependent if the output of q can be used as an input of p. Note that the ontology (i.e., the domain model) is used for helping the tool find "correct" input-output matches. Parameter relaxation, concept hierarchy relaxation, instance relaxation, and property relaxation are used for inferring flow dependencies. Empirical dependencies are used when prior knowledge of relations between Web services exists. In particular, we can infer empirical dependencies from stages in the method base that integrate different work units. OPOSSUM handles the following constructs for inferring empirical dependencies: sequence, if-then-else, repeat-until, split, and split+join.

When working with OPOSSUM, the method engineers define queries that specify the situations to which methodologies have to be created: the different types of tailoring info attributes are presented to the method engineers and they need to choose the relevant characteristics and their suitable values. Furthermore, the method engineers can decide whether the tailoring info will be checked for every method component or for complete compositions using aggregated functions, such as min, max, sum, avg, and count. The method base is first searched for method components that satisfy the component-related tailoring info conditions. Then, OPOSSUM runs on the retrieved

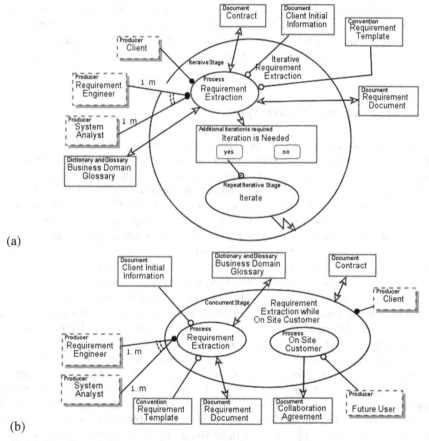

(a)

(b)

Fig. 5. (a) The "Iterative Requirement Extraction" stage. (b) The "Requirement Extraction while On Site Customer" stage.

method components, yielding a ranked list of possible compositions. These compositions are presented to the method engineers as stages that tailor the different work units. The sequence construct, for example, is represented by the sequential stage, the split+join construct is represented by the concurrent stage, and the repeat-until construct is represented by the incremental or iterative stages, depending on the resolution of the work products that it modifies. Fig. 5 exemplifies two tailoring results: in Fig. 5 (a) the "Requirement Extraction" process is tailored iteratively since this process appears so in the context of other methodologies, such as RUP, causing OPOSSUM infer an empirical dependency between an iterative stage and the requirement extraction process. In Fig. 5 (b), the same process is tailored concurrently to the "On Site Customer" work unit, taken from XP [4]. These components are tailored in parallel due to the absence of matching between their inputs and outputs. Note that the similar triggers and effects of these work units (e.g., Client and Contract) are percolated to the wrapping stage "Requirement Extraction while On Site Customer", improving the model readability. In both figures, the "signature" of the requirement extraction process is the same and is achieved by out-zooming Fig 4 (a).

After yielding the ranked list of compositions from OPOSSUM, compositions that violate the composition-related tailoring info are removed. The method engineer, for example, may require getting compositions in which the maximal project duration of their work units is 10 years. Compositions that violate this constraint are removed at this step.

5   Conclusions and Future Work

As there is no single universally applicable development methodology, the importance of SME approaches that support representing, retrieving, and tailoring method components to given situations has been increased. The proposed holistic ADOM-SME approach, whose roots are in domain engineering, overcomes several main shortcomings of existing SME approaches. First, ADOM-SME enables specifying both structural and behavioral aspects of the method components, as well as expressing the relationships between them. Second, the tailoring info attributes, defined in the methodology layer and used in the endeavour layer, support defining situations to which a specific method component suits, while the stage concept provides ways to tailor method components. Third, using OPOSSUM, approximate method component compositions are achieved, enabling the method engineer manually gluing and developing the missing parts. Finally, the ADOM-SME approach is supported by a case tool that helps maintaining the diagrams consistent and enables validating the endeavour models against the methodology models.

As for the future, we plan to extend the repository of method components with methodologies from the literature and from the industry. We further plan to improve and empirically test the tailoring activity. Currently OPOSSUM treats the method components as close boxes (services) and does not refer to their inner structure and behavior. Looking into the method components may enable other, more sophisticated tailoring options. These options and their suitability to different situations will be questioned with experts and practitioners.

References

1. Ankolekar, A., Martin, D.L., Zeng, H.J.R., Sycara, K., Burstein, P.M., Lassila, O., Mcilraith, S.A., Narayanan, S., Payne: DAML-S: Semantic markup for web services. In: Proceedings of the International Semantic Web Workshop (SWWS), pp. 411–430 (2001)
2. Brinkkemper, S., Saeki, M., Harmsen, F.: Assembly techniques for method engineering. In: Pernici, B., Thanos, C. (eds.) CAiSE 1998. LNCS, vol. 1413, pp. 381–400. Springer, Heidelberg (1998)
3. Dori, D.: Object-Process Methodology – A Holistic System Paradigm. Springer, Heidelberg (2002)
4. Extreme Programming Web Site (2006), http://www.extremeprogramming.org
5. Gonzalez-Perez, C.: Supporting Situational Method Engineering with ISO/IEC 24744 and the Work Product Pool Approach. In: Proceedings on Situational Method Engineering: Fundamentals and Experiences, pp. 7–18 (2007)
6. Gonzalez-Perez, C., Henderson-Sellers, B.: A work product pool approach to methodology specification and enactment. J. Syst. Software (2007), doi:10.1016/j.jss.2007.10.001
7. Gonzalez-Perez, C., Henderson-Sellers, B.: Notation for ISO/IEC 24744,
   http://www.sqi.gu.edu.au/sc7-mirror/N3751-N3800/
   07N3781%20MOS-006%20ISO_IEC%2024744%20Notation%
   20-%20NWI%20Form%20V1.0.pdf
8. Gonzalez-Perez, C., McBride, T., Henderson-Sellers, B.: A metamodel for assessable software development methodologies. Software Qual. J (in press, 2004)
9. Graham, I., Henderson-Sellers, B., Younessi, H.: The OPEN Process Specification. Addison-Wesley, Reading (1997)
10. Grundmann, M.: A CMMI Maturity Level 2 assessment of RUP, http://
    www.ibm.com/developerworks/rational/library/dec05/grundmann/
11. Henderson-Sellers, B.: SPI – A Role for Method Engineering. In: Proceedings of the 32nd EUROMICRO Conference on Software Engineering and Advanced Applications (2006)
12. Humphrey, W.S.: Managing the Software Process. MA.ISO/IEC, 2004. ISO/IEC 15504-1. Software Process Assessment – Part 1: Concepts and Vocabulary. Addison-Wesley, Reading (1989)
13. ISO/IEC. ISO/IEC 24744, Software Engineering – Metamodel for Development Methodologies, 1st edn. (2007)
14. Mirbel, I., de Rivieres, V.: Adapting Analysis and Design to Software Context: the JECKO Approach. In: Bellahsène, Z., Patel, D., Rolland, C. (eds.) OOIS 2002. LNCS, vol. 2425, pp. 223–228. Springer, Heidelberg (2002)
15. Mirbel, I., Ralyté, J.: Situational method engineering: combining assembly-based and roadmap-driven approaches. Requirements Engineering 11(1), 58–78 (2006)
16. Mirbel, I.: Rethinking ISD methods: Fitting project team members profiles. I3S technical report I3S/RR-2004-13-FR (2004),
    http://www.i3s.unice.fr/~mirbel/publis/im-isd-04.pdf
17. Mirbel, I.: Method chunk federation (2006),
    http://www.i3s.unice.fr/~mh/RR/2006/RR-06.04-I.MIRBEL.pdf
18. OMG, Software Process Engineering Metamodel Specification, Version 1.1 (2005),
    http://www.omg.org/docs/formal/05-01-06.pdf
19. OOSPICE, http://www.oospice.com/
20. OPCAT inc. OPCAT web site, http://www.opcat.com/,
    http://www.objectprocess.org/
21. OPEN Process Framework (OPF) Web Site, http://www.opfro.org/

22. Punter, H.T., Lemmen, K.: The MEMA-model: towards a new approach for Method Engineering. Information and Software Technology 38(4), 295–305 (1996)
23. Ralyté, J., Deneckere, R., Rolland, C.: Towards a generic model for situational method engineering. In: Eder, J., Missikoff, M. (eds.) CAiSE 2003. LNCS, vol. 2681, pp. 95–110. Springer, Heidelberg (2003)
24. Reinhartz-Berger, I., Dori, D.: A Reflective Metamodel of Object-Process Methodology: The System Modeling Building Blocks. In: Green, P., Rosemann, M. (eds.) Business Systems Analysis with Ontologies, pp. 130–173. Idea Group, Hershey (2005)
25. Reinhartz-Berger, I., Sturm, A.: Enhancing UML Models: A Domain Analysis Approach. Journal on Database Management (JDM) 19(1), 74–94 (2007); special issue on UML Topics
26. Schach, S.R.: An Introduction to Object-Oriented Analysis and Design with UML and the Unified Process. McGraw-Hill/Irwin (2004)
27. Soffer, P., Golany, B., Dori, D., Wand, Y.: Modelling Off-the-Shelf Information Systems Requirements: An Ontological Approach. Requirements Engineering 6(3), 183–199 (2001)
28. Soffer, P., Reinhartz-Berger, I., Sturm, A.: Facilitating Reuse by Specialization of Reference Models for Business Process Design. In: The 8th Workshop on Business Process Modeling, Development, and Support (BPMDS 2007), in conjunction with CAiSE 2007 (2007)
29. Software Engineering Institute, CMMI-SE/SW/IPPD/SS, V1.1, Continuous. CMMI for Systems Engineering/Software Engineering/Integrated Product and Process Development/Supplier Sourcing, Continuous Representation, version 1.1 (2002)
30. Sturm, A., Reinhartz-Berger, I.: Applying the Application-based Domain Modeling Approach to UML Structural Views. In: Atzeni, P., Chu, W., Lu, H., Zhou, S., Ling, T.-W. (eds.) ER 2004. LNCS, vol. 3288, pp. 766–779. Springer, Heidelberg (2004)
31. Toch, E., Gal, A., Reinhartz-Berger, I., Dori, D.: A Semantic Approach to Approximate Service Retrieval. ACM Transactions on Internet Technology 8(1) (2007), OPOSSUM is available at: http://dori.technion.ac.il/
32. Zowghi1, D., Firesmith, D.G., Henderson-Sellers, B.: Using the OPEN Process Framework to Produce a Situation-Specific Requirements Engineering Method. In: Proceedings of SREP 2005, pp. 29–30 (2005)

RETUNE: Retrieving and Materializing Tuple Units for Effective Keyword Search over Relational Databases

Guoliang Li, Jianhua Feng, and Lizhu Zhou

Department of Computer Science and Technology, Tsinghua University,
Beijing 100084, P.R. China
{liguoliang,fengjh,dcszlz}@tsinghua.edu.cn

Abstract. The existing approaches of keyword search over relational databases always identify the relationships between tuples on the fly, which are rather inefficient as such relational relationships are very rich in the underlying databases. Alternatively, this paper proposes an alternative way by retrieving and materializing tuple units for facilitating the online processing of keyword search. We first propose a novel concept of *tuple units*, which are composed of the relevant tuples connected by the primary-foreign-key relationships. We then demonstrate how to generate and materialize the tuple units, and the technique for generating the tuple units can be done by issuing SQL statements and thus can be performed directly on the underlying RDBMS without modification to the database engine. Finally, we examine the techniques of indexing and ranking to improve the search efficiency and search quality. We have implemented our method and the experimental results show that our approach achieves much better search performance, and outperforms the alternative literatures significantly.

1 Introduction

Keyword search is a proven and widely accepted mechanism for querying in textual document systems and World Wide Web. The database research community has recently recognized the benefits of keyword search and has been introducing keyword search capability into relational databases [4,6,20], XML databases [7,10,17,18,27,29], graph databases [11,15], and heterogenous data sources [19,21].

Traditional query processing approaches on relational and XML databases are constrained by the query constructs imposed by the query languages such as SQL and XQuery. Firstly, the query languages themselves are hard to comprehend for non-database users. Secondly, these query languages require the queries to be posed against the underlying, sometimes complex, database schemas. These traditional querying methods are powerful but unfriendly to the non-expert users. Fortunately, keyword search is proposed as an alternative means for querying the underlying databases, which is simple and yet familiar to most internet users as it only requires the input of some keywords. Although keyword search has been

Q. Li et al. (Eds.): ER 2008, LNCS 5231, pp. 469–483, 2008.
© Springer-Verlag Berlin Heidelberg 2008

proven to be effective for textual documents (e.g. HTML documents), the problem of keyword search on the structured data (e.g. relational databases) and the semi-structured data (e.g. XML documents) is not straightforward.

The alternative approaches of keyword search over relational databases can be broadly classified into two categories: those based on candidate networks; and others based on Steiner trees. The Steiner tree based methods first model tuples in the relational database as a graph, where nodes are tuples and edges are primary-foreign-key relationships, and then identify the minimum Steiner trees to answer keyword queries. The Steiner tree based methods have been proved to be an NP-hard problem [6]. The candidate network based methods generate and extend the candidate networks to identify the answers. However, most of the existing literatures always compute the relevant tuples on the fly and neglect that the relevant tuples can be identified and materialized off-line. Alternatively, we generate and materialize the relevant unites off-line so as to facilitate the online processing of keyword queries.

Based on above observations, in this paper, we emphasize on the efficiency and effectiveness of keyword search over relational databases by summarizing and indexing tuples in the underlying relational databases. We propose the concept of *tuple units* to effectively answer keyword queries. We generate and materialize the tuple units, which are composed of relevant tuples connected by primary-foreign-key relationships. We identify the most relevant and meaningful tuple units to answer keyword queries. Moreover, we examine the techniques of indexing and ranking to enhance the search efficiency and search accuracy. To achieve our goal, we propose RETUNE, Retrieving and matErialized Tuple UNits for Effective keyword search over relational databases, to effectively and efficiently answer keyword queries. To summarize, we make the following contributions:

- We propose the concept of *tuple units* to efficiently and effectively answer keyword search over relational databases. We generate and materialize the tuple units off-line so that we can efficiently identify the most relevant tuple units to answer keyword search online according to the materialized units.

- We introduce the technique of generating the tuple units by issuing SQL statements, which can be performed directly on the underlying RDBMS without modification to the database engine and thus can be easily incorporated into RDBMS.

- We examine the techniques of indexing and ranking to enhance the search efficiency and search quality.

- We have implemented RETUNE in MYSQL and SQL Server. The experimental results show that RETUNE achieves better search efficiency and accuracy, and outperforms state-of-the-art methods significantly.

The remainder of this paper is organized as follows. We review related work in Section 2. Section 3 presents our proposal RETUNE. In section 4, we examine the techniques of indexing and ranking to improve the search efficiency and quality. Section 5 reports some experimental results. We make a conclusion in Section 6.

2   Related Work

The alternative approaches of keyword search over relational databases can be broadly classified into two categories: those based on candidate networks [4,12,13]; and others based on Steiner trees [6,8,11,15,23,25]. DISCOVER [13], BANKS [6] and DBXplorer [4] are systems built on top of relational databases. DISCOVER and DBXplorer output trees of tuples connected through primary-foreign-key relationships that contain all the input keywords of a given keyword query, while BANKS identifies the connected trees, namely, Steiner trees, in a labeled graph by using an approximation to the Steiner tree problem, which is proved to be an NP-Complete problem. Hristidis et al [12] studied the problem of keyword proximity search in terms of disjunctive semantics. Kacholia et al [15] presented a technique of bidirectional expansion to improve the search efficiency. Liu et al [22] proposed a novel ranking strategy to solve the effectiveness problem for relational databases, which employs the phrase-based and concept-based models to improve the search effectiveness. Sayyadian et al [25] introduced schema mapping into keyword search and proposed a method to answer keyword search across heterogenous databases. Ding et al [8] employed a technique of dynamic programming to improve the search efficiency of identifying the Steiner trees. He et al [11] proposed a partition based method to improve the search efficiency by adopting a novel BLINKS index. Guo et al [9] proposed data topology search to retrieve meaningful structures from much richer structural data - biological databases. Markowetz et al [24] studied the problem of keyword search over relational data streams.

However, the existing methods always compute the relevant tuples on the fly and neglect that the relevant tuples can be identified and materialized off-line so as to facilitate the online processing of keyword queries. Although Su et al [28] proposed a technique of indexing relational databases to improve the search efficiency, their proposal is orthogonal to our work. Firstly, they modeled the relational databases as a tree structure by connecting the tables through primary-foreign-key relationships, joined the relational tables based on the tree structures, and took the tuples in the joined result as the answers. Alternatively, we group the relevant joined tuples and identify the most meaningful and relevant *tuple units* as the answers instead of the scattered tuples. Secondly, they only consider the document relevance in IR literature to rank answers but neglect the rather rich structural information, which is at least as important as the textual information, and even more crucial in most of cases. Instead, we propose a novel ranking method by taking into both the textual information from the IR point of view and the structural information from the DB viewpoint. Finally, our techniques of indexing and ranking can be performed directly on underlying RDBMS without modification to the database engine and thus can be incorporated into RDBMS.

Our prior work EASE [21] and SAILER [19] studied the problem of effective keyword search on heterogenous data sources. We presented a novel technique of progressive ranking for effective keyword search over relational databases [20].

3   Materializing Tuple Units

The existing methods of keyword search over relational databases usually identify the relevant tuples connected through primary-foreign-key relationships by retrieving the Steiner trees or by computing candidate networks on the fly. However, they are inefficient as it is rather hard to identify the answers on the fly which capture rather rich structural information. In this paper, we propose an alternative method to identify and materialize the relevant tuples off-line so as to facilitate the online processing of keyword queries.

3.1   Notations

This section introduces some notations for ease of presentation. Given a database $\mathcal{D}$ with m relational tables, $\mathcal{R}_1,\mathcal{R}_2,\cdots,\mathcal{R}_m$, let $\mathcal{R}_i \overset{\kappa}{\to} \mathcal{R}_j$ denote that $\mathcal{R}_i$ has a foreign key κ which refers to the primary key of $\mathcal{R}_j$. Two relational tables $\mathcal{R}_i$ and $\mathcal{R}_j$ are connected, denoted as, $\mathcal{R}_i \leadsto \mathcal{R}_j$, if, i) $\mathcal{R}_i \overset{\kappa}{\to} \mathcal{R}_j$; or ii) $\mathcal{R}_j \overset{\kappa}{\to} \mathcal{R}_i$; or iii) $\exists \mathcal{R}_k$, $\mathcal{R}_i \leadsto \mathcal{R}_k$ and $\mathcal{R}_k \leadsto \mathcal{R}_j$. Without loss of generality, we suppose any two relational tables are connected in this paper. If some relational tables are not connected, we decompose the tables into some groups of connected tables and apply our method on the decomposed groups.

The relational table $\mathcal{R}_i$ is called a *link relational table* if there is no relation table $\mathcal{R}_j$, such that, $\mathcal{R}_j \overset{\kappa}{\to} \mathcal{R}_i$. That is, $\mathcal{R}_i$ only contains foreign keys to connect other relational tables but does not contain any primary key.

For example, consider the database with three relational databases in Table 1, we have Write $\overset{\text{AID}}{\longrightarrow}$ Author and Write $\overset{\text{PID}}{\longrightarrow}$ Paper; and Write $\leadsto$ Paper. Write is a link relational table as it has no primary key.

3.2   Tuple Units

Given a database $\mathcal{D}$ with m connected relational tables, $\mathcal{R}_1,\mathcal{R}_2,\cdots,\mathcal{R}_m$, for each tuple $t_i \in \mathcal{R}_i$, we generate the *tuple units* composed of the relevant tuples which have close relationships with t_i, i.e., the tuples connecting with t_i through the primary-foreign-key relationships. To formally describe the tuple unit, we introduce a concept as follows.

Definition 1. *(Tuple Unit) Given a database $\mathcal{D}$ with m connected relational tables, $\mathcal{R}_1,\mathcal{R}_2,\cdots,\mathcal{R}_m$, and a tuple $t_i \in \mathcal{R}_i$, the tuple unit w.r.t. t_i are composed of the tuples in $\bowtie_{j \neq i} \mathcal{R}_j \bowtie \mathscr{R}_i$, where $\mathscr{R}_i$ is the table with only a tuple of t_i.*

We note that $\bowtie_{j \neq i} \mathcal{R}_j \bowtie \mathscr{R}_i$ denotes the join results of t_i with the other relational tables (except $\mathcal{R}_i$). $\bowtie_{j \neq i} \mathcal{R}_j \bowtie \mathscr{R}_i$ can be obtained through iteratively joining the connected tables with t_i as follows. We first find the relational tables which have primary-foreign-key relationships with $\mathcal{R}_i$, and then join $\mathscr{R}_i$ with such tables to generate an intermediate table, where $\mathscr{R}_i$ is a table with only a tuple of t_i. Subsequently, we identify other tables which have primary-foreign key relationships with the intermediate table and join them together. Iteratively,

Table 1. An Example Database

Author

AID	Name
a1	X. Zhou
a2	X. Lin
a3	J. Yu
a4	L. Guo
a5	J. Shanmugasundaram
a6	F. Shao
a7	V. Hristidis
a8	Y. Papakonstantinou
a9	A. Balmin

Write

AID	PID
a1	p1
a2	p1
a2	p2
a3	p2
a4	p3
a4	p4
a5	p3
a6	p4
a7	p5
a7	p6
a8	p5
a9	p6

Paper

PID	Title	Conf	Year
p1	Spark: Top-k keyword query in relational databases	SIGMOD	2007
p2	Finding top-k min-cost connected trees in databases	ICDE	2007
p3	Topology search over biological databases	ICDE	2007
p4	XRank: Ranked keyword search over xml documents	SIGMOD	2003
p5	Discover: Keyword search in relational databases	VLDB	2002
p6	Keyword proximity search on xml graphs	ICDE	2003

Table 2. Tuple Units

(a) Tuple Units on Table *Author*

Tuple Unit	AID	Name	PID	Title	$\cdots$
Ta1	a1	$\cdots$	p1	$\cdots$	$\cdots$
Ta2	a2	$\cdots$	p1	$\cdots$	$\cdots$
		$\cdots$	p2	$\cdots$	$\cdots$
Ta3	a3	$\cdots$	p2	$\cdots$	$\cdots$
Ta4	a4	$\cdots$	p3	$\cdots$	$\cdots$
		$\cdots$	p4	$\cdots$	$\cdots$
Ta5	a5	$\cdots$	p3	$\cdots$	$\cdots$
Ta6	a6	$\cdots$	p4	$\cdots$	$\cdots$
Ta7	a7	$\cdots$	p5	$\cdots$	$\cdots$
		$\cdots$	p6	$\cdots$	$\cdots$
Ta8	a8	$\cdots$	p5	$\cdots$	$\cdots$
Ta9	a9	$\cdots$	p6	$\cdots$	$\cdots$

(b) Tuple Units on Table *Paper*

Tuple Unit	PID	Title	AID	Name	$\cdots$
Tp1	p1	$\cdots$	a1	$\cdots$	$\cdots$
Tp2	p2	$\cdots$	a2	$\cdots$	$\cdots$
		$\cdots$	a3	$\cdots$	$\cdots$
Tp3	p3	$\cdots$	a4	$\cdots$	$\cdots$
		$\cdots$	a5	$\cdots$	$\cdots$
Tp4	p4	$\cdots$	a4	$\cdots$	$\cdots$
		$\cdots$	a6	$\cdots$	$\cdots$
Tp5	p5	$\cdots$	a7	$\cdots$	$\cdots$
		$\cdots$	a8	$\cdots$	$\cdots$
Tp6	p6	$\cdots$	a7	$\cdots$	$\cdots$
		$\cdots$	a9	$\cdots$	$\cdots$

for each tuple $t_i \in \mathcal{R}_i$ ($1 \leq i \leq m$), we can identify the tuple unit w.r.t. t_i through navigating and joining the connected tables.

We observe that the tuple unit w.r.t. t_i contains the most relevant information of t_i, and each tuple unit represents a meaningful and integral unit and thus can be adopted to answer keyword queries. To better understand the concept of *tuple units*, we give a running example as described in Example 1.

Example 1. Consider the database in Table 1. Given tuple t_{a2} in *Author*, to generate the tuple unit w.r.t. t_{a2}, we first identify the tables which have primary-foreign-key relationships with *Author*, i.e., *Write*, and join t_{a2} with *Write*. We then iteratively find the table, *Paper*, which has primary-foreign-key relationships with *Write*. Finally, we join them together and get the tuple unit w.r.t. t_{a2}, i.e., $\mathcal{R}_{a2} \bowtie Write \bowtie Paper$ as illustrated in Table 2. Similarly, we can get all such tuple units as shown in Table 2. We note that the tuple unit $Ta2$ w.r.t. t_{a2}

Table 3. Views and Tuple Units

(a) View				
AID	PID	Name	Title	...
a1	p1	...	...	...
a2	p1	...	...	...
a2	p2	...	...	...
a3	p2	...	...	...
a4	p3	...	...	...
a4	p4	...	...	...
a5	p3	...	...	...
a6	p4	...	...	...
a7	p5	...	...	...
a7	p6	...	...	...
a8	p5	...	...	...
a9	p6	...	...	...

(b) Group on *AID*				
AID	PID	Name	Title	...
a1	p1	...	...	...
a2	p1	...	...	...
	p2	...	...	...
a3	p2	...	...	...
a4	p3	...	...	...
	p4	...	...	...
a5	p3	...	...	...
a6	p4	...	...	...
a7	p5	...	...	...
	p6	...	...	...
a8	p5	...	...	...
a9	p6	...	...	...

(c) Group on *PID*				
AID	PID	Name	Title	...
a1	p1	...	...	...
a2		...	...	...
a2	p2	...	...	...
a3		...	...	...
a4	p3	...	...	...
a5		...	...	...
a4	p4	...	...	...
a6		...	...	...
a7	p5	...	...	...
a8		...	...	...
a7	p6	...	...	...
a9		...	...	...

contains the overall information related to Author $a2$. While the tuple unit $Tp1$ w.r.t. t_{p1} contains the overall information with respect to Paper $p1$.

More importantly, the number of tuple units w.r.t. a tuple t_i is no larger than the number of tuples in the underlying database. We give the upper bound of the number of tuples in any tuple unit as formalized in Lemmas 1 and 2.

Lemma 1. *The number of tuples in the tuple unit w.r.t. t_i is no larger than* $\sum_{j \neq i} |\mathcal{R}_j|$.

Proof. (Sketch) We first prove that, given any two relational tables, $\mathcal{R}_p$ and $\mathcal{R}_q$, such that $\mathcal{R}_p \overset{\kappa}{\to} \mathcal{R}_q$, we have $|\mathcal{R}_p \overset{\kappa}{\bowtie} \mathcal{R}_q| \leq (|\mathcal{R}_p| + |\mathcal{R}_q|)$, as for each tuple $t_p \in \mathcal{R}_p$, there is one and only tuple $t_q \in \mathcal{R}_q$, t_p and t_q are connected. Accordingly, it is easy to figure out that $|\bowtie_{j \neq i} \mathcal{R}_j \bowtie \mathcal{R}_i| \leq \sum_{j \neq i} |\mathcal{R}_j|$.

Lemma 2. *The total number of tuples in all tuple units is no larger than* $m \sum_{i=1}^{m} |\mathcal{R}_i|$.

Proof. Based on Lemma 1, the number of tuple units w.r.t. a relation table is no larger than $\sum_{i=1}^{m} |\mathcal{R}_i|$. Hence, the total number of tuples in all tuple units is no larger than $m \sum_{i=1}^{m} |\mathcal{R}_i|$.

Generally, the number of tuple units is much smaller than the total number of tuples in the underlying databases, as tuple units group relevant tuples together. Recall Example 1, we note that the tuple units w.r.t. the tuples in *Write* can be omitted, as such tuple units are subsumed by the tuple units w.r.t. the tuples in *Author* or *Paper*. This is because *Write* only contains the foreign key but does not contain any primary key. Based on these observations, we only need to preserve the tuple units w.r.t. the tables that have primary keys, i.e., those *non-link* relational tables.

Lemma 3. *Given a database $\mathcal{D}$ with m connected relational tables, $\mathcal{R}_1, \mathcal{R}_2, \cdots,$ $\mathcal{R}_m$. Consider $\mathcal{R}_i$ is a link relational table and $\mathcal{R}_i \overset{\kappa}{\to} \mathcal{R}_j$. Given any tuple $t_i \in \mathcal{R}_i$,* suppose $t_i \xrightarrow{\kappa} t_j$ $(t_j \in \mathcal{R}_j)$, we have $\mathcal{T}_{t_i} \subseteq \mathcal{T}_{t_j}$, where $\mathcal{T}_{t_i}$ and $\mathcal{T}_{t_j}$ respectively represent the tuple units w.r.t. t_i and t_j. $\mathcal{T}_{t_i} \subseteq \mathcal{T}_{t_j}$ denotes that tuples in $\mathcal{T}_{t_i}$ must be in $\mathcal{T}_{t_j}$.

Proof. As $t_i \xrightarrow{\kappa} t_j$, it is easy to figure out that, for any tuple $t_k \in \mathcal{R}_k (1 \leq k \leq m)$, if t_k is connected with t_i, t_k must be connected to t_j through primary-foreign-key κ. Thus, the tuples in $\mathcal{T}_{t_i}$ must be in $\mathcal{T}_{t_j}$. Hence, $\mathcal{T}_{t_i} \subseteq \mathcal{T}_{t_j}$.

Based on above observations, we need not preserve the tuple units for the link relational tables as they are contained in other tuple units as formalized in Lemma 3. For example, given the database in Table 1, the tuple units w.r.t. *Write* must be contained in those of *Author* and *Paper*. Hence, we only preserve the tuple units w.r.t. *Author* and *Paper* as shown in Table 2 and Table 3.

3.3   Views and Tuple Units

As described in above sections, we can identify the tuple units through navigating and joining the connected relational tables. In this section, we propose an alternative method to identify the tuple units using views.

We first join all the connected relational tables through the primary-foreign-key relationships to create a view $\mathcal{V}$[1]. It is easy to figure out that each tuple in $\mathcal{V}$ represents a meaningful and integral unit. We then group the tuples in $\mathcal{V}$ according to the primary keys in underlying databases, and each group is exactly a tuple unit. Finally, we materialize the grouped results to preserve the tuple units for facilitating the online processing of keyword queries.

For example, in Table 1, we can join the three tables to create a view as shown in Table 3(a). There are two primary keys, *AID* and *PID*. We group the tuples in the view based on *AID* and *PID*, and accordingly get the tuple units as illustrated in Table 3(b) and Table 3(c).

Note that we only need to create views on the top of underlying relational databases but do not maintain the physical data. For each primary key, we group the tuples in the view so as to maintain the tuple units w.r.t. the primary key. More importantly, we note that the database-enabled method has the following key features,

1. We can use SQL-based methods to create and materialize the tuple units, which are views on top of the underlying relational databases.
2. The interrelationships between tuples connected by primary-foreign keys are identified and materialized off-line, and thus RETUNE can facilitate the online processing of keyword search over relational databases.
3. The tuple units are more meaningful to answer keyword queries over relational databases as they capture the meaningful and integral information.

---

[1] We may also employ left-join or right-join in some cases. For example, given two relational tables, $\mathcal{R}_i$, $\mathcal{R}_j$, and $\mathcal{R}_i \xrightarrow{\kappa} \mathcal{R}_j$. If there exists a value v in attribute κ of $\mathcal{R}_j$, but v is not referred by any value of attribute κ in $\mathcal{R}_i$, we right-join $\mathcal{R}_i$ with $\mathcal{R}_j$.

4 Indexing and Ranking

We have presented how to identify and materialize the tuple units in Section 3. This section proposes a novel technique of indexing and ranking to improve the search efficiency and search quality.

A straightforward way to score and rank the tuple units is to employ the $TF \cdot IDF$-based method. We can model every tuple unit as a document and take the terms in the tuple units as keywords, and accordingly the technique of indexing and ranking in IR literature can be borrowed and incorporated to answer keyword queries over tuple units.

Suppose that we have gotten the total set (denoted as $\mathcal{U}$) of the tuple units in a given underlying relational database, and there are p distinct tuple units and q keywords in $\mathcal{U}$. Given a tuple unit $u \in \mathcal{U}$ and a keyword k_i ($1 \leq i \leq q$) in u, we denote $tf(k_i, u)$ as the term frequency of k_i in u, which is the number of occurrences of k_i in u; we denote $idf(k_i)$ as the inverse document frequency of k_i, where $idf(k_i) = \frac{p+1}{O_{k_i}+1}$ and O_{k_i} is the number of such tuple units which contain k_i; we denote $ntl(u)$ as the normalized term length, where $ntl(u) = \frac{|u|}{\frac{\sum_{u' \in \mathcal{U}} |u'|}{n}}$ and $|u|$ denotes the number of terms in u.

In traditional IR literature, the ranking methods usually integrate the three metrics to score a tuple unit w.r.t. a keyword query $\mathcal{K} = \{k_1, k_2, \cdots, k_n\}$, as illustrate in Equations 1 and 2, where s is a constant and usually set to 0.2 [22].

$$\text{SCORE}_{\text{IR}}(\mathcal{K}, u) = \sum_{k=1}^{n} \text{SCORE}_{\text{IR}}(k_i, u) \tag{1}$$

$$\text{SCORE}_{\text{IR}}(k_i, u) = \frac{(1 + ln(1 + tf(k_i, u))) * ln(idf(k_i))}{(1 - s) + s * ntl(u)} \tag{2}$$

However, the $TF \cdot IDF$-based method in IR literature may induce ineffectiveness, as the tuple units capture some structural information, which is rather rich in relational databases, as opposed to the textual information in text documents. Moreover, the structural information is at least as important as the textual information, even much more crucial in most of cases. To address this issue, we propose a novel ranking method in Section 4.1.

4.1 Structural Relevance Ranking

This section introduces a novel ranking approach, structural relevance ranking, to score the relevant tuple units so as to effectively answer keyword queries.

Besides the document relevance in IR literature, we should also incorporate the structural compactness of a tuple unit into the ranking function, which evaluates the overall compactness of tuple units. Given a tuple unit u and any two terms in u, t_x and t_y. We can classify t_x and t_y into three categories according to their relationships in the tuple unit as follows.

(i) t_x and t_y are in the same tuple/record and share the same attribute;
(ii) t_x and t_y are in the same tuple/record but are not in the same attribute;
(iii) t_x and t_y are in different tuples/records in u.

It is easy to figure out that, t_x and t_y in category (i) are much more relevant than those in category (ii), which in turn are more relevant than those in category (iii). Based on this observation, we set the distance between two keywords k_i and k_j in a tuple unit u, denoted as $d^u(t_x, t_y)$, as described in Equation 3.

$$d^u(t_x, t_y) = \begin{cases} 0 & t_x \text{ and } t_y \text{ in category } (i); \\ 1 & t_x \text{ and } t_y \text{ in category } (ii); \\ 2 & t_x \text{ and } t_y \text{ in category } (iii). \end{cases} \qquad (3)$$

Accordingly, given a pair of keywords t_x and t_y in a tuple unit u, we evaluate their relevance $\text{REL}^u(t_x, t_y)$ by considering the distance between t_x and t_y.

$$\text{REL}^u(t_x, t_y) = \frac{1}{(d^u(t_x, t_y) + 1)^2} \qquad (4)$$

We note that, given two input keywords k_i and k_j, there may be multiple corresponding terms in the tuple unit. We take the sum of all the $\text{REL}^u(t_x, t_y)$ as the relevance of k_i and k_j w.r.t. u, denoted as $\text{SCORE}_{\text{DB}}^u(k_i, k_j)$, as formalized in Equation 5, where t_x and t_y is the occurrences of k_i and k_j respectively.

$$\text{SCORE}_{\text{DB}}^u(k_i, k_j) = \sum_{t_x \in Occur(k_i), t_y \in Occur(k_j)} \text{REL}^u(t_x, t_y). \qquad (5)$$

where $Occur(k_i)$ denotes the set of occurrences of k_i in tuple unit u.

Accordingly, we can compute the structural compactness of a tuple unit u w.r.t. a keyword query $\mathcal{K} = \{k_1, k_2, \cdots, k_n\}$ as follows,

$$\text{SCORE}_{\text{DB}}(\mathcal{K}, u) = \sum_{1 \le i < j \le n} \text{SCORE}_{\text{DB}}^u(k_i, k_j) \qquad (6)$$

We not that the relevance function, i.e., Equation 4, has a key feature that if t_x and t_y, and t_y and t_z are highly relevant, we have t_x and t_z are also highly relevant as formalized in Lemma 4. Thus, the relevance function is a good metric to capture the structural compactness.

Lemma 4. *Given three terms in any tuple unit u, t_x, t_y and t_z, we have*

$$\text{REL}^u(t_x, t_z) \ge min(\text{REL}^u(t_x, t_y), \text{REL}^u(t_y, t_z)). \qquad (7)$$

Proof. Without loss of generality, we suppose $\text{REL}^u(t_x, t_y) \le \text{REL}^u(t_y, t_z)$.

If t_x and t_y are in category (iii), it is obvious that,
$$\text{REL}^u(t_x, t_z) \ge min(\text{REL}^u(t_x, t_y), \text{REL}^u(t_y, t_z)),$$
as $\text{REL}^u(t_x, t_z) \ge \text{REL}^u(t_x, t_y) = \frac{1}{(d^u(t_x, t_y) + 1)^2} = \frac{1}{9}$.

If t_x and t_y are in category (ii), t_y and t_z are in category (i) or (ii), as $\text{REL}^u(t_x, t_y) \le \text{REL}^u(t_y, t_z)$, thus t_x and t_z are in category (i) or (ii). Hence,

$$\text{REL}^u(t_x, t_z) \geq min(\text{REL}^u(t_x, t_y), \text{REL}^u(t_y, t_z)).$$

If t_x and t_y are in category (i), t_y and t_z must be in category (i), as $\text{REL}^u(t_x, t_y)$ $\leq \text{REL}^u(t_y, t_z)$, thus t_x and t_z must be in category (i). Hence,
$$\text{REL}^u(t_x, t_z) \geq min(\text{REL}^u(t_x, t_y), \text{REL}^u(t_y, t_z)). \qquad \square$$

We integrate the two scores, SCORE_{IR} (Equation 1) and SCORE_{DB} (Equation 6), to rank the relevant tuple units as described in Equation 8, which takes into consideration the document relevance from the IR point of view and also considers the structural compactness of a tuple unit from the DB perspective.

$$\text{SCORE}(\mathcal{K}, u) = \text{SCORE}_{\text{IR}}(\mathcal{K}, u) + \text{SCORE}_{\text{DB}}(\mathcal{K}, u) \qquad (8)$$

4.2 Indexing

Traditional IR literatures usually employ the inverted lists to index the tuple units. The entries of inverted lists are keywords and each entry keeps the tuple units, which contain the keyword, and the corresponding score. The tuple units w.r.t. entry k_i are sorted by $\text{SCORE}_{\text{IR}}(k_i, u)$ in descending order, where $u \in \{u_j | u_j$ contains keyword $k_i\}$.

In addition, to preserve the structural information, we maintain the inverted lists for any keyword pair. For each keyword pair k_i and k_j, we preserve the tuple units, which contain the two keywords and the corresponding score. Similarly, the tuple units are also sorted by $\text{SCORE}_{\text{DB}}^u(k_i, k_j)$ in descending order.

Accordingly, given a keyword query $\mathcal{K} = \{k_1, k_2, \cdots, k_n\}$, we first retrieve the inverted lists of $\mathcal{I}_i(1 \leq i \leq n)$, which is composed of the tuple units that contains keyword k_i, and then get the inverted lists of $\mathcal{I}_{(i,j)}(1 \leq i < j \leq n)$, which is composed of the tuple units that contains both k_i and k_j. Then, we compute the score of each relevant tuple unit and get the *top-k* answers by maintaining a heap. The heap preserves the tuple units with the *top-k* highest scores. If a new tuple unit u has a score larger than that of u' with the minimal score in the heap, we replace u' by u; otherwise, we discard u. Iteratively, we can get the *top-k* answers.

Alternatively, to improve the search efficiency, we employ the database capability to effectively and progressively compute the top-k answers. We maintain a relational *score table* according to the assigned scores so as to facilitate the on-line processing of keyword queries. The *score table* preserves the scores, and the attributes of *score table* are keywords and keyword pairs, and the tuples/records are the corresponding scores of each tuple unit.

To answer a keyword query $\mathcal{K} = \{k_1, k_2, \cdots, k_n\}$, we construct a view $\mathcal{V}_{\mathcal{K}}$ on top of *score table* by taking $k_1, k_2, \cdots, k_n$ and $<k_1, k_2>, <k_1, k_3>, \cdots, <k_{n-1}, k_n>$ as the attributes, and the score of each tuple on them as the tuples/records. Thus, we can issue a SQL statement to answer query $\{k_1, k_2, \cdots, k_n\}$,

> SELECT top k <u>Unit</u> FROM $\mathcal{V}_{\mathcal{K}}$
> ORDER BY sum($k_1, k_2, \cdots, k_n, <k_1, k_2>, <k_1, k_3>, \cdots, <k_{n-1}, k_n>$) DESC.

Accordingly, we can employ the capabilities of RDBMS to identify the top-k answers and seamlessly incorporate our method into RDBMS. We note that there

Table 4. Score Table

SCORE	Keyword	Search	Database	⋯	<Keyword,Search>	<Database,Keyword>	<Database,Search>	⋯
Tp1	0.49	0.19	0.49	⋯	0	1	0	⋯
Tp5	0.54	0.54	0.54	⋯	1	1	1	⋯
Ta4	0.43	0.43	0.17	⋯	1+0.11	0.11	0.11+1	⋯
⋯	⋯	⋯	⋯	⋯	⋯	⋯	⋯	⋯

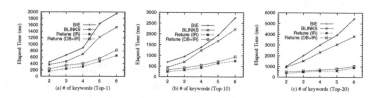

Fig. 1. Search Efficiency on DBLP

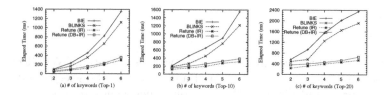

Fig. 2. Search Efficiency on IMDB

are many studies of answering top-k queries in relational databases [5,14,26]. We can borrow them to return the top-k answers. Moreover, the score table is a sparse table as there are many zeros, thus we can employ our techniques [30] to get the top-k answers in the sparse table.

Example 2. Consider the database in Table 1, we construct the score table as shown in Table 4. To answer keyword query $\mathcal{K}=\{$Keyword, Search, Database$\}$, we create the view $\mathcal{V}_\mathcal{K}$ by projecting the six columns from the score table, and then we can return the top-k query by issuing a SQL statement,

> SELECT top k <u>Unit</u> FROM $\mathcal{V}_\mathcal{K}$ ORDER BY sum (Keyword, Search, Database, <Database,Keyword>, <Keyword,Search>, <Database,Search>) DESC.

5 Experimental Study

We have implemented our proposal in real database systems, such as MYSQL 5.0.22 and SQL Server 2005. We reported some obtained experiential results on MYSQL [3] in this section[2]. We compared our algorithm with state-of-the-art algorithms, Bidirectional Expansion approach (abbreviated as BIE) [15], and BLINKS [11]. We employed the DBLP [1] and IMDB (a movie database) [2]

---

[2] We omitted the experimental results on SQL Server 2005 due to space constraints.

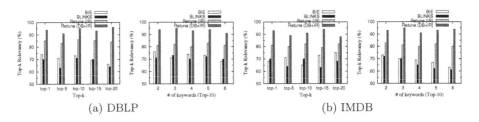

(a) DBLP   (b) IMDB

Fig. 3. Search Accuracy

datasets to compare these algorithms. The raw file of DBLP is about 420MB. IMDB contains about one million anonymous ratings of approximately 3900 movies made by 6040 users. All the experiments were conducted on an Intel(R) Core(TM)2@2.0GHz computer with 2GB of RAM running Windows XP, and all the algorithms were implemented in C++.

5.1 Search Efficiency

This section evaluates the search efficiency of various algorithms. We selected one hundred keyword queries for each dataset and evaluated the selected algorithms on them. Figure 1 and Figure 2 illustrate the experimental results.

To better understand the performance of our ranking method, we tested our algorithm with IR ranking method (RETUNE (IR)) and DB+IR ranking method (RETUNE(DB+IR)). We observe that our algorithms achieve better search performance than the existing state-of-the-art methods, which gives us rich confidence that the materialized views can improve the search efficiency as we need not identify answers on the fly by discovering the relationships between tuples. Moreover, we employ the database capability to improve the search efficiency. Although RETUNE (DB+IR) costs a little longer time than RETUNE (IR), RETUNE (DB+IR) archives better search quality than RETUNE (IR), which will be described in Section 5.2.

5.2 Search Quality

This section evaluates the quality of a search technique in terms of accuracy and completeness using standard precision and recall metrics, where the correct results are the answers returned by the corresponding schema-aware languages such as SQL. Precision measures search accuracy, indicating the fraction of results in the approximate answer that are correct, while recall measures completeness, indicating the fraction of all correct results actually captured in the approximate answer. To compute precision and recall, we first selected one hundred SQL queries and then transformed them to keyword queries by taking the terms of SQL queries as keywords. Finally, we took the answers of SQL queries as the accurate results to compute the precision and recall. As users are usually interested in the Top-k answers, we employed the metric, Top-k precision

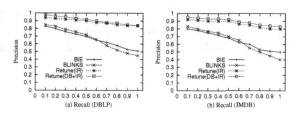

Fig. 4. Precision-Recall Graph

to evaluate the usability, which measures the ratio of the number of relevant answers among the first k answers with highest scores of an algorithm to k.

The obtained experimental results of the average Top-k precision for those selected queries are illustrated in Figure 3. As expected, RETUNE (DB+IR) always achieves more than 90% precision, which is about 10-30% higher than the existing alternative literatures for various queries and different datasets. We note that RETUNE(DB+IR) achieves the best performance. This reflects the effectiveness of our ranking method by taking into account both structural compactness from DB viewpoint and textual relevancy from IR perspective.

To further evaluate the ranking mechanism, we compared the overall precision and recall. Figure 4 shows the precision/recall graph. We observe that RETUNE outperforms alternative methods and always achieves higher precision than state-of-the-art proposals on whatever values of recall. Moreover, the precision of alternative methods falls sharply with the increase of recall, while that of RETUNE varies slightly. This demonstrates the effectiveness of our method.

6   Conclusion

We have studied the problem of effective keyword search over relational databases by retrieving and materializing tuple units. We proposed the concept of tuple units to answer keyword queries, which contain the most relevant tuples and thus can be taken as the answers of keyword queries. Tuple units can be identified and materialized off-line, and thus can improve the search efficiency significantly. More importantly, we can use the capabilities of RDBMS to effectively identify the tuple units and our proposed methods can be easily incorporated into the traditional RDBMS. We also presented a novel ranking method by taking into consideration the structural compactness of relevant tuple units from database point of view. We have implemented our proposal in real systems, and the experimental results show that our method achieves the best performance and outperforms state-of-the-art approaches significantly.

Acknowledgement

This work is partly supported by the National Natural Science Foundation of China under Grant No.60573094, the National High Technology Development

863 Program of China under Grant No.2007AA01Z152 and 2006AA01A101, the National Grand Fundamental Research 973 Program of China under Grant No.2006CB303103, and Basic Research Foundation of Tsinghua National Laboratory for Information Science and Technology (TNList).

References

1. http://dblp.uni-trier.de/xml/
2. http://www.grouplens.org/
3. http://www.mysql.com/
4. Agrawal, S., Chaudhuri, S., Das, G.: Dbxplorer: A system for keyword-based search over relational databases. In: ICDE, pp. 5–16 (2002)
5. Arai, B., Das, G., Gunopulos, D., Koudas, N.: Anytime measures for topk algorithms. In: VLDB (2007)
6. Bhalotia, G., Hulgeri, A., Nakhe, C., Chakrabarti, S., Sudarshan, S.: Keyword searching and browsing in databases using banks. In: ICDE, pp. 431–440 (2002)
7. Cohen, S., Mamou, J., Kanza, Y., Sagiv, Y.: Xsearch: A semantic search engine for xml. In: VLDB, pp. 45–56 (2003)
8. Ding, B., Yu, J.X., Wang, S., et al.: Finding top-k min-cost connected trees in databases. In: ICDE (2007)
9. Guo, L., Shanmugasundaram, J., Yona, G.: Topology search over biological databases. In: ICDE (2007)
10. Guo, L., Shao, F., Botev, C., Shanmugasundaram, J.: Xrank: Ranked keyword search over XML documents. In: SIGMOD, pp. 16–27 (2003)
11. He, H., Wang, H., Yang, J., Yu, P.: Blinks: Ranked keyword searches on graphs. In: SIGMOD (2007)
12. Hristidis, V., Gravano, L., Papakonstantinou, Y.: Efficient ir-style keyword search over relational databases. In: VLDB, pp. 850–861 (2003)
13. Hristidis, V., Papakonstantinou, Y.: Discover: Keyword search in relational databases. In: VLDB, pp. 670–681 (2002)
14. Hua, M., Pei, J., Fu, A.W.C., Lin, X., Leung, H.-F.: Efficiently answering top-k typicality queries on large databases. In: VLDB (2007)
15. Kacholia, V., Pandit, S., et al.: Bidirectional expansion for keyword search on graph databases. In: VLDB, pp. 505–516 (2005)
16. Kimelfeld, B., Sagiv, Y.: Finding and approximating top-k answers in keyword proximity search. In: PODS (2006)
17. Li, G., Feng, J., Wang, J., Zhou, L.: Efficient keyword search for valuable lcas over XML documents. In: CIKM (2007)
18. Li, G., Feng, J., Wang, J., Zhou, L.: Race: Finding and ranking compact connected trees for keyword proximity search over xml documents. In: WWW (2008)
19. Li, G., Feng, J., Wang, J., Zhou, L.: Sailer: An effective search engine for unified retrieval of heterogeneous XML and web documents. In: WWW (2008)
20. Li, G., Feng, J., Zhou, L.: Progressive ranking for efficient keyword search over relational databases. In: BNCOD (2008)
21. Li, G., Ooi, B.C., Feng, J., Wang, J., Zhou, L.: Ease: An effective 3-in-1 keyword search methord for unstructured, semi-structured and structured data. In: SIGMOD (2008)
22. Liu, F., Yu, C., Meng, W., Chowdhury, A.: Effective keyword search in relational databases. In: SIGMOD, pp. 563–574 (2006)

23. Luo, Y., Lin, X., Wang, W., Zhou, X.: Spark: Top-k keyword query in relational databases. In: SIGMOD (2007)
24. Markowetz, A., Yang, Y., Papadias, D.: Keyword search on relational data streams. In: SIGMOD (2007)
25. Sayyadian, M., LeKhac, H., Doan, A., Gravano, L.: Efficient keyword search across heterogeneous relational databases. In: ICDE (2007)
26. Schnaitter, K., Spiegel, J., Polyzotis, N.: Depth estimation for ranking query optimization. In: VLDB (2007)
27. Shao, F., Guo, L., Botev, C., Bhaskar, A., Chettiar, M., Yang, F., Shanmugasundaram, J.: Efficient keyword search over virtual xml views. In: VLDB (2007)
28. Su, Q., Widom, J.: Indexing relational database content offline for efficient keyword-based search. In: IDEAS (2005)
29. Xu, Y., Papakonstantinou, Y.: Efficient keyword search for smallest lcas in XML databases. In: SIGMOD, pp. 527–538 (2005)
30. Yu, B., Li, G., Sollins, K., Tung, A.K.H.: Effective keyword-based selection of relational databases. In: SIGMOD, pp. 139–150 (2007)

Model Driven Specification of Ontology Translations[*]

Fernando Silva Parreiras[1], Steffen Staab[1], Simon Schenk[1],
and Andreas Winter[2]

[1] ISWeb — Information Systems and Semantic Web,
Institute for Computer Science, University of Koblenz-Landau
Universitaetsstrasse 1, Koblenz 56070, Germany
{parreiras,staab,sschenk}@uni-koblenz.de
[2] Institute for Computer Science, Johannes-Gutenberg-University Mainz
Staudingerweg 9, Mainz 55128, Germany
winter@uni-mainz.de

Abstract. The alignment of different ontologies requires the specification, representation and execution of translation rules. The rules need to integrate translations at the lexical, the syntactic and the semantic layer requiring semantic reasoning as well as low-level specification of ad-hoc conversions of data. Existing formalisms for representing translation rules cannot cover the representation needs of these three layers in one model. We propose a metamodel-based representation of ontology alignments that integrate semantic translations using description logics and lower level translation specifications into one model of representation for ontology alignments.

1 Introduction

The reconciliation of data and concepts from different ontologies and data repositories in the Semantic Web requires the discovery, the representation and the execution of ontology translation rules. Though most research attention is now devoted to the discovery of alignments between ontologies, a shallow inspection of ontology alignment challenges already reveals that there does not exist *one* easily accessible way of representing such alignments as translation rules [1].

The reason is that alignments must address ontology translation problems at different layers [2] [1]:

1. At the *lexical layer* it is necessary to arrange character sets, handling token transformations.
2. At the *syntactic layer* it is necessary to shape language statements according to the appropriate ontology language grammar.
3. At the *semantic layer* it is necessary to reason over existing ontological specifications and data in both the source and the target ontologies.

---

[*] This work is supported by CAPES Brazil and EU STReP-216691 MOST.

Q. Li et al. (Eds.): ER 2008, LNCS 5231, pp. 484–497, 2008.
© Springer-Verlag Berlin Heidelberg 2008

For addressing ontology translation problems at the semantic layer, existing frameworks provide reasoning in one or several logical paradigms, such as description logics [3] [4] or logic programming [5] [6] [7]. For addressing ontology translation problems at lexical and syntactic layers, alignment frameworks take advantage of platform-specific implementations, sometimes abstracted into translation patterns [8] [9] or into logical built-ins [7].

Such hybrid approaches, however, easily fail to provide clarity and accessibility to the modelers who need to see and understand translation problems at semantic, lexical and syntactic layers. Indeed, modelers need to manage different languages: (1) an ontology translation language to specify translation rules and (2) a programming language to specify built-ins, when the ontology translation language does not provide constructs to completely specify a given translation rule. This intricate and disintegrated manner draws their attention away from the alignment task proper down into diverging technical details of the translation model.

Filling the gap in ontology translation domain between ontology mapping languages and general purpose programming languages helps to improve productivity, since modelers will not have to be aware of platform-specific details and will be able to exchange translation models even when they use different ontology translation platforms. Moreover, maintenance and traceability would be facilitated because mapping knowledge is not longer embedded in source code of programming languages anymore.

We propose an platform independent approach for ontology translation based on model-driven engineering (MDE) of ontology alignments. The framework includes a language to specify ontology translations, the Model-Based Ontology Translation Language (MBOTL). In order to reconcile *semantic* reasoning with idiosyncratic *lexical* and *syntactic* translations, we integrate these three different translation problems into a representation based on a joint metamodel. The joint metamodel comprises, among others, the OWL-DL metamodel and the OCL metamodel to support specification, representation and execution of ontology translations.

The paper is organized as follows: The running example and the requirements for ontology translation approaches are explained in Section 2. Our solution is described in Section 3, followed by examples in Section 4. In Section 5 we discuss the requirements evaluation and in Section 6 we present related work. The conclusion, Section 7, finishes the paper with an outlook to future work.

2   Running Example and Requirements

We consider two ontologies of bibliographic references from the test library of the Ontology Alignment Evaluation Initiative (OAEI) [1] to demonstrate the solution presented in this paper: the reference ontology (#101) and the Karlsruhe ontology (#303). Canonical mappings covered by examples in this paper and snippets of the source and target ontologies using the Manchester OWL Syntax are shown in Fig. 1. Please refer to OAEI for complete ontologies.

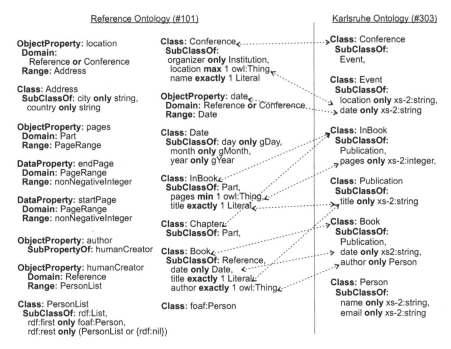

Fig. 1. Ontology mapping challenge for the running example

By examining the mapping between ontology #101 and ontology #303, it becomes clear that translations are required in order to completely realize the mapping. Individuals of the classes Chapter and InBook in ontology #101 are translated into individuals of the class InBook in the ontology #303. Values of the object property month having a Gregorian month, e.g., ''--01'', are translated into the equivalent unabbreviated form, e.g., ''January''. Values of the data property pages in ontology #303 can be calculated by subtracting the value of the data property initialPage from the value of the property endPage in ontology #101.

We define the translation rules explained above by the following logical rules. All variables are treated as universally quantified and prefixed with a question mark. Let *builtin: notShortened* be a built-in function that returns the unabbreviated month, *builtin: toUpper* be a built-in function to capitalize strings, *builtin:* − be a subtractor function, *s* be the namespace prefix of the source ontology #101, and *t* be the namespace prefix of the target ontology #303, the translation rules can be written as follows:

$$t: InBook(?x) \land t: month(?x, ?m) \land t: title(?x, ?n) \land t: pages(?x, ?p) \leftarrow$$
$$(s: InBook(?x) \lor s: Chapter(?x)) \land s: month(?x, ?y) \land$$
$$builtin: notShortened(?y, ?m) \land s: title(?x, ?z) \land builtin: toUpper(?z, ?n) \land$$
$$s: pages(?x, ?w) \land s: startPage(?w, ?a) \land s: endPage(?w, ?e) \land$$
$$builtin: -(?e, ?a, ?p). (1)$$

The translation rule of authors is not trivial as well. While in ontology #101 the authors are collected by recursively matching the property `first` of the class `PersonList`, in ontology #303 it is a matter of cardinality of the object property `author`. Let *list:contains* be the built-in able to filter a list structure into object properties, the referred rule can be written as follows:

$$t: Book(?x) \land t: author(?x, ?u) \leftarrow$$
$$s: Book(?x) \land s: author(?x, ?y) \land list: contains(?y, ?u). \qquad (2)$$

However, built-ins are black boxes that conceal knowledge about algorithms, compromising traceability and maintenance. Therefore, an approach able to specify rules and built-ins without code specifics is required.

From inspecting these examples, we illustrate requirements for a platform independent ontology translation approach addressing translation problems at the following ontology translation layers proposed by Corcho and Gómez-Pérez [2] based on Euzenat [1]: the lexical layer, the syntactic layer, the semantic layer and the pragmatic layer. Since the pragmatic layer addresses the meaning of representation in context, it is similar to the semantic layer from the point of translation decisions. In this paper, we refer to both layers as semantic layer.

1. The lexical layer deals with distinguishing character arrangements, including:
   (a) *Transformations of element identifiers.* They are required when different principles are applied to name objects, for example, when transforming the value of the data property `title` into capital letters (Rule 1).
   (b) *Transformations of values.* They are necessary when source and target ontologies use different date formats, for example transforming a Gregorian month into an unabbreviated form (Rule 1).
2. The syntactic layer covers the anatomy of the ontology elements according to a defined grammar. The syntactic layer embraces:
   (a) *Transformations of ontology element definitions.* They are needed when the syntax of source and target ontologies are different, e.g., when transforming from OWL 1.0 RDF syntax[1] into OWL 1.0 XML syntax[2].
   (b) *Transformations of datatypes.* They involve the conversion of primitive datatypes, e.g., converting string datatype to date datatype.
3. The semantic layer comprises transformations dealing with the denotation of concepts. We consider two different aspects:
   (a) *Inferred knowledge.* Reasoning services are applied to deduce new knowledge, for example, inferring properties from class restrictions.
   (b) *Transformations of concepts.* It takes place when translating ontology elements using the same formalism, e.g, translating a concept from Karlsruhe's OWL ontology for bibliographic references into on or more concepts in the INRIA's OWL ontology.

---

[1] http://www.w3.org/TR/rdf-syntax-grammar/
[2] http://www.w3.org/TR/owl-xmlsyntax/

The translation problems are classified in non-strict layers, e.g., one rule commonly addresses more than one translation problem. For example, in Rule 2, the built-in `toUpper` solves a translation problem at the lexical layer, the translation of months happens at the syntactical layer and is achieved by the built-in `notShortened` and, finally, the translation of the union of individuals of the classes `Chapter` and `InBook` in ontology #101 into individuals of the class `InBook` in ontology #303 appears at the semantic layer.

An orthogonal classification of ontology translation problems is given by Dou *et al.* [6]. From their point of view, ontology translation problems comprise dataset translation, ontology-extension generation and querying through different ontologies. This paper concentrates on dataset translation, i.e., translation of instances, leaving the model driven engineering of the remaining problems for future work.

3   A Model Driven Framework for Ontology Translations

The proposed ontology translation approach relies on advances in Model Driven Engineering (MDE) with support for Description Logic reasoning services [10] [11]. We define here the Model-Based Ontology Translation Language (MBOTL) comprising (1) a textual concrete syntax used to write translation rules, (2) an integrated metamodel as abstract syntax to represent the translation rules as models, (3) an extensible model library to provide built-in constructs, (4) model transformations yielding translational semantics and (5) a pilot implementation with model transformations to the target framework implementing ontology translation, in this case SPARQL and Java. Please, refer to the project web site [12] for complete specifications of these artifacts.

3.1   Concrete Syntax

While visual notations are effective in communicating models, textual notations are preferable to express more complex structures. The following subsections present the anatomy of the translations rules, alluding to the requirements presented in Section 2.

Dealing with Translation Problems at Semantic Layer. In order to extract information from the source ontology, we need a query language able to determine which datasets are to be translated. We use OCL expressions to formulate queries. Indeed, OCL has been used in MDE for specifying constraints and queries that are side effect free operations. As OCL is originally designed to be used with UML or MOF, we have extended OCL to be used with OWL [11], i.e., to support reasoning operations.

Ontology translation problems at the semantic layer are treated by querying individuals of the source ontology using OCL queries and matching target individuals. Queries are part of the input pattern in a transformation rule, that has an output pattern as well with variables binding the elements. Variables are declared and used as in classical programming. These assumptions have been used by model transformation languages like OMG MOF Query/View/Transformation (QVT) and the Atlas Transformation Language (ATL) [13]. We base MBOTL upon the ATL concrete syntax to specify ontology translations because it is simpler and more intuitive.

The example depicted in Fig. 2 illustrates the concrete syntax. A rule `Conference2Conference` is defined for translating individuals of the class `Conference` in ontology #101 into individuals of the class `Conference` in ontology #303.

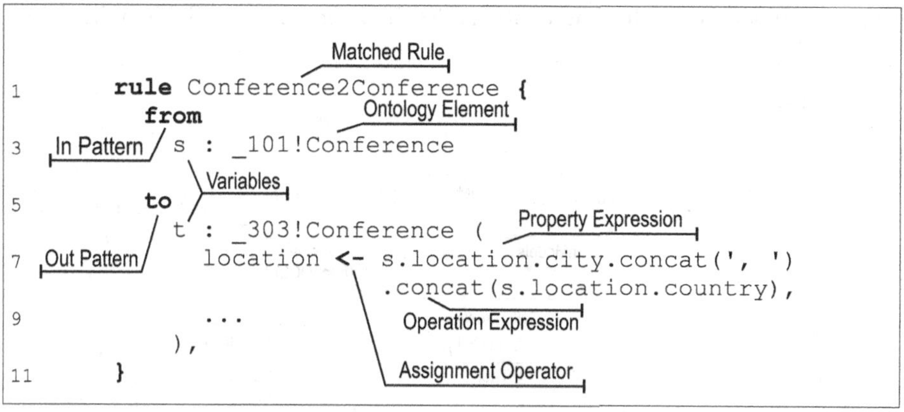

Fig. 2. Example of a Translation Rule

In OCL, a dot-notation is used to navigate through properties. In the scope of our extension of OCL, a property can be an OWL data property, an OWL object property, a predefined operation or a helper. A helper is an user defined side effect free query operation belonging to a defined class in one of the given ontologies.

For example, in the expression `s.location`, `s` is a reference to an individual of the class `Conference` with `location` resulting in a value of the class `Address`. The navigation can also end with an operation evaluation, as depicted in Fig. 2, where the operation `concat` is used to concatenate the properties `city` and `country`.

Addressing Translation Problems at Lexical and Syntactic Layers. Ontology translation problems at lexical and syntactic layers are supported by means of employing operations or helpers. For example, for the type `string`, the operation `toUpper()` returning an string object with capital letters is available. Thus, the evaluation of `s.title.toUpper()` capitalizes the value of the property `title`.

The operation `toUpper()` is an example of predefined operation. The set of predefined operations is available in the OCL library (M1 layer). These operations are applicable to any type in OCL. Additionally, it is possible to specify *ad hoc* operations, the so-called helpers.

3.2 Metamodels

The textual concrete syntax for ontology translation specification presented in the previous section has an integrated metamodel as equivalent abstract syntax. The integrated metamodel consists of the following metamodels: MOF metamodel, OCL metamodel, OWL metamodel [14], and part of the ATL metamodel [13]. As a matter of space, we do not present the complete metamodels in this paper, but noteworthy fragments. A detailed version is available online [12].

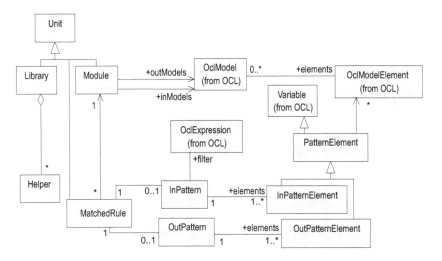

Fig. 3. Fragment of the ATL Metamodel

The translation metamodel (Fig. 3) allows for describing translations between two ontologies by means of a model. A translation is characterized as a `Module` relating source ontologies (`inModels`) and target ontologies (`outModels`). A `MatchedRule` is a specific translation rule that has a pattern for the input model (`inPattern`) and a pattern for the output model (`outPattern`). The `InPattern` has one or more elements that are OCL variables (`Variable`). Variables are bound to model elements (`OclModelElement`). The `InPattern` has an `OclExpression` acting as query to refine individuals of the `OclModelElement`.

Since each expression in OCL has a type, we need a type metamodel (Fig. 4). The expression evaluation produces a value of type of the expression . The type `TUClass` is the particular composition of the OWL class with the MOF class. This composition allows for applying side effect free operations into individuals of OWL classes, e.g., reasoning operations.

Figure 4 depicts additionally another part of the integrated metamodel, namely the package `Expressions` of the extended OCL metamodel. The class

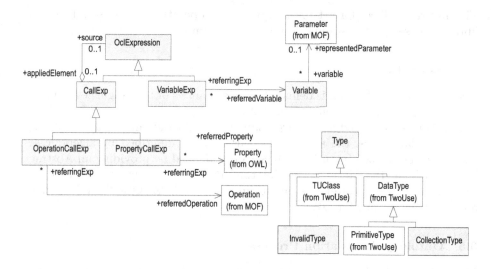

Fig. 4. Snippet of the package **Type** and package **Expressions** of the OCL metamodel

OclExpression enables MBOTL to define the abstract syntax for OCL expressions. The integration with the OWL metamodel is accomplished by expressions of type **PropertyCallExp**. Such expression allows for navigating through OWL properties, as explained in Sect. 3.1.

The operation call expressions (**OperationCallExp**) support the declaration of built-in operations and helpers. An operation call expression evaluates to the result of a class operation, providing that such operation is side effect free. This resource is particularly relevant in the scope of ontology translation, i.e., it enables queries to invoke built-in reasoning operations or helpers.

3.3   Model Libraries

The model libraries define a number of datatypes, class identifiers and operations that must be included in the implementation of MBOTL. These constructs are instances of an abstract syntax class. The foundation library exists at the M1 level, where the abstract syntax (metamodel) exists at M2 level. The foundation library is composed of the XML Schema Datatypes library, the RDF library, the OWL library and the OCL library.

Examples of M1 objects of the XML Schema datatypes library are the datatypes gDay, gMonth and gYear, having the M2 class RDFS::RDFSDatatype as metaclass. In the RDF library, for example, the M1 object nil has the M2 class RDFS::RDFList as metaclass. In the OWL library, interesting M1 objects are Thing and Nothing, both having the M2 class OWL::OWLClass as metaclass. These three libraries are based on the foundation library for RDF and OWL described in the ODM specification [14].

An example of M1 object of the extended OCL library is the construct oclAny. All types inherit the properties and operations of oclAny, except collection types.

This invariant allows for attributing predefined operations to classes. The OCL library is based on the standard OMG OCL library.

3.4   Semantics

The semantics of MBOTL is defined by the semantics of the languages comprising the integrated metamodel (Sect. 3.2).

MBOTL is translated into a target language (SPARQL and Java). Regarding the target languages, the semantics of SPARQL is described by algebraic semantics whereas the semantics of Java can be defined by providing an Abstract State Machine [15]. More specifically, the SPARQL basic graph pattern is described according to an entailment regime. Indeed, SPARQL-DL [16] provides an entailment regime for OWL-DL.

3.5   Ontology Translation Process

In order to guide the user from the ontology translation specification until the running code, the ontology translation process covers the following steps:

1. *Specification of Ontology Translation.* The ontology translation rules and helpers are specified by the user using MBOTL.
2. *Specification of Model Transformations.* In order to have a running implementation of ontology translation, the ontology translation specification model is transformed into models for a given platform. The model transformation specification mapping the MBOTL model onto platform specific models must be specified here. Our framework provides model transformations from MBOTL into SPARQL and Java as target platforms. Notice that other target platforms like F-Logic (Ontobroker) can be considered.
3. *Transformation into Target Platform.* Three transformations take place at this step. Firstly, the ontology translation specification in the concrete syntax (MBOTL file) is injected into a model conforming with the integrated metamodel, i.e, the ontology translation specification model. The second transformation is responsible for generating models according to the target metamodels, e.g., SPARQL and Java metamodels. Thirdly, SPARQL queries in the SPARQL concrete syntax and Java code are extracted from the SPARQL and Java MOF-based models.

3.6   Implementation

The implementation comprises (1) the environment to specify ontology translations and (2) transformations into ontology translation engines in order to realize ontology translation.

We have an implementation covering the MDE process for parts of MBOTL and we are currently working towards a comprehensive solution. Our implementation uses the Generative Modeling Technologies (GMT) project [17] under the Eclipse Modeling Framework. The Textual Concrete Syntax component (TCS)

[18] of the Eclipse GMT is used to specify the concrete syntax used to write dataset translations (1). Furthermore, such component allows for automatically translating the specification into a model conforming with the proposed integrated metamodel, i.e., the ontology translation specification model.

Taking the ontology translation specification model as source model, we use the Atlas Transformation Language [13] framework including Textual Concrete Syntax (TCS) to define model transformations into models for an ontology translation platform (2). We are currently using SPARQL and Java as target languages and the Jena framework as ontology translation solution. The Jena framework includes an API for OWL ontologies and reasoners, as well as a SPARQL engine.

Elements of the ontology translation specification model concerning translation problems at the semantic layer are transformed by ATL into SPARQL CONSTRUCT queries. The SPARQL engine can be extended using custom SPARQL filter functions — as foreseen as an extension hook in the SPARQL standard, but also using so called *predicate functions*. Predicate functions are not matched against the knowledge base like normal RDF predicates, but evaluated in Java code. Filter and predicate functions are used to handle translation problems at the lexical and syntactic layer. These functions are defined in the ontology translation specification model and have the Java code automatically generated by the ATL transformation.

The next section illustrates our approach by addressing the translation problems presented in Section 4, specifying the translation rules and transforming the ontology translation specification into SPARQL and Java code.

4   Application

This section presents rules integrating translations problems at semantic, syntactic and lexical layers, according the problems presented in Section 2. For further details and examples please refer to the Technical Report [12].

The classes **Chapter** and **InBook** in ontology #101 are translated into the class InBook in the ontology #303. The translation rule uses a helper to transform a Gregorian month, e.g., ''--01'', into its equivalent unabbreviated form, e.g., ''January''. This helper is applicable only to the gMonth datatype. Using MBOTL, we can specify both the rule and the helper — and hence lexical, syntactical and semantical translations — using an integrated framework. The helper is shown on top of listing 1.1, followed by the translation rule.

Listing 1.1. Semantic, syntactic and lexical translations with MBOTL

```
1 helper context _101!gMonth
    def: notShortened() : String =
      Sequence{'January','February','March'}->at(
        Sequence{'--01','--02','--03'}->indexOf(self.toString()))
5
    rule ChapterInBook2Inbook {
      from
```

```
          s  :  _101 ! Part  (s.owlIsInstanceOf(Chapter)  or
                                s.owlIsInstanceOf(Inbook))
10    to
          t  :  _303 ! Inbook  (
                title  <- s.title.toUpper(),
                pages  <- s.pages.endPage - s.pages.startPage,
                month  <- s.date.month.notShortened(),
15        )
      }
```

After we have been able to specify all aspects of the mapping in MBOTL, it is translated into suitable languages for execution. Our implementation uses SPARQL queries for semantic mappings and Java code for syntactic translations.

As we can see from the examples, helpers are used for lexical and syntactical translations and semantic translations.

5   Requirements Evaluation and Discussion

In response to the requirements deduced in Sect. 2, Table 1 shows use cases according to each requirement and where to find the corresponding examples in this paper.

Table 1. Satisfying ontology translation requirements

Requirement (Sect. 2)	Use Case	Implementation
1.(a)	converting to capital letters	Listing 1.1, Line 12
1.(b)	converting date formats	Listing 1.1, Line 14
2.(b)	converting gMonth to String	Listing 1.1, Line 14
3.(a)(b)	Union of Chapter and InBook	Listing 1.1, Line 8-9

Translation problems of lexical nature, like converting a string to an upper case string, are managed by using predefined OCL operations applied to specific types of objects, in this example a string type. It is also possible to write functions, i.e., helpers, to perform *ad hoc* operations. For example, the helper notShortened (Listing 1.1) allows for converting date formats, i.e., replacing a value of gMonth type to the unabbreviated form.

Translation problems inherent in the syntactic layer are handled distinctly. While datatype conversions are achieved by invoking predefined operations, like toString() (Listing 1.1), the translation from OWL RDF/XML to OWL XML can be accomplished by injectors and extractors to serialize the models (not shown in this paper).

Translation problems at the semantic layer, regarding datasets of ontologies with different vocabularies but the same formalism is demonstrated by the running example. In Listing 1.1, the individuals of the class Chapter in ontology

#101 and the individuals of the class InBook are translated into individuals of the class InBook in ontology #303.

Limitations. Our approach has some restrictions reflected by the ATL meta-model, i.e., it is possible to realize only unidirectional translations. A bidirectional translation must be accomplished by two unidirectional translations.

Moreover, at the current state of development, it is not possible to validate translation models. In other words, it is not possible to test the translation model without transforming it into the target platform (SPARQL and Java).

6   Related Works

Since a lot of work has been done in the field of ontology alignment, we group works according to semantic, syntactic and lexical layers.

Among works covering lexical and syntactic translations, Model transformation languages like OMG QVT and ATL [13] allow for defining how to transform MOF-based models using declarative and imperative constructs. Nevertheless, their semantics does not support reasoning over OWL ontologies. Our contribution extends ATL by integrating with the OWL metamodel and rewriting OCL semantics to support querying OWL ontologies.

The work of Atzeni *et al.* [19] is based on a metamodel approach with models described in terms of the constructs they involve, taken from a given set of predefined ones. However, the work is in the scope of databases and does not support reasoning at the semantic layer.

Among works covering semantic reasoning capabilities, C-OWL [3] and the ontology mapping system proposed by Haase and Motik [4] are formal solutions for ontology mapping with DL expressiveness. The mappings are based on subsumption relationships of concepts between ontologies. Notwithstanding, the usage of built-ins to express lexical and syntactic translation problems is not possible. A metamodeling-based approach of Haase and Motik [4] is provided by Brockmans *et al.* [20]. Although the usage of built-ins in mapping rules is allowed, the latter approach does not provide means do specify built-ins without recourse to programming languages, whereas MBOTL allows for specifying *ad hoc* functions by means of helpers.

Covering lexical, syntactic and semantic translations, MAFRA [8] and RDFT [9] are frameworks enabling dataset translations. Nonetheless, both are based on RDF Schema and neither they provide the expressiveness of OWL-DL nor support reasoning capabilities of DL inference engines.

OntoMorph [5] and the framework proposed by Dou [6] for ontology translation rely on First Order Logic (FOL) expressiveness to specify translation rules. Our approach counts on the decidable subset of FOL, i.e., Description Logics with complete and sound automated reasoning services for addressing semantic translation problems. Moreover, while the first solution relies on PowerLoom and the latter on Web-PDDL, we propose a platform independent model-based translation language, flexible enough to be used with different knowledge representation system.

OntoMap [7] is a mapping solution allowing for visual specification of mappings, with a limited number of translation functions. Snoogle [21] is an ontology translation tool that enables the use of SWRL rules to express translations and alignments between geospatial ontologies. While in both approaches it is possible to use custom plug-ins, the user has to write functions using Java and the Jena framework. In contrast, our approach allows for specifying mapping rules and functions in a platform independent and integrated way.

Corcho and Gómez-Pérez [22] propose ODEDialect, a set of declarative languages to specify ontology translations. However, it is platform specific approach based on Java that exposes users to complexity of programming languages, whereas MBOTL allows modelers to concentrate on business logics instead.

7   Conclusion

This paper presents a solution for ontology translation specification that aims at being more expressive than ontology mapping languages and less complex and fine-grained than programming languages. The solution is comprised of a concrete syntax, an integration metamodel covering OWL, MOF, OCL and ATL metamodels and model transformations from MBOTL into SPARQL and Java. We validate our solution against canonical ontology translation problems grouped into three layers: lexical, syntactic and semantic.

Future Work. Future areas of investigation involve different ontology translation problems like query translation and ontology-extension generation. The application of the proposed solution in networked environments is of particular interest for the field of distributed ontologies as well as the integration with the ontology mapping metamodel. Therefore, we plan to integrate the Eclipse Plug-ins into the Neon toolkit[3].

References

1. Euzenat, J., Shvaiko, P.: Ontology Matching. Springer, Heidelberg (2007)
2. Corcho, Ó., Gómez-Pérez, A.: A layered model for building ontology translation-systems. Int'l Journal on Semantic Web & Information Systems 1(2), 22–48 (2005)
3. Bouquet, P., Giunchiglia, F., van Harmelen, F., Serafini, L., Stuckenschmidt, H.: C-OWL: Contextualizing Ontologies. In: Fensel, D., Sycara, K.P., Mylopoulos, J. (eds.) ISWC 2003. LNCS, vol. 2870, pp. 164–179. Springer, Heidelberg (2003)
4. Haase, P., Motik, B.: A mapping system for the integration of OWL-DL ontologies. In: Proc. of IHIS 2005, pp. 9–16. ACM Press, New York (2005)
5. Chalupsky, H.: OntoMorph: A Translation System for Symbolic Knowledge. In: Proc. of KR 2000, Colorado,USA, pp. 471–482. Morgan Kaufmann, San Francisco (2000)
6. Dou, D., Macdermot, D., Qi, P.: Ontology translation on the semantic web. LNCS Journal of Data Semantics 2(3360), 35–57 (2004)

---

[3] http://www.neon-toolkit.org/.

7. Maier, A., Schnurr, H.P., Sure, Y.: Ontology-based information integration in the automotive industry. In: Fensel, D., Sycara, K.P., Mylopoulos, J. (eds.) ISWC 2003. LNCS, vol. 2870, pp. 897–912. Springer, Heidelberg (2003)
8. Omelayenko, B.: RDFT: A mapping meta-ontology for business integration. In: Proc. ofWorkshop on Knowledge Transformation for the Semantic for the Semantic Web (KTSW 2002) at ECAI 2002, pp. 77–84 (2002)
9. Maedche, A., Motik, B., Silva, N., Volz, R.: MAFRA - a mapping framework for distributed ontologies. In: Gómez-Pérez, A., Benjamins, V.R. (eds.) EKAW 2002. LNCS (LNAI), vol. 2473, pp. 235–250. Springer, Heidelberg (2002)
10. Brockmans, S., Colomb, R.M., Kendall, E.F., Wallace, E., Welty, C., Xie, G.T., Haase, P.: A model driven approach for building OWL DL and OWL full ontologies. In: Cruz, I., Decker, S., Allemang, D., Preist, C., Schwabe, D., Mika, P., Uschold, M., Aroyo, L.M. (eds.) ISWC 2006. LNCS, vol. 4273, pp. 187–200. Springer, Heidelberg (2006)
11. Silva Parreiras, F., Staab, S., Winter, A.: TwoUse: Integrating UML models and OWL ontologies. Technical Report 16/2007, Universität Koblenz-Landau (2007), http://isweb.uni-koblenz.de/Projects/twouse/tr16.2007.pdf
12. Parreiras, F.S., Staab, S., Schenk, S., Winter, A.: MBOTL - A Model-based Ontology Translation Language (2008), http://isweb.uni-koblenz.de/Research/MBOTL
13. Jouault, F., Kurtev, I.: Transforming models with ATL. In: Bruel, J.-M. (ed.) MoDELS 2005. LNCS, vol. 3844. Springer, Heidelberg (2006)
14. OMG: Ontology Definition Metamodel (October 2006), http://www. omg.org/cgi-bin/doc?ptc/07-09-09.pdf
15. Gurevich, Y.: Sequential abstract-state machines capture sequential algorithms. ACM Trans. Comput. Logic 1(1), 77–111 (2000)
16. Sirin, E., Parsia, B.: SPARQL-DL: SPARQL Query for OWL-DL. In: Proceedings of the OWLED 2007, Innsbruck, Austria, June 2007, vol. 258, CEUR-WS.org (2007)
17. The Eclipse Foundation: GMT Project (2007), http://www.eclipse.org/gmt/
18. Jouault, F., Bézivin, J., Kurtev, I.: TCS: a DSL for the specification of textual concrete syntaxes in model engineering. In: Proc. of 5th Int. Conf. of Generative Programming and Component Engineering, GPCE 2006, pp. 249–254. ACM, New York (2006)
19. Atzeni, P., Cappellari, P., Bernstein, P.A.: Model-Independent Schema and Data Translation. In: Ioannidis, Y., Scholl, M.H., Schmidt, J.W., Matthes, F., Hatzopoulos, M., Böhm, K., Kemper, A., Grust, T., Böhm, C. (eds.) EDBT 2006. LNCS, vol. 3896, pp. 368–385. Springer, Heidelberg (2006)
20. Brockmans, S., Haase, P., Stuckenschmidt, H.: Formalism-Independent Specification of Ontology Mappings - A Metamodeling Approach. In: Meersman, R., Tari, Z. (eds.) OTM 2006. LNCS, vol. 4275, pp. 901–908. Springer, Heidelberg (2006)
21. Ressler, J., Dean, M., Benson, E., Dorner, E., Morris, C.: Application of ontology translation. In: Aberer, K., Choi, K.-S., Noy, N., Allemang, D., Lee, K.-I., Nixon, L., Golbeck, J., Mika, P., Maynard, D., Mizoguchi, R., Schreiber, G., Cudré-Mauroux, P. (eds.) ASWC 2007 and ISWC 2007. LNCS, vol. 4825, pp. 830–842. Springer, Heidelberg (2007)
22. Corcho, O., Gómez-Pérez, A.: ODEDialect: a set of declarative languages for implementing ontology translation systems. In: Int.Workshop on Semantic Intelligent Middleware for the Web and the Grid at ECAI 2004, Valencia, Spain (2004)

Dealing with Usability in Model Transformation Technologies[*]

Jose Ignacio Panach[1], Sergio España[1], Ana M. Moreno[2], and Óscar Pastor[1]

[1] Technical University of Valencia
Department of Information Systems and Computation
Camino de Vera s/n, 46022, Valencia, Spain
{jpanach,sergio.espana,opastor}@dsic.upv.es
[2] Technical University of Madrid
Computing Science School
28660 Boadilla del Monte, Madrid, Spain
ammoreno@fi.upm.es

Abstract. Nowadays, the concept of Model Transformation Technology (MTT) is widely accepted in the Software Engineering community. These technologies have the capability of generating software code (solution space) from a conceptual model that specifies the system abstractly (problem space). Most MTTs disregard interaction modelling (and specifically usability modelling), even though usability is as important as functionality to produce high-quality software. The issue of ensuring usability has been researched from several perspectives. One of these perspectives is based on elaborating the information to be discussed with the user to gather usability needs and the modifications to be done in software design to support those needs. We adopt this perspective by using guidelines to capture usability requirements and architectural usability patterns. The main contribution of this paper is to propose a strategy to include existing usability features inside a complete Model Transformation Technology, from abstract modelling to code generation. In order to reach this goal, new conceptual primitives have to be defined using as a source the description of the usability features. The analyst uses these primitives to model the functionality of the usability features. Once the strategy is defined in general terms, it is applied to a specific Model Transformation Technology: the OO-Method.

1 Introduction

If we look back on software development history from a global perspective, the abstraction level has been continuously rising from the solution space to the problem space. At the beginning, software systems were built in a low-level, machine-understandable code. Then, new programming languages got progressively closer to the developer's cognitive models and provided a higher abstraction level, with the objective of improving efficiency and understandability. According to this evolution,

---

[*] This work has been developed with the support of MEC under the projects SESAMO TIN2007-62894. co-financed by FEDER and TIN2005-00176.

Q. Li et al. (Eds.): ER 2008, LNCS 5231, pp. 498–511, 2008.

modern Software Engineering (SE) is interested in providing strategies based on sound Model Transformation Technologies, where the main idea is to obtain the final software product by means of a transformation process. Model Transformation Technology bridges the gap between the models at different abstraction levels. In essence, Model Transformation Technologies take a model as input and generate another model as output. Model Transformation Technology is a part of the Model Driven Development (MDD) approach. MDD is simply the notion that we can construct a model of a system that we can then transform into the real thing [16]. In many MDD approaches, the system is modelled by means of a conceptual model. The modelling language that supports the conceptual model offers a set of conceptual primitives[1]. A model compiler is an automated tool that receives the conceptual model and generates the software system code. This idea is represented by different proposals, such as the MDA standard [15], the Conceptual-Schema Centric-Development challenge [22], and the Extreme Non-Programming approach [18]. More importantly, tools have started to enter the game with industrial solutions (OlivaNOVA [5], AndroMDA [1]).

In this work, within this context of elevating the abstraction level in software development, we are interested in the study of a basic aspect for software quality [11]: *usability*. ISO 9241-11 [10] defines usability as "the extent to which a product can be used by specified users to achieve specified goals with effectiveness, efficiency and satisfaction in a specific context of use". Usability benefits have been pointed out by several authors [3][8]. However, in the SE community, the main focus is generally placed on data and functional modelling, disregarding usability aspects [3].

Usability is a very wide concept. Human-Computer Interaction literature provides many different recommendations to improve the usability of a software system. In [12], authors present three groups of recommendations:

1. Usability recommendations with impact on the user interface (UI). These recommendations refer to presentation issues with slight modifications of the UI design (e.g. buttons, pull-down menus, colours, fonts, layout).
2. Usability recommendations with impact on the development process. These can only be taken into account by modifying the whole development process. For example, those that intend to reduce the user cognitive load require involving the user in the software development.
3. Usability recommendations with impact on the architectural design. These involve building certain functionalities into the software to improve user-system interaction. These set of usability recommendations are referred to as **Functional Usability Features** (FUFs). Examples of these FUFs are providing cancel, undo and feedback facilities. A big amount of rework is needed to include these features in a software system, unless they are considered from the first stages of the software development process [12]. User needs related to FUFs can be gathered by means of requirements elicitation guidelines [14] and the architectural design that they involve can be described by means of design patterns (aka architectural usability patterns) [13].

---

[1] In the context of this paper, a conceptual primitive is an element of the modelling language that allows to abstractly represent some aspect of the system. For instance, in a class diagram, the class is the main conceptual primitive; furthermore, we also consider conceptual primitives the class attribute and the class service.

In this paper, we will focus on FUFs. We are interested in studying how to incorporate FUFs in Model-Driven Development (MDD) approaches. In order to incorporate the FUFs, their corresponding usability requirements guidelines and architectural usability patterns have been studied. As a result, a set of changes to extend the modelling language with new conceptual primitives and to modify the model compiler have been identified.

One of the most remarkable benefits of using an MDD approach to address FUFs is the ease with which the system usability is improved: whenever a usability defect is found once the software system has been generated, the developer does not need to change the architecture of the system nor fix the defect in the source code, as in classical approaches. In our approach, the defect can be fixed by changing the conceptual model; that is, using the usability-related conceptual primitives. Then, the model compiler will generate the software again, now including components that fulfill the desired usability features. In this way, architectural usability patterns and the functionality that supports the business logic are appropriately intertwined in the code.

This paper takes the OO-Method [23] as an example of Model Transformation Technology. The OO-Method is an MDA-compliant, object-oriented software production method that generates computerised information systems automatically. We have chosen it because an industrial tool called OlivaNOVA [5] supports the method, thus allowing us to perform challenging experiments in practice.

The paper is structured as follows. Section 2 reviews the literature on usability modelling. Section 3 explains the MDA paradigm. Section 4 describes our approach to include usability modelling in a MTT. Section 5 shows a practical application of this approach to the OO-Method. Finally, section 6 shows the conclusions of this work.

2   Usability Modelling in the Literature

As far as authors know, there is no model transformation-based software development method that treats features directly in a Usability Model that is independent of the rest of the models that make up the conceptual model. Normally, methods deal with usability indirectly, via the models that represent the user-system interaction. Some modelling tools offer a model to represent the interaction that leads to improve particular usability features. Many modelling techniques and tools follow this trend and propose the task model as an abstract interaction model from which an abstract interface model is derived. DiaTask [28] derives a dialog graph from a task model. The dialog graph is composed by views and transitions. Each view is an abstraction of a single subdialog of the described user interface. A transition is a directed relation between an element of a view and a view. An interface prototype that reflects the navigational structure is generated from the dialog graph. UI Pilot [26] enables designers to create the initial specifications for the screens of website, desktop or mobile applications. UI Pilot is based on the use of wireframes (simple annotated descriptions of interface elements). Wireframes have proven effective in communicating requirements between design and engineering teams. UsiXML [30] is an XML-based interface description language. Their authors propose a task model as a primary interaction model that is used to derive interface models later. The UsiXML suite of tools allows interface sketching and generation.

Many tools support the Concur Task Tree (CTT) notation [24] for interaction modelling. The UsiXML suite supports CTT models. TERESA (Transformation Environment for inteRactivE Systems representAtions) [19] is a tool that supports CTT modelling and generates interfaces for different types of devices. In turn, SUIDT (Safe User Interface Design Tool) [2] is a tool that automatically generates interfaces using several interrelated models, some of which are based on the CTT notation. The above mentioned tools are only focused on interface modelling, disregarding the modelling of the software system functionality. CTT notation is widely employed in the Human Computer Interaction community, but it does not support functionality modelling. We advocate integrating three axes of system descriptions, as the OO-Method does: system memory, system reaction and user-system interaction.

Another tool that is worth mentioning is VAQUITA [4], which is aimed at web environments. The tool uses mapping rules to reverse-engineer an HTML page and obtains an interface model. Then, the interface model can be modified in order to improve usability. However, the holistic perspective of modelling and a precise model transformation-based, complete software production process is missing.

Finally, there are several UML-based approaches where interaction and functionality modelling have been integrated. This is the case of UMLi [29] and WISDOM [21]. UMLi is a set of user interface modelling primitives that extend UML to provide greater support for UI design. This way, some usability attributes can be improved. However, UMLi models are so detailed that the modelling turns out to be very difficult, thus hampering its industrial application. WISDOM is a software engineering approach that enriches UML with the necessary stereotypes to allow user-centred development. It also has a detailed user interface design. Three of its models are concerned with interaction modelling at different stages: the Interaction Model (analysis), the Dialog Model and the Presentation Model (both in design). The WISDOM notation simplifies the application of UML with regard to UMLi. However, neither of the two methods considers the generation of full functional systems.

3 MDA Environments

In 2001, the Object Management Group proposed an increasingly popular paradigm: the Model Driven Architecture (MDA) [15]. This de facto standard defines how to apply Model Driven Development. Three viewpoints were proposed:

1. A Computation Independent Model (CIM) focuses on the environment and the requirements of the system.
2. A Platform Independent Model (PIM) focuses on the operation of the system, which stays constant across any possible technological platform.
3. A Platform Specific Model (PSM) aims to provide the platform-dependent viewpoint with those features that are specific to a platform.

As defined by the Object Management Group, a model transformation is the process of converting one model to another model of the same system [15]. Commonly, the target model is in a lower abstraction level than the source model and, therefore, it is closer to the final implementation. By means of consecutive transformations, we end up with an executable model of the system: the Code Model.

Transformations can be applied manually, with computer assistance, or automatically. Transformation rules have to be unambiguously specified using some language, regardless of the degree of automation. Again there is a wide choice, ranging from natural language descriptions to QVT [17] specifications. Among the several model transformation approaches that can be used, the Metamodel Transformation deserves our special attention (see Figure 1). The definition of transformation rules is a hard task but it benefits analysts in many ways:

- Complete support for the software life cycle from requirements to maintenance.
- Reduction of software development costs. Analysts put their main effort in the analysis stage. Subsequent stages are facilitated by automatically deriving initial models that are refined by the analysts. This saves time and resources.
- Quality improvement. Code generation reduces the possibility of error.
- The same model can be transformed into code for several programming languages.

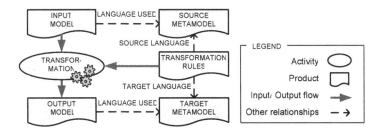

Fig. 1. Metamodel Transformation

The advantages of using a model transformation approach have more weight than the effort required to define transformation rules. For this reason, several Model Transformation Technologies have recently appeared in order to generate code from conceptual models [22][6]. We could say that "conventional" SE focuses on system structure and system behaviour, but it does not do a good job from the interaction modelling perspective in general, and from the usability point of view in particular. Some proposals such as [27][6] aim to integrate the usability engineering process with the SE process. These proposals show that these two perspectives (interaction and SE) do not often understand the goals and needs of others, pointing at several integration problems: lack of coordination; lack of provision for change; lack of synchronization of development schedules; lack of communication among different developer roles; lack of constraint mapping and dependency checks.

In the next section, we provide a concrete proposal that contributes to solve these problems and to accomplish the integration of interaction modelling and SE.

4   Projecting Usability to an MDA-Based Method

This section explains a strategy for adapting an MDA-based software development method in order to address usability. Our proposal is focused on Functional Usability Features (FUFs) because they have a wide impact on design [12]. At the requirements stage, analysts use requirements guidelines to elicit user needs regarding FUFs [13]. At the design stage, architectural usability patterns help developers to support the FUFs [14]. All in all, the rationale behind our approach is the following:

- Usability requirements guidelines contribute to define the different configuration possibilities of a specific usability feature (the details of the user needs). Feature configuration has to be modelled by means of conceptual primitives. Consequently, usability requirements guidelines have been studied to define conceptual primitives that represent FUF configurations.
- Architectural usability patterns offer an abstract design solution to include, in the system architecture, the components that support the usability feature. This proposal can be used to define the code generation strategy of the MTT.

As Figure 2 shows, we have proposed a four-step strategy to embed these FUFs in an MDA-based method. The first step is to study how the usability features can improve the usability of the generated systems. To fulfil this goal, we study the usability requirements guidelines to identify Ways of Use (WoU in Figure 2). The same feature may have several applications in the system. We define **Way of Use** as a specific application of a FUF in the final interface. We take the *Structured Text Entry* FUF as an example. It allows the specification of restrictions on data entry. Three Ways of Use are defined for this FUF: (1) this FUF can specify the widget type to enter data with a specific format (checkbox, radiobutton, listbox, etc.); (2) this FUF can define a mask that specifies the required format of an input text; (3) also, this FUF can define default values in order to help the user to enter information.

The second step is the definition of one or several usability properties for each Way of Use. **Usability properties** are options of the FUF that are used to adapt it to the user's requirements related to usability. For example, in the first Way of Use of the *Structured Text Entry* FUF, we can define a usability property for selecting the type of widgets and another one for organizing the widgets on the screen. We consider two types of usability properties:

- **Non-configurable usability properties** have the same value in all generated systems. It is unnecessary to configure these properties because they do not offer any alternative. For example, if commonly accepted usability guidelines determine that each action should be accompanied by a progress bar to indicate when it will finish, the analyst's decision is not involved. This is a non-configurable usability property of the *Progress Feedback* FUF.
- **Configurable usability properties** with different configuration alternatives that depend on the analyst's decisions. For example, in the *Structured Text Entry* FUF, the analyst decides the type of the widget and its organization on the screen. Therefore, this FUF has two configurable usability properties.

The third step for including usability features in an MDA environment is to specify which models (or views) have to be modified in order to support each usability property. The conceptual model may be composed of several views. Each view models the system from one perspective. For instance, in a given MDA-based method, one view may be used to model persistence and another view to model interaction. Usability properties are modelled in these views by means of conceptual primitives. Each con

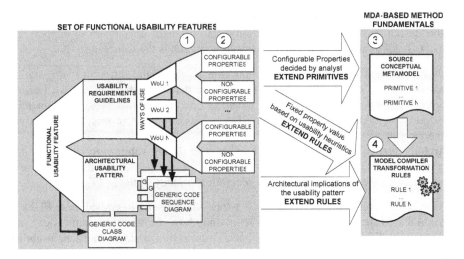

Fig. 2. Strategy to include Functional Usability Features in a MTT

figurable usability property requires the definition of new conceptual primitives. In other words, the source metamodel of the MDA-based method has to be enriched with new conceptual primitives. For instance, the configurable usability property of the *Structured Text Entry* which represents the type of the widget is represented by means of a conceptual primitive. This primitive specifies the widget type in the view which represents the interaction of the system. Non-configurable usability properties do not need new conceptual primitives because the knowledge to generate code to support their corresponding functionality can be embedded in the model compiler.

The fourth and last step is to improve the transformation rules of the model compiler in order to ensure that it can generate code that supports the functionality of the usability features, taking the conceptual model as input. For that aim, architectural usability patterns can be helpful. The incorporation of usability features involves adding new classes and services to the generated code. Both types of properties imply changes in the model compiler. With regard to configurable properties, new transformation rules have to be defined to map the new conceptual primitives to programming language code. With regard to non-configurable properties, the model compiler will also generate their corresponding code. For instance, the non-configurable property of the *Progress Feedback* which states that all actions should have a progress bar implies including code to calculate the remaining time of the action execution.

We can conclude that the incorporation of usability features concerns the entire code generation process of an MDA environment. Once the usability features are addressed, all the code that implements the functionality of these features together with the business logic can be generated automatically by means of the model compiler.

5   A Practical Application in the OO-Method

This paper applies the Functional Usability Features to the OO-Method. The main advantage of the OO-Method is that an industrial implementation of the method

(OlivaNova [5]) provides a model compiler that generates fully functional systems from the OO-Method conceptual model. Moreover, the OO-Method conceptual model is abstract and platform-independent. These characteristics make it the most appropriate MDA environment to illustrate our proposal.

5.1 The OO-Method, an MDA Environment

This section argues that the OO-Method [23] is MDA [15] compliant. Following the MDA paradigm, the OO-Method is based on the creation of abstract models and the application of model transformations. The equivalence between the OO-Method and the MDA models is the following:

- The OO-Method conceptual model corresponds to the MDA Platform Independent Model. The OO-Method conceptual model is composed of four views:
- The *Object Model* specifies the system structure in terms of classes of objects and their relations. It is modelled as an extended UML class diagram.
- The *Dynamic Model* represents the sequences of events that can occur to a class of objects and the interaction between object classes.
- The *Functional Model* specifies how events change object states. The behaviour of the system is modelled by the Functional and Dynamic Models working together.
- The *Interaction Model* models the interaction between the system and the user. This model has two views: the Abstract Interaction Model and the Concrete Interaction Model [25]. The *Abstract Interaction Model* defines the interface without taking into account concrete aspects of visualization. It represents the interface independently of the types of interaction and the peculiarities of the platform. The *Concrete Interaction Model* specifies details of the interface. It is a user-interface model that specifies the interface representation in terms of elements that can be perceived by the end user. The Concrete Interaction Model is not supported yet by OlivaNOVA because it is currently under research.
- The architectural knowledge embedded in the model compiler corresponds to the MDA Platform Specific Model.
- The MDA Code Model corresponds to the generated code that supports the system.

5.2 Dealing with Usability in the OO-Method

This section shows an instantiation of the strategy to include FUFs in the OO-Method Model Transformation Technology. To achieve this goal, it is necessary to adapt the FUFs to the OO-Method. We explain this adaptation, following the steps defined above: (1) define the Ways of Use of the FUFs; (2) define the usability properties of each Way of Use; (3) extend the conceptual model with new conceptual primitives in order to model configurable usability properties; (4) extend the model compiler to support the new conceptual primitives and non-configurable usability properties.

For the sake of brevity, this section focuses on the changes implied by a usability feature called *Warning*. This feature is used to specify which information needs to be elicited and specified in order to ask for user confirmation in case the action requested has irreversible consequences. This FUF contributes to prevent user errors. The requirements guidelines of the FUF elicits the information necessary to identify the actions where this feature should be applied and how to prevent the user for the consequences of those actions (generally by means of a message asking the user to accept or reject the action execution). The architectural usability pattern proposes to the developer a set of software components to include such feature in a software design.

5.2.1 Defining the Ways of Use of the FUF

Studying the requirements guidelines of the Warning FUF we can state that this feature only has one Way of Use: action warning - to notify the user before executing a potentially erroneous action. Some business rules recommend advising the user before executing an erroneous or irreversible action whenever a certain condition is satisfied. For example, in an invoicing system, the system should advise the user if an invoice with a total amount greater than 10.000 € is going to be emitted; this amount is infrequent, so it could be an error. This Way of Use is not currently supported by the OO-Method.

5.2.2 Defining the Usability Properties of the Way of Use

After studying the corresponding requirements guideline, the following usability properties have been defined for the action warning Way of Use: the business service associated to the warning, the condition, the text to show, and a set of format options for text visualization (see next step for more detail).

5.2.3 Extending the Conceptual Model with New Conceptual Primitives

All the usability properties of this Way of Use are configurable by the analyst. Therefore, the OO-Method conceptual model needs to be extended to support these properties. Two views are affected by the Warning FUF: the Object Model and the Concrete Interaction Model.

- Object Model: this view is extended with new conceptual primitives to model the following configurable usability properties:
- The service in which the FUF is applied.
- The condition that should be satisfied to show the warning message.
- The text that will be shown to the user when the condition holds true.
- Concrete Interaction Model: this view needs new conceptual primitives to model the following configurable usability properties:
- Whether or not the window is obtrusive[2].
- The window type: alert, information or error.
- Text font.
- Size.
- Colour.
- Alignment.

In order to facilitate the analyst's work, these conceptual primitives should have a default value in case the analyst does not want to configure them. Default values should be the values that are most frequently used for each conceptual primitive. The analyst can change these default values to adapt the conceptual primitives to the

---

[2] The term obtrusive is used to define a window that does not allow any other user interaction until the window is closed. Sometimes this is referred to as 'modal'.

user's requirements. By default, the Warning feature is implemented by an obtrusive window of the alert type, with Arial font, size 10, black colour and centred alignment.

The inclusion of these conceptual primitives in the OO-Method implies changes in OlivaNOVA [5], the industrial tool that implements the OO-Method. Changes related to the *Warning* FUF affect the Object Model and the Concrete Interaction Model:

- Object Model. This view should allow specifying which services have an associated warning message, the condition, and the text for this message. Figure 3 shows a window prototype[3] where the analyst can model these usability properties.
- Define the condition that, if fulfilled, triggers the warning message. The condition is edited using a wizard and the following elements can participate: (1) class attributes; (2) arguments of the service or transaction related to the warning message; (3) user functions defined by the analyst; (4) standard functions that are already included in OlivaNOVA to work with basic data types such as boolean, numeric, string and date types; (5) operators for basic data types.
- Define the warning message that the system shows if the condition holds true.
- Define explanatory commentaries for the developing team.

Concrete Interaction Model. Once the analyst has modelled the functionality of the Warning FUF in the Object Model, the next step is to model by means of the Concrete Interaction Model how the warning message is shown to the user. Figure 4 shows a non-functional prototype with the conceptual primitives used by the analyst to model the warning visualization. The tree view on the left-hand side shows the services that have an associated warning message. For each warning message, the analyst can change the primitives on the right-hand side.

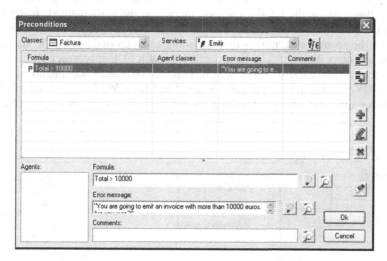

Fig. 3. Prototype to model the Warning usability feature in the Object Model

---

[3] These non-functional prototypes are only meant to illustrate the changes needed in the OlivaNOVA tool to support the Warning FUF.

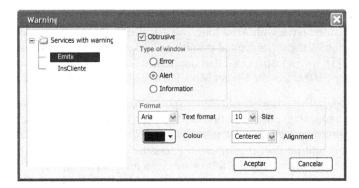

Fig. 4. Prototype to model the Warning usability feature in the Concrete Interaction Model

5.2.4   Extending the Model Compiler

Every conceptual primitive that composes the OO-Method conceptual model at the problem-space level is mapped to a piece of software code that represents it at the solution-space level. The architectural usability pattern can help in this task. The new conceptual primitives that are included to deal with the usability features should be related to a set of transformation rules in order to generate code that implements their functionalities. Although non-configurable properties do not have associated conceptual primitives, they need transformation rules too. Both facts imply changes in the automatic code-generation strategy. In order to abstractly represent these changes, we have used two types of diagrams (Figure 2): *Class Diagram* and *Sequence Diagram*. Class diagrams are used to represent the (software) classes associated to an architectural usability pattern, the relations among them, and the class methods that will implement the functionality offered by the usability feature. Sequence diagrams are used to express the sequence of actions that are going to be carried out by the classes that appear in the class diagram. The functionality of each FUF is represented by a single class diagram, while each Way of Use is represented by a sequence diagram.

OlivaNOVA can generate applications in C# and Java. We have focused on C#. To illustrate our approach, we offer the diagrams for the *Warning* feature (Figures 5 and 6).

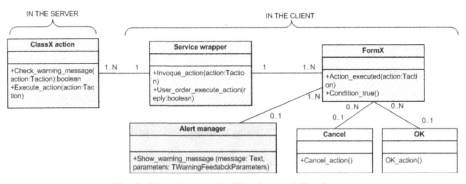

Fig. 5. Class diagram for Warning usability feature

New (software) classes needed to implement the feature appear with grey background. Classes with some methods that have been modified to add the usability feature appear with a background crossed by diagonal lines. Finally, those classes that do not change appear with white background. These classes are:

- ClassX action. For each class of the Object Model (at the analysis stage), the model compiler creates a class of this type (at the implementation stage). We have informally used the letter X to abstractly represent the set of all these classes. This class checks the condition associated to the warning message.
- FormX. There is a class of this type for each service modelled in the conceptual model. The class *FormX* represents the set of all the forms used by the user to execute services. This class receives a notification from *ClassX action* when the condition holds true, and it invokes *Alert manager* to show the warning to the user.
- Alert manager. This new class is created from scratch to show a window in which the user can decide whether or not she/he wants to execute the action.

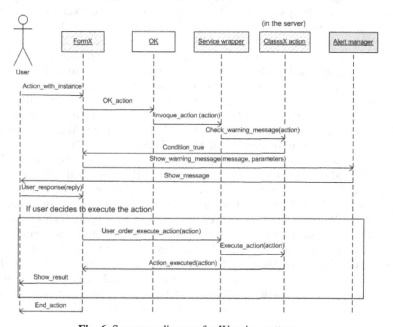

Fig. 6. Sequence diagram for Warning pattern

Figure 6 shows the sequence diagram (which represents the Way of Use of the Warning feature) whenever the condition to show the message holds true. When a user wants to execute an action, the *Service wrapper* class receives the request. This class launches the request to the *ClassX action* (which is implemented in the server). This class is in charge of verifying whether any warning message associated with the action exists; if so, it checks whether the condition is satisfied. When the condition is satisfied, the class *Alert manager* asks the user whether or not she/he wants to execute the action. If the user decides to execute the action, the class *FormX* will trigger the action. These changes in the model compiler make it possible to generate code to support the functionality of the Warning feature.

6 Conclusions

This paper discusses a strategy for including usability features with functional implications in a Model Transformation Technology. Our proposal is based on the use of already existing Functional Usability Features (FUF) that contain the information needed to specify and design such features. This method is based on the idea of abstracting the information contained in such usability features in order to include it in a conceptual model. Thanks to this abstraction, a model compiler can automatically generate the code for a specific programming language taking as input the conceptual model. This code supports the functionality of the usability features together with the functionality of the whole system. This automation reduces the development rework in case a usability defect is found in the implemented system. Notice how this proposal clearly helps to provide practical support to the existing tendency of addressing the treatment of usability in the early stages of the software development process. Therefore, it represents a starting point to improve the integration of usability and SE.

The proposed strategy consists of four steps that have to be taken for each FUF: (1) to study the FUF usability requirements guideline and to identify Ways of Use: each Way of Use is a particular application of the feature in a system; (2) to identify usability properties in each Way of Use: briefly, each property is an option of the FUF; (3) to extend the conceptual model with new conceptual primitives to represent configurable usability properties abstractly; (4) to change the transformation rules of the model compiler to support the code generation related to the new primitives and the non-configurable usability properties, using as input the architectural usability pattern.

This approach has been applied to the OO-Method using the Warning feature. The OO-Method is chosen as an example of Model Transformation Technology due to the high level of abstraction of its conceptual model. Taking as input the OO-Method conceptual model, a model compiler generates fully functional software systems. Both the OO-Method conceptual model and the model compiler need to be modified to incorporate the functionality of the usability features. The paper discusses the inclusion of the Warning FUF. Moreover, the changes to support such feature in OlivaNOVA (a industrial suite of tools that supports the OO-Method) are detailed.

As future work, this strategy should be applied not only to the Warning but also to the rest of the Functional Usability Features in order to incorporate them in the OO-Method. The inclusion of all these usability features should improve the usability of the systems generated with the OO-Method. To assess this issue, an empirical evaluation will be made. It will consist of usability tests with end users.

References

1. AndroMDA (2008) (Last visit: March 2008), http://www.andromda.org/
2. Baron, M., Romania, G.P.: SUIDT: A task model based GUI-Builder. Task MO-dels and DIAgrams for user interface design (TAMODIA), 64–71 (2002)
3. Bias, R.G., Mayhew, D.J.: Cost-Justifying Usability. An Update for the Internet Age (2005)
4. Bouillon, L., Vanderdonckt, J., Souchon, N.: Recovering Alternative Presentation Models of a Web Page with VAQUITA. CADUI 2002, France, pp. 311–322 (2002)
5. CARE Technologies S.A (2008) (Last visit: March 2008), http://www.care-t.com
6. Ceri, S., Fraternali, P., Bongio, A.: Web Modeling Language (WebML): a modeling language for designing Web sites. In: WWW9, Amsterdam, pp. 137–157 (2000)

7. Chrusch, M.: Seven Great Myths of Usability. In: Interactions, pp. 13–16 (2000)
8. Donahue, G.M.: Usability and the Bottom Line. IEEE Softwa. 18(11), 22–30 (2001)
9. Ferré, X., Juristo, N., Moreno, A.: Framework for Integrating Usability Practices into the Software. In: Bomarius, F., Komi-Sirviö, S. (eds.) PROFES 2005. LNCS, vol. 3547. Springer, Heidelberg (2005)
10. ISO 9241-11: Ergonomic Requirements for Office work with Visual Display Ter-minals. Part 11: Guidance on Usability (1998)
11. ISO/IEC 9126-1 (2001): Software engineering - Product quality - 1: Quality model
12. Juristo, N., Moreno, A.M., Sánchez-Segura, M.: Analysing the Impact of Usability on Software Design. Journal of System and Software 80(9), 1506–1516 (2007)
13. Juristo, N., Moreno, A.M., Sánchez-Segura, M.: Guideliness for Eliciting Usability Func-tionalities. IEEE Transactions on Software Engineering 33(11), 744–758 (2007)
14. Juristo, N., Lopez, M., Moreno, A., Sánchez-Segura, M.: Improving Software Us-ability Through Architectural Patterns. In: ICSE Workshop Bridging the Gaps Between Software Engineering and Human-Computer Interaction, Portland, USA, pp. 12–19 (2003)
15. MDA Guide V1.0.1 (2008) (Last visit: March 2008),
    http://www.omg.org/docs/omg/03-06-01.pdf
16. Mellor, S.J., Clark, A.N., Futagami, T.: Guest Editors' Introduction: Model-Driven Devel-opment. IEEE Software 20, 14–18 (2003)
17. MOF QVT (Last visit: March 2008), http://www.omg.org/cgi-bin/apps/doc?ptc/05-11-01
18. Morgan, T.: Business Rules and Information Systems-Aligning IT with Business Goals (2002)
19. Mori, G., Paterno, F., Santoro, C.: Design and Development of Multidevice User Inter-faces through Multiple Logical Descriptions. IEEE Transactions on Software Engineering
20. Nielsen, J.: Return on Investment for Usability. Alertbox (2003),
    http://www.useit.com
21. Nunes, N.J.: Wisdom: a software engineering method for small software development companies. Software 17(5), 113–119 (2000)
22. Olive, A.: Conceptual Schema-Centric Development: A Grand Challenge for Information Systems Research. In: Pastor, Ó., Falcão e Cunha, J. (eds.) CAiSE 2005. LNCS, vol. 3520, pp. 1–15. Springer, Heidelberg (2005)
23. Pastor, O., Molina, J.: Model-Driven Arquitecture in Practice, Valencia. Springer, Heidel-berg (2007)
24. Paternò, F.: ConcurTaskTrees: An Engineered Notation for Task Models. In: Diaper, D., Stanton, N., Stanton, N.A. (eds.) The Handbook of Task Analysis for Human-Computer Inter-action, London, United Kingdom, pp. 483–501. Lawrence Erlbaum Associates, Mahwah (2004)
25. Pederiva, I., Vanderdonckt, J., España, S., Panach, I., Pastor, O.: The Beautification Process in Model-Driven Engineering of User Interfaces. In: Baranauskas, C., Palanque, P., Abascal, J., Barbosa, S.D.J. (eds.) INTERACT 2007. LNCS, vol. 4663. Springer, Heidelberg (2007)
26. Puerta, A., Micheletti, M., Mak, A.: The UI pilot: a model-based tool to guide early inter-face design, San Diego, California, USA, pp. 215–222. ACM Press, New York (2005)
27. Pyla, P., Pérez-Quiñones, M., Arthur, J., Hartson, H.: Towards a Model-Based Framework for Integrating Usability and Software Engineering Life Cycles. In: INTERACT 2003 (2003), eprint arXiv:cs/0402036
28. Reichart, D., Forbrig, P., Dittmar, A.: Task models as basis for requirements engineering and software execution. In: Conference on Task models and diagrams, Prague, Czech Re-public, pp. 51–58. ACM Press, New York (2004)
29. Silva, P.P., Paton, N.W.: User Interface Modeling in UMLi. IEEE Software 20(4), 62–69 (2003)
30. Vanderdonckt, J., Limbourg, Q., et al.: USIXML: a User Interface Description Language for Specifying Multimodal User Interfaces. In: Proceedings of W3C Workshop on Multi-modal Interaction WMI 2004, Sophia Antipolis, Greece (2004)

Ontology Coordination: The iCoord Project Demonstration*

Silvana Castano, Alfio Ferrara, Davide Lorusso, and Stefano Montanelli

Università degli Studi di Milano
DICo - Via Comelico, 39, 20135 Milano - Italy
{castano,ferrara,lorusso,montanelli}@dico.unimi.it

The increasing complexity of knowledge-intensive applications, such as information integration, semantic search, semantic web services, collaborative knowledge sharing and exchange, demands more and more for ontology coordination systems with functionalities for knowledge discovery and acquisition to enable enhanced ontology design, maintenance, and querying functionalities [1,2].

Goal of the demo is to show iCoord, a comprehensive peer-oriented ontology coordination system. iCoord provides a suite of complementary and inter-related components where three *coordination services*, namely the harvesting engine, the matching engine, and the assimilation engine, are exploited to support the processes of ontology design, ontology alignment, and knowledge discovery and assimilation (see Figure 1). The knowledge & mapping repository is used for storing and maintaining over time the knowledge of the peer, also coordinated with outside peers through ontology mappings. For knowledge coordination, iCoord provides a coordination GUI to enforce i) *similarity-based search*, where both local and remote data can be accessed by exploiting the knowledge & mapping repository, ii) *ontology alignment*, where the discovered mappings with outside peers

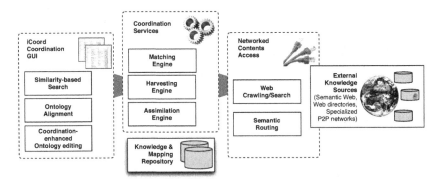

Fig. 1. Architectural overview of iCoord

---

* This paper has been partially funded by the BOEMIE Project, FP6-027538, 6th EU Framework Programme.

can be refined/recomputed through the matching engine, and iii) *coordination-enhanced ontology editing*, where the expert-user is supported in the process of visualizing/changing/evolving its own local knowledge by relying on external knowledge using the harvesting and assimilation engines.

Demonstration organization. We will focus on the iCoord functionalities for coordination-enhanced ontology design. Starting from a *probe query* defined by the expert-user and abstracting a concept skeleton that is missing in the local peer knowledge, iCoord invokes the harvesting engine to discover those outside peers that are capable of providing similar knowledge (see Figure 2(A)). Collecting the results of harvesting, we will show how iCoord will support the selection of the most interesting external contents by using the HMatch ontology matching engine [3]. Finally, we will show how the local peer knowledge can be interactively enriched through reuse/integration of concept/data retrieved from outside by relying on the assimilation engine (see Figure 2(B)) [1].

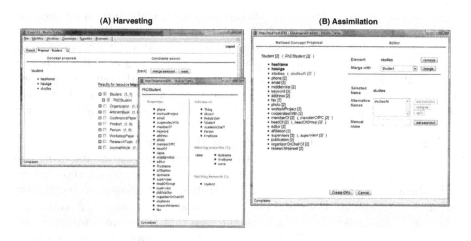

Fig. 2. iCoord screenshots: (A) harvesting and (B) assimilation

References

1. Bouquet, P., Serafini, L. (eds.): Proceedings of the ISWC Workshop on Meaning Coordination and Negotiation (MCN 2004), Hiroshima, Japan (2004)
2. De Baer, P., Kerremans, K., Temmerman, R.: Facilitating Ontology (Re)use by Means of a Categorization Framework. In: Proc. of the OTM Workshop on Agents, Web Services and Ontologies Merging (AweSOMe 2006), Montpellier, France (2006)
3. Castano, S., Ferrara, A., Montanelli, S.: Matching Ontologies in Open Networked Systems: Techniques and Applications. Journal on Data Semantics V (2006)

---

[1] A prototype version of iCoord is available on-line for this demonstration at the following URL: http://islab.dico.unimi.it/iCoord-demo/.

Designing Similarity Measures for XML

Ismael Sanz, María Pérez, and Rafael Berlanga

Universitat Jaume I de Castelló, Spain
{isanz,maria.perez,berlanga}@uji.es

Abstract. In this demonstration we will show a series of tools that support a methodology [1] for the design of complex similarity functions in the context of heterogenous XML systems.

1 Introduction

The existence of highly complex, publicly available XML-based databases has motivated research into multi-similarity XML applications, which support multiple notions of similarity to tailor queries to users with diverse information needs. Such applications arise e.g. in the integration and merging of highly heterogeneous XML databases, and in systems handling objects with complex structures such as protein data, music retrieval systems, or shape databases. Until now, little attention has been paid to the problem of designing suitable similarity measures for such applications.

[1] introduces a methodology to support the design of similarity functions for heterogeneous XML-based information systems, based on the following four steps: (1) Characterize a set of relevant XML collections and queries that describe the information needs of users. (2) Establish a candidate set of similarity measures. (3) Evaluate the suitability of the candidate measures. According to the result of this assessment it may be the case that (i) the measure may need some adjustment, which implies a change in the measure and the re-evaluation of the candidate set; or that (ii) deficiencies in the specification of the information needs are detected, which may cause the candidate set to change completely. (4) Finally, the final set of measures is obtained, and the indexing requirements are established and targeted for physical implementation and optimization

2 Outline of the Demonstration

We have implemented a set of tools, the *XML Collection Workshop*, which uses techniques that help in each of the steps of the previously sketched methodology. We will use two different collections: The ASSAM[1] highly heterogeneous collection, whose documents span several different domains, and a collection of large, publicly-avaliable XML databases containing Bioinformatics-related data

The demonstration will proceed through the following steps:

---

[1] http://moguntia.ucd.ie/repository/datasets/

Q. Li et al. (Eds.): ER 2008, LNCS 5231, pp. 514–515, 2008.

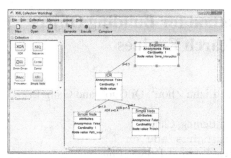
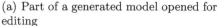

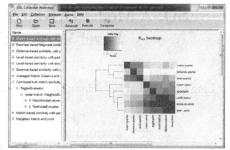

(a) Part of a generated model opened for editing

(b) Correlation between candidate measures, shown as a heatmap and a corresponding hierarchical clustering

Fig. 1. Screenshots of the XML Collection Workshop

1. *Characterization of XML collections.* Using the ASSAM collection as a case study, we will demonstrate how to create a simplified, probabilistic model of a highly complex XML collection using a probabilistic model described in [2].

2. *Design of test collections and associated queries.* We will show how to use a GUI-based tool, depicted in Figure 1(a), to display the model generated by the previous step, and edit it interactively to generate an XML test collection and a a set of queries which are suitable for testing candidate measures.

3. *Semi-automatic selection of measures.* The selected candidate measures will include a representative set of features: structural matching, text retrieval approaches, and Bioinformatics-specific algorithms. Using the Bioinformatics-based use case, we will show how to select appropriate measures using several assessment criteria. First, we will use a correlation measure to prune redundant candidates; for example, Figure 1(b) graphically displays a clustering of a set of candidate measures based on the the K_{min} distance [3], after performing a run of experiments on the collection and queries generated in the previous step. Then, we will apply standard techniques such as the F_1-measure to study the quality of the remaining candidates.

References

1. Sanz, I., Pérez, M., Berlanga, R.: Measure selection in multi-similarity XML applications. In: Third International Workshop on Flexible Database and Information System Technology (FlexDBIST-2008) (2008)
2. Sanz, I., Mesiti, M., Guerrini, G., Berlanga, R.: Fragment-based approximate retrieval in highly heterogeneous XML collections. Data & Knowledge Engineering 64(1), 266–293 (2008)
3. Fagin, R., Kumar, R., Sivakumar, D.: Comparing top-k lists. SIAM Journal on Discrete Mathematics 17(1), 134–160 (2003)

SESQ: A Model-Driven Method for Building Object Level Vertical Search Engines

Ling Lin[1], Yukai He[1], Hang Guo[1], Ju Fan[1], Lizhu Zhou[1], Qi Guo[2], and Gang Li[2]

[1] Tsinghua University, Beijing, China
linling03@mails.tsinghua.edu.cn
[2] Sohu Research and Development Division, Beijing, China
glassguo@sohu-rd.com

Abstract. In vertical search engine research, many works have been reported. But most of them focus on its key issues such as crawling, extraction, and query and few of them give a total solution for building a complete vertical search engine from scratch in a systematic method. To address this issue, we propose a model-driven method and its supporting tool SESQ. Based on a user defined ER schema for a target domain, the tool can help to build a complete search engine by integrating tasks of crawling, extraction, data management and query within one unified framework.

Keywords: model-driven method, schema, object-level vertical search engine.

1 Introduction

Object-level vertical Search Engine (OVSE for short)[1] is a computer system capable of finding data of a specific domain from the Web and presenting the data in a structured format. Many successful systems such as MSN Shopping, Yahoo! Shopping, Libra, and related techniques for Web crawling[2,3] and data extraction[4-6] have been reported; however few of them give a total solution for building a complete vertical search engine from scratch in a systematic method. To address this problem, we propose a model-driven method for OVSE building and its supporting tool SESQ system. With limited user input of schema, crawling seeds and extraction rules, SESQ helps to build an OVSE in an easy and stepwise way [7,8,9].

The whole model-driven method and the supporting role of SESQ depicted in Fig.2 for the building process can be summarized as follows. (1) First, the user defines the ER model schema of interested domain. (2) Second, using model-aligned data instances and keywords as crawling seeds and extraction patterns, the *Searcher* harvests web pages and the *Extractor* extracts relevant objects and relationships from the Web. (3) Next, the extracted data are organized in local databases managed by the *Storage Manager* and *Query Manager*. (4) Finally, the interactive user interface for data query and navigation are customized according to the schema and the OVSE is ready for use. Fig. 1 shows the interactive GUI of querying book instances acquired from online book shopping websites. The domain schema is illustrated on the GUI to help the users understand the data structure and compose a structured query easily.

Q. Li et al. (Eds.): ER 2008, LNCS 5231, pp. 516–517, 2008.

2 Demonstration Plan

Part 1. Vertical Search Engine Building Demo. We plan to take the C-BOOK search engine as an example to illustrate how to build a vertical search engine. We will first input the schema definition, seeds and extraction rules of C-BOOK to SESQ, and then run SESQ on sampling Web pages and illustrate the process of crawling, extraction and database materialization.

Part 2. User Interface Demo. This part will show the functions supported by query interface using C-PAPER (a scientific paper OVSE built by SESQ) and C-BOOK. It will include keyword and structured queries, navigation of entities through relationship, entity ranking, categorization and statistical analysis as well.

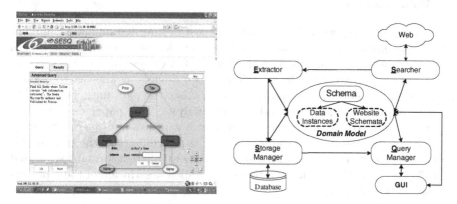

Fig. 1. Query GUI of C-BOOK   **Fig. 2.** Architecture of SESQ

References

1. Nie, Z., Zhang, Y., Wen, J.R., Ma, W.Y.: Object-Level Ranking: Bringing Order to Web Objects. In: WWW 2005 (2005)
2. Chakrabarti, S., Berg, M., Dom, B.: Focused Crawling: a new Approach to Topic-Specific Web Resource Discovery. In: WWW 1999 (1999)
3. Ester, M., Kriegel, H.P., Schubert, M.: Accurate and Efficient Crawling for Relevant Websites. In: VLDB 2004 (2004)
4. Crescenzi, V., Mecca, G., Merialdo, P.: Automatic Web Information Extraction in the RoadRunner System. In: Workshop DASWIS of ER 2001 (2001)
5. Zhu, J., Nie, Z., Wen, J.R., Zhang, B., Ma, W.Y.: Simultaneous record detection and attribute labeling in web data extraction. In: SIGKDD 2006 (2006)
6. Zhao, H., Meng, W., Wu, Z., Raghavan, V., Yu, C.: Fully Automatic Wrapper Generation for Search Engines. In: WWW 2005 (2005)
7. Lin, L., Li, G., Zhou, L.: Meta-Search Based Web Resource Discovery for Object-Level Vertical Search. In: WISE 2006 (2006)
8. Guo, Q., Zhou, L.: Schema driven topic specific web crawling. In: DASFAA 2005 (2005)
9. Lin, L., Zhou, L.: Leveraging Webpage Classification for Data Object Recognition. In: IEEE/WIC/ACM Web Intelligence 2007 (2007)

HealthSense: An Application for Querying Raw Sensor Data*

Fabrice Camous, Dónall McCann, and Mark Roantree

Interoperable Systems Group,
School of Computing, Dublin City University,
Dublin, Ireland
{fcamous,dmccann,mroantree}@computing.dcu.ie

1 Background

New sensing technologies and the decreasing cost of Information and Communication Technologies (ICTs) make possible the development of electronic Health (eHealth) monitoring systems. The challenges of such systems include the representation of data extracted from various sensor devices by knowledge workers through semantic enrichment and integration. Also, the data must be stored in a format suitable for querying and further analysis. This paper describes the demonstration of the HealthSense system which captures and queries personal health data extracted from wearable sensors. Figure 1 illustrates the transformation process. There are 4 layers, representing data in different formats, separated by the 3 processors that transform them. A detailed description of the 3 processors was presented in [1].

2 The HealthSense Demonstration

The demonstration includes:

- the wearing of sensor devices and recording of data,
- the extraction of sensor data to a laptop,
- the use of HealthSense to enrich, integrate, and store sensor data, and
- the querying of the stored data from an XML database using XPath.

2.1 The Sensor Devices

- **Polar S625X™ heart-rate monitor:** this consists of a fabric band which fits around a person's chest and detects and logs their *heart rate.*
- **BodyMedia SenseWear®:** this sensor array is worn around the upper arm and measures. It uses motion sensors and *galvanic skin response* sensors to measure activity.
- **Deluxe Wrist Blood Pressure Monitor HL168JC:** this device can store up to 90 blood pressure and pulse readings.
- **iPod Nano 4G with Nike®+ IPod Sport kit:** this sensor records the distance covered during a walk or run and caloric consumption.

---

* The RSS SENSE project is funded by Enterprise Ireland Ref. PC/2007/112.

Q. Li et al. (Eds.): ER 2008, LNCS 5231, pp. 518–519, 2008.

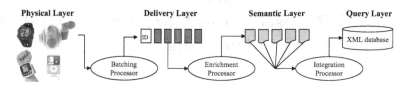

Fig. 1. System Architecture

2.2   Data Extraction, Enrichment and Integration

Device-specific software is used to extract and store the raw sensor data on the laptop hard disk. At this point, data is in a raw format not yet queryable in a standard way. The HealthSense application running on the laptop is used to batch, semantically enrich, integrate, and store the data locally in a XML database. Processing time depends on the size of the files. Table 1 shows examples of processing times from file upload to database storage for different groups of files. A complete analysis of processing times for enrichment and integration is found in [1]. For storage, we use the eXist XML database [2]. Our innovation arises from the fact that we can enrich data from any sensor device using our generic device manager, and our integration process can pivot on a number of different characteristics including time, individuals or sensor readings [1]. Once the data is stored in eXist, it is directly queryable using the XPath query language.

Table 1. Processing times from file upload to database storage

Raw Sensor Files	Upload to Storage (sec)	Stored File Size
1 Polar (3KB), 1 BodyMedia (173KB)	3.90841	388KB
1 Nike iPod (8KB), 1 Polar (13KB), 1 BodyMedia (437KB)	7.31041	1060KB
1 Nike iPod (8KB), 2 Polar (23KB), 1 BodyMedia (1099KB)	12.22107	2424KB

References

1. Camous, F., McCann, D., Roantree, M.: Capturing Personal Health Data From Wearable Sensors. In: Proc. of the 2nd Intl. Workshop on SensorWebs, Databases and Mining in Networked Sensing Systems (to appear, 2008)
2. Meier, W.: Index-Driven XQuery Processing in the eXist XML Database. In: XML Prague 2006 (2006)

Visual SQL:
Towards ER-Based Object-Relational Database Querying

Bernhard Thalheim

Computer Science Institute, Christian-Albrechts-University Kiel,
Olshausenstrasse 40, 24098 Kiel, Germany
thalheim@is.informatik.uni-kiel.de

Database Querying and Programming Based on Visual SQL

Query formulation is still a difficult task whenever a database schema is large or complex. The user has to entirely understand the schema before a correct and complete formulation of the query will be found. Furthermore, users may overlook types in the SQL schema that must be used in the query. Visualization based on Visual SQL leads to higher conceptual correctness and conceptual completeness.

Visual SQL is at the same time

- as powerful as SQL-2 and SQL:1999,
- is well-founded and has a well-defined semantics [Tha03],
- simpler to use and to comprehend, and
- less error-prone in complex settings.

Visual SQL shows what we would gain after realization of Chen's dream on ER database systems. It demonstrates the power of visual programming already for existing database technology. There have already been reported several project (for the analysis of these projects, proposals and tools see [Tha03]) but none of them covered the complete SQL:1999 or SQL-2 standard. It is more powerful than the editors for MS Access and Oracle.

Visual SQL eases *usability* (understandability, learnability, operability, attractiveness) [JT03]. Users do not have to have the ability to formulate a query while having complete understanding of a large database schema, of the impact of specific values such as null values and of the integrity constraints.

The Cottbus and Kiel teams have developed the Visual SQL editor and a re-translator from SQL-2 to Visual SQL. The editor has been used in a number of projects and for teaching purposes in universities and high schools in Germany and New Zealand. It has a German, English and Chinese version. The database schema is typically given on the basis of DBMain schemata. The re-translator has been used in project aiming to document already existing SQL code. The largest SQL query that has been cracked through the re-translator consists of more than 250 dense lines of SQL code. The version 1.5 of the system has been

Q. Li et al. (Eds.): ER 2008, LNCS 5231, pp. 520–521, 2008.
© Springer-Verlag Berlin Heidelberg 2008

exhibited at CeBIT 2006. The version 1.6 is available from teaching path of the website `http://www.informatik.uni-kiel.de/~fiedler/`.

A Demonstration Example

Let us compare the facilities of Visual SQL with SQL-92 based on the database schema used in [Tha00].

We consider the following query:

Provide data on students who have successfully completed those courses which have successfully been given or which are currently given by the student's supervisor?

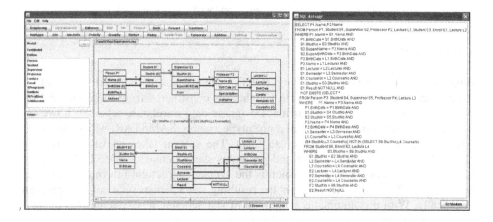

Fig. 1. Comparison of Visual SQL query formulation and SQL-2 representation

References

[JT03]   Jaakkola, H., Thalheim, B.: Visual SQL - high-quality er-based query treatment. In: Jeusfeld, M.A., Pastor, Ó. (eds.) ER Workshops 2003. LNCS, vol. 2814, pp. 129–139. Springer, Heidelberg (2003)

[Tha00] Thalheim, B.: Entity-relationship modeling – Foundations of database technology. Springer, Berlin (2000)

[Tha03] Thalheim, B.: Visual SQL - An ER-based introduction to database programming. Technical Report Preprint I-8/2003, Institut für Informatik, BTU Cottbus (2003)

SAMSTAR: An Automatic Tool for Generating Star Schemas from an Entity-Relationship Diagram

Il-Yeol Song[1], Ritu Khare[1], Yuan An[1], Suan Lee[2], Sang-Pil Kim[2], Jinho Kim[2], and Yang-Sae Moon[2]

[1] College of Information Science and Technology, Drexel University,
Philadelphia, PA19104, U.S.A.
{songiy,rk84,yuan.an}@drexel.edu
[2] Department of Computer Science, Kangwon National University,
192-1 Hyoja-dong, Chuncheon, Kangwon 200-701, Korea
{salee,spkim,jhkim,ysmoon}@kangwon.ac.kr

1 Introduction

While online transaction processing (OLTP) databases are modeled with Entity-Relationship Diagrams (ERDs), data warehouses constructed from these OLTP DBs are usually represented as star schema. Designing data warehouse schemas, however, is very time consuming. We present a prototype system, SAMSTAR, which automatically generates star schemas from an ERD. The system takes an ERD drawn by ERwin Data Modeler as an input and generates star schemas. SAMSTAR uses the Connection Topology Value [1] which is the syntactic structural information embedded in an ERD. SAMSTAR displays the resulting star schemas on a computer screen graphically. With this automatic generation of star schema, this system helps designers reduce their efforts and time in building data warehouse schemas.

2 The System Architecture

The SAMSTAR system consists of three modules: Graphic Input Module, Star Schema Generation Module, and Graphic Output Module. The overall architecture of the system is shown in Fig. 1.

The *Graphic Input Module* reads an ERD in a graphical form drawn by ERwin Data Modeler, in which the ERD is stored in the XML file format. The module transforms XML files for the ERD into DOM (Document Object Model) trees by an XML parser of JAXP (Java API for XML processing) of Sun Microsystems, Inc. It then extracts entities, relationships, and attributes through JAXP methods from the DOM trees.

The *Star Schema Generation Module* extracts facts and dimensions of star schemas from an ERD by using the SAMSTAR algorithm introduced in our early work [1]. This algorithm utilizes syntactic structural information, called Connection Topology Value (CTV), for each entity in ERDs. The CTV of an entity is calculated by the function of the topology value of direct and indirect M:1 relationships. The algorithm automatically selects entities with higher CTVs as facts, because a fact in star schema is connected by many dimensions.

Q. Li et al. (Eds.): ER 2008, LNCS 5231, pp. 522–523, 2008.
© Springer-Verlag Berlin Heidelberg 2008

The resulting star schemas are graphically displayed on the screen by the Graphic Output Module. This module is implemented by using JGraph which is an open source for graphic visualization library [2].

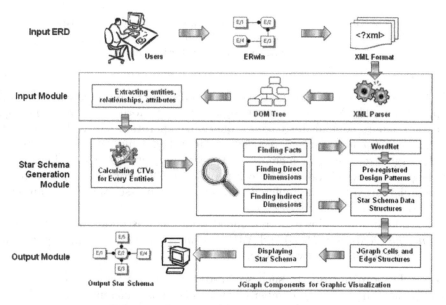

Fig. 1. The Overall Architecture of the System

3 Demonstration Plan

This demonstration shows both the process that the system extracts star schemas from an ERD and resulting star schemas in real time. We will use several ERDs used by other authors who published star schema design methodologies. Users will be able to compare the resulting star schemas automatically extracted by our system with the results of those previous works, which need much human interaction. These comparisons will help users appreciate how effective the resulting star schemas of our system are and how efficient the system is in constructing star schemas.

References

1. Song, I.-Y., Khare, R., Dai, B.: SAMTAR: A Semi-Automated Lexical Method for Generating Star Schemas from an Entity-Relationship Diagram. In: 10th ACM Int'l Workshop on Data Warehousing and OLAP (DOLAP 2007), pp. 9–16. ACM, New York (2007)
2. JGraph site, http://www.jgraph.com

Constraint-Aware XSLT Evaluation[*]

Ming Li, Murali Mani, and Elke A. Rundensteiner

Department of Computer Science, Worcester Polytechnic Institute
Worcester, MA 01609, USA
{minglee,mmani,rundenst}@cs.wpi.edu

XML has been widely accepted as the standard data representation for web applications. The XML Stylesheet Language for Transformations (XSLT) [7][3] is an increasingly popular language for query-like operations on XML documents, including data filtering and reconstruction. When handling XML documents with large size, the main memory buffer requirement in XSLT evaluation can be significant, which also leads to a significant CPU consumption due to the manipulation cost on the buffered data and the processor thrashing caused by excessive use of virtual memory.

XML input data followings pre-defined semantic constraints such as the *Document Type Definition (DTD)* and *XML schema* [1] in many real-life applications, shown by the following two scenarios:

News Dissemination. In such scenario, the news server retrieves and integrating news from a large number of sources (such as different reporter devices, different broadcast agencies and government sources) and disseminates messages to subscribers. The sources may all agree with a pre-defined schema.

Network Record Archiving. In such scenario, the archiving system collects statistics from different network traffic monitors. The statistic records, represented as XML documents, are usually generated by a work-flow engine or simply a customized program, which follow a pre-defined schema.

Such semantic knowledge of the XML data enables us to on the fly predict the non-occurrence of a given pattern within a bound context, which helps to avoid data buffering and thus achieving a minimized memory footprint in XSLT evaluation. Let us consider an XSLT program as below:

```
<xsl : template match = ''/''>
<html> <head> <title> News Data </title> </head>
<body> <table> <xsl : apply-templates  select = ''root/news''/> </table> </body>
</html> </xsl : template>
<xsl : template match = ''news''>
<xsl : for-each select = ''location[contains(@name,'Boston')]''> <tr>
<td> <table> <xsl : apply-templates  select = ''entry''/> </table> </td>
<td> <table> <xsl : apply-templates  select = ''comment''/> </table> </td>
</tr> </xsl> </xsl : template>
<xsl : template match = ''entry''> <xsl : value-of  select = ''.''/> </xsl : template>
<xsl : template match = ''comment''> <xsl : value-of  select  = ''.''/> </xsl : template>
```

When processing XML documents, most prevalent XSLT processors applied a DOM-based processing strategy [3] or a streaming-based processing strategy [5],

---

[*] This work has been partially supported by the National Science Foundation under Grant No. NSF IIS-0414567.

Q. Li et al. (Eds.): ER 2008, LNCS 5231, pp. 524–525, 2008.

where the latter is more advanced memory-wise. With a streaming-based processing strategy, while semantic knowledge is not available, the earliest we can perform predicate filtering on *locations*, output the extracted *entry* and *comment* fragments then release the corresponding buffer for each bound *news* element is after the *news* has been completely received.

Assume we are given the semantics of the *news* element type as the DTD below:

```
<!ELEMENT news ( ( location, entry, advertisement )*, advertisement*, comment* )>
```

By such XML constraint knowledge, if two consecutive *advertisement* subelements are met within an *news* element, no more *location* can occur under this *news* can be guaranteed. If none of the received *locations* within the *news* is equal to "Boston", buffered *entries* of the binding can be purged from memory and furtherly parsed *comments* can be directly dropped without any buffering because this *news* is guaranteed to be unqualified. More examples on such semantic optimization can be referred in [4].

State-of-the-Art. [5] proposes a streaming-based processing model using document projection techniques, which can be applied in XSLT evaluation. However, semantic optimization is not considered in their work. A limited number of XML processing engines [6][2] have looked at the semantic optimization opportunity for XML query processing, which can be utilized in XSLT evaluation. However, these methods do not fully support the possible optimizations arisen by given constraint knowledge.

CALF System. We propose **CALF** (**C**onstraint-**A**ware Engine for Evaluating XS**L**T with Minimized Memory **F**ootprint) in this demonstration. Given the DTD of the input XML document, CALF processes the document in a streaming fashion. It on the fly detects the *Pattern Non-Occurrence* (*PNO*) constraints [4] and then adjusts the evaluation strategy dynamically to achieve better buffering and CPU performance.

References

1. Bray, T., Paoli, J., Sperberg-McQueen, C.M., Maler, E., Yergeau, F.: Extensible markup language 1.0, 4th edn. (2006), http://www.w3.org/TR/REC-xml/
2. Koch, C., Scherzinger, S., Schweikardt, N., Stegmaier, B.: Schema-based scheduling of event processors and buffer minimization for queries on structured data streams. In: VLDB, pp. 228–239 (2004)
3. Li, C., Bohannon, P., Korth, H.F., Narayan, P.P.S.: Composing xsl transformations with xml publishing views. In: SIGMOD Conference, pp. 515–526 (2003)
4. Li, M., Mani, M., Rundensteiner, E.A.: Semantic query optimization for processing xml streams with minimized memory footprint. In: EDBT Workshops (2008)
5. Marian, A., Siméon, J.: Projecting xml documents. In: VLDB, pp. 213–224 (2003)
6. Su, H., Rundensteiner, E.A., Mani, M.: Automaton meets algebra: a hybrid paradigm for xml stream processings. DKE Journal, 576–602 (2006)
7. W3C. XSLT Tutorial, http://www.w3schools.com/xsl

A Quality Circle Tool for Software Models

Hendrik Voigt and Thomas Ruhroth

Universität Paderborn, Institut für Informatik
33098 Paderborn, Germany
{hvoigt,ruhroth}@uni-paderborn.de

Abstract. The quality management of software models is an important issue. As a preparative task, the quality circle requires quality planning. After that a software model can repeat the sequence: quality measurement, quality analysis, and quality improvement. Until now, existing tools lack support for all these activities at once. Therefore, we developed and implemented concepts that provide the full quality circle for software models. The considered models are mainly represented in the syntax of UML class and statechart diagrams and their semantics are formally defined. The formal semantics of the considered software models allows us to improve them while preserving their external behavior.

1 Introduction

The quality management of software models should take place as early as possible during software development. This helps to reduce costs for the detection and correction of defects, since it would be more expensive later on.

Concerning the quality management of software models, we focus on four strongly interrelated activities: quality planning, quality measurement, quality analysis, and quality improvement. Quality planning is the process of developing a quality plan for a project by establishing quality objectives, documenting desired qualities, and describing how these are measured. Quality measurement is concerned with deriving values for measures that quantify or qualify certain quality attributes. The measurement results are analyzed in order to diagnose certain quality problems. The correction of the detected quality problems is performed during the quality improvement activity.

If both the quality plan and the software model are available then the software model can enter the quality circle and repeat the quality measurement, quality analysis, and quality improvement activities.

Our tool features all these quality management activities (tool and its documentation available at: http://www.cs.uni-paderborn.de/index.php?id=7425). In the next section we briefly introduce the basic concepts that we have applied to the quality management activities described above.

2 Quality Circle

Quality Planning: For the development of *quality plans* we apply the Model Quality Plan (MQP) approach (cp. [4]). First, the context factors of a software

Q. Li et al. (Eds.): ER 2008, LNCS 5231, pp. 526–527, 2008.

model are documented to find out what is specific to the considered software model (e.g. used modeling language, diagram types, development phase or development dependencies). Second, the context factors are used for identifying information needs specified by goals and questions. Third, the quality model is defined. Forth, the measurement of the bottom level of the quality model is documented by Object Constraint Language (OCL) queries.

Developing Software Models: Before the quality measurement can take place, at least one software model must be available. We consider software models that are based on the modeling language UML/Z. The syntax of UML/Z is mainly derived from UML class and statechart diagrams. Its semantic is formally given by CSP-OZ [1].

Quality Measurement: After the software models that should be evaluated and an applicable MQP are specified, the MQP can be used to process the *quality measurement.* Our tool determines values for measures by interpreting OCL queries. Subjective measurements that involve human judgment are not supported, yet.

Quality Analysis: The purpose of the *quality analysis* is to find out, how the defects of a software model indicated by the quality measurement can be corrected. More generally spoken, we deal with the symptom/therapy constellation. Our quality measurement provides indicators that help us to diagnose symptoms. The quality improvement includes the therapies. The indicators (symptoms) given by the quality measurement are linked to these therapies in order to suggest possible solution strategies.

Quality Improvement: Refactoring is one widely used therapy technique in quality improvement. Applying refactorings means that you change the internal structure of a program or of a software model, but you don't chance its external behavior. While many works ensures the property of behavior preserving using tests (e.g. [2]), we use refactorings that are proven correct a priori.

The formal semantic definition of UML/Z models given by CSP-OZ enables us to prove the preservation of behavior by reusing refactorings for CSP-OZ specifications [3]. These refactorings can simply be transformed to refactorings for UML/Z models.

References

1. Fischer, C.: Combination and Implementation of Processes and Data: from CSP-OZ to Java. PhD thesis, University of Oldenburg (2000)
2. Fowler, M., Beck, K., Brant, J., Opdyke, W., Roberts, D.: Refactoring: Improving the Design of Existing Code. Addison-Wesley Professional, Reading (1999)
3. Ruhroth, T.: Refactoring Object-Z Specifications. In: 18th Nordic Workshop on Programming Theory (2006)
4. Voigt, H., Engels, G.: Kontextsensitive qualitätsplanung für software-modelle. In: Kühne, T., Reisig, W., Steimann, F. (eds.) Modellierung 2008, 12.-14. März 2008, Berlin, GI- (edn). Lecture Notes in Informatics, LNI, pp. 165–180 (2008)

Generating and Optimizing Graphical User Interfaces for Semantic Service Compositions

Eran Toch[1], Iris Reinhartz-Berger[2], Avigdor Gal[1], and Dov Dori[1]

[1] Faculty of Industrial Engineering and Management
Technion - Israel Institute of Technology
`erant@tx.technion.ac.il`, `dori@ie.technion.ac.il`, `avigal@ie.technion.ac.il`
[2] Department of Information Systems
University of Haifa
`iris@mis.hevra.haifa.ac.il`

1 Background

Semantic Web service composition is a discovery process in which a given set of requirements are fulfilled by dynamically locating and assembling semantically annotated services [5,6]. Semantic annotation of Web services is a set of models that describe its properties (e.g., inputs, outputs, process), in a formal language such as OWL-S [2]. These models provide an unambiguous description of service properties by relating them to concepts belonging to Web ontologies. While dynamic service composition provides a flexible applications which can change according to service failures and other factors, it raises several questions regarding the way users interact with the generated applications. Specifically, it raises a challenge for *usability*, which is defined as the effectiveness, efficiency and satisfaction in which users perform tasks using a given system [1].

In traditional software development processes, the user interface is manually designed, implemented and tested in order to ensure its usability. In contrast, in dynamically composed applications, the functionality is not established during the design of the system. Therefore, the user interface cannot be designed, let alone tested, for usability. The conclusion is that the user interface should be generated dynamically as well, reflecting the temporal functionality of the application.

The field of automatic generation of user interfaces attempts to formally define the elements of user interfaces, including presentation and interaction [4]. However, they do not deal with usability optimization as they presume the models are designed with usability in mind. Therefore, this approach will not suffice for dynamic compositions, as these compositions are not optimized for usability. The contribution of our work is in suggesting a method for optimizing the usability of dynamically composed applications, using formal methods.

2 Optimization by Model Transformation

In order to address the problem of usability in dynamically-created compositions, we present **Liquid-Interface**, a framework for user-interface generation and

Q. Li et al. (Eds.): ER 2008, LNCS 5231, pp. 528–529, 2008.
© Springer-Verlag Berlin Heidelberg 2008

optimization[1]. The framework generates Web-based user interfaces by analyzing the semantic properties of compositions defined in OWL-S [2]. Liquid-Interface applies an optimization technique to improve the usability of the user-interface, and specifically the way users navigate the applciation.

Liquid-Interface derives semantic concepts from the service description, visually expressing them using interface widgets. For example, concepts that express dates are displayed using a calendar, and concepts that have a bounded set of values (e.g. countries or currencies) are displayed as combo-box lists. Other semantic characteristics are expressed using user interface elements, including cardinality, concept generalization, multi-lingual concepts, and input validity checks.

Navigation optimization modifies the process execution order of the original OWL-S [2] model according to a set of user interaction design patterns [3]. We created a taxonomy of user interaction design patterns, which are relevant to navigation, and expressing them using formal mathematical models. For example, the *Flat and Narrow Tree* design pattern defines optimal measures to link distribution between the pages. The patterns are used in order to assign a *usability score* to a configuration of the application's navigational properties. These properties include the number of links between processes, the number of fields within a process, and so fourth. The optimization process searches for a configuration with an optimal accumulative score. Heuristic methods are used in order to bound the search space. The Liquid-Interface framework exhibit an open architecture that allows new design patterns to be defined and added dynamically to the optimization process. Preliminary results prove the feasibility of our approach, and reveal interesting relations between design patterns, including patterns that contradict, or reinforce, each other.

References

1. ISO 9241-11. Ergonomic requirements for office work with visual display terminals, part 11: Guidance on usability (1998)
2. Ankolekar, A., Burstein, M., Hobbs, J.R., Lassila, O., Martin, D.L., McIlraith, S.A., Narayanan, S., Paolucci, M., Payne, T., Sycara, K., Zeng, H.: Daml-s: Seman- tic markup for web services. In: Proceedings of the International Semantic Web Workshop (SWWS), July 13 2001, pp. 411–430 (2001)
3. Borchers, J.: A Pattern Approach to Interaction Design. John Wiley & Sons, Inc., Chichester (2001)
4. Khushraj, D., Lassila, O.: Ontological approach to generating personalized user interfaces for web services. In: International Semantic Web Conference, pp. 916–927 (2005)
5. Klusch, M.: Semantic service coordination. In: Schuldt, H., Schumacher, M., Helin, H. (eds.) CASCOM - Intelligent Service Coordination in the Semantic Web, ch. 4, Birkhaeuser Verlag (2008)
6. Toch, E., Gal, A., Reinhartz-Berger, I., Dori, D.: A semantic approach to approximate service retrieval. ACM Trans. Inter. Tech. 8(1), 2 (2007)

---

[1] The Framework can be used and downloaded at: http://dori.technion.ac.il/liquidInterface

REMM-Studio⁺: Modeling Variability to Enable Requirements Reuse

Begoña Moros[1], Cristina Vicente-Chicote[2], and Ambrosio Toval[1]

[1] Departamento de Informática y Sistemas
Universidad de Murcia, 30100 Espinardo (Murcia), Spain
{bmoros,atoval}@um.es
[2] Departamento de Tecnologías de la Información y las Comunicaciones
Universidad Politécnica de Cartagena, 30202 Cartagena (Murcia), Spain
cristina.vicente@upct.es

Abstract. Requirements reuse has been recently pointed out as one of the most pressing needs and grand challenges in Requirements Engineering. To cope with this demand, this work presents a systematic requirements reuse approach in the Model-Driven Software Development context. The proposal revolves around REMM, a Requirements Engineering MetaModel, which has been recently extended to provide variability modeling mechanisms, which enable requirements reuse. The REMM-Studio⁺ graphical modeling tool, built to support the new modeling capabilities of REMM, now enables the specification of both (1) catalogs of reusable requirements models (modeling *for reuse*), and (2) specific product requirements, by reusing previously defined requirements (modeling *by reuse*).

Keywords: Model-Driven Software Development, Requirements Engineering, Requirements MetaModel (REMM), Requirements Variability and Reuse.

1 Motivation for Building REMM-Studio⁺

It is well known that the higher the level of abstraction at which reuse takes place, the larger its benefits. Moreover, requirements reuse has been recently pointed out as one of the most pressing needs and grand challenges in Requirements Engineering (RE) [1]. The proposal we present here is aimed at coping with this demand. It is based on the adoption of a Model-Driven Software Development (MDSD) approach for RE, which revolves around the definition of a requirements metamodel, called REMM (*Requirements Engineering MetaModel*) [2, 3]. REMM allows designers to explicitly model (1) the main concepts involved in the RE process and the relationships existing between them, and also (2) the variation points of a requirements specification to enable its reuse [3]. The REMM-Studio⁺ graphical modeling tool, presented here, has been implemented on top of REMM, and it is aimed at enabling requirements modeling, validation and reuse.

Q. Li et al. (Eds.): ER 2008, LNCS 5231, pp. 530–531, 2008.

2   Requirements Reuse in REMM-Studio⁺

REMM-Studio⁺ is an improved version of the tool already presented in [2], which now provides two new model editors, as detailed next. Both editors provide model validation facilities against REMM and against some OCL and JAVA constraints.

2.1 Modeling *for Reuse* in REMM-Studio⁺

The graphical editor supporting requirements modeling *for reuse*, allows requirements engineers to define a repository, which contains reusable requirements models organized in catalogs. These catalogs store reusable requirements belonging to the same domain or profile. Variation points can be introduced in reusable requirements models by including any number of parameters in their specification. Each parameter is characterized by a name and a type, which could be a number, a string or a value from an enumerated set of values. Further details can be found in [3].

2.2 Modeling *by Reuse* in REMM-Studio⁺

The graphical editor supporting requirements modeling *by reuse*, allows requirements engineers to specify new product requirements. Product requirements can be created from scratch or from a reusable requirement specification, imported from a previously defined repository. In the last case, the tool provides the means for: (1) loading the repository and importing any of the reusable requirements stored in its catalogs, (2) selecting the requirements to be reused, and (3) instantiating their parameters (if any). When a reusable requirement is selected, all those related to it are also automatically included in the current product catalog. Thus, inter-requirements relationships are explicitly taken into account at reuse time. Further details in [3].

Acknowledgments

This work has been partially funded by the Spanish CICYT projects DEDALO (TIN2006-15175-C05-03) and MEDWSA (TIN2006-15175-C05-02).

References

1. Cheng, B.H.C., Atlee, J.M.: Research Directions in Requirements Engineering. In: ICSE 2007, Minneapolis, USA, pp. 285–303 (2007)
2. Vicente-Chicote, C., Moros, B., Toval, A.: REMM-Studio: an Integrated Model-Driven Environment for Requirements Specification, Validation and Formatting. JOT 6(9), 437–454 (2007)
3. Moros, B., Vicente-Chicote, C., Toval, A.: Metamodeling Variability to Enable Requirements Reuse. In: EMMSAD 2008, Montpellier, France (2008)

A Conceptual-Model-Based Computational Alembic for a Web of Knowledge*

David W. Embley[1], Stephen W. Liddle[2],
Deryle Lonsdale[3], George Nagy[4], Yuri Tijerino[5],
Robert Clawson[1], Jordan Crabtree[1], Yihong Ding[1], Piyushee Jha[4],
Zonghui Lian[1], Stephen Lynn[1], Raghav K. Padmanabhan[4], Jeff Peters[1],
Cui Tao[1], Robby Watts[1], Charla Woodbury[1], and Andrew Zitzelberger[1]

[1] Department of Computer Science
[2] Department of Information Systems
[3] Department of Linguistics and English Language
Brigham Young University, Provo, Utah, 84602
[4] Department of Electrical, Computer, and Systems Engineering
Rensselaer Polytechnic Institute, Troy, New York, 12180
[5] Department of Applied Informatics
Kwansei Gakuin University, Kobe-Sanda, Japan

The current web is a web of linked pages. Frustrated users search for facts by guessing which keywords or keyword phrases might lead them to pages where they can find facts. Can we make it possible for users to search directly for facts embedded in web pages? Instead of a web of human-readable pages containing machine-inaccessible facts, can the web be a web of machine-accessible facts superimposed over a web of human-readable pages? Ultimately, can the web be a WoK (a Web of Knowledge) that can provide direct answers to factual questions and support these answers by referencing and highlighting relevant base facts embedded in source pages?

Answers to these questions call for distilling knowledge from the web's wealth of heterogeneous digital data. But how? Our computational alembic must turn raw symbols contained in web pages into knowledge and make this knowledge accessible via the web. Further, the computational alembic must successfully break down barriers to WoK creation and usage. Currently, several barriers are too high: the barrier of creating machine-readable content (i.e., of creating populated ontologies); the barrier of annotating human-readable, web-page content with respect to ontologies; and the barrier of learning to query machine-readable content. Thus, WoK creation and usage faces three main technical challenges: (1) automatic or sufficiently easy creation of ontologies, (2) automatic or sufficiently easy annotation of web pages with respect to these ontologies, and (3) simple, but accurate, query specification, usable without specialized training. Meeting these basic challenges can simplify WoK content creation and access to the point that the vision of a web of knowledge can become a reality.

* This material is based upon work supported by the National Science Foundation under grant no. 0414644 and grant no. 0414854.

Q. Li et al. (Eds.): ER 2008, LNCS 5231, pp. 532–533, 2008.

Conceptual modeling plays a foundational role in creating a computational alembic to actualize these ideas. An ontology is a conceptualization of a real-world domain in terms of objects, relationships, generalizations, specializations, and aggregations with constraints over these conceptualizations. Indeed an ontology can be thought of as a conceptual model grounded formally in a logic system. Automatic and semi-automatic ontology generation from data-rich, semi-structured web pages is akin to reverse engineering structured data into conceptual models. Automatic and semi-automatic annotation of web pages can proceed bottom-up—can occur as a by-product of ontology generation via reverse engineering. Or annotation can proceed top-down—can come from extraction ontologies in which instance recognizers attached to conceptual object sets and relationship sets extract data on web pages with respect to conceptual models comprised of these object and relationship sets. For query processing, conceptual models grounded in description logics form a template to which free-form queries can be matched to yield formal queries that can be processed by standard query engines.

Conceptual-modeling research can help actualize the WoK vision by:

- providing an answer to the question about how to turn syntactic symbols into semantic knowledge;
- showing how to establish a workbench with toolkits to convert heterogeneous digital data into knowledge under the auspices of an ontology;
- exploring the synergistic interplay among ontology, epistemology, and logic for the advancement of knowledge to provide new ways to think computationally about what knowledge is and how knowledge is acquired; and
- providing a basis for untrained users to query and reason over fact-filled ontologies.

Our WoK Demo[1] illustrates the foundational presence of conceptual modeling in creating a WoK. Specifically, it shows how to create ontologies and annotate pages with respect to these ontologies, and it shows how to query and display annotated content. Ontology creation and usage in HTML-page annotation can be automatic, semi-automatic, or human specified in a user-friendly mode of interaction. User confirmation and correction is always possible, so that the user has the last say, but in many cases, automatically created ontologies and automatically annotated web pages are immediately usable within the WoK. Query specification can range from free-form conjunctive queries to a formal query language. Applications include scientific data (e.g., genes), geopolitical data (e.g., Canadian demographic statistics), family-history data (e.g., genealogical information), and commodity sales and services (e.g., car sales and apartment rentals).

---

[1] See www.deg.byu.edu and www.tango.byu.edu.

MDBE: Automatic Multidimensional Modeling

Oscar Romero and Alberto Abelló

Universitat Politècnica de Catalunya
Dept. Llenguatges i Sistemes Informàtics
{oromero,aabello}@lsi.upc.edu

Abstract. The goal of this demonstration is to present MDBE, a tool implementing our methodology for automatically deriving multidimensional schemas from relational sources, bearing in mind the end-user requirements. Our approach starts gathering the end-user information requirements that will be mapped over the data sources as SQL queries. Based on the constraints that a query must preserve to make multidimensional sense, MDBE automatically derives multidimensional schemas which agree with both the input requirements and the data sources.

Keywords: Multidimensional Design, Design by Examples, DW.

1 Introduction

Traditionally, the design of the *multidimensional* (MD) conceptual schema of a data warehouse (DW) has been performed manually, but automating this process is essential to not depend on the expert's ability to apply the methodology chosen, and to avoid the tedious task of analyzing the data sources. Nowadays, some methodologies to derive the MD conceptual schema from the data sources have been presented, but most of them must be carried out manually and just a few of them automate the process. Automatable methods always rely on a thorough analysis of the relational sources, and they mainly share three limitations: end-user requirements are not considered, design patterns used to identify potential subjects of analysis are based on weak heuristics and they demand data source schemas normalized up to third normal form.

Our methodology [1] was conceived to overcome these limitations. The *MDBE* tool automatically derives MD conceptual schemas from relational sources bearing in mind the end-user requirements. Thus, being able to compare information requirements with actual information availability. Our approach starts gathering the end-user *information requirements* since a DW must give support to the information necessities of a decision maker. These requirements, properly formalized, are mapped over the data sources, and based on the constraints they must preserve to make MD sense, MDBE automatically derives conceptual schemas fulfilling the input requirements. Moreover, MDBE is able to identify implicit MD knowledge according to how the relational concepts are related in the logical schema. In short, MDBE properly tag factual and dimensional data with formal rules derived from the requirements and because of this, it is also able to cope with denormalized schemas.

Q. Li et al. (Eds.): ER 2008, LNCS 5231, pp. 534–535, 2008.

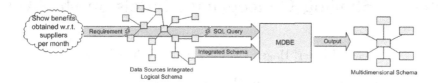

Fig. 1. MDBE overview

2   A MDBE Overview

The MDBE tool demands the MD requirements to lead the whole process. To do so, it is compulsory to translate them to a formal language understandable by computers. In our approach, requirements are translated into SQL queries over the relational data sources of the organization. Each SQL query, altogether with the data sources logical schema, would be the input of MDBE (see Fig. 1). As output, MDBE presents a MD schema derived from the data sources, which allows to retrieve data demanded in the input information requirement.

First step decomposes the input query and creates a *MD graph* corresponding to the query (i.e., relational tables and attributes as well as those relationships among them stated in the query). Our objective in this first step is to identify MD roles (i.e. *facts, measures, dimensions and levels*), whereas the second step aims to analyze the relationships among concepts to infer if indeed, this graph (i.e. the input query) makes MD sense. We say a query makes MD sense if it retrieves data derived from a valid sequence of MD operators over a MD schema. For this purpose, we carried out a study to identify which constraints should be guaranteed by a query in order to represent a combination of MD operators. These constraints may be summarized as follows: data retrieve should be (1) free of data summarizability anomalies, and (2) able to be placed in a MD space. If these constraints are guaranteed then, we may find a set of MD operators retrieving that data from the schema represented by the current graph. Eventually, the output MD schema is directly derived from the graph created along the process. Notice, however, that each query gives rise to a potential MD schema and the last step (not yet implemented) would embrace to conciliate those results in a minimum set of conceptual schemas meeting all the requirements.

Acknowledgments

This work has been partly supported by the Ministerio de Educación y Ciencia under project TIN 2005-05406.

Reference

1. Romero, O., Abelló, A.: Multidimensional Design by Examples. In: Tjoa, A.M., Trujillo, J. (eds.) DaWaK 2006. LNCS, vol. 4081, pp. 85–94. Springer, Heidelberg (2006)

Oryx – Sharing Conceptual Models on the Web

Gero Decker, Hagen Overdick, and Mathias Weske

Hasso-Plattner-Institute, University of Potsdam, Germany
{gero.decker,hagen.overdick,weske}@hpi.uni-potsdam.de

In recent years, the complexity of software systems has risen sharply, so that the role of conceptual modeling is more important than ever. To capture this complexity, different groups of individuals are now involved in modeling different aspects of the system, rather than a few people modeling internals of a software system. These different groups of persons concentrate their modeling effort on different aspects of the system and use different modeling techniques, for instance UML structure diagrams and the Business Process Modeling Notation.

Conceptual models are developed in a collaborative way, models are shared, reviewed, and finally agreed upon. In process modeling, for instance, experts from different companies discuss their business processes and how these interact.

In this paper we report on Oryx, an extensible modeling framework that makes use of Web 2.0 technologies. In Oryx, each model artifact is identified by a URL, so that models can be shared by passing references, rather than by exchanging model documents in email attachments. Since models are created using a browser and models are just "a bookmark away", contribution and sharing of conceptual models is eased. Oryx is realized as web-oriented solution that runs in off-the-shelf web browsers. Oryx supports the following use cases.

Support for Multiple Languages. Modeling takes a central role in various disciplines of computer science. They are domain-specific abstractions used for documentation and exchange of ideas, decisions, and operation guidelines, but also as blueprint for system design and development. Even within one individual domain there is a wide range of notations in use.

Meta-Information and Feature Extensions. Much effort is spent on using models for building new systems. An obvious example is a process model, which is instantiated by a workflow engine resulting in a system behavior according to the encoded process specification. Execution environments typically require large sets of meta-information augmenting. For instance, in case Web service are used to execute processes, technical configurations need to be represented. To do so, there must be a strategy how to extend models and how to provide plugins operating on these extensions.

Data Portability. Models are relevant to many stakeholders, e.g. system architects, developers, customers, and end-users. Their individual use-cases for models varies to a large extent. Consequently, stakeholders will use different tools when working with a model, e.g. the software architect needs an editor, the analyst uses a validator, the developer wants input to a code-generator, and end-users need a viewer to get an understanding of the model. Data portability means to use well documented data formats that can be used by different tools.

Q. Li et al. (Eds.): ER 2008, LNCS 5231, pp. 536–537, 2008.

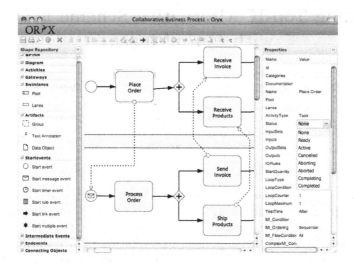

Fig. 1. Oryx supports the Business Process Modeling Notation

Oryx itself is realized as set of Javascript routines loaded into a modern web browser. Models are represented in RDF format.

Language Support via Stencil Sets. Stencil sets provide explicit typing, connection rules, visual appearance, and other features differentiating a model editor from a generic drawing tool. While there currently is a focus on business processes, it is also possible to create stencil sets for other modeling languages.

Feature Extensions via Plugins. Plugins allow for both generic as well as notation specific extensions. E.g. even element selection and cut & paste are plugin features, as they are not needed for an Oryx viewer. More advanced plugins realized allow for complex model checking.

Data Portability beyond Oryx. Any model element is addressable via a URI. The returned representation will normally turn into an Oryx editor. Yet, the same representation can be accessed and processed by other systems.

Oryx is an extensible framework for conceptual modeling on the web. In research collaborations, extensions have already been added easily. Oryx is available under MIT license. The Oryx homepage can be found at `http://oryx-editor.org`. Interested parties are welcome to use Oryx and to contribute to it.

Acknowledgements. The authors thank the Oryx team at HPI for their work.

References

1. Business Process Modeling Notation (BPMN) Specification, Final Adopted Specification. Technical report, Object Management Group (OMG) (February 2006)
2. Vossen, G., Hagemann, S.: Unleashing Web 2.0: From Concepts to Creativity. Morgan Kaufmann, San Francisco (2007)

Providing Top-K Alternative Schema Matchings with $\mathcal{O}nto\mathcal{M}atcher$

Haggai Roitman, Avigdor Gal, and Carmel Domshlak

Technion - Israel Institute of Technology
Haifa, 32000 Israel
{haggair@tx,avigal@ie,dcarmel@ie}.technion.ac.il

Uncertainty management at the core of data integration was motivated by new approaches to data management, such as dataspaces [2] and the use of fully-automatic schema matching takes an increasingly prominent role in this field. Recent works suggested the use, in parallel, of several alternative schema matching, as an uncertainty management tool [3,1]. We offer in this work $\mathcal{O}nto\mathcal{M}atcher$, an extension of the OntoBuilder [4] schema matching tool to support the management of multiple (top-K) schema matching alternatives.

Figure 1 provides an illustration of the $\mathcal{O}nto\mathcal{M}atcher$ architecture, putting it in the perspective of the OntoBuilder matching tool. In Phase 1, OntoBuilder generates a dictionary of terms by extracting labels and field names from Web forms, and then it recognizes unique relationships among terms, and utilize them in its matching algorithms (Phase 2).

Phases 3 and 4 are at the focus of this demonstration. The result of Phase 2 is a set of similarity matrices, one for each selected matcher. Each matrix represents the matcher's similarity scores between fields of Web forms (selected in Phase 1). In Phase 3, $\mathcal{O}nto\mathcal{M}atcher$ allocates queues to maintain a ranked list of local best matchings between the pair of Web forms, as ranked by a single matcher. $\mathcal{O}nto\mathcal{M}atcher$ accesses (possibly in parallel) the set of matching queues and generates a set of K matchings with the highest similarity scores from the set of local best matchings in the queues. $\mathcal{O}nto\mathcal{M}atcher$ associates a probability with

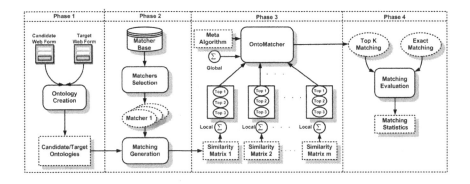

Fig. 1. $\mathcal{O}nto\mathcal{M}atcher$ Architecture

Q. Li et al. (Eds.): ER 2008, LNCS 5231, pp. 538–539, 2008.

each matching, estimating the chance of this matching being the exact matching. Using a predefined human-judged exact matching, that can be generated using a user-friendly utility tool integrated in OntoBuilder, $\mathcal{O}nto\mathcal{M}atcher$ can evaluate (Phase 4) the generated matchings from Phase 3 against the exact matching and report the precision and recall of each generated matching.

We demonstrate algorithms to provide a user with top-K alternative schema matchings, in a decreasing order of confidence. Given a user defined K, the system produces K alternative mappings and assigns a probability estimate based on the similarity measure, as assigned by an ensemble of matchers.

To justify our method, we use the monotonicity principle, as formally introduced in [5,6]. Intuitively speaking, a schema matcher is *monotonic* if its ranking of all possible matchings is "similar" to that of some oracle, ranking matchings according to the number of correct attribute correspondences in a matching.

We demonstrate the applicability of our ideas using deep-Web schemata. The demo user can select the schemata of choice, determine which matching algorithms to use and how to set up the matcher ensemble. $\mathcal{O}nto\mathcal{M}atcher$ can be configured to use different local aggregation functions and allows to define a global aggregation function over the set of local matching similarity values to determine the ranking score of each matching that the tool generates. $\mathcal{O}nto\mathcal{M}atcher$ further allows to select the number of required schemata alternatives.

We provide a visualization tool, to demonstrate the differences between the alternative matchings. Our online presentation (available from OntoBuilder site http://ie.technion.ac.il/OntoBuilder) shows the $\mathcal{O}nto\mathcal{M}atcher$ user-friendly GUI that dynamically illustrates how the different Top-K probabilistic matchings are generated. The demo provides a detailed view of the current top-ranked matching in every matcher's local queue, including the details of current local and global matching scores. The GUI provides also the details of each Top-K generated matching including the global scores of each matched pair, a view of the matching as a bipartite graph, and its precision and recall compared to the exact matching. Finally, the user can select to view the probability pie-chart of the Top-K generated matchings.

References

1. Dong, X., Halevy, A., Yu, C.: Data integration with uncertainty. In: Proceedings of the International conference on Very Large Data Bases (VLDB), pp. 687–698 (2007)
2. Franklin, M., Halevy, A., Maier, D.: From databases to dataspaces: a new abstraction for information management. SIGMOD Record 34(4), 27–33 (2005)
3. Gal, A.: Managing uncertainty in schema matching with top-k schema mappings. Journal of Data Semantics 6, 90–114 (2006)
4. Gal, A.: Why is schema matching tough and what can we do about it? SIGMOD Record 35(4), 2–5 (2007)
5. Gal, A., Anaby-Tavor, A., Trombetta, A., Montesi, D.: A framework for modeling and evaluating automatic semantic reconciliation. VLDB Journal 14(1), 50–67 (2005)
6. Gal, A., Modica, G., Jamil, H., Eyal, A.: Automatic ontology matching using application semantics. AI Magazine 26(1), 21–32 (2005)

Role and Request Based Conceptual Modeling – A Methodology and a CASE Tool

Yair Wand, Carson Woo, and Ohad Wand

Sauder School of Business,
The University of British Columbia
yair.wand@ubc.ca, carson.woo@ubc.ca, ohad.wand@gmail.com

Abstract. This paper contains a brief description of the R^2M (Role and Request Modeling) method and its supporting visual modeling CASE (Computer Assisted Software Engineering) tool. R^2M is a modeling method for creating Conceptual Models of work systems using a combination of ontological and object-oriented concepts. The ontological principles serve to define the meaning of modeling constructs in terms of domain semantics, and to derive rules guiding the modeling process. The R^2M CASE tool is a graphical software tool that supports the creation of models according to the R^2M method. Guided by the principles of R^2M, the tool helps assure the semantic integrity of models, and enables management of complex models via decomposition (i.e. including more details at lower abstraction levels). The tool can help ensure consistency between different modelers and completeness of models.

Keywords: conceptual modeling, business analysis, CASE tool.

The object-oriented approach is arguably the most common design and implementation paradigm now in use. This is evidenced by the popularity of UML (the Unified Modeling Language). However, the use of object-concepts in Conceptual Modeling of organizational domains has not been widely adapted. A main reason is that there are no generally accepted semantics of objects as constructs to model organizational domains [1].

To address the issue of assigning organizational domain semantics to object-oriented constructs we have used ontological principles. These principles can be used both to define the meaning of object-oriented concepts and to suggest rules to guide ontologically-sound modeling. Specifically, we suggest that objects represent active things (actors) and object classes represent organizational roles. In an organizational context the actors (human or otherwise) interact to accomplish a goal. The dynamics of the modeled domain can then be represented in terms of state changes of individual actors and of interactions between actors that assume certain roles. This view led us to suggest a set of modeling rules which address two issues: first - the mapping of domain phenomena to a model; and second - semantic integrity constraints over the constructed models. Based on these rules, we developed a modeling procedure – *Role and Request Modeling (R^2M)* – that assures the ontological validity of constructed models and assists the modeler in identifying situations that require further clarifications about the domain (thus leading to "domain exploration rules"). The R^2M approach is notation independent.

Q. Li et al. (Eds.): ER 2008, LNCS 5231, pp. 540–541, 2008.
© Springer-Verlag Berlin Heidelberg 2008

To facilitate the use of R^2M we have developed a CASE tool that provides a graphical environment for modeling organizational work systems. Models are created by placing shapes on a canvas and adding connections between them. Shapes represent roles and the connections represent interactions or relations between the roles. The models in the CASE tool are not merely pictures where the meaning is provided only by the user. Rather, the CASE tool is "aware" of the semantic meaning of the model, and embeds rules that reflect the ontological concepts and principles of the R^2M method. These can be used to validate the created models and enforce their semantic correctness. Therefore, to a model user, the shapes and connections in models always have a precise semantic and domain meaning.

The semantic validation capability of the CASE tool identifies errors within the model and provides explanatory messages to the user. As the errors are corrected by the user, the model becomes semantically correct and the messages disappear.

Organizational work systems may be complex, including many roles and interactions. R^2M provides decomposition to manage such complexity. Decomposing a "composite" role displays its constituent "component" roles and the interactions between them that are necessary to fulfill the composite's services. These components are not visible at the level where the composite interacts with other roles. Conversely, only roles with which the components interact are visible at the decomposition level. The CASE tool supports decomposition to any level of detail and ensures model integrity between levels.

Experience with the R^2M method and CASE tool in both teaching situations and practical cases has shown that the method led to consistency of models across modelers. Furthermore, semantic errors identified by the tool were often an indication to seek additional information about the modeled domain, thus leading to more complete and accurate models. The domain mapping, semantic integrity, decomposition, and domain exploration rules facilitate more effective and efficient creation of models with improved consistency and quality.

R^2M supported by the CASE tool can be used in the context of early requirements discovery in projects that require an understanding of how an organizations' work systems function. Additional uses of R2M can be seen in references [2] and [3].

References

1. Wand, Y., Woo, C.: Object-Oriented Analysis - Is It Really that Simple? In: Proceedings of the Third Workshop on Information Technologies and Systems WITS 1993, Orlando, Florida, pp. 186–195 (1993)
2. Wand, Y., Woo, C., Hui, S.: Developing Business Models to Support Information System Evolution. In: Proceedings of the Ninth Workshop on Information Technologies and Systems WITS 1999, Charlotte, North Carolina, pp. 137–142 (1999)
3. Wand, Y., Woo, C., Jung, D.: Object-Oriented Modeling: From Enterprise Model to Logical Design. In: Proceedings of the Tenth Annual Workshop on Information Technologies and Systems WITS 2000, Brisbane, Australia, pp. 25–30 (2000)

AutoMed Model Management

Andrew Smith, Nikos Rizopoulos, and Peter McBrien

Dept. of Computing, Imperial College London,Exhibition Road, London SW7 2AZ

Abstract. **Model Management** (**MM**) is a way of raising the level of abstraction in metadata intensive application areas. The key idea behind Model Management is to develop a set of *generic algorithmic operators* that work on schemas and mappings between schemas, rather than individual schema elements. In this demonstration we present a new approach to the implementation of MM operators based on schema transformation that provides some important advantages over existing methods.

1 Introduction

Current work on MM is focused on instance based implementation of the MM operators [1]. The tool presented in this demonstration, extends the AUTOMED data integration system [2] to create a schema transformation-based **Model Management System** (**MMS**) that supports *instance* based semantics, and is capable of manipulating schemas from a wide range of modelling languages. AUTOMED has the following advantages over existing systems: (i) ModelGen is designed in a manner that is readily applicable to a wide range of data modelling languages [3], ER, SQL, XML and CSV schemas can be translated by the prototype used in this demonstration; (ii) the implementation of Match allows for a wider set of semantic correspondences, eg. equivalence, disjointness and incompatibility, than other methods [4]; (iii) mappings in our mapping language can be composed by simply adding them together, whereas in other approaches this composition is a complex task.

2 Demonstration

We use the data integration technique **Both-As-View** (**BAV**) [5] as the mapping language in our MMS. A BAV mapping is made up of a sequence of *bidirectional* transformations that together describe precisely how *instances* of each **schema object** in the source schema are mapped to *instances* in the target schema and vice verse. BAV has a number of advantages over other mapping languages currently used in MMSs [1]. BAV mappings are bidirectional so their inverse is directly available. BAV also allows us to differentiate between partially and completely defined schema objects, by providing two primitives for both addition and deletion. add and delete are used when we can completely define the extent of the object we wish to add or remove, and extend and contract are used when we cannot. We can take advantage of the detailed information contained in BAV mappings when implementing the MM operators. For example, the algorithm to implement Extract which returns those instances of a schema that takes

Q. Li et al. (Eds.): ER 2008, LNCS 5231, pp. 542–543, 2008.

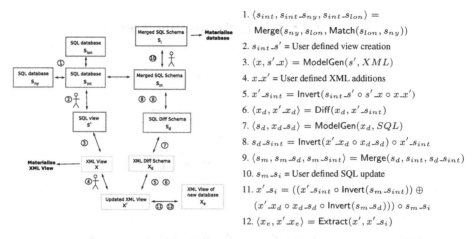

1. $\langle s_{int}, s_{int}\_s_{ny}, s_{int}\_s_{lon} \rangle =$
   $\qquad \text{Merge}(s_{ny}, s_{lon}, \text{Match}(s_{lon}, s_{ny}))$
2. $s_{int}_s' = $ User defined view creation
3. $\langle x, s'\_x \rangle = \text{ModelGen}(s', XML)$
4. $x_x' = $ User defined XML additions
5. $x'\_s_{int} = \text{Invert}(s_{int}\_s' \circ s'\_x \circ x\_x')$
6. $\langle x_d, x'\_x_d \rangle = \text{Diff}(x, x'\_s_{int})$
7. $\langle s_d, x_d\_s_d \rangle = \text{ModelGen}(x_d, SQL)$
8. $s_d\_s_{int} = \text{Invert}(x'\_x_d \circ x_d\_s_d) \circ x'\_s_{int}$
9. $\langle s_m, s_m\_s_d, s_m\_s_{int} \rangle = \text{Merge}(s_d, s_{int}, s_d\_s_{int})$
10. $s_m_s_i = $ User defined SQL update
11. $x'\_s_i = ((x'\_s_{int} \circ \text{Invert}(s_m\_s_{int})) \oplus$
    $\qquad (x'\_x_d \circ x_d\_s_d \circ \text{Invert}(s_m\_s_d))) \circ s_m\_s_i$
12. $\langle x_e, x'\_x_e \rangle = \text{Extract}(x', x'\_s_i)$

Fig. 1. Demonstration Example

part in a given mapping, need only investigate schema objects added to the schema with the **extend** primitive.

Fig. 1 illustrates the example scenario shown in the demonstration along with the MM script that we will run. Our system includes a GUI that allows inspection and querying of all the schemas and mappings created by the script. To consolidate the details of all employees working in an organisation local databases in the NY and London offices are integrated using the **Match** and **Merge** operators to create s_{int}. A view of s_{int} is created that contains only the IDs and names of the employees which is translated into XML using the **ModelGen** operator to give to another department. This schema is changed by that department to better meet their needs to produce schema x'. These changes need to be incorporated into the original database. The **Diff** operator followed by a **ModelGen** is used to produce an SQL schema that contains the instances of x' that do not appear in s_{int}. This is then combined with the original schema using **Merge**. The merged schema, s_m, is improved by a database designer to produce schema s_i. The XML view used in the other department must now be updated so that it only contains data that can be derived from s_i. The **Extract** operator creates this new XML view.

References

1. Bernstein, P.A., Melnik, S.: Model management 2.0: manipulating richer mappings. In: SIG-MOD Conference, pp. 1–12 (2007)
2. Boyd, M., Kittivoravitkul, S., Lazanitis, C., McBrien, P.J., Rizopoulos, N.: AutoMed: A BAV Data Integration System for Heterogeneous Data Sources. In: Persson, A., Stirna, J. (eds.) CAiSE 2004. LNCS, vol. 3084, pp. 82–97. Springer, Heidelberg (2004)
3. Smith, A., McBrien, P.: A generic data level implementation of modelgen. In: BNCOD (to appear, 2008)
4. Magnani, M., Rizopoulos, N., McBrien, P., Montesi, D.: Schema integration based on uncertain semantic mappings. In: Delcambre, L.M.L., Kop, C., Mayr, H.C., Mylopoulos, J., Pastor, Ó. (eds.) ER 2005. LNCS, vol. 3716, pp. 31–46. Springer, Heidelberg (2005)
5. McBrien, P., Poulovassilis, A.: Data integration by bi-directional schema transformation rules. In: ICDE, pp. 227–238 (2003)

QUINST: A Metamodeling Tool

Xavier Burgués[1], Xavier Franch[1], and Josep M. Ribó[2]

[1] Universitat Politècnica de Catalunya (UPC)
Jordi Girona 1-3 (Campus Nord, A0). E-08034 Barcelona, Catalunya, Spain
{diafebus,franch}@lsi.upc.edu
[2] Universitat de Lleida (UdL)
Jaume II, 69. E-25001 Lleida, Catalunya, Spain
josepma@diei.udl.cat

Abstract. We present a metamodeling tool to support a modeling methodology which we have succesfully applied in the field of software quality. As a distin- guishing and general purpose functionality, it implements the concept of in- duced associations, which are introduced by the tool when the user instantiates metaclasses related by inducing metaassociations in the metamodel.

1 Introduction

Software quality is a topic of highest relevance in the current practice of software engineering, not only at the product level but also at the process level. That is, not only the software developed but all software-related artifacts (such as specifications, designs, testing documents...) are in the scope of software quality. As a result, we may find a huge number of proposals to deal with quality, so diverse in nature such as software process assessment and improvement, analysis of data models like UML class diagrams or ER models, measurement of OO designs, and so on.

All of these proposals share a core of common concepts, e.g. metrics, quality factor, etc., but it is not obvious to identify similarities and differences between them. This difficulty hampers the understanding of the quality frameworks, their further extension or evolution, and their comparison when it becomes necessary to choose one in a given context. Several authors claim that ontologies, conceptual models or similar descriptions are needed in order to precisely define the concepts, processes, languages and tools related to software quality [1, 2]. In this context, we propose in [3] a conceptual frame- work for structuring quality models. The framework is integrated into the Meta Objects Facility (MOF) architecture [4] as an extension of the UML metamodel. It benefits from the concept of *induced associations* [5], a mechanism that is not easy to get imple- mented by existing tools.

To support the framework, the stepwise construction of quality models following the methodology outlined in [3] and to implement induced associations, we have developed the software tool QUINST (Quality models by instantiation) which is the object of this paper.

Q. Li et al. (Eds.): ER 2008, LNCS 5231, pp. 544–546, 2008.

2   The Modeling Methodology

Our framework to address software quality is based on a generic model which is, in fact, a metamodel defined as an extension of the UML metamodel. Taking the generic model as the root, a hierarchy of quality (meta)models may be defined step by step, defining new models starting from previous ones. Each step may add a new class as an instantiation of some metaclass of the generic model, perform a refinement (adding a specialisation of some existing class or a new association) or combine two or more previously defined models. As a consequence of the existence of inducing metaassociations in the generic model, these steps may imply the addition of induced associations in the model being constructed.

From the generic model, we may obtain virtually hundreds of reference models, one for each consolidated approach that has been defined in the software quality literature. The important thing is that each of these reference models takes as few assumptions as possible, not compromising therefore its use unnecessarily. These first-level reference models can then be refined to introduce details. This allows to structure quality proposals in such a way that details are introduced progressively, making understanding easier.

A general strategy we have adopted is to use first-level reference models to represent the general structure of the approach, and second-level ones to indicate particular elements. Another strategy consists on using this refinement concept for distinguishing among normative or mandatory parts of a proposal (defined at the first-level) from optional or recommended parts (defined at lower levels). Once the target level of detail has been reached, we can combine the lower-level reference models to obtain new ones embracing all the aspects of quality.

We think that this modeling methodology is a general purpose one, not only useful in the software quality domain. As the second version of QUINST allows changing the metamodel we will be able to check if our approach is or not suitable to some other contexts.

3   The Metamodeling Tool

QUINST's functionally is suited to follow the methodology explained in section 2. During edition, there are two class diagrams available to the user. The model at the left is the generic model and the one in the right is the model being edited. In this situation, the user may:

- Instantiate metaclasses of the generic model. A new class is incorporated into the model, together with any induced association depending on the already existing classes.
- Add a new class as a specialisation of an existing one. As before, the new class will be automatically related with others if induced associations must be generated. In this case, QUINST will also generate the corresponding association ends redefinitions as specified in [5].
- Add a new association.
- Save the model in its current state.

QUINST allows also performing the combination of two existing models taking into account the inclusion of new induced associations if required between a class of a model and a class of the other one.

Models may be retrieved and navigated forward and backward following the hierarchy of instantiation/refinement/combination steps. Searching may be done depending on the software domain of application of the models.

The tool is able to work with MOF-M0 objects and links also: the user may edit a model, choose a class and create instances of it. He may also create links between instances of classes related by some association.

Used in metamodeling mode, the tool allows the modification of the metamodel, adding or deleting metaclasses and metaassociations. When a metaassociation is introduced, it may be defined as an inducing or non-inducing one.

Packaging of the tool and instructions in order to make it easy to download and install is ongoing and will be available from http://www.lsi.upc.edu/~diafebus/QUINST/index.html.

4   Conclusions

We have presented a methodology to create a hierarchy of quality models in an incremental way. The starting point is a metamodel which serves as the guide to QUINST, a tool that assist in the construction of the hierarchy and that deals with induced associations. We think, as we argue in [5], that this concept is useful to improve the accuracy of metamodels. We also think that this hierarchical organisation is a suitable way to deal with situations where there is a set of approaches to some domain that share a couple of concepts and it is desirable to clarify similarities and differences between the approaches.

References

1. Olsina, L., Martín, M.A.: Ontology for Software Metrics and Indicators: Building Process and Decisions Taken. In: Koch, N., Fraternali, P., Wirsing, M. (eds.) ICWE 2004. LNCS, vol. 3140. Springer, Heidelberg (2004)
2. Kitchenham, B., Hugues, R., Linkman, S.G.: Modeling Software Measurement Data. IEEE Transactions on Software Engineering 27(9) (2001)
3. Burgués, X., Franch, X., Ribó, J.M.: A MOF-compliant approach to software quality modeling. In: Delcambre, L.M.L., Kop, C., Mayr, H.C., Mylopoulos, J., Pastor, Ó. (eds.) ER 2005. LNCS, vol. 3716. Springer, Heidelberg (2005)
4. MOF 2.0 Core Final Adopted Specification. Document ptc/03-10-04
5. Burgués, X., Franch, X., Ribó, J.M.: Improving the accuracy of UML metamodel extensions by introducing induced associations. Software and Systems Modeling (July 2007), doi:10.1007/s10270-007-0062-z

An Implementation of a Query Language with Generalized Quantifiers*

Antonio Badia, Brandon Debes, and Bin Cao

University of Louisville
{abadia,b.debes,bin.cao}@louisville.edu

1 Generalized Quantification

It is well known that SQL's syntax sometimes forces users to write queries in an awkward way. Together with the danger of formulating an incorrect query, complex queries pose a challenge to the optimizer. A well studied example is that of *universal quantification* [1,2]. As an example, assume two relations: `student(sid)` and `teaches(pid,sid)`, which denotes that professor `pid` is a teacher of student `sid`. Consider the question "find the professors teaching **all** students." Since SQL does not directly support the quantifier **all**, most textbooks express this question using two subqueries, NOT EXISTS and NOT IN.

Generalized quantification is an extension of traditional first-order languages by the introduction of quantifiers as a definable class; that is, one where different symbols with different meanings are introduced in the language to go beyond the traditional existential and universal quantifier. Intuitively, English determiners and noun phrase modifiers (like **most, all but 2, half, at least 3,**...) can be seen as quantifiers. The language QLGQ is designed to express queries using these GQs. For instance, the example above would be expressed with the quantifier **all** in a very simple way:

$$\{y \mid \textbf{all}(\{x \mid student(x)\}, \{x \mid teaches(y, x)\})\}.$$

2 Implementation to Be Demonstrated

The goal of our implementation is to provide a method for defining quantifiers and a process that accepts as input a query written in QLGQ and returns as output an equivalent SQL query. Our system can also run the query against a specified database, using ODBC or, by default, our local TPC-H instance.

We offer an interface (fig. 1) where users can define their own quantifiers in a simple language. Our interpreter uses these definitions to generate the correct relational algebra expression for each QLGQ query. Thus our language is extendible [3]. The process of running a query, then, consists of three essential steps performed in sequence: **parse**, **interpret**, and **transform/run**.

First, upon submission from the query interface (fig. 2), the user's query is run through a QLGQ parser. Syntactic errors are caught and the query is checked

---

* This research was sponsored by the NSF under grant CAREER IIS-0347555.

Q. Li et al. (Eds.): ER 2008, LNCS 5231, pp. 547–548, 2008.

against the database to verify that relations exist and have correct arities. A valid query results in a parse tree that is used as the input to the next phase.

In the second step, the valid QLGQ parse tree is translated into relational algebra extended with aggregation and grouping. Since we allow the users to define their own quantifiers, the formulas for the quantifiers are retrieved here and used in the translation. In some cases, depending on the definition of the quantifier used, optimizations are performed on this tree before proceeding.

For the final phase of the process, the software walks the extended relational algebra tree from root to leaves transforming it to standard SQL recursively. As an option of this step the resultant query can be run against the database. The result of each of these intermediate steps is retained and presented to the user to provide a degree of transparency into the workings of the query process. The generated SQL queries are deeply optimized but quite complex and unlike what most users would write, nicely demonstrating the motivation for a language that expresses such quantified questions in a more concise way.

We will demonstrate for session participants the current features of our software as well as discuss with them some possibilities for future development. We will also make our full source code available to interested parties and discuss with them the technical details of our approach.

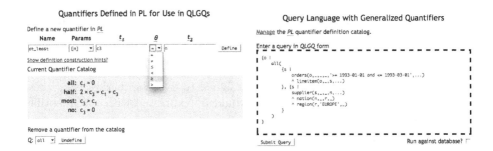

Fig. 1. Quantifier definition interface   **Fig. 2.** QLGQ query entry interface

References

1. Graefe, G., Cole, R.: Fast algorithms for universal quantification in large databases. ACM Trans. Database Syst. 20(2), 187–236 (1995)
2. Rantzau, R., Mangold, C.: Laws for rewriting queries containing division operators. In: Proc. of ICDE, p. 21 (2006)
3. Badia, A.: Extending description logics with generalized quantification. In: Proc. of ISFIS, pp. 94–102 (1999)

Author Index

Abelló, Alberto   534
Aharoni, Anat   455
Ahn, Gail-Joon   183
Akoka, Jacky   142
Ali, Raian   169
An, Yuan   114, 369, 522
Antón, Annie I.   154

Badia, Antonio   547
Barbosa, Simone D.J.   355
Bédard, Yvan   383
Bejaoui, Lotfi   383
Bellahsene, Zohra   341
Berlanga, Rafael   514
Bodenstaff, Lianne   216
Borgida, Alex   55
Bowers, Shawn   41
Breaux, Travis D.   154
Breitman, Karin K.   355
Burgués, Xavier   544

Cai, Yi   69
Calì, Andrea   326
Camous, Fabrice   518
Cao, Bin   547
Casanova, Marco A.   355
Castano, Silvana   512
Cherfi, Samira Si-Saïd   142
Clawson, Robert   532
Combi, Carlo   397
Comyn-Wattiau, Isabelle   142
Cordy, James R.   154
Crabtree, Jordan   532

Dalpiaz, Fabiano   169
Debes, Brandon   547
Decker, Gero   536
Degani, Sara   397
Ding, Yihong   532
Domshlak, Carmel   538
Dori, Dov   528
Dumas, Marlon   199

Embley, David W.   532
Ermolayev, Vadim   98
España, Sergio   498

Fan, Ju   516
Feng, Jianhua   469
Ferrara, Alfio   512
Franch, Xavier   544
Furtado, Antonio L.   355

Gal, Avigdor   528, 538
Gangemi, Aldo   128
Giorgini, Paolo   169
Gordijn, Jaap   216
Gottschalk, Florian   199
Greco, Sergio   311
Guizzardi, Giancarlo   83
Guo, Hang   516
Guo, Qi   516

He, Yukai   516
Hilsbos, Margaret   114
Hornung, Thomas   265

Iwaihara, Mizuho   183

Jensen, Christian S.   397
Jha, Piyushee   532
Jiang, Lei   55

Keberle, Natalya   98
Khare, Ritu   114, 522
Kim, Jinho   522
Kim, Sang-Pil   522
Kiyavitskaya, Nadzeya   154
Koschmider, Agnes   265

La Rosa, Marcello   199
Lausen, Georg   265
Lee, Suan   522
Leung, Ho-fung   69
Li, Chen   248
Li, Gang   516
Li, Guoliang   469
Li, Ming   524
Lian, Zonghui   532
Liddle, Stephen W.   532
Lim, Lipyeow   294
Lin, Ling   516
Lonsdale, Deryle   532

Lorusso, Davide   512
Lynn, Stephen   532

Madin, Joshua S.   41
Mani, Murali   524
Martinenghi, Davide   326
Matzke, Wolf-Ekkehard   98
McBrien, Peter   412, 542
McCann, Dónall   518
Mendling, Jan   199
Mich, Luisa   154
Molinaro, Cristian   311
Montanelli, Stefano   512
Moon, Yang-Sae   522
Moreno, Ana M.   498
Moros, Begoña   530
Murakami, Kohei   183
Mylopoulos, John   55, 154

Nagy, George   532
Ng, Wilfred   26
Norrie, Moira C.   15

Overdick, Hagen   536

Padmanabhan, Raghav K.   532
Panach, Jose Ignacio   498
Papastefanatos, George   440
Pardillo, Jesús   426
Pastor, Óscar   1, 498
Pérez, María   514
Peters, Jeff   532
Pijpers, Vincent   216
Pinet, François   383
Presutti, Valentina   128

Reichert, Manfred   232, 248, 279
Reinhartz-Berger, Iris   455, 528
Ribó, Josep M.   544
Rinderle-Ma, Stefanie   232, 279
Rizopoulos, Nikos   542
Roantree, Mark   518
Roitman, Haggai   538
Romero, Oscar   534
Ruhroth, Thomas   526
Rundensteiner, Elke A.   524

Saleem, Khalid   341
Sanz, Ismael   514
Schenk, Simon   484
Schildhauer, Mark P.   41
Schneider, Michel   383
Sheth, Amit   12
Silva Parreiras, Fernando   484
Simitsis, Alkis   440
Smith, Andrew   542
Song, Il-Yeol   114, 369, 522
Staab, Steffen   484

Tao, Cui   532
ter Hofstede, Arthur H.M.   199
Thalheim, Bernhard   520
Tijerino, Yuri   532
Toch, Eran   528
Toval, Ambrosio   530
Trujillo, Juan   426

Vassiliadis, Panos   440
Vassiliou, Yannis   440
Vicente-Chicote, Cristina   530
Voigt, Hendrik   526

Wagner, Gerd   83
Wand, Ohad   540
Wand, Yair   540
Wang, Haixun   294
Wang, Min   294
Watts, Robby   532
Weber, Barbara   232, 279
Weske, Mathias   536
Wieringa, Roel   216
Winter, Andreas   484
Wombacher, Andreas   248
Woo, Carson   540
Woodbury, Charla   532

Yoshikawa, Masatoshi   183

Zeni, Nicola   154
Zhou, Lizhu   469, 516
Zitzelberger, Andrew   532

Lecture Notes in Computer Science

Sublibrary 3: Information Systems and Application, incl. Internet/Web and HCI

For information about Vols. 1– 4810
please contact your bookseller or Springer

Vol. 5270: A. Pirhonen, S. Brewster (Eds.), Haptic and Audio Interaction Design. X, 131 pages. 2008.

Vol. 5266: T.J. Cova, H.J. Miller, K. Beard, A.U. Frank, M.F. Goodchild (Eds.), Geographic Information Science. XII, 393 pages. 2008.

Vol. 5262: J. Domingo-Ferrer, Y. Saygın (Eds.), Privacy in Statistical Databases. XI, 335 pages. 2008.

Vol. 5240: M. Dumas, M. Reichert, M.-C. Shan (Eds.), Business Process Management. XIII, 399 pages. 2008.

Vol. 5237: A. Popescu-Belis, R. Stiefelhagen (Eds.), Machine Learning for Multimodal Interaction. XII, 364 pages. 2008.

Vol. 5231: Q. Li, S. Spaccapietra, E. Yu, A. Olivé (Eds.), Conceptual Modeling - ER 2008. XIX, 550 pages. 2008.

Vol. 5224: C. Baroglio, P.A. Bonatti, J. Małuszyński, M. Marchiori, A. Polleres, S. Schaffert (Eds.), Reasoning Web. VII, 269 pages. 2008.

Vol. 5207: P. Atzeni, A. Caplinskas, H. Jaakkola (Eds.), Advances in Databases and Information Systems. XII, 321 pages. 2008.

Vol. 5187: A. Hameurlain (Ed.), Data Management in Grid and Peer-to-Peer Systems. VII, 121 pages. 2008.

Vol. 5186: M. Takizawa, L. Barolli, T. Enokido (Eds.), Network-Based Information Systems. XII, 324 pages. 2008.

Vol. 5184: M.A. Wimmer, H.J. Scholl, E. Ferro (Eds.), Electronic Government. XIII, 390 pages. 2008.

Vol. 5183: G. Psaila, R. Wagner (Eds.), E-Commerce and Web Technologies. XII, 145 pages. 2008.

Vol. 5182: I.-Y. Song, J. Eder, T.M. Nguyen (Eds.), Data Warehousing and Knowledge Discovery. XIV, 434 pages. 2008.

Vol. 5181: S.S. Bhowmick, J. Küng, R. Wagner (Eds.), Database and Expert Systems Applications. XIX, 853 pages. 2008.

Vol. 5176: S. Hartmann, X. Zhou, M. Kirchberg (Eds.), Advances in Web Information Systems Engineering. XV, 185 pages. 2008.

Vol. 5175: J. Bailey, D. Maier, K.-D. Schewe, B. Thalheim, X.S. Wang (Eds.), Web Information Systems Engineering - WISE 2008. XVIII, 460 pages. 2008.

Vol. 5173: B. Christensen-Dalsgaard, D. Castelli, B. Ammitzbøll Jurik, J. Lippincott (Eds.), Research and Advanced Technology for Digital Libraries. XVI, 457 pages. 2008.

Vol. 5159: W. Jonker, M. Petković (Eds.), Secure Data Management. X, 229 pages. 2008.

Vol. 5152: C. Peters, V. Jijkoun, T. Mandl, H. Müller, D.W. Oard, A. Peñas, V. Petras, D. Santos (Eds.), Advances in Multilingual and Multimodal Information Retrieval. XXI, 922 pages. 2008.

Vol. 5149: W. Nejdl, J. Kay, P. Pu, E. Herder (Eds.), Adaptive Hypermedia and Adaptive Web-Based Systems. XVIII, 438 pages. 2008.

Vol. 5145: F. Li, J. Zhao, T.K. Shih, R. Lau, Q. Li, D. McLeod (Eds.), Advances in Web Based Learning - ICWL 2008. XIII, 554 pages. 2008.

Vol. 5120: S. Helal, S. Mitra, J. Wong, C.K. Chang, M. Mokhtari (Eds.), Smart Homes and Health Telematics. XV, 220 pages. 2008.

Vol. 5105: K. Miesenberger, J. Klaus, W.L. Zagler, A.I. Karshmer (Eds.), Computers Helping People with Special Needs. XXVIII, 1350 pages. 2008.

Vol. 5094: V. Atluri (Ed.), Data and Applications Security XXII. IX, 347 pages. 2008.

Vol. 5093: Z. Pan, X. Zhang, A. El Rhalibi, W. Woo, Y. Li (Eds.), Technologies for E-Learning and Digital Entertainment. XVII, 791 pages. 2008.

Vol. 5080: Z. Pan, D.A.D. Cheok, W. Müller, A. El Rhalibi (Eds.), Transactions on Edutainment I. X, 305 pages. 2008.

Vol. 5075: C.C. Yang, H. Chen, M. Chau, K. Chang, S.-D. Lang, P.S. Chen, R. Hsieh, D. Zeng, F.-Y. Wang, K.M. Carley, W. Mao, J. Zhan (Eds.), Intelligence and Security Informatics. XXII, 522 pages. 2008.

Vol. 5074: Z. Bellahsène, M. Léonard (Eds.), Advanced Information Systems Engineering. XVII, 588 pages. 2008.

Vol. 5071: A. Gray, K. Jeffery, J. Shao (Eds.), Sharing Data, Information and Knowledge. XI, 293 pages. 2008.

Vol. 5069: B. Ludäscher, N. Mamoulis (Eds.), Scientific and Statistical Database Management. XIII, 620 pages. 2008.

Vol. 5068: S. Lee, H. Choo, S. Ha, I.C. Shin (Eds.), Computer-Human Interaction. XVII, 458 pages. 2008.

Vol. 5066: M. Tscheligi, M. Obrist, A. Lugmayr (Eds.), Changing Television Environments. XV, 324 pages. 2008.

Vol. 5061: F.E. Sandnes, Y. Zhang, C. Rong, L.T. Yang, J. Ma (Eds.), Ubiquitous Intelligence and Computing. XVI, 763 pages. 2008.

Vol. 5053: R. Meier, S. Terzis (Eds.), Distributed Applications and Interoperable Systems. XI, 303 pages. 2008.

Vol. 5039: E. Kapetanios, V. Sugumaran, M. Spiliopoulou (Eds.), Natural Language and Information Systems. XIX, 386 pages. 2008.

Vol. 5034: R. Fleischer, J. Xu (Eds.), Algorithmic Aspects in Information and Management. XI, 350 pages. 2008.

Vol. 5033: H. Oinas-Kukkonen, P. Hasle, M. Harjumaa, K. Segerståhl, P. Øhrstrøm (Eds.), Persuasive Technology. XIV, 287 pages. 2008.

Vol. 5024: M. Ferre (Ed.), Haptics: Perception, Devices and Scenarios. XXIII, 950 pages. 2008.

Vol. 5021: S. Bechhofer, M. Hauswirth, J. Hoffmann, M. Koubarakis (Eds.), The Semantic Web: Research and Applications. XIX, 897 pages. 2008.

Vol. 5017: T. Nanya, F. Maruyama, A. Pataricza, M. Malek (Eds.), Service Availability. XII, 225 pages. 2008.

Vol. 5013: J. Indulska, D.J. Patterson, T. Rodden, M. Ott (Eds.), Pervasive Computing. XIV, 315 pages. 2008.

Vol. 5006: R. Kowalczyk, M. Huhns, M. Klusch, Z. Maamar, Q.B. Vo (Eds.), Service-Oriented Computing: Agents, Semantics, and Engineering. X, 154 pages. 2008.

Vol. 5005: V. Christophides, M. Collard, C. Gutierrez (Eds.), Semantic Web, Ontologies and Databases. VII, 153 pages. 2008.

Vol. 4997: B. Monien, U.-P. Schroeder (Eds.), Algorithmic Game Theory. XI, 363 pages. 2008.

Vol. 4993: H. Li, T. Liu, W.-Y. Ma, T. Sakai, K.-F. Wong, G. Zhou (Eds.), Information Retrieval Technology. XIII, 685 pages. 2008.

Vol. 4976: Y. Zhang, G. Yu, E. Bertino, G. Xu (Eds.), Progress in WWW Research and Development. XVIII, 699 pages. 2008.

Vol. 4969: R. Kronland-Martinet, S. Ystad, K. Jensen (Eds.), Computer Music Modeling and Retrieval. XII, 508 pages. 2008.

Vol. 4956: C. Macdonald, I. Ounis, V. Plachouras, I. Ruthven, R.W. White (Eds.), Advances in Information Retrieval. XXI, 719 pages. 2008.

Vol. 4952: C. Floerkemeier, M. Langheinrich, E. Fleisch, F. Mattern, S.E. Sarma (Eds.), The Internet of Things. XIII, 378 pages. 2008.

Vol. 4950: A. Kerren, J.T. Stasko, J.-D. Fekete, C. North (Eds.), Information Visualization. IX, 177 pages. 2008.

Vol. 4947: J.R. Haritsa, R. Kotagiri, V. Pudi (Eds.), Database Systems for Advanced Applications. XXII, 713 pages. 2008.

Vol. 4936: W. Aiello, A. Broder, J. Janssen, E.E. Milios (Eds.), Algorithms and Models for the Web-Graph. X, 167 pages. 2008.

Vol. 4932: S. Hartmann, G. Kern-Isberner (Eds.), Foundations of Information and Knowledge Systems. XII, 397 pages. 2008.

Vol. 4928: A.H.M. ter Hofstede, B. Benatallah, H.-Y. Paik (Eds.), Business Process Management Workshops. XIII, 518 pages. 2008.

Vol. 4918: N. Boujemaa, M. Detyniecki, A. Nürnberger (Eds.), Adaptive Multimedia Retrieval: Retrieval, User, and Semantics. XI, 265 pages. 2008.

Vol. 4903: S. Satoh, F. Nack, M. Etoh (Eds.), Advances in Multimedia Modeling. XIX, 510 pages. 2008.

Vol. 4900: S. Spaccapietra (Ed.), Journal on Data Semantics X. XIII, 265 pages. 2008.

Vol. 4892: A. Popescu-Belis, S. Renals, H. Bourlard (Eds.), Machine Learning for Multimodal Interaction. XI, 308 pages. 2008.

Vol. 4882: T. Janowski, H. Mohanty (Eds.), Distributed Computing and Internet Technology. XIII, 346 pages. 2007.

Vol. 4881: H. Yin, P. Tino, E. Corchado, W. Byrne, X. Yao (Eds.), Intelligent Data Engineering and Automated Learning - IDEAL 2007. XX, 1174 pages. 2007.

Vol. 4877: C. Thanos, F. Borri, L. Candela (Eds.), Digital Libraries: Research and Development. XII, 350 pages. 2007.

Vol. 4872: D. Mery, L. Rueda (Eds.), Advances in Image and Video Technology. XXI, 961 pages. 2007.

Vol. 4871: M. Cavazza, S. Donikian (Eds.), Virtual Storytelling. XIII, 219 pages. 2007.

Vol. 4868: C. Peter, R. Beale (Eds.), Affect and Emotion in Human-Computer Interaction. X, 241 pages. 2008.

Vol. 4862: N. Fuhr, J. Kamps, M. Lalmas, A. Trotman (Eds.), Focused Access to XML Documents. XII, 456 pages. 2008.

Vol. 4858: X. Deng, F.C. Graham (Eds.), Internet and Network Economics. XVI, 598 pages. 2007.

Vol. 4857: J.M. Ware, G.E. Taylor (Eds.), Web and Wireless Geographical Information Systems. XI, 293 pages. 2007.

Vol. 4853: F. Fonseca, M.A. Rodríguez, S. Levashkin (Eds.), GeoSpatial Semantics. X, 289 pages. 2007.

Vol. 4836: H. Ichikawa, W.-D. Cho, I. Satoh, H.Y. Youn (Eds.), Ubiquitous Computing Systems. XIII, 307 pages. 2007.

Vol. 4832: M. Weske, M.-S. Hacid, C. Godart (Eds.), Web Information Systems Engineering – WISE 2007 Workshops. XV, 518 pages. 2007.

Vol. 4831: B. Benatallah, F. Casati, D. Georgakopoulos, C. Bartolini, W. Sadiq, C. Godart (Eds.), Web Information Systems Engineering – WISE 2007. XVI, 675 pages. 2007.

Vol. 4825: K. Aberer, K.-S. Choi, N. Noy, D. Allemang, K.-I. Lee, L. Nixon, J. Golbeck, P. Mika, D. Maynard, R. Mizoguchi, G. Schreiber, P. Cudré-Mauroux (Eds.), The Semantic Web. XXVII, 973 pages. 2007.

Vol. 4823: H. Leung, F. Li, R. Lau, Q. Li (Eds.), Advances in Web Based Learning – ICWL 2007. XIV, 654 pages. 2008.

Vol. 4822: D.H.-L. Goh, T.H. Cao, I.T. Sølvberg, E. Rasmussen (Eds.), Asian Digital Libraries. XVII, 519 pages. 2007.

Vol. 4820: T.G. Wyeld, S. Kenderdine, M. Docherty (Eds.), Virtual Systems and Multimedia. XII, 215 pages. 2008.

Vol. 4816: B. Falcidieno, M. Spagnuolo, Y. Avrithis, I. Kompatsiaris, P. Buitelaar (Eds.), Semantic Multimedia. XII, 306 pages. 2007.

Vol. 4813: I. Oakley, S. Brewster (Eds.), Haptic and Audio Interaction Design. XIV, 145 pages. 2007.